W9-BGH-091

IF THE ISSUE YOU ARE LOOKING FOR IS NOT
CONTAINED IN THIS VOLUME, WE DID NOT
RECEIVE IT. YOU MAY BE ABLE TO ORDER IT
THROUGH OUR INTERLIBRARY SERVICES DEPART-
MENT. FORMS FOR ORDERING CAN BE FOUND IN THE
REFERENCE DEPARTMENT.

September-October 1992

FAA Aviation News

A DOT/FAA FLIGHT STANDARDS SAFETY PUBLICATION

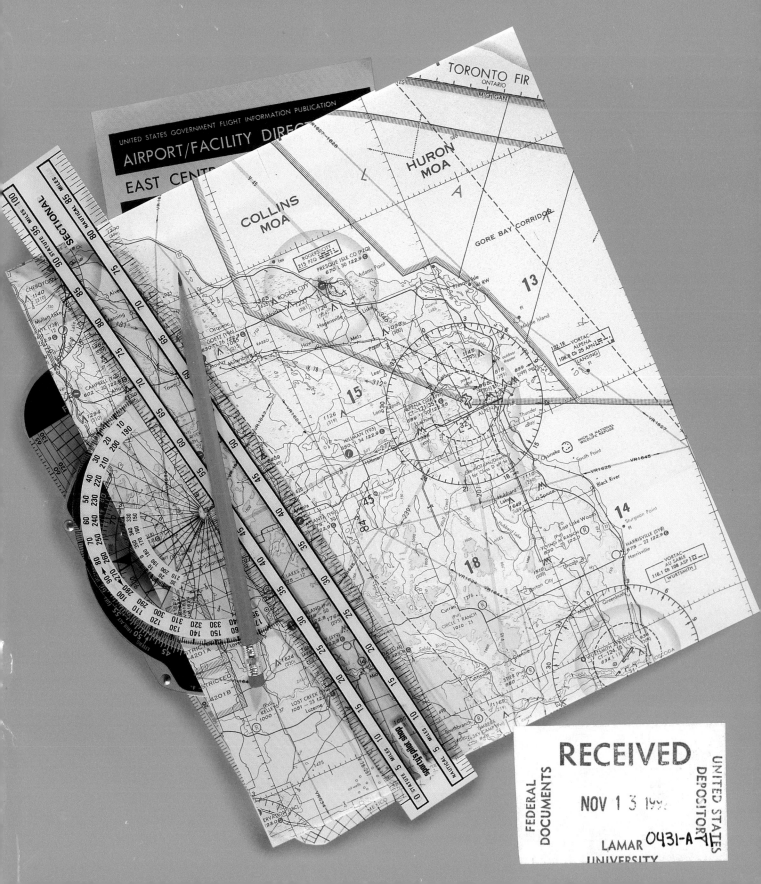

U.S. Department
of Transportation

**Federal Aviation
Administration**

Andrew H. Card, Jr., *Secretary of Transportation*
Thomas C. Richards, *FAA Administrator*
Joseph M. Del Balzo, *Executive Director*
  for System Operations
Anthony J. Broderick, *Associate Administrator*
  for Regulation and Certification
Thomas C. Accardi, *Director,*
  Flight Standards Service
Robert A. Wright, Manager, *General Aviation (Acting)*
Roger M. Baker, Jr., *Manager,*
  Accident Prevention Program Branch
Phyllis A. Duncan, *Editor*
Louise C. Oertly, *Senior Associate Editor*
H. Dean Chamberlain, *Associate Editor*

The FAA's Flight Standards Service, General Aviation and Commercial Division, Accident Prevention Program Branch, AFS–810, Washington, DC 20591, publishes FAA AVIATION NEWS in the interest of flight safety. The magazine promotes safety in the air by calling the attention of airmen to current technical, regulatory, and procedural matters affecting the safe operation of aircraft. Although based on current FAA policy and rule interpretations, all printed material herein are advisory or informational in nature and should not be construed to have regulatory effect. The FAA does not officially endorse any goods, services, materials, or products of manufacturers that may be mentioned. **Certain details of accidents described herein have been altered to protect the privacy of those involved.**
  The Office of Management and Budget has approved the use of funds for the printing of FAA AVIATION NEWS.

SUBSCRIPTION SERVICES

The Superintendent of Documents, U.S. Government Printing Office, Washington, DC 20402–9371, sells FAA AVIATION NEWS on subscription. Use the self-mailer form in the center of this magazine to subscribe. Cost: $8.00 ($10.00 foreign) for one year; $16.00 ($20.00 foreign) for two years. Prices are subject to change by the Government Printing Office without prior notice.
  Change of Address or Subscription Problems: Send your label with correspondence to Sup Doc, Attn: Chief, Mail List Branch, Mail Stop: SSOM, Washington, DC 20402–9373.
  To keep subscription prices down, the Government Printing Office mails subscribers only one renewal notice. You can tell how many copies are left in your subscription by checking the number that follows "ISSDUE" on the top line of your mailing label. For example, when this number is 003, it means you have three issues left in your subscription, and GPO will send you a renewal notice. The number 000 means you have received your last issue. To be sure that your service continues without interruption, please return your renewal notice promptly.

FAN SMITH 212J ISSDUE003 R 1
JOHN SMITH
212 MAIN ST
FORESTVILLE, MD 20747

September–October 1992

FAA Aviation News

Volume 31   Number 5

FEATURES

DEPARTMENTS

On the Cover:
No, there is nothing wrong with this chart. It is a portion of the Lake Huron sectional chart prototype showing the new charting changes. For more information see the article on page 12.

On the Back Cover:
One of ballooning's major events, the annual Albuquerque International Balloon Fiesta, is October 3–11, 1992, in Albuquerque, NM. This colorful scene from last year shows the number of balloons at the event. Photogragh courtesy of Roger M. Baker, Jr.

The FAA/Industry Partnership

by Thomas C. Accardi, Director, Flight Standards Service

Over the past 10 issues of *FAA Aviation News* we have featured a series of articles called the "FAA/Industry Partnership." We are about to put that series "on hiatus" for a few issues to begin our series on FAA's partnership with aviation education organizations. So, perhaps this is a good time to reflect on just what that series has meant—that is, what is the FAA/Industry partnership?

There has always been a relationship between the aviation industry and its regulatory body; it has not always been perceived as a partnership, however, by either partner. It may be perfectly natural for the regulated to believe there can only be an adversarial relationship with the regulator. In many areas of business that may truly be the case, but in the aviation industry both sides have a common interest that intrinsically draws them together. That common interest is the desire to provide the public with the safest aviation services in the world. The FAA/industry partnership has certainly achieved that, and both continue to search for new ways to improve that record.

When I requested that the staff of *FAA Aviation News* begin a series on the FAA/industry partnership, the FAA was just beginning to implement its Compliance for the 90's policy. We were coming off an unprecedented and demoralizing time in the long relationship between FAA and the aviation industry. Levels of trust and confidence had eroded. The reasons are varied; perhaps it is more a cyclical phenomenon than anything. Regardless, FAA felt it had to change its compliance posture in order to fulfill the other portion of its Congressional mandate—fostering aviation. More importantly, industry had blocked reception of FAA's safety message, and restoring those lines of communication was of the most vital importance. The Compliance for the 90's program—remedial training and self-disclosure—were only the beginning. When there are barriers to communication, one party has to take the lead in re-establishing

a two-way flow. We decided to reach out to industry by offering to feature the major aviation organizations in Flight Standards' safety magazine.

The Aviation News Staff tells me that when they initially approached several organizations, those organizations were skeptical. After all, some of these same organizations had just spent the last several years lambasting the FAA in their own publications. Was FAA merely returning the "favor?" The staff explained that what we wanted to present to people was the fact that these organizations very often have worked *with* the FAA in major safety initiatives. FAA wanted to recognize the efforts of the industry in a partnership whose existence they perhaps did not accept or realize.

We found about what we expected—that the industry put safety first, even ahead of that supposed adversarial relationship with the FAA. From AOPA's "trip planning" to HAI's "fly neighborly" program to NAAA's "Operation SAFE," along with many others, the industry was striving to keep the world's best safety record the best. All along what the aviation industry was doing right far outstripped the occasional incidents of non-compliance we found during surveillance. That, of course, makes our job easier and much more comfortable for everyone concerned.

The reason we are not finishing our FAA/industry partnership series is that there will always be new facets to that partnership. This series of articles has taught us many new and interesting things about our aviation organizations. Hopefully, those organizations and their members have learned a little about the FAA as well. We intend to keep up our side of the partnership for safety, and we have no doubts about our partners. ■

Mr. Accardi.

Mr. Accardi is a former airline and corporate pilot and flight instructor with more than 6,500 flight hours. In the FAA, he has been an air traffic controller, a Principal Aviation Safety Inspector, an Air Carrier Specialist, and Regional Flight Standards Division Manager before becoming Flight Standards Service Director.

Each season brings a new set of problems for a pilot to be aware of—in winter it is ice and snow.

Avoiding Frigid Flight Fright

by Wayne Phillips

About the time that this edition of the *FAA Aviation News* finds its way into mailboxes around the country, northern states aviators are rediscovering the exhilarating experiences of clawing through layers of wing frost with fingernails, thawing cryonic Lycomings and Continentals back to life for flight, and discovering that some cockpit heaters provide as much warmth as a match in a mineshaft. With proper preparation, though, flight during the winter months can be a zestful, invigorating encounter with winter. Density altitude is rarely a consideration, and, believe it or not, velvet smooth flight is possible at mid-day as blankets of snow snuff the thermals and their batterings that are all too common in the heat of August.

Winter flight, whether in Rhinelander, Wisconsin (the home of righteous, soul warming chili at the terminal restaurant) or in Aspen, Colorado (the home of soul warming skiwear) requires a different approach and attitude. There are hazards that are unique to frigid flying, and the pilot in command should become reacquainted with winter coping techniques.

CLOTHES MAKE THE PILOT

Preparation begins in the clothes closet! A December flight from a Minnesota airport requires much more than a pair of loafers, a sweater, and a country club golf jacket. A thorough winter pre-flight inspection takes more time and effort than in warm weather. In some instances, longjohns, a parka with hood, fur-lined gloves and boots, and a scarf around the face is the battle armor against a 30-minute engagement with blustery north winds and sub-zero wind chills. Take some good advice from hot air balloonists who will always caution passengers to dress in layers. All that "heavy gear" can be shed down to sweater and pants if the on-board stove can produce a reasonable amount of BTU's. Otherwise, pilot and passengers will be swimming in perspiration with a resultant loss of body heat. Footwear is also especially important not only for warmth but for negotiating icy ramps. Hand-towing an airplane on ice without foot traction can result in an unceremonious and hazardous "home plate slide" into the nose gear with a strong possibility of losing some facial skin to the prop blade.

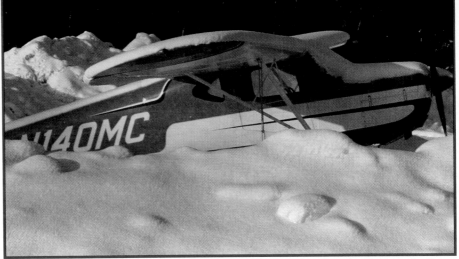

An ice and snow-covered airplane presents a challenge to the pilot who wants to fly. If a heated hangar is not available, pilots have been known to resort to a variety of unorthodox removal techniques.

PREFLIGHTING, PREHEATING, AND STARTING

After you have outfitted yourself properly, preparing the machinery for flight is another matter for extraordinary care. While most FBO's will routinely provide pre-heating services for their own rental equipment, the pilot flying his or her own plane will find that FBO's may charge them for the same pre-heating service. With the cost of flying being fairly pricey already, the frostbound pilot might be tempted to grind the engine's TBO down a few hours by attempting to start in subfreezing temperatures without the benefit of pre-heating. Before you make that decision based on cost alone, consult the aircraft's manual and do what the manufacturer recommends.

That aircraft manual is the authority for pre-heating advice. Typically, a turbo-charged engine will require external heat when the temperature falls to 20 °F. A light single may get by without pre-heating down to 15 °F. Turbine engines usually do not require heat, although a power cart should be used in cold weather because reduced battery capacity can lead to slow turbine speeds and hot starts.

Almost every pilot from Student to ATP is mindful of the dangers of attempting flight with frost and old snow adhering to the airframe. When the white stuff is thick and stubborn, aviators have developed unorthodox ways of removal. These range from chopping with ice scrapers to bathing the airplane in windshield washer fluid to throwing hot water on the snow and ice encrusted areas. Of course, each of these methods can produce more harm than good. The best solution is to either hangar the machine the night before or de-ice it and dry it in a heated hanger before flight. Failure to remove all the liquid moisture can result in frozen control surfaces once the aircraft is wheeled into the subfreezing outdoors.

If pre-heating or hangar storage is part of the pre-flight planning, engine starting will probably be normal. However, if such services are not available and the motor refuses to yield to the usual starting routine and prayers, opening the pilot operating handbook will reveal a section called "Cold Weather Starting," which includes procedures for flooded engine starts. If a fuel-injected plane is the equipment of the day, the book should be handy on the lap. Chances are, it will be needed since fuel-injected engines are notorious for difficult cold weather starting.

In the event of a dead battery, become familiar with the manufacturer's recommendation for using an external or auxiliary power unit (APU). Procedures for starting with an APU may differ from aircraft to aircraft, and using the wrong procedure could damage the electrical system. For example, on the Beech *Baron*, the battery switch should be ON, other electrical switches should be OFF, and a battery must be in the system before connecting an APU, but for the Cessna 182, the master switch has to be turned ON before tying into an APU.

GROUND OPERATIONS

Ground operations warrant more than casual thought. With glass-slick ramps, taxiways, and runways, brakes can become worthless.

Consider that most flooded engine techniques normally require that the mixture control be set at idle cut-off while the throttle is advanced full forward. In this situation, not only does the PIC require an extra hand to manipulate ignition, mixture, and throttle, but imagine the potential for a pirouette into a nearby fuel truck as the tach launches from zero to 2500 RPM in a heartbeat and the wheels are locked on a banana peel surface. Of course, the same slip-sliding away can happen during the run-up when the power is increased for the magneto check.

Although we have all learned that the FAA recommended taxi speed is described as a "brisk walk," a quartering surface wind of 15 knots will dictate a "slow crawl," especially if a high wing airplane is making its way to or from the runway. A review of aileron and elevator positioning to offset the wind's upsetting tendencies during taxi will never come at a better time. Exercise extreme caution when taxiing downwind on an icy taxiway since taxi speed can increase considerably even at idle RPM. Slowing to little more than a full stop well before the end of the taxiway can eliminate the need for a plow and a tug.

Cockpit heater operation might best be viewed as a pre-flight checklist item. Although heaters and defrosters in single engines are simple to operate (Two positions: frostbite and Frigidaire), multi-engine pilots will need to become familiar with the proper operation of heaters. Some heater start and shutdown procedures can be complicated in twins. Any time when using the aircraft's heater, it is important to recall the potential for carbon monoxide poisoning and how to recognize its symptoms.

UP, UP, AND AWAY—AT LAST

A definite "heads up" disposition is required for take-off on icy runways with strong winds. There will be times when the pilot will have no directional control while accelerating on the runway other than with ailerons and rudder. Certain winter conditions will mandate that a take-off not be initiated at all. The best action is a very sssll-looooooowwww taxi back to the ramp.

Once airborne, the VFR pilot will not only be exposed to the beauty that winter aviating can provide, but also the tricks that it can play. The lake that was such a great checkpoint enroute to some distant destination last June suddenly becomes blurred with snow. Is that the lake, or is it just one of so many fields that slide under the wings during cross-country flight? Familiar roads can disappear under drifts. Airports become invisible.

And what about the destination airport? Is it closed for snow removal? Closed for the winter? Since winter days are shorter, will required services be available for the cross-country trip that might arrive after the early sundown? Although the Flight Service Specialists do their absolute best to provide current and valid NOTAM's concerning airport conditions and other information, a telephone call to the destination FBO might well be worth the long distance charge.

One winter on an IFR flight to Rifle, Colorado, controllers at Denver Center would not authorize an instrument approach to the airport because it had been NOTAMed closed for snow removal. The pilot, however, had called the FBO before departure and learned that the snow removal operation had been completed. After a conversation with the controller and the supervisor on the frequency and a quick confirmation telephone call to the airport by Denver Center, the controller granted an approach clearance.

WINTER WEATHER— NOT SUCH A WONDERLAND

From November through March, the seasons can produce weather that can snare and scare the fair weather pilot.

Snow squalls, icing, mountain obscuration, and severe turbulence associated with the more southerly jet stream are just samples of nature's offerings during the winter months. The thorough pilot will devote more time deciphering weather information during the winter season when changes occur so rapidly.

Westbound cross-countries can produce near hover flight for mini-power flying machines thanks to the "Northwest Express." In some parts of the country, particularly in the Rockies and other rugged terrain, 9,000-foot winter winds aloft can exceed 60 knots on crystal clear days, not only undermining the best ETA and fuel require-

---

SURVIVAL KIT

This can be a commercially prepared item, or something you put together yourself. It need not weigh more than a few pounds altogether, and you may never use it—but some "bare" essential components of a winter survival kit are:

• **Shelter.** A high visibility plastic tube tent, with emergency space blankets (these fold into a space no bigger than a deck of cards).
• **First Aid.** A complete first aid kit.
• **Food.** High-energy dehydrated food, enough to last at least three days per person.
• **Warmth.** An all weather fire starter kit. (Matches too, of course, but these alone are not good enough).
• **Signalling.** Heliographic mirror, aluminum foil, aerial flares, a hand-held transmitter.
• **Outdoor living.** A strong knife, a good compass, cable saw, tin pot (to melt snow in for drinking water), candles.

Equipment of this kind is designed for minimal weight and can be bought at outdoor or camping stores. Get the best you can afford.

---

ments planning but also creating the dreaded mountain wave.

Training manuals pay little attention to the mountain wave phenomenon. Whether the Appalachians, the Cascades, the Smokies, or the Rockies, the effects of rivers of cascading air can totally deplete the flight capability of many light aircraft when caught in the downward rush. Under just the right conditions, the mountain wave can impact a flight hundreds of miles downwind of the peaks.

Turbulence is almost always associated with strong winter winds. Recall the significance of tightly spaced isobars on the surface analysis chart (if you can find one). Reading and interpreting winds aloft forecasts is a skill that should be revitalized during winter months. Committing maneuvering speeds to memory and knowing their significance is not a bad idea either.

Whether a flight is VFR or IFR, review communication procedures with weather data providers while in flight. All too often, flyers will conduct a long VFR or IFR cross-country flight relying solely on the pre-takeoff weather briefing. With the whims of winter weather, updates should be obtained frequently while enroute. It is surprising to learn that many pilots are unaware that Flight Watch is not available in all parts of the country and at all hours of the night or that communicating with an FSS through a VOR requires an understanding that the "122.1R" listed at the VOR facility box means that the FSS *receives* on that frequency, not the pilot.

IFR flights during the winter months expose the pilot to a medley of meteorological challenges, such as lake effect squalls and obscuration from snow and blowing snow. Add ice pellets and freezing drizzle to the menu. Of all the wintertime traps lurking in the murk, icing is potentially the most lethal and a healthy respect for it is essential for surviving winter IMC flight. Instrument pilots should invest time addressing go/no go decision-making. In the winter virtually all Area Forecasts have the standard disclaimer: "Chance of light to moderate icing in cloud and precipitation," which seems to render the instrument rating useless during the winter. However, through careful observation of freezing level reports, PIREP's, top

Snow clouds—rotor induced or otherwise originated—are potentially capable of bringing about pilot incapacitation from flicker vertigo. Rotor blade movements, in the presence of landing lights or other illumination reflected by snow, have caused pilots to become dizzy to the point of losing consciousness—another compelling reason for avoiding whiteouts, especially when alone at the controls.

reports, ceilings, low pressure and frontal positions, a reasoned decision with "escape options" can be made.

In order to make reasonable icing decisions, you must study the conditions ripe for the formation of ice, including an examination of the cloud types that produce rime, clear, or mixed ice. Of course, icing hazards come in two varieties: induction and structural.

Induction icing can present itself as either carburetor ice or a blocked air intake. While carburetor icing remedies (see article on page 8) are generally discussed and practiced during the first hours of flight training, the instrument pilot flying rented equipment might not be aware of an alternate induction air source or its operation. Likewise, the aircraft's anti-ice and de-ice systems, if installed, require familiarization.

As far as *structural icing* is concerned, ice avoidance techniques in flight must be an integral part of winter risk management. A simple matter of getting into the habit of requesting an unrestricted climb clearance to on-top conditions can mean the difference between an uneventful flying excursion or an anxious predicament caused by meandering around in icy clouds. Icing exiting maneuvers should be contemplated. For example, if while on an instrument flight in wintertime IMC you encounter icing in stratus clouds, a simple change in altitude of a thousand feet or so can normally bring relief since icing layers in stratus clouds are usually thin. On the other hand, a bout with clear ice in cumulus clouds may require an immediate, controlled descent to the nearest airport with an instrument approach if circumnavigation is not possible. If necessary, you should declare an emergency to expedite a descent and approach clearance. (A noteworthy point to make is to be certain that a current set of approach charts covering all possible alternates for the route to be flown is available—just in case.) The essential wisdom is this: If you encounter icing, do something now! This bit of advice must be carved into the mind of the IFR pilot.

WINTER LANDINGS AND SHUT-DOWN

No matter if the flight concludes at the end of an approach to minimums or after hours in exquisite, pristine blue sky, wintertime landings can press piloting skills to the max. As with the takeoff, a landing on a sheet of ice can bring the flight to an embarrassing conclusion. If wind conditions allow, touchdown should be made at a low speed to avoid skating the length of the runway only to be stopped by the fence at the far end. If braking is nil, a go-around may be the more savory alternative to a nose-over into the fluff.

Brisk crosswinds are especially testy during landings on glass-like runways. Alertness and positive control use is imperative with little reliance on the brakes or the nosewheel steering. The pilot should understand that a landing at another airport where the wind is more aligned with the runway is probably a prudent decision if prevailing conditions at the home airport are beyond the skill level.

The rusty winter flyer may want to practice approaches and landings to a strip with an inch or three of fresh snow. Not only will the exercise illustrate the value of soft-field landing procedures, but the pilot will soon recall the difficulty of flare altitude judgement resulting from whiteout.

Once the airplane is gingerly taxied into its outdoor space, if inside storage is unavailable, securing the aircraft well is important. Although a medium breeze would have little affect on a 152 on dry pavement, a loose Cessna on ice propelled by wind could produce a delicate meeting with an insurance adjuster.

If you plan to continue the flight after a short stay on the ground, engine heat preservation is an important consideration. An old horse blanket or ragged quilt secured around the cowling might retain enough heat to avoid the pre-heating charge when it is time to get up and go again.

On the market there are many fine weather flying books which provide some extra winter flying insights. Such pearls of knowledge as "heavier icing is generally found in new clouds more so than in old clouds," or "icing is typically more severe in the northeast quadrant of a low" come from writers who have been there. The conscientious pilot might direct his or her reading activities to such publications for practical solutions to winter weather risk management.

A final thought when preparing for winter flying: Take some advice from mountain search and rescue pilots who increase their chances for winter survival in the event of an off-airport landing by carrying both a survival kit and a sleeping bag on every winter flight. The Colorado Civil Air Patrol can speak of a tragedy near Snowmass recently where two airline pilots on a sightseeing tour in their *Comanche* crashlanded. They survived the landing but succumbed to the elements.

Wintertime flying can be a rewarding adventure. There is no need to become a homebound couch potato when the mercury slides to sub-freezing. To borrow the well-worn motto, all that is required is to, "Be Prepared!"

Thorough preparation is the absolute best way to avoid Frigid Flight Fright! ∎

Doing It in the Dark

The city lights at night can be spectacular, but how are you at landing in the dark?

by Bruce Edsten, Accident Prevention Program Manager, Louisville, Kentucky, Flight Standards District Office

Daylight is becoming a scarce commodity as we approach and pass the autumnal equinox. As winter nears our night currency may need some touching up after those long, lazy, hazy days of summer. FAR § 61.57(d) requires three night-time takeoffs and landings to a full stop within the preceding 90 days for a PIC to be considered night current. Three take-offs and landings while staying in the pattern at your local, familiar airport may meet the intent of the rule but are you ready to navigate at night or handle an emergency at night? The following article, reprinted from the Accident Prevention Program Newsletter published by the Louisville FSDO, offers some food for thought about night flying. **—Editor**

Night flying has lots of advantages. It is almost always cooler, and that usually means smoother air, so it is a lot more comfortable all the way round. If you fly rental airplanes, the selection is better at night so your favorite mount is more likely to be available. There are fewer folks up there in the sky with you, and that makes for fewer communications and traffic hassles. On top of that, it is fun and just plain pretty looking down on all the twinkling lights!

Of course, if you have not flown at night for a while you will need to get current, and any opportunity to get an instructor up with you can be very educational—far beyond the obligatory three takeoffs and landings. For instance, when was the last time you did a DF Steer? Or a no-gyro approach or maybe a Precision Approach Radar (PAR) approach? These are great practice exercises and are almost invariably easier to accomplish at night when the ground personnel are not quite so busy.

If you are going out there with an instructor, you might want to try some lights-off landings. With a little practice these are actually fun, and they are a great hedge against that day when your entire electrical system goes kaflooey. (Those of us who are intimately familiar with Murphy's Law know that the Busted Electrical System Corollary states that your flashlight will also pick the same time to quit.) I usually start students off with some airwork without cockpit lights to get them listening and feeling for clues about airspeed, power, etc. Next is a series of landings with emphasis on outside visual references, eventually working into landings with no landing lights and no cockpit lights. It is not as tough as it sounds. Night landings are pretty easy at the

> *"Probably the most important item to be considered in planning a night flight is YOU, the pilot. Flying at night requires a bit more attention to the task at hand than flying in the daytime, so you want to be sure you are up to it."*

huge international airports because it never really gets DARK there. The effect of a lights-out landing can be heightened by selecting a remote airport without a lot of bright city lights around it. That is how it should be done.

Is night flying more dangerous? Some folks think so. In most places outside the U.S., night VFR is prohibited unless you are IFR-rated, equipped, and filed as soon as the sun goes down. Some places further restrict night operations to multi-engine aircraft only, in addition to the VFR prohibition. How come? The problem is our eyes. We just do not have what it takes to operate in the dark like cats and owls and other nocturnal critters. To operate an airplane effectively at night, humans must compensate with technology and brains.

At night, the see-and-avoid concept depends on aircraft lights. You need to have the navigation lights and anti-collision lights in good working order. It is also handy to have cockpit and instrument lighting, and a trusty flashlight is a must (though not FAR Part 91-required) for your flight bag in case any of the other lights fail. As a rule, I have two flashlights in the bag and a spare set of batteries as well. This equipment should all be carefully preflighted, and you best not go if all are not working!

Another part of your preflight planning is an appropriate weather briefing. Many night accidents are a result of running into some unexpected weather and not being able to handle it. A cloud formation that would give you no trouble whatsoever in the daytime may not even be visible at night until you are inside it!

The dark also hides terrain features, so careful planning of your route of flight is very important. As a rule, you can expect such things as buildings and radio towers to be properly lighted, but there is a lot of high-level real estate out there that has nothing on it at all. Consult the appropriate charts, and give hills and mountains a wide berth.

Another consideration in selecting a route is fuel—specifically, how much do I need, and where can I get some more? The FAR require that you plan for a 45-minute reserve at night, but remember that is a MINIMUM. The prudent pilot will carry some extra, just in case. (One pilot's spouse insists upon an extra 15 minutes of fuel for each family member on board.) A check of the Airport/Facility Directory will show you which airports are attended after dark and whether they have the kind of fuel you need. A quick phone call to that planned fuel stop can be worth a lot, just to be sure they are really going to be open. The airports that are most likely to be open at night are the ones near the larger cities where airplane traffic is a 24-hour occurrence. Planning a night flight to one of those airports has another advantage, since the larger airports are easier to find—all those lights and major highways provide additional references for pilotage.

Lights play a big role once you get to the airport, too. Without a rotating beacon, many airports would be difficult or impossible to find. Does your destination airport have one? You can also find airports by looking for other lighting aids such as Runway End Identifier Lights (REIL), Approach Light Systems (ALS), or High Intensity Runway Lights (HIRL). In many case these and other lighting aids can be turned up to extra bright by the tower or FSS. Increasingly, airport lighting aids are operated by Pilot Controlled Lighting (PCL) devices. This can be a BIG help in picking the airport out the clutter of city lights. Check the *Airport/Facility Directory* and current charts for details.

How about landing aids such as VASI or PAPI? Within limits these approach aids will provide obstruction clearance through your descent and final approach if you remain on slope. Use them whenever you can. You may want to select a different runway or even a different airport to assure you can take advantage of these aids. In any case, be sure to check NOTAM's to see if the lights you are counting on are working tonight.

Probably the most important item to be considered in planning a night flight is YOU, the pilot. Flying at night requires a bit more attention to the task at hand than flying in the daytime, so you want to be sure you are up to it. Fatigue brought on by a full day at work (or play!) can significantly reduce your capacity to the point where you are simply no longer a safe pilot. The problem is the eyes, remember? We have enough trouble seeing at night when we are rested and healthy, and it only gets worse with fatigue. The effects of altitude will only make thing still worse; oxygen is very important to good night vision. Section 8–2 of the *Airman's Information Manual* even states that, "For optimum protection, pilots are encouraged to use supplemental oxygen above 10,000 feet during the day, and above 5,000 feet at night." Be realistic about your abilities, and leave the trip for another time if you are tired.

Doing it in the dark can be very rewarding. Proper attention to planning and pilot currency will make it safe. ∎

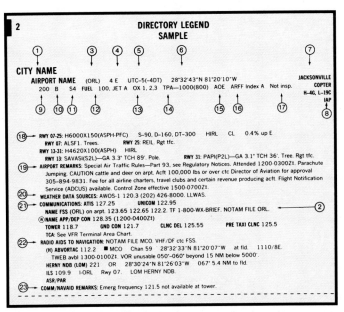

Page from Airport/Facility Directory. If you are not sure how to read the airport entries, check the legend sample on page 2 of the Directory. Number 12 indicates fueling information and number 18 indicates lighting information.

Carburetor Icing!

by Rand M. Sanders

WHAT IS CARBURETOR ICE?

- The formation of ice in the carburetor that may form at the fuel discharge nozzle, in the venturi, on or around the butterfly valve, or in the passages from the carburetor to the engine.

WHY IS CARBURETOR ICE DANGEROUS?

- Because it may restrict the power output of the engine or even cause the engine to quit operating.

WHAT CAUSES CARBURETOR ICE?

- Carburetor ice forms during the vaporization of fuel, combined with the expansion of air as it passes through the carburetor, both of which cause a sudden cooling of the mixture.
- If water is present, this cooling may reduce the temperature in the carburetor below freezing. If so, the moisture will be deposited as frost or ice inside the carburetor passages.
- The temperature drop in the carburetor can be as much as 40 °C (104 °F) but is usually 20 °C (68 °F) or less.

IS CARBURETOR ICE A PROBLEM IN FUEL INJECTION SYSTEMS?

- It is NOT a problem for fuel injected engines because such systems do not use a carburetor, i.e., fuel is vaporized by other means.

WHAT ARE THE IDEAL CONDITIONS FOR CARBURETOR ICE?

- When the cooling effect in the carburetor is sufficient to bring the temperature inside the carburetor down to 0 °C (32 °F) or colder and if moisture is visible in the air.
- When the relative humidity of the outside air is high, ice can form inside the carburetor in cloudless skies and when temperatures are

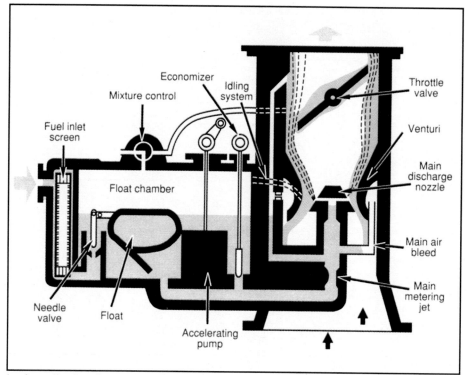

Ice formation in a float-type carburetor

as high as 25 °C (77 °F). It sometimes forms with outside air temperatures as low as –10 °C (14 °F).
- When the temperature and dewpoint approach 20 °C (68 °F).
- When the temperature is between –7 °C (20 °F) and 21 °C (70 °F) with visible moisture or high humidity.
- During low or closed throttle settings, an engine is particularly susceptible to carburetor ice.

HOW DO YOU DETECT CARBURETOR ICE?

- Because carburetor ice may restrict the power output or cause the engine to quit operating—
- For an airplane with fixed-pitch props the first indication of carburetor icing is a loss of engine RPM.
- For an airplane with constant speed props, the first indication of carburetor icing is usually a drop in manifold

pressure. There will be NO reduction in RPM.
- Engine roughness.
- In aircraft equipped with a carburetor air temperature gauge, a needle in the yellow arc (–15 °C to 5 °C) indicates the carburetor air temperature at which carburetor icing is most likely to occur.

HOW CAN YOU PREVENT/ REMOVE CARBURETOR ICE?

[Editor's note: Follow the procedures indicated in the POH for your aircraft, which may differ slightly from the generic procedures offered below.]

- Use carburetor heat, which is an anti-icing device that preheats air before it reaches the carburetor.
- Carburetor heat is usually adequate to prevent icing but it may not always clear ice which has formed.

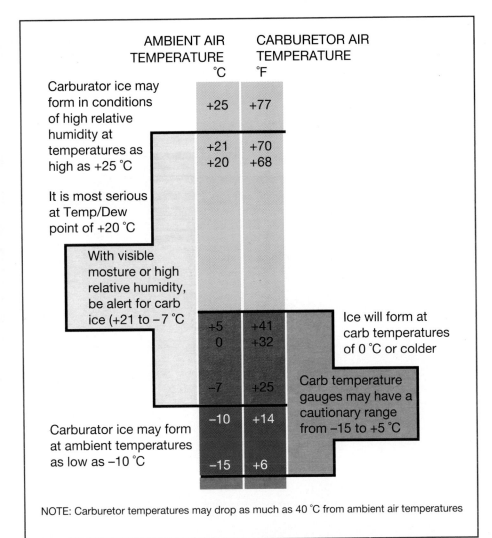

AMBIENT AIR TEMPERATURE °C	CARBURETOR AIR TEMPERATURE °F
+25	+77
+21	+70
+20	+68
+5	+41
0	+32
−7	+25
−10	+14
−15	+6

Carburator ice may form in conditions of high relative humidity at temperatures as high as +25 °C

It is most serious at Temp/Dew point of +20 °C

With visible mosture or high relative humidity, be alert for carb ice (+21 to −7 °C

Carburator ice may form at ambient temperatures as low as −10 °C

Ice will form at carb temperatures of 0 °C or colder

Carb temperature gauges may have a cautionary range from −15 to +5 °C

NOTE: Carburetor temperatures may drop as much as 40 °C from ambient air temperatures

Comparison of Ambient and Carburetor Air Temperatures

When the carburetor air temperature gauge needle is in the yellow arc, carburetor icing is most likely to occur.

- Make periodic checks for carburetor icing when conditions are conducive to its formation.
- When detected or suspected, full carburetor heat should be applied immediately and should be left "on" until all ice has been removed.
- If ice is present, applying partial carburetor heat or leaving it on for an insufficient time might aggravate the situation.
- If a pilot suspects carburetor icing conditions and anticipates closed throttle operations, the carb heat should be applied "full on" before closing the throttle and left on during the closed throttle operation. Periodically, open the throttle smoothly for a few seconds to keep the engine warm, otherwise, the carburetor heater may not provide enough heat to prevent icing.

SAY AGAIN, HOW DO YOU CHECK FOR ICE AND WHAT DO YOU DO IF ICING IS PRESENT?

Apply Carburetor Heat:

- There will be a drop in RPM for fixed-pitch propeller aircraft or manifold pressure for constant speed propeller aircraft.
- If ice is present and as it clears, RPM or manifold pressure will rise, often accompanied by engine roughness as the water is ingested.

Turn off Carburetor Heat only when ice is clear:

- RPM or manifold pressure will rise to a setting greater than that before application of carburetor heat.
- The engine should run more smoothly after the ice has been removed. ∎

Editor's Note: *Mr. Sanders is a Technical Sergeant in the U.S. Air Force Reserves where he flies as a boom operator on KC-10A's. He is an airline transport pilot, CFI, and flies with the North Carolina Wing of the CAP. He promises to write some time in the future about how misfueling caused both engines to quit on the Convair 240 in which he used to fly air freight.*

Sir Hiram Maxim

The crewmembers of Maxim's "aerial steamship" ready it for its trial run on its dual rail tracks. The craft had a 108-foot wingspan with twin 18-foot steam driven pusher propellers and a gross weight of 8,000 pounds. (The first successful Wright Flyer in 1903 weighed only 605 pounds.)

"Maxim speaks of Lilienthal as a parachutist, and likens him to a flying squirrel.... Lilienthal after alluding to the unwieldiness of Maxim's machine, says, 'After all, the result of his labors has been to show us how not to do it.' If any two men should be friends rather than foes, these are the two. Each has certain ideas and publications which the other lacks and it is the greatest of pities that they cannot clasp hands over the watery channel."

Sir Hiram Maxim and His Forgotten Legacy to Aviation

by Louise Oertly, Associate Editor

James Means, an American aeronautical enthusiast and publisher of the influential *Aeronautical Annual*, wrote this editorial in 1895. He was talking about two of the better known aviation figures of his day, Otto Lilienthal and Sir

Hiram Maxim, remembered today for their gliders and—machine guns?

That's right. Maxim's chance interest in the automation of guns led him to invent the first efficient machine gun. However, when the U.S. War Department called the gun ingenious but impractical, he showed his invention to the British War Office who immediately saw its possibilities in helping the British maintain their widespread empire. That is why U.S.-born Maxim was eventually knighted by Queen Victoria after he became a British subject.

Born in Sangerville, ME on February 5, 1840, Maxim inherited his mechanical ability and interest in aviation from his

In 1891 Maxim built this machine for testing the efficiency of the screw-propeller and the lifting power of his airplane design.

father, who designed a two-rotor helicopter. The craft was never built because a practical engine was not available—a fact that would later influence Maxim aeronautical experiments. With less than five years of formal education, Maxim left home and wandered the eastern U.S. and Canada working at a variety of jobs, studying science and engineering in his spare time. By the time he was 24 he was in New York working as a draftsman at his uncle's iron works.

He carried out important pioneering work in the field of electric lighting and was on the verge of producing a practical incandescent light bulb in 1879 when Thomas Edison patented his famous "light in a vacuum." This interest had been spurred by his job with one the first electric companies in the U.S. Eventually his mechanical ability and fertile imagination led him to form a company which produced everything from mousetraps to automatic sprinkler systems. With his gun factory in England a financial success, he was now able to pursue an interest of long standing–aeronautics.

Over the years the thought of flight had intrigued Maxim, so in 1891 he took a scientific approach to studying the problem of flight. He first studied wing forms and propellers using a whirling arm, then a wind tunnel to determine the best configurations for flight. The next step was to solve the problem of engine power, maintaining that "without a doubt the motor is the chief thing to be considered. Scientists have long said, give us a motor and we will very soon give you a successful flying machine." With this in mind he developed a light-weight 180 horsepower steam engine—he was skeptical about the reliability of the internal combustion engine. Two of these steam engines would be required to power the design that came off Maxim's drawing board.

The gigantic multi-engine craft measured roughly 200 feet from front to back and had a 108-foot wingspan and two 18-foot propellers. With a gross weight of 8,000 lbs., including the three person crew, the craft would have a total lifting surface of 4,000 square feet. Maxim calculated that his two steam engines would produce a combined thrust of 2,000 lbs. and, at 40 mph with wings at 7¼° pitch, a total lift force of 10,000 lbs.

Keeping in mind the money, time, and work involved in his craft, Maxim installed an elevator fore and aft and set outer wing panels at a dihedral angle to provide stability. He maintained, unlike Lilienthal, that human skill was totally inadequate for maintaining equilibrium. To further protect his craft, he built a 1,800' dual rail "runway" that consisted of a lower heavy steel rail for the craft's four red-painted cast iron wheels and a upper guiderail of 3 by 9 inch Georgia pine to keep the craft from escaping into uncontrolled flight.

Experiments began in late 1892 and journalist H.J.W. Dam described his 1893 flight in Maxim's craft this way. "A rope was pulled, the machine shot forward like a railway train, and, with the big wheels whirling, the steam hissing, and the waste pipes puffing and gurgling, flew over the 1,800 feet of track in much less time then it takes to tell it." Although Maxim's test runs were marred by a series of breakdowns and mishaps, none were serious enough to stop his experiments—not until July 31, 1894, that is. On this day his craft lifted off the ground as usual—only this time one of the upper guiderails snapped allowing the machine to float through the air. But not for long. The flight came to an abrupt end when a piece of the broken rail smashed into one of the propellers. It is interesting to speculate how long his enormous machine would have sustained powered flight if it had not been for that chunk of wood.

Even though Maxim had proved his theory that a powerful engine could lift a heavy object, investors were not willing to put more money into the project, and Maxim was too involved with his other affairs to continue his experiments. But he was optimistic about the future of aviation. In 1893 before his experiments came to an abrupt halt, he told a journalist, even "under the most unfavorable circumstances aerial navigation will be an accomplished fact inside of ten years."

Once upon a time there were two gentlemen from Dayton at a place called Kitty Hawk… ■

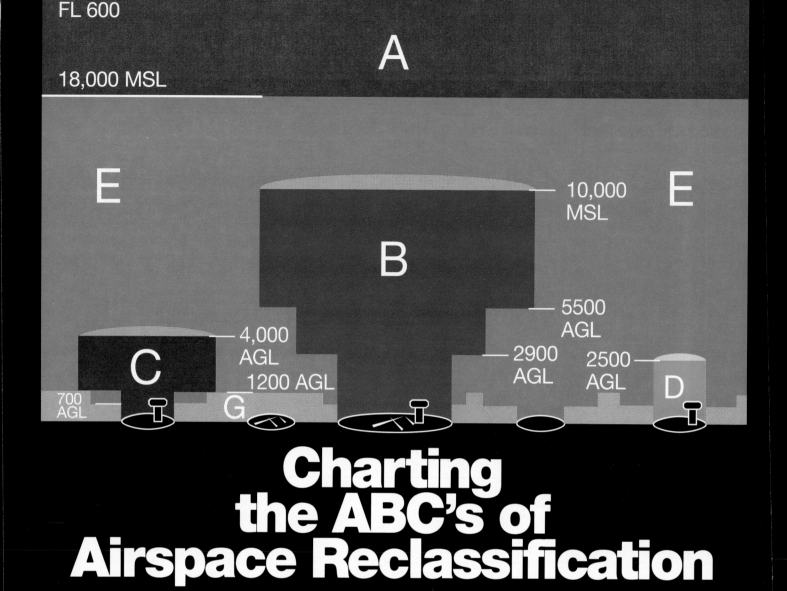

FL 600

A

18,000 MSL

E

E

10,000 MSL

B

5500 AGL

4,000 AGL

2900 AGL

2500 AGL

C

1200 AGL

D

700 AGL

G

F

Charting the ABC's of Airspace Reclassification

by Louise Oertly, Associate Editor

J ust in case you have been busy with election year politicking and not heard yet, on September 16, 1993, a new rule on airspace reclassification goes into effect—an event most airspace users are apprehensive about. Instead of the more familiar acronyms (ATA, TCA, etc.), the rule will establish six classes of U.S. airspace that will be designated by a single letter of the alphabet—A, B, C, D, E, and G (but no F; the International Civil Aviation Organization's Class F—ATC provides separation service to IFR aircraft so far as practical—has no equivalent in U.S. airspace). As daunting as this may sound, in fact there are very few changes to the FAR and those

changes that have been made are favorable to pilots. Basically, the airspace reclassification rule eliminates much of the overlapping airspace confusion. The main problem will be the re-education of all airspace users from the low-time student to the high-time ATP. FAA and industry will soon have videos and publications ready for Accident Prevention Program meetings.

In our March/April 1992 issue, the article, "The ABC's of Airspace Reclassification," explained how the rule came about. To help you make a smoother transition into the new system, this article explains each class; compares VFR and IFR operations; lists any rule changes; and shows how it will appear

on aeronautical, planning, and route charts. The first phase of airspace reclassification goes into effect on October 15, 1992, when changes begin appearing on VFR charting products. An insert explaining these changes will be provided with the charts, but we have printed them in this article grouped with the airspace they affect.

The FAA's goal in reclassifying the airspace is to simplify the airspace designations and to standardize equipment and pilot requirements for operation in U.S. airspace, not to confuse you. And this thought may help—you are not alone—even FAA's inspectors and air traffic controllers have to be re-educated too.

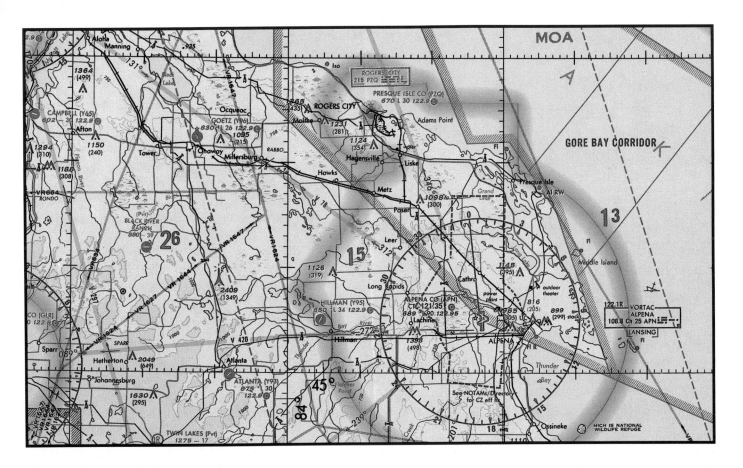

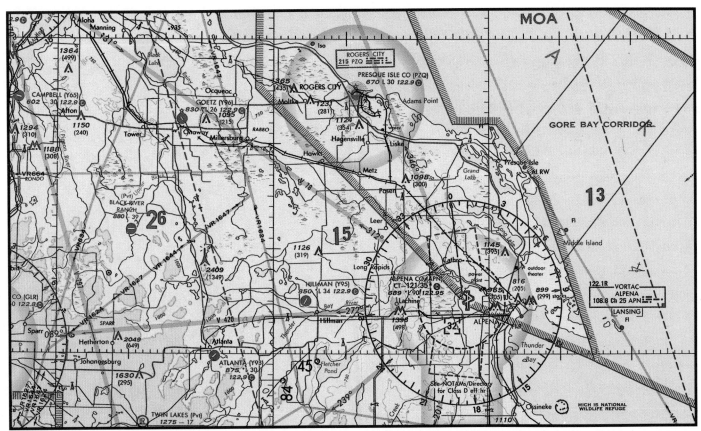

Look familiar? Above is a portion of the Lake Huron sectional chart with the old symbology for the control zone at Alpena. As of October 15, that same portion of the chart (below) will have a different look. The new symbology tells you that it is a control zone with a tower and with arrival extensions without communications requirements. (NOT TO BE USED FOR NAVIGATIONAL PURPOSES.)

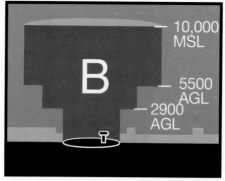

CLASS A
[Positive Control Area (PCA)]

- JET ROUTES
- AREA HIGH ROUTES
- OFFSHORE ADDITIONAL CONTROL AREAS AT OR ABOVE 18,000' MSL

CLASS A AIRSPACE	IFR	VFR
Operations Permitted	Yes	No
Entry Prerequisites	ATC Clearance	n/a
Minimum Pilot Qualifications	Instrument Rating	n/a
Two-way Radio Communications	Yes	n/a
Aircraft Separation	All	n/a
Differs from ICAO	No	n/a
Changes Existing Rule(s)	No	n/a

CHART INFORMATION

Not Pertinent to VFR Chart.

CLASS B
[Equivalent—Terminal Control Areas (TCA)]

CLASS B AIRSPACE	IFR	VFR
Operations Permitted	Yes	Yes
Entry Prerequisites	ATC Clearance	ATC Clearance
Minimum Pilot Qualifications	Instrument Rating Certificate	Private or Student
Two-way Radio Communications	Yes	Yes
Aircraft Separation	All	All
Traffic Advisories	Yes	Yes
Safety Alerts	Yes	Yes
Minimum Flight Visibility	n/a	3 Statute Miles
Minimum Distance from Clouds	n/a	Clear of Clouds
Differs from ICAO	Yes*	Yes*
Changes Existing Rule(s)	No	Yes**

* ICAO does not have speed restriction in Class B. U.S. will retain 250 KIAS rule below 10,000' MSL.
** Reduces cloud clearance from standard to clear of clouds.

CHART INFORMATION

There are no charting symbology changes. However, beginning on October 15, 1992, the control zones associated with any airport in the Terminal Control Area (TCA) surface area will cease to be charted. The control zones will continue to legally exist until the TCA's become Class B airspace on September 16, 1993. See page 16 for the new symbology for Part 93— Fixed Wing Special VFR Flight. On a VFR chart a box indicates Part 93 and "No SVFR" indicates that fixed wing SVFR operations are prohibited.

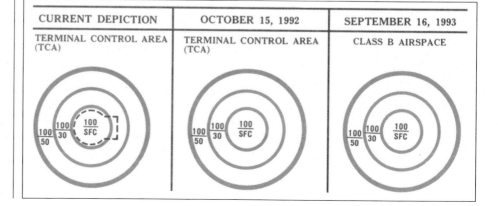

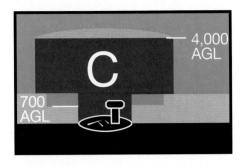

CLASS C
[Equivalent—Airport Radar Service Areas (ARSA)]

CLASS C AIRSPACE	IFR	VFR
Operations Permitted	Yes	Yes
Entry Prerequisites	ATC Clearance	Radio Contact
Minimum Pilot Qualifications	Instrument Rating	Private or Student Certificate
Two-way Radio Communications	Yes	Yes
Aircraft Separation	All	Between IFR & VFR
Traffic Advisories	Yes	Yes
Safety Alerts	Yes	Yes
Minimum Flight Visibility	n/a	3 Statute Miles
Minimum Distance from Clouds	n/a	500'Below, 1,000'Above 2,000' Horizontal
Differs from ICAO	Yes*	Yes**
Changes Existing Rule(s)	No	No

* ICAO does not have speed restriction. U.S. will retain 250KIAS rule below 10,000' MSL and 200KIAS below 2,500' AGL within 4NM of the primary airport.
** ICAO requires ATC clearance.

CHART INFORMATION

On April 2, 1992, Terminal Radar Service Areas (TRSA) began to be depicted with a solid black line. This interim conversion will be completed August 20, 1992. TRSA's, as entities, will not become an airspace class on September 16, 1993. Beginning on October 15, 1992, the solid magenta line formerly used for TRSA's is used for Airport Radar Service Areas (ARSA). This change will be completed on sectional and terminal area charts by March 4, 1993. Also beginning on October 15, 1992, the Control Zones associated with any airport in the ARSA surface area will coincide with the ARSA surface area and cease to be charted. The ARSA's will become Class C airspace on September 16, 1993. Any extension of a control zone that exceeds an ARSA surface area will be depicted with a magenta segmented line. The magenta segmented line denotes controlled airspace extending upward from the surface to the overlying or adjacent controlled airspace. Such extensions will become Class E airspace on September 16, 1993. There are no operating rule changes. Pilots may continue to operate VFR underneath the ARSA/Class C shelf without contacting air traffic control.

CURRENT DEPICTION	OCTOBER 15, 1992	SEPTEMBER 16, 1993
AIRPORT RADAR SERVICE AREA (ARSA)	AIRPORT RADAR SERVICE AREA (ARSA)	CLASS C AIRSPACE

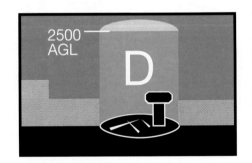

CLASS D
[Equivalent—Airport Traffic Areas (ATA) and Control Zones (CZ)]

- **AIRSPACE REQUIRING COMMUNICATIONS WITH ATC BY VFR AIRCRAFT**
- **TOWERED CONTROL ZONES**
- **TOWERED AIRPORTS WITHOUT STANDARD INSTRUMENT APPROACH PROCEDURES**

CLASS D AIRSPACE	IFR	VFR
Operations Permitted	Yes	Yes
Entry Prerequisites	ATC Clearance	Radio Contact
Minimum Pilot Qualifications	Instrument Rating	Student Certificate
Two-way Radio Communications	Yes	Yes
Aircraft Separation	IFR & SVFR	n/a
Traffic Advisories	Workload Permitting	Workload Permitting
Safety Alerts	Yes	Yes
Minimum Flight Visibility	n/a	3 Statute Miles
Minimum Distance from Clouds	n/a	500'Below, 1,000'Above 2,000' Horizontal
Differs from ICAO	No	Yes*
Changes Existing Rule(s)	Yes**	Yes**

* ICAO requires ATC clearance.
** Generally, the upper limits of the Control Zone lowered from 14,500' MSL to 2,500' AGL and Air Traffic Area lowered from 2,999' AGL to 2,500' AGL. Communications required.

CHART INFORMATION

Those Control Zones (CZ) with an operating control tower will continue to be depicted with a blue segmented line. The vertical limit, in MSL, in now charted in hundredths of feet. The Air Traffic Area (ATA) and its communications requirement with air traffic control remains until September 16, 1993, at which time a like communications requirement for all aircraft within the Class D airspace is established.

Arrival extensions will either be charted as part of the basic surface area with the blue segmented symbology or as a separate surface area indicated by the magenta segmented line. Communications with air traffic control are not required within the airspace encompassed by the magenta lines which will be Class E airspace.

CURRENT DEPICTION	OCTOBER 15, 1992	SEPTEMBER 16, 1993
CONTROL ZONE	CONTROL ZONE WITH TOWER	CLASS D AIRSPACE
CONTROL ZONES ARE SHOWN ON ALL VFR CHARTS	CONTROL ZONE WITH TOWER AND EXTENSION WITHOUT COMMUNICATIONS REQUIREMENT	CLASS D AIRSPACE WITH ASSOCIATED CLASS E AIRSPACE

18,000 MSL

E

CLASS E
[Equivalent—Controlled Airspace—General]

- **NONTOWERED CONTROL ZONES**
- **700 FOOT TRANSITION AREAS**
- **1,200 FOOT TRANSITION AREAS**
- **FEDERAL AIRWAYS**
- **OFFSHORE CONTROL AREAS BELOW 18,000' MSL**
- **ADDITIONAL CONTROL AREAS BELOW 18,000' MSL**
- **CONTINENTAL CONTROL AREA**

CLASS E AIRSPACE	IFR	VFR
Operations Permitted	Yes	Yes
Entry Prerequisites	ATC Clearance	None
Minimum Pilot Qualifications	Instrument Rating	Student Certificate
Two-way Radio Communications	Yes	No
Aircraft Separation	IFR & SVFR	n/a
Traffic Advisories	Workload Permitting	Workload Permitting
Safety Alerts	Yes	Yes
Minimum Flight Visibility	n/a	3 Statute Miles*
Minimum Distance from Clouds	n/a	500' Below,** 1,000' Above 2,000' Horizontal
Differs from ICAO	No	No
Changes Existing Rule(s)	No	No

* Operations at or above 10,000' MSL—5 statute miles.

** Operations at or above 10,000' MSL—1,000' below, 1,000' above, 1 statute mile horizontal.

CHART INFORMATION

Beginning October 15, 1992, Control Zones (CZ) without an operating control tower will be depicted with a magenta segmented line which denotes controlled airspace extending upward from the surface to the overlying or the floor of the adjacent controlled airspace; therefore, the vertical limit is not depicted.

Effective October 15, 1992, the blue vignette (light-blue shaded) line will not be used to depict the 1,200 foot or above airspace, unless it abuts uncontrolled airspace. Where the outer edge of the 700 foot transition area (magenta vignette) ends, the 1,200 foot or greater area automatically begins. Effective September 16, 1993, these areas become Class E airspace extending upward from other than the surface.

New symbology will be used beginning October 15, 1992, to depict the boundary of controlled airspace with floors other than 700 feet or 1,200 feet. This symbology will also be used to distinguish the floors of the domestic offshore areas and the offshore control areas beyond 12 NM of the U.S. coast.

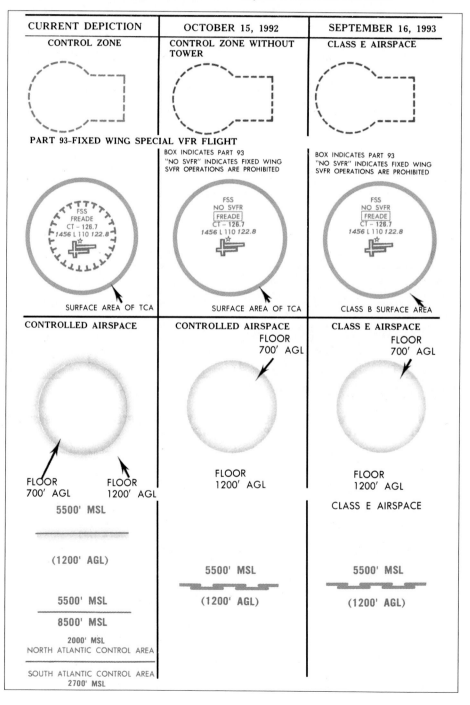

14,500 MSL

CLASS G

[Equivalent—Uncontrolled Airspace] As noted in the illustrations, there will continue to be airports in Class G airspace. At those airports with an instrument approach procedure, the floor of controlled airspace will generally be a Class E area extending upward from 700' AGL. There are no charting or operating rule changes.

CLASS G AIRSPACE	IFR	VFR
Operations Permitted	Yes	Yes
Entry Prerequisites	None	None
Minimum Pilot Qualifications	Instrument Rating	Student Certificate
Two-way Radio Communications	No	No
Aircraft Separation	None	None
Traffic Advisories	Workload Permitting	Workload Permitting
Safety Alerts	Yes	Yes
Minimum Flight Visibility	n/a	1 Statute Mile*
Minimum Distance from Clouds	n/a	Clear of Clouds**
Differs from ICAO	No	Yes***
Changes Existing Rule(s)	No	No

* Operations at or above 10,000' MSL—5 statute miles; Night operations below 10,000' MSL—3 statute miles; day or night operations at or above 10,000'MSL—5 statute miles.

** Operations more than 1,200' AGL, but less than 10,000' MSL–500' below, 1,000' above, 2,000' horizontal. Operations at or above 10,000' MSL—1,000' below, 1,000' above, 1 statute mile horizontal.

*** ICAO requires 3 statute miles visibility

CURRENT DEPICTION	OCTOBER 15, 1992	SEPTEMBER 16, 1993
UNCONTROLLED AIRSPACE	UNCONTROLLED AIRSPACE	CLASS G AIRSPACE
1200' OR GREATER CONTROLLED AIRSPACE	1200' OR GREATER CONTROLLED AIRSPACE	1200' OR GREATER CLASS E AIRSPACE

The pilot of this Piper Cheyenne III *flies away safe in the knowledge of the new airspace reclassification systems. How about you?*

International Altimetry

by Perry Thomas, ASRS Analyst

This is the first in a series of articles reprinted from ASRS Directline, a quarterly publication that addresses particular areas of safety that appear in pilot reports received by NASA's Aviation Safety Reporting System. (ASRS Directline is free from ASRS, NASA-Ames Research Center, Moffett Field, CA 94035.) More and more private aircraft are making international flights, so if you are contemplating such a journey and a hectopascal sounds foreign to you, read on. **—Editor**

The use of Hecto Pascal or Millibars by some countries has, on occasion, caused experienced international flight crews, who are accustomed to inches of mercury, to incorrectly set their aircraft altimeters.

Europe

"[A] three-man, wide-body type aircraft flight crew experienced in European operations" was engaged in a difficult (nine degrees drift over water in heavy rain) VOR-DME approach to an MDA of 420 feet. The transition altitude had been 4,000 feet so the experienced, but weary, flight crew was late receiving ATIS, reducing the time available for completing their landing data. QNH was given as 9–9–1."

The first officer was flying the approach, and the captain called 1,000 feet MSL in descent. Shortly thereafter, the second officer called, "300 feet radar altitude—go around!" A missed approach was flown, and the "captain questioned the tower about [the] altimeter setting. . .29.91. . .this was confirmed. A second voice, however, corrected that statement to 991 *millibars*" [emphasis added].

The aircraft's altimeters were reset from 29.91 to 991 millibars—a 640-foot difference (see Figure 1). The flight crew later calculated they had come within 160 feet of hitting the water.

Was this merely an isolated incident? Here is another occurrence from the other side of the world.

The Orient

It was the end of a long overwater flight:

"Approach control gave the altimeter as 998 hectopascal. I read back 29.98. [The] approach controller repeated his original statement. Forgetting that our altimeters have settings for millibars and hectopascal (which I had only used once in my career and that was six months ago), I asked where the conversion chart was. 'Old hand' captain told me that approach meant 29.98. Assuming that he knew what he was doing, I believed him. We were a bit low on a ragged approach, and I knew we were awfully close to some of the hills that dot the area. . . but it was not until we landed and our altimeters read 500 feet low that I realized what had happened."

Quotes from Other ASRS Reports

"Never having used mb before, the significant of 971 mb wasn't apparent to me until I read the equivalent Hg 26.68."

"Dealing in millibars did not make an impression. . . [because of] the very low [atmospheric] pressure."

The "copilot who had copied the ATIS gave me 2997 when I asked for QNH. Gusty winds and [the controller's] thick accent weren't helping things. [Obstructions] seemed unusually close to our altitude. [The] copilot had assumed 9–9–7 to be 29.97." (500 feet low)

"[Given] altimeter of niner-seven-eight hPa. The [words] hPa were somewhat muted. We set 29.78 [inches]." (900 feet low)

Factors

Several human and procedural factors appear to increase the possibility of incorrectly set altimeters in international operations.

The Question of Q's

We all tend to forget things we either have not used in a while or that we do not use very often. For those of us who need a memory refresher, here are three important "Q" altimeter settings.

QNE: The standard altimeter setting of 29.92 inches of mercury (Hg) or 1013.25 hectopascal (hPa) or 1013.25 millibars (mb). (See the sidebar "What's a Pascal" on p. 19 to find out why hPa and mb are the same.)
- ON THE GROUND—a variable elevation reading that is above or below actual elevation (unless the station pressure happens to equal 29.92 Hg).
- IN THE AIR—positive separation by pressure level but at varying actual or true altitudes.

QNH: Height above sea level when corrections are applied for local atmospheric pressure that is above or below the standard altimeter setting of 29.92 Hg. QNH is the altimeter setting provided in the ATIS information and by ATC.
- ON THE GROUND—the actual elevation above sea level when the aircraft is on the ground.
- IN THE AIR—the true height above sea level without consideration of temperature.

QFE: An altimeter setting that is corrected for actual height above sea level and local pressure variations.
- ON THE GROUND—zero elevation when the aircraft is on the ground. Thus, for an aircraft at the gate at Denver (actual airport elevation above sea level, 5,333 feet) the aircraft altimeters would read zero if set to QFE.
- IN THE AIR—the height above ground without consideration of temperature.

Fatigue

International flights from the United States are generally of long duration through several time zones. The element of fatigue in long distance flights is inescapable.

Workload on Approach

Transition from standard altimeter setting flight levels (QNE) to sea level altimeter setting altitudes (QNH) are at generally much lower altitudes than in the United States. Many countries provide altimeter settings corrected for actual height above sea level and local pressure variations (QFE) which alone can cause significant confusion for pilots used to flying QNH. Obtaining altimeter setting and landing data closer to the approach segment complicates the task of preparing data for landing at the very time the flight crew may be most fatigued.

Language Difficulties

Rapid delivery of clearances coupled with unfamiliar accents and contraction of hectopascal (hPa) or millibars (mb) increase the potential for error.

Communication Procedure

Only *one* person receiving the approach and landing data then passing that information to the rest of the crew means that a misconception or misunderstanding is less likely to be detected until too late.

Cockpit Management

There is often inadequate crew briefing for approach and landing with no mention of how the altimeter setting will be expressed—that is, Hg, mb, or hPa. Flight crews also may not adequately review approach charts for information. Some airlines do not provide the second officer with approach plates. Unless he or she makes an extra effort to look at one of the pilot's charts, the altimeter setting standard may be unknown.

Experience Level and Currency

At least one airline experiences a constant turnover in the international group as senior pilots retire and other crew members bid off international schedules to upgrade to captain or first officer. Many of the international reports submitted to ASRS mention that at least one flight crew member is new to the operation. Airline training is

---

What's a Pascal?

The term "hectopascal" is derived partly from the name of a 17th century philosopher and mathematician and partly from the Greek.

Blaise Pascal was born in 1623 in France. A youthful genius in mathematics, at age 21 he developed and built the first digital computer. Pascal's Law of Pressure was developed in 1647 and is the principle that created hydraulic lifts and eventually the hydraulic brakes in our automobiles. Using Evangelista Torricelli's work on the principle of the barometer, Pascal developed his own method of measuring barometric pressure.

Hecto is an irregular contraction of the Greek word for hundred from the metric system of measurement— hence hecto pascal, often abbreviated to HP or hPa. In common usage, one hPa equals one millibar.

---

usually reported as being adequate, but some of the training for international operations may not be used or need to be recalled for months after the training is received.

Recommendations

- Review approach charts before the descent, approach, and landing phase. Each flight crew member should pay particular attention to whether altimeter settings will be given in inches (Hg), millibars (mb), or hectopascal (hPa).

- Use precise radio phraseology; confirm with ATC any radio communication that is not fully understood. (Radio phraseology considered "acceptable" in one country may not be accepted or understood in another.)

- Keep more than one flight crew member in the communications loop—including for ATC clearances and ATIS messages.

- Practice good cockpit management technique. Include in the approach briefing how the altimeter setting will be expressed.

- Observe proper crew coordination. Flight crews need to cross check each other for accurate communication and procedure. Question anything that does not seem right.

Some of the aspects involved, such as fatigue, will be more difficult to overcome. Implementing sterile cockpit procedures, avoiding distractions during periods of high cockpit workload, and getting adequate crew rest and nourishment will help to avoid those famous last words—I ASSUMED. ■

The Aviation Safety Reporting System is a cooperative program established by the FAA's Office of the Assistant Administrator for Aviation Safety and administered by the National Aeronautics and Space Administration.

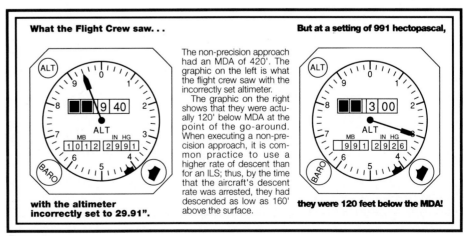

What the Flight Crew saw . . .

But at a setting of 991 hectopascal,

The non-precision approach had an MDA of 420'. The graphic on the left is what the flight crew saw with the incorrectly set altimeter.

The graphic on the right shows that they were actually 120' below MDA at the point of the go-around. When executing a non-precision approach, it is common practice to use a higher rate of descent than for an ILS; thus, by the time that the aircraft's descent rate was arrested, they had descended as low as 160' above the surface.

with the altimeter incorrectly set to 29.91".

they were 120 feet below the MDA!

Figure 1

Aviation Maintenance Technician
Awards Program

by Bill O'Brien, National Resource Specialist–Sport Aviation Airworthiness, AFS–310

We rarely appreciate someone who is always there—the man or woman who works alongside us, giving a hundred percent, whose only thanks most of the time is the satisfaction in a job well done. Unbelievably, sometimes we put these people down because their job might not be as glamorous or as neat and clean as our own.

Aircraft mechanics and technicians must surely be at the top of the list of professionals who are taken for granted. Why is this so? There are probably several reasons, but if we have to blame someone, maybe it would be Hollywood for the creation of the stereotypical greasy mechanic in the movies or perhaps the producers of the TV sit-com *Wings* who created "Lowell," the room temperature IQ mechanic. It's about time for a change!

To initiate that change, on October 1, 1992 the FAA will implement the Aviation Maintenance Technician Awards Program. This new awards program will recognize the maintenance technician when he or she completes a certain number of hours of training every year. However, the FAA will also put a different "spin" on this awards program by also recognizing the maintenance technician's employer's investment in recurrent training. Why? It is the employer who must bear the burden of training costs and the short-term loss of productivity.

The awards for both the technician and employer are broken down into five phases, and qualifications for each phase get progressively more extensive.

Awards Program Overview

The awards program is actually two separate programs—one for technicians and one for employers. The technician's award will be in the form of an FAA "Certificate of Training" and a tie tack/lapel pin for each phase successfully completed, similar in spirit to the Accident Prevention Program's "Wings" (and not to be confused with that aforementioned sitcom). The employer's award will be in the form of an FAA "Certificate of Excellence" and will be based on the percentage of maintenance technicians who have received any one of the five FAA Certificates of Training in the past calendar year. Both the technician and the employer awards are divided into Phases I–V.

The program is designed so that each additional phase (award) is more demanding than the preceding one. In order to be eligible for an award the requirements for the particular phase must be completed within a calendar year.

History of the Aviation Maintenance Technician Award Logo

The logo that will be used for the Aviation Technician Awards Program lapel pins was one of 11 designs submitted by mechanics and technicians in response to articles in *FAA Aviation News* (November/December 1990) and *Aviation Equipment Magazine* (September 1990). Over 300 mechanics who attended maintenance seminars in Lafayette, LA, Pittsburgh, PA, and Trenton, NJ were asked to choose the best logo from the 11 designs submitted. The design was chosen because of the following reasons:

- It is the exact size and shape of a standard AN-5 fastener (1/2 inch across); this represents the strength in maintaining a common standard of integrity and trust.

- The two perfect circles within the hexagon represent the continuing cycle of maintenance and inspection which must be unbroken and perfect today and every day to ensure aviation safety.

- The formula—Knowledge + Professionalism = Safety—is not only the aviation maintenance industry's commitment to maintaining the aircraft entrusted to their care but a personnel commitment as well.

- The two aircraft located in the center of the logo represent the 1903 Wright Brothers flyer superimposed over the proposed 2001 space plane. The Wright Flyer represents the maintenance community's proud past by the fact that the Wright Brothers mechanic, Mr. Charles Taylor, the first aircraft mechanic, was there at the very beginnings of aviation. The space plane, with its technological advancements and low orbit capability represents our bright future of the maintenance profession.

The aviation maintenance community and the FAA believe that this symbol represents the best of what the aviation maintenance industry has to offer. It will take hard work to earn it. It should be worn with pride!

Eligibility Requirements for Technician and Employers

The following individuals are eligible for the technician award:

1. An FAA-certificated mechanic or repairman.
2. A student in a FAR Part 147 school who is maintaining a course average of C or better.
3. FAR Part 147 school instructors.
4. Avionics, propeller, and instrument technicians.
5. Any individual who is employed full-time by a FAR Part 121, 135, or 145 operator who actively performs maintenance on aircraft or their component parts.

To be eligible for the employer's award the employer must:

1. Be involved full-time in the business of maintaining or repairing aircraft and/or their component parts.
2. Employ at least five full-time technicians.

Phase Requirements and Description for Technicians

A technician may apply for one of the five awards as long as the following requirements are satisfied.

For the Phase I or Bronze award, the technician must have completed at least four hours of FAA or industry training in the prescribed calendar year.

The Phase II or Silver award requires that the technician attend one FAA or industry maintenance seminar, and satisfactorily complete eight hours of FAA or industry training.

The technician receives the Phase III or Gold award when he or she has attended one FAA or industry maintenance seminar, and has satisfactorily completed a three-day FAA or industry training seminar.

The Phase IV or Ruby award comes when the technician has attended one FAA or industry maintenance seminar, and has satisfactorily completed a five-day FAA or industry training seminar or has taught a three-day (15-hour) maintenance course on aircraft systems.

For the final award, Phase V or Diamond, the technician must have attended one FAA or industry maintenance seminar, have satisfactorily completed a five-day FAA or industry training seminar or have taught a three-day (15-hour) maintenance course on aircraft systems, and have satisfactorily completed a college-level course in either management or technical subjects

Phase Requirements for Employers

When a specific percentage of employees in a maintenance organization has received any one of the five phases of awards within the calendar year, that employer becomes eligible for one of the five "Certificates of Excellence." The percentages are as follows:

5% for a Bronze Certificate of Excellence
10% for a Silver Certificate of Excellence
15% for a Gold Certificate of Excellence
20% for a Ruby Certificate of Excellence
25% for a Diamond Certificate of Excellence

Applying for an Award

At any time during the calendar year any eligible technician can apply either in person or by letter to the local FAA Flight Standards District Office (FSDO) for an award. The technician must show that he or she is eligible. First, there must be acceptable proof that the individual is indeed an aviation maintenance technician. This proof may be in the form of either an FAA mechanic or repairman certificate, a statement from a FAR Part 147 school certifying that the student is maintaining at least a C average, a statement from a FAR Part 147 School certifying that the individual is an instructor at that school, or a statement from a FAR Part 121, 135, or 145 operator certifying that the individual is employed by that operator to maintain aircraft or related components.

The second required item is a short, signed and dated letter to the local FSDO describing the phase requested, where the training was received, who did the training, what training was received, how long the training was in hours, and the date of the training.

The third required item is some form of proof that the training was received. Copies of a certificate of training, attendance, or graduation are acceptable as long as they corroborate the information supplied in the letter.

At any time during the calendar year an eligible employer can apply by letter to the local FSDO for an award. The employer's letter should state the award requested, that the organization works full-time on aircraft or their component parts, and that the total number of technicians working full-time is at least five. The employer should attach copies of employees' FAA Certificates of Training dated for the applicable calendar year.

Both the technician and employer should allow at least 30 days for the FSDO to process the award request. But this small delay in recognition is short considering the U.S. Government has been certificating mechanics for 66 years. The time has come to recognize these hard-working, dedicated people who play a large part in the achievement of the outstanding safety record of U.S. registered aircraft.

And on October 1, 1992, we will! ■

Definitions

Training Seminar is defined as a formal meeting at least four hours in length in which technical training is conducted. Seminar training sessions at least an hour long may be combined to meet the four-hour requirement.

Validation means proof of attending a maintenance seminar in the form of a certificate that shows the date, instructor, location, and subjects covered.

For the purpose of this awards program, ***calendar year*** is defined as the period of time from October 1 of one year to September 30 of the following year.

STATUS OF THE FAR

As promised, the *FAA Aviation News* is publishing an annual listing of the Federal Aviation Regulations (FAR) in loose-leaf form and their latest changes and prices. Many of the FAR are reprinted commercially, some in book form. It is important to keep in mind that the rules are amended often in some cases, and existing provisions may be nullified or changed by this process unless they are updated continuously. Commercial publications may or may not provide updates.

The FAR are sold in two ways by the Superintendent of Documents—subscription and single sales. When you order a subscription, for which there is an annual change, the changes will be sent to you automatically as they are issued. Single sales are a different matter. The changes to these parts are infrequent, and no direct notice of a change is sent out. Therefore, you must order and pay for each change as it is issued.

Another way of obtaining the FAR is to purchase the bound volumes of the U.S. Code of Federal Regulations. Three volumes of Title 14 contain the Federal Aviation Regulations:

Parts 1–59	(SN 869–017–00042–6)	$25.00
Parts 60–139	(SN 869–017–00043–4)	$22.00
Parts 140–199	(SN 869–017–00044–2)	$11.00

These volumes are only updated annually, so the latest changes would have to be obtained from another source.

The following pages contain the current status and price list for the loose-leaf FAR. Color highlighting indicates those rules considered of special interest to general aviation pilots. To order any of the FAR parts, send check, money order, or credit card number to the Superintendent of Documents, U.S. Government Printing Office, Washington, DC 20402–9325. Add a 25% charge for foreign mailing on the single sale items. Remember to use the stock number.

Parts Sold on Subscription Service

Part	Title	Code Letter	Price Domestic	Foreign	Changes Issued
1	Definitions and Abbreviations	FA001	30.00	37.50	—
11	General Rule-making Procedures	FA011	30.00	37.00	—
13	Investigative and Enforcement Procedures	FA013	30.00	37.50	12
21	Certification Procedures for Products and Parts	FA021	34.00	42.50	35
23	Airworthiness Standards: Normal, Utility, Acrobatic, and Commuter Category Airplanes	FA023	35.00	43.75	30
25	Airworthiness Standards: Transport Category Airplanes	FA025	39.00	48.75	31
27	Airworthiness Standards: Normal Category Rotorcraft	FA027	35.00	43.75	23
29	Airworthiness Standards: Transport Category Rotorcraft	FA029	36.00	45.00	25
33	Airworthiness Standards: Aircraft Engines	FA033	27.00	33.75	9

Parts Sold on Subscription Service

Part	Title	Code Letter	Price Domestic	Foreign	Changes Issued
36	Noise Standards: Aircraft Type and Airworthiness Certification	FA036	32.00	40.00	23
43	Maintenance, Preventive Maintenance, Rebuilding, and Alterations	FA043	32.00	40.00	—
45	Identification and Registration Marking	FA045	30.00	37.50	16
47	Aircraft Registration	FA047	28.00	35.00	8
61	Certification: Pilot sand Flight Instructors	FA061	36.00	45.00	27
63	Certification: Flight Crewmembers Other Than Pilots	FA063	33.00	41.25	13
65	Certification: Airmen Other Than Flight Crewmembers	FA065	30.00	37.50	15
71	Designation of Federal Airways, Area Low Routes Controlled Airspace, and Reporting Points, Jet Routes, and Area High Routes[3]	FA071	29.00	36.25	—
91	General Operating and Flight Rules *Preamblefree	FA091	53.00	66.25	—
93	Special Air Traffic Rules and Airport Traffic Patterns	FA093	31.00	38.75	27
103	Ultralight Vehicles	FA103	32.00	40.00	5
108	Airplane Operator Security	FA108	29.00	36.25	10
121	Certification and Operations: Domestic, Flag, and Supplemental Air Carriers and Commercial Operators of Large Aircraft	FA121	60.00	75.00	82
125	Certification and Operations: Airplanes Having a Seating Capacity of 20 or More Passengers or a Maximum Payload Capacity of 6,000 Pounds or More	FA125	32.00	40.00	20
127	Certification and Operations of Scheduled Air Carriers With Helicopters	FA127	31.00	38.75	22
129	Operations:Foreign Air Carriers and Foreign Operators of U.S.-Registered Aircraft Engaged in Common Carriage	FA129	30.00	37.50	22
135	Air Taxi Operators and Commercial Operators	FA135	45.00	56.25	40
137	Agricultural Aircraft Operations	FA137	32.00	40.00	8
139	Certification and Operations: Land Airports Serving Certain Air Carriers	FA139	29.00	36.25	3
145	Repair Stations	FA145	29.00	36.25	10
150	Airport Noise Compatibility Planning	FA150	30.00	37.50	2
152	Airport Aid Program	FA152	31.00	38.75	12
159	National Capital Airports	FA159	30.00	37.50	13
161	Notice and Approval of Airport Noise and Access Restrictions	FA161	29.00	36.25	—

* Not included with subscription. For a particular FAR Part 91 preamble, write to DOT, M–443.2, Washington, DC 20590.

Parts Sold on Single Sale Basis

Part	Title	Price[1]
31	Airworthiness Standards: Manned Free Balloons (SN 050–007–00246–7)	2.25
	Change 1 (050–007–00361–7)	1.75
	Change 2 (050–007–00559–8)	4.50
	Change 3 (050–007–00842–2)	1.25
34	Fuel Venting and Exhaust Emission Requirements for Turbine Engine Powered Airplanes (SN 050–007–00883–0)	1.00
35	Airworthiness Standards: Propellers (SN 050–007–00247–5)	2.75
	Change 1 (050–007–00363–3)	3.25
	Change 2 (050–007–00369–2)	3.00
	Change 3 (050–007–00558–0)	4.50
	Change 4(050–007–00845–7)	1.25
39	Airworthiness Directives[2] (SN 050–007–00229–7)	1.75
49	Recording of Aircraft Titles and Security Documents (SN 050–007–00232–7)	1.75
	Change 1 (050–007–00336–6)	2.00
	Change 2 (050–007–00792–2)	1.00
67	Medical Standards and Certification (SN 050–007–00248–3)	3.50
	Change 1 (050–007–00341–2)	1.75
	Change 2 (050–007–00611–0)	4.50
	Change 3 (050–007–00617–9)	2.75
	Change 4 (050–007–00861–9)	1.00
	Change 5 (050–007–00882–1)	1.25
73	Special Use Airspace[3] (SN 050–007–00274–2)	1.75
	Change 1 (050–007–00291–2)	2.00
	Change 2 (050–007–00402–8)	1.75
	Change 3 (050–007–00815–5)	1.00
	Change 4 (050–007–00850–3)	1.00
	Change 5 (050–007–00889–9)	1.00
	Change 6 (050–007–00891–1)	1.00
75	Establishment of Jet Routes and Area High Routes[3] (SN 050–007–00275–1)	2.75
	Change 1 (050–007–00326–9)	2.00
	Change 2 (050–007–00941–1)	1.75
77	Objects Affecting Navigable Airspace (SN 050–007–00276–9)	4.50 *
	Change 1 (050–007–00855–4)	1.00
95	IFR Altitudes[3] (SN 050–007–00277–7)	1.75
	Change 1 (050–007–00285–8)	1.75
97	Standard Instrument Approach Procedures[4] (SN 050–007–00278–5)	3.00
	Change 1 (050–007–00471–1)	1.75
99	Security Control of Air Traffic (SN 050–007–00830–9)	1.75
	Change 1 (050–007–00831–7)	1.00
	Change 2 (050–007–00873–2)	1.75
101	Moored Balloons, Kites, Unmanned Rockets, and Unmanned Free Balloons (SN 050–007–00223–8)	1.75
	Change 1 (050–007–00242–4)	1.75
105	Parachute Jumping (SN 050–007–00315–3)	3.25
	Change 1 (050–007–00344–7)	1.75
	Change 2 (050–007–00431–1)	3.00
	Change 3 (050–007–00663–2)	1.25
	Change 4 (050–007–00696–9)	1.00
	Change 5 (050–007–00700–1)	1.25
	Change 6 (050–007–00744–2)	1.25

Parts Sold on Single Sale Basis

Part	Title	Price[1]
107	Airport Security (SN 050–007–00468–1)	3.50
	Change 1 (050–007–00588–1)	2.50
	Change 2 (050–007–00607–1)	2.25
	Change 3 (050–007–00736–1)	1.25
	Change 4 (050–007–00814–7)	1.25
	Change 5 (050–007–00836–8)	1.50
	Change 6 (050–007–00917–8)	2.00
109	Indirect Air Carrier Security (SN 050–007–00512–1)	1.75
	Change 1 (050–007–00856–2)	1.00
133	Rotorcraft External–load Operations (SN 050–007–00318–8)	1.75
	Change 1 (050–007–00365–0)	3.50
	Change 2 (050–007–00380–3)	2.00
	Change 3 (050–007–00389–7)	1.75
	Change 4 (050–007–00450–8)	1.75
	Change 5 (050–007–00748–5)	2.00
	Change 6 (050–007–00843–1)	1.25
	Change 7 (050–007–00874–1)	1.25
141	Pilot Schools (SN 050–007–00322–6)	3.50
	Change 1 (050–007–00620–9)	2.25
	Change 2 (050–007–00844–9)	1.75
	Change 3 (050–007–00900–3)	2.75
143	Ground Instructors (SN 050–007–00249–1)	3.00
147	Aviation Maintenance Technician Schools (SN 050–007–00250–5)	3.50
	Change 1 (050–007–00350–1)	2.25
	Change 2 (050–007–00437–1)	2.25
149	Parachute Lofts (SN 050–007–00221–1)	1.75
151	Federal Aid to Airports (SN 050–007–00261–1)	5.00
153	Acquisition of U.S. Land for Public Airports (SN 050–007–00262–9)	1.75
	Change 1 (050–007–00858–9)	1.00
154	Acquisition of U.S. Land for Public Airports Under the Airport and Airway Development Act of 1970 (SN 050–007–00269–6)	1.75
	Change 1 (050–007–00388–9)	1.75
	Change 2 (050–007–00549–1)	1.75
155	Release of Airport Property from Surplus Property Disposal Restrictions (SN 050–007–00270–0)	1.75
	Change 1 (050–007–00550–4)	1.75
157	Notice of Construction, Alteration, Activation, and Deactivation of Airports (SN 050–007–00279–3)	2.75
	Change 1 (050–007–00879–1)	1.00
	Change 2 (050–007–00895–3)	1.00
	Change 3 (050–007–00911–9)	1.00
158	Passenger Facility Charges (SN 050–007–00906–2)	1.25
169	Expenditure of Federal Funds for Non–Military Airports or Air Navigation Facilities Thereon (SN 050–007–00280–7)	2.25
	Change 1 (050–007–00851–1)	1.00
170	Establishment and Discontinuance Criteria for Airport Traffic Control Services and Navigational Facilities	1.25

Parts Sold on Single Sale Basis

Part	Title	Price[1]
	(SN 050–007–00892–9)	
171	Non–Federal Navigation Facilities (SN 050–007–00281–5)	4.50
	Change 1 (050–007–00297–1)	3.75
	Change 2 (050–007–00619–5)	5.00
	Change 3 (050–007–00676–4)	1.00
	Change 4 (050–007–00734–5)	1.50
	Change 5 (050–007–00832–5)	2.75
	Change 6 (050–007–00849–0)	1.00
183	Representatives of the Administrator (SN 050–007–00233–5)	3.00
	Change 1 (050–007–00352–8)	1.75
	Change 2 (050–007–00398–6)	1.75
	Change 3 (050–007–00503–2)	1.75
	Change 4 (050–007–00527–0)	1.75
	Change 5 (050–007–00634–9)	3.50
	Change 6 (050–007–00862–7)	1.00
185	Testimony by Employees and Production of Records in Legal Proceedings and Service of Legal Process and Pleadings (SN 050–007–00237–8)	1.75
	Change 1 (050–007–00859–7)	1.00
187	Fees (SN 050–007–00234–3)	2.75
	Change 1 (050–007–00618–7)	2.75
189	Use of Federal Aviation Administration Communication System (SN 050–007–00235–1)	2.75
	Change 1 (050–007–00867–8)	1.00
191	Withholding Security Information From Disclosure Under the Air Transportation Security Act of 1974 (SN 050–007–00359–5)	1.75
	Change 1 (050–007–00502–4)	1.75
	Change 2 (050–007–00857–1)	1.00

[1] Add 25% for foreign handling.

[2] Due to their length, complexity, and frequency of issuance, individual Airworthiness Directives (AD's) are published separately in the Federal Register. Microfiche or paper copies of the AD's in summary form are sold by DOT/FAA for the Superintendent of Documents. Ordering information is in Advisory Circular 39–6P, "Announcement of Availability—Summary of Airworthiness Directives," (free from DOT, M–443.2, Washington, DC 20590) or call 405–680–6901 for an order form.

[3] Due to their length, complexity, and frequency of issuance, individual airspace designations, airways descriptions, restricted areas, jet route descriptions, and IFR altitudes are not included in the publication of these basic Parts. Such descriptions are published in the Federal Register and depicted on appropriate aeronautical charts. Aeronautical charts can be obtained from the Distribution Branch, N/CG33, NOS, NOAA, Riverdale, MD 20737–1199.

[4] Standard Instrument Approach Procedures are published in the Federal Register by reference to FAA documents which are available for examination in the Rules Docket (AGC–10) and the National Flight Data Center, FAA Headquarters, Washington, DC, and at the appropriate FAA regional offices and Flight Inspection District Offices. These Instrument Approach Procedures Charts can be obtained from the Distribution Branch, N/CG33, National Ocean Service, NOAA, Riverdale, MD 20737–1199.

* This change incorporates Amendment 75–5 which removes and reserves Part 75, effective December 1991.

Remedial Training's New, "Blameless" Policy

FAA Administrator Richards announces new policy at Oshkosh '92.

Before the implementation of FAA's Remedial Training Program in 1990, many pilots reacted to contact with the FAA much in the same way they would a trip to the dentist. (Some might say they would prefer the dentist!) Remedial Training has gone a long way to enhance lines of communication between the FAA and its customers; yet, many potential participants still had one small, sticking point—that they had to admit to the non-compliance before being considered eligible for remedial training. Comments from aviation groups and letters like the one following, convinced us that Remedial Training should be offered to any pilot who feels he or she needs it and not be withheld in an attempt to assign blame. Consequently, FAA Administrator Thomas Richards announced on August 3 at the EAA Fly-in at Oshkosh, WI that pilots would no longer be required to admit to a violation in order to be considered eligible for the Remedial Training Program. All the other eligibility requirements remain the same, including demonstrating a cooperative attitude toward the remedial training. It really does not matter whose fault it is when non-compliance occurs; what matters is returning a safe airman to the national airspace system. If there was ever any doubt about the validity of remedial education over arbitrary punishment, read on:

FAA
Flight Standards Service

Dear Sir/Madam:

This letter is in response to the Remedial Training Program I was given for my having entered the San Diego TCA inadvertently. I feel compelled to address the real benefit of this program for its educational value rather than a penalty or punishment for an accident event. I have been a private pilot for nearly 30 years. During this time span I have accumulated only 400 hours as pilot in command. I realize that flight training and licensure were not as difficult in the 1960's as they are now. The last 250 hours of my flight time has been in the last five years in my Cessna 210. I have also maintained currency by reading magazines, the FAR, and the AIM.

I had heard terrible reports of what would happen to me if I "busted the TCA" and, therefore, approached the Letter of Investigation from the FAA Flight Standards District Office with great concern. I wasn't going to admit to anything, and I was prepared with legal counsel if things started looking serious. I truly believe the people who fly airplanes are all serious, safe pilots. None of us would intentionally fly dangerously. I realized the purpose of the TCA but tried to stay clear of it so I wouldn't be hassled. What a mistake!

Having had this experience of remedial training has been one of the best things that has happened in my flying career. The flight instructor assigned me was extremely knowledgeable and able to get his message across in a clear, concise manner. The five hours I spent with him were priceless in terms of the knowledge I gained. Now I know how to *use* the TCA, TRSA, and ARSA and how to get all the information I need to be really safe in our busy skies. After the flight instruction and ground school, I spent some time with the controllers at Miramar Naval Air Station. This experience put everything together with what I had experienced in the flight training. This also showed me the other side of whom I was talking to and how eager they are to help.

In summary I want to recommend the Remedial Training Program to all pilots before they break into the TCA or are involved in some other rule infraction. In fact, I think every VFR pilot should get some training every five years or so to encourage them to become instrument-rated. You can be sure that's my next move.

Once again, thank you for the *"severity"* of your punishment for my infraction—I had a ball and truly needed this experience.

Very sincerely,

Robert D. Rens, DDS

Flight**FORUM**

• AD's On-line
The reason I am writing is to ask if there is an on-line service, such as DUATS, that I can access with a computer to find specific airworthiness directives (AD) on aircraft, as well as special type certificates. I have limited space and the cost of buying AD's is prohibitive—not to mention the constant updates required to keep them current. I just purchased a new laptop computer with a modem which allows me to access DUATS and other libraries of information and I just love it. I believe the possibilities are endless and feel that an on-line service is needed.

William A. Tuite III
Alvin, TX

Presently, the FAA sells AD's only in paper copy or microfiche form and has no immediate plans to put them on-line. However, there are several private companies that have advised the FAA that they are available to do individual AD research for a fee. The FAA office that publishes the AD's does not recommend one company above another.

AOPA	1–800–654–4700
Frederick, MD	
Aircraft Technical Publishers (ATP)	1–800–227–4610
Hawthorne, CA	
Aviation Compliance Services	1–800–783–0327
Atlanta, GA	
Flightline	1–800–842–1716
Malvern, PA	
UNICOM	214–644–1158
Richardson, TX	

• Alternate Weather
In your response to the continuing saga of use of alternate airports wherein area forecasts may be utilized to determine forecast alternate weather conditions...you state that the airport may not be authorized for use as an alternate airport if weather observing and reporting capability is not available. In some western sections of this country there are few instrument airports, and alternates according to your standards are sometimes beyond useful cruising distances. The use of a nearby non-instrument airport is certainly feasible under the regulations, FAR § 91.169 (c)(2). This would certainly allow area forecasts in such instances. The symbol A NA applies to airports with published instrument approaches.

Gordon S. Hall
Memphis, TN

You are right. FAR § 91.169(c)(2) states, "If no instrument approach procedure has been published in FAR Part 97 of this chapter for that airport, the ceiling and visibility minimums are those allowing descent from the MEA, approach, and landing under basic VFR." Pilots must be careful to

ensure that any weather conditions that might make their filed destination airport go below minimums is not wide spread enough to make their alternate go below minimums.

• Citylad Reminder
I believe that there are many pilots out there that truly realize the importance of pilot reports (Re: May/June 1992 News/Brief article, "PIREP's—Standardizing Turbulence?") However, when I pick up the "weather phone" everyday, I hardly ever hear the word "PIREP" or see the letters "UA." I think the problem comes down to. . . we don't know what to say or how to say it. So here is a little acronym (oh no! Not another one!) that I derived from the AIM and use as a guide.

Just remember, "a **c**ityla**d** *reports turbulence!"*
Clouds *(in cloud/precip?)*
Intensity *(light, moderate, severe, extreme?)*
Time
t**Y**pe *(of aircraft)*
Location
Altitude
Duration *[occasional (–1/3), intermittent (1/3–2/3), continuous (+2/3)]*
I'm no "citylad," but I still do PIREP's.

Mark D. Merritt
Norman, OK

FAA AVIATION NEWS welcomes comments from its readers. We may edit letters for style and/or length. We will select one representative letter from those on the same topic for publication, and, because of our bimonthly publishing schedule, responses may not appear for several issues. We will send personal replies only upon request. We will not print anonymous letters, but we will withhold names upon request. Address: Editor, FAA AVIATION NEWS, AFS–810, Washington, DC 20591.

• Stall/Spin Recovery
I am writing to congratulate you on recovering the camera and film from the wreckage of N66315 so that you could print the picture on page 14. With only 110 feet of altitude, 42 mph airspeed, a 20° bank and 180 ft/min descent rate, it is obvious that the plane must have crashed. Fortunately, it apparently did not burn. Tough way to illustrate an article on Stall/Spins.

A.E. McLaughlin, Jr.
Long Island, NY

• Setting the Record Straight
As President of the International Aerobatic Club (IAC), I read with interest your article on "Airshows" and the November/December 1991 news brief on "Helping Set the Media Straight." Your introductory paragraph in the latter article accurately expresses the frustrations we in the sport aerobatics field have felt for a long time.

Your recommendation toward education [of the media] is exactly what the IAC has been about since its formation in 1970. It is a constant uphill battle, but one in which each of us needs to be actively engaged in order to present accurate impressions of the safety of aviation. Thanks for your part in this effort.

Steven E. Morris
Oshkosh, WI

The article "Helping Set the Media Straight" promoted a brochure published by the Aircraft Owners and Pilots Association (AOPA) called "The ABC's of Aviation: A Glossary of Aviation Terms." The brochure is designed for non-aviation media and provides definitions of nomenclature common to us but maybe foreign to non-pilots. Copies of the brochure are free from AOPA; call (301) 695-2162. We and AOPA suggest that you get copies and pass them along to your local or national media.

• Birds of a Feather
I have a medium-sized bird who is domesticated but frequents the skies often. He has read the Kamikaze article (March/April 1992) by Cmdr. Danielson and begs to differ with him. He has informed me that the majority of the birds wish no harm to any aircraft. It is only a small, very radical collection of feathered foes that give all the birds a bad name. These birds believe they will go straight to animal heaven if they die for their cause. He apologizes for them but wishes to inform all pilots that they will not lay down their beaks until the skies are once again theirs and theirs alone.

Robert & Fluffy
Oklahoma City, OK

Flight**FORUM**

• ATP Instruction

*I have three questions regarding FAR §
61.169, Instructor in Air Transportation
Service.*

*1. Can ATP's (without CFI ratings) instruct
students or rated pilots under FAR Part
61 or 141 operations?*

*2. When can an ATP (without CFI ratings)
instruct other than in "air transportation
service"?*

*3. What is the definition of air transportation
service since FAR Part 1 does not define it,
or does it simply apply only to Part 121 or
Part 135 operations?*

Clifford Moriarty, III
Langley AFB, VA

1. No. FAR § 61.169 states in part, "An airline transport pilot may instruct other
pilots in air transportation service in aircraft of the category, class, and type for
which he is rated." It then limits the type
of instruction by stating, "Unless he has
a flight instructor certificate, an airline
transport pilot may instruct only as provided in this section."

2. An ATP may give flight instruction to a
person only if the recipient is engaged in
air transportation service.

3. The Federal Aviation Act of 1958, FAR
Parts 1, 121, and 135 define air transportation service indirectly by defining
the various types of air commerce and
air transportation as well as the types of
aircraft used in each type of service. FAR
Part 1 defines air carrier, air commerce,
and air transportation for interstate,
intrastate, and foreign operations. FAR
Parts 121 and 135 define the aircraft
requirements for each type operation.

• Alaska Tale

*Just a note to tell you what a great arti-
cle in the January/February FAA Aviation
News you had on "Flying to Alaska"
because it was so thorough. It is the first
time I've seen the "Information Source"
printed anywhere, for example. Also,
emphasis on knowing how to track ADF is
so important up there. Down in the 48, we
hardly ever need it.*

*I've flown the route from St. Paul, MN to
both Anchorage and Fairbanks several
times—the most recent this past summer
(1991)—using both the airways and the
highway. Every trip was an incredibly great
trip. (My wife puts a blanket over her head
when we fly the airways.) My original first
aid kit was expanded after I started flying
over remote territory. It now includes bigger
adhesive bandages, stronger pain killers,*

Keopectate, burn cream, etc. Also,
although handguns are not allowed in
Canada, rifles are. I carry a heavy caliber
rifle just in case one goes down where
there are no streams or lakes and land
game may be the only food one can get.

*Keep up the good work. Every page of the
FAA Aviation News is always good.*

Kent Hadrits
Woodbury, MN

Thank you for your kind words. We
always like to hear about our readers' flying
experiences, be it in letter or article form.
We also might suggest that your wife
remove the blanket from her head and help
you spot traffic and landmarks.

• Learning your ABC's

*You reported the new alphabet (A, B, C,
etc.) designation for airspace, effective
September 1993. The old acronyms (e.g.
TCA = Terminal Control Area) told us what*

they are. Now there will emerge "memory
association" phrases to help recall what type
of airspace the new alphabet letters signify.

*Suggestions from us at AIR CHART
Systems are:*

*A = Altitude (Positive Airspace above
18,000')*

*B = Busy, close second was Bust N' Rue
(for TCA's)*

*C = Contact 20 (for ARSA's where calling
20 nm out is requested)*

*D = Destination (for Airport Traffic Areas
and Control Zones)*

*E = Elsewhere (for all other controlled
airspace)*

G = Go for it! (for all uncontrolled airspace)

Howie Keefe
Venice, CA

Thanks for your suggestion. One pilot
suggested that B should stand for "Be careful" and that the "Elsewhere" is not used
as in the old CAR (pre-FAA) terminology—
controlled, uncontrolled, and elsewhere.

INSTRUMENT CORNER

• Weathering CZ's

*I would appreciate your comments on
FAA policy regarding FAR § 91.155(c),
which states that, "Except as provided in
FAR § 91.157, no person may operate an
aircraft, under VFR, within a control zone
beneath the ceiling when the ceiling is less
than 1,00 feet."*

*The control zone at Waco, TX, has two
airports within it. Waco Regional is a Fed-
eral-tower facility with 24-hour national
weather reporting. The other airport, Waco
T.S.T.I., is a non-Federal-tower facility without weather reporting.*

*When the ceiling being reported at
Waco Regional is less than 1,000 feet, can
a pilot take off or land at T.S.T.I. without
obtaining an IFR or special VFR clearance
when:*

*a. A pilot reports no cloud formation at
T.S.T.I.*

*b. A pilot reports a cloud formation at T.S.T.I.
with the base at or above 1,000 feet.*

Name withheld

The answer to both of your questions
is no. The pilot would need an ATC clearance based upon FAR § 91.157, Special
VFR Weather Conditions, to operate at
T.S.T.I. under the conditions you listed.
Control zones are designated to provide
controlled airspace for terminal operations conducted under instrument meteorological conditions at the airport for
which the control zone was established
and extend upward from the surface of
the earth to a designated altitude or to
the adjacent or overlying controlled
airspace. The primary airport's ceiling
affects the type of operations that may be
conducted throughout the control zone.
When the ceiling is reported to be less
than 1,000 feet at the primary airport, no
VFR operations may be conducted in the
control zone below the altitude of that
ceiling, regardless of any PIREPS. However, it is reasonable to expect an aircraft
to be in the control zone, operating above
the reported ceiling of the primary airport,
in visual meteorological conditions and
operating under visual flight rules as provided for in FAR § 91.155. The key factor
in determining whether a SVFR clearance
is required is the reported ceiling at the
primary airport in the control zone. For
more information on control zones, you
can review the Airman's Information Manual (AIM) which discusses control zones
and weather reporting in paragraph 3-26.

Thomas C. Richards
New FAA Administrator

Thomas C. Richards, a veteran pilot and retired Air Force four-star general who served on the President's Commission on Aviation Security and Terrorism, was sworn in as Administrator of the Federal Aviation Administration on June 27.

FAA Administrator Richards

Richards, who retired from the Air Force in October 1989, began his military career in the Army in 1948 and served as an infantryman in the Korean War. In Korea he rose to the rank of platoon sergeant and was wounded twice. After his discharge, he attended Virginia Polytechnic Institute where he enrolled in the Air Force ROTC program. He graduated in 1956 and was awarded a commission as a second lieutenant in the Air Force and was sent to flight school. Since earning his wings, he has flown over 15 different aircraft and logged more than 5,000 flight hours which includes the 624 combat missions he flew during the Vietnam War.

When he retired from the Air Force he was deputy commander-in-chief of the U.S. European Command. Before that he was commander of the Air University at Maxwell Air Force base in Alabama; vice-commander of the 8th Air Force, Strategic Air Command, at the Barksdale Air Force base in Louisiana; and commandant of cadets at the Air Force Academy in Colorado.

Richards, who was born in San Diego, is married and has six children.

Details on Important AIM Change

In the recent issue of the *Airman's Information Manual* (AIM), there are several changes and modifications. The following are a few that are of particular interest to pilots.

Paragraph 4–56's title was changed to USE OF RUNWAYS/DECLARED DISTANCES and a section c. was added to clarify declared distances. It now reads:

"c. At some airports, the airport proprietor may declare that sections of a runway at one or both ends are not available for landing or takeoff. For these airports, the declared distance of runway length available for a particular operation is published in the *Airport/Facility Directory*. Declared distances (TORA, TODA, ASDA, and LDA) are defined in the Pilot/Controller Glossary. These distances are calculated by adding to the full length of paved runway any applicable clearway or stopway and subtracting from that sum and sections of the runway unsuitable for satisfying the required takeoff run, takeoff, accelerate/ stop, or landing distance."

Paragraph 4–70 was modified to clarify the responsibilities of the pilot after landing and exiting the runway. It now reads:

"4–70 EXITING THE RUNWAY AFTER LANDING

"The following procedures should be followed after landing and reaching taxi speed.

"a. Exit the runway without delay at the first available taxiway or on a taxiway as instructed by air traffic control (ATC).

"b. Taxi clear of the runway unless otherwise directed by ATC. In the absence of ATC instructions the pilot is expected to taxi clear of the landing runway even if that requires the aircraft to protrude into or cross another taxiway, runway, or ramp area. This does not authorize an aircraft to cross a subsequent taxiway/runway/ ramp after clearing the landing runway.

"4–70b NOTE—The tower will issue the pilot with instructions which will normally permit the aircraft to enter another taxiway, runway, or ramp area when required to taxi clear of the runway.

"c. Stop the aircraft after clearing the runway if instructions have not been received from ATC.

"d. Immediately change to ground control frequency when advised by the tower and obtain a taxi clearance.

"4–70d NOTE 1—The tower will issue instructions required to resolve any potential conflictions with other ground traffic prior to advising the pilot to contact ground control.

"4–70d NOTE 2—A clearance from ATC to taxi to the ramp authorizes the aircraft to cross all runways and taxiway intersections. Pilots not familiar with the taxi route should request specific taxi instructions from ATC."

Paragraph 7–78 is new. It reads:

"7–78 EMERGENCY AIRBORNE INSPECTION OF OTHER AIRCRAFT

"a. Providing airborne assistance to another aircraft may involve formation flying. Most pilots receive little if any formal training or instruction in formation flying. Formation flying after a face to face planning session is difficult enough. Formation flying without sufficient time to plan (i.e., an emergency situation), coupled with the stress involved in a perceived emergency can be hazardous.

"b. The pilot in command of the aircraft experiencing the problem/emergency must take the lead in coordinating the airborne intercept and inspection and take into account the unique flight characteristics and differences of the category(s) of aircraft involved.

"c. Some of the safety considerations are:

"1. Direction and speed of intercept;

"2. Minimum separation distance;

"3. Communications requirements, lost communication procedures; and

"4. Emergency actions to terminate intercept.

"d. Close proximity, in-flight inspection of another aircraft is uniquely hazardous. The pilot in command of the aircraft experiencing the problem/ emergency must not relinquish his/her control of the situation and jeopardize the safety of his/her aircraft. The maneuver must be accomplished with minimum risk to both aircraft."

The *Airman's Information Manual* is the official FAA guide to basic flight information and ATC procedures and is issued every 112 days. It is sold by the Superintendent of Documents (U.S. GPO, Washington, DC 20402–9371) and its yearly subscription cost is $26 ($32.50 foreign).

Charting a New Appearance

On October 15, a new cycle for printing VFR aeronautical charts begins and with it begins the implementation of charting changes for VFR products. An insert will be included in all new sectional and WAC charts to explain the charting changes. The majority of them are the result of the airspace reclassification, but not all. The Air Defense Identification Zone (ADIZ) is changing symbology size and color. Special Use Airspace and Military Operations Area (MOA) are changing symbology. As these are not a class of airspace, it was not appropriate to include them in the airspace reclassification article that appears on page 12, but we wanted our readers to know about them (below).

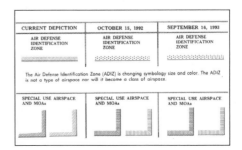

CURRENT DEPICTION	OCTOBER 15, 1992	SEPTEMBER 16, 1993
AIR DEFENSE IDENTIFICATION ZONE	AIR DEFENSE IDENTIFICATION ZONE	AIR DEFENSE IDENTIFICATION ZONE

The Air Defense Identification Zone (ADIZ) is changing symbology size and color. The ADIZ is not a type of airspace nor will it become a class of airspace.

SPECIAL USE AIRSPACE AND MOAs	SPECIAL USE AIRSPACE AND MOAs	SPECIAL USE AIRSPACE AND MOAs

NOS Chart Users

If you use NOS instrument approach charts—before you depart on your next flight—check to see that the charts you are planning to use are actually in the book. An air taxi operator advised us that when he got to his destination, the charts he needed had been left out of his book during the printing process. Further, a collating error had misfiled several pages. This operator said this is the second time this year this has happened to him. BE ALERT! If you find this problem with your charts, be sure to call the 800 number in the back of the chart book to aid in the quality control process.

Physiological Training

The Federal Aviation Administration (FAA) is offering a one-day course on physiological training, primarily for pilots and other national airspace personnel. Physiological training is a program directed toward understanding and surviving in the flight environment. It covers the problem of high altitude exposure and recommends procedures to prevent or minimize human factor errors that occur in flight.

The physiological training course covers many topics. They include the environment to which the flyer is exposed, physiological functions of the body at ground level, and alteration of some of these functions by changes in the environment. The higher one flies, the more critical the need for supplemental oxygen becomes. This need is discussed so that the trainee will understand why a pilot cannot fly safely at altitudes in excess of 12,500 feet for a prolonged period without some aid, either supplemental oxygen or a pressurized aircraft. When humans are suddenly confronted with stressful or threatening situations, there is a tendency to breathe too rapidly or hyperventilate, so instructors discuss hyperventilation and methods of control. They also discuss and explain the causes of ear pain on descent.

The course addresses the potential consequences of alcohol, tobacco, and drug use as they apply to flying. Instructors discuss and demonstrate pilot spacial disorientation (vertigo) so that the trainee will understand why a VFR pilot or a noncurrent instrument pilot should never attempt to fly in clouds or other weather situations where visibility is significantly reduced. The course includes an altitude chamber flight where the trainees experience individual symptoms of oxygen deficiency as well as decompression. The chamber flight demonstrates the following: proper oxygen equipment and its use protects you from oxygen deficiency; experiencing and recognizing symptoms that are the same as those found in actual flight and therefore take the necessary action to prevent loss of judgement and consciousness; and decompression, which is not dangerous provided proper actions have been planned and taken when necessary.

The physiological training course is offered in several U.S. locations. The fee

FAA Instructor Roger Storey prepares a physiological training class for a "flight" in the FAA's Civil Aeromedical Institute's high altitude chamber.

H. Dean Chamberlain

is $20, unless taken at the FAA Aeronautical Center, Oklahoma City, OK, where no fee is required. For further information about how to register, specific course dates and locations, and qualifications of eligibility to receive physiological training, contact the FAA, Civil Aeromedical Institute; Airman Education Programs Branch, AAM–420; Post Office Box 25082; Oklahoma City, OK 73125: or phone (405) 680–4837.

Accident Prevention Program Seminars

If you are going to be a "leaf peeper" this fall and head for New England to take in Nature's show of changing colors, consider attending one the Bedford, MA FSDO's General Aviation Safety Seminars or CFI Workshops. Accident Prevention Program Manager John F. Hemmer has provided the following schedule.

Mr. Hemmer notes that the locations and topics are subject to change and suggests that you give him a call for additional information and current scheduling. His telephone number is (617) 274–7130.

GENERAL AVIATION SAFETY SEMINARS

SUNDAY, SEPTEMBER 6, 8:00 a.m.
Plymouth Fun Day
Plymouth Municipal Airport, Plymouth, MA

THURSDAY, SEPTEMBER 10, 7:00 p.m.
Pilot Judgement/Human Factors
Westerly, RI

TUESDAY, SEPTEMBER 15, 7:00 p.m.
Aviation Security
Beverly, MA Airport

SATURDAY, SEPTEMBER 26
Helicopter Safety Seminar
Westford Regency, Westford, MA

SAT.-SUN., SEPTEMBER 26–27 9:00 a.m.–5:00 p.m.
Expo 92/Airfair 92
Hanscom Field, Bedford, MA

SATURDAY, OCTOBER 3, 8:00 a.m.
Glider Safety Seminar
Pepperell, MA Sport Center

TUESDAY, OCTOBER 13, 7:00 p.m.
Safety Seminar
Hanscom AFB "O" Club, Bedford, MA

THURSDAY, OCTOBER 15, 7:00 p.m.
Accident Review
TF Green Airport, Providence, RI

TUESDAY, OCTOBER 20, 7:00 p.m.
Corporate Aviation Safety Seminar
Jet Aviation, Hanscom AFB, Bedford, MA

TUESDAY, OCTOBER 27, 7:00 p.m.
Maintenance Topics for Pilots
Hyannis, MA

CFI WORKSHOPS

TUESDAY, SEPTEMBER 8, 7:00 p.m.
Helicopter Safety/CFI Workshop
Jet Aviation, Hanscom AFB, Bedford, MA

WEDNESDAY, SEPTEMBER 9, 7:00 p.m.
Bridgewater State College
Bridgewater, MA

THURSDAY, SEPTEMBER 17, 7:00 p.m.
High Altitude Flight
Newport Airport, Newport, RI

TUESDAY, OCTOBER 6, 7:00 p.m.
Stowe/Minuteman Airport
Stowe, MA

THURSDAY, OCTOBER 15, 7:00 p.m.
Analysis of Maneuvers
Bridgewater State College, Bridgewater, MA

THURSDAY, OCTOBER 22, 7:00 p.m.
Multiengine Procedures, CCRI
Warwick, RI

National Aerospace Teacher of the Year Award

by TSgt. Donnie R. Veasey, HQ CAP-USAF Public Affairs

Susan Broderick frequently conducts her first grade class aboard the space shuttle. On other days, class may convene in the cockpit of a Navy jet catapulting off a aircraft carrier. And if her frisky first graders are up to it, Broderick holds class high above the earth in an eye-catching, multi-colored hot air balloon.

Okay, so the Head Elementary School first grade teacher cannot get 25 six-year-old children in those lofty confines. But by experiencing those aerospace treats herself, with an innate ability to transfer the raw feel of these experiences to her students, and through judicious use of imagination, she helps her students get excited about school and learning.

This imagination and enthusiasm, plus an unrivaled desire to give children the ultimate learning experience, contributed to Broderick's earning the 1992 A. Scott Crossfield National Aerospace Teacher of the Year Award. The Award was presented in a special ceremony at the 25th Annual National Congress on Aviation and Space Education held recently in Oklahoma City. The Civil Air Patrol, Federal Aviation Administration, and National Aeronautics and Space Administration sponsor this annual congress. The award, named for famed aviation test pilot and aerospace pioneer A. Scott Crossfield, was started in 1986 to recognize and reward education teachers for outstanding accomplishments in aerospace education and for demonstrated dedication to their students.

Broderick's unquenchable interest in the aerospace world and her dedication in providing education and positive direction for youngsters during their formative years is not unique. What separates her efforts from others in that category is the fervor in which she pursues those goals. She strives to provide the perfect learning environment for her students. As mentioned earlier, Broderick routinely partakes in a myriad of "wild" aerospace adventures, and then translates them into interesting learning avenues. Some of her other aerospace adventures include: afterburner climbs in an Alabama Air National Guard F-16 jet fighter, attending the week-long Space Camp in Huntsville, AL, test flying flight simulators at Delta Operations in Atlanta, and

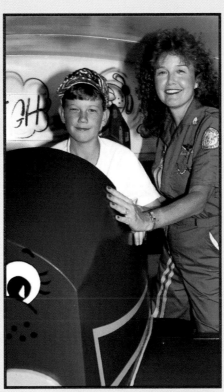

Susan Broderick and one of her students in her mobile aerospace classroom—a converted bus.

flying in a 1941 open cockpit trainer and landing on a grass runway. These adventures are completed on her own time and in many cases, she foots the bill for the experience.

"I wanted to find something in my classroom that would touch children in a way that would build a foundation for learning specific skills of life and for learning other ways to gather knowledge. Aerospace education does that," the Montgomery, AL, native explained.

The 1975 Auburn University graduate first got involved in the aerospace education world some six years ago, when the Alabama Department of Aeronautics and Education needed someone to field-test the use of aerospace curricula in the classroom. Broderick's excitement about being the first teacher to have this opportunity has carried over to her students.

After winning a Christa McAuliffe Fellowship Grant, Broderick immediately pursued her dream to have the first mobile aerospace classroom. One year later, Broderick and her husband, Tim, converted an old bus into this mobile classroom, complete with a flight simulator. Broderick's teaching skills and her aerospace bus are in demand throughout the state.

Her efforts in the education world earned Broderick selection as a participant in the teacher-in-residence program in the School of Education, Auburn University of Montgomery. Her two-year stint in that position ends in 1993. Many of Broderick's other awards are even more lofty. They include: the 1989 Federal Aviation Administration's National Administrator's Award for Excellence in Aviation Education, the 1990 Christa McAuliffe Fellow for Alabama, and the 1991 Learning Magazine and Oldsmobile's National Professional Best Leadership Award.

Broderick says that the best thing to come out of winning awards is that it lets the public see that, "There are good things going on in classrooms all around America. We need to shine more light on those people who do good jobs," she said. "There are teachers out there who just give their lives to kids. They wake up in the morning and they dream all night about what they are going to do in their classroom," she said. "I am one of those teachers."

DO NOT DELAY—CRITICAL TO FLIGHT SAFETY!

November–December 1992

FAA Aviation News

A DOT/FAA FLIGHT STANDARDS SAFETY PUBLICATION

U.S. Department
of Transportation

**Federal Aviation
Administration**

Andrew H. Card, Jr., *Secretary of Transportation*
Thomas C. Richards, *FAA Administrator*
Joseph M. Del Balzo, *Executive Director
    for System Operations*
Anthony J. Broderick, *Associate Administrator
    for Regulation and Certification*
Thomas C. Accardi, *Director,
    Flight Standards Service*
Robert A. Wright, Manager, *General Aviation (Acting)*
Roger M. Baker, Jr., *Manager,
    Accident Prevention Program Branch*
Phyllis A. Duncan, *Editor*
Louise C. Oertly, *Senior Associate Editor*
H. Dean Chamberlain, *Associate Editor*

The FAA's Flight Standards Service, General Aviation and
Commercial Division, Accident Prevention Program Branch,
AFS–810, Washington, DC 20591, publishes FAA AVIA-
TION NEWS in the interest of flight safety. The magazine
promotes safety in the air by calling the attention of airmen
to current technical, regulatory, and procedural matters
affecting the safe operation of aircraft. Although based on
current FAA policy and rule interpretations, all printed material herein are advisory or informational in nature and should
not be construed to have regulatory effect. The FAA does
not officially endorse any goods, services, materials, or
products of manufacturers that may be mentioned.
**Certain details of accidents described herein have
been altered to protect the privacy of those involved.**
    The Office of Management and Budget has approved
the use of funds for the printing of FAA AVIATION NEWS.

SUBSCRIPTION SERVICES

The Superintendent of Documents, U.S. Government
Printing Office, Washington, DC 20402–9371, sells FAA
AVIATION NEWS on subscription. Use the self-mailer
form in the center of this magazine to subscribe. Cost:
$8.00 ($10.00 foreign) for one year; $16.00 ($20.00 foreign) for two years. Prices are subject to change by the
Government Printing Office without prior notice.
    Change of Address or Subscription Problems: Send
your label with correspondence to Sup Doc, Attn: Chief,
Mail List Branch, Mail Stop: SSOM, Washington, DC
20402–9373.
    To keep subscription prices down, the Government
Printing Office mails subscribers only one renewal
notice. You can tell how many copies are left in your
subscription by checking the number that follows "ISS-
DUE" on the top line of your mailing label. For example,
when this number is 003, it means you have three
issues left in your subscription, and GPO will send you a
renewal notice. The number 000 means you have
received your last issue. To be sure that your service
continues without interruption, please return your
renewal notice promptly.

FAN SMITH 212J ISSDUE003 R 1
JOHN SMITH
212 MAIN ST
FORESTVILLE, MD 20747

November-December 1992

FAA *Aviation* News

Volume 31   Number 6

FEATURES

DEPARTMENTS

On the Cover:
*Is the pilot of this Piper Arrow set up for an altitude
bust? To learn how to avoid the altitude deviation
"trap" see p. 2. Photo courtesy of Piper Aircraft.*

On the Back Cover:
*A Cessna 172 comes in for a landing with flaps
extended. Any number of factors dictate the use or
non-use of flaps. If you don't know what they are,
see p. 16. Photo courtesy of Cessna Aircraft.*

FAA's Best Kept Secret

by Phyllis A. Duncan

Did you know that what you are holding in your hot little hands right now is FAA's "Best Kept Secret?" What I'm talking about is *FAA Aviation News.* We didn't make it secret; in fact, we don't want it to be a secret, but it apparently is. I get a lot of letters (not surprisingly since that is where "letters to the editor" go) from people who say, "FAA's new magazine is great! I just saw my first copy of *FAA Aviation News,* and I'm glad the FAA is finally doing something like that." They teach you in Editor's School to be polite to readers, so I can't say, "Are you blind? Look at the inside front cover where it says 'Volume 31, Number 6.' Volume 31 means 31 years!"

Actually, I don't really care if the reader thinks *FAA Aviation News* is brand new. What counts is that he or she is reading it now, and that is what's important. It means that another person may read something that somewhere down the line may save a life, any life.

But deep down where editor's ulcers grow, I'm a little upset that more people don't know about this publication that FAA's Flight Standards produces for the aviation public. The fine print on the page to the left of this one contains some very bureaucratic language about the content and purpose of this publication. The Office of Management and Budget requires us to put that in, but, quite simply, our sole purpose is to keep airmen from making the mistakes that may cost

them their right to fly, the use of their equipment, or, most seriously, their very lives.

More people need to know about us, and we're doing some things differently in order to accomplish that. We're sending a complimentary copy to anyone who calls in or writes in. (If you do that expect to get a subscription push from us.) We're sending copies to major aviation events across the country and doing many other promotional activities. But you can also help us. When you are finished with this magazine, pass it on to a friend and explain why you subscribe. If you are like many of our readers who keep their back issues in their personal aviation library, you can at least use the order form to purchase a gift subscription for someone—it *is* the holiday season, after all! If you are reading this at an airport or FBO and the subscription form is missing from the middle, call us at (202) 267–8017 or write us at *FAA Aviation News,* AFS–810, 800 Independence Ave., S.W., Washington, DC 20591, and we will send a complimentary copy. Or contact your Accident Prevention Program Manager (listed on p. 22), and he or she will tell you how to subscribe.

Increased subscriptions mean that we are serving more aviation customers, and I can ease up on the antiacid. Joking aside, secrets can be bad or good, but some secrets aren't meant to be kept.
—*The Editor* ■

Ms. Duncan is a commercial pilot and flight instructor with 13 years in the FAA. Her ulcers are only figurative—for now.

This is the second in a series of articles reprinted from ASRS Directline, *a quarterly publication that addresses particular areas of safety that appear in pilot reports received by NASA's Aviation Safety Reporting System and which have been identified by safety analysts as "significant."* ASRS Directline *is free from ASRS, NASA-Ames Research Center, Moffett Field, CA 94035. Altitude busting is of significance to all pilots, not just the airliners. According to the following, the crucial altitudes for deviations appear to be 10,000 and 11,000 feet. Read on to find out why.* —Editor

One-Zero Ways to Bust an Altitude Or... Was That 11?

by Don George, ASRS Analyst

Here I am, the PIC (passenger in coach) on a coast-to-coast wide body, cruising along at flight level 350. I am in seat 25B (one of the cheap ones), feeling fairly comfortable after recovering from an earlier incident which involved the guy in 24B suddenly tilting his seat to the full recline position and spearing me with my very own tray table. In any decent football league, that would have been a 15-yard penalty, but I didn't even get an "excuse me."

No cracked ribs, so I try to relax, but I can't because now I'm already worrying about the fact that we will have to descend in a couple of hours, and I know from reading a lot of ASRS reports that our chances of getting down through 11,000 and 10,000 feet without an incident of some sort are pretty remote. I conjure up in my mind a scenario that runs something like this ...

The controller will say, "Descend and cross three zero miles west of Gulch VOR at one-one-thousand, reduce to two five zero knots, report leaving flight level two zero zero, Podunk altimeter three zero zero five." With all those zeros now implanted into the flight crew's heads, one of them will undoubtedly read back "Descend to one-zero-thousand" along with the other values, and the controller will fail to note the wrong altitude in the readback.

Shortly thereafter, we will change over to Approach Control and report "... out of one eight thousand for one-zero-thousand." Again a busy controller will miss the incorrect altitude.

As we start to level off, the controller sees our altitude readout, questions us, and tells us to climb back up to one-one-thousand, where we belong. At the same time, there are a couple of departing aircraft heading in our direction, also at 10,000 feet. We evade them by making some steep turns and climbing rapidly. Not much harm done

except a few spilled drinks, and the possible creation of some future paperwork.

Pretty soon, I hear the announcement for flight attendants to prepare for landing. This is the favorite part of the trip for me because it means that the guy in 24B must put his seat back into the upright position, and it also indicates that we have gotten down through 11,000 and 10,000 feet without hitting another aircraft. Both of these occurrences allow me to breathe a lot easier.

Okay... so I made up all this stuff about the guy in 24B and the dogfights with other aircraft, but it all could have really happened, because, seriously, there is a real-life 10K/11K problem. I just wanted to get your attention so that we could talk about it.

Why do a lot of altitude deviations occur at 10,000 and 11,000 feet?

In the preparation of this article, I reviewed hundreds of ASRS reports which involved a mix-up with these two altitudes. The reports reveal several causal factors that show up in nearly all of the incidents. These incidents, however, do not usually occur as a result of a single cause. Rather, they almost always reflect a combination of two or more of them.

Similar Sounding Phrases

Pilots misunderstand a clearance, and controllers misunderstand the read back because of expectation and the similar sounding phrases "one-zero-thousand" and "one-one-thousand."

"I believe it is very easy to confuse one-one-thousand with one-zero-thousand and vice versa."

"I don't know if the controller said 10,000 but intended to say 11,000 or if he said 11,000 and I thought he said 10,000."

Readback/Hearback

Controllers fail to note incorrect altitudes in pilot readbacks—the old "hearback" bugaboo.

"Voice tape reading showed that the clearance was to 11,000 feet but readback by [the] captain of 10,000 feet went uncorrected."

"Controller said, 'Oh, I should have checked your readback.'"

Too Many Numbers

Controllers include several (sometimes, too many) numbers in the same radio transmission.

"The controlling agency, in rapid manner, told us to turn to 310 degrees, slow to 210 knots, and I understood him to say 'maintain 10,'"

"Very often controllers issue four to five instructions in the same breath, such as 'turn left 330 degrees, maintain 2,000 feet till established, cleared for ILS 30 approach, contact tower 119.4 at the outer marker, and maintain 160 knots until five mile final.'"

Similar Numbers

Altitude crossing points stated in miles may be similar to the altitude to which the flight is cleared.

"Were we cleared to 10,000 feet 11 miles west of ARMEL or 11,000 feet 10 miles, or 10,000 feet 10 miles, or 11,000 feet 11 miles?"

"Center cleared us to cross 10 DME NE PVD 11 thousand, 250 knots. I read back 11 miles NE PVD 10 thousand, 250 knots. At 10,100 feet I questioned center, and they said 10 north east at 11,000, 250 knots. We climbed back up to 11,000 feet."

250 Knots at 10,000 Feet

Pilots tend to associate a 250-knot speed restriction with a 10,000-foot altitude assignment since civil aircraft are normally restricted to a speed of 250 knots or less below 10,000 feet.

"A clearance for 250 knots generally makes a pilot think about 10,000 feet [because of] the association of 250 knots below 10,000."

"We think the 250-knot restriction could have led us to assume 10,000 feet because the majority of locations use 10,000 feet/250 knot crossings in their STAR's."

Spring Loaded

Pilots may anticipate receiving a certain clearance but get something just a little different. Perhaps the last SID or STAR they executed had speed and altitude crossing restrictions that were similar but not exactly the same as the one they are currently flying. Noted an air carrier pilot who initiated a premature descent to 10,000 from 11,000 feet:

Piper Aircraft

"I may have anticipated being given 10,000 feet after seeing [an air carrier aircraft] pass below me."

Failing to Question the Unusual

Pilots may or may not be familiar with normal ATC procedures in a particular area and may, in either case, neglect to question an abnormal altitude assignment.

"Next time in and out of DEN we will be aware that the inbound aircraft are normally at 11,000 feet and departure aircraft normally restricted to 10,000 feet."

"The usual clearance for this arrival is 11,000, but we both followed my error blindly to 10,000 feet."

The Ten Mindset

Pilots and controllers get what is referred to as a "number 10 mindset" after hearing a lot of zeros. It seems like one-zero-thousand then becomes the altitude assignment.

"I do think the number of tens in the clearance was a contributing factor."

"Flight crew read back 'one-one-thousand' but somehow had mindset of one-zero-thousand."

Reduced Monitoring

Cockpit duties and distractions may result in only one flight crew member monitoring the ATC frequency. Similarly, controller workload and frequency congestion may be factors which affect the ability of controllers to monitor pilot readbacks closely.

"This type of situation has occurred with this crewmember 3 or 4 times since flying two-man crew aircraft when one crewmember is busy reviewing approach plate and procedures and is distracted from hearing conversation between [the] other crewmember and controller."

Cockpit Management

Cockpit management and flight crew coordination may be less than optimum, and crew members fail to monitor each other adequately in such tasks as altitude alert setting or readback of clearances.

"Center cleared our flight from 17,000 feet to 11,000 feet MSL. This was acknowledged by me, however the first officer understood 10,000 feet and placed that altitude in the selector."

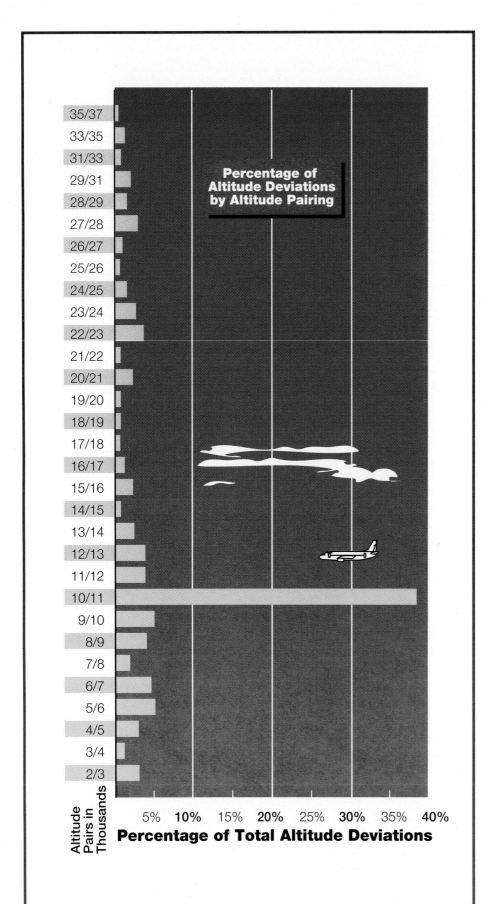

Percentage of Altitude Deviations by Altitude Pairing

Altitude Pairs in Thousands:
35/37, 33/35, 31/33, 29/31, 28/29, 27/28, 26/27, 25/26, 24/25, 23/24, 22/23, 21/22, 20/21, 19/20, 18/19, 17/18, 16/17, 15/16, 14/15, 13/14, 12/13, 11/12, 10/11, 9/10, 8/9, 7/8, 6/7, 5/6, 4/5, 3/4, 2/3

5% 10% 15% 20% 25% 30% 35% 40%

Percentage of Total Altitude Deviations

Analysis of the ASRS database indicates that there are far more clearance misinterpretations involving the altitude pair of 10/11 thousand feet than any other altitude combination—fully 38% of the sample data set. The next largest category accounted for less than 5% of the total deviations.

The sample data on which this finding is based is composed of 191 ASRS reports describing incidents with the following characteristics: (1) an assigned altitude was overshot or undershot, (2) a misinterpreted clearance contributed to the occurrence, (3) the event occurred between 1987 and 1990, and (4) the deviating aircraft attained an altitude 1,000 feet above or below its assigned altitude (2,000 feet when above FL290). The search was confined to ASRS full-form records since only these contain all of the necessary data elements.

The accompanying figure is based on an analysis of these data. Each category relates to a pair of altitudes that were confused with another, leading to an altitude overshoot or undershoot on either climb or descent.

"I will have to watch the music closer while the other guy is playing the piano."

Radio Technique

Very often controllers and/or pilots fail to use proper techniques. I consider this to be the "big one" when in comes to causative factors. Yessir, old number one-one (that's eleven) is a really critical factor.

"The controller was busy--a lot of traffic. Contributing factors: Fast talking, bad radios, long clearances, a lot of numbers--given too fast to comprehend or write down."

"I don't know who was correct, but I know that I was incorrect in not requesting a confirmation of the clearance since some doubt existed."

Confusing Phraseology

Controllers and pilots are frequently misunderstood because of their use of improper phraseology.

"We had understood and read back 'descending to 10,000.' Phraseology contributed to this incident."

"To correct future problems like this, the altitude should be given in the form of 'ten thousand' or 'eleven thousand,' instead of saying 'one-zero' or 'one-one-thousand.' There is

Dean Chamberlain

too much of a chance of error. We are used to hearing ten or eleven or twelve in everyday life."

So...what are you going to do about it? Here are a few starter suggestions.

Saying it Twice—Differently

Controllers and pilots are encouraged to use both single digit and group form phraseology in order to reinforce altitude assignments whenever there is the possibility of misunderstanding. Consider the following examples:

Controller transmission: "(Ident) descend and maintain one-zero-thousand. That's ten (with emphasis) thousand."

Pilot transmission: "Roger (callsign), leaving one-seven thousand for one-one thousand. That's eleven (with emphasis) thousand."

Note: A recent Air Traffic Procedure Handbook (FAA Order 7110.65) change allows controllers to use this phraseology to reinforce an altitude assignment. Many "old" pilots have used this technique for a long time and find that it helps.

Radio Technique

Take a good hard look at your radio communication techniques. Do you check to make sure the frequency is clear before transmitting? Do you activate the transmitter before starting to speak? Do you use your full and correct callsign? Do you use an acceptable speech rate? Do you enunciate, and emphasize when necessary for clarity? Do you ask the other party to repeat if transmission was not clear or may have been stepped on? Do you listen for similar callsigns?

These are just a few of the questions you should ask yourself. I'm sure you can think of many other good radio technique questions.

Area Familiarity

Pilots should work to improve their "situational awareness" skills. For instance, you often fly in the Dallas/Ft. Worth area and have observed that normally the departures are restricted to 10,000 feet and the arrivals are held up to 11,000 feet or higher until arrival and departure routes have crossed. You probably should question any altitude assignment which appears to be in conflict with these normal ATC procedures. Most terminal ATC facilities use standard routes and altitudes, and your situational awareness can help prevent an incident.

Reduce the Number of Numbers

Controllers can help make a conscientious effort to defeat the hearback problem by being aware of the nasty effects of including too many numbers in the same transmission and by using named intersections when possible rather than a number of miles when issuing crossing restriction.

Summary

Let's take a final look at some of the reasons for the 10K/11K altitude problem. Factors include:

- Similarity in the sound of one-zero and one-one-thousand, particularly when other numerical information is being transmitted at the same time.

- Pilots may be spring-loaded to expect a 250-knot airspeed in conjunction with a 10,000 foot altitude, this a clearance for an airspeed of 250 knots may lead the flight crew to assume an altitude requirement of 10,000 feet by mistake.

- Failure to question an unexpected or unusual clearance; anticipating 10 when hearing a lot of zeros; flight crew and controller distraction; and breakdown in cockpit management.

- The 10K/11K quandary seems to be rooted in confusing phraseology and improper radio technique—compounded by the Readback/Hearback problem.

The solution to the 10K/11K problem lies in realizing the potential for error when descending or climbing through or near the 10,000- and 11,000-foot boundaries and in using both single digit and group forms to express these altitudes. Be prepared to question a clearance that seems unusual. If pilots and controllers use clear, concise radio technique, paying particular attention to the hearback phase, the potential for error will be reduced. ∎

No doubt there are a good many readers of this article who are actively engaged in training activities, and you may want to consider this problem as the subject of a lesson or two. If you are interested in obtaining a small package of ASRS reports (about 20) on which to base training sessions, please write ASRS (address on the first page of this article) and request the 10K/11K Report Package. It will be sent at no charge.

The Aviation Safety Reporting System is a cooperative program established by the FAA's Office of the Assistant Administrator for Aviation Safety and administered by the National Aeronautics and Space Administration.

Answers to the Piloting IQ Quiz
1. b. December 21
2. b. high speed. Weather, 92
3. 3–1=c., 3–2=a., 3–3=b., and 3–4=d. Weather, 93
4. a. cloudy. Weather, 92
5. d. all of the above. Weather, 99
6. d. mountainous areas. Weather, 102
7. e. all of the above. Weather, 102.
8. c. always. Weather, 103
9. a. related. Weather, 92
10. a. and c. adjusted as per the handbook or if no information is provided, increased. Weather, 104
11. True. AIM, Para. 7–5c5. Note
12. True. AIM, Para. 7–5e.
13. True. AIM, Para. 7–5g.
14. d. any one of the above. Weather, 103/104, AIM, Para. 7–20b.
15. 15–1=a., 15–2=d., 15–3=c., 15–4=b. AIM, Para. 7–20b.

A Statement on Altitude Deviation

The following is a behind-the-scenes account of a corporate aviation crew who faced enforcement action as a result of an altitude deviation. This incident occurred on a routine, daylight, VFR flight. The crew filed a NASA ASRS form immediately after the incident. Their statement is printed with permission from Business Aviation Issues, *a publication of the National Business Aircraft Association.*

From an intermediate level off at 10,000 feet, we were given climb clearance to what I thought was Flight Level two-two-zero. I'm certain as the pilot flying that I stated, "Climbing to two-two-zero" and confirmed it by a glance at the altitude alerter preselect which had 2-2-0-0-0 selected. The first officer, having set the altitude alerter, was also certain that we were cleared to Flight Level two-two-zero. At some point in the climb, the controller issued traffic at 10 to 11 o'clock position, six miles, eastbound, which was descending to Flight Level two-one-zero. We were given a heading change of 15 degrees to the left for that traffic. The heading change added to my certainty that the controller was providing separation from that traffic as we climbed to Flight Level two-two-zero. With traffic in sight, and after watching it pass in front of us, my thought was, "This is pretty close proximity under radar control." It wasn't until passing Flight Level two-zero-seven, when the controller asked us to confirm level Flight Level two-zero-zero, that I questioned Flight Level two-two-zero as a clearance. Since we had the other aircraft in sight, I knew a descent was not required for collision avoidance. The traffic had passed well ahead and above us. The controller immediately cleared us to Flight Level two-three-zero.

The fact that the first officer believed we had been cleared to Flight Level two-two-zero was evident by her response on radio, stating, "I read back two-two-zero." She

also said we had the traffic in sight. I thought the controller had made the mistake in altitude assignment. It was not until three days later, when I heard the ARTCC tape, that I was convinced that we were cleared to Flight Level two-zero-zero. My first conversation was with the Manager of Quality Assurance at the controlling ARTCC. Over the telephone I listened to the tape of the incident and for the first time admitted that the crew was indeed in error. I was invited to tour the controlling ARTCC. He [The manager] implied that this action would be viewed positively by the FAA investigator and would indicate that my approach is constructive rather than resistant.

When I made the inquiry to two Washington-based trade associations I got the idea that I should be noncommittal and refrain from making a statement to the investigator upon initial contact and let the legal process take its course. My other source of advice was a retired FAA air carrier inspector who is familiar with current enforcement philosophy and investigative procedures. He encouraged me to be repentant and cooperative in my approach to the impending investigation.

The [company] Director of Aviation, who was very supportive and encouraging at all times, insisted on maintaining a positive approach to the investigation. Both he and the Training Captain began seeking measures our aviation department could take to prevent similar occurrences in the future. The first step was to review and revise the flight procedures manual to include a clarification of procedures to be used concerning altitude clearances.

Both crewmembers visited the controlling Air Route Traffic Control Center to become more familiar with the operations of Air Traffic Control and to discuss pilot/controller communications. Both crewmembers, with the Training Captain, attended a well-known training organization's refresher course in Cockpit Resource Management.

Before receiving the letter of investigation, someone from the FAA's investigating office called to gather personal data on both crewmembers and to offer an opportunity to make a statement concerning what happened from my perspective. Even though I declined to make a statement, I did indicate that I would fully cooperate with their office throughout the investigation. After receiving the letter of investigation, on the advice of the retired inspector, I called the investigating office to arrange an informal interview at which time both crewmembers could sit down and discuss the incident openly.

During the interview both crewmembers were present, and we each told the interviewer what we recalled of the incident. We admitted our mistake but expressed why we thought we were innocent at the time. Then we presented all the steps that had been taken to prevent similar occurrences. Also, we pointed out published articles reporting on the hearback problem that noted both pilots and controllers have the tendency to confuse altitudes such as "one-zero-thousand" versus "one-one-thousand" as well as "Flight Level two-zero-zero" versus "Flight Level two-two-zero."

Since the FAA is currently attempting to use remedial training whenever possible, and since we had taken all the steps that they would have required of us, the following statements (from letters to each pilot involved) sum up [the FAA's] thoughts on the investigation:

"Discussions with you have indicated that your attitude concerning this incident is cooperative and constructive... In consideration of the measures you have taken to prevent similar occurrences in the future, we have concluded that the matter does not warrant legal enforcement action. In lieu of such action, we are issuing this letter which will be made a matter of record for a period of two years, after which the record will be expunged."

IHC staff (left to right) Paul McConnell, Craig Brant, Keith McCutchen, and President Steve Kinnaman accepts the first Flight Standards Safety Award from Director of Flight Standards, Tom Accardi.

Awarding Safety...
... In Deed and Attitude

by Phyllis Duncan, Editor

For years, aviation pundits touted hopping aboard a helicopter from a hub airport for a short trip to "downtown" anywhere as the wave of future business commuting. Then, on May 16, 1977, the worn-out landing gear of a Sikorsky S-61 collapsed atop the Pan Am Building in New York City. Debris rained down on Madison Avenue 808 feet below. Five people died, and seven were seriously injured. Citizens of New York City cried that the middle of a highly congested city was no place for helicopters. The New York City government agreed and shut down the heliport immediately after the accident; it has never reopened. The accident increased public fear of city heliports all over the nation, and others across the country were closed down by municipal governments.

In the years after the New York accident, FAA and industry experts tackled the problem of how to fit a heliport in with the bustling downtown of major cities. And a need for such heliports was rapidly becoming apparent with the growth of a new segment of the helicopter industry—emergency medical service (EMS). On May 9, 1985 in Indianapolis, IN, FAA and city officials dedicated the first heliport developed under FAA's National Prototype Demonstration Heliport Program. The Indianapolis Downtown Heliport came to be the example for others to follow. Unlike its rooftop ancestor in New York City, this heliport had the wholehearted support of the municipal government, which saw its convenient location as attractive to business interests for Indianapolis.

In mid-July 1992, FAA and city officials again gathered at the Indianapolis Downtown Heliport, not for another dedication but for an awards ceremony to honor the heliport's operator, Indianapolis Helicopter Corporation (IHC). IHC, one of the country's major providers of Hospital-based Emergency Medical Service (HEMES), was the recipient of Flight Standards' first "Flight Safety Award" for its remarkable safety record. In 1986 when IHC received the contract to provide service at the Indianapolis Downtown Heliport, its management indicated its commitment to serving the public and its customers safely. IHC sought and received a FAR Part 135 air taxi certificate for its all-weather, HEMES operation. This meant IHC would be adhering to the higher safety standard FAA prescribes for certificated operators holding out to the public for transportation.

So, what was so special to warrant an FAA safety award? Quite simply, IHC has amassed over 11,000 hours of accident- and incident-free, single-pilot air ambulance operations since 1986. This record held while the company expanded to six satellite locations in five states, using 12 helicopters, and employing 30 pilots and 20 aircraft maintenance technicians. IHC accrued this record at a time when the overall EMS industry was experiencing an alarming accident rate. (After reaching an overall high in 1986, the accident rate has steadily improved.)

The numbers, however, were not the only aspect of the operation that FAA found noteworthy. The Indianapolis FSDO, manager of IHC's air taxi certificate, cited the company's attitude toward regulatory compliance as well: IHC and its pilots and mechanics have had no incidences of noncompliance. IHC company policy requires all pilots to participate in the Pilot Proficiency Award Program ("Wings"). IHC has all pilots undergo semi-annual, independent contractor-supplied instrument refresher training and provides specific factory aircraft training for all newly hired pilots. The company has also maintained its own internal audit program, similar to the FAA's program for FAR Part 121 and 135 operators.

IHC's record and safety attitude came to Flight Standards' attention through the efforts of Ms. Bernadette Bauer, Manager of the Indianapolis FSDO, Ms. Holly Geiger, former APPM now Geographic Unit Supervisor, and Aviation Safety Inspector Lewis Owens. They passed the information on to Regional Flight Standards Division Manager David Hanley who in turn advised Flight Standards Director Thomas Accardi. Mr. Brian Calendine of the Air Taxi and Commuter Branch in FAA Headquarters proposed the idea of the award after conferring with the Indianapolis FSDO and Aviation Safety Inspectors Ed Robinson and Al Michaels, who oversaw IHC's original certification. The award, first of its kind, was presented to IHC President Steven Kinnaman at a ceremony which included current and previous employees of the company. Kinnaman accepted the award but said, "This belongs to every IHC employee, past and present, who made our safety record possible."

In addition to the Flight Safety Award, Mr. Kinnaman and three members of his "safety team" also received recognition from Flight Standards. They included Lead Mechanic Craig Brant, Director of Operations Herbert McCutchen, and Director of Maintenance John Paul McConnell.

There are many other EMS operators whose dedication to safe transportation of patients in need of critical care is equally deserving of recognition. To them and IHC, thanks for the life-saving service you provide. ∎

The increase in the use of the versatile helicopter in EMS has had some growing pains in the form of a high accident rate. In the January/February 1993 issue of FAA Aviation News, we will provide an in-depth article on the history and current status of EMS and FAA's and industry's efforts to improve the safety record. —Editor.

Prefright

by Bruce Edsten, Accident Prevention Program Manager, Louisville, Kentucky, Flight Standards District Office

Looks like I just spelled it wrong, but it was intentional. Happily, it is not as big a problem as it might be, but too often a poor or non-existent pre*flight* does indeed result in a major, big-time *fright*.

Some Amusing Anecdotes

Probably the classic example is the tale of the two good ol' boys who were partners in a Piper *Tri-Pacer*. This particular airplane was a relatively high-time bird and in need of some tender loving care, particularly in the area of the fabric cover. Several spots had already been patched, and the boys knew they were going to have to spring for a re-cover job pretty soon. Most likely, it would not get through the next Annual, so maybe the coming winter would be a good time to take bird apart and fix her up.

Well, one day when good ol' boy #1 came to fly, he noticed another place on the rudder that needed some immediate help. Now patching the fabric cover is really a bit beyond what pilot/owner types can do on their own, but #1 takes the rudder off and hauls it home for a quick bandaid treatment anyway. Not being especially flush, these guys can only afford to keep the bird in a dirt-floored T-hangar with no doors. They are trying to keep their maintenance costs down as much as possible, too. Like down to ZERO.

Of course, it is a beautiful day for flying, so good ol' boy #2 shows up at the airport, too, and decides to go commit aviation. He checks the gas (got some) and the oil (showin' on the stick). He also notes that it still has three more or less properly inflated tires, so he climbs in and fires it up right there in the hangar. After all, it flew in here, right? What could go wrong?

After a quick mag and carb heat check, our hero swings onto the active and unleashes the fury of all 150 (more or less) of those Lycoming horses, and the *Tri-Pacer* starts down the centerline. Actually, everything went pretty well until

The first step in a safe flight—a thorough preflight.

he raised the nose, since the *Tri-* has good nosewheel steering. With the nosewheel off the ground, however, the front end starts for the tall weeds on the left side of the runway in a big hurry. In response, our intrepid aviator mashes the right pedal for all he is worth but only gets about 12 feet of slack cable for his trouble.

As the plane starts down the drainage ditch, trailing three runway lights behind it, the pilot decides to yank the power off (about time) and grab the brake handle, but it is already too late. All concerned parties come to rest in the cornfield about 50 feet from the runway, with the left main and the left wing acting as the primary shock absorbers. Fortunately, the pilot had hooked up his seat belt, so he climbs out of the bird without a scratch. Looks like the new fabric job is going to come a bit earlier than anticipated.

Of course, the FAA comes out to see what happened, and as the inspector starts into the corn, the first thing he sees is the tail of the *Tri-Pacer* prominently sticking up in the air because of the wrinkled gear. Conspicuously absent from said tail is the rudder. The inspector asks the pilot where the rudder is, and the response is, "Beats me! I had one when I started, so it musta fell off." On closer inspection, however, it is found that good ol' boy #1 had put all the nuts and bolts back in the hinges and the turnbuckles so they would not get lost. Pretty tough to lose a rudder with all the hardware in place.

Just about this time, good ol' boy #1 shows up in his pick-up truck and drives over to see what all the commotion is about. In the back is the rudder with a new patch in place—so fresh the dope is still wet. Well, as you could imagine, the Inspector had a few well-chosen words for these two.

If you re-read this story a few times, you can probably conjure up some really humorous images, but every once in a while the punch line is a lot more serious. And it is not always a couple of good ol' boys, either. Airliners take off with the landing gear safety pins in place and inspection panels hanging open. Crewmembers have even been left behind.

General aviation has a bunch more airplanes—about 220,000 versus about 6,000 for the airlines—so you would expect that we would see a lot more preflight incidents. How about the *Bonanza* driver who forgot to untie the tail when he started home from the Bahamas? Seems he was parked in the sand alongside a taxiway and figured the reason he needed full power to leave the parking spot was because of having settled into the sand a bit. Actually, he pulled about 10 feet of yellow nylon rope and the concrete block clean out of the sand and flew all the way back to West Palm Beach with it! Lotsa nose down trim.

Late model Piper *Aztecs* come with a huge towbar that folds in the middle so it will fit in the baggage compartment. It attaches pretty securely to the nose gear, so it usually will not even touch the ground. You can see what is coming next, right? I was waiting for takeoff one day when this *Aztec* shows up, and the tower notices something about five feet long hanging down from the nose. The *Aztec* makes a low pass down the runway so the tower can look him over and as he does, I can clearly see what it is. The pilot drops the gear, makes a really good soft-field landing, and does not even scratch towbar. However, there is a really interesting pattern in the rear portion of the nose gear doors where they closed over the towbar.

Causes of "Prefright"

Seriously, though, a lot of preflight items go undone or are done in such haste that the effect is the same. Why is this? Actually, I think the problem has two components. On the one hand, we have complacency and, on the other, dependence on others.

Complacency is sort of a "familiarity breeds contempt" thing. As a pilot gains some experience, his or her thought pattern begins to sound like this, "Heck, I've done this at least a half a gazillion times, and it's always the same, and I never find anything, and I've flown this particular airplane sixty-eleven times, and I wanna FLY not grow old on the ramp, and like that, etc., etc." You get the idea, right?

The other side is dependence on others. We all have to do this to a certain extent, but some folks do a little too much. There is a strong tendency to think that the last guy who flew this thing would surely have written it up if anything were wrong. Of course the mechanic who did the last inspection certainly would not have let the thing out if it were not perfect, either. But, having the most conscientious group of people in the world going before you still will not guarantee that something has not happened in the interim or that something was not overlooked. How about the birds that built a nest in the cowling overnight? Or the new fueler that squirted your *Skyhawk* full of jet fuel and/or backed into your elevator without noticing it? Perhaps that last pilot was not too familiar with this type of airplane and thought the brakes were always like that?

Mechanics make an occasional booboo, too. I am presently the owner of a really good pair of diagonal cutters that I found *on top of the engine* when I opened the cowling to explain a point to a student. Never did find out who left

'em there. Guess the mechanic they belonged (past tense) to figured he had better buy some new ones rather than own up to having left them where he left them. A while back I watched a pilot nearly crash a DeHavilland *Beaver* that had just come out of annual, and the reason he almost lost it was that the ailerons had been rigged backwards. The mechanic messed up, to be sure, but the pilot compounded the error with an incomplete preflight.

Preflighting with a Purpose

What actually prompted me to write this article, though, was watching the many preflight contests held at airshows and safety seminars. I really thought that most of the participants would do better than they did. Perhaps they were not taking it all very seriously because they all knew they would not have to fly the thing, but I am sure that some of it was sloppy preflighting also. One year at Sun 'n' Fun the ones who put the competition together got really sneaky, and put in some stuff that nobody found. But having the seatbelts in backwards? Or would you have noticed that Page 7 was missing from the Approved Flight Manual? Wow! Super sneaky! However, many people missed a rag stuck in the cowling, a broken safety wire on the brakes, screws missing from the wingtips, and lots of other pretty obvious stuff. Not sneaky at all.

The scene was repeated at Oshkosh, and then I got involved in setting one up myself at a local airshow. Once again, we set up some really sneaky stuff, but mostly the items were obvious ones, like no airworthiness certificate, a sparkplug wire hanging loose, and things like that. We told all the participants that there were 10 items to find, but we actually had 12, and the best score was nine. I am quite sure that some of this poor showing was because of having some really hard-to-spot items and some because of assumptions about the paperwork, but a good deal of it was because of *not looking*, and that is the whole answer.

You have to look closely! Having and using a preflight checklist is a big help, too, but simply reciting the items and not really looking will not get the job done. Even really looking is not enough without also knowing what you are looking for. Because of the considerable differences in airplanes, there simply is not enough space here to get into *all* the fine details of what to look for, but

an example might be useful. [See "First Check for Safety—The Preflight Inspection," in the September/October 1991 issue of *FAA Aviation News.—Editor*]

Take tires, for instance. When you look at the tire you are looking for proper inflation but also for the general condition of the tire. How about the tread? Any cord showing? Are the sidewalls cracking and checking? Is the valve stem in good condition? How about the slip indicator, that little strip of paint that crosses the rim and the tire? Are both paint marks lined up?

See what I mean? How many of us just glance at the tire without ever bending down to take a good look?

About the only way to get to know all the fine details about your airplane is to spend some time with a flight instructor or a mechanic who knows the airplane like the back of a hand. If you are really lucky, you may have a detailed owner's manual or an approved flight manual, but even the good ones leave out some of the details. Take a few minutes to poke around your favorite mount, whether you own it or rent it, and ask questions.

When you get really sharp, you may want to test your skills at one of the preflight contests that are sure to come up in the future. I know they will come up because it is an area that needs work. I promote them at every opportunity. They usually draw a lot of attention, and people stay up nights thinking of truly incredible things to do to the subject aircraft. Of course, they have the advantage of using an airplane that can be tied up for weeks and can then be handed back to the mechanics for restoration to airworthy status. Some people have painted different N-Numbers on each side of the fuselage. Would you believe a recent upholstery job with cloth that did not meet the current fire-resistance standards? Would you catch a trim tab that was rigged backwards? Heavy stuff, dude!

It is not likely that the contest at your local airport will get that wild, but there is still a lot of underhanded stuff that I did not mention. Do not be afraid to try one of the contests when the next one comes up in your area because everybody is going to miss something. You will not be alone. Plus, you will undoubtedly learn something about looking at your airplane.

And, when it comes to preflighting your air machine, let us paraphrase our national motto: **IN GOD WE TRUST. EVERYTHING ELSE, *WE CHECK!*** ■

STOP, LOOK, AND LISTEN

Situational Awareness and the Ground Collision at LAX

by Dean Chamberlain, Associate Editor

At 6:07 pm PST, February 1, 1991, 34 passengers and crewmembers were killed when two planes collided on runway 24L at Los Angeles International Airport (LAX). One plane, Skywest Flight 5569, a Fairchild *Metroliner* (SA–227–AC), had been cleared to taxi into position and hold on 24L at Intersection 45. The other aircraft, USAir Flight 1493, a Boeing 737-300 (B–737), had been cleared to land on 24L. The resulting crash killed all 10 passengers and two crewmembers on the *Metroliner* and 20 passengers and two crewmembers on the B-737.

The National Transportation Safety Board's (NTSB) report on the accident identified several factors that the NTSB felt needed to be brought to every pilot's attention. One of those factors was that the local controller working the two aircraft made a mistake and cleared both aircraft onto the same runway. Although the Board's complete report discusses the controller's workload and training, airport lighting, ATC procedures, and several other factors, the report highlighted the fact that controllers as well as pilots can and occasionally do make mistakes. Because mistakes happen, every pilot operating an aircraft should maintain *an awareness of all of the events affecting his or her aircraft's safe operation.*

In a letter about the accident to the FAA Administrator, NTSB said, "Inherent in the 'see and avoid' concept to avoid collision is a need for pilots to be alert and vigilant in monitoring air traffic communications for situations that may lead to conflicts with other aircraft." Also in the letter the Safety Board expressed a concern that the relatively low number of runway incursions may lead to a relaxed vigilance and a decrease in the high state of situational awareness of pilots that is so critical to their performance.

Complacency in a Radar Environment?

In the radar environment of an approach and after having received specific landing clearance, pilots may relax their attentiveness in listening to communications that are not specifically directed to their aircraft. In addition, they may reduce efforts to scan for aircraft between their position and the intended landing runway. As a consequence, pilots of aircraft on an active runway or on final approach to landing should be especially attentive in listening for information about the runway they occupy or expect to occupy. It is essential that pilots monitor the ATC system to the fullest extent possible to detect unsafe practices or conditions that

may affect their flight and to take action to protect themselves from dangerous practices or conditions before they result in accidents. This is not always as easy as it sounds. The Board recognizes the "challenging, inherent difficulties in monitoring the flow of information that is intrinsic to high-density environments." The Board noted that more than 60 ATC transmissions took place in the three minutes and 43 seconds from the time USAir 1493 came on the local controller's frequency until the accident.

Effective training, planning, and resource management may be able to diminish the effects of limitations on the ability of pilots to detect time-critical information. As a result of the LAX accident NTSB has recommended that general aviation and air carriers should take steps to ensure that their respective training programs, including crew resource management (CRM) training and flight operating procedures, place sufficient emphasis on the need for pilots to monitor ATC communications for potential traffic conflicts with their aircraft, especially when on active runways and during final approach/landing segments. All aircrews, therefore, need to develop an increased *situational awareness*.

CRM training is the cornerstone of aircrew preparation for air carriers, and a story on the subject of crew resource management in general aviation operations appeared in the September-October 1991 issue of *FAA Aviation News*. The article, a reprint from *Flight Training* magazine, discussed the need for CRM training, CRM elements, and the CFI's role in CRM training for general aviation. The article highlighted the fact that CRM is as important in a single-pilot cockpit as it is in a crew environment. The article concluded with a list of additional articles and sources of information on CRM training and concepts for general aviation pilots.

In addition to its comments on CRM, the Board also discussed the need for better use of standard words and conversational phraseology between pilots and controllers to avoid any misunderstanding that could cause an accident. At the moment, the FAA is reviewing the question of proper phraseology when pilots request an intersection takeoff and when controllers issue "position and hold" instructions. Any changes will be addressed in a future edition of the *Airman's Information Manual* (AIM).

Responsibilities versus Workload?

But what do developing an increased situational awareness and using proper phraseology really mean? Basically, it means that every pilot is responsible for his or her own safety. Although this accident occurred at a major, towered airport, it highlights the fact that, statistically, the most dangerous segment of flight is on or near an airport. Part of this is because of the number of aircraft operating around, converging on, or departing from the airport. Add to this the extra workload pilots are subject to while starting, taxiing, doing runups, taking off, or preparing to land, and you can understand why a pilot could make an error that may cause an accident. Multiply the number of aircraft operating at a given moment either on the airport or in its vicinity by the number of required ATC radio transmissions and the decisions that the controller has to make, and you can perceive the workload of the controllers responsible for the facility. Throw in the problems of pilots having to navigate and communicate with ATC while operating their aircraft, and you can begin to comprehend why flight at or near airports can be accident prone. The increasing complexity of today's airspace and the resulting number of ATC communications involved in today's operating environment, as noted by NTSB in its discussion of the LAX crash, all add to the problems and stress involved in today's flight operations for both pilots and controllers. Together, all of these factors add up to a lot of distractions that can, as in the case of the LAX crash, result in an accident.

So how can you, as pilot in command, prevent a similar occurrence at LAX or at your own local community airport? We will discuss a few suggestions based upon the NTSB LAX report and general safe flying concepts that may help you avoid this type of accident. If you have any suggestions or ideas that we did not list, please send them to us for possible use in future articles. Listen and Avoid?

First, all pilots and controllers must operate in accordance with the Federal Aviation Regulations (FAR), local airport procedures, and other FAA procedures. The reason is obvious; every pilot must be able to anticipate what another pilot is going to do, and every controller and pilot must be able to anticipate each others' actions. Everyone must be careful, though, not to anticipate an action and do it without authorization. When someone does not follow procedures there is always the potential for an accident.

Listen and Avoid?

So how can a pilot try to avoid an accident? By being aware of what is happening around your aircraft—what we have termed situational awareness. The general aviation pilot is well versed—or should be—in situational awareness. Just consider your actions during a recent weekend of nice weather at a busy non-towered airport that boasts several flight schools, numerous transients, and mixed aircraft operations. You not only broadcast your position when entering and circuiting the traffic pattern, you *listen* for the broadcasts of others as well. When you get through announcing that you are left base and number one for landing then hear some one else make the *same* announcement, your awareness of your situation really heightens—as well as the hackles on the back of your neck. Then, there are the not-so-professional pilots who are too busy or too unconcerned to announce themselves. You have to anticipate their arrival in the traffic pattern when you would otherwise least expect it. This same situational awareness applies both to flight and ground operations at towered *and* non-towered airports.

TIPS ON BEING SEEN

In addition to stressing the need for increased emphasis on monitoring ATC communications, especially when on the runway or landing, and the need for increased situational awareness when in those flight segments, the Board outlined several other good ideas that all pilots should think about. First, the accident report highlighted the fact that in testimony and flight tests after the accident there may have been a problem in the USAir crew being able to see the *Metroliner* on the runway. According to the report, in tests which simulated the accident conditions, the test crews had problems in differentiating a similar *Metroliner* from the lighted runway environment at LAX. And according to testimony of the surviving flight crewmember when asked to account for the fact he did not see the *Metroliner* earlier, he testified, "It wasn't there. It was invisible."

As a result of the flight tests and testimony NTSB made the following recommendations: (1) "The visual approach exercises also indicated that the likelihood of detecting an aircraft from the rear on an active runway by an approaching aircraft can be increased if the first aircraft is displaced from the runway centerline lighting by approximately 3 feet. Moreover, when this offset procedure was used in conjunction with high-energy strobe lighting and anticollision and navigation lighting, aircraft conspicuity was enhanced." (2) "The Safety Board considers that the use of strobe lighting, along with the practice of displacing the aircraft off the centerline lighting, would significantly enhance the ability of pilots and air traffic controllers to visually detect traffic conflict situation." (3) Aircraft operators should upgrade their aircraft anticollision lighting installations on those aircraft certificated before September 1, 1977, to meet current standards. The installation of higher-standard lighting systems would help increase the nighttime conspicuity of the aircraft, particularly while on the ground. It should be noted that aircraft position and anticollision lighting is primarily designed for inflight use, not to maximize conspicuity on the ground.

Seeing and Being Seen?

The Board also emphasized the need for pilots to "see and avoid" other aircraft. You might say, "see and avoid" is a two-part problem. One part is seeing. The other part is being seen. One part is teaching pilots how to look and scan for other aircraft. The other part is thinking of ways of making your aircraft more "seeable" to other pilots. "Operations Lights On" is one way to help—i.e., turn on the aircraft navigation lights, rotating beacon, and strobes when in a terminal area. Of course, strobes should be *off* when in clouds, and at night at a busy well-lighted airport, your lights may become just another shining spot in the background. This is where situational awareness in reverse comes in— you want other pilots and any controllers to be aware of where you are situated. This is again why takeoff and landing announcements are so important at non-towered airports. At towered airports, do not be hesitant to remind a controller of your position if a significant amount of time has passed between ATC transmissions. At towered airports with simultaneous operations off multiple runways, there is no problem with reminding ATC that you are "ready for take-off on 18" after a position and hold clearance. Your transmission requires a response and may serve as a life-saving memory jogger. That transmission on frequency to ATC helps also to make you more "seeable" to other pilots—if they hear you, they will look for you.

Stop, Look, and Listen?

The need for increased situational awareness might be paraphrased by saying all pilots should, stop, look, and listen before putting themselves at risk. Before someone says that you cannot stop an aircraft in flight, think of airborne stopping as not entering a block of airspace without knowing for certain that it will be clear of another hard object, such as another aircraft or a mountain. This can also apply to ground operations but requires that single pilots and aircrews spend as much time as possible protecting their airspace block as best they can. They can do this by knowing their position at all times and knowing where they are going. The time-honored "see and avoid" concept has always meant that pilots must look outside of their aircraft as much as possible, but pilots must also listen to ATC communications for possible conflicts in their airspace whether in flight or while waiting to takeoff and while landing.

One way pilots can do this is through increased training and proficiency. By knowing their aircraft and their flight operating environment, pilots can maximize their "look and listen" time without jeopardizing flight safety. Knowing your aircraft is important. Remember the last time you got checked out in a new aircraft and the amount of time you spent looking for gauges, controls, and other items in the new cockpit? Now remember the amount of time you have to spend looking inside the cockpit of the aircraft you fly frequently. The time you can save by being familiar with your aircraft and its systems is time you can spend looking outside the aircraft for your own safety. Another example of how you can save valuable time for looking outside your aircraft is by having studied the airport diagram and departure procedures, including radio frequencies, before starting engines at a strange airport. If you do not review this information before starting engines, you will have to spend valuable time looking inside the cockpit at charts, etc., instead of looking outside the aircraft for possible problems. The same is true when preparing to land at a new airport. Simply stated, being prepared maximizes the time you can dedicate to safety.

SOP versus Creativity?

Whether departing or landing, pilots also need to follow standard procedures when operating on or near an airport. This includes using standard radio phraseology and reporting procedures. Your own protection depends upon other aircraft knowing exactly where you are at any given moment. Being creative on final or downwind is not the way to avoid an accident. Save being creative for those times that need creativity; otherwise, follow standard procedures whenever possible. For example, how many of you have heard pilots reporting their downwind position using non-standard terms, e.g., CB lingo? How many of you have heard someone reporting their position, and, when you looked to find them, they were not where they had said they were. As we all know, communication requires that everyone knows and follows the same set of guidelines. In the complex world of aviation, pilots and controllers must be able to understand each other. The *Airman's Information Manual* (AIM) not only defines proper airport operating procedures, it has a pilot/controller glossary of aviation terms with their meanings. Since the AIM and its glossary are subject to change, all pilots need to review the current edition of the AIM to ensure compliance with the latest procedures

In addition to reviewing the latest AIM, another safety item is that pilots must use the latest charts and facility information. Before a flight, a pilot should review the latest *Notices to Airmen* publication as well as checking with Flight Service for all changes to charts (both IFR and VFR) facilities, and procedures.

In summarizing some of its recommendations from the LAX accident, the NTSB said that—

- Pilots should remain alert at all times when operating their aircraft, especially when on the runway or when landing.

- Pilots should do all they can to increase the conspicuity of their aircraft either through improved lighting equipment or through such NTSB recommended techniques as offsetting from a runway's centerline lighting when operating in reduced visibility, e.g., during periods of darkness or other periods of reduced visibility.

- Pilots should monitor all ATC communications that could affect their aircraft, and we will add, not just ATC communications but also UNICOM or CTAF transmissions at non-towered airports.

Hopefully through better pilot training and increased situational awareness and, using such techniques as crew resource management, accidents such as the one on the night of February 1, 1991, at LAX can be prevented. ■

INDEX of *FAA Aviation News*

Articles 1991–1992

by Kris Kjos, DOT Management Intern and Louise Oertly, Associate Editor

Flaps *or No Flaps?*

by Fred G. DeLacerda, owner/operator of Delta Aviation, Stillwater, OK.

Cleared for takeoff, the commercial airliner started its takeoff roll with 149 passengers and six crew members on board. Less than a second after takeoff, the MD-80 was in trouble. The airplane climbed slowly, rolling slightly then sharply. Fourteen seconds after takeoff the airplane was less than 50 feet above the ground. At this point first contact was made with a ground obstacle. The ensuing crash left only one survivor.

Approximately one year later the official report by the National Transportation Safety Board (NTSB) stated that the high-lift devices—the wing's leading edge slats and trailing edge flaps—were retracted. Hence, the airplane was not properly configured for takeoff, and, as a result, the airplane's climb performance was severely limited. In an effort to gain altitude, the climb pitch was too high, causing a decrease in roll stability. This resultant roll further degraded climb performance.

The purpose of citing this accident is not to show fault, either human or mechanical, but rather to illustrate how slat and flap configuration affect the performance of a particular airplane. Improper flap configuration can be equally disastrous for less complex airplanes. Consider, for example, a Cessna 182, equipped with a short field takeoff and landing (STOL) kit. The pilot took off with the flaps extended to 35 degrees; however, the pilot thought the flaps were extended to only 20 degrees. Consequently, the pilot established a climb at a pitch angle that exceeded the critical angle of attack for the flap configuration. At an altitude of approximately 100 feet, the airplane stalled and crashed.

A contributing factor in many airplane accidents is the misuse of flaps. Pilots involved in these accidents range from the novice with minimal flight time to the veteran with many hours. Although flap misuse is relatively rare in large air carrier-type airplanes, the failure to use flaps properly on a jet airliner can have tragic results. Misuse of flaps on light airplanes do not necessarily cause an accident, but failure to recognize the effects of a particular flap configuration on the flight characteristics of a certain airplane is a contributing factor to some accidents.

Flaps are used only during a small portion of flight—the takeoff and landing of the airplane. Therefore, the use of flaps becomes either a mechanical process whereby a certain flap setting is used for a particular flight operation or else the pilot relies on judgement as to when, where, and how much flaps to use. In either case the pilot should understand the general effects of flaps, and the specific effects relative to the airplane's design. Unfortunately, some pilots of general aviation airplanes may lack this comprehensive understanding of flaps. This is may be because of a superficial treatment of the subject during flight training, simply because some instructors may not consider flaps an indispensable item for flight safety.

Despite the fact that flaps are used for only two flight conditions, takeoff and landing, these flight conditions are critical because of the airplane's proximity to the ground. Any alteration in the control configuration of the airplane during these flight conditions must be understood by the pilot. The purpose of this article is to provide a detailed analysis of flap operation so the pilot is aware of the complexities involved in the design and use of a seemingly simple control device. Such an awareness could remove "misuse of flaps" as a probable cause or contributing factor to certain accidents.

Airplane Design

It is possible to tell by looking at a parked airplane whether it was designed to fly fast or slow. High speed requires thin, moderately cambered airfoils with a small wing area, whereas the high lift needed for low speeds is obtained with thicker, highly cambered airfoils with a larger wing area. Many attempts have been made to compromise this conflicting requirement of high cruise and slow landing speeds.

Since an airfoil cannot have two different cambers at the same time, one of two things must be done. Either the airfoil can be a compromise, or a cruise airfoil can be combined with a device for increasing the camber of the airfoil for low-speed flight. One method for varying an airfoil's camber is the addition of devices to the leading edge (slats) and/or trailing edge (flaps). Engineers call these devices a high-lift system.

While the flap/slat high-lift system increases wing area and drag, the drawback is the added weight and complexity of the system. In the interest of simplicity, trailing edge flaps only are used on most general aviation airplanes.

Function of Flaps

Flaps work primarily by changing the camber of the airfoil since deflection adds aft camber. Flap deflection does not increase the critical (stall) angle of attack, and in some cases flap deflection actually decreases the critical angle of attack. The traditional definition of angle of attack seems to contradict the decrease in critical angle of attack with flap deflection. Every pilot learns early in flight training that the angle of attack is defined as the angle of the chord line to the relative wind. The chord line is a straight line drawn from the leading edge to the trailing edge of the airfoil. Exceeding a specific angle of attack for a given airfoil, called the critical angle of attack, results in a stall.

The definition of a chord line does not remain the same when flaps are defected despite the degree of deflection being defined relative to the chord line. Chord line is referenced with the zero-lift line, this being a straight line that starts at the leading edge of the airfoil and is parallel to the relative wind when the airfoil angle of attack is such that no lift is produced. Now the angle of attack is redefined relative to

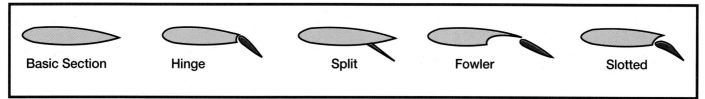

Figure 1. Shown are the four basic types of flaps: plain (hinge), split, Fowler, and slotted.

Basic Section   Hinge   Split   Fowler   Slotted

the zero-lift line so that as the flaps move, the zero-lift line also moves, changing the angle of attack. Hence, as flaps are deflected lift is increased without change in the pitch attitude. The greater the camber, the greater the lift although the angle of attack does not increase.

Deflection of trailing edge control surfaces, such as the aileron, alters both lift and drag. With aileron deflection there is asymmetrical lift (rolling moment) and drag (adverse yaw). Wing flaps differ in that deflection acts symmetrically on the airplane. There is no roll or yaw effect, and pitch changes depend on the airplane design.

Pitch behavior depends on flap type, wing position, and horizontal tail location. The increased camber from flap deflection produces lift primarily on the rear portion of the wing. This produces a nose-down pitching moment; however, the change in tail load from the downwash deflected by the flaps over the horizontal tail has a significant influence on the pitching moment. Consequently, pitch behavior depends on the design features of a particular airplane.

Flap deflection of up to 15 degrees primarily produces lift with minimal drag. The tendency to balloon up with initial flap deflection is because of lift increase, but the nose-down pitching moment tends to offset the balloon. Deflection beyond 15 degrees produces a large increase in drag. Drag from flap deflection is parasite drag and, as such, is proportional to the square of the speed. Also, deflection beyond 15 degrees produces a significant nose up pitching moment in most high wing airplanes because the resulting downwash increases the airflow over the horizontal tail.

Flap Effectiveness

Flap effectiveness depends on a number of factors, but the most noticeable are size and type. In most general aviation airplanes, the flap length depends on the size aileron required because the flaps are located between the ailerons and the fuselage. Consequently, the length of most flaps are approximately 40% of the wingspan. Effectiveness increases with increase in flap chord up to about 40% of the wing chord; however, general aviation airplanes have a flap chord approximately 20 to 25% of the wing chord.

The type of flaps used on general aviation aircraft are limited by structural and weight considerations to trailing edge flaps of four basic types: Plain (hinge), split, slotted, and Fowler. (Figure 1)

The *plain* or *hinge flap* is the simplest in terms of structural requirements since it is a hinged section of the wing. The structure and function are comparable to the other control surfaces—ailerons, rudder, and elevator. The *split flap* is more complex. It is the lower or underside portion of the wing; deflection of the flap leaves the trailing edge of the wing undisturbed. It is, however, more effective than the hinge flap because of greater lift and less pitching moment, but there is more drag. Split flaps are more useful for landing, but the par-

tially deflected hinge flaps have the advantage in takeoff. The split flap has significant drag at small deflections, whereas the hinge flap does not because airflow remains "attached" to the flap. Split flaps can increase the maximum lift coefficient as much as 1.0 compared to .9 for the hinge flap.

The *slotted flap* has a gap between the wing and leading edge of the flap. The slot allows high pressure airflow on the wing undersurface to energize the lower pressure over the top of the flap thereby delaying flow separation. The slotted flap has greater lift than the hinge but less than the split, but, because of a higher lift-drag ratio, it gives better takeoff and climb performance. The slotted flap can give a maximum lift coefficient of 1.2. Small deflections give a higher drag than the hinge flap but less than the split. This allows the slotted flap to be used for takeoff.

The *Fowler flap* deflects down and aft to increase the wing area. This flap can be multi-slotted making it the most complex of the trailing edge systems. This system does give the maximum lift coefficient—as much as 1.7. Drag characteristics at small deflections are much like the slotted flap. Because of structural complexity and difficulty in sealing the slots, Fowler flaps are most commonly used on larger airplanes.

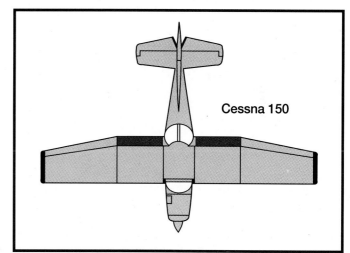

Cessna 150

Figure 2. Cessna 150

One Airplane's Example

It would be overwhelming to compare the many airplane/flap design combinations, but the Cessna 150 is a good example to discuss here because it has a fairly complex flap system for a two-place airplane. The Cessna 150 (Figure 2) is a high-wing trainer with a conventional tail and a compromise wing—rectangular inboard and tapered outboard. The flaps, a single slot Fowler type (Figure 3), are located on the rectangular portion of the wing. They move aft eight inches when fully extended. Flap actuation is by electric motor which allows any degree of deflection from zero to 40

Figure 3. Located on the inboard portion of the wing of this Cessna 150 is a single slot Fowler-type flap. Airplane courtesy of the Professional Flight Service, Ft. Washington, MD.

degrees. Full extension requires nine seconds and retraction six seconds. The flaps represent 11.5% of the total wing area, 17.1% of the wing span, and 30% of the wing chord. Full flap extension decreases the stall speed by 12.7%. The first 20 degrees of deflection lowers the stall speed six mph while the second 20 degrees lowers it only one.

The Cessna manual indicates that normal landing approaches can be made with flaps up or down. When landing in a strong crosswind, the manual recommends that a minimum setting be used as required by runway length. For short field landings, an approach with 40 degrees of flaps is recommended with a power-off touchdown. No more than 10 degrees should be used for takeoff. The 10 degrees shortens the ground roll but hinders the climb.

A go-around requires an immediate 20-degree retraction. It takes approximately two seconds to accomplish this. Any remaining flap retraction is restricted to 10-degree increments, thereby allowing the airplane to accelerate to a speed adequate for a safe climbout.

During the long production life of the Cessna 150 several significant changes were made to the flap system. The early models had mechanically actuated flaps for four positions of deflection at 10-degree increments. The speed for deflection was controlled somewhat by dynamic air pressure on the flaps, but retraction was assisted by this air pressure. Consequently, full flap retraction could be accomplished very rapidly, so rapidly that on low-level go-arounds the loss of lift could allow the airplane to make ground contact. The mechanical flap system was replaced with an electrical system that had a controlled rate of extension and retraction, but even then the manufacturer was specific regarding flap retraction during a go-around. Rather than four positions the electrical system allowed any degree of flap deflection over a range of 40.

Although the geometrical design of the Cessna 152 flaps remained the same as the Cessna 150, there were two significant changes. First, the flap switch was changed for flap settings at 10-degree increments. Second, flap deflection was limited to 30 degrees. The latter design change resulted from pilot problems during go-around. With a 40-degree deflection of the flaps, the application of full power produced a significant increase in airflow over the flap portion of the wing. The sudden increase in lift caused the airplane to pitch up rapidly, requiring significant forward yoke pressure in order to prevent a takeoff/departure stall.

As stated earlier, the position of the horizontal tail relative to the wing determines pitch reaction with flap extension or retraction. The Cessna 150 horizontal tail is below the wing so that with 40 degrees of flaps there is a large downwash over the tail causing a pitch up, a condition that addition of power and nose-up trim aggravated. Therefore, in a go-around, application of full power while simultaneously raising the nose to climb will quickly produce a power-on stall that can be complicated by failure to compensate for torque with the appropriate rudder pressure.

Operational Procedures

As we said, it would be impossible to discuss all of the many airplane design and flap combinations, but the discussion of the Cessna 150 illustrates the importance of the pilot's operating handbook (POH) for a given airplane. However, while some handbooks are specific as to operational use of flaps, most are lacking, particularly for light general aviation airplanes. Hence, flap operation makes pilot judgement of critical importance. In addition, flap operation takes place for landings and takeoffs, operations with the airplane in proximity to the ground where the margin for error is small.

Since the recommendations given in the POH are based on the airplane and the flap design combination, the pilot must relate the manufacturer's recommendation to the aerodynamic effects of flaps. This requires that the pilot have the basic background knowledge of flap aerodynamics and geometry presented earlier. With this information the pilot must make a decision as to the degree of flap deflection and time of deflection based on runway and approach conditions relative to the wind conditions.

The time of flap extension and degree of deflection are related. Large flap deflections at one single point in the landing pattern produce large lift changes that require significant pitch and power changes in order to maintain airspeed and glide slope. Consequently, the deflection of flaps at certain positions in the landing pattern has definite advantages. Incremental deflection of flaps on downwind, base, and final allow smaller adjustment of pitch and power compared to extension of full flaps all at one time. Should the need arise to make a go-around, the degree of flap retraction required will depend on one's position in the landing pattern.

A soft or short field landing requires minimal speed at touchdown, so the flap deflection that gives the minimal ground speed is the flap setting of choice. If obstacle clearance is needed, then the flap deflection that gives the steepest angle of approach is used. It should be noted that the flap setting that gives the minimal speed at touchdown does not necessarily give the steepest angle of approach; however, maximum flap extension gives the steepest angle of approach and minimum speed at touchdown. Maximum flap extension particularly beyond 30 to 35 degrees, gives a large amount of drag. This requires higher power settings than used with partial flaps. Because of the steep approach angle combined with power to offset drag, the flare with full flaps becomes critical. The drag produces a high sink rate that must be controlled with power, yet failure to reduce power at a rate so that it is at idle at touchdown allows the airplane to float down the runway. A reduction in power too early results in a hard landing.

Wind conditions include not only the velocity but the crosswind component and the degree of turbulence. As stated previously, touchdown speed should be at a minimum, but one must be reminded that airspeed and ground speed are not necessarily the same. The stronger the headwind at touchdown the slower the ground speed will be. The greater the flap deflection the slower the ground speed at touchdown for a given headwind component. This is particularly true when the flap setting exceeds 30 to 35 degrees. Needless to say, maximum flap extension on final approach in a strong headwind would require a high power setting, the setting dependent on the velocity of the headwind. There reaches a point in a strong headwind approach where the pilot must consider the merits of flap setting versus power setting. There is little need to use maximum flaps if the wind condition makes full power a requirement to make the runway. This is a case where pilot judgement, based on airplane performance and manufacturer recommendations, is the determining factor.

A crosswind component is another factor to consider in the degree of flap extension. The deflected flap presents a surface area for the wind to act on, and the more the degrees of deflection, the more surface area that is affected by the wind. In a crosswind the "flapped" wing on the upwind side is more affected than the downwind wing. This is, however, eliminated to a slight extent in the crabbed approach since the airplane is more nearly aligned with the wind. In a wing low approach the lowered wing partially blankets the windward flap, but the dihedral of the wing combined with the flap and wind make lateral control more difficult. Lateral control becomes more difficult as flap extension reaches maximum and the crosswind becomes perpendicular to the runway.

Crosswind effects on the "flapped" wing become more pronounced as the airplane comes closer to the ground. The wing, flap, and ground form a "container," so to speak, that is filled with air by the crosswind. With the wind striking the deflected flap and fuselage side and with the flap located behind the main gear, the airplane tends to lift the windward wing and turn into the wind. Therefore, proper control position and flap retraction upon positive ground contact is essential for maintaining runway alignment.

Gusty and turbulent wind must also be considered when making a decision about flap settings. Generally, approach speeds are increased during gusty and turbulent wind conditions. When gusty and turbulent air strikes the "flapped" wing asymmetrically, lateral control of the airplane becomes more difficult. Such wind conditions call for minimum flap settings or per the recommendations in the POH.

The go-around is another factor to consider when making a decision about degree of flap deflection and about where in the landing pattern to extend flaps. Because of the nose down pitching moment produced with flap extension, trim is used to offset this pitching moment. Application of full power in the go-around increases the airflow over the "flapped" wing. This produces additional lift causing the nose to pitch up, a motion that does not diminish completely with flap retraction because of the trim setting. Expedient retraction of the flaps is desired to eliminate drag, thereby allowing rapid increase in airspeed; however, retraction of flaps also decreases lift so that the airplane sinks rapidly.

The degree of flap deflection combined with design configuration of the horizontal tail relative to the wing requires that the pilot carefully monitor pitch and airspeed, carefully control flap retraction to minimize altitude loss, and properly use the rudder for coordination. Considering these factors, it is important to extend flaps the same degree of deflection at the same point in the landing pattern. This requires that a consistent traffic pattern be used. Therefore, the pilot can have a pre-planned go-around sequence based on the position in the landing pattern.

There is no single formula to determine the degree of flap deflection to be used on landing, simply because a landing involves variables that are dependent on one another. The aircraft's POH will contain the manufacturer's recommendations on flap usage for some landing situations. On the other hand, POH information on flap usage for takeoff is more precise. The manufacturer's requirements are based on the climb performance produced by a given flap design. Under no circumstances should a flap setting given in the POH be exceeded for takeoff.

Although pilots receive considerable emergency training, there is very little given for flap malfunctions. Although highly reliable, flap systems do fail. While a flapless landing is not necessarily a problem, there are certain factors to be considered. First, the pitch angle is higher for the airspeeds normally used in the pattern, making detection of traffic more difficult on some models of aircraft. Second, the landing speed will be higher, thereby requiring more runway. Because of the increased pitch angle, the pilot has difficulty seeing the runway, hence, there is a tendency to lower the nose, which in turn increases the approach speed.

A more critical emergency situation is the asymmetrical flap deflection. Such a condition immediately produces a rolling moment that must be countered with aileron opposite to the rolling moment and rudder opposite to the aileron to offset the yaw produced by the one deflected flap. Again, consult the POH's emergency section to see if there are specific procedures for this situation. If there is not, the pilot is faced with a critical decision: Continue with the asymmetrical flap extension or retract the flaps. Unless the pilot has increased the airspeed, the sudden retraction of the down flap at a low airspeed and low to the ground could result in a stall. In either case, a stall must be avoided. With asymmetrical flaps an uncontrollable roll in the direction of the "unflapped" wing will probably produce a stall and subsequent spin if the airspeed slows below stall speed. The unflapped wing will stall at a lower angle of attack than the flapped wing. The differential in lift on the two wings at stall produces the yaw needed for spin entry. To ensure against a stall, approach speeds should be higher than normal, at least 30% greater. Of course, this will require a longer than usual landing distance.

Conclusion

Full flaps or partial flaps? The answer depends on consideration of the following factors: 1) flap aerodynamics, 2) airplane and flap design combinations, 3) manufacturer recommendations, 4) runway and approach conditions, and 5) wind conditions. Pilot judgement based on a working knowledge of these factors ensures safe flight—and flap—operations. ∎

We Are Here to Help You

by Dean Chamberlain, Associate Editor

When was the last time you called the FAA for something other than a flight plan or weather briefing? If you cannot remember, something is wrong. Either your memory is failing or you have been avoiding the FAA. Avoiding the FAA is easy. What with DUATS, electronic flight plan filing, consolidated Flight Service Stations, designated pilot examiners, and computerized airman testing, today airmen can go years without ever meeting anyone from the FAA except after an incident, accident, or inspection.

This article is a reminder for airmen to get to know their local FAA aviation safety inspectors (ASI) and Accident Prevention Program Managers (APPM) before they have to meet them officially. The reason is simple. Your local inspectors and APPM can provide you with a lot of good aviation information. Since help is only a telephone call or visit away, you owe it to yourself to take advantage of all of the FAA services and information available. You should be proactive and go meet your local FAA representatives, and one of the easiest ways to do that is through the Accident Prevention Program. To find out more about the Program call or visit your local APPM. And while you are talking to the APPM, you can ask about the next FAA safety meeting in your area. So the next time you are near your local Flight Standards District Office (FSDO) stop in and say hello. Some pilots do, but more do not.

Why is that? Fear may be one of the reasons more airmen do not routinely visit their local FSDO. Apparently, there are still a few intrepid airmen across

National Manager of the Accident Prevention Program, Roger M. Baker, Jr., speaking at the EAA fly-in at Oshkosh, WI.

the country who are willing to risk their lives by gulping their coffee, jumping over small restaurant tables, leaping tall counters, crashing security gates, and flying through open T-Hangars just to get across the airport to avoid an FAA inspector walking on the ramp near the airport's restaurant. Why these brave airmen would want to risk spilling their coffee or risk life and limb to avoid an inspector looking for a cup of coffee remains a mystery. If nothing else, they could take a taxi to the other side of the airport, but that is not the point of this article. The point is many airmen avoid the very people who can help them fly or work safer. In many cases, unless these airmen work for a large company that can afford the high cost of keeping up with the constantly changing information in aviation, the local FAA safety inspectors and Accident Prevention Program Manager may be the best and only free source

of information about new rule changes, airworthiness directives (AD), and other changes in the industry. After all, the FAA works for you. Your tax dollars pay the bills, so you should make sure you get your money's worth. If you have been avoiding the FAA for years or are a new airmen, you may not know what services are available. The following article briefly lists some of the services the Accident Prevention Program and its parent organization, the Flight Standards Service, offer airmen. For instance, we know many airmen do not know about the new FAA Maintenance Technician Awards Program discussed in our September-October 1992 issue. Why the emphasis on Flight Standards? Because it is responsible for airmen certification, aircraft maintenance and airworthiness issues, aircraft operations, and many other areas that impact all airmen.

Flight Standards Service

For those airmen not familiar with the Flight Standards Service, its mission as stated in its most recent five-year management plan is "To provide the public with accident-free aircraft operations through the highest standards in the world." That plan, the *Strategic Management Plan, 1992-1997,* outlines the Service's eight strategic goals it plans to accomplish during the next five years. One of the goals addresses safety. Another addresses quality service and productivity. One safety goal the Service wants to accomplish is to continue to increase safety though a partnership with the aviation industry, a partnership that stresses voluntary industry compliance with appropriate regulations and safety procedures rather than through FAA enforcement. At the same time, the Service wants to improve the quality of service it offers the public by anticipating customer needs and responding in the public interest.

As it strives to accomplish its stated goals, Flight Standards will continue to perform its traditional role of ensuring safety within the aviation industry through the certification and surveillance of: air carriers, commercial and general aviation operators and air agencies; airmen and their proficiency; maintenance programs for U.S. aircraft; operational use of instrument flight procedures and aviation weather services; through management of the Accident Prevention Program; and through its investigatory role in aviation accidents, incidents, and regulatory non-compliance.

Flight Standards is involved in all segments of aviation involving airmen and aircraft. To manage such a wide range of activities, the Service is divided into major functional areas or divisions at FAA Headquarters in Washington D.C. Each division then provides the Service, the FAA Administrator, and the industry the expertise, policy guidance, and support needed within its specialized area. The names of the specialized headquarters divisions tell what industry segments they serve. The divisions are: Air Transportation, Aircraft Maintenance, Technical Programs, Field Programs, and General Aviation and Commercial. The divisions are then organized into branches and other offices to serve the unique needs within an industry group. For example, the Accident Prevention Program Branch (AFS-810) is a branch within the General Aviation and Commercial Division (AFS-800). That Division's other branches include the Operations Branch (AFS-820) which deals with general aviation pilot and aircraft operating procedures under FAR Parts 91, 103, 105, 125, 133, and 137; the Certification Branch (AFS-840) which deals with airmen certification and training; and the Regulations Branch (AFS-850) which deals with general aviation regulatory matters, including rulemaking and exemptions.

The divisional concept is also reflected in a somewhat modified form down through each of the FAA's nine Regional Offices to the Service's field operating units, the 90-plus national Flight Standards District Offices. The Service's Washington Headquarters organizational structure is representative of the way Flight Standards provides support at the FSDO level. Each FSDO has specialists assigned who can handle most of the questions and problems that an airman (which includes organizations and operators as well as individual airman) may have. Quick service is why airmen should contact their local FSDO's whenever they have a question or need help in resolving any FAA or aviation matter. If your question cannot be answered at the FSDO level, the person handling your question will forward it to the appropriate level, the respective regional office or FAA Headquarters, that has the expertise or authority to answer your question.

General Aviation and Commercial Division

This division serves the needs of general aviation, which is normally defined as all segments of aviation other than the FAR Part 121 Air Carrier operators and Part 135 Air Taxi Operators. To put the Division's responsibilities into perspective, we must review the size and scope of general aviation. According to the division's 1992-1997 *General Aviation Action Plan* (GAAP), general aviation accounts for about 97% of all of the nation's pilots and aircraft. It also provides about 530,000 jobs and contributes about $38 billion to the nation's economy. In 1990, about 700,000 general aviation pilots operated about 220,000 general aviation aircraft a total of about 35 million flight hours. These numbers show that general aviation pilots, maintenance technicians, and the industry supporting them represent a significant national investment in terms of operations, equipment, and economic impact. Since general aviation means every operation other than air carrier, air taxi, and commercial operators, the general aviation fleet ranges from the historic Piper J3 *Cub* flown by a new recreational pilot from a grass strip to the pipeline patrol pilot flying a Cessna *Skyhawk* to the latest business jet (which in some cases can be a Boeing 747) flown by a crew of seasoned pros.

This diversity of types of pilots, flying, and aircraft can cause difficulties. It created a safety problem for the in-dustry and the FAA in the 1950's and 1960's. General aviation's accident rate skyrocketed out of sight. As a result, the FAA, working with industry, organized the Accident Prevention Program in the early 1970's to try to reduce the accident rate through education. Because of the support of the aviation industry and dedicated airmen everywhere, the Program has been very successful. Since its founding nearly 20 years ago, the Accident Prevention Program and the dedicated people supporting the concept, both within industry and the FAA, have all worked together to reduce the general aviation accident rate from the deadly rates of the 1950's and 1960's to its lowest rate ever last year. The diversified Accident Prevention Program means different things in different parts of the country, but within the Program there is a common goal: Accident Prevention through education.

Accident Prevention Program

A National Accident Prevention Program Manager and staff provide resource support and policy guidance to the nine Regional Accident Prevention Program Managers (RAPPM) who direct the activities of the APPM's working at the various FSDO's. Although most FSDO's have an APPM assigned, some of the satellite FSDO's and specialty offices do not. In those cases, the safety needs within their areas are served by the nearest APPM. An interesting point many airmen may not know is that each APPM is an experienced Aviation Safety Inspector (ASI) and a well qualified pilot and instructor. Although every ASI is dedicated to aviation safety, each APPM's full-time job is promoting safety within his or her area. This is why your local APPM should be your first point of contact at your FSDO for access to all of the FAA's safety information and related products. Each APPM has access to safety films, video tapes, pamphlets, and other safety material that can be used in safety presentations or meetings. In addition, because of their safety work, APPM's normally know of both FAA and industry experts within their respective areas who are willing to provide safety help and advice when needed. APPM's also have access to a wide range of other types of information, including *FAA Aviation News,* to support their local programs. And since the APPM's work closely with many of the aviation trade and membership groups, they can normally tell you about the types of safety information available from these groups as well. As you can see, your local APPM is a valuable information resource waiting to serve your needs.

In addition to the direct support your APPM can provide you or your group, he or she may also refer you to one of the many volunteer Accident Prevention Counselors (APC) who support and make the Accident Prevention Program work. The Accident Prevention Program would not be the success it is today without the 3,000-plus APC's across the country who volunteer their time and aviation knowledge and expertise to help their fellow airmen. Although the volunteer support the APC's provide the Program is critical to its success, in many cases, they seldom receive the public recognition they deserve. As a result, many airmen may not even know about the help and support available from their local APC's. But without the APC's, the Accident Prevention Program could not provide the quality support that airmen have come to expect and rightly deserve over the last 20 years.

This lack of public awareness of the support and dedication of the APC's and APPM's to aviation safety and of the Accident Prevention Program in general is why we are listing the names and addresses of the following APPM's by their respective FSDO's and regions. Because of the number of APC's nationwide, we cannot list their names and addresses. Airmen should contact their local APPM for the names and telephone numbers of APC's within their areas.

When you combine the APC's and APPM's knowledge of the unique pilot operating requirements within their respective geographical areas and their aviation expertise with your own skills and knowledge, you have a winning safety combination that cannot be beat for your next flight. For example, before your next extended cross-country flight you could contact the APPM at each FSDO along your route of flight with any questions you might have about his or her respective area. While we are not proposing that you contact

an APPM or APC in lieu of your obtaining proper preflight information required by the FAR, we are suggesting that APPM's or APC's be contacted for such information that is not provided elsewhere. Such information might include tips on how to fly safely in mountainous terrain if you have never flown in the mountains, or how to safely fly over-water from Florida to the Bahamas, or similar questions on pilot techniques or operating procedures such as how to fly in or near a TCA or some other question that is bothering you. In addition, since most APC's are flight instructors, you may want to arrange a local checkout with one of them when you visit the area. APPM's can also answer your questions about other flight safety areas such as when the next FAA safety seminar will be held in your area or in the area you are planning to visit. Simply stated, everyone within the FAA and the Accident Prevention Program is dedicated to providing you with the safety tools and information necessary to ensure your next trip or operation is a safe one. The necessary resources to manage your own personal safety program is only a telephone call or visit away. And if you have any questions about pilot certification, airworthiness issues, or such diverse subjects as how to start an air taxi operation, arrange a flight test, or how to hold an airshow, please contact your local ASI or APPM. They are there to help you.

And no discussion of the Accident Prevention Program would be complete without mentioning its Pilot Proficiency Awards Program, or "WINGS Program," for short. If you do not know about the program, or how it can be used to satisfy your FAR Part 61 Flight Review requirement, call your local APPM.

Although FSDO addresses and telephone numbers are printed in various FAA publications, and are listed in the *Airport/Facility Directory* and under the U.S. Government/Department of Transportation/Federal Aviation Administration in the telephone directory for example, we are printing the names of all of the current APPM's and FSDO's by region, including those FSDO's without APPM's for your information and ease of access. We will update the list as space permits. Remember to fly safely. ∎

NATIONAL ACCIDENT PREVENTION PROGRAM STAFF

Manager:
Roger M. Baker
Federal Aviation Administration
AFS-810
800 Independence Avenue, S.W.
Washington, DC 20591
Telephone: (202) 366–6321

Staff:
Reneé Ostopoff
Branch secretary
Telephone: (202) 366–6321
FAX: (202) 366–7060

Milt Gilmore
Program specialist
Telephone: (202) 366–6384

Judy Ashby-Adams
Program specialist
Telephone: (202) 366–6378

FAA AVIATION NEWS staff:

Phyllis Duncan,
Editor
Telephone: (202) 267–8017

Louise C. Oertly,
Associate editor
Telephone: (202) 267–7953

H. Dean Chamberlain,
Associate editor
Telephone: (202) 267–7956

FAA Aviation News
FAX: (202) 267–5219

ALASKAN REGION

RAPPM: Valerie Aron
FAA Flight Standards
Division, AAL–204
222 West 7th Avenue, Box 14
Anchorage, AK 99513–7587
Telephone: (907) 271–5912
FAX: (907) 276–6207

APPM: Dennis Ward *(General Aviation)*
Donald Nelson *(Air Carrier)*
Flight Standards District Office–01
6348 Old Airport Way
Fairbanks, AK 99709
Telephone: (907) 474–0276
FAX: (907) 479–9650

APPM: Tom Eldridge
Flight Standards District Office–03
4510 West International Road,
Suite 302
Anchorage, AK 99502–1088
Telephone: (907) 243–1902
FAX: (907) 243–0884

APPM: Patty Mattison
Flight Standards District Office–05
1910 Alex Holden Way, Suite A
Juneau, AK 99801
Telephone: (907) 789–0231
FAX: (907) 789–1833

CENTRAL REGION

RAPPM:
Randy Robinson
FAA, ACE–250A
Federal Office Building
601 E. 12th Street, Room 1664
Kansas City, MO 64106
Telephone: (816) 426–3426
FAX: (816) 426–6811

APPM: Roger Clark
Flight Standards District Office–01
3021 Army Post Road
Des Moines, IA 50321
Telephone: (515) 285–9895
FAX: (515) 285–7595

APPM: Fred P. Harms
Flight Standards District Office–03
10801 Pear Tree Lane, Suite 200
St. Ann, MO 63074
Telephone: (314) 429–1006
FAX: (314) 429–6367

Flight Standards District Office–05

525 Mexico City Avenue
Kansas City International Airport
Kansas City, MO 64153
Telephone: (816) 243–3818
FAX: (816) 243–3819

APPM: Richard Perigo
Flight Standards District Office–07
1801 Airport Road
FAA Building, Room 103
Mid-Continent Airport
Wichita, KS 67209
Telephone: (316) 941–1208
FAX: (316) 946–4420

APPM: Larry T. Craig
Flight Standards District Office–09
General Aviation Building
Lincoln Municipal Airport
Lincoln, NE 68524
Telephone: (402) 437–5485
FAX: (402) 474–7013

EASTERN REGION

RAPPM:
George V. Strickland
FAA, AEA–264
JFK International Airport
Fitzgerald Federal Bldg. 111
Jamaica, NY 11430
Telephone: (718) 553–1374
FAX: (718) 244–0386

APPM: Mark Furman
Flight Standards District Office–01
Albany County Airport
CFR & M Building
Albany, NY 12211
Telephone: (518) 869–8482
FAX: (518) 869–5267

APPM: Darrell Miller
Flight Standards District Office–03
12 Allegheny County Airport
Administration Bldg., Room 213
West Mifflin, PA 15122–2656
Telephone: (412) 462–5507
FAX: (412) 466–3749

APPM: Jim Ryan
Flight Standards District Office–05
Allentown–Bethlehem Easton Airport
3405 Airport Road North
Allentown, PA 18103
Telephone: (215) 264–2888
FAX: (215) 264–3179

APPM: Doug Lundgren
Baltimore Flight Standards

District Office–07
890 Airport Park Rd.
Glen Burnie, MD 21601
Telephone: (410) 787–0040
FAX: (410) 787–8708

APPM: David Burgess
Flight Standards District Office–09
Yeager Airport, Room 144
301 Eagle Mountain Road
Charleston, WV 25311
Telephone: (304) 343–4689
FAX: (304) 343–2011

APPM: Betty Jo Ault
Flight Standards District Office–11
Administration Building, Suite 235,
Route 110, Republic Airport
Farmingdale, NY 11735–1583
Telephone: (516) 755–1300
FAX: (516) 694–5516

APPM: Warren Green
Harrisburg Flight Standards
District Office–13
Room 201, Admin. Building
Capitol City Airport
New Cumberland, PA 17070
Telephone: (717) 774–8271
FAX: (717) 774–4918

APPM: William Miller
Flight Standards District Office–17
Scott Plaza #2, 2nd Floor
Philadelphia, PA 19113
Telephone: (215) 596–0673
FAX: (215) 521–4893

APPM: Harry L. Watson
Flight Standards District Office–21
Richmond International Airport
Terminal Bldg., 2nd Floor
Sandston, VA 23150–2594
Telephone: (804) 222–7494
FAX: (804) 222–4843

APPM: David Fosdick
Flight Standards District Office–23
Rochester–Monroe County Airport
1 Airport Way, Suite 110
Rochester, NY 14624
Telephone: (716) 263–5880
FAX: (716) 436–2322

APPM: George Strickland
Flight Standards District Office–25
150 Fred Wehran Drive, Room 5
Teterboro Airport
Teterboro, NJ 07608
Telephone: (201) 393–6700
FAX: (201) 288–7308

APPM: James Jacobsen
Flight Standards District Office–27
P.O. Box 17325
Washington Dulles International Airport
Washington, DC 20041–0325
Telephone: (703) 661–8160
FAX: (703) 661–8744

GREAT LAKES REGION

RAPPM:
Michael G. Beiriger
FAA, AFS–204
2300 East Devon Avenue
Des Plaines, IL 60018
Telephone: (312) 694–7154
FAX: (312) 694–7884

APPM: Denis Caravella
Flight Standards District Office–03
31W 775 N. Ave., Dupage Arpt.
West Chicago, IL 60185–1056
Telephone: (708) 377–4500
FAX: (708) 584–0274

APPM: Martha Lunken
Flight Standards District Office–05
Lunken Airport Executive Bldg.
4242 Airport Road, Ground FL.
Cincinnati, OH 45226
Telephone: (513) 533–6104
FAX: (513) 533–8420

APPM: Richard Fischer
Flight Standards District Office 07
3939 International Gateway, 2nd FL.
Port Columbus Int'l Airport
Columbus, OH 43219
Telephone: (614) 469–7476
FAX: (614) 231–0920

APPM: Christine Winzer
Flight Standards District Office–09
P.O. Box 888879
Grand Rapids, MI 49588–8879
Telephone: (616) 456–2427
FAX: (616) 940–3140

APPM: Lew Owens
Flight Standards District Office–11
6801 Pierson Drive, Int'l Airport
Indianapolis, IN 46241
Telephone: (317) 247–2491
FAX: (317) 247–2498

APPM: Jimmy Szajkovics
Flight Standards District Office–13

4915 South Howell Avenue
Milwaukee, WI 53207
Telephone: (414) 747–5531
FAX: (414) 747–0244

APPM: Verdon Kleimenhangen
Flight Standards District Office–15
6020 28th Ave., South Rm 201
Minneapolis-St Paul Int. Airport
Minneapolis, MN 55450
Telephone: (612) 725–4288
FAX: (612) 725–4290

APPM: Don Hales
Flight Standards District Office–17
1843 Commerce Drive
South Bend, IN 46628
Telephone: (219) 236–8480
FAX: (219) 236–8486

APPM: John Blohm
Flight Standards District Office–19
#3 North Airport Drive
Capital Airport
Springfield, IL 62708
Telephone: (217) 492–4238
FAX: (217) 492–4447

APPM: Les Ellingson
Flight Standards District Office 21
1801 23rd. Avenue N., Rm 216
Fargo, ND 58102
Telephone: (701) 232–8949
FAX: (701) 235–2863

APPM: Alfred Hunt
Flight Standards District Office–23
Willow Run Airport, East Side
8800 Beck Road
Belleville, MI 48111
Telephone: (313) 487–7207
FAX: (313) 487–7221

APPM: Ron Drake
Flight Standards District Office–25
Federal Facilities Bldg., Rm. 131
Cleveland Hopkins Int'l. Airport
Cleveland, OH 44135
Telephone: (216) 265–1374
FAX: (216) 265–1379

APPM: Al Neal
Flight Standards District Office–27
Rural Rt. 2, Box 4750
Rapid City, SD 57701
Telephone: (605) 393–1359
FAX: (605) 393–0876

NEW ENGLAND REGION

RAPPM:
George M. Gabriel
FAA Regional Office, ANE–204
12 New England Executive Park
Burlington, MA 01803–5299
Telephone: (617) 273–7132
FAX: (617) 273–0837

APPM: John Hemmes
Flight Standards District Office–01
L.G. Hanscom Field
Civil Air Terminal, 2nd Floor
Bedford, MA 01730
Telephone: (617) 273–7231
FAX: (617) 274–6725

APPM: Bob Martens
Flight Standards District Office–03
Bldg. 85–214, 1st Floor
Bradley International Airport
Windsor Locks, CT 06096–1009
Telephone: (203) 654–1002
FAX: (203) 654–1009

APPM: William Gianetta
Flight Standards District Office–05
Portland International Airport
2 Al McKay Avenue
Portland, ME 04102
Telephone: (207) 780–3263
FAX: (207) 780–3296

APPM: John Hemmes
FAA/ANE Flight Standards
Field Office–02
Logan International Airport
Massachusetts Tech Center, Rm 306
East Boston, MA 02128
Telephone: (617) 561–5789
FAX: (617) 561–5792

NORTHWEST MOUNTAIN REGION

RAPPM:
David Miller,
(ANM–204 OPS);
Lou Lerda
(ANM–204A Airworthiness)
1601 Lind Ave., SW
Renton, WA 98055–4056
(Miller) Telephone: (206) 227–2263
(Lerda) Telephone: (206) 227–2924
FAX: (206) 227–1200

APPM: Escott Gardiner
Seattle Flight Standards

District Office–1
1601 Lind Ave., SW
Renton, WA 98055–4056
Telephone: (206) 227–2880
FAX: (206) 227–1810

APPM: Herbert Wilson
Denver Flight Standards
District Office–03
5440 Roslyn Street
Suite #201
Denver, CO 80216–6026
Telephone: (303) 286–5405
FAX: (303) 286–5430

APPM: Jimmie C. Herzfeld
Casper Flight Standards
District Office–4
Terminal Building, 2nd Floor
Natrona County International Airport
Casper, WY 82604
Telephone: (307) 261–5425

APPM: Denny L. Bridges
Helena Flight Standards District Office–5
FAA Building, Room 3
Helena Airport
Helena, MT 59601
Telephone: (406) 449–5270
FAX: (406) 585–5275

APPM: James Pyles
Salt Lake City Flight Standards District
Office–07
116 North 2400 West
Salt Lake City, UT 84116
Telephone: (801) 524–4247
FAX: (801) 588–5329

APPM: John Goostrey
Boise Flight Standards District Office–8
Boise Airport
3975 Rickenbacker Street
Boise, ID 83705
Telephone: (208) 334–1238
FAX: (208) 334–9158

APPM: James E. Laird
Portland Flight Standards
District Office–9
Portland–Hillsboro Airport
3355 NE Cornell Road
Hillsboro, OR 97124
Telephone: (503) 326–2104
FAX: (503) 648–6729

SOUTHERN REGION

RAPPM:
Robert Henrich
FAA, ASO–204
P.O. Box 20636
Atlanta, GA 30320
Telephone: (404) 763–7145
FAX: (404) 763–7601

APPM: Bruce Edsten
Flight Standards District Office–01
Kaden Bldg., 5th Floor
6100 Dutchman's Lane
Louisville, KY 40205
Telephone: (502) 582–5941
FAX: (502) 582–6735

APPM: Jerald L. Ritchey
Flight Standards District Office–03
2 International Plaza Drive, Suite 700
Nashville, TN 37217
Telephone: (615) 781–5437
FAX: (615) 781–5436

APPM: Thomas N. Jones
Flight Standards District Office–05
8025 North Point Blvd., Room 250
Winston-Salem, NC 27106
Telephone: (919) 631–5147
FAX: (919) 631–5014

APPM: St. Elmo ("Buz") M. Massengale
Flight Standards District Office–07
FAA Building, Suite C
120 N. Hangar Drive
Jackson International Airport
Jackson, MS 39208
Telephone: (601) 965–4633
FAX: (601) 965–4636

APPM: James E. Toombs
Flight Standards District Office–09
6500 43rd Avenue, North
Birmingham, AL 35206–4197
Telephone: (205) 731–1641
FAX: (205) 731–0939

APPM: Larry E. Payne
Flight Standards District Office–11
1680 Phoenix Parkway, 2nd Floor
College Park, GA 30349
Telephone: (404) 994–5279
FAX: (404) 994–5679

APPM: Richard Hitt
Flight Standards District Office–13
103 Trade Zone Drive
Building C, Suite 30–C
West Columbia, SC 29170
Telephone: (803) 765–5931
FAX: (803) 253–3999

APPM: Obie S. Young
Acting Asst. William L. Hoenstine
Flight Standards District Office–15
9677 Tradeport Drive, Suite 100
International Airport
Orlando, FL 32827–5397
Telephone: (407) 648–6840
FAX: (407) 648–6916

APPM: Donald J. Muzeroll
Flight Standards District Office–17
Ft. Lauderdale–
Hollywood International Airport
286 SW 34th Street
Ft. Lauderdale, FL 33315
Telephone: (305) 356–7526
FAX: (305) 356–7531

APPM: Millard ("Mac") McChesney
Flight Standards District Office–19
P.O. Box 592015
Miami, FL 33159
Telephone: (305) 526–2776
FAX: (305) 526–2698

APPM: Abel Mirabel
Flight Standards District Office–21
5000 Carr 190
Carolina, PR 00979–7450
Telephone: (809) 253–4690
FAX: (809) 253–4578

SOUTHWEST REGION

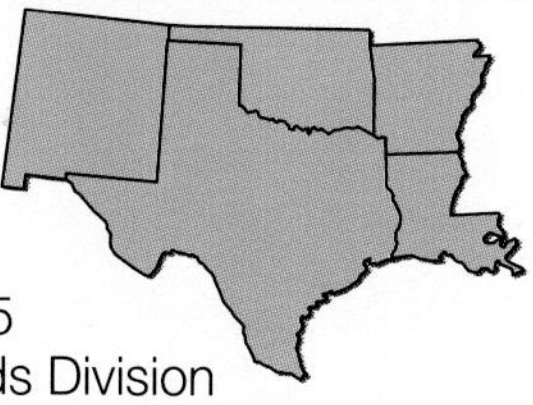

RAPPM:
David A.
Robinson
FAA, ASW–205
Flight Standards Division
Fort Worth, TX 76193–0205
Telephone: (817) 624–5268
FAX: (817) 740–3393

APPM: Berlin H. Blair
Flight Standards District Office–01
ABQ International Airport
1601 Randolph Road, S.E.
Suite 200 N
Albuquerque, NM 87106
Telephone: (505) 764–1222
FAX: (505) 766–1217

APPM: Maurice K. Fulkerson
Flight Standards District Office–03
FAA Building, Ryan Airport
9191 Plank Road
Baton Rouge, LA 70811
Telephone: (504) 358–6800
FAX: (504) 358–6875

APPM: John H. Jarchow
Flight Standards District Office–05
7701 No. Stemmons Freeway
Suite 300, Lockbox 5
Dallas, TX 75247
Telephone: (214) 767–5850
FAX: (214) 767–5859

APPM: Patricia K. Mathes
Flight Standards District Office–09
Hobby Airport
8800 Paul B. Koonce Dr., Rm. 152
Houston, TX 77061–5190
Telephone: (713) 640–4400
FAX: (713) 640–4459

APPM: Jarrett McFarlin
Flight Standards District Office–11
1701 Bond Street
Adams Field
Little Rock, AR 72202–5733
Telephone: (501) 324–5565
FAX: (501) 324–5598

APPM: J. Lamont Williford
Flight Standards District Office–13
Lubbock International Airport
Route 3, Box 51
S. End Old Terminal Bldg.
Lubbock, TX 79401
Telephone: (806) 762–0335
FAX: (806) 743– 7677

APPM: Glenn J. Nelson
Flight Standards District Office–15
The Parkway Building
1300 S. Meridan, Suite 601
Oklahoma City, OK 73106
Telephone: (405) 231–4196
FAX: (405) 231–4810

APPM: Owen M. Russell
Flight Standards District Office–17
International Airport
10100 Reunion Place, Suite 200
San Antonio, TX 78216–4118
Telephone: (512) 341–4374
FAX: (512) 229–5128

APPM: Angelo Spelios
Flight Standards District Office–19
Fort Worth Alliance Airport
2260 Alliance Boulevard
Fort Worth, TX 76177
Telephone: (817) 491–5000
FAX: (817) 491–5014

WESTERN–PACIFIC REGION

APPM:
Vacant
FAA, AWP–204
P.O. Box 92007
Worldway Postal
Center
Los Angeles, CA
90009–2007
Telephone: (310) 297–0118/0698
FAX: (310) 643–9753

APPM: Barry McCoy
Flight Standards District Office–01
16501 Sherman Way Suite 330
Van Nuys, CA 91406
Telephone: (818) 904–6291
FAX: (818) 786–9732

APPM: None Assigned
Flight Standards District Office–03
831 Mitten Road
Building B, Room 105
Burlingame, CA 94010–1303
Telephone: (415) 876–2771
FAX: (415) 697–7231

APPM: Kevin Clover
Flight Standards District Office–5
2815 E. Spring Street
Long Beach, CA 90806–2485
Telephone: (310) 426–7134
Fax: (310) 424–4439

APPM: Jack Christopherson
Flight Standards District Office–07
15041 North Airport Drive
Scottsdale, AZ 85260
Telephone: (602) 640–2561
FAX: (602) 948–9372

Acting APPM: Thelma Bullinger
Flight Standards District Office–09
8525 Gibbs Drive, Suite 120
San Diego, CA 92123
Telephone: (619) 557–5281
FAX: (619) 279–3241

APPM: Richard Angelo
Flight Standards District Office–11
210 S. Rock Blvd.
Reno, NV 89502
Telephone: (702) 784–5321
FAX: (702) 856–0672

APPM: George Combs
Flight Standards District Office–13
90 Nakola Place, Room 215
Honolulu, HI 96819–1850
Telephone: (808) 836–0615
FAX: (808) 836–8163

APPM: Howard Manning
Flight Standards District Office–14
P.O. Box 2397, Airport Station
Oakland, CA 94614
Telephone: (510) 273–7155
FAX: (510) 632–4773

APPM: Don Warren
Flight Standards District Office–15
1250 Aviation Ave. Ste. 295
San Jose, CA 95110–1119
Telephone: (408) 291–7681
FAX: (408) 279–5448

APPM: Richard Hague
Flight Standards District Office–17
Fresno Air Terminal
4955 E. Anderson, Suite 110
Fresno, CA 93727
Telephone: (209) 487–5306
FAX: (209) 454–8808

APPM: Dennis Michael Murphy
Flight Standards District Office–19
6020 S. Spencer Street, Suite A7
Las Vegas, NV 89119
Telephone: (702) 388–6482
FAX: (702) 798–4999

APPM: Carl A. Christopher
Flight Standards District Office–21
6961 Flight Road
Riverside Municipal Airport
Riverside, CA 92504
Telephone: (714) 276–6701
FAX: (714) 689–4309

APPM: James Whitehead
Flight Standards District Office–23
5885 W. Imperial Highway
Los Angeles, CA 90045
Telephone: (310) 215–2150
FAX: (310) 645–3768

APPM: Ray Steinkraus
Flight Standards District Office–25
Sacramento Executive Airport
6650 Belleau Wood Lane
Sacramento, CA 95822
Telephone: (916) 551–1721
FAX: (916) 551–1741

FlightFORUM

• Curtiss not Wright

Congratulations on producing a publication which turns a dull and dreary, yet important, subject into a sparkling pleasure to peruse. However, on page 27 of the July/August issue the striking photo from Oshkosh '91 is captioned as a replica Wright Flyer. It is really Vern Dallman's Curtiss Pusher—even the logo on the rudder appears to be Curtiss! So we now may have three of our oldest aviation pioneers whirling in their graves.

Also in the May/June "Famous Flights" the first blind flight by Jimmy Doolittle was mentioned. He had much more instrumentation than the three items listed. He had something on the order of eleven instruments including marker beacon and I/r needle.

Charley Hayes
Park Forest, IL

You are correct; the airplane is a Curtiss. Our apologies to Messrs. Wright, Curtiss, and Doolittle for not doublechecking our facts.

• Fueling Headwinds

Please explain what "headwinds" have to do with fuel endurance as stated on page 11 of your July/August 1992 article, "Rescued by the FAA."

George Vogler
Bakersfield, CA

Headwinds have nothing to do with endurance. What the author meant was range, which is reduced by headwinds. Thank you for the catch.

• Log Jam

I am writing so that you can resolve a debate among instructors, examiners, and my local FSDO personnel regarding the definition and logging of cross-country flight time. I have heard three different interpretations of what is a cross-country flight. I will use the attached box diagram to illustrate my point. The distance from Point A to Point B is 100 miles. The following scenarios illustrate the three different interpretations.

1. A pilot flies from Point A to Point B in a C-172. En route the pilot does some airwork, flies over the airport at Point C, then

flies over the airport at Point D, and finally lands at Point B. The total flight time from the takeoff at Point A to the landing at Point B was three hours. One group, including the FAA's Airman Certification branch at Oklahoma City, says the pilot can log three hours cross-country flight time.

2. Another group says the pilot can log only one hour cross-country flight time, or the direct flight time from Point A to B. This group would not allow any deviation or loitering flight time to be included in their interpretation of "cross-country" flight time.

3. Finally, a third group would only allow the three hours of cross-country flight time if the pilot's original intent was to fly from Point A to Point B. If the pilot took off with the intent to do some airwork, then decided to land at say Point C after three hours to be able to log the time as cross-country time, then this group would not allow the total flight time to be logged as cross-country time.

My problem is one FSDO is not allowing certain ATP candidates' total cross-country flight time to be counted because the office is using example 2 as the basis for determining cross-country flight time. The FAR only refer to certain minimum distances regarding cross-country flight time needed for the various pilot certificates. The FAR does not mention "intent" in defining cross-country flight time.

Please clarify the definition of "cross-country" flight time.

James R. Waydula
Maple Grove, MN

Interpretation number one is correct. The FAR do not specifically address the questions you are asking. The FAR only discuss the type of cross-country flights (normally in terms of distances) needed to meet specific pilot certification requirements such as those for the private pilot or instrument pilot ratings. The key to your question can best be answered by remembering aircraft flight time is "block-to-block" time. Time starts from the moment the aircraft first moves under its own power for the purpose of flight

until the moment it comes to rest at the next point of landing. Only pilot certification requirements specify how far that point must be from the point of original departure to qualify as cross-country time. The determining criteria is distance, not time. Remember the purpose of a certification cross-country flight is either pilot training or for the pilot to demonstrate the various levels of piloting skills required to meet the minimum qualifications specified for a particular certificate.

Under current FAA policy, distance is not a factor when determining ATP cross-country flight time after the commercial pilot has met all of the appropriate cross-country requirements through the commercial pilot rating. Once those commercial pilot requirements are met, the ATP applicant has no minimum cross-country distance requirement. The only ATP cross-country requirement is a landing at a point other than the airport of departure.

• Battery Replacement

Can an owner/pilot replace ELT batteries under FAR Part 43, Appendix A Section C, Preventive Maintenance? Some people have argued that this rule doesn't apply to ELT's because Appendix A was written before ELT's existed. Before Appendix A was revised in 1982, item (24) read, "Replacing batteries and checking fluid level and specific gravity." The change to "Replacing and servicing batteries" was apparently intended to include ELT batteries. This seems reasonable since replacing ELT batteries is a simple operation, not requiring the expertise of a mechanic and ensures that ELT's are ready for an emergency. ELT batteries that involve complex assembly operations should be changed by an A&P, but the average pilot can easily replace the battery in most ELT's.

Robert K. Henry
Kingsport, TN

You are correct. According to FAR Part 43, Appendix A, Section C, an owner/pilot can replace ELT batteries, but FAR §§ 43.9(a) and 91.207(c)(2) must also be complied with by making the proper maintenance record entry and by placarding the exterior of the ELT with the new battery expiration date.

• Caption Missing

The "Spin or Not to Spin, Part 1" article in the May/June 1992 issue of FAA Aviation News, inadvertently left off the illustration credit line on page 12. It should have read: "Figure 1 reprinted by permission from The Flight Instructor's Manual by William Kershner by the Iowa State University Press, Ames Iowa 50010. Our thanks to Mr. Kershner for letting use his illustration.

FAA AVIATION NEWS welcomes comments from its readers. We may edit letters for style and/or length. We will select one representative letter from those on the same topic for publication, and, because of our bimonthly publishing schedule, responses may not appear for several issues. We will send personal replies only upon request. We will not print anonymous letters, but we will withhold names upon request. Address: Editor, FAA AVIATION NEWS, AFS–810, Washington, DC 20591.

AV**NEWS/BRIEFS**

Changes in Latitudes— and Longitudes

If you are still using out-of-date Terminal Area Charts, here is a good reason to recycle them for the most current editions: The horizontal geodetic referencing system is changing. No, the earth's axis has not shifted, but what has happened is that the datum used by the National Oceanic and Atmospheric Administration (NOAA) for charting has been updated. As of October 15, 1992, all chart and chart products produced by NOAA will now be drawn according to the North American Datum of 1983. Lest you wonder why NOAA is "updating" to a nearly 10-year old reference, be aware that its previous reference was the North American Datum of 1927 (NAD27). Technological advances in Global Positioning Systems (GPS) now allow satellites to pinpoint locations much more accurately by a reference to the center of the earth. NAD27 used a reference point in Kansas for all North American latitude and longitude control points.

The greatest coordinate shifts will be in Alaska and Hawaii, where latitudes will move by as much as 1,200 feet and longitudes will move by up to 950 feet. In the *conterminous* U.S., the maximum changes will be approximately 165 feet of latitude and 345 feet of longitude. However, this shift will not be significant enough to change the latitude and longitude grids on sectional charts or WAC's, but it could affect TCA charts, helicopter charts, and sectional insets and will most definitely affect airport diagram charts. All digital products sold by the National Oceanic Service (NOS) or FAA and coordinates in the Digital Aeronautical Chart Supplement, the *Airport/Facility Directory,* the Pacific and Alaska Chart Supplements, and on Enroute navigation charts will be affected.

Users of digital data from NOS or FAA must purge their entire data bases when the new datum (NAD83) comes into use. If you have questions about charts and chart products, call 1–800–626–3677. For technical questions on the datum conversion, contact Mr. Doyle at the National Geodetic Survey on (301) 443-8684. For questions about the FAA's conversion efforts, contact David Thompson on (202) 267–9303.

Computer-based Testing

FAA has approved Sylvan Learning Systems as the third organization authorized to give computer-based FAA airmen written tests. Recreational pilot, private pilot, commercial pilot, instrument rating, flight instructor, flight engineer, airline transport pilot, mechanic-general, airframe, and powerplant computerized written tests are available at over 100 Sylvan Technology Centers around the country. The computerized tests are graded upon completion of the test, and applicants are given certified score sheets as soon as the test is graded.

Applicants are reminded that they must have a certified test score form issued by Sylvan for the test results to be accepted by either a designated pilot examiner or FAA inspector as proof of passing the appropriated written test.

Airmen wanting additional information on Sylvan's airmen testing services can call 1-800-967-1100 for the location of the nearest Sylvan testing center.

AD Summary Available

The FAA has announced the sale of the *Summary of Airworthiness Directives* for the cycle beginning in 1992 and ending in May 1994. The AD summaries are published in four books and are available to the public in paper or microfiche.

The *Small Aircraft and Rotorcraft* Books 1 and 2 relate to aircraft of 12,500 pounds or less maximum certificated takeoff weight and to all rotorcraft and balloons, regardless of weight. The *Large Aircraft* Books 1 and 2 pertain to aircraft of more than 12,500 pounds maximum certificated takeoff weight (except for rotorcraft). Book 1 of both editions contain AD's issued from the 1940's through December 1979. Book 2 of both editions contain AD's published from January 1980 to December 1991.

New subscribers for the paper edition should be aware that full AD coverage can only be obtained by having both Books 1 and 2 and the *Biweekly Supplements.* U.S. subscribers may purchase the *Biweekly Supplements* in paper format only without ordering a new Book 2. However, Book 2 has been revised and is available. The January 1992 *AD Index* reflects these revisions and the page references are those found in the revised Book 2. Neither *Small Aircraft and Rotorcraft* Book 1 nor *Large Aircraft* Book 1 was revised. The 1990 revisions of both Book 1's are current and do not have to be reordered. Subscribers to the 1992 microfiche edition of the *Summary of AD's* will not see any changes but should note the subscription will expire in May 1994, the same as the paper subscription.

Anyone interested in subscribing may obtain ordering and cost information from Advisory Circular 39–6P, "Announcement of Availability—Summary of Airworthiness Directives." AC 39–6P is available from the DOT Utilization and Storage Section, M–443.2, Washington, DC 20590. You may also obtain information from: FAA Manufacturing Standards Section, AVN–113, P. O. Box 26460, Oklahoma City, OK 73126–0460, Telephone: (405) 680–4103, FAX: (405) 680–4104.

EAA'S Young Eagles Program

Do you remember your first airplane ride? Most pilots clearly remember the day when they first soared into the air. In fact, many pilots have become "hooked" on aviation as a result of their first airplane ride, whether they were five years old or 50! The Experimental Aircraft Association (EAA) is well aware of the excitement experienced during first flights by young people in particular. With the slow decrease in general aviation activity during past years and concern about the lack of young people entering aviation, the EAA has created the "Young Eagles Program" to spark youngsters' interest in aviation and to demonstrate aviation's accessibility.

The premise of the "Young Eagles Program" is this: EAA and the EAA Aviation Foundation will lead the aviation community into its second century by providing 1,000,000 young people a personal flight experience by the year 2003, the 100th anniversary of powered flight and the 50th anniversary of EAA. The first Young Eagles, who are primarily between the ages of eight and 18, "spread their wings" at the EAA OSHKOSH '92 Fly-in Convention in Oshkosh, WI. These young people made friends, met aviation "mentors," and were introduced to exciting future possibilities of personal flight. To enhance their flight experience, the "Eagles" participated in forums, workshops, and in other educational activities.

The "Young Eagles Program" will continue its success during the next 10 years at airports, museums, in classrooms, and in the air all over America. The FAA is equally eager to expand aviation opportunities and education for young people, and will support and join with the EAA as "mentors" for the Young Eagles.

For more information on the "Young Eagles Program" write to the EAA, P.O. Box 3065, Oshkosh, WI 54903–3065 or call 414–426–4800.

TEST YOUR PILOTING IQ:
Icing Quiz

Test your icing knowledge. Choose the correct answer or answers. More than one answer may apply. Answers are on page 5. Information sources: *FAA's Aviation Weather* (AC 00-6A) handbook and the FAA *Airman's Information Manual* (AIM). The answers include reference and location.

1. The first day of winter is?
   a. November 27
   b. December 21
   c. December 25
   d. I don't care; how many days until summer?

2. The following is not a requirement for structural icing in flight
   a. flight through visible moisture
   b. high speed
   c. aircraft external surface temperature at or below freezing
   d. ambient air temperature a degree or two above freezing

3. Match the following definitions with the type of icing
   a. Rime
   b. Mixed
   c. Clear
   d. Cloudy

   3–1__ Hard, Glossy, and Heavy
   3–2__ Brittle and Frost-like
   3–3__ Hard Rough Conglomerate
   3–4__ Not a Type of Icing

4. This is not a type of structural ice
   a. cloudy
   b. clear
   c. rime
   d. mixed

5. Cloud factors affecting icing include
   a. drop size
   b. drop distribution
   c. aerodynamic effects of the aircraft
   d. all of the above

6. Icing is more hazardous in
   a. flatland areas
   b. desert areas
   c. ocean areas
   d. mountainous areas

7. Icing can occur in
   a. winter
   b. spring
   c. summer
   d. fall
   e. all of the above

8. Frost should be removed from an aircraft before flight
   a. sometimes
   b. never
   c. always
   d. only at gross weight

9. Stall speed and icing are
   a. related
   b. not related
   c. somewhat related
   d. none of the above

10. Approach speed when "iced up" should be
   a. adjusted as per the aircraft handbook
   b. decreased
   c. increased
   d. none of the above

11. A Convective SIGMET implies severe icing
   __ True
   __ False

12. SIGMETS are issued for severe icing
   __ True
   __ False

13. AIRMETS are issued for moderate icing
   __ True
   __ False

14. When icing conditions are encountered what action/s should be taken
   a. depart the area
   b. climb to above freezing temperature
   c. descend to above freezing temperature
   d. any one of the above depending upon circumstances

15. Match the following PIREP icing terms with their respective definitions
   a. Trace
   b. Light
   c. Moderate
   d. Severe

   15-1__ Ice becomes perceptible. Rate of accumulation is slightly greater than the rate of sublimation. It is not hazardous even though deicing/anti-icing equipment is not used unless encountered for an extended period of time (over 1 hour).
   15-2__ The rate of accumulation is such that deicing/anti-icing equipment fails to reduce or control the hazard. Immediate flight diversion is necessary.
   15-3__ The rate of accumulation is such that even short encounters become potentially hazardous and use of deicing/anti-icing equipment or flight diversion is necessary.
   15-4__ The rate of accumulation may create a problem if flight is prolonged in this environment (over 1 hour). Occasional use of deicing/anti-icing equipment removes/prevents accumulation. It does not present a problem if the deicing/anti-icing equipment is used.

DO NOT DELAY—CRITICAL TO FLIGHT SAFETY!

January-February 1993

FAA Aviation News

A DOT/FAA FLIGHT STANDARDS SAFETY PUBLICATION

U.S. Department
of Transportation

**Federal Aviation
Administration**

Andrew H. Card, Jr., *Secretary of Transportation*
Thomas C. Richards, *FAA Administrator*
Joseph M. Del Balzo, *Executive Director
for System Operations*
Anthony J. Broderick, *Associate Administrator
for Regulation and Certification*
Thomas C. Accardi, *Director,
Flight Standards Service*
Robert A. Wright, *Manager, General Aviation (Acting)*
Roger M. Baker, Jr., *Manager,
Accident Prevention Program Branch*
Phyllis A. Duncan, *Editor*
Louise C. Oertly, *Senior Associate Editor*
H. Dean Chamberlain, *Associate Editor*

The FAA's Flight Standards Service, General Aviation and Commercial Division, Accident Prevention Program Branch, AFS–810, Washington, DC 20591, (telephone 202 267–8017) publishes FAA AVIATION NEWS in the interest of flight safety. The magazine promotes safety in the air by calling the attention of airmen to current technical, regulatory, and procedural matters affecting the safe operation of aircraft. Although based on current FAA policy and rule interpretations, all printed material herein are advisory or informational in nature and should not be construed to have regulatory effect. The FAA does not officially endorse any goods, services, materials, or products of manufacturers that may be mentioned. **Certain details of accidents described herein have been altered to protect the privacy of those involved.**
The Office of Management and Budget has approved the use of funds for the printing of FAA AVIATION NEWS.

SUBSCRIPTION SERVICES

The Superintendent of Documents, U.S. Government Printing Office, Washington, DC 20402–9371, sells FAA AVIATION NEWS on subscription. Use the self-mailer form in the center of this magazine to subscribe. Cost: $8.00 ($10.00 foreign) for one year; $16.00 ($20.00 foreign) for two years. Prices are subject to change by the Government Printing Office without prior notice.
Change of Address or Subscription Problems: Send your label with correspondence to Sup Doc, Attn: Chief, Mail List Branch, Mail Stop: SSOM, Washington, DC 20402–9373.
To keep subscription prices down, the Government Printing Office mails subscribers only one renewal notice. You can tell how many copies are left in your subscription by checking the number that follows "ISS-DUE" on the top line of your mailing label. For example, when this number is 003, it means you have three issues left in your subscription, and GPO will send you a renewal notice. The number 000 means you have received your last issue. To be sure that your service continues without interruption, please return your renewal notice promptly.

FAN SMITH 212J ISSDUE003 R 1
JOHN SMITH
212 MAIN ST
FORESTVILLE, MD 20747

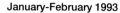
FEATURES

DEPARTMENTS

On the Covers:
It does not matter if you are rated in a Learjet 31A, such as the one on the cover flying over San Francisco Bay, or in a Piper Warrior, as on the back cover, when an emergency happens—are you ready for it? Photos courtesy of Learjet and Piper Aircraft.

Aviation Safety Through Flight Proficiency

by Lauren D. Basham, *FAA Aviation Safety Inspector*

Someone once said, "Look to the future; that's where you'll spend the rest of your life." How significant this statement is. How important it really is for each of us to consider what lies ahead, what new experience is "just around the corner" to cope with.

In this dynamic industry in which we find ourselves, we can readily predict much of the experience that is in store for us "just around the corner." We can also prepare in advance to meet this eventuality with insight, confidence, and, most of all, with the knowledge that we can handle whatever it is. So, maybe some day we do have an engine malfunction. Through training, practice, and experience the *successful outcome* of this minor problem is predictable. Radio problems? No sweat—through training and knowledge of procedures the *successful outcome* of this minor problem is also predictable. Gear malfunction? Through training and knowledge of emergency extension procedures, the *successful outcome* of this minor event is predictable. Unforecast inclement weather? Through training, knowledge, and proper preflight planning the *successful outcome* of this minor irritation is easily predictable.

Come what may—rain, snow, sleet, wind, engine, radio, gear, etc, etc.—our best insurance for a *successful outcome* is thorough initial training and then recurrent training to obtain new knowledge; review and practice; and a complete understanding of ourselves and the complexity of the systems we use. Complacency, overconfidence, lack of knowledge, or an "I don't give a

Lauren D. Basham

d**n" attitude predict damage, injury, and, worst of all, widows, widowers, and orphans. Don't misunderstand; we in the FAA have nothing against widows, widowers, or orphans. We do not appreciate the manner in which we in aviation produce them.

Now, what this all adds up to is this: If you take this advice, I will predict something for you. If you will take just a couple of hours of your time to visit and fly with your favorite flight instructor and take his or her advice regarding your need for additional training and practice, learn your aircraft's limitations as well as your own, and then promise yourself and your loved ones you will operate within these limitations, *I predict* that you can become what all pilots long to become—an Old Pilot. The future, starting today, is the time for you to become a "Pro." Pro is short for proficiency. No matter what type of certificate you now hold, you can only benefit from recurrent training, and you will make your insurance company happy, too. Drop us a card letting us know that you are working to become a Pro. We would appreciate it. ∎

If any of you reading this are from Montana and this sounds familiar, you received this message from your Accident Prevention Specialist in the Helena, Montana General Aviation District Office some 22 years ago. This, of course, was written in the days before biennial flight reviews and the "Wings" program, before GADO's became FSDO's, and before Accident Prevention Specialists became APPM's, but its message has not faded over the two decades since Mr. Basham thought enough of his "Montana Pilots" to mail it to them. Now, as a specialist in the Airman Certification Branch of the General Aviation and Commercial Division in FAA headquarters, Mr. Basham can spread the word to a larger audience—be a Pro! —**The Editor**

Shaping Aviation's Future

by Dean Chamberlain, *Associate Editor*

Education. The word means different things to different people, but to a select group of students education is their key to enter the exciting world of aviation. Their education may open the door to a cockpit career, provide them the opportunity to help design the next generation aircraft, give them the chance to solve the latest aircraft maintenance problem, or give them the opportunity to resolve the latest management crisis. For all, it means making hard career decisions, selecting the right school, finding tuition money, graduating, and finding a job. For the successful, their aviation education offers them the opportunity to follow their dreams in which the sky is not a limitation but an opportunity. For them, the sky is their future.

If you are wondering why we are writing about education instead of safety, the answer is simple. Education contributes to safety. We are also branching off our FAA/industry partnership series by highlighting the Federal Aviation Administration's ongoing partnership with the aviation education community and the vital role education plays in aviation safety. In our last series, we discussed how representative aviation membership groups and the FAA work together to promote aviation safety. Now we are emphasizing

the role education plays in aviation and aviation safety. This first article in the series is introductory in nature and discusses how tomorrow's aviation professionals are being trained and the role the FAA plays in that training. The series will eventually highlight several representative types of educational programs at schools around the country to show there is a curriculum available to meet every student's needs. So, in recognition of the unique challenges schools face in training tomorrow's aviation professionals, we would like to dedicate this series to all of the schools training today's students to meet tomorrow's aviation/aerospace needs.

FAA and Education

Few people realize how much money the FAA contributes to aviation education. We are not talking about federal student loans. We are talking about millions of dollars given as grants to schools for buildings and equipment that support aviation-related educational programs. This money is disbursed through the Airway Science Grant Program to support the Airway Science Program (AWS). According to Ms. Margaret Powell, Manager, AWS Curriculum Program, AWS is a series of FAA-approved, four-year degree programs at various colleges and universi-

ties nationwide. The programs are designed to meet the aviation training and employment needs of both FAA and the aviation industry.

Ms. Virginia Hancock Krohn, Manager, Airway Science Grant Program, said the FAA AWS Grant Program's objective is to help defray the high cost of Airway Science Program needs through federal grants. The monetary goal of the AWS Grant Program is to enhance student educational opportunities through use of state-of-the-art instructional facilities and equipment.

Although we are highlighting the FAA's role in the AWS Program, we cannot ignore the support provided by private industry. Well-known aerospace and high-tech companies have for years recognized the long-term benefits of supporting aviation-related programs at colleges and universities around the country. Their support includes cooperative educational programs, internships, and the hiring of AWS graduates and others with a strong background in aviation-related subjects.

Helping colleges train students for careers in aviation is one way FAA fulfills its Congressional mandate to "encourage and foster" civil aviation. The FAA's Airway Science Curriculum Program was developed in partnership with the University Aviation Association and the

Airway Science Curriculum Committee in the early 1980's to fill the need for college-trained aviation professionals. AWS's FAA-approved aviation curriculum was designed to train aviation students to meet the FAA's and the aviation industry's needs. Based upon a common core of subjects similar to those required for every college degree, the 2,157 students enrolled in AWS programs today are specializing in one of the following five areas: Airway Science Management, Airway Computer Science, Aircraft Systems Management, Airway Electronic Systems, or Aviation Maintenance Management. Each program consists of at least 40 semester hours of specialized training in a group of courses known as a program's Area of Concentration (AOC) and a minimum number of supporting courses called Core Subject Area (CSA) courses. For example, the Airway Computer Science AOC's minimum requirement is met by studying 40 hours of computer science courses. The Aircraft Systems Management AOC involves flight training as well as aviation related flight subjects as part of its program.

In addition to meeting the AOC minimum requirement, each program also requires a student to complete the common Core Subject Area requirement, which is at least a minimum of 80 semester hours needed to meet the FAA-general curriculum requirement. The following is a breakdown of each student's common Core Subject Area requirement: At least 24 to 30 semester hours of General Studies, 21 to 28 hours of Math and Science/Technology, nine hours of Computer Science, nine to 12 hours of Management, 15 hours of Aviation, and 30 hours of General Electives or a total sufficient to meet the school's graduation requirements and meet the 80-hour minimum Core Subject Area requirement. As you can see, each program option emphasizes math, science, computer, and management courses. Courses designed to help students succeed in today's technological aviation arena.

In addition to the four-year AWS college programs, the FAA in conjunction with the University Aviation Association is now developing a new two-year AWS Program to satisfy the needs of those programs that may not require a four-year college degree. Details on the new two-year program should be available soon from the FAA AWS Program resource managers listed at the end of this article.

AWS Support

Since we have briefly reviewed the AWS Program, and the FAA's role in helping develop it, it is time to discuss some of the ways the FAA supports the program. Although the FAA hires a limited number of AWS graduates each year and participates in cooperative education programs for AWS students, FAA's greatest contribution to the program is through monetary grants to AWS schools. Over the years, Congress, through the FAA, has appropriated millions of dollars to fund grants for AWS schools. From Fiscal Years (FY) 1982 through 1991, FAA awarded more than $61 million to 35 AWS schools. About 24 percent of those grants went to minority schools. During FY 1992, $20 million was available for AWS support. Of that amount, $16.2 million was awarded through seven Congressionally designated awards to specific schools. FAA is in the process of competitively awarding the remaining $3.8 million. Thirty million dollars in Congressionally designated awards will be distributed by the FAA to designated schools during FY 1993.

We have included a list of AWS schools (see p.5) to help students interested in pursuing an aviation education identify AWS schools. Students seeking information about a particular school should contact the school directly. School officials interested in learning more about the AWS Program should contact the FAA's Office of Training and Higher Education in Washington, DC. The address for AWS information is Higher Education and Advanced Technology Staff, 400 7th Street S.W., AHT-30, Washington, DC 20590.

Aviation Research

In addition to helping support the AWS Program, FAA also funds aviation-related research at many colleges and universities. The research plays an important role in both adding to the industry's scientific data base and in promoting safety. According to Mr. James Remer, Grants Officer, FAA Office of Research and Technology, the FAA is developing and expanding its new Aviation Research Grant Program. The program, established by two recent Public Laws, PL-101-508 and PL-101-604, has awarded 30 grants for more than $20 million for research at various schools. One example of the FAA's commitment to certain long-term research projects is its establishment of a new joint research project at the Georgia Institute of Technology and Rutgers, the State University of New Jersey. The $1.5 million project established the first FAA Center of Excellence in Computational Modeling of Aircraft Structures at the schools. The schools will use crash scenario modeling and aircraft structural modeling for FAA aircraft certification related research and to study the long-term effects of metal fatigue and corrosion on aging aircraft. Both areas of study are of importance to the FAA as it explores the use of new technology in aircraft design as well as preserving the aircraft already flying. The new Center of Excellence concept provides the FAA the means to support long-term research in specific subject areas at select schools that have the expertise to be designated as Centers of Excellence. Together with traditional research funding the new Centers of Excellence program will provide the FAA-sponsored research information the aviation industry and the FAA need to ensure America remains competitive in today's and tomorrow's global aviation environment. An indirect benefit of these FAA supported research projects is the challenging educational opportunities the projects provide students participating in the studies. The value of these various programs is reflected in the number of past projects that have become important household names in the aviation industry. Cockpit/crew resource management, controller-pilot interaction, aging aircraft studies, composite construction materials and techniques, and wind shear studies are but a few of the names of research projects airmen have benefitted from. Institutions and companies interested in submitting research grant proposals to the FAA can contact Mr. Remer at the Office of Research and Technology Applications, ACL-1, FAA Technical Center, Atlantic City International Airport, NJ 08405. A voice mail telephone number is also available for requesting research grant information, solicitation, or application

K THROUGH 12 PROGRAMS

Although we are focusing on post-high school educational programs supported in part by the FAA in this series, FAA also supports elementary and high school programs for grades K through 12 by providing a wide range of educational material, both for teachers and students, for classroom use. The material, which includes such items as curriculum guides and a wide range of other types of aviation-related educational materials, is designed to help teachers explain to students the important role aviation plays in their daily lives. The material is so designed that no specialized aviation knowledge is required of the teacher wanting to use the material. To help distribute its educational materials the FAA has established Aviation Education Resource Centers at selective sites around the country. The Centers serve as central distribution points for printed material, videotapes, slides, computer materials, and other types of aviation material. The dedicated Center coordinators and their staff members also serve as valuable information resources for both the program and aviation subjects. Educators and media representatives are encouraged to contact the Centers for help or materials as needed. A list of Aviation Education Resource Centers (see p.5) is provided for your convenience.

In addition to the Aviation Education Resource Centers and the nine FAA Regional Headquarters that provide educational support within their respective areas, the FAA's Office of Public Affairs Aviation Education Program and the FAA's Office of Training and Higher Education, both in Washington, DC, provide information on many of the FAA's educational and funding programs. Their addresses are also listed on page 5.

FAA REGIONAL AWS COORDINATORS

NAME	REGION	TELEPHONE
Sharron Feland	FAA Aeronautical Center Oklahoma City, OK	405 680–5295
Dave Bruebaker	Alaskan	907 271–5375
Lovia Riding	Central	816 426–2928
Bruce Wynn	Eastern	718 553–1968
Myrna Rivera	Great Lakes	312 694–7893
Katrina Newlin	New England	617 273–7322
Maureen Coulter	Northwest Mountain	206 227–2012
George Burnette	Southern	404 763–7916
Donna Thayer	Southwest	817 624–5839
William Green	FAA Technical Center Atlantic City, NJ	609 484–6615
Barbara Keller	Western Pacific	213 297–0501

packages. The number is (609) 484-4761.

AWS and Safety

Although the AWS Program is important to the FAA, as a safety magazine, *FAA Aviation News* is more interested in how the AWS Program contributes to aviation safety. As we said, one of the obvious ways the program supports safety is through the academic contributions the various schools make to the industry's overall scientific data base. Research projects are a good example of some of these safety applications. There is another equally important way that may not be as apparent as scientific data and research projects, and that is the way the schools instill an attitude of professional responsibility in the hearts and minds of their AWS students. Only when knowledge, technical skill, and professional responsibility are combined do we really have a true aviation professional.

We think everyone will agree that education has always played an important role in aviation and aviation safety. Every airman is familiar with the FAA's long standing interest in airmen training and certification. So why our current interest in education? Simply stated, times have changed. In the past, maintenance technicians, pilots, and others, could have very successful careers in aviation with just their respective FAA certificates. In today's highly competitive business and work environment, many jobs now require advanced training and knowledge that goes beyond the basic FAA airmen certification requirements. This requirement for more education and training was one of the reasons the FAA worked with the education community and the aviation industry to help develop college-level degree programs to satisfy this need. A quick review of some of the schools participating in the AWS Program shows there is a type of school to meet every student's needs and budget. The key is identifying and matching each student's personal and professional goals with the type of school that can best fulfill them.

Preparing for the Future

But before we start our series on the various types of schools with AWS Programs, no discussion about education and aviation would be complete without a reminder for the next generation of airmen and teachers. We want to remind our younger readers that while there are many fine schools available that can provide each of you a quality education when you are old enough to attend, the time to start preparing to follow your aviation dream is now, before you graduate from high school and start pursuing your career goals. Like every profession, the secret for a successful career in aviation includes making good grades while you are in school and getting a quality education which includes taking all of the higher-level science and math courses you can. If you are planning on going to college that also means enrolling in a college preparatory program, working hard, developing perseverance, and having a certain amount of luck. Although FAA may not be able to improve your luck, the FAA may be able to help you obtain the education you need to make your own luck. And when you make the grade, the aviation industry will be waiting for you.

In our March 1993 issue we will highlight the first of many fine higher aviation education institutions. The featured school will be Embry-Riddle Aeronautical University with campuses in Daytona Beach, Florida and Prescott, Arizona. ■

AWS INSTITUTIONS

Federal Aviation Administration Airway Science Recognized Institutions with their Airway Science Areas of Concentration. Areas of Concentration are as follows: MGT=Airway Science Management; CSC=Airway Computer Science; SYS=Aircraft Systems Management; ELE=Airway Electronic Systems; and MNT=Aviation Maintenance Management.

Arizona State University, MGT:SYS
Tempe, AZ 85287
Dr. Laurence E. Gesell
Dept. of Aeronautical Technology
602/965–7775

Auburn University, MGT:SYS
162 Wilmore Lab
Auburn University, AL 36849
Mr. Emmett F. Johnson
Aerospace Engineering
205/844–6848

Averett College, MGT
420 West Main Street
Danville, VA 24541
Mr. David Ruev
Asst. Prof of Aviation
804/791–5615

Baylor University, SYS
P.O. Box 97440
Waco, TX 76798–7440
Dr. Max Shauck
Project Chairman
817/848–5050

Bridgewater State College, MGT:SYS
Bridgewater, MA 02325
Mr. William L. Anneseley
Aviation Science Coordinator
617/697–1395

Central Missouri State University, ELE
Technology Complex 210
Warrensburg, MO 64093
Dr. Tim Brady
Chair., Dept. of Power & Transportation
816/543–4975

Central Washington University,
MGT:SYS:ELE:MNT
Hebeler 101, Ellensburg, WA 98926
Dr. Robert M. Envick
Industrial & Engineering Technology
509/963–3691

Chadron State College, MGT:CSC:ELE
Chadron, NE 69337
Dr. M. L. Gramberg
Div. of Vocational & Tech. Education
308/432–6365

Daniel Webster College, MGT:CSC
20 University Drive
Nashua, NH 03063
Mr. Thomas Teller
Airway Science Coordinator
603/883–3556

Delaware State College, MGT:SYS
1200 North DuPont Highway
Dover, DE 19901
Dr. Pamela McDermott
Chair., Airway Science Department
302/739–3535

Delta State University, MGT:SYS
Box 3203
Cleveland, MS 39833
Mr. Robert H. Ryder
Commercial Aviation
601/846–4206

Dowling College, MGT:CSC:SYS
Idle Hour Boulevard
Oakdale, NY 11769
Dr. Paul Whelan
Dean, School of Aviation and Trans.
516/244–3077

Edward Waters College, MGT
1658 Kings Rd., Jacksonville, FL 32209
Mr. Charles Mount
Business Administration Division
904/366–2739

Elizabeth City State University, CSC
ECSU Box 823 Elizabeth City, NC 27909
Mr. William Barker
Director, Airway Science Program
919/335–3290

Embry-Riddle Aero. University FL,
MGT:CSC:SYS:MNT
600 So. Clyde Morris Blvd.
Daytona Beach, FL 32114–3900
Dean William A. Martin
Dean, College of Aviation Tech.
904/226–6215

Embry-Riddle Aero. University Prescott, SYS
3200 N. Willow Creek Rd.
Prescott, AZ 86301
Mr. Dan Carrell
Department Chairman, Aero. Science
602/776–3856

Florida Institute of Technology, MGT:SYS
150 W. University Blvd.
Melbourne, FL 32901
Mr. Alan Devereaux
School of Aeronautics
407/768–8000

Florida Memorial College, MGT:CSC
15800 NW 42nd Ave., Miami, FL 33054
Mr. J. Anthony Sharp
Director, Airway & Computer Science
305/623–4277

Hampton University, MGT:CSC:SYS:ELE
Hampton, VA 23668
Mr. Herbert B. Armstrong
Department of Airway Science
804/727–5417

Henderson State University, MGT:SYS
HSU Box 7611, Arkadelphia, AR 71923
Dr. Jerry L. Robinson
Director of Aviation Programs
501/246–5511

InterAmerican University of Puerto Rico,
MGT:CSC:SYS:ELE
Metropolitan Campus, Box 1293
San Juan, PR 00919–1293
Dr. Eleazar Lamboy
Coordinator, Airway Science Program
809/250–1912

Jackson State University, ELE
1400 John R. Lynch St,
Jackson, MS 39217
Dr. Raphel Lee
Chairman,, Dept. of Tech. & Indus. Arts.
601/968–2466

Kent State University,
MGT:CSC:SYS:ELE:MNT
4020 Kent Rd., Stow, Ohio 44224
Dr. Eugene G. Ripple
Director, Kent State Airport
216/672–2640

Lewis University, MGT:CSC:SYS:MNT
Route 53, Box 282, Romeoville, IL 60441
Mr. Humphrey Abeh
Asst. Prof. of Aviation
815/838–0500

Louisiana Tech University, MGT:CSC:SYS
P.O. Box 3181 Tech Station
Ruston, LA 71272–9989
Prof. Richard J. Ozment
Dept. of Professional Aviation
318/257–2691

Metropolitan St. College of Denver,
MGT:SYS:MNT
P.O. Box 173362, Campus Box 30
Denver, CO 80217–3362
Mr. Robert Mock
Chairman,, Aerospace Science Dept.
303/556–2982

Middle Tennessee State University,
MGT:CSC:SYS:ELE:MNT
Box 67
Murfreesboro, TN 37132
Dr. Wallace R. Maples
Chairman, Dept. of Aerospace
615/898–2788

Morris Brown College, CSC
643 Martin Luther King, Jr. Dr. SW
Atlanta, GA 30314
Mr. Floyd Campbell
Dept. of Computer Science
404/220–0159

National University,
MGT:CSC:SYS:ELE:MNT
4141 Camino del Rio South
San Diego, CA 92108
Mr. Ernie Bonderheyden
School of Tech. & Computer Science
619/563–7355

Norfolk State University,
CSC:ELE
2401 Corprew Avenue
Norfolk, VA 23504
Mr. Darryl Stubbs
Computer Science Department
804/683–9447

Northeast Louisiana University,
MGT:CSC:SYS
Monroe, LA 71209
Mr. William T. Hemphill
Department of Aviation
318/342–1780

Ohio University, ELE
Athens, OH 45701
Ms. Joan E. Mace
Chairperson, Aviation Department
614/698–2028

Oklahoma State University,
MGT:CSC:SYS
300 North Cordell
Stillwater, OK 74078–0422
Mr. Glen Nemecek
Coordinator, Aviation Education
405/744–5856

Parks College of St. Louis University
MGT:CSC:SYS:ELE:MNT
St. Louis University
Cahokia, IL 62206
Dr. Peggy Baty
Associate Vice President and Dean
618/337–7500

Purdue University, MGT
West Lafayette, IN 47906
Dr. William P. Duncan
Department of Aviation Technology
317/494–9950

Rocky Mountain College, SYS
1511 Poly Drive
Billings, MT 59102
Mr. David G. Kimball
Director of Aviation Studies
406/657–1060

San Jose State University,
MGT:MNT
One Washington Square
San Jose, CA 95192–0081
Dr. H. Gene Little
Department of Aviation
408/924–6582

So. Illinois University at Carbondale,
MGT:CSC:SYS:ELE:MNT
Carbondale, IL 62901
Dr. David A. NewMyer
Coordinator, Aviation Mgt. & AWS
618/453–8898

St. Cloud State University, MGT
HH 101–SCSU
St. Cloud, MN 56301
Dr. Hope B. Thornberg
Department of Technology
612/255–4167

St. Francis College, MGT
180 Remsen St.
Brooklyn, NY 11201
Prof. Stanley G. Maratos
Chairman, Aviation Management
718/522–2300

Suffolk University, CSC:ELE
8 Ashburton Place
Boston, MA 02108
Dr. John L. Sullivan
Coordinator, Aviation Programs
617/723–4700

Tennessee State University, ELE
3500 John Merrit Boulevard
Nashville, TN 37209–1561
Mr. T. Ledwith
AIT Acting Department Head
615/320–3287

Texas Southern University, MGT:CSC
3100 Cleburne Ave.
Houston, TX 77004
Prof. I. Richmond Nettey
Director, Airway Science
713/639–1847

The Ohio State University,
MGT:CSC:SYS:ELE
2160 W. Case Road
Columbus, OH 43210–0022
William E. Pippin
Prof. & Chairman, Dept. of Aviation
614/292–5593

University of Alaska Anchorage, MGT
3211 Providence Drive
Anchorage, AK 99508
Mr. Gary E. Cox
Associate Dean
907/786–4661

University of Maryland Eastern Shore,
MGT:CSC:ELE
Airway Science Program
Princess Anne, MD 21853
Mr. Abraham D. Spinak
Director
301/651–2200

Univ. of Nebraska at Kearney,
MGT:CSC
West Center Building E202
Kearney, NE 68849
Mr. Larry Carstenson
Director of Airway Science Program
308/234–8570

University of Nebraska at Omaha,
MGT:CSC:SYS
Omaha, NE 68182–0508
Mr. James E. Crehan
Aviation Institute
402/554–3424

University of North Dakota,
MGT:CSC:SYS:ELE:MNT
Box 8216 University Station
Grand Forks, ND 58202
Prof. John Bridewell
Airway Science Coordinator
701/777–3034

Utah State University, ELE:MNT
Industrial Science 112E
Logan, Utah 84322–6000
Dr. Maurice G. Thomas
Head, Dept. of Ind. & Tech. Ed.
801/750–1795

Western Michigan University, MGT
2043 Kohrman Hall
Kalamazoo, MI 49008
Mr. Thomas L. Deckard
AWS Coordinator
616/387–6586

Winona State University, MGT:CSC
Johnson and Sanborn
Winona, MN 55987
Dr. George Bolon
Physics/Aviation
507/457–5260

WHAT GOES UP...
...Must Come Down

Knowing when to declare an emergency

by Bill Richards, *ASRS Analyst*

This is the third in a series of articles reprinted from ASRS Directline, a quarterly publication that addresses particular areas of safety that appear in pilot reports received by NASA's Aviation Safety Reporting System and which have been identified by safety analysts as "significant." ASRS Directline is free from ASRS, NASA-Ames Research Center, Moffett Field, CA 94035. Declaring an emergency is not something to be taken lightly, nor should it be considered a sign of weakness to do so when the appropriate time arises. Just remember, the air traffic system cannot respond accordingly to your emergency unless they know it is an emergency. **— Editor**

A three-engine wide-body air carrier aircraft climbing to flight level 410 experienced a compressor stall and had to shut down an engine just before leveling off. The flight crew ". . . advised center [that they were] descending, [had] shut down an engine, and need[ed] 24,000 feet."

The controller cleared the stricken aircraft for a descent to flight level 370, but the flight advised ". . . advised twice we had to get down [to yet a lower altitude]." Because of traffic at flight level 350, the controller was unable to approve their request, and so stated. The flight crew kept repeating their request for a lower altitude, and the controller kept repeating that he was "unable."

Controller's Dilemma

It is well-publicized that air carrier aircraft will flying very well with one and, in some cases, two engines shut down. What is not made clear is that this is not true at higher altitudes such as 37,000 feet; thus, it is possible that the controller in this incident did not realize the urgency of the need for a lower altitude. It is, however, more likely that the controller fully understood the seriousness of the flight crew's situation, but the controller's hands were tied.

An air traffic controller's primary function is to maintain certain minimum separation standards between aircraft. The controller was undoubtedly trying to provide the requested descent clearance as quickly as possible, but until he could clear traffic from below the troubled aircraft, the flight could not be issued a clearance to descend. An air traffic controller cannot issue a clearance that will result in a loss of standard separation but can and will provide assistance in the form of traffic call-outs and/or recommendations intended to increase separation between conflicting traffic.

Meanwhile the flight crew had lost control of their airplane. Minus the power of the failed engine, they were descending, and there was nothing they could do to prevent it. This was certainly an emergency situation, yet the crew never declared an emergency. The controller was finally able to vector the traffic out of the way and to clear the stricken aircraft for a continued descent, but by this time the aircraft had already descended slightly below flight level 370.

Emergency

I will not speculate why the flight crew did not declare an emergency; however, they may have neglected to assess properly the effect of their descent on other traffic in the vicinity and thus ATC's potential difficulty in maintaining traffic separation. Given the declaration of an emergency, the controller could have pointed out conflicting traffic to all involved and provided traffic advisories even though a loss of standard separation might result from the flight crew's actions.

A Different Twist

In another incident, a trans-Atlantic wide-body aircraft was forced to descend and reverse course after shutting down an engine. The flight crew advised the Center controller of the nature of their problem, requested a lower altitude, and stated they wanted to return to their departure airport. They made their situation, intentions, and altitude capability very clear. They also *declared an emergency*, but for some reason, Center did not acknowledge their declaration of an emergency. The crew began the "contingency procedure," announcing their intentions in the blind to all other traffic. Center was ". . . a bit slow at re-clearing us back towards [the departure airport] thereafter."

Upon changing to the next Center sector an hour later, the flight crew discovered that Center was treating the whole thing as a routine change of destination and that "no emergency existed in the ATC view." In this case, no apparent conflicts arose. It can only be assumed that had Center understood that an emergency had been declared, their service would have been much more prompt. As with all ATC/aircraft communications, if a flight crew is not sure that a transmission or request has been properly understood, they should repeat their message and make sure that they receive a proper acknowledgement. In this instance, the fact that the flight was over water and using high frequency (HF) radio surely added to the breakdown in communications. Nonetheless, the flight crew must share the responsibility for accuracy in the information exchange.

The Pilot's Toolbox

There seems to be great reluctance among pilots to declare an emergency. It is not uncommon for reporters to the ASRS to indicate that they believe that declaration of an emergency will bring the wrath of the FAA down upon them and cause them innumerable hours of tedious paperwork. FAR § 91.3(c) states that "Each pilot-in-command who deviates from a rule under paragraph (b) of this section shall, *upon the request* [emphasis added] of the Administra-

tor, send a written report of that deviation to the Administrator." In most cases, the report of irregularity that the captain has already written for the company should provide all the information the FAA might need if they request it, and no further paperwork would be required. For a non-airline pilot, a telephone call to the chief of the ATC facility handling the emergency to explain the need for the special handling may suffice for a written report.

When determining if an emergency condition exists, flight crews need to consider the implication of their potential inability to conform to ATC instructions. Pilots should not frivolously declare emergencies, of course, but declaring an emergency is something in the pilot's "toolbox" that can be put to use if it is needed.

DON'T OVERLOOK IT. ∎

The Aviation Safety Reporting System is a cooperative program established by the FAA's Office of the Assistant Administrator for Aviation Safety and administered by the National Aeronautics and Space Administration.

G. S. Livack

178 SECONDS TO LIVE

Spatial Disorientation can be a Killer

by Verdon Kleimenhagen, Ron Keones, and James Szajkovics *of FAA* and Ken Patz of *MN/DOT Office of Aeronautics*

If you are ever tempted to take off in marginal weather and you do not have an instrument rating or are not instrument current, read this article before you make your GO/NO-GO decision. If you decide to go anyway and subsequently lose visual contact with the ground, start counting down from 178 seconds. —Editor

How long can a pilot, with or without a *current* instrument rating, expect to live after experiencing SPATIAL DISORIENTATION? Researchers at the University of Illinois found the answer to this question. Twenty student "Guinea pigs" in ground trainers flew into simulated instrument weather, and all went into graveyard spirals or rollercoaster-like oscillations. The outcomes differed in only one respect: The time required until control was lost. The interval ranged from 20 seconds to 480 seconds. The average time was 178 seconds—*just two seconds short of three minutes!!!* Here is the fatal scenario...

The sky is overcast and the visibility poor. That reported five-mile visibility looks more like two, and you cannot judge the height of the overcast. Your altimeter says you are at 1,500 feet, but your chart tells you there is terrain as high as 1,200 feet in this sector. There might be a tower nearby because you are not sure how far off course you are. But you have flown in weather worse than this, so you press on. You find yourself unconsciously easing back just a bit on the controls to clear those none-too-imaginary towers. With no warning, you are in the soup. You peer so hard into the milky white mist that your eyes hurt. You fight the feeling in your stomach. You swallow only to find your mouth dry. Now you realize you should have waited for better weather. The appointment was important but not that important. Somewhere a voice is saying, "You've had it. It's all over."

You Now Have 178 Seconds To Live!

Your aircraft feels on an even keel, but your compass turns slowly. You push a little rudder and add a little pressure on the controls to stop the turn, but this feels unnatural and you return the controls to their original position. This feels better, but your compass is now turning a little faster and your airspeed is increasing slightly.

You scan your instrument panel for help, but what you see looks unfamiliar. You are sure this is just a bad spot. You will break out in a few minutes (but you do not have a few minutes left...).

You Now Have 100 Seconds To Live!

You glance at your altimeter and are shocked to see it unwinding. You are already down to 1,200 feet. Instinctively you pull back on the controls, but the altimeter still unwinds. The engine RPM is into the red and the airspeed nearly so.

You Now Have 45 Seconds To Live!

Now you are sweating and shaking. There must be something wrong with the controls; pulling back only moves the airspeed further into the red. You can hear the wind tearing at the aircraft.

You Now Have 10 Seconds To Live!

Suddenly you see the ground. The trees rush up at you. You can see the horizon if you turn your head far enough, but it is at an unusual angle—you are almost inverted. You open your mouth to scream but...

You Now Have No Seconds Left!!

You have just become a victim of Spatial Disorientation.

UNDERSTANDING SPATIAL DISORIENTATION

Pilots have taken the subject of Spatial Disorientation far too lightly. If you look at the material presented on the test preparation for the Private Certificate and Instrument Ratings and the questions on the FAA examinations, this subject is the easiest to respond accurately to and yet the least understood.

Recent statistics from the National Transportation Safety Board indicate that Spatial Disorientation is the **number one cause of fatal accidents.** Most pilots think "Pilot Error" and "Weather" were the most common causes. Therefore efforts have been concentrated on adding better weather information systems. Example: FSS' computer briefing formats, DUAT, Kavouras, Pan Am, and a host of others that are now available. We promote courses in cockpit resource management and decisionmaking—all of these new information systems and training methodologies are great and have reduced the accident rates over the last 10 to 20 years. We do not emphasize the limitations of the human anatomy.

Pilots need to experience spatial disorientation in a controlled setting. Why? Because we have to dispel some common misconceptions and illustrate why flying aircraft is different than other two dimensional modes of transportation.

1. **Myth:** "Just Believe Your Instruments."

   Truth: Many pilots have no idea that some types of spatial disorientation are so incapacitating. Though the pilot knows something is wrong, the sensory conflict is so great that the thinking process breaks down and the pilot is unable to recover the aircraft. This may be compounded by the inability to obtain visual information due to blurring of vision (nystagmus).

2. **Myth:** "I'm an instrument-rated pilot, all of this spatial disorientation information doesn't really apply to me because I've already demonstrated my ability to fly in instruments."

   Truth: FAA Accident Reports tend to contradict this statement. Many instrument pilots experience spatial disorientation every year with fatal consequences.

3. **Myth:** "Continued flight into adverse weather, or flying VFR into IMC conditions are the real causes of many of the aviation accidents."

   Truth: What really caused the accident was spatial disorientation. Maybe this sounds a little like who came first, the "chicken or the egg." The pilot wouldn't have experienced spatial disorientation if it wasn't for the weather. However, again statistics still seem to indicate that just because we improve our weather information systems we still don't prevent this kind of accident. What pilots often don't understand is that weather, especially poor visibility, leads to spatial disorientation. Because pilots have never experienced spatial disorientation in a controlled situation, they do not know how incapacitating it can be, or how to avoid it.

Case in Point: A private non-instrument-rated pilot, flying an aircraft that was not IFR equipped, departed an airport on his way home from Oshkosh, WI. After having been briefed thoroughly about the marginal weather along his route of flight he departed in limited visibility and crashed killing himself and his passenger about an hour and one-half later. It is hard to believe that if the pilot had known the risks associated with spatial disorientation, he would have made the decision to make this flight.

THE INNER EAR

Most problems related to disorientation can be traced to the inner ear, a sensory organ about the size of a pencil eraser. It may well be the most well-protected organ in the human body, and for good reason. It is the key to our ability to balance when on the ground or to remain oriented in space when we fly.

The inner ear is similar to a three-axis gyro. It detects movement in the roll, pitch, and yaw axes that pilots know so well. When the sensory outputs of the inner ear are integrated with appropriate visual references and spatial cues from our bodies, there is little chance to experience disorientation.

The inner ear consists of an auditory and non-auditory portion. The latter, primarily associated with equilibrium, contains the three semicircular canals. The semicircular canals are filled with fluid and are located at approximately right angles to each other. One end of each canal is enlarged and in this area is found a mound of sensory hair cells. Movement or rotation of the body tends to move the fluid of the semicircular canal, thereby causing displacement of the hair cells. The hairs, or cilia, which project into the

ANGULAR ACCELERATION AND THE INNER EAR

The semicircular tubes are arranged at approximately right angles to each other, in the roll, pitch and yaw axes.

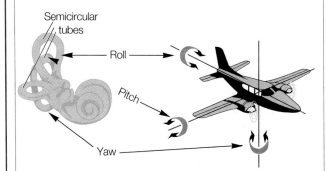

Semicircular tubes

Roll

Pitch

Yaw

A sensory organ, which consists of small sensory hairs that project into a gelantinous substance, is located in each tube. When the head starts to turn (angular acceleration), or speeds up, slows down, or stops its turning, the sensory hairs in the tube in the axis of turning are temporarily deflected due to the motion of the fluid lagging behind the motion of the tube wall. This causes the sensation of turning.

Sensory hairs tube

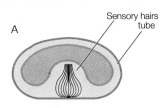
A

NO TURNING
No sensation

B

START OF TURN
Sensation of turning as moving fluid deflects hairs

C

CONSTANT RATE TURN
No sensation after fluid accelerates to same speed as tube wall

D

TURN STOPPED
Sensation of turning in opposite direction as moving fluid deflects hairs in opposite direction

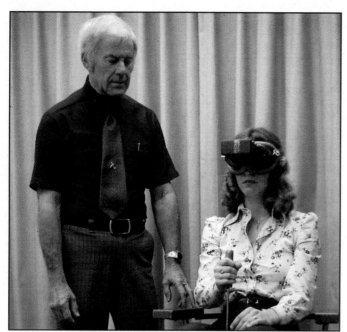

The Barony chair or "spatial spinner" demonstration helps pilots gain an understanding of how disorientation is induced and how to avoid it.

fluid are extremely fine and light and bend with the fluid's movement. The cilia transmit messages to your brain, telling it which way they are displaced, and your brain figures out the direction of your rotation. Since each canal lies in a different plane, the semicircular canals can report on rotation in three dimensions.

The problem occurs when the outside visual input is obscured, and the seat of the pants input is ambiguous. Then you are down to just the output from the inner ear. That is when trouble can start because fluid in the inner ear reacts only to *rate* of change not a sustained change.

For example, when you initiate a banking left turn, your inner ear will detect the roll into the turn. This system works fine for short turns, but if you hold the turn constant, your inner ear will compensate and rather quickly, although inaccurately, sense that it has returned to level flight. Therefore, if a constant rate turn continues for more than 15 seconds, the motion of the fluid in the canals catches up with the canal walls (stabilizes in the canals), the hairs are no longer bent, and your brain receives false impression that the turning has stopped. *Thus, after a few seconds, it is impossible for your semicircular canals to detect that you are in a turn, especially if it is a gentle turn.*

As a result, when you finally level the wings, that new change will cause your inner ear to produce signals that make you believe you are *banking to the right*. This is the crux of the problem you have when flying without instruments in low visibility weather.

Even the best pilots will quickly become disorientated if they attempt to fly without instruments when there are no outside visual references. That is because vision provides the predominant and coordinating sense we rely upon for stability.

Perhaps the most treacherous thing under such conditions is that the signals the inner ear produces—incorrect though they may be—feel right! These sensory illusions occur because flight is an unnatural environment our senses are not capable of providing reliable signals that we can interpret and relate to our position in three dimensions without visual reference.

As to "risky weather decisions," all pilots should understand that, unless they are thoroughly trained and CURRENT in instrument flying techniques, they are basically *incapable of safely operating in reduced visibility*. The accident statistics attest to this. Unless understanding is brought to the consciousness of every pilot, no substantial reduction in fatal weather accidents is likely to be achieved in the foreseeable future.

In addition, a change of bank, pitch or yaw may be too slow to be perceived by a pilot. In other words, acceleration may be below the threshold of perception. In the course of normal cockpit duties a pilot may be surprised to look up and find the airplane in a bank when it was not previously in a bank.

Although the problem of spatial disorientation is as old as aviation itself, its significance in flight safety is clearly underplayed. For example, in flight training and throughout general aviation a great deal of attention is given to weather and the movement of weather fronts. But little or no mention is made about the connection between weather and spatial disorientation. In the *Pilot's Handbook of Aeronautical Knowledge* (AC 61-23B) the student pilot can obtain a wealth of information on weather. We have made tremendous progress with improving aircraft design, power plants, radio aids and navigational techniques. Safety in flight however, is still subject to conditions of limited visibility. An NTSB study of fatal weather-involved general aviation accidents shows spatial disorientation as a frequent cause. Many of the fatal, weather-involved, general aviation accidents are caused by the pilot's mistaken idea of his or her ability to cope with flight in reduced visibility.

The FAA's *Aviation Instructor's Handbook* (AC 60-14) discusses the desirability of "integrated flight instruction" from the first time each maneuver is introduced. When this training technique is used, instruction in the control of an airplane by outside visual references is integrated with instruction in the use of flight instrument indications for the same maneuver. This handbook states that such instruction

"provides the student with the ability to control an airplane in flight for limited periods if outside references are lost. This ability could save the pilot's life or those of the passengers in an actual emergency."

The real hazard of loss of visual references, i.e., spatial disorientation, is not specifically identified and such identification is important if both pilots and flight instructors are to more successfully deal with this flight hazard. Another source of information is chapter 13 of the *Flight Training Handbook* entitled "Emergency Flight by Reference to Instruments."

REMEMBER !

A flight into reduced visibility or Instrument Meteorologic Conditions (IMC) may be...**LETHAL !!!**

For the opportunity to experience *Spatial Disorientation* for yourself and learn what your limitations are, contact the Accident Prevention Program Manager at your local Flight Standards District Office for a Spatial Spinner (Barony Chair) demonstration in your area. Find out why you CANNOT fly "by the seat of your pants." ■

This table lists the common OTC's and outlines some of their possible side-effects that could affect flying abilities. As with all drugs, side-effects may vary with the individual and with changes in altitude and other flight conditions.

MOST COMMONLY EXPERIENCED SIDE EFFECTS AND INTERACTIONS OF OTC MEDICATIONS

	MEDICATIONS	SIDE-EFFECTS	INTERACTIONS
PAIN RELIEF/ FEVER	ASPIRIN Alka-Seltzer Bayer Aspirin Bufferin	Ringing in ears, nausea, stomach ulceration, hyperventilation	Increased effect of blood thinners
	ACETAMINOPHEN Tylenol	Liver toxicity (in large doses)	
	IBUPROFEN Advil Motrin Nuprin	Upset stomach, dizziness, rash, itching	Increased effect of blood thinners
COLDS/ FLU	ANTIHISTAMINES Actifed Drixoral Benadryl Nyquil Cheracol-Plus Chloritrimetron Contac Sinarest Dimetapp Sinutab Dristan	Sedation, dizziness, rash, impairment of coordination, upset stomach, thickening of bronchial secretions, blurring of visions	Increased sedative effects of other medications
	DECONGESTANTS Afrin Nasal Spray Sine-Ald Sudafed	Excessive stimulation, dizziness, difficulty with urination, palpitations	Aggravates high blood pressure, heart disease, and prostate problems
	COUGH SUPPRESSANTS Benylin Robitussin CF/DM Vicks Formula 44	Drowsiness, blurred vision, difficulty urination, upset stomach	Increased sedative with effects of other medications
BOWEL PREPARATIONS	LAXATIVES Correctol Ex-Lax	Unexpected bowel activity at altitude, rectal itching	
	ANTI-DIARRHEALS Imodium A-D Pepto-Bismol	Drowsiness, depression,blurred vision (See Aspirin)	
APPETITE SUPPRESSANTS	Acutrim Dexatrim	Excessive stimulation, dizziness, palpitations, headaches	Increases stimulatory effects of decongestants, interferes with high blood pressure medications
SLEEPING AIDS	Nytol Sominex	(Contains antihistamine) Prolonged drowsiness, blurred vision	Causes excessive drowsiness when used with alcohol
STIMULANTS	CAFFEINE Coffee, tea, cola, chocolate	Excessive stimulation, tremors, palpitations, headache	Interferes with high blood pressure medications

Summary Advice

- READ and follow label directions for use of medication.

- If the label warns of side effects, do not fly until twice the recommended dosing interval has passed. So, if the label says, "Take every 4-6 hours," then wait at least 12 hours to fly.

- Remember, the condition you are treating may be as disqualifying as the medication.

- When in doubt, ask your physician or Aviation Medical Examiner for advice.

- As a pilot, you are responsible for your own personal "preflight." Be wary of any illness that requires medicine to make you feel better.

- If an illness is serious enough to require medication, it is also serious enough to prevent you from flying.

- Do not fly if you have a cold—changes in atmospheric pressures with changes in altitude could cause serious ear and sinus problems.

- Avoid mixing decongestants and caffeine.

- Beware of medications that use alcohol as a base for the ingredients.

This article is based on the pamphlet, "Over the Counter Medications and Flying," published by FAA's Civil Aeromedical Institute (CAMI). CAMI is the medical certification, research, education, and occupational health wing of the FAA's Office of Aviation Medicine. For copies of the pamphlet, write to CAMI, Aeromedical Education Division, AAM–400, P. O. Box 25082, Oklahoma City, OK 73125.

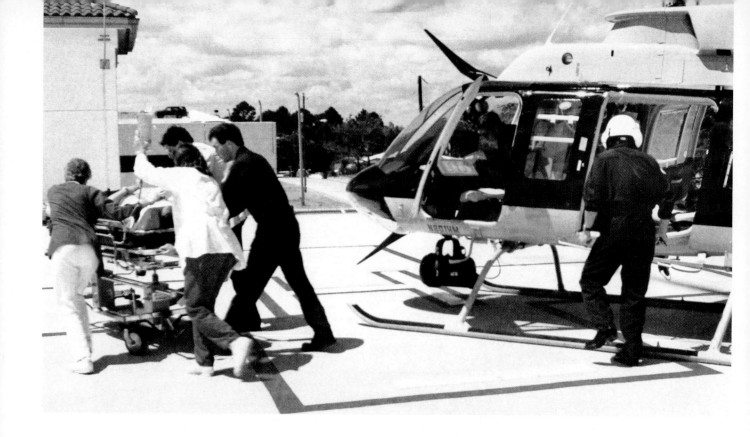

Hospital-based Emergency Medical Evacuation Services

by Phyllis A. Duncan, *Editor*

Dedicated to the EMS pilots, mechanics, flight nurses, doctors, paramedics, emergency medical technicians, and other personnel whose hard work and commitment have saved countless lives.

On a slick, rain-wet highway, a paramedic works frantically to stabilize the victim of an automobile accident. The patient has head injuries, and the paramedic knows her efforts will be for nought unless the victim is hospitalized immediately. But the nearest trauma center is one hour away by ambulance.

In the aftermath of a snowstorm that has closed the secondary roads, a woman on a remote farm goes into premature labor. When the baby is born, its chances of survival are slim unless it can be rushed to a neo-natal center some 150 miles away. But the roads will not be plowed open for hours or even days.

A middle-aged man who has suffered a heart attack arrives at a small, rural treatment center but needs to go to the cardiac care unit of a hospital in the next state. Unless he soon receives appropriate care, cardiac arrest is likely, but the CCU is a half a day's trip by ambulance.

Is the above the *TV Guide* description of an upcoming episode of "Rescue 911?" No, they are simply examples of the dilemmas health care providers face everyday. For many years the outcomes of such emergencies were not the uplifting ones shown on supposedly truth-based television programming. Because an essential piece of medical equipment was not available, the accident victim, the pre-mature baby, and the cardiac patient would have died in that first "golden hour" of opportunity that health care givers tell us is so important to recovery from trauma. That "essential piece of medical equipment" is the helicopter.

"M*A*S*H" and "China Beach"

Those of us who watched the Vietnam War from our living rooms became accustomed to the sight of wounded soldiers who had been initially stabilized on the battlefield by medics and then flown by helicopter to special medical units for life-saving surgery. Many a helicopter medevac pilot received medals and commendations for rescues and transportation under fire, but the helicopter's use for mercy missions as well as for combat goes back to its very beginnings in

World War II and the Korean Conflict. This usage was popularized by Hollywood in American culture by television programming such as "M*A*S*H" in the 1970's and "China Beach" in the 1980's.

It was only natural, then, as more and more civilian uses evolved for the helicopter, that it should be pressed into service as an "air ambulance." In the early 1970's the occasional use of a police or military helicopter to transport an accident victim became a full-fledged industry. Transportation of patients via helicopter moved out of the public sector to the private sector, where FAA-certificated air taxi operators provided the service for a fee.

Airplanes Were First but not Always Best

Aircraft and medical assistance have long mixed. In World War II, many airplanes that were to enjoy a post-war heyday in civilian flying, were used to move wounded soldiers from the front lines to hospitals and recovery centers a "safe" distance away. (If not for the C-47 (similar to the DC-3) that brought my father—cocooned in a full body cast—home strapped to its floor, you might not be reading these words under my byline today.) The term "medevac" was coined in the Korean Conflict era when front lines were less easy to define, and, as a result, hospitals were very far away or on ships offshore.

In civilian medical evacuation, airplanes were also the first to be used, but they soon showed their limitations in terms of size and versatility. Airplanes needed a runway or a sizable open field (preferably free of woodchuck holes and rocks) to operate in and out of. This was not a problem provided the accident or medical emergency occurred next to a convenient airport or a long, straight piece of highway. Helicopters could take off and land in a space many times smaller, often right next to the accident or emergency site. Most of the airplanes readily available for civilian medevac use were smaller than the venerable DC-3, and their size and weight-bearing capacity left little room for anything except a stretcher or litter and no adequate door to allow its ingress or egress, much less an accompanying nurse or doctor and his or her equipment. Helicopters had these wonder-

fully large doors that swung or slid out of the way, and they had been combat-designed to carry substantial loads, like gurneys and other medical equipment as well as personnel. Helicopters could also be landed on hospital rooftops or nearby parking lots, unlike airplanes, which required an ambulance ride from the airport.

Airplanes still remain the call for long-distance flights cross-country or across several states and especially for the transport of organs for transplantation, but for the short-haul trips for rapid emergency care or ease of patient transfer, helicopters seem made for airborne emergency medical service.

Genesis of an Industry

In the 1970's and 1980's conditions in the U.S. were ripe for this offshoot of the helicopter industry. For some time we had seen helicopters used in police work, in traffic spotting, in offshore oil-rig transport, in fire fighting, but there were several factors which inevitably led to the civilian helicopter medevac industry.

First, there were large numbers of Vietnam-era medevac pilots who had witnessed firsthand the benefits of evacuating patients by helicopter. Eager to keep flying in the only business many of them knew and most of them loved, they were a workforce waiting to be tapped. Second, Vietnam had also proved the helicopter's versatility and durability and had inspired manufacturers to design and build larger turbine-powered helicopters capable of lifting more people and heavier loads. Although surplus military helicopters were available for public

use (police and fire departments), manufacturers were geared to manufacture newer, more specialized 'copters for civilian entrepreneurs. Since the pilots and their equipment were already available, what was needed was something to bring them together. Again, a spin-off from the Vietnam War would provide the catalyst.

Young doctors enured in the MASH units of Korea and Vietnam had learned that when critically injured people were stabilized (bleeding stopped, shock averted, heartrate and blood pressure maintained, etc.) within the first hour after their trauma, their survival rate dramatically improved. This is why aid stations and surgery units were placed as close as possible to the front lines. Doctors treated wounded soldiers on the basis of a pre-operative triage (separating patients according to the seriousness of their condition) and stabilized them before they were sent to hospital ships, Japan, or stateside for further, more extensive treatment. When the interval between the wounding and the treatment was reduced by using helicopters to evacuate patients quickly, survival rates soared. Massive trauma that was certain death in World War II was being treated successfully in Korea and later Vietnam.

When these "Hawkeye Pierces" and "Trapper John McIntires" returned to civilian practice, they put this knowledge to good use. They convinced hospital administrators to create highly specialized emergency rooms called "shock-trauma units." These trauma centers, staffed by the most highly qualified doctors and nurses specializing in emergency medicine and supplied with state-of-the-art equipment, were all but useless unless patients could get to them within that first "golden hour" after injury. So, the next logical addition to the trauma center's staff and equipment were a pilot and a helicopter.

Accident and Regulatory History

The early 1980's saw the real burgeoning of EMS using helicopters, but the mid-1980's brought a surprising and alarming jump in fatal accidents in EMS helicopter operations. In 1984 there were three accidents with two fatalities, but in the following year, 1985, there were 11 accidents with 12 fatalities. Then, 1986 was even worse—4 accidents and 13 fatalities.

Although EMS hours flown were not calculated as with other aircraft operations, i.e., 100,000 hours flown, the NTSB in a 1988 safety study on commercial EMS helicopter operations was able to extrapolate some distressing figures. From 1980 through 1985, commercial EMS helicopter operations had an estimated accident rate of slightly more than 12 accidents per 100,000 hours flown. This rate was twice that of nonscheduled FAR Part 135 helicopter operations and one and one-half times that of all turbine-powered helicopters. The fatal accident rate for EMS helicopters was 5.4 per 100,000 hours flown—three and one-half times greater than the fatal accident rate for nonscheduled FAR Part 135 helicopter air taxis. This situation was surprising because the people involved were so professional and the record had started out so promising; alarming because the very people these operations were trying to save were becoming the fatalities.

FAA and the helicopter industry immediately began examining the problem and looking for solutions. No one really wanted to go for the easiest one: Have the FAA put a halt to EMS operations—a solution that was really a non-solution given the potential for saving lives. What everyone wanted was to isolate the causes of these accidents and use that to prevent future ones from occurring, all without compromising regulations, patient safety, or the business' ability to compete in the marketplace.

Accident Analysis

As a result of accident analyses conducted by FAA and NTSB and of studies conducted by a national EMS task force (consisting of EMS pilots, flight nurses, paramedics, and industry representatives from the National EMS Pilots Association (NEMSPA) and the Helicopter Association International), a number of causal factors came to light, some of which were not really unique to EMS helicopter operations. That is, they were causal factors that could affect any aircraft operation—weather, mechanical failure, lack of pilot experience. However, one area that seemed unique to EMS operations was *pilot fatigue brought on by long duty hours*. During a study of 166 commercial aeromedical operators in 1987, FAA had discovered that the typical shift for an EMS pilot was 24 hours, but some operators used a 48-hour or 72-hour shift on the high end as well as the low end of 12 hours. Of course, the pilot did not fly for 24 hours or 48 hours straight, but he or she would be "on call" for that entire time, perhaps with sleep patterns disrupted or interrupted or with no opportunity to obtain meaningful rest.

Rest Requirements

FAR § 135.271 sets rest and flight time requirements for HEMES (Helicopter-based Emergency Medical Evacuation Services). Basically, no flight crewmember can accrue more than eight hours of flight time during any 24 consecutive hours of a HEMES assignment. Any flight crewmember who exceeds this eight hours must be relieved of duty until he or she obtains 12 consecutive hours of rest for a 48-hour HEMES shift or 16 consecutive hours of rest for a shift more than 48 hours. A flight crew-member must also receive eight consecutive hours of rest during a 24-hour period of a shift. If the flight crewmember does not obtain eight consecutive hours of rest, he or she must be relieved of duty. Also, during each calendar year, an operator must assure that flight crewmembers receive 13 rest periods of at least 24 consecutive hours.

Human Factors

FAA also believed that emotional stress may have played an important part. The old adage of "fly the airplane first" may be difficult to keep in perspective when the pilot realizes that the patient he or she is carrying may be a child the same age as his or her own or a person similar to a spouse or parent. The overwhelming urge is to get that person to help as fast as possible, and the memory of combat missions ("Get it done at all costs regardless of the risks—you're saving a life.") may also induce a sense of exigency that is not appropriate to typical civilian rescue missions.

Another factor was that often the helicopter crew was dealing with emergency personnel at the site of accident who may have a distorted image of the capabilities of a helicopter. The landing area set aside may have obstructions that would place the helicopter and its "cargo" at undue risk or the surface may not support a landing. Also, when the call comes for a medevac mission, there is little time for checking weather or flight planning, and the crew may literally have to "wing it" and in some cases fly into an unfamiliar area. Add non-IFR equipped aircraft, maybe non-instrument rated pilots, nighttime, and quite possibly the weather conditions that caused a ground accident in the first place, and the scene would be set for disaster.

Another often-discussed but unproven factor may have been simple business competition. The services these companies supplied had to be competitive—who can get the patient there the fastest. On-scene rescue crews would sometimes call a second operator after the first one had refused the mission for safety reasons, and the second operator would jump at the chance to take business away from a competitor. In addition, the hospitals that contract with FAR Part 135 operators for air ambulance services may have placed stress on pilots by emphasizing the need to take every call and not heed the weather, the helicopter's condition, or their own fatigue. In many cases, hospital admin-

---

EMS ACCIDENT OVERVIEW

From 1978 to 1991 there were **80** EMS accidents:

40 were fatal accidents

76 involved helicopters

4 involved fixed wing aircraft

42 occurred at night

52 were classified as caused by pilot error

22 were classified as caused by mechanical failure

22 were classified as caused by weather

12 involved striking objects

Of the 76 helicopter accidents only
22 were considered "on scene;"
45 were inter-hospital transfers.

istrators responsible for EMS operators had no aviation background and could not understand the safety reasoning behind an operator's refusal to provide a service the hospital had paid good money for. After all, if this company could not do it, there were dozens of others in a locality that could.

The Industry's Response

The industry EMS task force came to about the same conclusion as the FAA and the NTSB about what needed changing in EMS operations: appropriate equipment (IFR capable helicopters and instrument rated and current pilots), staffing schedules (limits on duty times), training for pilots, and government regulation of this aspect of the industry. Working with insurance carriers many operators responded without impetus from the FAA: They hired and trained more pilots so that shifts could be shorter; they established training programs that emphasized both initial and recurrent training especially in the areas of night flight and all-weather flight; they established minimum operating conditions that in some cases were more restrictive that those required by FAR Part 135, and they required their pilots to adhere to them; they established procedures that kept pilots from knowing who they were flying or what condition they were in; they contacted police and fire departments to offer training on the types of situations helicopters could not handle; they worked with hospital administrators to re-think business philosophies and emphasized that the safety margin was just as important as the profit margin; and they made their helicopters IFR capable. The rest—establishing and enforcing operating standards—as always was up to the FAA.

FAA's Role

Like any air taxi operator carrying passengers for a fee, EMS helicopter operators must have FAA certification under FAR Part 135. FAR Part 135 has extensive requirements for management personnel, training, operating procedures and conditions, and so on. Certificated EMS helicopter operators must adhere to all appropriate aspects of FAR Part 135. (Public-use aircraft operated by police and fire departments do not have to have a FAR Part 135 certificate and may not have to

adhere to all of the FAR that apply to air taxi operators.) Once certificated, EMS helicopter operators are subject to FAA inspection and surveillance of their personnel, equipment and facilities to ensure compliance with the regulations.

Yet, EMS helicopter operators are a unique facet of FAR Part 135 commercial operators. An EMS operator may be only one part of a larger FAR Part 135 operator whose main business is the carriage of passengers not in need of medical assistance; that is, the EMS operation is only a minor part of the overall business. Or, EMS operations may be the only business that the FAR Part 135 operator conducts. FAA has had to respond to each of these situations so that a level of safety can be maintained without burdening either type of operator. Indeed, after the increase in accidents in the mid-1980's, there were calls for heavy-handed FAA response; e.g., to require that only twin-engine helicopters be used, to require two-pilot crews, or to require all operations to be conducted under IFR. These actions may or may not have improved the accident record, but the industry and FAA knew that such drastic measures would put most EMS operators out of business.

FAA's approach was to explain that the existing standards in FAR Part 135 were sufficient, but what was needed was education on how to apply them appropriately to EMS operations. For example, the training program required by FAR § 135.341 would have to be "customized" to EMS operations. The

FAR Part 135 operator for whom EMS was only a "sideline" of the overall operation would have to consider pulling the EMS pilots out of the regular training program and/or supplementing it with material directed at EMS flights. The EMS operator who flew nothing but EMS missions would have to design its entire training program around EMS considerations. FAA principle inspectors for such operators would have to be very aware of the operators' unique operating situations.

FAA and Industry Standards

The EMS industry, through its several professional organizations, not only demonstrated a strong commitment to self-improvement of its safety record but also recognized that it had to work with the FAA in improving and maintaining a clean record and a good reputation. While the EMS industry was working on its internal improvements (see above), FAA was keeping up its end. In 1988 FAA published Advisory Circular (AC) 135–14, "Emergency Medical Services/Helicopters." This AC outlined some crucial definitions concerning EMS operators as well as explained certification requirements, training programs, and operational requirements. It described a suggested safety program and provided a sample of flight and duty time records, a sample of operations specifications, and a sample weight and balance loading schedule. The AC also suggested types of additional equipment, detailed manual requirements and flight following/dispatch procedures,

and offered suggested VFR weather minimums for dispatch as well as types and numbers of personnel. The EMS industry had aided FAA in drafting the AC and were generally pleased with the information and advice it offered. In 1989 FAA updated the AC, adding definitions of the two types of air ambulance services offered—Basic and Advanced—among other additions. (In December 1990 FAA also issued AC 135-15, "Emergency Medical Services/Airplanes," which followed a similar format for airplane air ambulance services. Airplane EMS operations have grown in their own way, advancing from DC-3's and King Airs to corporate jets. Airplane EMS operations are also moving into the international arena.)

FAA worked closely with EMS industry representatives in the development of the AC's and in the development of the next logical regulatory step to enhance air ambulance safety: Air ambulance operations specifications. FAA issues every FAR Part 135 operator a set of *operations specifications* which outline in detail the kinds of operations that can be conducted and the conditions under which they can be conducted. No FAR Part 135 operator can legally operate outside these "ops specs;" discovery could mean legal enforcement action from the FAA and possibly loss of certification. In 1992 FAA developed the first set of EMS specific ops specs. By sometime in 1993 in order to conduct EMS operations, a FAR Part 135 operator will have to have an "air ambulance paragraph" in its ops specs; otherwise, the operator cannot hold out to the public

as a provider of air ambulance services. This will not only help FAA to identify EMS operators more accurately for surveillance and tracking purposes, it will also help to reduce the likelihood of unscrupulous FAR Part 135 operators taking an EMS flight they may not be trained or equipped to handle. No one—the public, the FAA, or the EMS industry—wants to encounter an operator who pulls seats out in order to shove an unsecured gurney inside.

The cooperation between the FAA and the EMS industry in the regulation of and policy development for air ambulance services using helicopters is one of the better examples of an ever-growing safety partnership, a continuing partnership that is now working on enhanced safety and training programs for EMS operators. For its part, FAA will continue to strive in partnership with the EMs industry to structure future rules and policies that will maintain public safety and enhance economic growth. The FAA is also encouraging EMS operators to participate in its *voluntary disclosure* or "self-audit" program, which allows operators to identify potential or existing problems and work with the FAA to correct them without fear of legal enforcement action.

EMS Lessons for All Pilots

The helicopter EMS aspect of the aviation industry has experienced the highs and lows that any innovation has to endure in order to prove itself. The advantages of the use of helicopter in medical transport—emergency or routine—far outweigh the prospect of

having to do without them in such a service. Through its preponderance in HEMES operations, the helicopter has once again been vindicated as an integral part of civil aviation.

The reaction of the EMS industry to its mid-1980's accident rate and an aberrant spike in the number of accidents in the early 1990's (solvable, FAA and industry believes, with the enhanced training programs now being devised) is an example of how everyone in aviation needs to react to safety crises: Safety issues will not go away by being ignored; they have to be addressed proactively by the FAA and the industry in partnership.

The predominant causes of EMS accidents can give any pilot in any operation some food for thought:

- Don't fly when you are tired; get plenty of rest *before* entering the cockpit.

- Don't fly when you are stressed; leave daily stresses behind before flying for work or pleasure.

- Don't succumb to "corporate pressure" or "get-home-itis" and fly when your better judgement says not to.

- Know and follow the regulatory weather minimums and abide by them or establish your own, stricter minimums.

- Maintain your instrument currency and proficiency if you are instrument rated.

- Get an instrument rating if you don't have one.

- Above all, fly the aircraft first and foremost; don't let distraction take over the controls.

We all do our best to avoid accidents of any kind, but if a catastrophe avoidably occurs, the beat of the rotor blades during that "golden hour" is something we all want to hear. ∎

To obtain copies of AC 135–14A or 135–15, contact DOT, M–443.2, Washington, DC 20590. A copy of the NTSB safety study NTSB/SS–88/01, "Commercial Emergency Medical Service Helicopter Operations," is available from the National Technical Information Service,Springfield, VA 22161. Special thanks go to FAA's Air Taxi and Commuter Branch, to FAA Aviation Safety Inspector Edwin Robinson, and to the Helicopter Association International for their assistance in the preparation of this article. Photos courtesy of Bell Helicopter Textron, Inc.

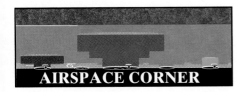

AIRSPACE CORNER

The word has been out on airspace reclassification just long enough for the questions to start coming in. The way we would like to handle them is in a regular "Airspace Corner" column, similiar to our "Instrument Corner." For future editions of "Airspace Corner" we would welcome questions, comments, or subjects that the readers feel need clarification. —Editor

The first of the new visual charts (Sectional and Terminal) appeared October 15th. By the time you read this, the December charts will be out, and we will be halfway through the first cycle. We have received several calls regarding the charted vertical limits of control zones at non-TCA/ARSA airports with operating control towers, and we would like to share those questions and their answers with you—you may have had the very same thoughts!

Question: *Was the airport traffic area (ATA) lowered to the same height of the control zone?*

Answer: No! Only the control zones were changed via rulemaking that was effective October 15th. The ATA's lateral limits continue to be a five-statute mile radius of the airport, and its vertical limits extend up to, but do not include, 3,000 feet AGL. The ATA's will be eliminated effective September 16, 1993, at which time the charted control zones become Class D airspace. Remember that the radius of the ATA probably does not coincide with the charted control zone boundary boundary and, in almost all cases, the 2,999 foot AGL limit will be higher than the control zone's upper limit. Based on the calls received to date, FAA's Air Traffic Service has updated the NOTAM on November 12th to further clarify this point.

Question: *At Sacramento Executive, the chart indicates the vertical limit of 2,500 feet MSL for the control zone and the Mather AFB ARSA is 1,600 feet MSL. Which altitude applies?*

Answer: For that portion of the control zone that underlies the ARSA, the vertical limit is up to, but does not include 1,600 feet MSL. The 2,500 foot MSL limit applies to that airspace outside the ARSA. Under the reclassification program, there is a hierarchy within the classes that prevents overlapping. In this case, the Mather ARSA (Class C) preempts the Executive control zone (Class D).

• Night Flight

The question of when can a pilot log night time has come up several times recently. The U.S. Federal Aviation Regulations (FAR) Part 1 and the Airman's Information Manual (AIM) glossary defines "night" time as "the time between the end of evening civil twilight and the beginning of morning civil twilight, as published in the American Air Almanac, converted to local time." Some pilots use FAR § 61.57(d) to define when they log night time. This paragraph states in part, "No person may act as pilot in command of an aircraft carrying passengers during the period beginning one hour after sunset and ending one hour before sunrise (as published in the American Air Almanac) unless, within the preceding 90 days, he has made at least three takeoffs and three landings to a full stop during that period in the category and class of aircraft to be used."

Which do I use?

Why is there a disparity?

I fly in Europe. Evening civil twilight here is defined as official sunset plus 30 minutes, and morning civil twilight is defined as official sunrise minus 30 minutes. Believe me, it is dark then.

Please, clarify when I can log night time.

> *Gregory J. Findlay*
> *APO AE*

First, if you are flying in Europe on the basis of your American pilot certificate in a U.S. registered civil aircraft, you must comply with FAR Part 91 Subpart H. Subpart H, Foreign Aircraft Operations and Operations of U.S. Registered Civil Aircraft Outside of the United States, states in part in FAR § 91.703 (a), "Each person operating a civil aircraft of U.S. registry outside of the United States shall- (1) Note: Part 1 deals with flight over the high seas and is not applicable here. (2) When within a foreign country, comply with the regulations relating to the flight and maneuver of aircraft there in force; (3) Except for §§ 91.307(b), 91.309, 91.323, and 91.711, comply with this part so far as it is not inconsistent with applicable regulations of the foreign coun-

try where the aircraft is operated or annex 2 of the Convention on International Civil Aviation." Based upon FAR § 91.703(a)(2) and (3) you must compare your host country's rules regarding night flying with the U.S. rules and apply the above guidance.

To answer your question about night time in the United States, FAR Part 1 defines official "night" so pilots can log the conditions of flight, day or night, required by FAR § 61.51(b)(3)(i). FAR § 61.57(d) defines a pilot proficiency requirement that must be complied with before the pilot can be pilot in command (PIC) of an aircraft carrying passengers during the period stated in the rule. The more restrictive pilot proficiency "night" definition is designed to ensure a greater degree of darkness. Pilots using the proficiency requirement of FAR § 61.57(d) to define "night" time for logging night time required by FAR § 61.51(b)(3)(i) may be cheating themselves out of night time required for meeting certain certificate requirements.

• Diving and Flying

I read with interest your brief article in the March-April issue regarding scuba diving and flying. Many divers operate under the misguided assumption that a pressurized plane has a cabin pressure of sea level and, further, do not consider the potential for a complete depressurization at 30-40,000 feet and the probable complications just after diving.

While diving in Florida and since, I made 15-20 dive trips to the Bahamas and the Florida Keys in non-pressurized, mostly single engine airplanes. Many of the trips were one day trips with two tank dives each trip. My friends and I used the "Tahoe Tables" in reverse to calculate a safety zone depth for our dives. That is, we calculated how deep we could dive based on the altitude correction in the Tahoe Table. The altitude used was the altitude we intended to use flying back to the states. We never had a problem, but I always wondered whether this was luck or whether the Tahoe Tables really worked for these types of situations. Can you folks validate this procedure as a practical approach?

> *Ken Brown*
> *Humble, TX*

Sorry. The FAA cannot validate your procedure. Although the *Airman's Information Manual* was changed to reflect the latest available information concerning scuba diving and flying, the specific approval you are asking for should be requested from diving experts familiar with high altitude diving. Possibly one of the diving certification associations, the Divers Alert Network (DAN), or a diving safety/medical journal article on the subject might be able to answer your question

Flight**FORUM**

• Logging PIC Time

Here we go again. I need clarification on the logging of PIC time. Can a non-instrument rated pilot log PIC time on an IFR flight plan, either IMC or VMC, with a current and qualified instrument pilot (not a CFII) in the right seat?
D. Chris Anderson
Columbia, SC

Yes, under the following conditions. First we must differentiate between the two meanings for PIC. One meaning for PIC is the FAR Part 1 definition of "the pilot responsible for the operation and safety of an aircraft during flight time." You can not be PIC on an IFR flight plan without being an instrument-rated pilot and holding the appropriate pilot and aircraft ratings. But you can log PIC time under the second definition of PIC which FAR § 61.51(c)(2)(i) defines in part as that time when the pilot is the sole manipulator of the controls of an aircraft for which the pilot is rated. FAR § 61.51(c)(4) then defines instrument time as being that time during which a pilot operates an aircraft solely be reference to instruments, under actual or simulated instrument flight conditions. As a result of the two definitions, you cannot be PIC (responsible for the flight), but you can log as PIC time that time during which you are the sole manipulator of the controls of the aircraft for which you are rated. This PIC time (sole manipulator) is creditable towards the minimum time needed to meet the flight experience requirements for an instrument rating under FAR § 61.65, Instrument Rating Requirements.

• VFR Restricted

I recently obtained my Airplane Single Engine Land rating from the local FAA in Frankfurt, Germany, via my military experi-ence. This rating was an add-on to my multi-engine/instrument. When I obtained this addition it came limited to VFR only. I know this would be correct for a multi addition. My question is: Is the VFR restriction correct for the addition of single engine land?
Emmett Tullia II
Manchaca, TX

If the circumstances are as indicated in your letter, then the VFR limitation should not have been issued, but check with FAA's Frankfort office to be sure. Usually a person who has a multi-engine rating with instrument privileges may, when issued an airplane single rating, exercise instrument privileges in that single engine airplane without further showing of competence.

Answers to Quiz: 1-E, 2-I, 3-C, 4-J, 5-B, 6-G, 7-A, 8-F, 9-L, 10-D, 11-H, 12-K

• VFR on Top

*There seems to be a misunderstanding between pilots and FAA air traffic controllers as to altitude requirements while flying VFR-on-top. The pilot/controller glossary in the Air-man's Information Manual (AIM) and the Air Traffic Control Handbook both state under "VFR-on-top" that a pilot must comply with the minimum IFR altitudes specified in FAR Part 91. Pilots are being advised in a popular, widely read aviation magazine that VFR-on-top (*Flying *magazine, October 1991, "Eyeball Separation" by J. Mac McClellan) allows pilots to descend below the minimum en route altitude (MEA). Controllers do not allow a VFR-on top aircraft to fly below MEA's or minimum IFR altitudes (MIA), yet many pilots expect to be able to do this. Who is correct?*
Mikhail H. John
Salt Lake City, UT

The FAR and controllers are correct. What may have confused some pilots is that there may be more than one FAA-approved IFR minimum altitude for a given route segment. Some minimum altitudes are published on charts. Others are only published for controller use. As a result, although IFR pilots operating on an IFR clearance must comply with FAR §§ 91.177, Minimum altitudes for IFR Operations, and 91.179, IFR Cruising Altitude or Flight Level, they may be able to request a lower "minimum" altitude than the published or derived MEA depending upon the route segment being flown and the type of navigation equipment being used.

Since VFR-on-top is an IFR clearance, the pilot requesting it must comply with the various IFR altitude rules in the FAR. For VFR pilots not familiar with the term, the AIM defines VFR-on-top as an "ATC authorization for an IFR aircraft to operate in VFR conditions at any appropriate VFR altitude (as specified in FAR and as restricted by ATC). A

INSTRUMENT CORNER

pilot receiving this authorization must comply with the VFR visibility, distance from cloud criteria, and the minimum IFR altitudes specified in FAR 91. The use of this term does not relieve controllers of their responsibility to separate aircraft in TCA's/TRSA's." As you can see, ATC may be able to authorize a lower-than-chart-published minimum en route altitude and still comply with the FAR.

To answer your question, *FAA Aviation News* contacted Mr. McClellan about his article. He said many people wrote him about his comments. Please see, "FlyingMail" in the December 1991 issue of *Flying* magazine for some of the comments. In his response to his readers, he clarified the difference between a "direct" clearance and flying between VOR's on an airway and how the difference between the two types of clearances determine the minimum en route altitude ATC can approve for a given route segment. As he said in his article, it may be possible to request a lower-than-published IFR en route altitude, and if one is available, and ATC authorizes the use of that altitude, the pilot can fly it.

Please remember the purpose of the FAR altitude rules are to protect pilots by providing them the minimum safe flight altitudes or means of determining minimum safe altitudes based upon terrain, known obstacles, and navigational requirements for the route segment being flown. What apparently confused some pilots about the *Flying* magazine article is that they did not know or remember that there may be several different IFR altitudes available to controllers and pilots for a given route segment depending upon what type of navigational equipment is being used for course guidance, i.e. VOR, radar, or RNAV. Aircraft distance from a fix or radar site may also be a factor in determining the minimum altitude available for a given route segment.

As a reminder to IFR pilots, examples of *some* of the different minimum IFR altitudes defined in the AIM include *minimum vectoring altitudes* (MVA) which are altitudes that can be used by radar controllers in certain circumstances depending upon the strength of the radar return. MVA's may be lower than a published MEA along an airway or J-route segment. *Minimum obstruction clearance altitudes* (MOCA) which provide obstacle clearance over the entire route but only ensures acceptable navigational signal coverage only within 25 statute (22 nautical) miles of a VOR. MOCA's may also be lower than MEA's. And then there is the *minimum en route altitude* (MEA), which most IFR pilots use in flight planning, that provides both obstacle clearance and navigational guidance between radio fixes. On unpublished direct routes the *minimum IFR altitude* (MIA) established by the ATC facility and the MIA for the pilot complying with the FAR may not be the same. Whenever the pilot is lower, action in the form of a clearance or restriction will be taken by the controller to ensure the operation is conducted at or above the facility sector MIA.

These and other minimum and maximum IFR altitudes are defined in the AIM. IFR pilots should review the AIM periodically as a reminder of the specific types of IFR altitudes available in the National Air Space (NAS) system, and by understanding them, IFR pilots may in fact be able to request a lower minimum altitude than the chart published MEA for a given route segment.

Turn Coordinators in Aerobatic Aircraft

An investigation into an aerobatic aircraft fatal accident has highlighted the fact that turn co-ordinators can give ambiguous indications during an inverted spin. A causal factor in the accident was the pilot's failure to recover from an inverted spin. It is probable that the pilot failed to identify correctly the spin mode and direction and hence failed to take the correct spin recovery action.

The aircraft was fitted with a modern turn co-ordinator. This instrument, unlike a conventional turn and slip indicator, does not have a turn needle. A turn co-ordinator measures both roll and yaw rates and will only give reliable indications of yaw direction in an erect spin. In an inverted spin, since the aircraft yaws in one direction and rolls in the other, a turn co-ordinator may give an incorrect indication of yaw direction to the pilot. A conventional turn (needle) indicator measures yaw rate only and therefore always indicates the correct yaw direction in both erect and inverted spins. If a pilot is disorientated in a spin, whether erect or inverted, reference to a turn needle will correctly confirm the spin direction and should insure that the correct recovery action is taken.

The provision of a turn indicator (i.e., turn needle) is strongly recommended for aircraft cleared for spinning and aerobatics in order to identify correctly the direction of spin in both erect and inverted spin modes.

Editor's Note: This article is reprinted with permission from the September 1992 British CAA General Aviation Safety Information Leaflet (GASIL).

Awards for the CFI and the AMT of the Year

"I have the world's smallest aerobatic school—one airplane, one sick sack, and an instructor (himself). Then last week a guy used the sick sack, and now I am in serious financial trouble," said the 1992 Certificated Flight Instructor (CFI) of the Year. The comments were made during ceremonies at FAA headquarters in Washington, DC on November 16 honoring the winners of the 1992 CFI and Maintenance Technician of the Year awards. Although everyone laughed at the joke

FAA Administrator Richards (left) with CFI of the Year William Kershner (center) and AMT of the Year John Canedo.

made by the owner/instructor of the "world's smallest aerobatic school," no one questioned his selection as the General Aviation Industry Awards Program's Certificated Flight Instructor of the Year for 1992. After all, Mr. William K. Kershner of Sewanee, TN, has taught students and pilots a thing or two about flying over the years. The 1992 Maintenance Technician of the Year, Mr. John Canedo of Herndon, VA, has an equally impressive record of accomplishments in General Aviation. Mr. Canedo is responsible for supervising the maintenance on six multi-million dollar jet aircraft for a major corporation. Both winners were recognized by the General Aviation Industry Awards Program for their life-long contributions to the industry.

Mr. Kershner is the well-known author of many flight training handbooks on aviation. His flying career dates back to 1945 when he first started flying in his hometown of Clarksville, TN. Since then, he has served as a Navy pilot during the Korean War and as the Experimental Flight Testing supervisor for Piper Aircraft. Since 1964 he has taught aerobatics in Sewanee, TN while writing the flight training manuals that have made him famous. In addition to his writing and flight instructing, he promotes aviation safety as a speaker at many aviation events and seminars.

Mr. Canedo's aviation career also started in the 1940's when he built and flew model aircraft. A commercial pilot, Mr. Canedo decided maintaining aircraft satisfied his mechanical appetites more than flying them. While pursuing his career in general aviation maintenance, he worked for several fixed-

based operators (FBO) over the years before joining the Gannett Company in 1986. At Gannett, he supervises eight A&P maintenance technicians who maintain a fleet of six jet aircraft. His dedication and interest in aviation maintenance have resulted in many of his aircraft modification ideas being incorporated in the work of his company and its aircraft manufacturer and other manufacturers.

Both men recognized the help and support provided by their families and colleagues over the years that contributed to their being selected for their respective honors. During the ceremony, in addition to receiving plaques from FAA Administrator Thomas C. Richards, the winners also received awards and gifts from many general aviation companies, associations, and industry groups. During their visit to Washington, the honorees and their families met privately with Secretary of Transportation Andrew H. Card, Jr. and the FAA Administrator as part of their industry-sponsored tour of Washington. This year's General Aviation Industry Awards Program was sponsored by the AOPA Air Safety Foundation, the General Aviation Manufactures Association, the National Business Aircraft Association, and the Federal Aviation Administration.

Cellular Phones

The latest Federal Communcations Commission (FCC) ruling on cellular phones does allow them to be used on an aircraft as long as it is still on the ground. Once the aircraft (this includes hot air balloons) leaves the ground, usage is prohibited, and violators are subject to a fine.

Accident Prevention Program Seminars

You have seen the commercials after the Super Bowl where the off-camera announcer says to the Most Valuable Player, "You've just won the Super Bowl! Where are you headed now?" The response is, "I'm going to Disney World!" So what does this have to do with flying? Now that we are in the depths of winter, many of us yearn for the sunshine and sandy beaches of Florida, but if we have young children, we end up at Disney World. If you load the spouse and kids into the family airplane and head for the "Mouse House," you (the pilot in the family) might want a little diversion. Why not continue your Accident Prevention Program education while you are in central Florida? Mr. Obie Young, Accident Prevention Program Manager in the Orlando, FL Flight Standards District Office, offers the following meetings in the upcoming months. If you need more detailed information, contact Mr. Young at (407) 648-6840.

WARNING—Autogas and Alcohol Don't Mix

We all know that drinking and flying are a no-win combination, but did you know that users of autogas could have a problem with automobile gasoline that has been blended with "oxygenates"—i.e., alcohol?

FAA inspectors in North Carolina learned that there was plenty of *unlabeled* blended automobile gasoline containing oxygenates available. Because these blends are unlabeled, the autogas user may unknowingly purchase what he or she believes to be regular autogas. Use of such blended autogas in an aircraft can create a potential safety problem, and Mr. John Colomy, Manager of FAA's Standards Office in the Central Region, wants us to "get the word out" about this likely hazard.

Both the Experimental Aircraft Association (EAA) and Peterson Aviation, the main holders of the autogas Supplemental Type Certificates (STC), prohibit the use of autogas blended with alcohol, and both STC holders state this prohibition on the placards installed next to the airplane's fuel filler caps. Both also sell kits to test autogas for the presence of alcohol. Neither STC holder addresses the use of

---

GENERAL AVIATION SAFETY SEMINARS

TUESDAY, JANUARY 12, 1993 7:30 P.M.
On Landings Part II
Tampa General Hospital, Tampa, FL

WEDNESDAY, JANUARY 13, 1993 7:30 P.M.
On Landings Part II
MSL Auditorium, St. Petersburg, FL

SATURDAY, JANUARY 16, 1993 9:00 A.M.
Ultralight Seminar
Lakeland, FL

THURSDAY, FEBRUARY 4, 1993 7:00 P.M.
Navaids
Savage Aviation, Sandford, FL

THURSDAY, MARCH 4, 1993 7:00 P.M.
Instrument Flight
Savage Aviation, Sanford, FL

SATURDAY, FEBRUARY 6, 1993 ALL DAY
General Aviation Pilots Association
Sanford, FL

SUNDAY, FEBRUARY 7, 1993 ALL DAY
General Aviation Pilots Association
River Ranch Resort, FL

TUESDAY, FEBRUARY 9, 1993 7:30 P.M.
On Landings Part III
Tampa General Hospital, Tampa, FL

WEDNESDAY, FEBRUARY 10, 1993 7:30 P.M.
On Landings Part III
MSL Auditorium, St. Petersburg, FL

WEDNESDAY, MARCH   3, 1993 6:30 P.M.
WEDNESDAY, MARCH 10, 1993 6:30 P.M.
WEDNESDAY, MARCH 17, 1993 6:30 P.M.
WEDNESDAY, MARCH 24, 1993 6:30 P.M.
WEDNESDAY, MARCH 31, 1993 6:30 P.M.
Airspace Reclassification*
Daytona Beach, FL

TUESDAY, MARCH 9, 1993 7:30 P.M.
Enforcement
Tampa General Hospital, Tampa, FL

WEDNESDAY, MARCH 10, 1993 7:30P.M.
Enforcement
MSL Auditorium, St. Petersburg, FL

SATURDAY, MARCH 20, 1993 8:00 A.M.
Wings Weekend
Orlando, Jacksonville, St. Petersburg, Melbourne, Punta Gorda, Flagler County, Fort Pierce, Sanford, Lakeland, and Crystal River

THURSDAY, APRIL 1, 1993 7:00 P.M.
Preflight
Savage Aviation, Sanford, FL

ALL WEEK, APRIL 18–24, 1993
Sun 'n Fun
Lakeland, FL

THURSDAY, MAY 6, 1993 7:00 P.M.
Ground Operations
Savage Aviation, Sanford, FL

THURSDAY, JUNE 3, 1993 7:00 P.M.
Communications/Manuevers
Savage Aviation, Sanford, FL

THURSDAY, JULY 1, 1993 7:00 P.M.
Weather and Airspace
Savage Aviation, Sanford FL

SATURDAY, AUGUST 14, 1993 9:00 A.M.
Corporate Aviation Seminar
Lakeland, FL

*Day two of a three-day Operation Raincheck

---

autogas blended with ether. The FAA's position at this time, is that methyl-tertiary-butyl ether (MTBE) and other oxygenates are not approved because no STC testing has been done. (To date, research conducted with autogas blended with MTBE have not uncovered any serious problems with this additive, and in the future the FAA may be in a position to approve the use of autogas blended with MTBE once STC testing has been addressed. If MTBE additives are approved without the need for hardware changes to airplanes, the STC holders may not have to revise their STC's.)

Tests conducted with autogas blended with alcohol (ethanol and methanol) have shown problems with corrosion of metal parts and deterioration of non-metallic seals and hoses. It is unlikely that FAA can approve alcohol blends without requiring hardware changes to the airplane's engine and fuel system. Consequently, FAA approval of STC's for alcohol blends is not in the foreseeable future.

At this time, the problem of unlabeled blended autogas does not require rescission of the autogas STC's. FAA's Office of Environment and Energy is working with the U.S. Environmental Protection Agency concerning the labeling of fuels blended with oxygenates. In the meantime, airplanes owners who use autogas under the STC's should purchase autogas from sources they know have been tested for alcohol or from sources that can document that oxygenates are not in the fuel. Autogas users can also test the fuel themselves using the available test kits.

FAA cautions against using autogas containing oxygenates until such time as they are approved for use in aircraft. The aircraft operator has the responsibility to determine if the fuel used meets the requirements of the STC. If the approved autogas is not available, there is always aviation grade gasoline.

Any autogas users with questions about blended autogas should contact EAA or Peterson Aviation.

TEST YOUR TRIVIA:
Denver International Airport Quiz

After reading the article on page 17, match the correct answer to the questions. *(Information provided by the Denver International Airport Public Affairs)* *(For the answer key see page 26.)*

1. What is the surface area of the new airport? ___

2. What is the concrete surface area of the first design phase of construction (six runways, ramps, and taxiways)? ___

3. How many dump truck loads of earth will be moved during construction? ___

4. If the earth in question 3 was put in a pile how large would the pile be? ___

5. The total earth being moved is equal to about half of the volume of what famous earthmoving project? ___

6. What is the total raw material, asphalt and cement, needed to build the first phase? ___

7. During the first phase of construction 36 million cubic yards of earth will be moved. This volume would fill a ditch 10 feet by 10 feet from Denver to what famous city? ___

8. How many square miles of airspace are involved in the Victor Airways changes being made to serve the Denver region? ___

9. How many square miles of airspace are involved in all of the jet airways, SID's, and STAR's being changed to serve the area? ___

10. What is the number of new or amended airway segments involved in the change? ___

11. What is the number of new approaches, STAR's, SID's, and departure procedures involved in the change? ___

12. What is the number of new or canceled intersections being made to support the new airport? ___

ANSWERS

A. New York City

B. The Panama Canal project.

C. Enough loads that if the trucks were placed end to end the line would reach 1.5 times around the world. The amount is about 100 million cubic yards of dirt.

D. 163

E. 53 square miles or twice the size of Manhattan Island in New York.

F. 25,000 square miles

G. In excess of 10 million tons or enough, for you football fans, to fill Mile High Stadium in Denver to the brim 10 times.

H. 140

I. The area is equivalent to a single-lane highway from Denver to Chicago.

J. A surface area of 32 city blocks by a quarter mile high.

K. 162

L. 164,000 square miles

DO NOT DELAY—CRITICAL TO FLIGHT SAFETY!

DO NOT DELAY—CRITICAL TO FLIGHT SAFETY!

TEST YOUR TRIVIA:
Denver International Airport Quiz

After reading the article on page 17, match the correct answer to the questions. *(Information provided by the Denver International Airport Public Affairs) (For the answer key see page 26.)*

1. What is the surface area of the new airport? ___

2. What is the concrete surface area of the first design phase of construction (six runways, ramps, and taxiways)? ___

3. How many dump truck loads of earth will be moved during construction? ___

4. If the earth in question 3 was put in a pile how large would the pile be? ___

5. The total earth being moved is equal to about half of the volume of what famous earthmoving project? ___

6. What is the total raw material, asphalt and cement, needed to build the first phase? ___

7. During the first phase of construction 36 million cubic yards of earth will be moved. This volume would fill a ditch 10 feet by 10 feet from Denver to what famous city? ___

8. How many square miles of airspace are involved in the Victor Airways changes being made to serve the Denver region? ___

9. How many square miles of airspace are involved in all of the jet airways, SID's, and STAR's being changed to serve the area? ___

10. What is the number of new or amended airway segments involved in the change? ___

11. What is the number of new approaches, STAR's, SID's, and departure procedures involved in the change? ___

12. What is the number of new or canceled intersections being made to support the new airport? ___

ANSWERS

A. New York City

B. The Panama Canal project.

C. Enough loads that if the trucks were placed end to end the line would reach 1.5 times around the world. The amount is about 100 million cubic yards of dirt.

D. 163

E. 53 square miles or twice the size of Manhattan Island in New York.

F. 25,000 square miles

G. In excess of 10 million tons or enough, for you football fans, to fill Mile High Stadium in Denver to the brim 10 times.

H. 140

I. The area is equivalent to a single-lane highway from Denver to Chicago.

J. A surface area of 32 city blocks by a quarter mile high.

K. 162

L. 164,000 square miles

March 1993

FAA Aviation News

A DOT/FAA FLIGHT STANDARDS SAFETY PUBLICATION

U.S. Department
of Transportation

**Federal Aviation
Administration**

Federico F. Peña, *Secretary of Transportation*
Joseph M. Del Balzo, *Acting FAA Administrator*
Carl B. Schellenberg, *Acting Executive Director
    for System Operations*
Anthony J. Broderick, *Associate Administrator
    for Regulation and Certification*
Thomas C. Accardi, *Director,
    Flight Standards Service*
Robert A. Wright, *Acting Manager,
    General Aviation and Commercial Division*
Roger M. Baker, Jr., *Manager,
    Accident Prevention Program Branch*
Phyllis Anne Duncan, *Editor*
Louise C. Oertly, *Senior Associate Editor*
Dean Chamberlain, *Associate Editor*

The FAA's Flight Standards Service, General Aviation and
Commercial Division, Accident Prevention Program
Branch, AFS-810, Washington, DC 20591, (telephone
202 267–8017) publishes FAA AVIATION NEWS in the
interest of flight safety. The magazine promotes safety in
the air by calling the attention of airmen to current technical, regulatory, and procedural matters affecting the safe
operation of aircraft. Although based on current FAA policy and rule interpretations, all printed material herein are
advisory or informational in nature and should not be
construed to have regulatory effect. The FAA does not
officially endorse any goods, services, materials, or products of manufacturers that may be mentioned. **Certain
details of accidents described herein have been
altered to protect the privacy of those involved.**
    The Office of Management and Budget has
approved the use of funds for the printing of FAA AVIA-
TION NEWS.

SUBSCRIPTION SERVICES

The Superintendent of Documents, U.S. Government
Printing Office, Washington, DC 20402–9371, sells FAA
AVIATION NEWS on subscription. Use the self-mailer
form in the center of this magazine to subscribe. Cost:
$8.00 ($10.00 foreign) for one year; $16.00 ($20.00 for-
eign) for two years. Prices are subject to change by the
Government Printing Office without prior notice.
    Change of Address or Subscription Problems:
**Send your label with correspondence to Sup Doc,
Attn: Chief, Mail List Branch, Mail Stop: SSOM,
Washington, DC 20402–9373.**
    To keep subscription prices down, the Government
Printing Office mails subscribers only one renewal
notice. You can tell how many copies are left in your
subscription by checking the number that follows "ISS-
DUE" on the top line of your mailing label. For example,
when this number is 003, it means you have three
issues left in your subscription, and GPO will send you
a renewal notice. The number 000 means you have
received your last issue. To be sure that your service
continues without interruption, please return your
renewal notice promptly.

FAN SMITH 212J ISSDUE003 R 1
JOHN SMITH
212 MAIN ST
FORESTVILLE, MD 20747

March 1993

FAA Aviation News

Volume 32   Number 2

FEATURES

DEPARTMENTS

On the Cover:
*Want to learn how to fly this cockpit? See page 2
for further details.*

On the Back Cover:
Photo courtesy of Embry-Riddle.

The Myth of the Superpilot

by Dean Chamberlain, *Associate Editor*

1992 marked the end of an era that many of us never thought would happen. Superman died. His demise was marked by a special commemorative issue and national TV commentaries. Many believe he will make a super comeback, as few can envision a world without the super hero. Time will tell. But in a way, Superman may have outlived his usefulness by a generation or more. Today, in our politically correct world, Superman would have to be a Superperson. And frankly, it is hard to imagine a Superperson saving the world from evil as did the man of steel time after time. Or maybe the world has changed so much since the arrival of that baby from another planet, that not even Superman could survive the disillusionment of our times after seeing such acts as carjackings, violence in the streets, and shootouts between teenage gangs on the nightly TV news. In Superman's glory days, it was easy to tell good from evil. Good guys wore white hats and bad guys wore black. Today, sometimes it is hard to tell the good guys (persons) from the bad guys (persons). Compounding the problem is the fact we must now face an uncertain future without our super hero.

So who is going to protect us from evil?

Or maybe the question should be rephrased to ask, "Do we need super heroes at all?" Maybe we no longer need them. Which leads in a super stretch of the imagination to the question of should the myth of the superpilot be laid to rest with Superman? Do we still need the image of general aviation (GA) pilots being able to leap off tall hangers in a single bound? So what if someone needs a running start to leap off small T-hangers, does that make

Dean Chamberlain

that pilot any less of a pilot? And what if maintenance technicians do not have X-ray vision, does that make them any less capable? And for that matter just how big, strong, and fast do men and women have to be to be good, safe, general aviation airmen? Although some young GA pilots aspire to be weapon platform managers in multi-million dollar flying weapons systems, not every middle-aged GA pilot aspires to fly the dawn patrol over the Western Front at sunrise. Many are happy just to fly the spouse and kids to the next airport for lunch; i.e., something else that does not require the skill of a super hero to perform well; something that can be done by a normal, everyday-type of person; someone that thinks aviation can be done just for fun. After all, not every boat is a cargo ship, nor is every vehicle on the highway a truck, nor every golf course a farm (although a few golf courses would make great GA airports). The fact is many different kinds of ordinary people enjoy general aviation. Pilots do not have to be super people to fly; pilots are just super people.

But like Superman, some doom and gloom forecasters would have us to believe that general aviation is dying or dead. Or is aviation, like Superman, just waiting for the right moment to take off and fly again? Only time will tell, but as we wait for the next chapter in the saga of Superman and general aviation, what are you doing for aviation while you wait? Because while you are waiting out the traditional bust or boom cycle of aviation, what you fail to do might be more important than what you do.

1992 not only saw the demise of Superman, it also saw a change in national politics. The Congress has

Continued on page 19

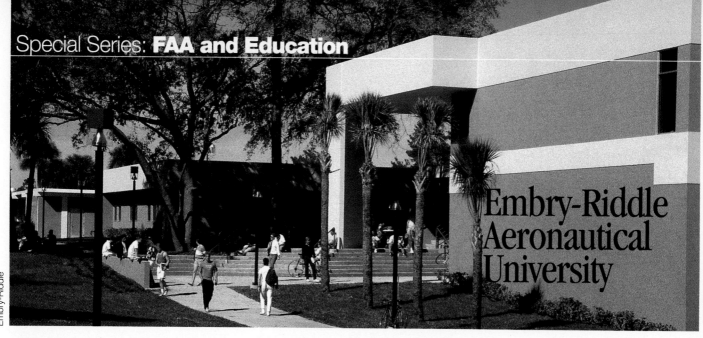

Embry-Riddle

Embry-Riddle Aeronautical University

by Dean Chamberlain, *Associate Editor*

We discussed in the previous issue the FAA's involvement in aviation education and research. Now it is time to start our series on representative Airway Science Program (AWS) schools by discussing one of the world's most famous universities dedicated to aviation and aerospace—Embry-Riddle Aeronautical University (ERAU) of Daytona Beach, Florida, and Prescott, Arizona. Known throughout the aviation world, it is also one of the largest universities dedicated solely to aviation. In describing the university's and its students' focus on aviation, the phase "Aviation is spoken here" may be a gross understatement. As one young ERAU student said when asked why she went to Embry-Riddle, "I wanted to learn to fly, and Embry-Riddle has a great reputation." Being able to study all phases of aviation at one of Florida's premier beach resorts has to be an added bonus. For students who prefer a western setting instead of the beach, there is ERAU's Prescott campus in Arizona. For students, especially military students, who cannot attend either campus, ERAU offers bachelors and masters degree programs at over 90 continuing education centers around the world.

For those not familiar with ERAU, it is a private, not-for-profit, co-educational university that traces its heritage to the early days of aviation. During the barnstorming days of the 1920's, two

aviation pioneers, T. Higbee Embry and J. Paul Riddle, founded an aviation school in 1926 at Lunken Airport in Cincinnati, Ohio. That school would later grow into ERAU. According to ERAU, the men started the school based upon the philosophy, "To teach every phase of flying, from the ground up to the sky."

Since then, ERAU has developed into a major aeronautical university that offers more than 20 aviation-related undergraduate and graduate level degrees. Although many of the degree programs at ERAU—such as its aerospace engineering; electrical engineering; engineering physics; aeronautical science (professional pilot, which also includes the FAA-sponsored Airway Science (AWS) curriculum); aerospace studies; aviation maintenance technology; avionics engineering; and computer science programs—may sound similar to other university programs, there is one significant difference between ERAU's programs and many of the others around the nation. Everything at ERAU has an aviation connection. While the flight portion of the AWS program at ERAU and other participating schools provides students the opportunity to earn their FAA-Commercial Pilot Certificate with Instrument and Single- and Multi-engine Ratings and the maintenance portion provides students the opportunity to earn their Airframe and Power-plant (A&P) certificates, ERAU's

commitment to aviation is seen throughout its campuses.

From the aircraft suspended from the ceiling of the Daytona campus' cafeteria to ERAU's classrooms and research labs to its flight lines, aviation seems to be the only subject at ERAU. Although ERAU students study a broad range of college subjects, the one attitude they all seem to have in common is that they all seem to live and breath aviation and aerospace. Their attitude about aviation is also shared by the professors and instructors at ERAU. One professor, Dr. Gerry Gibb, the Director of the Airway Science Simulation Lab, said although it may sound like the party line, aviation is everything at Embry-Riddle. According to Dr. Gibb what makes ERAU unique is how the school brings the various educational disciplines together to solve a particular classroom problem. The result, Dr. Gibb said, is that the aviation program at ERAU is more diversified and far more extensive in breath than anywhere else. One benefit of ERAU's unique approach to teaching, using computers, practical experience, mixed disciplines, and state-of-the-art teaching techniques and equipment, he said, is that it teaches students how to work together as a team that can meet milestones, resolve problems, and find solutions to problems. Vital skills not only in aviation, but in any environment.

Although ERAU offers a large number of programs at its various sites, because of the technical requirements of some courses, such as the need for specialized facilities, labs, and equipment, not all programs are offered at all locations. ERAU's Daytona Beach campus and its College of Continuing Education (CCE), which serves the needs of students at more than 90 locations around the world, offer programs at three degree levels—associate, bachelors, and masters. The Prescott campus offers only under graduate-level programs (but no associate degree). Both campuses offer flight training using a wide range of aircraft types.

In addition to the traditional use of aircraft for flight training, computer simulation plays an important role in ERAU's flight training program. One interesting aspect of Embry-Riddle's use of simulators is how it is using both flight and air traffic control simulators to teach students in both programs how to operate in a simulated "real-life" airspace environment. Student air traffic controllers "control" student pilots "flying" aircraft simulators in real-time situations. This type of training interaction with students talking and reacting to other students adds a degree of realism to the training that some other types of simulator training may lack. This is only one example of the use of computer-based training and simulators at ERAU. Another example is ERAU's new Airline Flight Crew Techniques and Procedures course which uses classroom, computer software-based training, and full-motion aircraft simulation to train select students in advanced, high speed, "glass cockpit" procedures based upon Boeing's B747–400 aircraft's "glass cockpit." The course starts with three weeks of ground school that uses Boeing's donated computer-based B747 training software to teach students the aircraft systems, operation, and flight procedures of the B747–400 and its glass cockpit. Students who complete the ground school then go to Northwest Aerospace Training Corporation (NATCO), a Northwest Airlines affiliate,

in Minnesota for additional classroom training and 32 hours of B727 and B747–400 full-motion simulator training. Throughout their training, students will train as part of a crew to learn and practice management and crew coordination skills as they prepare to take their place in tomorrow's electronic cockpits. This type of training program combines the best of traditional classroom, computer-based instruction, and state-of-the art aircraft simulation to train students in aircraft and crew resource procedures in a cost-effective manner.

As a leader in aviation education, research, and flight training, ERAU offers its students access to some of the latest state-of-the-art equipment available in such areas as aircraft simulation, computer modeling, weather forecasting, accident investigation, cockpit resource management, aircraft design, and other areas of study. With more than 4,500 students at Daytona Beach, about 1,500 students at Prescott, and more than 12,000 students enrolled in its CCE program world-wide, ERAU offers each of them one of the largest curricula dedicated to aviation in the world today. Its world-wide reputation is also recognized by the number of international students from more than 80 countries who attend ERAU to take advantage of its unique focus on aviation and learning.

Today, ERAU, in keeping with its founders' philosophy of "To teach every phase of flying, from the ground up to the sky" continues to teach that way, but now it teaches from the ground up to the sky and beyond as it does research for NASA, FAA, and major companies in the aerospace industry. Some of this research in such areas as PC-based simulation and pilot training, cockpit visual imagery simulation for approach and taxi use, and other aerospace research involving air traffic control, aircraft design, and other aerospace needs of the future. An important part of all of these studies is how the human element—the pilot, controller, or maintenance technician—fits into the overall hardware and software systems of the

ERAU's President, Steven M. Sliwa, Ph.D.

future. As ERAU prepares students for their future roles in space and beyond, a quote from the *Star Trek* TV series could be paraphrased to say, ERAU is preparing them to go where no one has gone before.

ERAU's commitment to the future is reflected in the views of its President, Dr. Steven M. Sliwa. When asked why anyone should pursue a career in aviation, he said although the short-term outlook for aviation may not look favorable now, aviation's long-term outlook is very good; especially, he said, if the United States takes a more international view and continues its leadership role in aviation and aerospace. According to Dr. Sliwa, there will be lots of growth opportunities for aviation in the new global economies being developed around the world. He said that growth will not just be in technology. "It will also be in the human infrastructure. You need to have the managers, you need to have the marketers, you need to have the pilots, the mechanics, the flight attendants. The whole airspace system has to be staffed. That is why people have the chance to be involved," he said.

He said there are two ways to get involved in an aviation/aerospace

(Above) Aerospace engineering majors learn to design, analyze, and test aircraft systems. Here students work with measurements for wind tunnel experiments. To keep up with the rapid technological advancements of aviation and aerospace, students and faculty conduct applied research projects on campus. (Below) The curricula stress computer literacy.

Embry-Riddle

Embry-Riddle

career. One way is to go to Embry-Riddle. The other way is to pursue a less focused aviation science degree program and then go into the aviation/ aerospace industry. But he said, "Our students are going to be incredibly competitive in the industry, be it the aviation insurance industry, engineering, computer science, legal, airport management, maintenance, or piloting. When students come here, especially to the Daytona Beach campus, where there are another 4,600 students here just like themselves who are passionate about aviation and aerospace, they learn a lot from each other's experi-

ences both in and out of the classroom.

"The second reason I think students should come to Embry-Riddle is a general rule of thumb I have for being successful. If you start out being successful, you will end up being successful. I think it is important when you get to college where it is really tough in general that you be successful. And it is a lot easier being successful when you enjoy what you are doing," he said. That is why when students come to Embry-Riddle and get involved with our faculty the students do incredibly well, he said. "They can realize their full potential here where they are able to

focus their energies and passion much more directly on their studies," he said. To prove his point, Dr. Sliwa told how well Embry-Riddle students did on two recent Florida state-wide college examinations. The State of Florida has a state-wide examination that covers a wide-range of subjects that public university students and private university students receiving financial aid must take between their sophomore and junior years. He said at the time of this interview, Embry-Riddle had scored number one in the state the previous two quarters. "I see that as a prime ingredient for why people would want to be involved in a place like Embry-Riddle," he said. As he said, Embry-Riddle teaches students how to learn. Apparently, Embry-Riddle students learn very well.

And Embry-Riddle students, instructors, and faculty not only learn and teach very well, they are willing to share their knowledge and enthusiasm with others. According to Mr. Obie S. Young, the FAA Accident Prevention Program Manager for the North Florida Flight Standards District Office in Orlando, Embry-Riddle takes an active part in the FAA's Accident Prevention Program. He said, facility members volunteer to be guest speakers at many area safety seminars, and ERAU flight instructors work closely with their students to promote safety. Speakers from ERAU are always in demand because of their aeronautical knowledge and experience, possibly because being involved on the leading edge of many research projects gives ERAU speakers an insight into aviation that others may lack. This willingness of ERAU facility members to get involved in their local aviation community's activities, the school's dedication to aviation, the quality of its students and facility, and its leading role in aviation research all combine to make ERAU a national leader in aerospace education. A role it cherishes as it prepares its students for the 21st Century.　■

For further information write to: Embry-Riddle Aeronautical University, 600 South Clyde Morris Boulevard, Daytona Beach, FL 32114–3900.

ASOS...
Coming Soon to an Airport near You!

by Harold Bogin, *National Weather Service*

Since the early days of aviation, the taking and dissemination of Surface Aviation Observations (SAO) at airports across the nation has been an essential function for the safe and efficient operation of aircraft. With the expansion of the National Airspace System in recent years, this activity has increased to the point that the National Weather Service (NWS), the Federal Aviation Administration (FAA) and the Department of Defense (DOD) collectively expend over 1,000 staff-years to take and disseminate SAO's across the United States.

With the advent of new reliable and sophisticated sensors and computer technology, it has become increasingly practical to automate many observing functions. This potential has come to fruition with the successful development and testing of the Automated Surface Observing System (ASOS) in the 1980's and its planned deployment by the NWS, FAA, and DOD at as many as 1,700 airports across the U.S. in the 1990's .

ASOS will gradually replace manual weather observations at approximately 250 NWS sites and 300 FAA flight service stations and air traffic control towers. By February 1992, 54 ASOS units were already providing test observations at airports in the central U.S. and at Atlantic City, NJ with an additional 118 units scheduled for installation across the U.S. by the end of 1992. When fully implemented, ASOS will more than double the number of full-time surface aviation weather observing locations and enable valuable human resources to devote greater attention to other vital tasks.

ASOS is designed to support aviation operations and weather forecast activities and, to the extent practical, general needs of the hydrometeorological, climatological, and meteorological research communities. ASOS provides minute-by-minute observations and performs the basic observing functions necessary to generate the SAO.

While the automated system and the human observer may differ in their methods of data collection and interpretation, both produce an observation quite similar in form and content. For the "objective" elements such as pressure, ambient temperature, dewpoint temperature, wind, and precipitation accumulation, both the automated system and the observer use a fixed location and time-averaging technique (e.g., temperature is measured at one location over a five-minute period). The quantitative differences between the observer and the automated observation of these elements are negligible. For the "subjective" elements, however, observers use a fixed time, spatial-averaging technique to describe the visual elements (sky condition, visibility, and present weather), while the automated systems use a fixed location, time-averaging technique. Although this is a fundamental change, the human and automated techniques yield remarkably similar results within the limits of their respective capabilities.

ASOS will automatically report the following weather elements in the SAO:

- Sky condition—Cloud height and amount up to 12,000 feet
- Visibility up to 10+ statute miles. (The maximum reported visibility may be changed to 10 miles.)
- Basic present weather information, i.e., type and intensity for rain, snow, freezing rain
- Fog, haze
- Pressure—Sea level pressure in Hectopascals (hPa) (Hectopascal is

ASOS sensor site

NWS

equivalent to a millibar (mb). For example: 1012 hPa = 1012 mb) and altimeter setting in inches of mercury (Hg)

- Ambient Temperature, dewpoint temperature (degrees Fahrenheit)
- Wind—Direction (tens of degrees—true), speed (knots), and character (gusts, squalls)
- Selected significant remarks including—variable cloud height, variable visibility, precipitation beginning and ending times, rapid pressure changes, pressure change tendency, wind shift, peak wind, etc.
- Precipitation accumulation (hundredths of an inch)
- In addition, ASOS will provide routine hourly and 15 minute threshold criteria precipitation totals in Standard Hydrometeorological Exchange Format.

ASOS is capable of accepting manual input (augmentation) to the automated observation. At staffed locations where NWS or FAA policy permits, thunderstorm information will be manually inserted into the SAO until this information can be obtained automatically.

ASOS' Technical Advantages

Extensive factory and field testing over a period of many years has given NWS every expectation that ASOS will perform its mission exceedingly well. The primary technical advantages of ASOS lie in its superior network resolution, objectivity, consistency, and enhanced dissemination.

Superior Network Resolution

NWS observers are skilled and dedicated professionals. However, they are only available to provide a "basic weather watch," since they must perform other high priority duties which preclude continuous weather monitoring. In contrast, ASOS provides a minute-by-minute weather watch, 24 hours a day, and automatically generates and disseminates hourly and special observations when required. This high temporal resolution will therefore substantially increase our capability to detect important small-scale changes in surface weather and hazards to aviation. With today's network, there are large surface data voids, particularly in the western U.S., between sunset and sunrise. The provision of ASOS to many smaller airports that are currently without weather observations or that maintain only part-time observing programs, will mean a significant increase in the density of the network.

Objectivity and Consistency

In contrast to human observations, which tend to vary from place-to-place and day-to-day because of subjective differences between observers, ASOS provides objective and consistent observations of the ever-changing atmosphere. For example, automated visibility and cloud readings at night are superior to estimates currently made by observers, since ASOS is not handicapped by human visual acuity differences. Moreover, ASOS observes from its vantage point near runways, in contrast to today's observing locations, which tend to be near brightly-lit terminal buildings and well-removed from the location of interest.

In addition, ASOS implementation provides the once-in-a-lifetime opportunity to install all observing sensors, insofar as possible, in accordance with siting criteria that are common to the Federal meteorological community. Adherence to these criteria ensures a consistent exposure that is not characteristic of today's network, which is the product of an *ad hoc* accrual process ongoing since the early days of aviation. ASOS implementation will also minimize errors caused by previously undocumented instrument and siting changes. Additionally, ASOS self-checking algorithms will minimize the effects of out-of-calibration and drift problems than can occur with meteorological sensors. Not to be overlooked is the fact aging observing equipment, increasingly difficult to maintain or obtain parts for, will be retired by ASOS.

Enhanced Dissemination

In addition to the automatic dissemination of hourly and special observations via the NWS and FAA communications networks, ASOS routinely and automatically provides computer-generated voice observations directly to aircraft in the vicinity of the airport, using the FAA ground-to-air radio. These messages are also available via a telephone dial-in port at the ASOS. This dissemination capability provides a level of real-time service that was not possible in the past, without an unacceptably large investment in costs to both NWS and FAA.

The Modernized Surface Observing Concept

The integration of a new technology, such as ASOS, into the operational flow of the NWS necessarily means certain procedural changes must be instituted. Although we are confident that "what ASOS does, it does very well," we know that no automated observing process can replicate the observer in every way. Hence, the modernized surface observing concept will become an important ingredient in NWS', modernized operations. In essence, this new observing concept entails the provision to users, by supplementary and complementary means, of required and enhanced observational data that ASOS cannot, or does not yet, provide. These data, in combination with ASOS, comprise the "modernized observation."

When fully implemented, the modernized observation will mean a richer and more versatile information flow to users of the surface observation, when contrasted to the single-point and subjective observation in use today.

Supplementary Component

The supplementary component consists of surface observing networks distinct from ASOS which provide specific data for forecasting and public service purposes. (Strictly speaking, this component is not new. What is different are the products in which much of these data will appear.) These networks include: severe weather spotter networks, hydrological reporting networks, synoptic and climatological observing networks, and cooperative observing networks. Supplementary observations will also be taken at more than 100 NWS-staffed offices scheduled to become Weather Forecast Offices (WFO) in the modernized NWS. Supplementary data are not disseminated as part of the ASOS observation, but are

instead provided as separate data sets or products. Examples of supplementary data are: severe weather reports (tornado/funnel cloud sightings) and information on clouds, dust, and other obstructions to vision, snowfall and snow depth, hail, ice pellets and volcanic ash.

Complementary Components

The complementary component to the modernized surface observation consists of data derived from non-ASOS remote sensing technologies. These technologies include:

—Satellite (including the Geostationary Orbital Environmental Satellite (GOES)

—Radar (including the Next-Generation Weather Radar, WSR–88D)

—Lightning detection system (LDS)

The data derived from these technologies will also be provided as separate data sets or products. The data in this category include thunderstorm coverage and intensity and total cloud cover information. These data are planned to be provided in near real-time.

Data Continuity

The implementation of ASOS means changes in sensor siting and sensor characteristics, as ASOS replaces the conventional observing equipment. In order to ensure data integrity and continuity, NWS is planning to provide overlapping observations to support an independent study of temperature and accumulated liquid precipitation compatibility. The purpose of the study is to determine if systematic differences exist between historical observing methods and ASOS, and, if so, to document the biases. The results of the comparative study should ensure the transition to automated observations without significant discontinuities in the historical record.

NWS-staffed locations will provide these comparative observations at up to 16 of the ASOS units to be deployed in central United States beginning in 1992. These comparative observations may be expanded to include other locations as well. This study will consist of at least one year of comparative manual observations and ASOS observations.

NEXRAD, new Doppler radar installation

The comparative observations will consist of daily liquid precipitation accumulation using the NWS' standard weighing rain gauges, daily maximum and minimum temperatures, and six hourly temperature and dewpoint temperature observations. Other elements may be observed as background data.

Summary

The successful and timely modernization of the NWS and FAA is widely accepted as a necessity. The transition to ASOS will be a critical and, at many locations, an initial step in that overall modernization and restructuring. ASOS will provide minute-by-minute, standardized and objective observations designed to meet the requirements of aviation, weather forecasting and warning services, and, to the extent practical, the nation's climatological record. The implementation of the modernized surface observing concept means that surface data from complementary technologies and supplementary networks, when combined with ASOS observations, will provide all users of the surface observation a more comprehensive and informative product. ∎

For further information on ASOS, write to: Department of Commerce, National Weather Service, NOAA, 1325 East-West Highway, #12166, Silver Spring, MD 20910, Attn: W/OSD14.

What about AWOS?

There are two types of automated observing systems in operational use in the United States: the National Weather Service developed Automated Surface Observing System (ASOS) and the commercially developed Automated Weather Observing System (AWOS). There are approximately 165 federal AWOS in operation and over 200 non-federal AWOS deployed by the states. Both systems are similar in operation and use the same basic algorithms for data processing. AWOS provides measurements of ceiling (cloud height), visibility, wind, temperature, dew point temperature, altimeter setting, and density altitude (when certain conditions are met).

"What Fools These Mortals Be"

by Bill Cuccinello, *Accident Prevention Program Counsellor, Bedford, Massachusetts*

Perhaps the title line should really be attributed to Lucius Annaeus Seneca (4BC—AD65) since he seems to be the first person on record associated with it. But more people seem to associate it with that impish Puck, who appeared in Shakespeare's *A Midsummer Night's Dream*. So for now, let us place ownership of the line to Puck, aka Robin Goodfellow.

For who knows, maybe Robin Goodfellow, the playful, mischievous fairy of old stories and legends knew something we do not. Maybe he knew, those many years ago, that the day would come when machines would fly through the skies and they would be driven by people called "pilots" who, in their every endeavors, would be out to prove their superhuman skills. And through it all, maybe Puck knew that some of those machines would fall from the skies because some of those very same pilots were not really superhuman—but mere mortals. And perhaps foolish mortals at that.

And so we wonder—why don't some of us mere mortals do *it*? After all:

Airline pilots do it.
Corporate pilots do it.
CFI's do it.
Even examiners
   (and FAA inspectors) do it.

So why does the average general aviation pilot—who probably flies less than 50 hours a year—NOT do it.

What is *it*? That is right, I am talking Refresher courses with a capital R—big time safety blankets for the average pilot.

Did you ever think how stupid we pilots can sometimes be? The Professional Pilot (be it airlines, corporate, charter, etc.) flies for a living, probably puts in some 450 flight hours a year, is continually updated, attends seminars or classes, and jumps into a simulator every six months. Despite the fact they are pushing those machines around for a living and are basically getting practice everyday, they still update themselves continually with extensive, comprehensive programs.

Yet, many of the average general aviation pilots, some who barely eke out their 90-day requirements, will continually rent planes, fly in marginal weather (oftentimes scaring the H*** out of their passengers, thereby creating another anti-aviation person) and then, very complacently tell many of their co-workers of their harrowing experience and how they summoned all their "macho-ness" to get the plane to the ground in one piece.

It is a fact that the accident rate for pilots with 100 to 400 hours is one of the highest in general aviation. Recurrent/refresher courses are essential for all pilots but especially for this category. But remember the difference: Recurrency courses are not required for pilots to meet the flight experience necessary to act as PIC as specified in FAR § 61.57. Refresher training usually may be more extensive since it might include several hours of ground and flight instruction, and it may be directed at

you if you have not been an active pilot for some time.

To be effective, the program should have basic objectives. If you would like to update yourself on the requirements, order a copy of AC 61-10A, *Private and Commercial Pilots Refresher Courses*. [Currently $3.75 from GPO, Superintendent of Documents, Washington, DC 20402.] The material inside will supply you with a refresher outline for the private, commercial, or instrument pilot. With this pamphlet in hand, go to your nearest instructor, and let him or her update you on some of the areas you feel you need to improve. In addition, try to fly more with other pilots. It is amazing how much more you can learn when you fly with other pilots, especially if they have a good amount of experience. Often, it is a good idea for several pilots to rent a plane together and take turns flying and navigating. It is not only a good learning experience; it is fun.

And while you are doing some refresher training, why not also refresh yourself with the POH. Try a weight and balance problem. Check on the plane's emergency procedures and systems. With your instructor (or another pilot) discuss airspace, aeromedical facts, and, above all, weather. Incidentally, while you are taking that refresher course, be certain to look over the new videotapes on weather, maneuvers, emergency procedures, etc., that most pilot schools now use as part of their curricula. If you have not looked at such tapes for a few years, you are in for a real treat. They have improved tremendously.

If you are IFR rated, by all means go over the rules and regulations. It is amazing how many instrument rated pilots actually "bust" minimums by descending below the glide slope or think the FAF is always at the outer marker.

If you enjoy the romance of night flying, by all means get a refresher with an instructor who is night current and proficient. After all, isn't it strange how altitude seems so different at night or how night distance changes the look of an airport? If nothing else, be certain you get some night emergency procedures—full or partial engine failures, landings without lights, etc. When night flying concentrate on a parallel downwind even more so than in the daylight. Keeping the runway edge lights near or under a certain point on the wing tips, you will know if you are getting wind drift or gaining or losing altitude. And be certain your instructor takes you to a few unfamiliar airports for some landings to a full stop.

I will never forget the comment by one of my students who was getting back into flying after being inactive for a few years. He originally had a commercial certificate with an instrument rating and just wanted to be checked out. After checking out day VFR, he decided he also wanted to be checked out for night VFR. Well, after some hours of night work, I suggested to him we do some stalls. He looked at me with the most quizzical look I had ever seen and said, "Stalls? In the dark? At night? In all the years I've been flying, I've never done a stall at night?" I looked at him and said, "Why? Airplanes can't stall at night? Only during the day?"

Needless to say, we not only did many stalls that night, but we also had the plane in "slow flight" for 360's, 720's, glides, turns, and everything else. When we landed, he told me he felt it was one of the most satisfying learning experiences he had ever encountered in his flying career and that it gave him the confidence he needed to fly the plane in any situation.

The moral is simple.

The Lucius Annaeus Seneca referred to in the first paragraph was a Roman philosopher, writer, and politician. The Seneca in the photo is a twin-engine airplane built by Piper Aircraft Corporation.

Have your instructor put you through the paces. If you do not feel completely at ease flying the plane, tell the instructor. Let the instructor work with you until you feel confident handling the plane in just about any circumstance.

Remember, instructors do not get rich by instructing, but they do get great satisfaction in knowing that they have made a pilot much more proficient. The greatest feeling an instructor gets is when he or she sees the student go for that "ride" and come back with a new rating or certificate. But the instructor feels doubly proud when the examiner says to the instructor, "You did a great job with this student. This student is not only proficient, but a good, safe pilot."

So, let us listen a little closer to the impish Puck. Let us agree that we are all super and macho (or macha) and everything else we want to believe. But deep down, let us also agree that we are mere mortals, and, as such, we can make mistakes. We are not infallible. However, flying does not allow for mistakes, so instead of wasting $50 or $60 for things we really do not need, set aside a "refresher budget" for training every three months, especially if you fly less than 100 hours a year. A two-hour refresher program with a good instructor will be the best and cheapest insurance you can ever buy.

Besides that, isn't it wonderful to complete a flight, feeling completely confident that you know every second where you are, what your machine can do, and exactly what approach you are going to make when the time comes? And isn't it wonderful to anticipate how ATC is going to direct you?

It really is amazing how much a simple refresher program can help you keep current. ∎

We might add that working on your "Wings"—Phases 1 through 10—is an excellent way of assuring yourself some well-used dual instruction. See your local FAA Accident Prevention Program Manager about "Wings," the Pilot Proficiency Award Program. This article was reprinted from the Communicator, *the Accident Prevention Program newsletter of the Bedford, MA FSDO. Our thanks to APPM John Hemmes.* —**Editor**

FULL POWER—Have You Got It?

by Mike Liversidge, *Area Manager, Prescott, AZ, AFSS*

In the mountainous west, pilots who operate aircraft with normally aspirated engines and fixed-pitch propellers are constantly measuring their aircraft's anticipated performance against the demands that will be placed upon them. Operating these aircraft requires a significant amount of careful *performance management*. This is especially true when short runways, heavy loads, high altitudes, or a combination of these or other factors that deter performance challenge these light aircraft.

Performance Management— Preflight

Flying safely under these conditions demands a painstaking approach to preflight activities. This starts with collecting appropriate background information, including but not limited to: airport elevation; runway length, orientation, gradient, and condition of surface; surface wind, temperature and other local weather factors; local terrain features; and, last but not least, computed density altitude. Next comes the task of weighing all of these data against your aircraft's performance tables. Under such circumstances, performance margins are frequently very narrow, and even a seemingly insignificant change in factors could completely erode a perceived safety margin. Also, while you are reviewing those aircraft performance tables, keep in mind that they

were based on a new, or nearly new, aircraft. If you are typical of most of our breed of light plane pilot, your aircraft is probably closer to 15 years old than it is to new. For this and other reasons, remember that we are talking about *anticipated* performance.

Performance Management— Run-up

The next critical step of performance management comes with the preflight inspection and run-up, with detailed use of the checklist. If you are about to depart a high altitude airport, the pretakeoff checklist should include your carefully following the engine manufacturer's recommended leaning procedures. [See "Thin Air Accidents" by Mr. Liversidge in the July/August 1992 issue for a discussion of leaning.] If performance margins are expected to be minimal, most mountain-wise pilots would elect to do a predeparture, full static run-up. Maximum power run-ups cannot be taken lightly, however. They require a great deal of care and alertness, with the pilot remaining aware of propeller wash and the real danger of breakaway (failure of the wheels brakes to hold the aircraft). The full throttle run-up itself would usually include adjusting the mixture control to achieve maximum static RPM. A more precise method for leaning would be with the use of an exhaust gas temperature (EGT) gauge and analyzer. In this case, the pilot would lean the

hottest cylinder to peak EGT indication while remaining at full throttle. Next, enrich the mixture slowly to achieve a temperature of approximately 100 degrees Fahrenheit on the rich side of peak EGT indications. In both of these cases, the aim is to attain peak available power during takeoff and initial climbout.

Performance Management— Takeoff

Well, now comes the moment of truth. . . you start your takeoff roll, the runway is slightly uphill, and the air is thin. Still, you did your homework, including a careful preflight and run-up, and all factors indicate that you should have a reasonable margin of safety. As you move down the runway an uneasiness starts to gnaw at you; you seem to be accelerating very slowly, and the RPM seems to be taking longer than normal to develop. You scan all of the gauges for reassurance that all is well, and it seems to be. Still, it is hard to shake that feeling and you start to ask yourself questions: "Am I really developing all of the available power for these conditions?" or "Is there something wrong with my engine?" Controls feel mushy and confidence erodes... time to abort. Things might be okay, but you are just not sure, so you did the wise thing and made a safe, aborted takeoff.

These are feelings we can all relate to and are part of the anxiety of flying a light, normally aspirated aircraft under these demanding conditions. We cannot make these feelings all disappear; they are called survival instincts, and any safe pilot needs them. On the other hand, the origin of much of this anxiety is the pilot's inability to determine the efficiency of power output in this class of aircraft accurately.

In this area we can offer some relief. Some pilots have added a relatively inexpensive instrument to their aircraft, an instrument that helps to determine the efficiency of power during most phases of operation, including run-up, takeoff, climb out, or any other full throttle application. This is strictly an auxiliary instrument to supply additional "now time" data, and in no way de-emphasizes the importance of other engine instruments. While this instrument is by no means unusual or hard to find, you would be hard pressed to find one in this class of aircraft. This instrument, believe it or not, is a twin engine manifold pressure gauge.

Twin Engine Manifold Pressure Gauge

By now I am sure you are asking yourself, "what on earth would I do with a twin engine manifold pressure gauge in my single engine, fixed prop, *Skyhawk*?" Your concern for my sanity is understandable! Actually I more or less stumbled onto the value of this instrument in my own aircraft, a Cessna 150/150. It started when a friend was doing the annual inspection on my aircraft; he was aware that I sometimes conducted high altitude operations and suggested installing a manifold pressure gauge. While I questioned its value, I told him to go ahead and install one as his past suggestions always turned out to be very helpful. When I picked up my aircraft a few days later, I was somewhat surprised to see a twin engine manifold pressure gauge had been installed. My friend told me not to worry as this was just a temporary arrangement until he got the appropriate gauge in. He explained that the number two needle was connected to the engine manifold, but the number one needle was connected to

This gauge will not tell you what is wrong, but it will tell you if the engine is right with the world this very minute.

nothing and reflected only static pressure. That was back in 1979, and my friendly mechanic is still trying to get his twin engine manifold pressure gauge back, but I simply will not part with it!

The real value to this instrument arrangement is the number one needle that is connected to nothing! It serves as a moving baseline of power for all phases of flight. If your engine is developing all available power, no matter how variable the conditions, the number two needle (manifold pressure) will indicate within two inches of the number one needle (static pressure). This is true for all full throttle operations, whether they be at sea level or at flight level one eight zero. If your air filter was plugged, if your mixture was too rich, if a mag was misfiring, if a cylinder has gone off line, or if the plugs were fouled, all would likely be indicated by a needle spread of more than two inches. This gauge will not tell you just what the problem is, but it will tell you quickly if a problem exists. Static minus two inches or less equates to a current state of all *available* power being on line (not to be confused with 100% of rated power). If full throttle operation exceeds two inches of needle spread, you have got a problem that requires your attention. During any takeoff roll, it only takes a few seconds for peak manifold pressure to be displayed. If needle spread exceeds two inches, you simply abort and return to the run-up area and investigate with a

full static run-up. If, on the other hand, all looks good and you continue your departure, you can monitor full throttle response throughout the climb. As the static pressure needle (#1) comes down, so will the manifold pressure needle (#2). Again, as long as we are using full throttle operation, the spread should remain within that two inches. If the spread starts to increase, check your mixture; it may require some leaning.

This gauge will not tell you what is wrong, but it will tell you if the engine is right with the world this very minute. *The key point to remember is that we are looking at your engine's current state only and not its future state.* For that you must maintain a watchful eye on all of the other engine instruments.

Other advantages to this arrangement come during normal cruise when you are operating at less than full throttle. Under these circumstances a quick glance at this gauge will provide a graphic display of how much power you are holding in reserve. If the needle spread is two and a half inches, you have not got much left; but if it is four inches, you should still have some power and performance left if you need it. When your aircraft approaches its operating ceiling limitations, that two inch spread will tell you if you have got all there is to give or not.

A twin engine manifold pressure gauge is clearly no cure-all for high altitude operations in this class of aircraft. It is not a reason to bypass any manufacturer's operating recommendations. It is, however, a tool which can be of considerable value to you, the pilot. After 12 years of mountain flying with this gauge installed in my aircraft, I would not be without it. If you operate your fixed pitch, normally aspirated aircraft under similar conditions, this instrument arrangement may add a significant amount of safety to your power management. ∎

Addition of a manifold pressure gauge must be accomplished by an appropriately rated mechanic who must make the required entries in the aircraft's maintenance record and weight and balance sheet, if applicable. —*Editor*

WORRIED ABOUT YOUR NEXT FLIGHT TEST?
RELAX—There Will Be No Surprises

by E. Allan Englehardt, *FAA Designated Pilot Examiner*

During the conduct of an FAA Private Pilot practical test, would it be proper for the examiner who is administering the test to expect the applicant to know the date of the Wright Brothers' first flight? Of course not! While this historic flight occurred on December 17, 1903—an important date to be sure—knowledge of this date certainly has no bearing on whether a Private Pilot can operate safely. How about requiring the applicant to describe the relationship of thrust, drag, lift, and weight on an aircraft operating in straight and level, unaccelerated flight? Again, while this type of information may be somewhat more relevant and is required knowledge for flight instructor certification, the facts are that such information is really not necessary in order for a Private Pilot to operate safely and is, therefore, not a required area of testing during the Private Pilot practical test.

Through a major overhaul of the testing system and the complete implementation of the "practical tests," as described by the FAA Practical Test Standards (PTS), we now have a true standardized practical flight test for pilot certification, one designed with a single purpose—to determine objectively if the applicant can satisfactorily perform the tasks required for the certificate or rating being sought. The present practical test—the one required for pilot certification—is no longer the individual examiner's concept of what a pilot should

know or how he or she should perform; it is a concept jointly developed by the FAA and industry for a practical test that is used to determine if an applicant should be certificated.

Today's applicant should understand that the areas required for testing are not chosen by the examiner and evaluated to the examiner's standards, but, rather, they are tasks chosen jointly by the FAA and industry with standards of satisfactory performance set by this same group and observed by the pilot examiner administering the practical test. The examiner is simply a "referee" who observes and determines if the applicant has been trained to perform to the standards set forth in the PTS. Since its implementation, the days are now gone when an applicant passes or fails a test based on a subjective evaluation. The present practical test has become totally objective, with required tasks clearly stated and with clear standards of acceptable performance.

As a pilot examiner I always find it disturbing to begin a practical test, a test for which the applicant has told me he or she has prepared and one where a flight instructor has signed the student's application—stating that the applicant is prepared for the test—and then only to find the applicant unable to pass the simplest knowledge tasks required for examination during the ground phase of the test. The tasks I am referring to are the ones clearly shown in the beginning of the PTS

under Area of Operation (I), Task (A), (B), (C), etc. As an example, in the Private Pilot PTS, Area of Operation (I) covers Preflight Preparation with Task (A) covering certificates and documents, Task (B) covering Obtaining Weather Information, Task (C) covering Determining Performance and Limitations, Task (D) covering Cross Country Flight Planning, Task (E) covering Airplane Systems, and, finally, Task (F) covering Aeromedical Factors.

Lack of Preparation

What is particularly discouraging to me is that many of the applicants who are unable to perform to the published standards for the practical test, fail the test not because they are poor pilots but because they are simply not prepared for the practical test they are taking. For example, I have found applicants that are completely confused about the most basic documentation and certificates required to prove an airplane and pilot properly certificated for flight. Other applicants are unable to tell me the visibility or the wind direction and velocity from a typical sequence weather report or to provide me with an accurate figure of how much fuel the airplane will burn in one hour or even where to find such information. Still others tell me that the aircraft static system is somehow connected to the vacuum driven attitude indicator. One applicant told me that the airplane has 10 gyros, and he later told me that carburetor heat is electric and that it heats the carburetor in much the same way a toaster heats a piece of bread. With answers like these I find it hard to believe that the applicant has been prepared for the test in accordance with the published PTS—after all the PTS lists all these subjects as required testing areas!

All the questions that I ask are as simple and as practical as I can make them while keeping the subject in line with the objective of the task required for testing. For example, I always ask what aeromedical concerns should be considered when the aircraft heater is in use. Surprisingly, I find applicants who are unable to tell me anything about carbon monoxide considerations.

On the other portions of the practical test, the flight portions, applicants seem to fail for any number of reasons, but in my experience the most common reason for failure at the Private Pilot level concerns crosswind landings. The applicants simply have not been trained to land in a direct crosswind of eight to 12 knots, certainly a practical and a necessary skill. If an applicant fails crosswind landings, he or she usually knows this without being told because he or she simply loses control of the airplane, and a recovery is necessary by the examiner. Sometimes an applicant has enough good sense to initiate a go-around when a safe landing is in doubt; however, it seldom makes any difference because if the pilot has not been trained for this task, the same problems will result during the next attempt.

Using the PTS to Prepare

When an applicant comes to the practical test unprepared in any of the required tasks as shown in the PTS, the examiner has no choice but to issue a "Notice of Disapproval," or "pink slip" as it is sometimes called. Such failures can sometimes occur without the applicant advancing far enough to have an opportunity to start the engine.

No examiner becomes one in order to fail pilots; in fact, in my opinion, the opposite is true: Examiners volunteer for this position because they enjoy issuing a new certificate to a qualified pilot. I believe that anyone who loves aviation receives pleasure in being part

of the certification process of a new pilot. All of us, then, will understand that a failure of the practical test is bad for everyone—the examiner, the instructor, and, most of all, the applicant.

Is there a solution to this problem? Yes, there certainly is, and I believe the solution is quite simple. The applicants must simply become more involved and must take it upon themselves to be certain that they are prepared for the practical test—as that test is shown in the PTS. *In other words, applicants must read the PTS and determine if they have been completely trained and can perform to the standards set forth.* And if they feel that their training has been inadequate, they must insist that their instructors prepare them to the published standards.

I am able to pass 80% of the applicants I test, and that tells me that the greatest percentage of instructors are properly preparing their students. What I am concerned about, of course, is the 20% of applicants who fail. In many of these cases, I feel the primary problem is the flight instructor who recommends an applicant for the practical test when that pilot's training is simply incomplete.

While an applicant should understand that the test will be conducted according to the PTS, in practice the student comes to trust that the instructor knows what is to be expected on the test. A student believes that an instructor's recommendation for the test must prove that the pilot is prepared. However, the facts seem to show something different. Too many pilots are not prepared for the test, and these pilots are failing. In order to assure a satisfactory performance on the practical test, it is necessary for the applicant to take an active part in making certain that all required testing areas have been thoroughly covered.

On a recent flight test I was forced to issue a "Notice of Disapproval" before the applicant completed the very first half of the "Preflight Preparation" ground phase of the test. The applicant never had the opportunity to yell, "Clear!" In this case I telephoned the instructor to see why the problem occurred. I can report that I was told something by this particular instructor

that I am afraid is all too common an attitude of flight instructors. The instructor told me that he felt the flight instructor's role was to teach the flight portion of the training, and that it is the applicant's responsibility to learn the other portions through ground school or self-study, and, after all, the student has already demonstrated understanding of this knowledge by satisfactorily passing the written test. This position, of course, is incorrect because of the fact that it is the *recommending* instructor whose name appears on the back of the application. It is the instructor's reputation that is on the line when he or she makes the written statement and signs his or her name certifying that the applicant is prepared to pass the practical test—every part of the practical test.

Using the PTS Checklist

In the back of the Private, Instrument, and Commercial PTS there is a checklist for use by the applicant, the instructor, and the examiner. This checklist shows all the required Areas of Operation and lists all the required Tasks for testing. I can assure you that all examiners use this list and administer the test according to the PTS. Please do not make the mistake of thinking that the tasks only exist in the mind of the examiner on that particular day. The truth is that the required tasks for each practical test are clearly listed in the PTS.

Please, before taking any test for a new certificate or rating, purchase the appropriate PTS and read the booklet thoroughly. Then, ask yourself, "Have I received the training necessary to perform to the standards shown?" If the answer is yes, the FAA practical test will be a pleasure and a chance to demonstrate your true ability as a pilot. The test will contain no surprises, and it is certainly possible for the examiner to be impressed enough to write a letter commending both you and your instructor on an outstanding FAA practical test. ∎

Mr. Englehardt is also an Accident Prevention Counsellor in the FAA's Great Lakes Region and a first officer for United Airlines. This copyrighted article was originally published in the March 1992 issue of AOPA Pilot and is reprinted with permission.

Between a Rock and a Hard Place
Weather Deviations

by Ed Ari, *ASRS Analyst*

This is the fourth in a series of articles reprinted from ASRS Directline, a quarterly publication that addresses particular areas of safety that appear in pilot reports received by NASA's Aviation Safety Reporting System and which have been identified by safety analysts as "significant." ASRS Directline is free from ASRS, NASA-Ames Research Center, Moffett Field, CA 94035. It is not too early to be thinking about dealing with thunderstorms, and deviation around weather is something every pilot will have to face at some point in a, hopefully, long aviation career. But the very request can raise the hackles of some controllers. Both groups need to understand the ramifications. **—Editor**

Each year both pilots and controllers are confronted with weather-related problems that have a significant impact on the safety of flight and on the air traffic system as a whole. Pilots want to deviate around build-ups they see and/or observe on their airborne weather radar as "red cells." In the face of weather-mandated route or altitude changes, the controller must maintain standard separation from other aircraft. Pilots frequently blame controllers for not understanding their need to deviate. Controllers, on the other hand, believe pilots have little idea of what is involved in granting such requests and the subsequent impact on other traffic.

Different Jobs, Different Viewpoints

The air traffic control system is designed to handle a large number of aircraft within a highly standardized route structure. Whenever weather becomes a factor, both the pilot's and the controller's workloads greatly increase. Since weather has little regard for the standardized route structure, the air traffic control system at that particular time and location demands non-standard remedies to reduce the negative impact on all aircraft. Controllers will, if they are able, approve deviation around the "red cells" for passenger comfort and, more importantly, for safety. Most of the time ATC can approve these deviations with minimal impact on the system; however, there are times when even slight deviations can create enormous problems for the controller. Adding to the controller's problem is the movement of the storm. It generally does not stay in one place long enough for the controller to work out some sort of routine with other sectors or positions.

The pilot has relatively few options when it comes to avoiding severe weather. The forces of nature can be extremely nasty at times. The instinct for survival tells the pilot that the weather ahead is bad stuff that he or she must absolutely, positively avoid. When ATC denies approval for deviation, both the pilot and the controller must work out and communicate solu-

tions and alternatives. Of course, all of this is taking place while the aircraft continues to head toward the problem.

Pilot's Perspective

The number one priority for the pilot is safety. A pilot bases a request to deviate around weather on known factors that tell him or her some sort of action is necessary to remain clear of the adverse weather conditions ahead—for the well-being of the aircraft and its occupants.

Pilots may believe that controllers do not appreciate the risks that confront pilots in heavy weather. One pilot who was not allowed to deviate around a thunderstorm system reported,

> "...I believe the situation occurred because ATC procedures do not change with the changing weather. ...Controllers should be given ground instruction in the effects of thunderstorms and windshears."

Many pilots believe there should be enough flexibility in the system to handle these adverse situations. They feel that if coordination with the next controller is necessary to allow an aircraft to deviate around weather, then the controller should go ahead and do it. The pilot does not want to play "20 questions" before the deviation is finally approved. The pilot may also be reluctant to declare an emergency when the controller denies a request to deviate. One reporter claims that a "...request to squawk 7700 is an invitation to paperwork." [The third article in this series, "What Goes up Must Come Down," which appeared in the January/February 1993 issue, discusses the effects of declaring an emergency on the air traffic system and reiterates that a written report to the FAA is not automatically required but required only upon request.—Editor]

Controller's Perspective

Many reports received by ASRS from controllers indicate that weather deviations have been responsible for losing separation between aircraft and have frequently resulted in the controller "being charged" with an operational error. What the pilot wants to do does not always conform to ATC handbook requirements and occasionally is contrary to ATC practices. Allowing pilots to deviate from standard routes greatly diminishes the controller's ability to provide effective, positive separation between aircraft—the separation provided by the standard route suddenly does not apply. Aircraft can easily enter the adjacent controller's airspace without coordination because of the sheer volume of traffic and distractions. There is little time to coordinate new headings and routes with other ATC facilities because of frequency and interphone congestion.

A controller may also be unable to stop other traffic from entering his or her airspace right away because of coordination requirements. Traffic flow cannot be turned on and off like a faucet. One controller involved in an operational error reported that,

"...at the time of the incident I was working 22+ aircraft with extreme weather conditions causing deviation and altitude changes ... frequency congestion was a factor..."[and] a loss of separation occurred.

The more aircraft that are deviating, the more problems the controller must contend with; the controller's ability to provide positive control to all aircraft under extreme conditions may be compromised.

The controller does not have authorization to use less-than-standard separation except in emergencies. When confronted with situations that limit their ability to provide positive control to all IFR aircraft, controllers encounter an increased risk of operational error. Operational errors are taken very seriously by the controller and the FAA. They may result in the controller being "off the boards" from two days to two weeks, and sometimes longer, while the investigation and recertification process is conducted.

Some Examples . . .

Restricted Airspace

An air carrier flight on an airway wanted to deviate to the left around a large thunderstorm, but the controller was reluctant because of a nearby restricted area.

"...We encountered a large area of thunderstorms on our route... [and]...advised Los Angeles Center that deviations would be necessary. We requested and had approved an easterly heading which would keep us north of the weather. Center appeared to be concerned that our required deviations might eventually cause a conflict with Edwards' [AFB] restricted airspace.... While we continued to deviate to remain clear of weather, we told Center several times that we could not turn right.... Center's only concern seemed to be to keep us away from restricted airspace.... Center said we could not enter the restricted airspace. The Captain declared an emergency.... We were then told by Center to 'turn hard right' because there were 'live rounds ahead'.... We were in trouble, and they were no help."

Conflicting Traffic

A center controller had aircraft deviating around thunderstorms during moderate to heavy traffic conditions. Two aircraft on conflicting courses were unable to comply with ATC instructions because of build-ups along their route of flight. A loss of separation occurred between the aircraft.

"... [The controller] told air carrier B to turn left 15 degrees, vector for traffic. Air carrier B refused to take the turn, saying it would put him right into a thunderbumper with tops at flight level 400. Radar man told air carrier A to make a left turn 15 degrees. Air carrier A said that would put him in the clouds... the radar man said, 'One of you is going to have to turn; you're

head on [at] flight level 370'.... Air carrier A said he would go left... but it became obvious it wasn't enough... [Separation] was later measured to be zero vertical, 1.9 miles lateral, but on the scope it looked much less than 'that. I respect the pilot's wishes not to fly into the clouds, but I sometimes think they don't take us seriously enough. A cloud may be a better choice than another aircraft."

A departing air carrier discovered thunderstorm cells on radar and requested deviation around them. The controller was unable to approve the request because of heavy departure traffic in front and behind.

"I noticed two thunderstorm cells on the radar... [and]... asked departure for deviations around the cells to the south. He told us 'unable.' We advised him that there was weather... and we needed to avoid it. He told us that there was a bunch of aircraft to our left, and he was unable to [approve a deviation] at this time.... At about 5 miles the large cells [were] painting solid red 30 degrees on either side of the centerline of the scope.... I asked the controller [again].... He said he would not and to maintain our present heading... Our heading was taking us into the center of the storm.... At 3 miles from the storm, I told departure that we needed a 30 degree right turn.... The controller seemed upset with us but granted us a turn... then told us to descend to 3000 feet and that we had traffic behind us overtaking.... I can accept the fact that he was busy with traffic and weather re-routes, but my responsibility is for the safety of my passengers and aircraft."

Reactions

The following comments indicate some typical reactions whenever requests cannot be granted by either the pilot or controllers:

"I believe the controller and his supervisor's attitude were extremely poor and very uncooperative, not to mention dangerous." (Pilot)

An operational error occurred "because [of a] vector to the west for traffic.... This was the primary factor which caused me to lose lateral separation." (Controller)

"The controller just did not understand the necessity to turn to avoid the thunderstorm." (Pilot)

"Thunderstorms are extremely difficult to work with." (Controller)

"Given the same situation [again], I would do it exactly the same way, and I [am] incredulous that any controller in his right mind would send any kind of aircraft through that kind of weather...." (Pilot)

Captain said, "I never heard a controller turn aircraft into a thunderstorm." Controller said, "You won't hear anything in a couple of minutes when you meet the other aircraft."

Weather Emergencies

ASRS reports indicate a reluctance on the pilot's part to declare an emergency whenever "all else" fails. In the following report, the flight crew needed to deviate around thunderstorms, but the controller could not approve the deviation since it would take the aircraft into a restricted area.

"[Our request to]... deviate north to avoid thunderstorms was denied. A vector... was assigned... [however] a line a thunderstorms mandated a more southerly deviation. The controller became upset over our proximity to the adjacent restricted area and attempted to vector us into the thunderstorms and make us squawk 7700. Neither request was complied with.... Vectoring the flight south with the knowledge that the range in the restricted area was hot might have been the root problem. I don't see this as a big deal... "

In another instance, a Center controller working aircraft with thunderstorm activity in the area approved a pilot's request to deviate but because of the heavy concentration of aircraft and limited flexibility in the airspace had to restrict where the aircraft could go.

"We observed a massive thunderstorm.... Weather radar was on and showed an extensive area of heavy precipitation and turbulence.... We informed the Center that we would be unable to continue... because of the storm. We were told we could alter our heading right of [the projected] course, but do not proceed east.... We informed Center that we would not be able to [comply on that heading] to avoid the storm condition.... We were told again to not fly east... 'under any circumstances.' We requested a higher altitude and were denied.... We then requested a right... to circumnavigate the storm

to the west, again denied. We were told that a left turn would be permitted. We informed ATC that a left was impossible because it would place [us in] the main intensity of the thunderstorm... Our explanation was not accepted... An air carrier preceding us told ATC... that no one can get through... The PIREP was disregarded by ATC. We made a slight turn and just skirted the storm. Ice and turbulence was encountered... I told my First Officer if ATC instructs a further left turn to declare an emergency."

Reducing the Impact

Timely communication can help the pilot avoid thunderstorms while still allowing the controller to provide separation from other traffic. Last minute requests are difficult to coordinate.

Pilots

- Do not assume that the controller knows where all the thunderstorm activity is located. Tell him or her what you want and what you can do, not what you cannot do, when making your request.

- Plan ahead—give the controller as much notice as possible so that the controller can accomplish inter/intra facility coordination in a timely manner.

- The pilot is responsible for the operation of the aircraft and the safety of the passengers. Timely PIREP's can help the controller work with the pilot in accomplishing this by formulating a traffic plan in advance and relaying this information to other aircraft.

Controllers

- Controllers need to minimize last minute surprises by finding out exactly what pilots have in mind when they request clearance to deviate. Carte blanche approvals can lead to problems.

- Controllers too should plan ahead. Developing a good plan for future traffic flow and letting flight crews know in advance what is going on will go a long way toward reducing conflicts and last minute surprises.

When All Else Fails...

- Since the controller is not authorized to go below minimum-required separation (unless a pilot declares an emergency) and will do whatever is necessary to ensure that separation loss does not occur, the final decision on the course of action rests with the pilot.

- Pilots are reluctant to declare an emergency. However, in certain situations, there may be no other alternative available to the pilot. FAR § 91.3(b) states that: "In an in-flight emergency requiring immediate action, the pilot-in-command may deviate from any rule of this part to the extent required to meet that emergency." The *Airman's Information Manual* (AIM), paragraph 6.2, states: "An aircraft is in at least an urgency condition the moment the pilot becomes doubtful about position fuel, endurance, weather, or any other condition that could adversely affect flight safety." The AIM goes on to say, "This is the time to ask for help, not after the situation has developed into a *distress* condition."

- Once the pilot declares an emergency, the controller can provide advisories and other services until the emergency situation no longer exists and normal radar or vertical separation can be re-established.

Summing Up

Good planning by both the pilot and controller, an awareness of adverse weather conditions, effective communications, the willingness to endure a little paperwork, and mutual cooperation are the key elements to reducing the impact of being "Between a Rock and a Hard Place." ∎

The Aviation Safety Reporting System is a cooperative program established by the FAA's Office of the Assistant Administrator for Aviation Safety and administered by the National Aeronautics and Space Administration.

Seaplane Right of Way

by Dean Chamberlain, *Associate Editor*

Several readers and the Seaplane Pilots Association wrote about the article "Water and Flying Do Mix Well When Pilots are Aware," which was published in the May-June 1992 issue of the magazine. They questioned an apparent contradiction between the article's "Right of Way Rules" listed on page 7, which states that the Coast Guard (USCG) considers seaplanes vessels once they land on water, and a statement made in the new FAA Advisory Circular (AC) 91-69, "Seaplane Safety for FAR Part 91 Operators," which says the Coast Guard does not consider seaplanes vessels once they land on water.

The article and AC are both correct. The Coast Guard considers a seaplane on the water a vessel. When afloat, as a vessel, seaplanes must comply with all of the appropriate Coast Guard Nautical Rules of the Road as well as the appropriate Federal Aviation Regulations (FAR). The apparent contradiction resulted because the AC failed to state clearly that the Coast Guard does not consider seaplanes afloat vessels only for the purpose of excluding seaplanes from having to meet the Coast Guard's personal flotation device (PFD) requirements for vessels. Simply stated, seaplane operators do not have to meet the same Coast Guard PFD (life preserver) requirements that other vessel operators have to meet. But seaplane operators must comply with all other applicable USCG regulations when operating on the water.

Although seaplane pilots are not required to comply with the same Coast Guard PFD requirements as other vessel operators, safety and common sense dictate that all seaplanes have some type of PFD on board for each occupant. The problem in selecting PFD's for seaplanes is that seaplanes can flip over in a crash and trap their passengers under water. Because of their bulk or buoyancy, certain types of Coast Guard-approved PFD's for vessels, if worn at the time of a seaplane accident, could possibly prevent the occupants from getting out of an overturned seaplane or any other type aircraft in water. The problems of exiting an aircraft in water is why airliners carry FAA-approved inflatable PFD's for passenger protection on overwater flights. Uninflated, inflatable PFD's allow their wearers to exit through smaller openings than other types of PFD's and to swim under water if necessary to clear the aircraft. This unique aviation need for inflatable PFD's is why the Coast Guard does not consider seaplanes vessels for PFD purposes and only for PFD purposes. The reason is current Coast Guard regulations do not allow inflatable PFD's to be used to meet minimum PFD requirements aboard vessels, hence the exclusion of seaplanes from the "vessel" PFD rule. But no matter what type of PFD you use in your aircraft, you should make sure the PFD's meet applicable FAA or USCG standards or the specific regulatory requirement for your operation.

If you plan on using inflatable PFD's aboard your aircraft, we recommend you use dual air chamber PFD's. The dual chambers provide redundancy in case one chamber is damaged. Also be aware that some inflatable PFD's on the market for boaters automatically inflate when sufficiently wet. They are designed to automatically protect someone thrown overboard who may be injured or unconscious. If this type of PFD is used in an aircraft, it may inflate before the wearer can exit a submerged aircraft. Then the wearer may have the same type of problems exiting the aircraft discussed earlier. Because of the number of types and models of PFD's on the market, both USCG and FAA approved and not approved, each pilot in command must decide based upon applicable regulations for the specific flight what is the best type of PFD for use in his or her operation. For additional information on PFD's and safety afloat, you can contact your local Coast Guard unit, local boating organization, or call the Coast Guard's Boating Safety Hotline, 1-800-368-5647. You can obtain a copy of AC 91-69 by writing to DOT Utilization and Storage Section, M443.2, Washington, DC 20590.

Another reader questioned the statement about powered and unpowered seaplane "sailing" in the article's sidebar discussion about one of the unwritten seaplane right of way rules. He said some seaplane pilots and boaters mistakenly believe that seaplanes are not simple powered vessels when on the water but are a separate category below that of conventional powered vessels. To set the record straight regarding these concerns, the Coast Guard does not consider seaplanes a separate vessel category under its nautical rules of the road. The deciding factors in determining right of way afloat involve the types of vessels involved and their particular operation at the time. Then the Coast Guard's nautical rules of the road determine right of way. Seaplane pilots must also follow appropriate FAR regarding right of way questions afloat.

One final comment on vessels (seaplanes, boats, and anything else that floats) and the nautical rules of the road is that not everyone afloat knows or follows the nautical rules of the road. Therefore, seaplane pilots afloat must always be prepared for the unexpected actions of others operating vessels near their aircraft. ∎

Smoking is one of the most controversial issues of our times. It seems almost daily that another study shows the detrimental effects of smoking or passive smoke. No one will argue that it is also a difficult habit to break, that its "hold" on smokers is a physical addiction; yet the health benefits of ceasing to smoke occur almost immediately. If you are still having trouble finding a good reason to quit, consider the following article about how smoking affects your ability to deal with stressful situations—which we all have once in a while when flying. By the way, the opinions expressed by Mr. Rand are his and not necessarily those of the FAA. —Editor

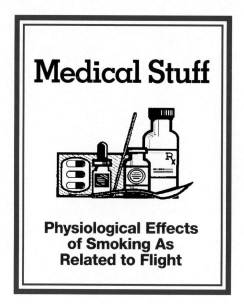

Medical Stuff

Physiological Effects of Smoking As Related to Flight

by Rand M. Sanders

Stress is an encompassing term that includes anything and everything that places a strain on an individual's ability to perform at his or her very best. The flyer whose health is impaired is often unable to adjust to stresses or to cope with the demands of flying. In about one-half of the accidents with a "human factors" label, there were no contributing factors such as weather or maintenance—just human fallibility, especially when stresses were involved. Stress comes from many sources, most of which we can learn to control by understanding what causes the stress. Any stress imposed on a pilot by a lack of knowledge or inattention to healthy living habits are unacceptable, because they may decrease a pilot's capabilities below the level necessary for the safe operation of the aircraft.

Aside from the long-term effects to health, the smoking of tobacco—"self-imposed stress"—constitutes immediate and on-going threats to health and safety of flight. A report from the United States Public Health Service stated that cigarette smokers are 20 times more likely to die of lung cancer than non-smokers, and six to 10 times more likely to die of cancer of the larynx (voice box). The report indicated cigarette smoking may be the cause of cancer of the esophagus and bladder and is strongly suspected of causing cancer of the pancreas.

Medical studies show us that cigarette smoking causes a relative deprivation of oxygen to the heart muscle and contributes to circulatory problems by constricting arteries; thus, it affects the cardiovascular system and is significant in the development of coronary heart disease. Cigarette smoking causes irritation to the lining of the respiratory tree (lungs and bronchial tubes) which, in turn, causes edema (accumulation of fluid) and swelling, preventing air from passing in and out freely. This and other factors lead to emphysema and permanent lung damage in many individuals.

Let us look at some of the individual components of cigarette smoke and the effects they have on the human body.

Tar

This is a catch-all term for the viscous residue left from cigarette smoke after the gasses and water vapor have been eliminated. In addition to its cancer potential, it causes swelling and tends to prevent the natural cleansing action of the lungs.

Nicotine

Pure nicotine, even in extremely small doses, is one of the most toxic substances in the world. Many years ago, rose growers used it to kill many stubborn insects on rose bushes. Nicotine primarily affects the nerves and muscle tissue. If the nicotine contained in two cigarettes were extracted from the tobacco and injected into the bloodstream, it could be fatal. Fortunately, nicotine in cigarette smoke is not completely absorbed in the respiratory tree. Nicotine can, however, cause weakness and twitching of the skeletal muscles and may result in abdominal cramping, nausea, and vomiting, particularly in those not habituated to its effects. In addition to altering nerve impulses and the circulation of the blood, it also alters the heart and respiratory rates. There is also evidence that nicotine in small amounts will decrease the body's ability to adapt to stress.

Carbon Monoxide

Carbon monoxide produced in cigarette smoking probably presents the most immediate harmful effects in tobacco smoking. Carbon monoxide is a colorless, tasteless, and odorless gas produced by incomplete combustion of any carbon-containing material. It combines with hemoglobin (the compound in red blood cells that transports oxygen) 250 times more readily than oxygen. The hemoglobin involved in this combination is not available for transporting oxygen to the tissues and produces a degree of *hypemic hypoxia* (hypoxia caused by the reduced capacity of the blood to carry oxygen). A pilot who smokes will normally have 5% to 10% of his or her total hemoglobin taken up by carboxyhemoglobin (a mixture of CO and O_2 in a red blood cell). This results in hypemic hypoxia and *lowers the pilot's altitude tolerance.* Flying at a cabin altitude of 10,000 feet with 10% carboxyhemoglobin is physiologically equivalent to 15,000 feet cabin altitude. (FAR § 91.211 requires the flight crew to use supplemental oxygen for flights above 12,500 feet MSL and up to and including 14,000 feet MSL cabin pressure altitude for that part of the flight that exceeds 30 minutes and continuously above 14,000 feet.) The chronic smoker who is breathing ambient air carries this additional hazard for several hours after the last cigarette. Lack of oxygen to the brain impairs judgement, so a smoker with hypemic hypoxia may suffer a diminished ability to make decisions about a flight even though he or she is not at the altitudes that require use of supplemental oxygen. Furthermore, this carbon monoxide hazard exists also for the non-smoker who is in the same area with the smoker.

Hypoxia resulting from CO poisoning affects visual acuity, brightness discrimination, and dark adaptation in the same way and extent as similar degrees of hypoxia that results from reduced oxygen partial pressure. *As little as 5% CO in the blood will affect the visual threshold and raise the physiological altitude.* Smoking three cigarettes in succession may cause a temporary CO level in the blood of 4% with an effect on visual sensitivity equal to that of an altitude of about 8,000 feet. This effect is greater when flying at night, since our night vision is far from perfect anyway.

What cannot be explained enough about quitting smoking is that reversal of these effects occurs almost at the moment you smoke your last cigarette. You will reduce your worry about developing smoking-related cancer; your heart and respiratory rate will get back to normal; your tissues will receive oxygen from your blood more efficiently—in short, you will feel better. You will have eliminated one stressor and left yourself better fit to deal with the "everyday" stresses encountered in flying. ∎

Mr. Sanders is a Technical Sergeant in the U.S. Air Force Reserves where he flies as a boom operator on KC-10A's. He is an airline transport pilot, CFI, and flies with the North Carolina Wing of the CAP. He wrote about carburetor icing in the September/October 1992 issue of *FAA Aviation News.*

Answers to Quiz:
1–T, 2–F (major repair), 3–T, 4–T, 5–F (major repair), 6–T, 7–F (major repair), 8–F (major repair), 9–T, 10–T, 11–T, 12–F (major alteration), 13–T, 14–T, 15–T, 16–F (major alteration)

Superpilot

Continued from page 1

confirmed President Clinton's appointment of Federico F. Peña as Secretary of Transportation. At some point in the political process of setting up a new administration, a new FAA Administrator will be appointed. Change was the campaign slogan of the new President, and as we said about Superman, only time will tell what changes will occur in our transportation system and the FAA as a result of President Clinton's election. But regardless of your political viewpoint, every airman has a responsibility to get involved in the aviation political process. Too many airmen sit back and do nothing, or they let one of their membership groups speak for them. In many cases, the groups may or may not speak for the majority of their members. My point is that so few airmen get involved in the process that determines how we all fly. It is a process which, once you are familiar with it, is so simple that it is an embarrassment that so few airmen participate. I am talking about the right of all airmen to comment on proposed rulemaking by the FAA, a right spelled out in Federal Aviation Regulations (FAR) Part 11 and in Advisory Circular 11–2A, *Notice of Proposed Rulemaking Distribution System.* (Available from DOT, M–443.2, Washington, DC 20590.)

Rulemaking is simple, although the results may not be. With the exception of emergency rulemaking, one of the most important rulemaking steps is the issuance of a notice of proposed rule making (NPRM). Published in the *Federal Register,* the U.S. Government's official public forum, the NPRM explains the proposed rule, the reasoning behind the proposed rule, and how the public can comment on the proposed rule. Each notice contains the name of the FAA person responsible for that particular rule. The problem is very few individuals comment on proposed rules, although most trade and membership groups do. But

regardless of how airmen become aware of NPRM's, few airmen respond. In fact, more airmen respond to the FAA's implementation of a final rule than during the public comment period when it was proposed as a NPRM.

This lack of public response is regrettable because the FAA is required by law to consider all responses it receives as it goes through the rule-making process. In many cases, a proposed rule has been changed or dropped because of the comments made by interested airmen and groups. In the political reality of life in Washington, comments made by citizens can and do have impact on every law and regulation. But many times, the political facts of life in Washington are that the vocal few are heard, the so-called silent majority are not. What this means in today's aviation environment is what normally benefits one group is done at a cost to another group. One group wins. One group loses.

As you prepare for another season of flying, you need put a new item at the top of your preflight checklist— Check NPRM's. As you kick off the 1993 flying season, make yourself a promise to make your voice heard in the rule-making process in Washington throughout the new year. Remember, a bad rule can ground you just like a bad mag check. The problem is bad rules take longer to fix. We don't know if Superman will ever fly again, but a careful preflight of your aircraft, your self, and appropriate NPRM's should keep you flying for years to come.

Have a safe 1993 flying season. ∎

If Mr. Chamberlain can't imagine a "person of steel" saving the world, he needs to read Wonder Woman—she flew an invisible airplane! Consult AC 11–2A for information on how to receive free copies of NPRM's. —*Editor*

Two faces of Amelia Earhart

This article is presented as part of the Federal Aviation Administration's celebration of National Women's History Month, March 1993. **—Editor**

"Good morning ladies and gentlemen. This is your Captain speaking, and on behalf of myself and the crew, I would like to welcome you to the flight. We are leveling out now at our cruising altitude of 28,000 feet and will reach our destination in about 55 minutes. The flight attendants will be serving breakfast shortly. Thank you for flying with us, and we hope your day is a pleasant one." After this cheerful greeting from the cockpit of the airline jet, a few of the passengers look surprised, if not down-right shocked. (And, no, it is not from the mystery breakfast being placed before them.) The voice of the captain coming over the intercom was that of a woman!

Today, it is not unusual for a woman to be an airline Captain. Although many of us have not flown with a woman at the controls, chances are we will as the number of women pilots increases in the 1990's. In 1991 there were over 1,225 female airline pilots in the United States and 1,600 worldwide. (This includes only women who fly under FAR Part 121 in aircraft in excess of 90,000 pounds gross weight.) Women currently make up close to 6% of airline pilots.

Through the Years

A Look at Attitudes toward Women in Aviation

by Kristine Kjos, *FAA Evaluation Specialist*

Women have participated in aviation since the first balloon rides in the late 1700's. Amelia Earhart, Anne Morrow Lindbergh, and Jacqueline Cochran are famous for their flying feats, but there were thousands more women who made spectacular contributions to aviation. So many of these women pilots or aviatrices, as they were called in the early decades of flight, are known only to small circles of aviation enthusiasts. The path for women aviators has not been an easy one, and women today are still breaking new ground for themselves and others in all aviation fields as they did when aviation was born.

EARLY AVIATION

In the days after the Wright Brothers historical first powered flight, women in aviation were scarce. Flying was still new, and most Americans had not even seen an airplane. Flying was usually considered "socially inappropriate" and "physically impossible" for women in the 1910's, and early aircraft were not known for being stable. Yet, despite societal disapproval, several women became well-known aviatrices during those early years.

On September 2, 1910, Blanche Stuart Scott became the first American woman to solo in a fixed-wing, heavier-than-air aircraft. However, there is debate as to whether this flight was accidental or intentional. Glenn Curtiss, the airplane's builder and Scott's instructor, agreed to give Scott flying lessons for monetary reasons, although he believed that the sky was no place for women. Curtiss, thinking he was clever, had wedged a piece of wood beneath the throttle to prevent the plane from becoming airborne. Scott discovered the wood, removed it, and finally soared into the air, making history for women. She went on to become a stunt pilot with various exhibition groups touring the country and was famous for flying upside down under bridges and for her "Death Dive" from 4,000 feet down to 200 feet above ground.

Some credit Bessica Raiche with the title of "First Woman Aviator of America," for her first flight on October 13, 1910. Raiche and her French husband built their own airplane in which she soloed without any prior instruction. A mechanic simply told her to pull the wheel back to go up and push the wheel in to go down. Raiche flew for years, and the husband and wife team went on to form the French-American Aeroplane Company which manufactured lightweight airplanes.

Harriet Quimby was the first American woman to earn her pilot's license on August 1, 1911. "Flying seems easier than voting," said Quimby to a crowd of women after her first solo flight. Quimby soon set the first woman's record by flying at night over New York City before a crowd of 20,000 spectators. On April 2, 1912, Quimby became the first aviatrix to pilot a plane across the English Channel. On July 1, 1912, in a tragic accident at a Boston air meet, Quimby lost control of her plane, fell out of the cockpit, and plunged to her death in the shallow water of the bay. She was not wearing a seat belt, as they were very uncommon at the time.

Other famous women of the era included Matilde Moisant, Katherine and Marjorie Stinson, and Ruth Law. Moisant, the second woman in the United States to receive a pilot's license, flew in various meets around

Matilde Moisant

the country. She last flew on April 14, 1912, when her plane burst into flames from a fuel tank leak. Moisant's clothes were afire, but her heavy tweed flying costume saved her life.

The Stinson sisters were both skillful pilots. The older of the two, Katherine, was the first woman to carry airmail and the first woman to loop-the-loop. She raised considerable money for World War I using her flying skills and opened a flying school in Texas with her family. Marjorie, the youngest woman pilot in the United States at the time, flew several exhibition flights and later focused on teaching at and running the Stinson Aviation School.

Ruth Law received her pilot's license on November 12, 1912. Soon she was making daily exhibition flights, carrying passengers, and looping-the-loop. In November 1916, Law set the American nonstop cross-country record, flying from Chicago to New York. She later

set a new women's altitude record of 14,700 feet in September 1917.

These first few pioneers were just the beginning in a long line of women who struggled their way into aviation. Slowly, it became more socially acceptable for single women to participate in aviation, although some women continued to disguise themselves as men or as other women when taking a flight. Advances in aircraft design lessened objections to women flying airplanes for physical reasons. Daring women ventured into the cockpit wearing pants and, although this was considered improper at first, it was eventually accepted because of the nuisance and danger caused by long skirts. Although some men encouraged women to fly, there remained an unwillingness to accept women pilots. Claude Grahame-White, a famous British aviator, feared women's lack of self-confidence would

Jacqueline Cochran

cause panic and loss of control in an emergency. He felt women were "temperamentally unfit, and when calamity overtakes them, and sooner or later it will," he said he would feel "in a way responsible for their sudden decease." This perception of women as panicky was all too common. As the 1920's came in with a roar, the aviatrices tried harder than ever to prove to men and to other women that they were competent pilots.

BARNSTORMING

Women pilots in the 1920's were more daring than ever. Many turned to barnstorming early in the decade because it was the only door open to them in aviation. Social disapproval continued, but women were determined to dazzle the doubtful with their daring barnstorming loops and dives.

Ruth Law's fame grew in the 1920's when she opened "Ruth Law's Flying Circus." "My trickiest [stunt] involved climbing out of the cockpit, and inching toward the center of the biplane's wing. The pilot would then make three loops with me standing on the wing," said Law. Law also made numerous plane-to-car transfers. Laura Bromwell astounded a crowd of 10,000 when she flew 199 consecutive loops, stopping only when she ran out of fuel. Phoebe Fairgrave was famous for her double parachute jumps. After the first chute opened, she cut it loose and free-fell further through the air before releasing the second chute.

Barnstormers knew well of the dangers their stunts could incur; fatal aviation accidents were common among male and female barnstormers. Bessie Coleman, the first black aviatrix, met the same fate as Harriet Quimby when her plane flipped during a nose dive in April 1926. Wearing neither parachute nor seatbelt, Coleman was thrown from the plane and plunged to her death. Laura Bromwell died two weeks after her loop record when she lost control of her plane in a loop and crashed. Some tragedies occurred on the ground. Gladys Roy, famous for dancing the Charleston on the upper wing of a plane, accidentally walked into a plane's spinning propeller. Some of these women risked their lives to make a meager living for themselves, but most of them flew because they had caught the "flying bug."

Record setting and air racing became popular as the decade progressed. After Lindbergh's successful crossing of the Atlantic Ocean in May 1927, the race was on for a woman to cross the same waters. It was not to be accomplished by a woman at the controls until Amelia Earhart's famous Atlantic crossing in 1932, although there were several attempts made by women before her. After one of the failed Atlantic crossing attempts, Dr. Katherine B. Davis, a sociologist, said "There is no woman alive today. . . equipped for such a flight."

Other women's records were set for endurance, altitude, and speed. Viola Gentry, Bobbi Trout, Louise Thaden, Elinor Smith, and others were famous for their endurance competitions. In January 1929 Trout and Smith teamed up and remained in the air for 45 hours and 5 minutes. At the close of the decade, Louise Thaden set speed and altitude records of 156 miles per hour and 20,260 feet respectively.

In August 1929, the Women's Air Derby, later called the "Powder Puff Derby," began in Santa Monica, California. The race lasted a week and ended in Cleveland, Ohio. Out of the 18 participants, 14 made it to Cleveland, three had accidents, and one woman, Marvel Crosson, died when she bailed out too low for her parachute to open. Crosson's death created an uproar of protests to cancel the race. "Women Have Conclusively Proven That They Cannot Fly," read one headline. But the women pressed on to prove that flying was no longer exclusive to men.

A male survey at the time showed that women pilots were considered "too emotional, vain, inconstant and frivolous— hazards to themselves and to others." Despite these kinds of comments, women had firmly established a niche for themselves in aviation and had formed an unbreakable bond. In

PROFILE: Mary Feik—mechanic, engineer, pilot

Mary Feik calls herself an aviation "anomaly." After overhauling her first engine when she was 13, Mary turned to airplane engines at age 18 and taught aviation mechanics at the U.S. Army Air Force Seymour Johnson Air Base at Goldsboro, N.C. during WWII. Mary became an expert on several WWII fighter planes before advancing to Wright Field in Dayton, Ohio where she is credited with becoming the first woman engineer in research and development for the Air Technical Service Command. One of Mary's primary assignments was to design and build

the "Captiveair," an apparatus used to train fighter pilots. "We mounted a real P–51C *Mustang* off the line on pylons, *(see photo above),* moved all the cockpit instruments back to an instructor's cubicle, leaving the pilot with remote indicators the instructor could operate to simulate operational situations and emergencies," described Mary. The "simulator" was a success and Mary helped other bases build "Captiveair's." To her great relief, Mary was finally allowed to fly the planes she worked on (after many secret early morning and middle of the night test flights) and flew

more than 5,000 hours during WWII and the Korean War as a B–29 flight engineer, engineering observer, and pilot in fighter, attack, bomber, cargo, and training aircraft.

The Smithsonian Air and Space Museum was lucky to recruit Mary in 1976, where she worked for many years as a docent, or guide, and antique and classic aircraft restoration specialist. Today, Mary continues to lend her restoration expertise to many and has now been restoring airplanes for 50 years. She gives lectures to the community about aviation history, women in aviation, and aircraft restoration, and is active in many aviation organizations, including the Civil Air Patrol (CAP), Experimental Aircraft Association (EAA), and the Potomac (MD) chapter Ninety-Nines, of which she is a charter member. Mary owns, flies, and maintains a 1962 PA–24 180 Piper *Comanche* and a 1952 PA–20 135 Piper *Pacer*, both in original condition, of course! When asked how she feels about aviation, Mary responds that "Flying is only half of it. No airplane flies safely if the maintenance is not good. There are a lot of women [mechanics] out there who are technically capable, but nobody ever hears about them." Needless to say, she feels that pilots should understand engines and can never know enough about the planes they fly. Mary sees herself as a "resource" for people seeking advice and enjoys sharing her knowledge about aviation. And if you need to find her, chances are she is out at the airfield working on one of her beautiful planes with a smile on her face.

1929, a women's aviation group called the Ninety-Nines was formed to promote women pilots and to serve as an information exchange network. The Ninety-Nines participated in air races, promoted aviation and related research, and supported other aviation causes. They were and continue to be instrumental in the aerial marking campaign. The campaign involves painting thousands of airport names on building

roofs around the country and indicating the direction and number of miles to these airports. This effort by the Ninety-Nines has assisted numerous lost pilots over the decades.

Also in 1929, federal regulations were established prohibiting low flying and hindering many barnstorming stunts. Some women retired from their flying careers, and some went on to set bigger and better records. A

famous quote by Amelia Earhart best described what many of these women were feeling at the time: "Now and then, women should do for themselves what men have already done—and occasionally what men have not done—thereby establishing themselves as persons, and perhaps encouraging other women toward greater independence of thought and action."

THE GLORIOUS THIRTIES

Records of all kinds continued to be set by men and women in "The Golden Years" of aviation. Flying was becoming a more reliable means of transportation and women were used to demonstrate its safety and ease to the public. They were seen in advertisements with anything to do with aviation. Women raced, toured, made promotional flights to demonstrate the safety of flight, sold airplanes, and instructed. Membership in the Ninety-Nines continued to grow. In 1932, there were 472 licensed women pilots in the United States, and by the end of the thirties, the number of women pilots was nearing 1,000.

There were some people who continued to doubt women's flying abilities, but others began to acknowledge their skills. A chief pilot for a flying service explained that women "are easier to teach, and learn quicker than men. Women usually think about flying for a long time before they start taking instruction. They leave the instruction to you. When you tell them their mistakes, they pay more attention, and often correct them faster."

Some of America's most famous women flew in the 1930's. Everybody knows of Amelia Earhart's famous ocean crossings and mysterious disappearance over the Pacific during an attempt to circle the world at the equator. Her bravery and strong beliefs in women's competence have fascinated people for decades. Earhart was a woman ahead of her time. In 1936, Louise Thaden and Blanche Noyes won the Bendix air race, a race previously limited to men. Laura Ingalls finished a surprising second.

Higher, faster, farther! As soon as one woman set a record, it was broken by another. Ruth Nichols, Amelia Earhart, Bobbi Trout, Frances Marsalis, and Elinor Smith are just a few women who set records in the 1930's.

In 1938, Jacqueline Cochran won the Bendix. Cochran was an amazing woman who climbed to an altitude of 30,052 feet with no heat, oxygen supply, or pressurization. She got frostbite,

PROFILE:
Velta Benn—pilot, CFI

The name Velta Benn is well-known in the Washington, D.C. aviation community. Velta has been a flight instructor since 1945 and is an FAA designated examiner. During WWII, she answered the call for women pilots to join the war effort and became a Women's Airforce Service Pilot or WASP. She was in the third to last class to graduate and flew for three months at Merced Army Airbase in California (now Castle Air Force Base), before the WASP's were disbanded. During this short time, Velta flew com-

bat returnees back for their "R and R" and also flew with these men for their four hour "R and R" currency requirements. When asked if she was disappointed about the WASP's being disbanded, Velta replied that she felt and still feels very grateful for the flying opportunity. It was a positive experience for her and an enormous boost to her flying career.

Velta's aviation record is pretty impressive. She has taught several Congressmen how to fly, as well as a Canadian General, and was even approached by former First Lady Mrs. Nixon who was interested in flying lessons (unfortunately, White House security did not permit the lessons). Velta says that she has been the chief flight instructor during most of her jobs and has "always been well-accepted." In the late 1960's and early 1970's, Velta was a partner in a company that wrote scripts for Navy training films. "I wrote training scripts about carrier landings, gunnery patterns, and high angle of attack and spin characteristics of high performance jets," described Velta. Ironically, creating the films brought Velta back into military cockpits, as the Navy let her fly the jets described in the films.

Today, Velta's love for aviation is as strong as ever. She enjoys giving check rides as an FAA pilot examiner and has no intentions of stopping anytime soon. Chances are she is in the air even as you read this!

ruptured a sinus blood vessel, and became very disoriented from lack of oxygen but was not one to let "little things" like these deter her efforts. Cochran was also famous for her unbelievable speed records. During and after WWII, Cochran would earn her title "The greatest woman pilot in aviation history."

Women who flew in the 1930's have fond memories of the "Golden Age." Louise Thaden described aviation in the 1930's: "It was the first time

women began to be accepted on their own merits as pilots. It was a time of growth and exploration, when all 'firsts' were really firsts. It was a time when camaraderie existed because words were not always necessary between fellow pilots, a time of instant friends and a spirit of cooperation, and a sense of something shared." The "camaraderie" Thaden describes became stronger than ever when women pilots were allowed to fly for the Army during WWII.

THE WASP's

When the United States entered World War II, major air races were suspended and flying was not permitted near the coastal areas. Everyone began to focus on the war effort. By 1942, women were not uncommon in commercial aviation and began filling in for the men who went off to battle the Axis powers. There were women pilots, mechanics, engineers, assembly line workers, flight instructors, flight attendants, and air traffic controllers. The men working in these fields were reluctant to hire women at first, but with the war progression and shortage of men, women were soon welcomed and encouraged to do their part in supporting the war effort.

Jacqueline Cochran saw the war as a golden opportunity for women to serve their country as ferry pilots. She suggested her idea to the Army and was rejected at first. Determined to form a group of women ferry pilots, Cochran organized and established an elite group of women ferry pilots who served in Great Britain. As the war continued, another influential pilot named Nancy Love proposed using a small number of well-qualified women pilots to ferry aircraft domestically under the Air Transport Command. Love's proposal was accepted and the Woman's Auxiliary Ferry Service (WAFS) was created on September 10, 1942, with Love as squadron commander.

Cochran was angry about the situation. She came back to the United States from Great Britain and convinced the Army to form a second group of women ferry pilots of whom Cochran was in charge. Love's WAFS had more flying experience and were an elite group. Cochran's group, called the Woman's Flying Training Detachment (WFTD) had fewer hours so she organized a huge operation to provide further training. The two groups were eventually combined into one called the Women's Airforce Service Pilots (WASP's), headed by Cochran.

Doubts about women being too weak to handle heavy equipment were dispelled as the WASP's flew every kind of military airplane all over the U.S. They flew 77 different types of planes, from the P–51 *Mustang* fighter to the B–29 *Superfortress*, for a total of 12,650 deliveries and 60 million miles travelled during their two years as WASP's. There were 1,074 WASP's, 76 of whom lost their lives in accidents. Surprising to some, the WASP's safety record was better than the men's record for the same types of missions. At first, the WASP's were responsible for ferrying planes to coastal ports for shipment to the war arenas. Eventually, the women served as test pilots for problem aircraft, towed targets to train ground-to-air gunners (real ammunition was fired at the targets and sometimes hit the planes), trained male cadets, flew simulated strafing and smoke-laying missions, and performed radar jamming and searchlight tracking missions.

The WASP program run by Cochran was very militaristic to guarantee top performance by the women. Despite long hours, marching and exercising, rustic quarters, and the sometimes dangerous and unsafe aircraft, most WASP's enjoyed their jobs. Comraderie was high as was pride. The situations that the WASP's found themselves in were sometimes amusing, sometimes dangerous, sometimes infuriating. Women were at first grounded during their menstrual cycles. (This rule was later revoked.) Some had to have physicals every month, unlike the men. This was also quickly revoked. Even sabotage was a scary possibility. One WASP was killed in a crash because somebody deliberately put sugar in the gas tank of the plane she was ferrying. But the danger and hassle endured by WASP's was worth it for most when they saw the looks of shock on ground crew's faces, as they climbed out of the fighter planes.

On December 20, 1944, the WASP program was deactivated. Loss of men in the war theaters was lower than predicted, and some male pilots began to return home. Many WASP's were disappointed at the loss of their jobs. They were of course happy that war losses were minimal, but they had worked so hard and come so far. They struggled to find other jobs in aviation, but jobs were scarce for men, let alone for women. At the last WASP graduation ceremony in Sweetwater, Texas, Cochran and the WASP's felt a great deal of pride and accomplishment when General Arnold (who doubted the WASP program at first) stated the following: "Frankly, I didn't know in 1941 whether a slip of a young girl could fight the controls of a B-17. You, and more than nine hundred of your sisters, have shown that you can fly wingtip to wingtip with your brothers. The entire operation has been a success. It is on the record that women can fly as well as men. . ."

But the WASP's were not properly recognized for their valiant efforts or fully incorporated into the Army. After years of protesting and negotiations with the Department of Defense, the WASP's were finally made veterans and thus eligible for appropriate benefits, on November 23, 1977, almost 40 years later. ∎

End of Part 1

Editor's Note: Part 2 of this article will appear in the April 1993 issue of *FAA Aviation News* and will cover the period from after WWII to the present. Ms. Kjos was a U.S. Department of Transportation Management Intern when she prepared this article as part of a developmental assignment on the Aviation News Staff. She is a student pilot who now works in FAA's Office of Contracting and Quality Assurance.

Author's Note: Special thanks to the Potomac (MD) Chapter of the Ninety-Nines for the help and encouragement given me on this article and towards getting my pilot's license, especially Patricia Garner, Evie Washington, Nancy Waylett, Mary Feik, and Linda Denett. Thanks also to Velta Benn, Jean Ross Howard, Pat Napier Adams, and JoEllen Casilio for their time and input. For others who have caught the "flying bug" as I have and who would like more information about women in aviation, I suggest visiting or contacting the Smithsonian Air and Space Museum in Washington, D.C.

FLIGHT**FORUM**

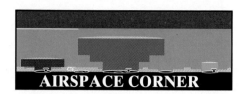

AIRSPACE CORNER

The word has been out on airspace reclassification just long enough for the questions to start coming in. The way we would like to handle them is in a regular "Airspace Corner" column, similar to our "Instrument Corner." For future editions of "Airspace Corner" we would welcome questions, comments, or subjects that the readers feel need clarification. —*Editor*

Question: *Since special VFR (SVFR) operations can only be authorized and conducted in a control zone, are we still going to be able to get an SVFR clearance in the new airspace?*

Answer: Yes. FAR Section 91.157a(1) has been amended, effective September 16, 1993, to allow SVFR operations to be conducted (with an ATC clearance) within the lateral boundaries of Class B, Class C, Class D, and Class E airspace surface areas up to, but not including 10,000 feet MSL.

Question: *In reading the new FAR's for SVFR, it appears that "through flights" are no longer authorized (§ 91.157). Also, VFR flight is now prohibited within the lateral boundaries of Class B, Class C, Class D, and Class E airspace surface areas anytime the ceiling is less than 1,000 feet (§ 91.155c). Am I reading these sections correctly?*

Answer: You are correct. However, in both cases, the rules were inadvertently changed. The FAA fully intended to continue to allow SVFR flights through Class B, Class C, Class D, and Class E surface areas. The revised rule prohibiting VFR flights within Class B, Class C, Class D, and Class E surface areas when the ceiling is less than 1,000 feet inadvertently dropped the phrase, "beneath the ceiling." One item our "eagle-eyed" reader missed was the title of Section 3, Appendix D to Part 91, Locations at which Special VFR operations are prohibited, did not include the phrase "fixed-wing." We did not intend to prohibit SVFR operations for helicopters. The FAA intends to initiate rulemaking action to correct these three administrative oversights prior to September 16, 1993.

Question: *What is a "surface area?"*

Answer: The term "surface area" has been selected as a generic replacement for "control zones" and/or "airport traffic areas" when there is application within more than one class of airspace. In a forthcoming change to the Pilot/Controller Glossary, we plan to define surface area as, "The use of the term surface area applies to the airspace within the lateral boundary of Classes B, C, D, and E airspace areas that begin at the surface and extends upward."

• Outer Marker Approach

According to FAR § 91.175(k) a compass locator or precision radar may be substituted for the outer marker or middle marker. DME, VOR, or NDB fixes that are authorized in the standard instrument approach or surveillance radar may be substituted for the outer marker. According to the inoperative components or visual aids table, if the middle marker is out and a compass locator or precision radar is not available for substitution, then we simply increase decision height by 50 feet for Cat. A, B, and C aircraft.

My question is, if the outer marker is out and there is no substitute available, can we still fly the approach? Since there is no inoperative components or visual aids table for outer marker failure, are there any adjustments necessary?

Kevin L. Davis
Honolulu, HI

The answer to your question is no. You can not fly an ILS approach if the outer marker is out and no other authorized means of defining the outer marker fix is available. Since the approach is not authorized without an outer marker, no adjustment is applicable.

• SVFR Operations

This is a request to either reprint or do a new article on the various conditions that permit special VFR operations (SVFR). I believe that there was an article done in the late 1970's or early 1980's that explained various unusual situations that allow SVFR.

One of these would be a VFR tower reporting -X9 OVC 4F. The control zone is IFR, but a pilot requests transition at 2,500 feet. If the pilot states that he is above the clouds and has five miles visibility the controller may authorize his transition without a SVFR clearance. Do you concur?

Second, a pilot is transitioning a control zone at 2,000 feet and cannot comply with VFR requirements below the clouds. Even though the zone is VFR, I believe that the pilot may request and be granted SVFR clearance through the control zone. This allows the pilot to deviate from the FAR's

and stay "clear of clouds." What is your opinion?

I believe that both pilots and controllers are generally unfamiliar with these situations and neither the Airman's Information Manual *or the controller handbook specifically address them.*

Leslie John Gaton
Isla Verde, PR

Yes, there was a control zone article published in the January/February 1985 issue of the then *FAA General Aviation News.* We currently are not planning on doing a special VFR article before the new airspace change scheduled for September 1993. We intend to focus our efforts on informing everyone about the new designations rather then writing about airspace that will change. We will be discussing how the current airspace procedures will be merged into the new system. For example, next year, control zones will become either Class B, C, D, or E airspace depending upon the establishment criteria for such airspace.

To answer your two questions, in the first example, if the pilot is able to maintain VFR at 2,500 feet and is outside the airport traffic area (ATA), the pilot does not have to talk to the controller at all to transition through the control zone assuming that the control zone is not within a TCA or ARSA. If the pilot plans on flying through an ATA, TCA, or ARSA the pilot must meet other requirements before entering such areas.

In your second example, a SVFR clearance does not allow a pilot to deviate from the FAR. A SVFR clearance simply lets the pilot meet another FAR standard that provides an adequate level of safety. Although we do not completely understand your question, if you mean can the pilot request a SVFR clearance under FAR § 91.157 to stay at 2,000 feet while maintaining less than the minimum VFR cloud separation in the control zone? The answer is yes. However, this operation would be subject to approval from the ATC facility responsible for the control zone. Remember, when the weather at the primary airport in the control zone is VFR, even with a SVFR clearance, the pilot, and pilots on IFR clearances, must be very alert for other VFR traffic in the zone. Control zones are designated to provide controlled airspace for terminal instrument operations at a primary airport and extend upward from the surface of the earth to a designated altitude or to the adjacent or overlaying controlled airspace when weather conditions are less than that required for visual flight rules (VFR) at the primary airport for which the control zone was established. When conditions are VFR at the primary airport, pilots can transition under VFR through a control zone without talking to a controller as long as the pilot is not going to penetrate an airport traffic area, TCA, or ARSA, which requires communication with ATC. Control zones are designated by rulemaking and are always in effect regardless of the weather. The only time a VFR pilot must be concerned with a control zone is when the weather is less than basic VFR.

Please note: FAR § 91.157(e) limits the use of Special VFR by pilots of fixed-wing aircraft to daylight hours except where the pilot is instrument rated and currently qualified and the aircraft is equipped for IFR flight.

• Emergency Frequencies

Simon Whitney's article, "Preflight Passenger Preparation" in the March/April issue provides an excellent outline for indoctrinating first flight passengers. However, the article does have one minor inaccuracy: Commercial airlines do not routinely monitor emergency frequency 121.5 MHz within the contiguous U.S. Airline aircraft do monitor this frequency when operating in oceanic airspace.

In addition, it is my understanding many FAA air traffic control facilities no longer monitor the emergency frequencies. It might be helpful to summarize in a future article what agencies and facilities still monitor the emergency frequency.

Glenn Morse
Director, Air Transport Association

According to FAA's Air Traffic Service, Flight Service Stations and the Civil Air Patrol continually monitor emergency frequencies.

• Contacting ATC

I am a private pilot with an instrument rating and a small plane. I was told in flight training that whenever I was receiving flight following or any other air traffic control (ATC) services, I didn't have to worry about contacting the towers of the airport traffic areas I was going through. ATC would coordinate the transition. This is precisely what the Airman's Information Manual (AIM) paragraph 3–61(b) says.

During a recent visit to an approach control facility, the controllers were surprised that some pilots relied on them to contact the towers. They said that nothing in their training contained a statement similar to AIM paragraph 3–61(b).

It seems that the AIM and pilot procedure should be amended so that whenever a pilot is approaching an airport traffic area he or she should either call the tower for approval to enter or ask ATC to do so and receive explicit verification that they have indeed secured permission for the pilot to enter. It is obviously very dangerous to be close to an airport without the tower knowing you're there.

John Paul Zima
Shaker Heights, OH

INSTRUMENT CORNER

• Missed Approaches

I have two questions about missed approaches. When flying a side-step maneuver on an ILS, such as the Oakland, CA, ILS RWY 27R procedure, if you have to make a missed approach at the side-step altitude, do you execute the missed approach procedure at that point on the glide slope, or do you continue to fly at the side-step altitude until expiration of the time from the final approach fix to the missed approach point like you would do for a non-precision approach?

If you are flying an ILS approach to a circling procedure, do you fly the glide slope down to the circling minimum descent altitude (MDA), or do you just ignore the glide slope and fly the localizer? If we use the glide slope, do we execute a missed approach at the MDA on the glide slope like we would do at the decision height on a full ILS approach, or do we continue to fly at the circling MDA until our time runs out? I am referring to the Livermore, CA, ILS RWY 25R circling procedure.

Thomas Klump
Oakland, CA

First, you must follow the procedures listed in FAR § 91.175 as to when you must execute a missed approach procedure. Then regarding your questions, the best answer is it is your choice. Just remember that although the glide slope provides good vertical guidance on a precision approach, when you are flying a non-precision approach, the use of elapsed time from the FAF to the MAP should normally put you closer to the runway. Both of the examples you mentioned show the MAP to be the end of the runway. If you go missed approach on the glide slope, you probably would not be as near the runway. Either way, you must comply with FAR § 91.175 as to whether you can land safely or must execute a missed approach.

An important safety point that must be made regarding any missed approach procedure that has an initial turn as part of the procedure is that no turns should be made until you are at either the DH on a precision approach or MAP on a non-precision approach. The reason is that missed approach procedures are designed only to protect you starting from the DH or MAP and not before. If a missed approach procedure involving a turn is executed before either of these points the only safe procedure is to climb and continue flying to the respective missed approach point before executing the missed approach instructions.

The AIM does not have to be amended. We checked with the facility Mr. Zima's mentioned in his letter. The appropriate manager contacted Mr. Zima, and the facility will provide the services outlined in the AIM. In a second letter to the magazine, Mr. Zima discussed the facility's telephone call and asked the magazine to ". . . disregard my first letter." But Mr. Zima's first letter provides us an opportunity to review some of the pilot and ATC responsibilities involved when pilots operate in certain airspace.

As Mr. Zima noted, AIM Paragraph 3–61(b) states, "FAR § 91.127 requires that unless a pilot is landing at or taking off from an airport in the airport traffic area (ATA) or authorized otherwise by ATC, the pilot must avoid the area. Generally, it is the pilot's responsibility to obtain the necessary authorization. Pilots operating under IFR or *receiving radar services from an ATC facility* (emphasis added) are not expected to obtain their own authorizations through each area. Rather, the ATC facility providing the service will coordinate with the appropriate control towers for the approval to transit each area." The requirement for air traffic controllers to coordinate with appropriate airport traffic control towers is contained in FAA Order

7110.65, *Air Traffic Control* paragraph 2–16b.

One important item for all VFR pilots to remember is that, in certain cases and areas, ATC services to VFR pilots are provided on a workload-permitting basis. Therefore, it is possible that ATC radar services could be terminated rather abruptly. If that happens, the VFR pilot would be told that radar services are terminated and to squawk 1200. From that moment on, the VFR pilot would be responsible for requesting his or her own authorization when planning to enter an ATA. This is why VFR pilots need to be aware of their position at all times and be prepared to resume their own navigation.

For detailed information on available ATC services, including emergency services, pilots should review the current edition of the AIM, which is the FAA's official guide to basic flight information and ATC procedures. The AIM also provides a glossary of pilot/controller terms to help improve the communication between pilots and ATC personnel.

Pilots can order the AIM from the Superintendent of Documents, U.S. Government Printing Office (GPO), Washington, DC 20402. GPO's Washington, DC telephone number is (202) 783–3238.

AV**NEWS/BRIEFS**

Looking to Aviation's Future

At the 1992 Experimental Aircraft Association's Fly In and Convention at Oshkosh, EAA launched the Young Eagle Program in an effort to introduce more young people to the world of aviation. EAA has gone a step further by introducing a new magazine, *Sport Aviation for Kids,* to its publication lineup. Aimed at the 17 and under audience, this bimonthly magazine fills a void previously ignored by featuring aviation personality profiles, history, games, and trivia. The magazine is available only to members of the Sport Aviation Club (annual membership fee $15). It will not be sold on the newsstand; however, participants of the Young Eagle Program will receive two complimentary issues.

MTBE Approved for Autogas STC

In the January/February "AvNews/Briefs," we reported about oxygenated fuels and the autogas STC. In the article we mentioned that FAA had not approved the additive methyl-tertiary-butyl-ether (MTBE) for aircraft fuel systems using autogas. As that story was going to press, FAA did approve MTBE's use.

As a blending agent, MTBE increases the antiknock index of autogas, and oil companies now add it to fuels to meet Environmental Protection Agency standards. Research conducted at FAA's Technical Center in Atlantic City, NJ with autogas blended with MTBE has not shown any safety related problems, nor have material compatibility and performance data supplied by the Experimental Aircraft Association and Petersen Aviation, the main

holders of autogas STC's, shown any safety related problems. FAA service difficulty reports do not reveal any material compatibility or safety issues. Accordingly, the FAA has determined that *autogas blended with MTBE can be used safely in aircraft that are approved for the use of autogas by STC.*

The existing prohibition on the use of alcohol additives remains in effect. It is the operator's responsibility to assure that autogas conforms to appropriate specifications. The policy guidance in Advisory Circular 23.1521–1A which prohibits the use of MTBE additives will be revised to reflect MTBE's approval.

Do You Know the Way to Sun 'n Fun

If you plan to attend the annual Sun 'n Fun Fly-In, reading a copy of the *Notices to Airmen* (NOTAM's) is strongly advised as part of your preflight planning. As an increase in traffic is expected, special procedures are in effect at Lakeland Airport from April 17 through 24.

To facilitate the flow of traffic, airplanes will arrive using the Lake Parker arrival procedures. Ultralights shall enter and exit from the south-southwest, and helicopters shall enter and exit from the southeast. For more details on IFR and VFR arrival and departure procedures, see NOTAM's.

Exclusion from the Mode C Veil rule for both Tampa and Orlando are defined in the Class II NOTAM's. Aircraft without electrical systems, balloons, and gliders are excluded (FAR § 91.215) from Mode C transponder requirement.

Limited grassfield operations can be accommodated. For "Special Grassfield Authorization and Procedures," contact: Sun 'n Fun (EAA) Fly-In, Inc., P.O. Box 6750, Lakeland, FL 33807, telephone (813) 644–2431. For those planning to fly an aircraft without a radio to Sun 'n Fun, a postcard should be sent to: Air Traffic Control Tower, Tampa International Airport, Tampa, FL 33607. Be aware that this postcard will indicate to ATC that you have read and understood all the procedures presented in NOTAM's for Lakeland Airport.

The Lakeland Linden Regional Airport Control Tower will be open and the control zone in effect from 6:30 a.m. to 9:30 p.m. However, these special procedures will be in effect ONLY from 7 a.m. to 7 p.m. on April 17 through 24.

Missing Something?

Several subscribers let us know that their copies of the January/February 1993 issue were missing pages. If this was the case for your copy, rest assured it is not bureaucratic cost-cutting but a binding error. Let us know *(see the inside front cover),* and we will try to replace your copy. But, our supply is *limited.*

News on the Move

The magazines with perhaps the best circulation are those that you find in the seat pocket in front of your airline seat. Unless an intrepid traveller takes the copy, you usually find the issue, well-thumbed by numerous readers, there for your entertainment. *FAA Aviation News,* thanks to Delta Air Lines, is taking a step in that direction. No, we won't be showing up in the seat back pocket of Delta planes, but one issue at least might be in a far more important place: the flight cases of Delta Air Lines' pilots. Mr. Bill Watts, Manager of Delta's MD-88 fleet, took the offer of a complimentary copy of the magazine, tendered in the November/December 1992 editorial, very seriously. He asked for 9,500 complimentary copies—one for every Delta pilot. Just after the first of this year, Delta mailed the copies with a cover letter encouraging pilots to subscribe. Flight Standards Director Thomas Accardi sent a letter of appreciation to Delta Air Lines, citing their interest in aviation safety and their generosity.

Being a pilot who sweats it out when she can't kick her own rudders, I might relax a little if I knew my captain and first/second officers had read the latest FAA safety news before takeoff. And just so that there are no hard feelings—we'll be happy to supply copies to any other airlines who want to follow Delta's example.

Is that southern hospitality or what?

—The Editor

New World Record Set

On October 3, 1992, 200 skydivers exited from six airplanes at approximately 18,000 feet over the skies of Myrtle Beach, SC, and successfully shattered the 150-way freefall formation record. It was their 24th attempt at complete a 200-way freefall formation. The jumpers used three DeHavilland DHC–4 *Caribous,* a DC–3, and two DeHavilland DHC–6 *Twin Otters.*

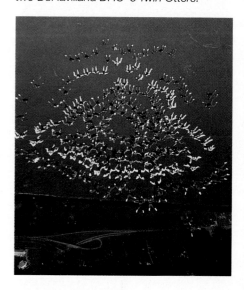

TEST YOUR PILOTING IQ: Preventive Maintenance Quiz

by Louise Oertly, *Associate Editor*

For those of you who have let your aircraft take a long winter's nap, the arrival of spring means preparing your aircraft for flight. Part of this preparation includes checking for bird, rodent, and insect nests in expected—and unexpected—places and conducting preventive maintenance. According to the Federal Aviation Regulations (FAR), the holder of a pilot certificate issued under FAR Part 61 may perform preventive maintenance on any aircraft owned or operated by that pilot which is not used under FAR Parts 121, 125, 127, 129, or 135.

The following quiz is to test your knowledge of what is considered preventive maintenance (provided it does not involve complex assembly operations). The answers are on page 19, but the complete list of preventive maintenance work can be found in FAR Part 43, Appendix A.

Answer the questions **True** or **False.**

___1. Replacing and servicing batteries.

___2. Repairs to deep dents, cuts, scars, or nicks on, and straighting of an aluminum propeller blade.

___3. Replenishing hydraulic fluid in the hydraulic reservoir.

___4. Replacing or cleaning spark plugs and setting of spark plug gap clearance.

___5. Calibration of radio equipment.

___6. Removal, installation, and repair of landing gear tires.

___7. Replacement of fabric on fabric-covered parts such as wings, fuselages, stabilizers, and control surfaces.

___8. Special repairs to structural engine parts by welding, plating, metalizing, or other methods.

___9. Replacing defective safety wiring or cotter keys.

___10. Trouble shooting and repairing broken circuits in landing light wiring circuits.

___11. Replacing bulbs, reflectors, and lenses of position and landing lights.

___12. Installation of structural parts other than the type of parts approved for the installation.

___13. Replacing wheels and skis where no weight and balance computation is involved.

___14. Servicing landing gear shock struts by adding oil, air, or both.

___15. Replacing safety belts.

___16. Installation of an accessory which is not approved for the engine.

DO NOT DELAY—CRITICAL TO FLIGHT SAFETY!

FAA Aviation News

A DOT/FAA FLIGHT STANDARDS SAFETY PUBLICATION

U.S. Department
of Transportation

**Federal Aviation
Administration**

Federico F. Peña, *Secretary of Transportation*
Joseph M. Del Balzo, *Acting FAA Administrator*
Carl B. Schellenberg, *Acting Executive Director
    for System Operations*
Anthony J. Broderick, *Associate Administrator
    for Regulation and Certification*
Thomas C. Accardi, *Director,
    Flight Standards Service*
Robert A. Wright, *Acting Manager,
    General Aviation and Commercial Division*
Roger M. Baker, Jr., *Manager,
    Accident Prevention Program Branch*
Phyllis Anne Duncan, *Editor*
Louise C. Oertly, *Senior Associate Editor*
Dean Chamberlain, *Associate Editor*

The FAA's Flight Standards Service, General Aviation and
Commercial Division, Accident Prevention Program
Branch, AFS–810, Washington, DC 20591, (telephone
202 267–8017) publishes FAA AVIATION NEWS in the
interest of flight safety. The magazine promotes safety in
the air by calling the attention of airmen to current technical, regulatory, and procedural matters affecting the safe
operation of aircraft. Although based on current FAA policy and rule interpretations, all printed material herein are
advisory or informational in nature and should not be
construed to have regulatory effect. The FAA does not
officially endorse any goods, services, materials, or products of manufacturers that may be mentioned. **Certain
details of accidents described herein have been
altered to protect the privacy of those involved.**
    The Office of Management and Budget has
approved the use of funds for the printing of FAA AVIA-
TION NEWS.

SUBSCRIPTION SERVICES

The Superintendent of Documents, U.S. Government
Printing Office, Washington, DC 20402–9371, sells FAA
AVIATION NEWS on subscription. Use the self-mailer
form in the center of this magazine to subscribe. Cost:
$8.00 ($10.00 foreign) for one year; $16.00 ($20.00 for-
eign) for two years. Prices are subject to change by the
Government Printing Office without prior notice.
    Change of Address or Subscription Problems:
**Send your label with correspondence to Sup Doc,
Attn: Chief, Mail List Branch, Mail Stop: SSOM,
Washington, DC 20402–9373.**
    To keep subscription prices down, the Government
Printing Office mails subscribers only one renewal
notice. You can tell how many copies are left in your
subscription by checking the number that follows "ISS-
DUE" on the top line of your mailing label. For example,
when this number is 003, it means you have three
issues left in your subscription, and GPO will send you
a renewal notice. The number 000 means you have
received your last issue. To be sure that your service
continues without interruption, please return your
renewal notice promptly.

FAN SMITH 212J ISSDUE003 R 1
JOHN SMITH
212 MAIN ST
FORESTVILLE, MD 20747

April 1993

FAA *Aviation* News

Volume 32   Number 3

FEATURES

DEPARTMENTS

On the Cover:
*Which type of fuel would you use in this aircraft?
See page 6 for further details.*

On the Back Cover:
*Sun 'n Fun in Lakeland, FL, on April 17 through 24
is not the only aviation event around.
See page 28 for more details.*

Doing the Right Thing

by Roger M. Baker, Jr., *Manager, National Accident Prevention Program Branch*

When I sat down to write this piece, I began to think about why we constantly strive to increase participation in the various events that we call the *National Accident Prevention Program.* I recalled a couple of examples I used in my "pep talks" to the ranks of the Accident Prevention Program Managers (APPM) around the country.

First, the FAA requires commercial aircraft to contain written checklists that the pilots must use. FAA then randomly conducts cockpit en route inspections (surveillance) to be certain that airline pilots use them. However, I like to think that all pilots follow their checklists for two far more important reasons: self-preservation and economy. "Failure to use checklist" has been cited as the cause of accidents and incidents which have resulted in fatalities, serious injuries, and economic losses. But this is no surprise to any of you; everyone knows that they should follow a checklist to keep any of the above from occurring. How do you know that? Throughout your flying career, whether for business or pleasure, you have seen and heard so much evidence—much of it from those safety seminars we send you yellow flyers about—that checklists are a good thing. Checklists have become a part of your everyday flying habits.

Second is the use of seatbelts in aircraft. No one asks anymore whether they should wear a seatbelt in either commercial or private aviation, but we still have some people who question the use in an automobile. Why? We wear seatbelts in aircraft (and use checklists) not because some regulation or inspector tells us to do so but because we have received and processed enough accident prevention

Roger M. Baker, Jr.

information over the years that we know it is the right thing to do.

In the Accident Prevention Program in our own subtle way, we are trying to convince all of you to do the right thing when it comes to weather, fueling, crosswinds, instrument currency, recurrent training, and many other topics. Back in our aviation past we learned that there were good self-preservation and economic reasons for following the FAR and approved procedures. As time has passed we may have forgotten some of those reasons; however, it doesn't matter why we forgot them; what matters is that we take every opportunity to relearn those "right to do" reasons again. Wouldn't it be great if someday we had reduced the fuel exhaustion or "VFR into IMC" accident rate to zero? We can, you know, if we are constantly reminded of the things we already learned that would keep us from having such accidents. That is where the Accident Prevention Program comes in; that is our purpose, from FAA headquarters to the regional offices to the FSDO's.

The FAA has been supporting the Accident Prevention Program for over 30 years with the sponsorship and support of every segment of the aviation industry. Now more than ever in this time of budget shortfalls and belt-tightening, we must rely on government/industry partnerships to keep the Program going.

But, you say, you are not part of any big industry group; what can you do? *You* are the aviation industry, for without you there would be no reason for such an industry to exist. And you can lend a hand in the Accident Prevention Program. Perhaps you can give some

Continued on page 8

Flight Instructor Responsibilities

by Richard Perigo, *FAA Aviation Safety Inspector*

Mr. Perigo is the Accident Prevention Program Manager for the Wichita, Kansas Flight Standards District Office. This article comes from the October 1992 edition of his newsletter, "FSDO Flyer." Although the situations he describes come from his district, the idea of instructors fulfilling their safety responsibilities to students is universal. —***Editor***

As an Accident Prevention Program Manager, I find that I get a very good picture of what is going well in the district and what is NOT going so well. Recently, I dealt with three situations that came under the heading of "not going so well." After reading them I hope you will agree with me that at the heart of the matter is *instructor responsibility.*

Situation Number One

Recently a CFI applicant arrived at the FSDO for his third attempt at obtaining his flight instructor certificate. Now, the third time is supposed to be the charm, but in this case it was not. He returned home with another addition to his already large collection of "pink slips." During a discussion between the examining inspector and the applicant's recommending instructor, the instructor made a statement something to the effect of, "Well, I didn't think he would pass, but I wanted to give him a shot at it." Wait a

minute. That is not what a CFI is in business for—"to give him a shot at it"!!

Let's review what the regulations say about sign-offs for practical tests. First, look at the sign-off for the CFI ride. FAR § 61.187(a) says of the applicant that "his logbook must contain an endorsement by the person who has given him instruction certifying that he has found the applicant competent to pass a practical test..." The regulation then lists six subparagraphs detailing the subjects in which the applicant must be competent. Notice there is no reference to "giving him a shot at it."

Please understand that with the system WE (as in, WE are all in this together) use is one where the CFI trains the applicant, and the FAA spot checks that training with the practical test or checkride, as we call it. When the applicant walks through our door, we consider that applicant to be of CFI competence. All we are doing is making him or her legal to perform the duties of an instructor. The instructor making the applicant's sign-off has said to us, in effect, "This person is a competent flight instructor now—today. Please confirm my finding and issue the proper governmental paperwork so he or she can begin instructing."

This concept does not apply just to the CFI practical test. Please note FAR §§ 61.98, 61.107, and 61.127, which deal with recreational, private, and commercial applicants. Concerning CFI's making endorsements for appli-

cants, the FAR say that the CFI shall certify that he or she "has found the applicant prepared to perform each of those operations competently" as a recreational, private, or commercial pilot. Notice in these endorsements that it does not even speak to the practical test but rather to the applicant's performing at the level of the certificate sought. Again, there is no wording about "giving him a shot at it." In the sign-off, you the CFI are saying that this pilot is competent as a pilot—whether recreational, private, or commercial. All you are asking the examiner to do is confirm your finding and do the paperwork to certificate the person.

Instructor responsibility, or lack thereof, is very apparent when the applicant fails a ride that the instructor expects him or her to fail. The real problem arises when that applicant slips by, and there is rejoicing back at the hangar because the applicant got lucky and passed. Think for a minute about what has just happened. A person, who a certificated flight instructor has concluded is at best questionable and at worst totally incompetent, has been certificated—certificated to share the airspace with you and me, to carry maybe my friends or his or her family in an airplane. In the case of a CFI practical test, that person has been certificated to teach other people how to fly—to share his or her incompetence with unsuspecting students.

This is why CFI responsibility goes to the very heart of aviation safety.

Situation Number Two

I recently had a conversation with a student pilot who had gotten lost as he "slipped the surly bonds of earth" over Kansas. It seems that he had carefully planned his solo cross-country route, plotting each line on the chart, marking off time-distance ticks, highlighting points of interest and things to avoid. He arrived at the airport with a chart that closely resembled a work of art. His regular instructor was on vacation at the time, and by previous arrangement, another very experienced CFI was to meet him and review his flight planning and sign him off in accordance with the FAR. During the review the instructor noticed that the student had plotted one leg of the course near a restricted area. The instructor advised that it would be better if the student gave that area a little wider berth. He recommended that the student separate that leg into two shorter legs by picking up a prominent road, follow that road to a rather large town, pick up an interstate highway at that town and follow the interstate, thus missing the restricted area by a very safe margin. The student agreed that this was the wisdom of Solomon and asked about replanning and replotting the flight on his chart. The instructor told the student something to the effect that since it was not a very large deviation and the road to be followed was very prominent it was not necessary to redraw all those lines on the chart and redo the calculations. All the student had to do was just follow the road.

As you can probably guess, the very prominent road to you or me proved not to be so prominent to the low-time student. The result was that the student found himself with no road to follow and no heading to fly. So, what's the point? Students are students because they lack the experience and skills. When they get the experience and skills, we call them pilots. What seems simple to the experienced instructor can seem like calculus to the student pilot. What is more, student

Is the student really ready to go it alone? It is the flight instructor's responsibility to be sure.

pilots do not always step up and say, "Gee, I don't understand that." This is especially true when they are dealing with a new or unfamiliar instructor. But most importantly, there is a reason that we have students turn a perfectly good chart into something that looks like a cross between modern art and a flight log for the last moon shot. It ensures that the student understands and has available all that he or she needs to make the flight safely. The instructor is *responsible* for making sure that happens.

Do you think the student in this situation really "got himself lost?" It seems like he had some help.

Situation Number Three

Another lost student on his solo cross-country. This one was an "invader" from the east—Missouri, to be exact. Having evaded our eastern front defenses, he headed straight for his designated target airport. The only problem was he ran out of sectional chart about 40 miles out and began using—what his instructor said would be okay—a WAC chart. You know the WAC. It is the wallpaper of choice for at least one wall of almost every fixed base operator in America. Now, I realize that nowhere in the FAR can it be found that a student must use a sectional chart. Nor can it be found that a student cannot use a WAC chart. I

guess the regs say nothing about using a Texaco road map either. (Come to think of it, I know a few folks who swear by them, but that's another story!)

Really, did the instructor fulfill his *responsibility* to the student when he said that a WAC would be okay? I know if you or I can get to within 40 miles of an airport and have a relatively good chart with us, we can find that airport. But, again, a student does not have the benefit of our experience. Remember, that's why we call them students. The CFI business—which, hopefully, is more a love than a business—is one of real responsibility.

But lest I close on a negative note, let me quickly add that in the last two situations, the students did exactly what they were supposed to do when they had trouble. They called and asked for help before they got into really bad trouble. There were no low-fuel situations, no airspace violations, and no near misses. The flight service people responded with the appropriate steer (DF rather Hereford or Angus), and the students were reoriented and on their way. Well done to the instructors who taught them to ask for help and how to ask for it. In that respect the instructors fulfilled their responsibilities to their students as they should have.   ■

Aviation Sign Language

by Dean Chamberlain, *Associate Editor*

For those airmen who have not seen a recent copy of the FAA's *Airman's Information Manual* (AIM), the good news is that part of it is now printed in color. The better news is that some of the color illustrates the new standardized airport signs for both pilots and ground personnel. The best news is that you have plenty of time to learn about the new signs before they go into effect.

FAR Part 139 airports must have the new signs installed by January 1, 1994. (FAR Part 139 airports are those land airports that serve scheduled or nonscheduled air carrier passenger operations that use aircraft with more than 30 passenger seats.) However, some of these airports started installing the new signs last summer. Because of the possibility of this on-going installation process, flight and ground personnel may find a mixture of old and new styles of signs at some FAR Part 139 airports between now and the end of 1993. As part of the sign installation some airports will be redesignating taxiways. Therefore, it is particularly important to use the latest airport diagram and have the latest NOTAM's and ATIS information when taxiing.

Although non-FAR Part 139 airports are not required to comply with the new sign format, many will probably install the new sign format as older signs are replaced. To acceler-

ate the installation of signs at these airports the FAA is developing a standard for retroreflective signs. These signs will appear to be the same as the ones being installed on the FAR Part 139 airports, but will not be lighted. Several state aviation agencies have expressed interest in assisting in the installation of the new signs at these airports. However, it is conceivable that a combination of the old and new signs could exist for many years at non-FAR Part 139 airports.

The new signs are explained in both FAA Advisory Circular (AC) 150/5340–18 (Standards for Airport Sign Systems), and paragraph 2–23, (Airport Signs) of the AIM. Both the AC and the AIM include color examples of the five new types of signs. Ordering information is provided below.

The first new type provides MANDATORY information. These RED SIGNS with WHITE INSCRIPTIONS may mark a runway holding position or other critical operating area, or aircraft prohibited areas.

The second type shows LOCATION. The signs will identify the taxiway or runway on which your aircraft is located. The taxiway and runway signs have YELLOW INSCRIPTIONS on a BLACK BACKGROUND with a YELLOW BORDER. Two other location signs may be seen as you exit a runway or clear an ILS critical area.

The runway boundary and ILS critical area boundary signs have BLACK INSCRIPTIONS depicting the pavement markings on YELLOW BACKGROUNDS. The runway boundary and ILS signs show you when you are clear of these areas. DIRECTIONAL signs are the third type. These YELLOW signs with BLACK INSCRIPTIONS use arrows to show the direction to various taxiways. If a sign contains more than one message, the messages are divided by a vertical message divider. Groups of signs are read from left to straight ahead to right. When a location sign is located in the array all signs for turns to the left will be located to the left of the location sign while signs for straight ahead or turns to the right will be to the right of the location sign. If it is just a simple intersection, i.e. one crossing taxiway, the location sign may be located to the left of the direction sign. Normally the direction signs will be located on the left side of the taxiway before an intersection. Runway exit signs will be located prior to and on the same side as the exit.

The fourth type of new sign shows direction to specific DESTINATIONS such as runways, terminals, FBO's, specific types of operating areas and other such locations. These YELLOW SIGNS with BLACK LEGENDS show direction several ways. An abbreviation (minimum of three letters) for the

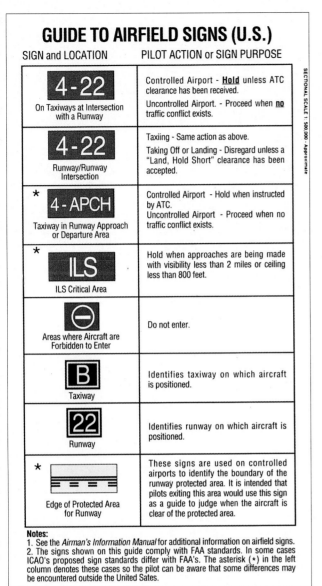

GUIDE TO AIRFIELD SIGNS (U.S.)

SIGN and LOCATION	PILOT ACTION or SIGN PURPOSE
4-22 On Taxiways at Intersection with a Runway	Controlled Airport - **Hold** unless ATC clearance has been received. Uncontrolled Airport. - Proceed when **no** traffic conflict exists.
4-22 Runway/Runway Intersection	Taxiing - Same action as above. Taking Off or Landing - Disregard unless a "Land, Hold Short" clearance has been accepted.
* **4-APCH** Taxiway in Runway Approach or Departure Area	Controlled Airport - Hold when instructed by ATC. Uncontrolled Airport - Proceed when no traffic conflict exists.
* **ILS** ILS Critical Area	Hold when approaches are being made with visibility less than 2 miles or ceiling less than 800 feet.
⊖ Areas where Aircraft are Forbidden to Enter	Do not enter.
B Taxiway	Identifies taxiway on which aircraft is positioned.
22 Runway	Identifies runway on which aircraft is positioned.
* Edge of Protected Area for Runway	These signs are used on controlled airports to identify the boundary of the runway protected area. It is intended that pilots exiting this area would use this sign as a guide to judge when the aircraft is clear of the protected area.

Notes:
1. See the *Airman's Information Manual* for additional information on airfield signs.
2. The signs shown on this guide comply with FAA standards. In some cases ICAO's proposed sign standards differ with FAA's. The asterisk (*) in the left column denotes these cases so the pilot can be aware that some differences may be encountered outside the United Sates.

SECTIONAL SCALE 1: 500,000 - Approximate

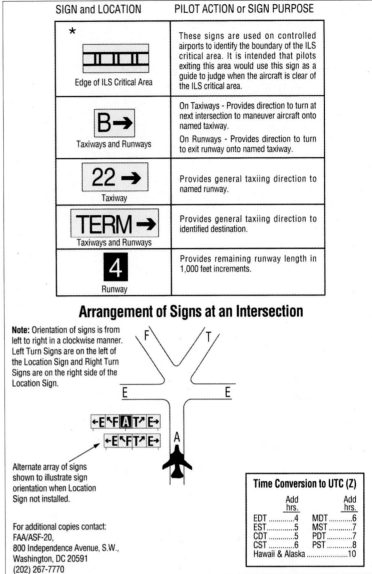

SIGN and LOCATION	PILOT ACTION or SIGN PURPOSE
* Edge of ILS Critical Area	These signs are used on controlled airports to identify the boundary of the ILS critical area. It is intended that pilots exiting this area would use this sign as a guide to judge when the aircraft is clear of the ILS critical area.
B→ Taxiways and Runways	On Taxiways - Provides direction to turn at next intersection to maneuver aircraft onto named taxiway. On Runways - Provides direction to turn to exit runway onto named taxiway.
22 → Taxiway	Provides general taxiing direction to named runway.
TERM → Taxiways and Runways	Provides general taxiing direction to identified destination.
4 Runway	Provides remaining runway length in 1,000 feet increments.

Arrangement of Signs at an Intersection

Note: Orientation of signs is from left to right in a clockwise manner. Left Turn Signs are on the left of the Location Sign and Right Turn Signs are on the right side of the Location Sign.

Alternate array of signs shown to illustrate sign orientation when Location Sign not installed.

For additional copies contact:
FAA/ASF-20,
800 Independence Avenue, S.W.,
Washington, DC 20591
(202) 267-7770

Time Conversion to UTC (Z)			
	Add hrs.		Add hrs.
EDT	4	MDT	6
EST	5	MST	7
CDT	5	PDT	7
CST	6	PST	8
Hawaii & Alaska			10

Although slightly larger than shown here, the "Guide to Airfield Signs" (U.S.) is available from your local APPM and is a handy reference for the new signage.

---

area with a directional arrow may be used. If two areas share the same direction such as two runways, the runway numbers will be separated by a dot. A directional arrow would then point in the common direction. If a sign shows separate routes for different locations, the information will be separated by a vertical black message divider line.

The last of the new standardized signs shows RUNWAY DISTANCE REMAINING. Although these signs are not required by FAR Part 139, many airports are installing them. The signs have a BLACK BACKGROUND with WHITE NUMERALS and may be installed on one or both sides of a runway. The signs indicate the remaining runway distance in thousands of feet with the last sign, showing the numeral 1, at least 950 feet from the end of the runway.

We have only shown a few of the new signage here. To make sure you are up on "the signs of the time," get a copy of the AC or AIM. A busy airport is no place to lose your way. ■

Copies of AC 150/5340-18 are available from Department of Transportation, *M-484.1, Distribution Requirements Section, Washington, DC 20590. Copies of the AIM can be purchased from the Superintendent of Documents, U.S. Government Printing Office, Washington, DC 20402. Telephone number (202) 783-3238. The AIM stock number is 750-001-00000-9.) Contact your local Accident Prevention Program Manager (APPM) to view a 25-minute videotape called "Aircraft Surface Movement—What every pilot should know about airport markings, lighting, and signs." You can also obtain copies of the reference card above called "Guide to Airfield Signs (U.S.)" from your APPM. And remember, at towered airports you can still ask ATC for progressive taxiing instructions.* **—Editor**

Misfueling of Aircraft

by Larry Craig, *Accident Prevention Program Manager, Lincoln, NE*

No, this is not a story about a new way to harvest corn in the midwest. Just about the time we thought we had pretty well solved the problem of misfueling aircraft, "Murphy's Law" strikes again.

The Piper PA 31–350 (*Navajo*) in the photograph had just taken off and was about a quarter of a mile off the end of the runway when both engines quit. Fortunately, the pilot was able to set it down in the cornfield. There were no injuries to the pilot or passengers.

Now, only two quick reasons come to mind when both engines on a piston-powered aircraft quit running: (1) no fuel, or (2) misfueled with jet fuel. In this case, the aircraft was misfueled with jet fuel. As I said, if there is a way for "Old Murph" to strike, he will, although in this case Old Murph had to work very hard to strike. So, how did the *Navajo* get fueled with jet fuel? It was not that easy, as you will see.

The story begins with the company that operated the *Navajo*. The company had previously owned a Piper PA–31T, a *Cheyenne*, with turbine engines that used jet fuel. Then the line person who normally fueled the *Cheyenne* quit the FBO. While this person was gone, the company sold the *Cheyenne* and bought the *Navajo* which was a piston-powered airplane that did not use jet fuel. However, the company had transferred the *Cheyenne*'s tail number to the *Navajo* and had painted the *Navajo* to look like the *Cheyenne*. Then the line person who used to fuel the *Cheyenne* returned to work for the FBO again. Soon after, the line person spotted a fuel ticket (You can see this coming, right?) with the *Cheyenne*'s old tail number on it, and fueled the *Navajo* with jet fuel. But this is only part of the story. Sometimes Old Murph really has to work at causing an accident. In this case the *Navajo* was equipped with jet-fuel-lockout devices and the jet-fuel truck was equipped with a flared jet-fuel nozzle. When FAA inspectors asked the line person how in the world was he able to get jet fuel in the *Navajo*, he replied, "Well, it took a long time."

The next question is, "Why didn't the pilot catch the misfueling during his preflight?" Obviously he did not. But then, how many of us would have checked for jet fuel during an early morning preflight, especially when the aircraft was equipped with jet-fuel-lockout devices. The question is how can similar misfueling accidents be prevented? Although, as this accident proves, there may be no absolute foolproof way of preventing an aircraft misfueling accident if Old Murph decides to intervene, the following ideas may reduce the risk of misfueling.

First, the FBO must ensure that line personnel are trained to recognize the different types of aircraft they may refuel and to know what type of fuel each requires. A rule should be made that if there is any doubt as to the proper type of fuel needed for an aircraft, the line person should wait and ask the pilot what type of fuel is required. Personnel writing up the fuel request must ensure that the proper type of fuel and desired quantity is listed correctly on the refueling order. Then the line person must ensure that clean, pure fuel of the correct type is put in the aircraft. Finally, the line person must accurately record both the type and quantity of fuel put in the aircraft on the refueling order.

The pilot in command (PIC) has the ultimate responsibility of ensuring the proper fuel was used to refuel the aircraft. If possible, the PIC should watch the aircraft being refueled. If the pilot can not be present during refueling, the pilot should closely check the fuel receipt for the type of fuel put in the aircraft and, if possible, verify with the line department that the proper type of fuel was put in the aircraft. Then the pilot should do a careful preflight.

Each aircraft fuel-filler port should be marked with the proper type of fuel required. There are placards available to put around or near fuel ports that tell what type of fuel the aircraft uses. If there is any chance of the aircraft being confused with an aircraft that uses jet fuel, jet-fuel-lockout devices should be installed on the fuel ports, especially if the aircraft is marked as a "turbo" aircraft. Since some line personnel may think "turbo" in an aircraft name means the aircraft is a turbine-powered aircraft that uses jet fuel, you might consider painting out the word "turbo" to avoid any possible confusion. But as this accident points out, even if the aircraft has jet-fuel-lockout devices and the jet-fuel truck has the proper jet-fuel nozzle, it is still possible for someone with the best of intentions to misfuel the aircraft. As this story points out, it was difficult but not impossible for the line person to misfuel the *Navajo*. So how do you prevent such an accident?

The PIC must check the tanks and sumps for fuel contamination during every preflight. Only by knowing the quantity, quality, and type of fuel on board can the PIC avoid a misfueling accident.

For additional information about how to avoid misfueling accidents, contact your local FAA Accident Prevention Program Manager at your local Flight Standards District Office. ∎

Many aircraft display decals next to their fueling port to eliminate the question of which fuel to use. All the line person has to do is match the color and legend with the design on the fuel pumps and nozzles. (see examples above)

How to detect misfueling problems.

by Dean Chamberlain, *Associate Editor*

Misfueling accidents are preventable. The means are simple: Do not let someone put the wrong fuel in your aircraft. If they do, you must detect the misfueling before takeoff. But if this is so simple, why do pilots continue to takeoff with the wrong fuel on board? According to National Transportation Safety Board (NTSB) statistics of fuel related problems in small general aviation aircraft for a recent five-year period, 21 general aviation aircraft were involved in accidents in which NTSB listed improper fueling as a finding. Four of the accidents involved misfueling piston-powered aircraft with JET A fuel. Three of the four aircraft were Piper PA 31–350 *Navajos*. This statistic indicates that pilots flying *Navajos* should be particularly careful when refueling. Although NTSB did not list improper fueling as a probable cause in all 21 accidents, in some cases the cause could not be determined and in other cases the NTSB listed one or more of its other findings. The accident investigations also revealed a wide-range of fuel related problems. Automotive gasoline was mentioned in 12 of the accidents. In most of the cases, the autogas was being used without an STC. In one case, the pilot had been warned by his mechanic not to use autogas. In another case, the pilot operating handbook said not to use autogas. In addition to the problems of JET A misfueling and the use of autogas without a STC, the NTSB report's narrative summary listed other such fuel problems as water contamination, old fuel, ice, mixed fuels, borrowed fuel, and in one case, it reported a carburetor float absorbed enough autogas to malfunction.

So what can be done to prevent such accidents? How can new, and not so new pilots, avoid a fuel-related accident?

Since safety starts with the pilot in command (PIC), each pilot, especially renter pilots, must know what type of fuel or fuels his or her aircraft is approved to use. (The reason we said types of fuel is some aircraft may be approved for more than one grade of fuel in case the primary fuel is not available.) The aircraft's pilot operating handbook (POH), aircraft flight manual (AFM), or pilot operating manual lists what type or types of fuel are approved for use in the aircraft.

Some aircraft use automobile gasoline. They have a Supplemental Type Certificate (STC) approving the use of certain types of automotive gasoline. So it is important to know what types of fuel are used in a given aircraft, not only for your own benefit, but also for the person refueling the aircraft.

The Line Personnel

Like pilots, people refueling aircraft have varying levels of experience. As a result, you cannot be sure the person refueling your aircraft knows what type fuel you want or need in your aircraft. As PIC, you must ensure the person refueling your aircraft puts in the correct fuel. An interesting (and true) anecdote illustrates that safety is no accident. At an FBO the line person put avgas in a turbine-powered Beechcraft *King Air* because it had propellers. Fortunately, someone saw what was being done and stopped the fueling before any major damage was done. Later, that same line person had to refuel a World War II fighter. After having made one mistake involving a big "prop" plane, the line person did not want to make the same mistake twice, so he asked the pilot if he wanted jet fuel. The pilot thought the question was a big joke, so he said, "Yes." The line person filled the aircraft with Jet A. The moral of the story is not every new refueler knows what type of fuel every aircraft uses and if that conscientious person asks you what type of fuel you want, do not jokingly tell him or her to fill your aircraft with the wrong fuel. Like the pilot in this example, you might get what you asked for. It could be a very expensive and even fatal joke on you.

The Preflight and the PIC

Preventing someone from putting the wrong type of fuel in your aircraft is only half of the battle against misfueling. The other half is not taking off with the wrong fuel on board. The only way to win the second half of the battle is for every PIC to do a "carefuel" preflight before every flight to check for the proper fuel.

The following are some "helpfuel" hints. First, as one petroleum industry bulletin says, "Aviation fuels should be 'clear and bright.'" Clear means being free of sediment or emulsion. Bright refers to the fluorescent appearance of fuel without any haze or cloudiness that could be caused by water droplets.

Color Test

Once a pilot has done an initial "clear and bright" check, the three common preflight fuel checks available to pilots are the color, smell, and feel tests. Avgas is color coded by octane grade: 80/87 red, 100 green, and 100LL blue. So the first avgas color test is looking for the correct color for the grade being used. Although color is an important test, the lack of color may be a more important color test. The explanation could be as simple as the approved use of autogas. If not, the lack of color could be mean mixed avgas grades. (If avgas grades have been mixed, check with your mechanic before flight.) Another more deadly explanation is that jet fuel, which is colorless or sometimes straw-colored, is in the aircraft. If jet fuel is on board, again check with your mechanic. Do not try to fly the aircraft. And according to one industry expert, a fuel sample that has been left out in the sun for a period of time can fade.

But in most cases, a colorless avgas sample probably only indicates the presence of aviation's most common fuel contaminate: water. If so, you should continue to take samples until you get a pure, color-coded fuel sample. If you have any doubts about hav-ing a good sample, check with your mechanic.

Smell Test

In addition to color, you can also do a "smell" test. Gasoline smells different from kerosene-based jet fuel, which has a very distinct smell. The best way to learn how to tell the difference is to smell pure samples of each.

Feel Test

Feel is the third common fuel test. Kerosene-based jet fuel has a more oily feel than gasoline. Again, the best way to develop a "feel" for the various fuels is to feel samples of each.

Paper Test

There is a "paper test" you can use to tell avgas from jet fuel. If you put a drop of avgas and a drop of jet fuel near it on a piece of clean, white paper, the gasoline will quickly evaporate and disappear. The oily and more slowly evaporating jet fuel will leave what can best be described as a halo spot on the paper as the fuel evaporates. Again, a test using pure samples is the best way to "see" how this test works.

You can learn more about fuel and fuel testing by going to your local FBO or instructor and talking with him or her about fuel. Another practical method is to buy some fuel samples from your FBO and experimenting. Try mixing various combinations of fuels and water to see how they look, smell, and feel. You should then be able to recognize a misfueling or water contamination problem if you ever have one. (If you do this at home or on the ramp, again observe proper disposal methods.)

For additional information on misfueling, you can contact your FAA Accident Prevention Program Manager (APPM) at your local Flight Standards District Office (FSDO)and ask to see a video entitled, "Basic Fuel Management." Remember accident prevention starts with a safe flight. And a safe flight starts with you. **—Editor**

Doing the Right Thing
Continued from page 1

of your time (precious, we know) to assist in a program or convince your corporation to support a safety seminar or donate a meeting room. Maybe you can help another pilot relearn some basic airmanship. Maybe you can become an Accident Prevention Program Counsellor—a major commitment of your time and energy, but the rewards are high.

In 1992 the Accident Prevention Program participated in nearly 14,000 safety seminars and clinics which were attended by more than 880,000 people, a *63% increase over the attendance from the year before.* Our approximately 100 FAA personnel dedicated full time to the Accident Prevention Program didn't increase those numbers alone. Your colleagues in aviation volunteered at every opportunity to help. I and they would encourage each one of you to volunteer to help in your own way.

It's hard to measure our success, but we know that over the years we have been successful. The accident rates have declined over the past 10 years, and participation in the Accident Prevention Program has increased. We believe there is a direct correlation. And that correlation may have come from your attendance at a safety seminar; from your watching a safety video or slide/tape presentation; from your reading an Accident Prevention newsletter, safety pamphlet, *FAA Aviation News,* or just a clever safety sign; from your being counselled by a volunteer; from your dialing up an electronic bulletin board; or by your taking a tour of an air traffic facility—all brought to you in some way by the Accident Prevention Program.

We could all make aviation even safer if we would just pass the word to one other pilot to join us in participating in Accident Prevention Program Activities. Bring an airman friend to the next meeting and help him or her to remember "the right things to do."

See you at a seminar! ∎

Our acknowledgement to film maker Spike Lee for the 1989 film "Do the Right Thing," which suggested this article's title. **—Editor**

Medical Stuff

"White Coat Hypertension" Nearly Grounds an Aviator's Career

by Jeffrey L. Nelson

It all started the day I had my first elevated blood pressure reading during my annual Air Force physical. From that day forward, the nerve impulse in my brain triggered a nervous impulse in my stomach every time this event would show up on the schedule. No other requirement of my military career could prompt the sweaty-palmed, cold-sweat, gut-tumbling reaction that developed when I awoke on "P day" (physical day)—because suddenly the synaptic connection had been formed.

My career, my enjoyment, and, indeed, my paycheck relied on this one simple medical procedure. And unlike flying an aircraft, which I had no problem flying by the numbers, trying to keep my blood pressure within the required numbers while sitting in the doctor's office became a real challenge.

White coat hypertension had reared its head and by the second year it was getting me anxious.

The anxiety over this one event just kept festering inside me. I would rather face a no-notice checkride in a 40-knot crosswind than get my annual checkup. I would start thinking about the dreaded blood pressure cuff the day before, then the week before, and eventually weeks before the event. I could get nervous about my physical, and it wouldn't really have any effect on my vision or hearing or chest x-ray. But the free-flowing adrenaline could surely fire up the ol' blood pressure, and I knew it but remained unable to control it.

I would always pass my physicals, but not until a follow-up five day blood pressure check confirmed that my skyrocketing pressure on the day of my physical was not the norm. This was the real frustration—I was in my mid-twenties, a paragon of health, yet unable to control a bodily condition because my mind was overriding the event.

The situation has improved over the years, but I know a great many pilots who face this same malady once or twice a year as their medical expiration date rolls near. I think the impetus behind the problem is twofold.

First, aviation is one of a few professions that requires medical certification in order to perform the job. Lose your medical and you lose your livelihood. That in itself creates a lot of pressure.

Second, pilots tend to be "controllers"—most pilot personality inventories reveal that pilots are strong-willed leaders who like to be in charge. They like to be in control of day-to-day situations, and that trait is denied when a pilot walks into the doctor's office. Now someone else is in control, not only of the event, but of the pilot's future as well.

I share this experience merely as a reminder for AME's. Any medical reading that does not fit into the established parameters should not be overlooked. There are factors that can cause an elevated blood pressure reading, and I'm not about to lecture to the professionals. But there is a factor that should be included in the list of excesses—i.e., salt, fat, and alcohol—and that is anxiety. It is easy to have an overabundance of anxiety when your career is on the line. I'm just thankful for the AME's who have the patience and understanding regarding this one day of hypertension a year.

There's an axiom for pilots who suffer from this syndrome—what goes up one day will probably come down the next, as long as they're not sitting in that darn doctor's office! ∎

Any episode of elevated blood pressure should be monitored by your AME. Mr. Nelson is a commercial pilot who formerly flew with the airlines. He is the Editor of the aviation safety newsletter, The Airworthy Aviator, which is published monthly by Aeromed Publications, 7900 Xerxes Ave. S., Suite 730, Minneapolis, MN 55431–1103. This article originally appeared in the Winter 1992 issue of The Federal Air Surgeon's Medical Bulletin, published by FAA's Civil Aeromedical Institute (CAMI). **—Editor**

TAKING CHARGE OF THE MACHINE

by Brian Jacobson

When it comes to responsibility for aircraft airworthiness, the buck stops with the pilot

Although many of us tend to regard our aircraft as living beings, they are, in truth, machines. They require regular maintenance like any other machine or piece of equipment. The FAR are quite explicit about how maintenance is to be performed and the time limits allowed for its completion.

The responsibility for assuring compliance with maintenance regulations rests on several shoulders. Traditionally, the *owner or operator* of an aircraft has the primary responsibility for maintaining his or her aircraft in an airworthy condition. The owner/operator must have the prescribed inspections completed, ensure that maintenance personnel make appropriate entries in records, and have any inoperative instrument or item of equipment repaired.

The *mechanic* making repairs or conducting an inspection must meet certain quality standards and must make required entries in the maintenance records of the aircraft before returning it to service.

Finally, FAR § 91.7 requires the *pilot in command* to determine whether the aircraft is airworthy before flying it.

If a particular airplane were never flown, it would not matter if it were in airworthy condition or not. However, once a pilot approaches that aircraft with the intention of flying it, that pilot must fulfill the requirements of FAR § 91.7, which states, in part, "The pilot in command of a civil aircraft is responsible for determining whether that aircraft is in condition for safe flight."

Therefore, while the FAR delegate airworthiness requirements to several parties, the ultimate responsibility for airworthiness rests squarely on the shoulders of the pilot in command. Unfortunately, not all pilots meet that responsibility. For example, I recently asked a pilot why he did not do a preflight when he came to pick up his aircraft after an annual inspection. He said it was not necessary because the mechanic who completed the inspection was better qualified than he is, and he expected that there was nothing wrong with the airplane. It never occurred to him that the mechanic who had worked on the machine may have made a mistake somewhere along the line.

Last Resort

The accident files show that mechanical malfunctions immediately after scheduled or unscheduled maintenance do occur more often than we would like to believe. A friend of mine was able to preclude such an occurrence by doing a thorough preflight after an annual inspection. She discovered that the mechanic had not replaced the oil in the engine. Had her preflight been hasty or nonexistent, the engine would have seized shortly after she applied full power. She was rightfully upset and let the mechanic know it. Her own inspection saved her from experiencing a very dangerous situation. Another friend was not so fortunate. She had a complete electrical failure at night after maintenance was done on her aircraft's alternator. Several years ago, I ferried a Cessna 150 to a mechanic for a pre-purchase inspection. When the cowling was removed, we found a half-inch-drive ratchet resting on top of the engine. There are other stories of mechanics not safety-wiring oil plugs, leaving cotter pins out of wheel nuts, leaving jack pads attached to the aircraft, tying cable bundles to a vacuum line, thereby constricting the line, and rigging ailerons backwards after a cable change.

Your mechanic is not infallible. He or she is human and can make mistakes, too.

With this in mind, I always ask the mechanic to accompany me during a preflight after maintenance. If I should spot something that does not look right, the mechanic can explain the apparent anomaly or make repairs.

Sometimes, the mechanic finds something missed earlier, before I see it.

Even if there is nothing to be found, having the mechanic accompany you on the preflight inspection will enable you to learn more about your aircraft. My experience has been that mechanics enjoy the opportunity to explain the workings of airplanes and their systems to customers.

Check the Records

Before flying an aircraft you are unfamiliar with, assure yourself that the required maintenance is complete and up to date. Last summer, while pursuing a purchase of a Cessna 172, I ran across two airplanes that had not been inspected within the last 12 months. Neither owner told me his airplane was not airworthy, and both had flown their airplanes recently. One of the airplanes was two years out of annual. When I asked the owner why it had been three years since the last annual, he explained that he had been "ripped off" by the mechanic who had done the last inspection and would not allow that to happen again. The owner of the other airplane, which was six months out of annual, claimed the inspection had been done but not recorded in the logs.

Potential Disaster

Many pilots do not preflight their airplanes or only do cursory walka-

Doing a careful preflight before each flight could avoid some unpleasant surprises once you get into the air.

rounds. There is a potential for disaster here. One airplane I fly is kept in a community hangar where each aircraft owner may move others to get one airplane out. It is possible that someone could do some damage to another airplane and not say anything about it. If I were to fly that aircraft without preflighting it, I would be inviting Murphy to knock on my cockpit door. Good preflights can also alert you to problems that require immediate attention, or discrepancies that could become problems in flight. If you find a discrepancy during a preflight, have a mechanic look at it.

Not long ago, I was preflighting a Cessna *Citation* and noticed that the oil in one of the engines was almost black. Jet engine oil is usually clear or straw-colored and seldom changes color very much. Suspecting a serious engine problem, I grounded the airplane and sought out a mechanic. It turned out that one of the engine's main bearings had "coked," contaminating the oil in the process. The engine had to be disassembled and the bearing replaced. That engine would have failed in the next several hours, had it been flown in that condition.

Another point to be made regarding preflight inspections is that one time around the airplane at the beginning of the day is not enough. At the very least, you should walk around the aircraft before subsequent takeoffs. Once, a pilot taxied his *Cherokee* into the tail of my Cessna 310. While he was inside looking for me, I was outside getting ready to leave. Had I not walked around the airplane, I might have taken off without knowing about the damage done to the tail section.

Fuel Checks

If you are not present when your airplane is refueled, make doubly sure you check the fuel and security of the caps. If jet fuel is put into a piston engine airplane's tanks, the engine will most likely quit shortly after takeoff. Jet

Oil is as important to the engine as fuel. Make sure the oil level and coloration are correct for your aircraft.

fuel is clear and has a thick, oily touch and smell. The best way to avoid a mixup in fuels is to stand by the airplane while servicing is in progress. Check the decals on the fuel truck and drain the airplane's sumps. Check the color and smell of the fuel samples. Being there during refueling will prevent the need for a time-consuming draining and cleaning of the tanks, to say nothing of the mess you would have if you took off with jet fuel in the tanks and had a forced landing just off the airport. [See the article on page 6 for detailed information on misfueling—Editor]

Several times a year, we hear stories of airplanes that had not been flown for long periods of time being involved in mishaps and, too often, fatal accidents. A lot of the crashes are caused by fuel contamination or lack of maintenance. I remember a pilot who showed me an aircraft he had just purchased. He boasted about the low-time engine and how it would last him years and years. A month later, he was doing a top overhaul because of a lack of compression in most of the cylinders. Piston engines that are not flown regularly will deteriorate. Cylinder walls can rust from lack of use, causing excessive ring and cylinder wear when put back to work. This particular engine was overhauled 10 years

before and had only been flown 50 hours since. Most engine operating manuals provide recommendations that should be followed if an airplane is not flown for long periods of time.

If you must fly an airplane that has not been flown for a long time, get a mechanic to inspect it and sign off the logs. The mechanic will check the fuel system for water or other contaminants and the airframe for control continuity, bird nests and other things that might present a problem during flight. If you are not a licensed mechanic, do not do this yourself. There are many reports of pilots who drained fuel until they were satisfied there was no more water, only to have the engine quit on takeoff.

Complying with AD's

Another thing to be aware of in any aircraft is compliance with applicable airworthiness directives (AD). AD's can be issued at any time and may ground an aircraft immediately or at some point in the future. Several months ago, a Cessna 180 took off from my home airport only to crash just off the airport property. While the official word is not out yet, it is possible the AD which affects most Cessna seat rails was overlooked. Investigators are checking the possibility that the seat

had not latched and slid backwards during the takeoff.

Mechanics must check AD's during each annual inspection. Some mechanics are more thorough than others when it comes to this tedious job. However, an AD issued against an aircraft or accessory will affect its airworthiness. It becomes the pilot's responsibility if he or she flies an aircraft affected by an AD that has not been complied with in the required time frame. Similarly, if you fly an aircraft after maintenance has been completed but before the appropriate entries have been made in the log books or aircraft records, your aircraft is not airworthy.

As mentioned earlier, the FAR require that a mechanic make the appropriate entries in the aircraft records before returning the aircraft to service. They also require an owner or operator to ensure that those entries have been made. An occasional review of the log books for the aircraft you fly will alert you to maintenance inspections that are coming due. It can also serve as a reminder for altimeter and encoder certification dates and other items that are often forgotten.

Summary

After maintenance has been done, make sure the mechanic has made the necessary entries. Be cautious when dealing with a "hangar queen" or an aircraft that has been sitting for a long period of time. Watch for AD's that affect the types of aircraft you fly. The required work should be accomplished within the time frames set forth in the directives.

Before you fly any aircraft, it is up to you to be certain that it is airworthy. In reality, it is more than just following the rules for the sake of the rules. It is following the rules so that you will have a safe, uneventful flight. ■

This article has been reprinted courtesy of Aviation Safety *magazine. For further subscription information, contact* Aviation Safety, *Subscription Services, P. O. Box 420234, Palm Coast, FL 32142; (800) 829–9162. The cost is $84 a year for 24 issues; $6 for single copies.* —**Editor**

STOP and GO

by Dean Chamberlain, *Associate Editor*

Seen any pink elephants lately? Well, what about pink circles? No, we haven't been off oxygen too long. We are talking about the pink circles (Shown above and officially known as geographical position or control point markings) along the taxiways at the Seattle-Tacoma International Airport as well as some special taxiway lighting and stop bar lighting there. Soon you may be able to see similar markings and lights at other airports around the country. It is all part of an ongoing FAA and industry demonstration project to increase airport safety and airfield operations.

As a result of several low visibility runway incursion accidents at airports in the U.S., the FAA and the aviation industry are testing several visual aids designed to reduce runway incursions during periods of low visibility as part of the FAA's national Runway Incursion Plan. The devices, based upon International Civil Aviation Organization (ICAO) standards, allow aircraft to operate in visibility conditions of 600 feet RVR or less depending upon aircrew certification and equipment. Under the plan, select crews can fly Category IIIb IFR approaches down to RVR 300 conditions. Seattle, the first demonstration airport, has IFR approaches approved down to 300 feet landing visibility.

Advisory Circular (AC) 120–57, "Surface Movement Guidance and Control System (SMGCS)," dated September 4, 1992, contains the requirements to operate in low visibility conditions using SMGCS and the new stop bar lighting plan. The AC provides guidance for airports wanting to operate in visibility conditions of less than 600 feet RVR and for all airports requesting Category III landing authorization. The AC's guidance will apply to all airports conducting operations in visibility conditions of less than 1,200 feet RVR by January 1, 1995.

In concept, when operated by air traffic control (ATC) during visibility conditions of 1,200 feet or less, SMGCS and its stop bars, wig-wag lights, and pink circles will all combine to provide aircrews and ground operators positive ATC guidance and control on select taxiways and runways during low visibility conditions. In addition to the use of special guidance and control lighting, SMGCS also calls for special control point markings to be painted on the taxiways approved for low visibility use. These pink circular numbered markings along the taxiways provide positive ATC control of aircraft and ground vehicles along low-visibility taxiways by providing a means of identifying known locations and holding positions along the route. Yellow, in-pavement lights will also identify the location of the taxiway holding points. Special flashing amber lighting (called Wig-Wags because of its two alternating flashing amber lights) mounted in boxes installed along side the pavement will identify an entrance to an active runway.

Although the special lights, markings, and airport charts will help guide aircraft to and from designated low-visibility runways, the key to SMGCS is its stop bars and their associated lead-on lights. As shown in the illustrations, the lights provide visual confirmation of ATC verbal approval for aircrews and vehicle operators to move onto or to cross a runway in low visibility conditions by turning on and off both the red stop bar lights and the green runway lead-on lights. Located at the instrument landing system (ILS) critical area holding location on illuminated taxiways, red stop bar lights are installed in the pavement across the hold line. The stop bars may also include two elevated edge lights at airports in the snow belt or for cockpit cutoff angle visibility considerations. When the stop bar lights are manually turned off by controllers in the tower, the lead-on lights come on to guide the aircraft onto the runway. The stop bars are reset on automatically after the aircraft crosses a sensor. This prevents a second aircraft from entering the runway without clearance. The stop bar lights confirm ATC instructions for aircraft to hold at the stop bar position by showing illuminated red stop lights to approaching aircraft and vehicles taxiing to the runway. In addition, the green lead-on lights leading from the hold line to the runway centerline will be off.

Figure 1 shows an aircraft, Aircraft 1, holding at the red stop bar lights. The

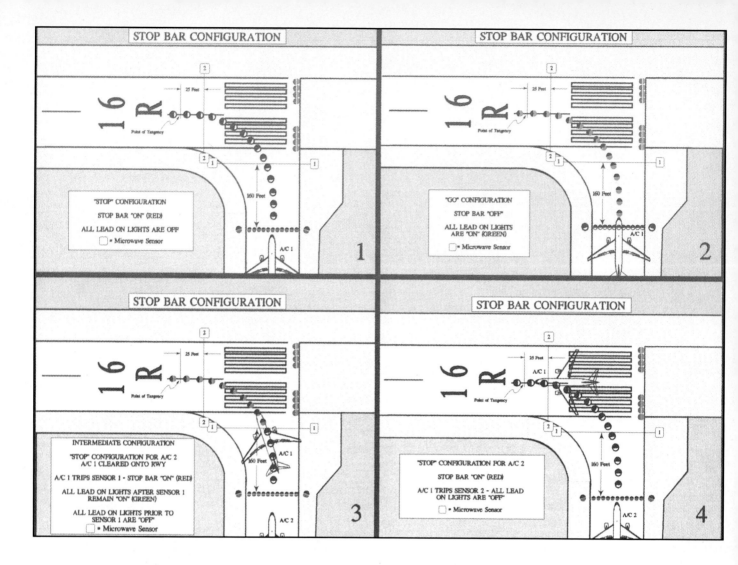

red stop lights across the taxiway are on. The green lead-on lights are off. In Figure 2, the tower has *verbally* cleared Aircraft 1 onto the runway and has manually turned the red stop lights off. All of the green lead-on lights are turned on. The green lead-on lights provide guidance to the runway centerline and confirms the aircraft is cleared to taxi to the centerline. Figure 3 shows Aircraft 1 at an intermediate position. As the aircraft crosses a sensor located at Point 1, the red stop bar lights automatically turn on behind the aircraft, and the green lead-on lights from Point 1 back to the stop bar lights turn off. The green lead-on lights from Point 1 to the runway centerline remain on to guide Aircraft 1 to the centerline. The "on" red stop bar lights now stop Aircraft 2 from taking the runway without ATC approval. The "black hole" left after the green lead-on lights have been turned off by the sensor at Point 1 serves as a reminder to the crew of Aircraft 2 not to

cross the now "on" red stop bar lights. Figure 4 shows Aircraft 1 aligned on the runway centerline. As Aircraft 1 takes its position on the runway centerline, it crosses a sensor at Point 2. The Point 2 sensor then turns off all of the remaining lit green lead-on lights from the centerline back to Point 1. The key safety point in the red stop bar concept is that no pilot or ground operator should taxi/drive over a lit red stop bar. Simply stated, red stop bar lights on—all aircraft/vehicles stop. Once ATC *verbally* clears an aircraft holding at a lit red stop bar onto the runway and turns off the red stop bar lights, the pilot can then follow the now "on" green lead-on lights to the runway centerline. Any questions regarding the meaning of the stop bar system must be resolved with ATC before an aircraft or vehicle moves onto the runway.

Pilots will also see stop bars at intersections which are not to be used for entering a runway. If these intersections

are not part of the published low visibility route, they will remain on and are not controlled by ATC. Some airports are using stop bars in all weather conditions to prevent pilots from taxiing the wrong way on a high-speed exit.

Combined with the other features being tested at Seattle and being developed at three other demonstration airports, SMGCS should reduce the runway incursion problem by providing positive ATC control of and positive position guidance for aircrews and ground operators on designated taxiways and runways during low visibility operations. The overall benefit for everyone will be increased safety and better use of the air transportation system. ∎

For more information, Advisory Circular 150/5340.1G, "Marking of Paved Areas on Airports," is available free from DOT M–443.2, Washington, DC 20590. —Editor

Answers to Quiz: 1–H, 2–F, 3–D, 4–E, 5–G, 6–C, 7–B, 8–A

WAIT...and Balance!

by Bruce Edsten, *Accident Prevention Program Manager, Louisville, Kentucky*

Just for a MOMENT, let me take you by the ARM and talk about aircraft LOADING. . . .

Volumes have been written on the subject of aircraft weight and balance! Just about every book you pick up on the subject of aviation has at least a full chapter on it, and several stand-alone issues have come out as well. Anything that even resembles an Airplane Flight Manual (AFM) for any airplane has an appropriate section, and even if your bird is old enough that no AFM was ever printed, the FAR require that the minimum information necessary to calculate a safe loading situation be on board.

Given all that, everybody ought to be totally familiar with all the possibilities and ramifications of proper and improper observance of weight and balance restrictions, right? Yeah, well, you'd think so, but it apparently doesn't work that way because people keep on wrinkling perfectly good airplanes through dumb loading.

Weight

Let's look at weight first. Most people are pretty well aware that their trusty old bird will actually lift a lot more than the listed gross weight. Somewhere they read that the structure is rated at three-point-something-or-other "G's," and they know that in a 60-degree bank, the wing has to produce lift equal to twice the weight of the airplane in order to maintain level

flight. So, given that, what harm could a teensy little overload do? If that wing will so easily hold up 4,000 pounds, a couple hundred pounds on top of that excessively conservative 2,000 pound max gross ought to be a piece of cake, right? Wrong!

Even a little overweight condition can get you in deep trouble, because the effects are hard to judge and probably cannot be extrapolated from aircraft documents such as the AFM or Pilot's Operating Handbook (POH). For instance, a 10% overweight condition may result in a 10% decrease in performance, but the degradation could be a lot greater. Then, too, the effect may be different for a different performance characteristic. For example, let's just list the factors that will be affected in a negative way by overloading:

Increased stall speed
Increased runway length for takeoff
Increased speed required for takeoff
Decreased rate of climb
Decreased maximum altitude
Decreased range
Degraded controllability and
  maneuverability
Increased approach speed
Increased runway length for landing
Decreased "G" tolerance

To what degree will each be affected? Well, if you are the adventuresome type, you could always get a brightly painted crash helmet and paint "EXPERIMENTAL" on the side of your

trusty old Cessna or Piper. In any case, when you start overloading, whether you mean to or not, you WILL be a test pilot! Then, you can go fly the machine and find out what effect the overload has, but, as they say, if you don't want to hear the answers, don't ask the question. Actually, in this case it's a matter of being prepared for the full range of possible answers!

Balance

Controlling the weight is important to be sure, but if you inadvertently mess up, weight—not balance—is the place. [Intentional overloading of any aircraft is never acceptable.—Editor] Structural integrity is designed into every aircraft to such a degree that many overloads go unnoticed. However, even an airplane that is loaded a very great deal below is maximum allowable gross weight can be totally unsafe to fly if the weight is in the wrong place.

The reason for this is elevator limitations, and it is almost exclusively elevator effectiveness that determines that airplane's center of gravity (CG) limits. For example, the forward CG limit must be established to ensure that the airplane can still be pitched up enough to flare at the minimum approach speed.

So, what will happen if your airplane is loaded too far forward? Let's look at a possible scenario. On takeoff, you notice that the normal application of back pressure does not raise the nose

Check the weight, don't gamble with fate (from April 1971 FAA Aviation News. *Congratulations to Mr. Robert Osborn on his 50 years of aviation safety cartooning.)*

in the normal fashion. "Hmmmmmm," says you, but there is no cause for alarm just yet, since there's still a couple thousand feet of runway ahead. Then, a few seconds later, the nose comes up, albeit a bit sluggishly, and at a few knots more airspeed than usual, but it does come up, and you're safely over the trees and gone.

On final approach to your destination airport, all goes apparently well until very short final. Now, you go for that last bit of nose up to make your customary "squeaker" landing, but the elevator control hits the stops, the nose stays about two degrees down, and you land nosewheel first, followed in rapid succession by the mains. Next is a huge bounce, and another really sharp pitch down, and a second "arrival." If you're lucky, it stops there, and the structural integrity saves your bacon. If this just is NOT your day, the second "arrival" (or third or fourth) could cause you to crunch the nosewheel, wheelbarrow off into the weeds, or simply collapse the whole machine in a heap in the middle of the runway. Uncool.

Bent and broken airplanes aside, most of these situation are survivable, and if the out-of-CG condition is not too bad the only damage may be to the airman's pride. Frequently, the lack of pitch up capability is noticed early on as the aircraft is slowed to pattern speed, or the pilot may simply be

aware of it because of a requirement for excessive "nose up" trim in cruise flight.

Elevators and Balance

Elevators do what they do through aerodynamic lift, of course, and lift is a function of angle of attack and airspeed. The elevator has fixed limits, so the angle of attack can only go to a certain maximum value, but the elevator can be more effective at the same deflection if it is operated at a higher airspeed. That's what happened above on the takeoff roll, right? The nose *eventually* came up as the airspeed got faster.

Of course, you should have paid enough attention to what you were doing so that you never got here in the first place, but now that you're here, and you *know* you have a pitch problem, what can you do about it? Landing at a higher speed may be your only way out. The use of an appropriate flap setting might be useful, too, depending on how flaps affect pitch on your particular airplane. Don't forget that the higher speed may require a flatter approach and will almost certainly require more runway, too!

Aft CG Limits

How about a pitch problem the other way around? This is the situation that really gives me goosebumps, makes the hair stand up on the back

of my neck, and produces that weird tingle at the base of my spine. Out-of-CG-AFT. Scaaaaaaar-eee! Well, I guess we don't need to be overly dramatic, but I have been fortunate (?) enough to have been an in-person observer of this situation and lived to tell about it. Unfortunately, the accident reports are full of accounts of those who did not because these accidents tend to be less survivable.

The aft CG limit is more critical because of the problem of stability. The further aft the CG goes, the less stable we get. Specifically, moving the CG aft will eventually result in an uncontrollable pitch up condition, which results in a stall that cannot be recovered from. The problem, of course, is the elevator. Simply not enough force available to get the nose down.

Once again, the elevator can only produce so much aerodynamic lift, so the aft CG limit has to be established to allow the elevator to do its thing down to and beyond the stall speed. As you will no doubt recall from stall training, the airplane is supposed to pitch down entirely on its own, even with full "up" elevator, upon reaching V_{so} or V_s1. In other words the airplane basically recovers from the stall by itself. This is good! Get that CG a little past the aft limit, and the airplane may need some help, like at least relaxing the back pressure. This is still not too bad. Go a bit further, and a lot more positive, decisive help may be necessary, like full forward elevator. This is NOT good! The next step is the one related above, where all the help available is not enough.

In many cases, this condition will be noticed before you even get in the airplane. The thing may have simply fallen on its tail or at least be looking like it's about to! If you're really lucky, the nose may come up immediately upon the start of the takeoff roll, giving you plenty of time to abort, but it could happen later in the trip down the runway, and the result is frequently disastrous. If there is enough airspeed to fly but not enough for the elevator to produce sufficient lift to hold the nose down, the airplane will lift off, pitch up, and stall back onto the runway.

An Example from Real Life!

As a very junior first officer with a commuter airline, I found myself looking at just about that position one day. The station personnel had produced a manifest which declared that our 19-seater was about two pounds below the 12,499-pound max gross and right up against the aft CG limit. Normally, this thing would leap into the air after about 1,200–1,500 feet of ground roll, but even taxiing out, it didn't feel right. We were so heavily loaded that the gear was bottoming out as we rolled over each of the expansion joints in the ramp!

Fortunately, the runway 35 we had before us was over 11,000 feet long, so we would have about 10 times what we needed (normally), and it's slightly downhill, too. Tower said go, so we stood up all the handles, shouted "Hi-yo Silver," and waited. Still didn't have flying speed passing the 5,000-foot marker, and I knew we were in trouble. (Bet you can't guess whose leg it was, can you?) Eventually, the airspeed got to the appropriate point, and I started back with the elevator, whereupon the nose popped up like a cork! I jammed the wheel full forward and hollered, "Trim!" The Captain sez, "Which way?" I said, "Down!" He sez, "How much?" I said, "All of it!" and we whistled off the end of the runway some two miles plus from brake release, about 50 feet up, and about a knot and a half above V_{mc}!

Happily, there are not a lot of obstacles close to that airport, and the route to the next stop was mostly over water, but we still had a problem! How slow can we get this thing before we run out of elevator? Some experimentation (We are now test pilots, remember?) showed that we would probably be okay as long as we landed about 30 knots fast, which is just what we did. I have no idea how far over gross we were or how far out of CG, but it was plenty! Basically, I was told not to worry about it, but I did, with ample justification.

AIRCRAFT
WEIGHT AND BALANCE

"NO ROOM FOR ERROR"

A year later, the company's policy caught up with it in St. Croix, U.S. Virgin Islands, when an almost identical situation produced a crash that killed the first officer and several passengers. It was found out that many manifests were, to put it mildly, pure fiction, and probably thousands of overgross and out-of-CG flights had been made through the years. The airplane that crashed had been loaded several hundred pounds over the limit but most importantly nearly 50% of the CG range beyond the rear CG limit!

Once again, you should never get there in the first place, but if you do about the only way out is the extra airspeed, which is the only way to get elevator to generate a bit more aerodynamic lift. Proficiency in flight at minimum controllable airspeed ("slow flight") will be a big help too, because you really don't want to stall this thing when it's out of CG. Much better to recover from "slow flight." And, worst of all, if you have the aft CG condition and allow it to progress beyond the stall and into a spin, there may be no way out at all, since aft CG conditions tend to make spins go flat.

An Ounce of Prevention...

Of course, you could do all your homework and still find yourself in one of these situations by accident. In any case, there are clues to look for, such as how does the airplane perform on takeoff, and how does it feel as you enter the pattern? Also, did it require excessive nose-up or -down trim in cruise? Pay attention to what your trusty air-machine is telling you. If everything is not normal, beware.

Most pilots get pretty familiar with a particular airplane and tend to overlook the actual weight and balance data once they have an idea about what it will take, but there is danger here, too. You should sit down and figure a problem in detail once in a while just to refresh your memory. Work it out to the last fraction of an inch-pound whenever you get close to any maximum.

There is no excuse for going flogging off into the blue with your airplane improperly loaded! ∎

This article originally appeared in the January 1993 edition of Mr. Edsten's Accident Prevention Program Newsletter. *If you are interested in attending Mr. Edsten's "Wings" Weekend in September, contact him at (502) 582–5941 for more information.* **—Editor**

Don't Let Your Radome Get You Down

by Ben Mackenzie

One of the least understood aspects of weather radar performance is the role of the radome. This is as true in general aviation as in air transport or military aircraft. The fact is, design and condition of the radome dramatically affect the range of the weather radar and how accurately its screen "paints" the weather ahead. In other words, the radome affects the radar's vision as the windshield does the pilot's.

A new Minimum Operating Performance Standard (MOPS) for weather radar radomes being developed by the Radio Technical Commission for Aeronautics (RTCA) will underscore this fact. The final draft has been reviewed by the industry and has been approved by the RTCA. The standard creates five categories for radomes: Class A for those radar systems requiring higher radome performance; for example, Forward Looking Wind Shear Detection/Avoidance; and Class B through E for applications where higher performance is not required; for example, Weather Detection. Side lobe levels are also addressed. (Side lobe refers to that portion of the radar energy that does not go out straight ahead. Pilots would recognize this as "scatter.") Category 2 (Classes B through E) essentially duplicates the requirements that have been used in the past for weather radar, while Category 1 (Class A) requires a tighter control over side lobes and is intended for predictive

wind shear radar applications requiring this level of performance. Side lobe levels are the same except if the plane has predictive wind shear which is rare in general aircraft.

Obviously, the new MOPS will affect those who elect to install these new radar systems in their general aviation aircraft. Persons involved in the design, operation, and maintenance of weather radar systems will also be affected. On the one hand, the new MOPS will set higher electromagnetic performance standards on new Class A weather radomes. On the other, for the first time it will also cover the radomes which have been designed to this specification after they are in service. The draft calls for retesting of radome transmission efficiency after any radome repair that could affect electromagnetic performance. Also, whenever Doppler radar for predictive wind shear detection is added, the installer will need to ensure that the radome he or she is installing will meet the Class and Category required by the radar manufacturer. The obvious plus side will be enhanced flight safety and a clearer, more accurate portrayal of weather further ahead over the entire life of the radome. The price of this is that radomes will have to be built, repaired, and tested to a standard over their entire operating life. The radome's electromagnetic characteristics must be kept within specification values in the

same way the radar system must for proper operation.

Radome electrical performance over life is a new notion in some areas of the aircraft industry. There have been no government regulatory standards directly addressing repairing and retesting radomes. FAR § 43.13 applies to radome repair, but the word radome is not present. Perhaps that is why knowledgeable people in the industry figure that half of the radomes in service today would not even meet the present standard. The main reasons are improper repair, excessive paint thickness, a lack of understanding about the harm moisture can cause, and how easily moisture can penetrate a radome, etc. More on these points later.

Standards and regulations aside, paying attention to the electromagnetic performance of radomes is, as Wilfred Brimley puts it, "the right thing to do." Certainly it's the safe thing to do. Let's look at a couple of recent cases in flight operations that point up the role of radomes in a weather radar's ability to perform.

About two years ago, pilots of a European commuter airline began regularly complaining of seeing storms two miles ahead of their aircraft on their radar indicators. This happened when flying in perfectly clear air at 10,000 feet. The problem occurred over their entire fleet of a particular make of aircraft equipped with a particular radar set. The problem was so severe, the fleet faced grounding by Swiss authorities unless the problem was resolved by a specific date. Making a long story short, the avionics shop manager for the airline naturally first suspected the radar systems. The radar systems checked out fine, and the radar manufacturer's field engineer suggested checking out the radomes at a radar test range in Ohio. Sure enough, the radomes typically checked out with only 78% transmission efficiency (the acceptable minimum at present is 85%).

Substandard transmission efficiency explained why the pilots were seeing non-existent storms on their screens. The radome was not "tuned" correctly and therefore the top portion acted like a partial mirror to the radar energy. It reflected a portion of the outgoing signal, producing a side lobe of energy 90° straight down. As a result, the screen was "painting" the ground 10,000 feet below the aircraft as a storm two miles ahead of the aircraft.

To solve the problem, new radomes were designed with a transmission efficiency of 93° including lightning diverters and paint. In operation, this improvement not only eliminated the false storm in front of the aircraft, but also translated to a doubling of the radar's range—without changing anything. The new radomes are now standard equipment on that particular make of aircraft and standard replacement radomes for the airline's entire commuter fleet. Also, the new design's structure has been strengthened to withstand a dive speed 110 knots beyond that of the present aircraft. (This allows for growth in the flight envelope for future aircraft designs.) The new design also includes a new state-of-the-art lightning diverter system that effectively stops lightning punctures through the front of the radome that had occurred with earlier designs.

The reverse can happen as well, sometimes with tragic results. At about the same time in the U.S., a radome went back into service after being field-repaired for damage on its front center area. However, the radome was not tested for transmission efficiency after the repair. The result of the repair was

satisfactory transmission efficiency left and right, but suspected degraded performance dead ahead. Two flights later, the aircraft was flown directly into a thunderstorm. It came apart and fell to the ground in pieces, killing all aboard. It is suspected that because of the radome, the radar screen painted a pattern of severe storms on either side and a corridor of less severe weather straight ahead. In this condition the pilot selected a route straight ahead, with the inevitable tragic result.

Clearly, the relationship between a weather radome's electromagnetic performance and flight safety is direct. Unless the radome is properly designed for the aircraft and the frequency of the radar system, the radar system simply cannot perform to the level it was designed for. This is one reason why radar manufacturers are happy with the new MOPS that have been developed. They contributed to it in a major way. The installation and operation manuals of most general aviation weather radar systems call for installation behind a radome with 90% average transmission efficiency.

So far, we've only discussed radome performance as it affects today's weather radar systems. The fact is, the approach of Doppler radar for predictive wind shear detection will place an even greater importance on radome electromagnetic design and performance. This type of radar system will require an antenna with very low side lobes (lobes of energy outside the main beam). Low side lobes prevent ground clutter from masking over the signal being reflected back from the wind shear event in front of the aircraft. For optimum radar performance a radome that will be used with this radar system must maintain the low side lobe level to the degree required in the new radome MOPS.

Creating such a radome is an issue for the radome designer. It is achieved by balancing radome material, dielectric constant, loss tangent, and type of construction with the electromagnetic, structural, and lightning protection needs of the application. Once the radomes go into service, it then becomes the responsibility for the

repair technicians to maintain the radome at the level required by the MOPS. In fact, it may be necessary to send such radomes to specialized repair and testing stations rather than attempting field repairs.

Moisture—the Main Enemy

Moisture in the radome is perhaps the most serious enemy of radar performance. The reason is simple: water is partially opaque to radar frequencies. Wherever water collects in the radome, the transmission efficiency could be reduced by as much as 30%, depending on the size of the affected area and the quantity of water present.

Water very readily penetrates even the smallest microcrack or pinhole on a radome surface—even through openings too small for the eye to see. The cracks may result from impact and pinholes from static burns. When the aircraft descends from cruise altitude in a wet environment, increasing air pressure equalizes through the hole and into the structure, taking water with it. During subsequent flights above the freezing level, the freezing water causes more microcracks... and the moist area enlarges. [Pilots should carefully inspect their radomes for visible cracks and pinholes as part of their daily preflight. —Editor]

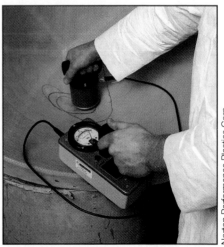

A technician scans a radome with a moisture meter to determine if moisture is present in the radome. Moisture scanning is a primary and simple trouble-shooting step, but radomes finished with antistatic coatings must be checked from the inside for accurate readings.

Norton Performance Plastics Corp.

Unless this moisture is removed during radome repairs, it can be encapsulated forever, making the impaired transmission permanent. This is why it is so important for maintenance technicians to run a moisture meter over the radome during maintenance checks and especially before repairing the radome. The procedure to remove the water, in most instances, is for the maintenance technician to first remove the inner skin behind the affected area and dry the area by placing the radome in an oven at 125°F. Then a new inner skin must be installed. Also note that if an anti-static primer or paint is on the radome, the moisture meter can show it as moisture when there is none present. In addition a reading of no moisture is not an indication that the radome is satisfactory. There could be an improper repair, excessive paint, or even a flawed design present that reduces the radome's performance below the radar manufacturer's requirements.

Repair—More than Structural

This brings us to repair. Unfortunately, all too few field repairs are made with any thought to how the repair affects transmission efficiency of the radome. One indication of this is the scarcity of proper test ranges at radome repair locations. Few U.S. airlines have radome test ranges and, to my knowledge, virtually no FBO's have them. Some of the airlines and FBO's send their radomes to appropriately equipped, FAA-certificated radome repair stations for repair and/or testing when they are not equipped to do this themselves.

The unfortunate fact is that, in a large number of cases, radomes are regarded—and repaired—as nothing more than a structural or aesthetic member of the airframe. Little or no regard is given to its electromagnetic function. That's a serious oversight. This is also the main contributor to the substandard transmission efficiency of most radomes now in service. Small wonder, then, that so many pilots don't fully trust the information on their radar screens.

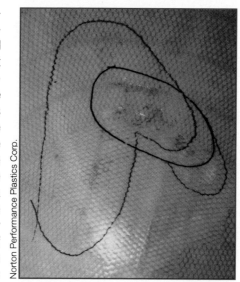

A look at the interior surfaces of a radome shows how damage inside can be greater than what appears outside. This is why thorough diagnostic procedures call for both interior and exterior examination.

Also overlooked is the issue of paint. Thickness and application of the paint on a radome can affect its transmission efficiency by several percentage points. Sometimes, paint can degrade performance exponentially. Advisory Circular (AC), 43–14, "Maintenance of Weather Radar Radomes," addresses radome maintenance quite well.

Seven Key Hints

What can the aviation pilot and maintenance technician do to keep radome transmission efficiency at its maximum?

1. Understand that the radome can directly and significantly affect the weather radar's ability to perform correctly.

2. Be sure to periodically check for moisture in the radome's internal structure. Be sure to check both inside and outside surfaces. Moisture is the main enemy. It can be present internally even if the surface looks perfectly fine. Good moisture meters are a very affordable for an avionics shop, and the procedure takes just a few minutes.

3. When repainting keep paint within the thickness limits. It is best to remove old paint layers, being

careful not to take off any of the radome structure itself. It is the thickness and composition of the entire material system—structure plus exterior coatings and lightning diverters—that determine the radome's overall performance.

4. Always have the radome tested for transmission efficiency after a major repair of a type which can degrade the radome's performance. Some radome repair stations rent "loaners" so you can keep flying while your repaired radome is being checked out.

5. Unless the repair is truly minor, consider having it done by an FAA-certificated radome repair and testing station. It can make a big difference in weather radar range and performance and, ultimately, in flight safety. Many repairs done by well-meaning technicians actually do more harm than good.

6. If the radar system bench checks normal and meets manufacturer's specifications but displays false targets or reduced range, suspect the radome, not the radar.

7. If your radome is beyond repair, check out an independent radome manufacturer for a replacement. You may get better prices, better delivery, and a better performing radome.

Obviously, radomes play more than a structural role in today's weather radar-equipped civil aircraft. Not so obviously, there's more to radome performance than meets the eye. ∎

Mr. Mackenzie is an aeronautical engineer, a designated engineering representative of the FAA in structures and systems and lightning protection for radomes and composite structures, an instrument rated commercial pilot, and an extra class amateur radio operator. He has been involved in radome design for 19 years and is on the RTCA committee that drafted the new radome MOPS. He is also on the steering committee of a joint international program on lightning and static charge protection of radomes and fairings. He is the Director of Technology and Engineering, Norton Performance Plastics Corporation Composites Operation, Ravenna, Ohio. —Editor*

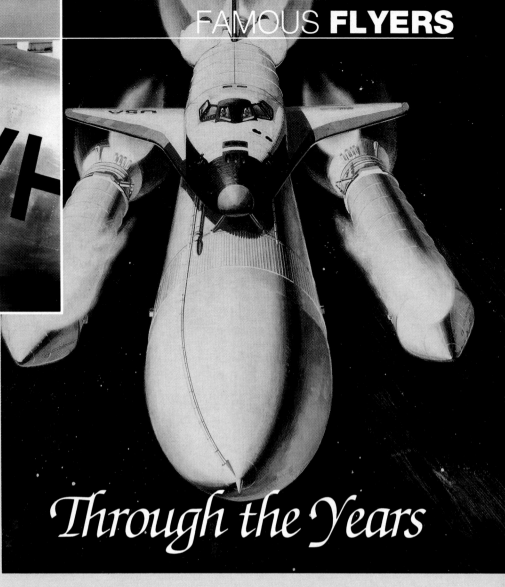

Women's changing role in aviation finds them everywhere from the FBO to the airline cockpit to the space shuttle—Amelia would have been proud.

Part 1 of this article appeared in the March 1993 issue of FAA Aviation News and covered women in aviation from the early part of the 20th Century through World War II. —**Editor**

Part 2

THE POST-WAR YEARS AND BEYOND

After World War II, the women who stayed in aviation-related jobs did not have much to choose from. Women were no longer a rarity in aviation, and this sometimes worked to their disadvantage when applying for jobs. A lucky few were able to do some flight instruction or fly for aviation businesses. Olive Ann Beech even headed Beech Aircraft Corporation with her husband. Most settled for support jobs, such as pumping gas, ferrying old surplus aircraft that were widely available after the war, doing secretarial work for companies, or working as flight attendants.

As technology advanced, women delved into new aviation areas. The increasing use and development of helicopters in the late 1940's broadened aviation capabilities enormously and caught the attention of some daring women aviators. People used heli-

Through the Years

A Look at Attitudes toward Women in Aviation

by Kristine Kjos, *FAA Evaluation Specialist*

copters to give tours, for military purposes, and for search and rescue. In 1947, Ann Shaw Carter was the first woman in the U.S. to earn a helicopter rating. Other women soon followed suit, including Jean Ross Howard, who in 1955 founded the Whirly-Girls, a group of women helicopter pilots whose primary aim was, and continues to be, to promote interest in helicopters. The group has provided scholarships to women for helicopter ratings, promoted aviation safety through publications and meetings (or "hoverings" as they are called by the Whirly-Girls), and has been active in

increasing the number of heliports in the United States.

Women continue to fly helicopters in all of the original ways, as well as for traffic reporting, air taxi, fire suppression, pipeline patrol, spraying, photography, and of course for instruction. Some women have even received their helicopter ratings before they received their driver's licenses. Kim Darst is such a woman. After obtaining her certificate in March 1987, Kim surprised her high school graduating class later that spring by landing a helicopter on the field at the ceremony. She now owns her own helicopter business.

OPPORTUNITIES IN THE MILITARY

During the 1950's and 1960's, opportunities for women in aviation increased steadily but not always quickly. Most women held jobs in the civilian sector but as the 1970's approached, women began to examine military aviation possibilities. As with all new areas that women have entered, questions arose about what women should and should not do. One question is still unresolved today: Should women be allowed to fly for combat purposes? The answer remains the same. According to the U.S. Code, "Federal law prohibits women...from directly engaging in aerial combat...delivery of munitions or other destructive material against an enemy and duties where enemy fire is expected and where risk of capture is substantial." Yet, some feel the reversal of this law is imminent. In 1991 Congress distanced itself from the issue by voting to allow the individual military organizations to set their own policy on women pilots performing combat roles.

The Navy was the first military branch to allow women pilots. In 1974, Barbara Ann Rainey was the first woman to earn Navy wings. Several other women soon joined Rainey in this honor. At the time, there were three "pipelines" or specialization areas that Navy pilots could enter—propeller, helicopter, or jets. Women were not allowed to enter the jet pipeline because jets were fighter planes. They were also not allowed to land on aircraft carriers because this would constitute "assignment to a combat vessel." Seen eventually as discrimination, the first woman was finally allowed to become carrier qualified (in props only) in 1975. In 1982, women were able to earn their wings in the jet pipeline. Today women land aircraft on carriers as a normal part of training. Also in 1974, the Army opened its doors to women aviators. Sally Murphy was the first woman in the Army to graduate from flight training. Murphy has worked her way up the ranks and

was given a battalion command in Japan in 1991. In Operation Desert Storm, women Army helicopter pilots flew on an air assault into Iraq, making history for women in combat zones. Women Army pilots are still excluded, though, from flying *Apache* or *Cobra* attack helicopters "that seek out and engage the enemy."

In 1976, the Air Force followed the Navy's and Army's leads and began to train women pilots. Eight years later, women finally qualified to fly tankers and continue to fly them today. Yet, the Air Force does not allow women to fly bombers or fighters.

MEDICAL CONSIDERATIONS

The controversy over military and civilian women flying grows more complicated still when the issue of pregnancy is introduced. Contradicting rules are currently in place for pregnant military pilots. The Navy restricts women from piloting aircraft during the last trimester of their pregnancy, the Air Force prohibits flying during the first and last trimesters, and the Army restricts flying for the entire pregnancy. The military is concerned about the effects of cockpit radiation on the unborn fetus. Surprisingly, the military does not restrict pregnant women from flying as passengers in aircraft and being exposed to the same amount of radiation in the passenger seat. Conversely, all civilian pregnancy restrictions have been rescinded. In 1939, the Civil Aeronautics Agency (CAA) had banned pregnant women from piloting aircraft. The CAA soon revoked this law but then imposed another—if a woman's pilot license expired during her "recovery" after birth, she would have to retake the written and flight tests. The Ninety-Nines had a strong hand in revoking these restrictions.

Whether it be military or civilian, women pilots have slowly entered every aviation field over the past few decades. Women are mechanics, airport managers, astronauts, fixed-base operators, and engineers. The Federal Government employs a large number of women in aviation-related positions,

such as in air traffic control and aviation safety inspector positions. Women work for museums and educate school children about aviation. The Ninety-Nines and the Whirly Girls have thousands of members who promote flying and women's contributions to aviation. Women are corporate jet pilots, agricultural pilots, flying traffic reporters, and instructors. They fly for air-charter services, air ambulance services, and for forestry, photography, survey, and pipeline patrol purposes. And as in the scenario in Part 1 of this article, women are airline captains, first officers, and flight engineers.

AIRLINE JOBS

Despite all of the accomplishments of women pilots over the century, especially those of the WASP's, it was not until the early 1970's that women began to fly for scheduled airlines. (The only exception to this is Helen Richey who was the first woman to fly for an airline during a short stint in 1934.) Emily Warner became the first American woman "in modern times" to fly for a scheduled airline when Frontier Airlines hired her as a co-pilot in January 1973. Initially uncertain of the public's response to a woman pilot, Warner and Frontier Airlines were pleased with the positive reactions they received. When asked about the attitudes she encountered overall, Warner said the following: "I've never had any sexual harassment. Flying is so intense and so professional, when you're working you forget the gender of the person sitting next to you. That is not to say there wasn't a sexist attitude, however. My first flight was awful. The Captain looked at me and said, 'Just don't say anything in the cockpit.' He was the boss." Warner flew as Captain on a United Parcel Service Boeing 727 before retiring in May 1990.

The first woman to fly for a major airline (Frontier was only a regional airline at the time) was Bonnie Tiburzi, who began working for American Airlines in March 1973. "Most of the pilots were wonderful and supportive," said Tiburzi. Most of the hostility she faced

PROFILE:
Evie Washington—pilot, educator, CFI

Pictured above is Evie Washington, a pilot and aviation educator who resides in Washington, D.C. Evie is active in the Potomac Chapter (MD) Ninety-Nines and spends much of her leisure time flying as a mission rated pilot and as a cadet flight orientation pilot for the Civil Air Patrol. Although flying is not a full-time career for Evie, she can never spend enough time in the cockpit . She has been flying since 1984 and just earned her certificated flight instructor (CFI) rating and multi-engine instructor (MEI) rating.

So what is so admirable about Evie? Everything! Evie has had some unusual experiences while attaining her ratings. She encountered hurricane force winds and witnessed a *Navajo* crash during her first long solo cross-country, had her commercial checkride canceled eight times before she could finally go, experienced a total electrical failure while on an actual IFR flight, and had the landing gear handle fall off in her hand during her multi-engine checkride. Yet, one of the most admirable qualities about Evie (besides her ability to handle unexpected situations), is her ability to teach school children of all ages about aviation and related careers. Evie frequently takes time off from her busy career as a Federal government employee and travels to Washington, D.C. area schools, often speaking to disadvantaged children. Evie says the number one question is "How much do you make as a pilot?" followed by questions about the difficulties facing minorities who want to enter aviation careers. The children are shocked when they find out that Evie often does not get paid to fly, but rather pays for aircraft rental! Evie tells the children that the sacrifices are well worth the effort. She is a wonderful role-model and her aviation stories are never soon forgotten!

was not from the pilots but from others who felt she was taking away a man's job. But Tiburzi enjoyed her job too much to be intimidated by such comments. Her dedication to flying has resulted in her Captain's stripes and several aviation awards.

Several more women were hired by the airlines in the 1970's and 1980's and other "firsts" occurred. Cheryl Peters captained the first all-female jet crew on a U.S. scheduled airline on July 10, 1982. On July 19, 1984, Lynn Rippelmeyer and Beverly Burns were the first women to captain the Boeing 747. On January 16, 1986, Lennie

Sorenson captained the first all-female crew on the 727. Sorenson again captained an all-female crew on a DC-10 wide-body jet in August 1987. Today, there are approximately 275 women captains flying for U.S. airlines.

Overall, women airline pilots feel they have been treated fairly. JoAnn Osterud, a flight engineer with United Airlines, describes her opinion of women in aviation: "It seems in aviation if you do your job right, eventually people don't really care what you are." Captain Denise Blankinship believes that the public has been "generally supportive." "[The public] realized that

we have to earn our credentials. We wouldn't be here if we weren't qualified. . ." Gay King, a pilot who began with Piedmont Airlines (now USAir) in March 1987, admits that there are still some male pilots "in the dark ages," but "most of the captains are younger and seem to have gotten used to the women's movement."

The women all have stories to tell about strange and sometimes rude reactions from crew members, passengers, and the public. A few people see a woman pilot sitting in the cockpit and refuse to fly, choosing to wait for the next flight with a "real" pilot or asking for a refund. But the funny comments and reactions are what these women remember most. Many passengers mistake women Captains for flight attendants, asking them for beverages or a magazine. Captain Lori Griffith, hired by Piedmont Airlines in 1984, has had several funny experiences on the job. Once an elderly lady who she had helped to a seat before the plane departed commented that it was nice of the Captain to let her sit up front with him, having seen Griffith sitting in the cockpit during the flight. "Once a woman ran to the galley as we were taxiing out to the runway to ask the flight attendant why we were taxiing when it was obvious that the pilots were left at the gate," said Griffith. "We had an all female crew and I'm not sure just what she thought we were doing up there." Kathy Sullivan, who flies Boeing 737's, was surprised one time when she and her all-female crew got a standing ovation from the passengers. Once, Captain Amy Correll (who was a flight engineer on a 727 at the time) was surprised when a man boarding the plane asked the captain about Correll's qualifications. "The captain calmly replied I had a Ph.D. in Astrophysics from MIT," Correll said. "I struggled to keep a straight face while the man took his seat."

CONCLUSION

So will there be future changes "in the air"? You bet! The percentage of women pilots continues to increase, and by the year 2000, it is predicted that the number of women airline pilots will more than double in size to approximately 15% of total airline pilots. As women become more commonplace in cockpits, negative or surprised reactions towards them will also decrease. More "firsts" will surely be set by women in all walks of aviation and new frontiers will be explored with women in the forefront. Women have permeated every aviation field, and they are there to stay.

Amelia Earhart would be proud.

Author's Note: Special thanks to the Potomac Chapter (MD) of the Ninety-Nines for the help and encour-

PROFILE:
Nancy Waylett—ATP, CPI

Flying is the only way of life for Captain Nancy Waylett. She has been a pilot with USAir for 10 years and was promoted to Captain three years ago. Determined to succeed in aviation, Nancy completed her instrument, commercial, certificated flight instructor (CFI), certificated flight instructor instrument (CFII), multi-engine, and multi-engine instructor ratings all in a six-month period. She passed the checkrides for all of these ratings within a two month period and began instructing. "I taught everybody," described Nancy. "I got to be an expert at teaching 'hard knocks'

cases, the cases nobody else could teach."

Soon after she began instructing, Nancy was hired by Milestone Petroleum as a corporate jet Captain. Then in 1983, she began with USAir as a Flight Engineer on Boeing 727's. It took only three months for Nancy to again move up the cockpit ladder to First Officer, a position she held for six and a half years. As a Captain now, Nancy is on reserve to fly Boeing 737's. The reserve schedule, for newly promoted Captains, involves being on-call to cover any additional or unexpected flights. A regular monthly schedule is approved for Captains after they have gained seniority during their initial years. Although the hectic schedule is sometimes difficult, Nancy believes the inconveniences are definitely worth the challenge and enjoyment that aviation and her career provide.

So what is Nancy's secret to becoming a successful airline pilot? "I had a very good basic instructor," she says. "I think that's the key to anyone learning how to fly. His philosophy was 'the way you fly the Cessna 150 is the way you'll fly a Boeing 747.' And he was right. If the basic skill, attitude, judgement, and thinking are there, that's the way you'll always fly."

Nancy encourages other women to fly professionally. Overall, she has been well accepted during her years as a woman pilot. Her favorite comment comes from "the 90-year-old woman," says Nancy, "who comes up and pats my hand and says, 'Dearie, I'm just so glad to see you up here.'"

agement given me on this article and towards getting my pilot's license, especially Patricia Garner, Evie Washington, Nancy Waylett, Mary Feik, and Linda Denett. Thanks also to Velta Benn, Jean Ross Howard, Pat Napier Adams, and JoEllen Casilio for their time and input. Also I would like to acknowledge Henry M. Holden's

book, *Ladybirds, for much of my background information.*

Ms. Kjos was a U.S. Department of Transportation Management Intern when she prepared this article as part of a developmental assignment on the Aviation News Staff. She is a student pilot and now works in FAA's Office of Contracting and Quality Assurance. —**Editor**

AIRSPACE CORNER

Question: *I really enjoy your magazine. However, please explain Class F airspace. I frequently fly to Canada, to the Bahamas, and to the Cayman Islands and I want to be in full compliance. No one at the FSDO level knows what "Class F" airspace is, and they keep giving me a FAA Aviation News reprint, "The ABC's of Airspace Reclassification," which does not address this issue.*

Answer: In International Civil Aviation Organization (ICAO) Class F airspace, air traffic control provides separation service to IFR aircraft so far as practical. As there is no equivalent in U.S. airspace, the FAA decided not to adopt Class F.

As for being in compliance, FAR § 91.703 requires that each person shall operate a civil aircraft of U.S. registry outside the U.S. in compliance with the regulations relating to the flight and aircraft operations in force within that country. Also, each person is expected to comply with FAR Part 91 if it does not conflict with the applicable regulations of that foreign country.

• Cross-country Requirements

FAR §§ 61.109(b)(2) and 61.129(b)(3)(ii) describe the aeronautical cross-country experience requirements for Private and Commercial (Airplane) Pilot certification. If all of the other cross-country requirements are met, and the applicant has exactly the minimum hours of cross-country experience required for the airplane rating, my questions are:

1. Do the applicants for these ratings meet the FAR requirements if within the cross-flight there is a landing between points less than 50 nautical miles (NM) apart?

2. Do the applicants for these ratings meet the FAR requirements if on the return to the original departure point, they make a stop at a point that is less than 50 nautical miles from the original departure point?

> Thomas E. Miller
> Ballston Spa, NY

The answer to both questions is yes, provided that the distances flown meet all of the stated FAR requirements and that at some point during each cross-country flight a landing is made at a point that is more than 50 nautical miles from the original departure point.

• Request for Change

I have been subscribing to FAA Aviation News for a few years and applaud the Administrator for the magazine. As a flight instructor working on my instrument flight instructor certificate, I would like to inquire if the FAA could change the illustration of "eights along a road" in the FAA's Flight Training Handbook (FTH) (AC 61–21A) to show the longest dimension of the eight over and along the road. Naturally, the "eights across a road" would also have to be changed.

Also, I would suggest changing FAR § 135.243 (Pilot in command qualifications) to allow newly licensed commercial pilots to fly as pilot in command in any airplane that does not require a type rating. Such a change would enable new and low-time pilots to enhance their flying careers by building flight time much more rapidly.

> W.R. Nofford
> Port Charlotte, FL

Thanks for the opportunity to tell you and our other readers how to comment on the various handbooks published by the FAA. Currently, the FAA is soliciting comments on four airman handbooks it plans on updating and republishing. Your suggestion about changing the illustration for "eights along a road" has been forwarded to the FAA office in Oklahoma City responsible for updating the handbooks. Your comments will be considered along with those of others in the aviation industry during the handbook updating process.

In addition to the Flight Training Handbook (AC 61–21A), the Pilot's Handbook of Aeronautical Knowledge (AC 61–23B), the Instrument Flying Handbook (AC 61–27C), and the Basic Helicopter Handbook (AC 61–13B) are being reviewed. Anyone wanting to submit comments about the handbooks or proposed changes to the handbooks should send their comments to FAA Operations Standards Development Section, AVN–131, P.O. Box 25082, Oklahoma City, OK 73125.

Regarding your second question, although many new, commercial pilots

---

FAA AVIATION NEWS welcomes comments from its readers. We may edit letters for style and/or length. We will select one representative letter from those on the same topic for publications, and because of our bimonthly publishing schedule, responses may not appear for several issues. We will send personal replies only upon request. We will not print anonymous letters, but we will withhold names upon request. Address: Editor, FAA AVIATION NEWS, AFS–810, Washington, DC 20591.

---

would probably welcome any change in FAR § 135.243 that would give them the chance to build flight time more quickly, the purpose of the FAR is to protect the flying and general public. The FAR does this by setting the minimum standards for PIC's engaged in air taxi and commercial operations that are necessary to ensure public safety. As you know, this particular FAR is only one of many that hold airmen engaged in air taxi and commercial operations to much higher standards and operating limitations than pilots operating under FAR Part 91. But new pilots should not be discouraged. Thousands of pilots have found the means over the years to build the flight time needed to meet the various higher commercial operating requirements such as those in this FAR. Please remember, one of the FAA's most important public obligations is ensuring that when the flying public puts their lives in the hands of the unknown airmen flying their aircraft, the pilot in command and crew have the necessary skill and experience to ensure a safe flight.

• Established by ICAO and PTS

I have subscribed to FAA Aviation News for several years. It is a very interesting magazine. I particularly like the "FlightForum/Instrument Corner." I would like to comment about the "An Established Meaning" article in the May/June 1992 issue. The International Civil Aviation Organization (ICAO) publishes a document on flight procedures (Doc. 8768 Vol.I) which states in Chapter 3,3.3.3.4 that when discussing approach segments, "Established" is considered as being within half full scale deflection for the ILS and VOR, or within +/-5 degrees of the required bearing for the NDB.

> Henrique Nunes
> ANA-EP Air Traffic Controller
> Santa Maria Area Control Centre
> Portugal

Thank you for providing us with ICAO's international definition for determining when one is established on an approach segment. Such a definition makes it easy to determine if one is established on course or not. For those pilots not familiar with ICAO, it is the world's civil aviation organization which sets the international aviation standards for all member states. The United States, as an ICAO member state, complies with ICAO procedures and polices.

In addition to the ICAO definition and our discussion in the May-June 1992 issue of the magazine on how to determine when you are established on course, there is an indirect method we have not discussed. The FAA's Practical Test Standards (PTS) for the various pilot certificates or ratings set the minimum acceptable pilot performance standards for the various tests. The Instrument Rating, and the Airline Transport Pilot (ATP) and Type Rating PTS each include instrument performance standards as part of their respective tests. Since the PTS set the minimum acceptable pilot performance standards for a given certificate or rating, by inference, the PTS must indirectly set the minimum instrument flying standards within the U.S. (The FAR set all flight standards, including being the basis for the PTS within the U.S.) Therefore, if you are navigating within the respective PTS tolerances for your certificate or rating on a specified IFR route segment, you must be established on course.

The PTS instrument standards are as follows. An Instrument Rating applicant is not permitted more than three-quarter-scale CDI or glide slope deflection during a VOR or ILS approach and no more than plus or minus 10 degrees deviation for an NDB approach. ATP or Type Rating applicants are allowed no more than one-quarter scale CDI or glide slope deflection during an ILS approach, less than half-scale CDI deflection for VOR approaches, and plus or minus 5 degrees for NDB approaches. So, although FAR Part 1 does not define the term "established," an instrument or ATP pilot flying IFR within his or her appropriate Practical Test Standards must be "established" on course when operating on an IFR route segment within those standards.

• What's Official

On the inside of the front cover, you make the following statement, "The magazine promotes safety in the air by calling the attention of airmen to current technical, regulatory, and procedural matters affecting the safe operation of aircraft. All printed materials herein are advisory or informational in nature and should not be construed as having regulatory effect." Does the above statement mean that the FAA Aviation News *provides the aviation community with the FAA's Official interpretation of technical, regulatory, and procedural matters? Am I, as an instructor to teach your interpretations and as a Designated Pilot Examiner to accept these interpretations as "Official?"*
Joe D. Parker
Vero Beach, FL

The material published in the magazine is only advisory or informational in nature and should not be construed as having regulatory effect, even though the magazine's articles are approved by the various policy-making organizations here at FAA Headquarters for compliance with current policy and guidelines. The magazine allows us to provide our readers an informal forum to ask

INSTRUMENT CORNER

• Visibility Defined

FAR § 91.175(c)(2) states that operation below decision height (DH) or minimum descent altitude (MDA) is only permitted if flight visibility is not less than the visibility prescribed in the approach being used. However, the visibility prescribed in the instrument approach procedure (IAP) either prevailing or runway visual range (RVR) is ground visibility. Is the value for ground visibility presumed to reflect the flight visibility? If not, can a pilot legally land the aircraft if he/she believes the flight visibility exceeds the prescribed ground visibility, even if the prescribed ground visibility, prevailing or RVR, is being reported as being below minimums?
Cyril Toker
Ponte Vedra Beach, FL

Reported ground visibility has no reflection on actual flight visibility. FAR Part 1 defines both flight and ground visibility, and there is a difference in the two meanings. Flight visibility means the average forward horizontal distance, from the cockpit of an aircraft in flight, at which prominent unlighted objects may be seen and identified by day and prominent lighted objects may be seen and identified by night. Ground visibility means prevailing horizontal visibility near the earth's surface as reported by the U.S. National Weather Service or an accredited observer. As you can see, no pun intended, flight visibility is the slant range visibility from the cockpit. In flight, flight visibility may be greater than ground visibility. But landing minimums are based upon ground visibility for a good reason. Many times it is possible when flying for the pilot to look down through a fog bank over an airport and see the ground, but when that pilot tries to land, the pilot can not see far enough down the runway through the fog to maintain directional control. This inability to see through a surface obscuration at ground level is the reason why FAR §91.175(d) states, "No pilot operating an aircraft, except a military aircraft of the United States, may land that aircraft when the flight visibility is less than the visibility prescribed in the standard instrument approach procedure being used." Also FAR Parts 121 and 135 specifically restrict operations if the visibility is below published minimums. Pilots landing in reported conditions less than that prescribed for the IAP being used may be investigated for non-compliance with the FAR.

questions about various FAA rules and policies without having to go through a typical, "official," bureaucratic process.

Regarding your question about the magazine being an official source, the FAA prints many "official" sources of information, such as the *Airman's Information Manual* (AIM), various training handbooks, and advisory circulars that are all non-regulatory in nature. They provide the public the FAA's officially recognized procedures or means for complying with its various regulatory requirements. As one such publication, the *FAA Aviation News* is Flight Standards Service's "official" safety magazine. That is as "official" as we can get. Although the information contained in FAA Aviation News conforms to the FAR and FAA policy, as an instructor and Pilot Examiner, your official regulatory guidance is contained in the Practical Test Standards (PTS), the FAR, your examiner's manual, and any other regulatory guidance you may receive.

• Supervising Simulator Time

Please answer a question that has caused some serious concern. FAR § 61.57(e)(1) states that a pilot may log up to three hours in an approved simulator to meet currency requirements. There is no mention of these hours having to be supervised by a CFI. Recently, a couple of trade magazines stated that CFI supervision is required. Realizing that Advisory Circulars (AC's) are non-regulatory, AC–61–98A, Para. 6a, states that the hours "may be done under the supervision. . . . " The statement begs the question as to whether the pilot may (author's emphasis) elect to use a simulator versus whether if he uses a simulator that a CFI may (author's emphasis) be used to supervise.
Name withheld by request

FAR § 61.51(c)(5) which deals with the logging of pilot ground trainer instruction is the basis for answering your question. All time logged in a ground trainer used to meet pilot currency, instruction, or skill requirements must be certified by an appropriately rated instructor from whom it was received. In the case of an approved instrument training device or simulator being used to meet IFR currency requirements, the IFR training must be signed off by an instrument flight instructor or ground instructor with instrument privileges. A similar question was answered in the May-June 1992 issue of the magazine.

I Wish I Hadn't Said That

The following is a selection of remarks made by pilots, controllers and others where it is clear that they had not engaged their brains before opening their mouths. Our thanks to the Editor and Staff of the U.K.'s *General Aviation Safety Information Leaflet* (GASIL) for sharing their particular favorites.

Pilot: "Golf Juliet Whisky requests instructions for takeoff."

Persons unknown: "Open the throttle smoothly, check temperatures and pressures rising, keep the aircraft straight using. . ."

Student Pilot (trying to disguise the fact that he is lost) to an airport which is presently overhead: "Unknown airport with Cessna 150 circling overhead, identify yourself."

Tower: "Alpha Charlie climb to and maintain 4,000 feet for noise abatement."

Aircraft: "Tell me how at 2,000 feet I can possibly be creating undue noise."

Tower: "At 4,000 feet you will miss the twin coming at you at 2,000 feet and that is bound to avoid one hell of a racket."

And finally, the GASIL Editor's favorite, involves a twin engine aircraft with fare-paying passengers on board which had a serious engine fire in flight. Even more unfortunately, the captain of the aircraft, realizing he had to inform both the airport of the hazard and the passengers of their impending diversion, regrettably operated the transmit/intercom switch the wrong way. While Air Traffic might have been mildly amused to be told, "Hello everybody, we're just going to make a landing at a nearby airport so you can all have a nice cup of tea," the amusement was not shared by the passengers, who were told over the intercom "Mayday, Mayday, Mayday, Golf Xray Xray engine fire. Emergency landing. Please have all emergency services including fire and ambulances available."

Replacing Lost or Destroyed Certificates

Airmen who need to replace their lost or destroyed certificates can no longer use the Western Union collect telegraphic service to obtain a telegram from the FAA confirming their status as holders of specified certificates and ratings. The Airmen Certification Branch and Aeromedical Division will now FAX you the required information to enable you to keep flying. For more information on this subject, contact the Airman Certification Branch, AVN–460 (telephone: 405–680–3205) or Aeromedical Certification Branch, AAM–300 (telephone: 405–680–4821) at P.O. Box 25082, Oklahoma City, OK 73125.

National Designated Pilot Examiner Registry

The Federal Aviation Administration (FAA) and the Experimental Aircraft Association (EAA) recently signed an agreement to initiate a National Designated Pilot Examiner Registry (NDPER) of pilot examiners authorized to check out pilots in certain large vintage, surplus military aircraft hereafter called vintage aircraft. This NDPER program will allow registry pilot examiners to check out applicants in the vintage aircraft for which the FAA may not have enough qualified inspectors to conduct either initial certification or proficiency tests required by the FAR for their operation.

Under the NDPER program, EAA will identify and recommend to the FAA pilots believed qualified in specific types of large, reciprocating engine, single and multi-engine vintage aircraft such as T28's, B17's, B25's, and P38's. The EAA will maintain a list of all of registry examiners approved by FAA and the aircraft make, model, and type, or series in which each registry examiner is authorized to give practical tests. EAA will also maintain a record of each registry examiner's FAA designation and initial and recurrent training given to ensure that registry examiners maintain currency in the aircraft in which they are authorized to give practical tests. As part of the FAA/EAA agreement, EAA will develop and oversee a training program found acceptable to the FAA for each registry examiner in vintage aircraft in which the examiner is authorized to conduct practical tests under the NDPER program.

A record of each practical test given by registry examiners will also be maintained by EAA along with the test results. Each record will include pilot data as well as the type of aircraft in which the practical test was conducted. EAA will also keep a current list of aircraft identified as vintage aircraft under the NDPER program.

Under this program, applicants will be able to contact either their local Flight Standards District Office (FSDO) or the EAA for the names of registry pilot examiners qualified in a particular vintage aircraft. Applicants can then contact a registry examiner of their choice to arrange the practical test needed without regard to FSDO or regional boundaries. The local FSDO will coordinate the required FAA flight test between the involved FSDO's and regions if the test is to be given outside of the local FSDO's area. The FAA may, at its discretion, elect not to observe the flight test when conducted.

Although the NDPER program will be facilitated by EAA, the FAA will monitor the program for compliance with appropriate FAR and FAA pilot examiner policy regarding airman certification and registry examiners activities. Working together, this cooperative program between EAA and FAA should ensure that the needs of all qualified airmen who wish to fly vintage aircraft are met. As the letter of agreement states, this is a model FAA/EAA partnership program designed to provide a service to the public by ensuring the continued preservation and static and flight display of a broad variety of ex-military vintage aircraft that might otherwise be lost to public view.

Updates on this subject will appear in a variety of FAA publications.

AV**NEWS/BRIEFS**

Improper Aircraft Exporting Procedures

Recently representatives from the Brazilian Civil Airworthiness Authority (CAA) visited FAA headquarters to discuss operation of aircraft bearing U.S. registration in Brazil. They brought along a list of 104 N-numbered aircraft currently operating in Brazil, some for as long as two years.

What's so unusual about that, you say? When FAA Maintenance Division ran the 104 N-numbers through the Aircraft Registration Branch in Oklahoma City, they found out that 48 of the aircraft had been previously deregistered, sold, and exported. Although these aircraft had been removed from U.S. registry, their owners had not assured that the U.S. registration numbers were removed as required by FAR § 45.33.

The FAA has received similar inquiries and reports from CAA's in the United Kingdom and many other countries. These countries have expressed concern about the increasing number of aircraft bearing U.S. markings operating in their airspace. Most member countries of the International Civil Aviation Organization (ICAO) do not, as a normal procedure, spot inspect or ramp check foreign-registered aircraft operating in their countries. They expect the country of registry to ensure proper registration and airworthiness.

Owners and operators of U.S.-registered aircraft must be aware of the regulatory requirements. At the time of official sale to a non-U.S. purchaser, FAR § 45.33 requires the registration certificate holder to remove permanently all U.S. registration marks from the aircraft. FAR § 47.41 requires that the Certificate of Aircraft Registration, AC Form 8050–3, be returned to the FAA Aircraft Registry with its reverse side completed. The address is:

FAA Aircraft Registration Branch
AVN–450
P. O. Box 25504
Oklahoma City, OK 73125

Previous owners of the aircraft involved in the Brazil incident included aircraft dealers, private individuals, and new aircraft manufacturers. Being aware of the regulatory requirements for deregistering aircraft and following the proper procedures will help aircraft owners and exporters to avoid confrontations with the FAA, U.S. Customs Service, the Drug Enforcement Agency, and other federal entities.

Prepared by Larry Kephart, Manager, FAA's General Aviation and Commercial Branch, Aircraft Maintenance Division.

Carrying You Back To Ol' Virginny

Going to Sun 'n Fun for a few days this April? Well, if you are, you might want to head home through the Commonwealth of Virginia. Why? To get your Wings, of course!

As a part of Virginia's annual Aviation Safety Week, there will be a Virginia "Wings Weekend" at Manassas Municipal Airport (HEF) on April 24 and 25. Manassas is located in a beautiful and historic part of Virginia not far from Washington, DC. It's about 14 miles south of Dulle International Airport and is the site of the country's only recycled control tower.

What is a "Wings Weekend?" A chance to participate in the Accident Prevention Program's Pilot Proficiency Awards Program and qualify for your "Wings" lapel pin all in one weekend. Continuous safety seminars will be going on hourly, and the ground and flight instruction will be provided at no charge. You can finish the requirements (one hour of airwork, one hour of takeoffs and landings, and one hour of instrument flight plus attendance at a seminar) in one day or do it more leisurely in two days. In addition to the seminars and flying aircraft, there will be aircraft on display, good food, and some interesting hangar talk. When you have completed your requirements, you'll receive your certificate and Wings on the spot. Remember, the Wings count as a biennial flight review.

You must pre-register to assure that you will be accommodated by the Capitol Area Association of Flight Instructors, who are volunteering their time for the weekend. For specific flying and driving arrival procedures and information on motels, contact Accident Prevention Program Manager Jim Jacobsen at (703) 661–8160.

Checked Your Plumbing Recently?

No, we are not talking about your bathroom at home. We are talking about the plumbing in your airplane. What? You say your trusty four place aeroplane doesn't have plumbing. It doesn't even have enough space for a portapottie. No, we have not flushed one too many times. We are talking about a method for some aircraft owners to check their aircraft's fuel system. A recent recommendation from the FAA's General Aviation and Commercial Branch, Aircraft Maintenance Division points out how pilots and mechanics can check their fuel system for leaks with a simple prestart test.

Depending upon type of aircraft (not all aircraft have the required fuel pumps and gauges) the fuel pressure check is done before engine start to avoid the possibility of an engine fire. This check is especially important after maintenance where the fuel system plumbing was disturbed or when braided hoses are moved or disturbed. (Please note, before conducting this type of check, pilots and mechanics must review the aircraft operating handbook/service manual to make sure there are no restrictions on doing this type of check. Appropriate safety procedures must always be followed when doing any kind of check.) The technique is to turn the magnetos off, master switch on, fuel boost pump on, place the throttle and mixture control full forward, and monitor the fuel pressure and flow. If the pressure is lower than what is indicated in the POH or aircraft manual as normal and the flow is above zero with the engine static, there is a good chance there is a leak in the system. If a leak is suspected, it should be checked out by an appropriately rated mechanic before engine start.

One way to avoid possible leaks in any plumbing system is to replace at recommended intervals any metal braided medium pressure hose that is subject to constant engine heat or flexing. The problem is the metal braid may hide small cracks or deterioration in the hose that may go unnoticed during a preflight check. Such defects could cause leaks. According to the recommendation, a good hose replacement would be one that meets the specifications of MIL H 8794 with a fire sleeve in areas where needed, but always remember the manufacturer's recommendations must be followed when replacing any aircraft item. Have a safe flight.

TEST YOUR piloting IQ:
Signage Quiz

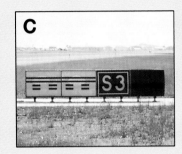

by Louise Oertly, *Associate Editor*

Now that you have read the article, "Aviation Sign Language," on pages 4 and 5, test yourself to see if you can read the following airport signs. Admittedly, not all airports will not be required to use these signs, but you should be familiar with them just in case you come across them in your travels. (The answers are on page 14.)

___1. Holding position line for ILS critical area

___2. Do not enter sign to indicate areas that aircraft are prohibited from entering

___3. Taxiway location sign collocated with taxiway direction sign for single crossing taxiway

___4. Outbound destination sign showing the same direction for two runways (Note: black dot should be read as "and")

___5. Inbound destination sign showing direction to apron

___6. Taxiway location sign collocated with boundary sign for runway safety area/obstacle free zone sign

___7. Holding position sign for taxiway located in approach area for a runway

___8. Location sign collocated with runway holding position sign

DO NOT DELAY—CRITICAL TO FLIGHT SAFETY!

May-June 1993

FAA Aviation News

A DOT/FAA FLIGHT STANDARDS SAFETY PUBLICATION

U.S. Department
of Transportation

**Federal Aviation
Administration**

Federico F. Peña, *Secretary of Transportation*
Joseph M. Del Balzo, *Acting FAA Administrator*
Carl B. Schellenberg, *Acting Executive Director
for System Operations*
Anthony J. Broderick, *Associate Administrator
for Regulation and Certification*
Thomas C. Accardi, *Director,
Flight Standards Service*
Robert A. Wright, *Acting Manager,
General Aviation and Commercial Division*
Roger M. Baker, Jr., *Manager,
Accident Prevention Program Branch*
Phyllis Anne Duncan, *Editor*
Louise C. Oertly, *Senior Associate Editor*
Dean Chamberlain, *Associate Editor*

The FAA's Flight Standards Service, General Aviation and
Commercial Division, Accident Prevention Program
Branch, AFS–810, Washington, DC 20591, (telephone
202 267–8017) publishes FAA AVIATION NEWS in the
interest of flight safety. The magazine promotes safety in
the air by calling the attention of airmen to current technical, regulatory, and procedural matters affecting the safe
operation of aircraft. Although based on current FAA policy and rule interpretations, all printed material herein are
advisory or informational in nature and should not be
construed to have regulatory effect. The FAA does not
officially endorse any goods, services, materials, or products of manufacturers that may be mentioned. **Certain
details of accidents described herein have been
altered to protect the privacy of those involved.**
 The Office of Management and Budget has
approved the use of funds for the printing of FAA AVIA-
TION NEWS.

SUBSCRIPTION SERVICES

The Superintendent of Documents, U.S. Government
Printing Office, Washington, DC 20402–9371, sells FAA
AVIATION NEWS on subscription. Use the self-mailer
form in the center of this magazine to subscribe. Cost:
$8.00 ($10.00 foreign) for one year; $16.00 ($20.00 for-
eign) for two years. Prices are subject to change by the
Government Printing Office without prior notice.
 Change of Address or Subscription Problems:
**Send your label with correspondence to Sup Doc,
Attn: Chief, Mail List Branch, Mail Stop: SSOM,
Washington, DC 20402–9373.**
 To keep subscription prices down, the Government
Printing Office mails subscribers only one renewal
notice. You can tell how many copies are left in your
subscription by checking the number that follows "ISS-
DUE" on the top line of your mailing label. For example,
when this number is 003, it means you have three
issues left in your subscription, and GPO will send you
a renewal notice. The number 000 means you have
received your last issue. To be sure that your service
continues without interruption, please return your
renewal notice promptly.

FAN SMITH 212J ISSDUE003 R 1
JOHN SMITH
212 MAIN ST
FORESTVILLE, MD 20747

May-June 1993

FAA Aviation News

| Volume 32 | Number 4 |

FEATURES

DEPARTMENTS

On the Covers:
*The decision to go or not to go is not always depen-
dent on the weather. Sometimes pilots can be more
dangerous to themselves than any thunderstorms.
See the series of articles on page 4 through 14.*

Cover photo by G. S. Livack

Product Liability: A Case Study

by John S. Yodice

Product liability is a continuing problem to general aviation—in terms of the overall problem and the conflicting interests that we have as aircraft owners and pilots. On the one hand, we want a fair compensation system for persons who may be injured or damaged by aviation products—usually aircraft owners and pilots and their families and friends. On the other hand, we would like to have the continued availability of aircraft and parts at reasonable cost, and product liability is driving the manufacturers out of business and driving up the costs of products.

A product liability case now working its way through the court system is gaining a lot of attention. There has already been one jury trial, a number of appeals, and there is the prospect of a second jury trial. The facts of the case and some of the law and procedure are interesting and potentially precedent-setting.

The accident happened in 1983 at a residential airpark in New Mexico. The pilot was attempting a takeoff in a Piper *Super Cub,* towing a sailplane. In the takeoff, the *Cub* struck a van intentionally parked on the runway by the airpark owner to prevent the takeoff. Apparently, there was some feud going on between the airpark owner and the sailplane operators because of alleged safety violations.

The reason for the flight was to photograph the sailplane for a television commercial. The pilot had the front seat (which had a shoulder harness) removed and had installed in its place a large movie camera on a camera mount. The camera was mounted in such a way that the cameraman had to sit on two-by-fours facing rearward toward the camera and with his back against the instrument panel. The pilot sat in the rear seat, which had no shoulder harness.

AOPA

John S. Yodice

When the *Cub* struck the van, the pilot's body jackknifed forward, and his head hit the camera mount, causing massive head injuries and brain damage. The camera operator was not seriously injured.

The pilot and his wife first sued the van driver for the pilot's injuries, and that case was settled for $600,000. The pilot and his wife then brought a product liability lawsuit against Piper Aircraft Corporation. They alleged that Piper was negligent in the design of the *Super Cub* for two reasons: One, that the *Super Cub* had inadequate rear-seat forward visibility during takeoff, which caused the collision, and two, that the injuries were caused by the lack of a rear-seat shoulder harness.

At a trial in 1986, a jury brought in a verdict in the amount of $2.5 million. At the request of the injured pilot's lawyer, the jury was asked to make two separate allocations of fault: first among the persons responsible for the collision (called the "original tortfeasors") and second among the persons responsible for the lack of a shoulder harness (called the "crashworthiness tortfeasors"). The jury decided that the collision was 42.5% because of the injured pilot, 41.7% because of Piper, and 15.8% because of the person who had approved the alterations to the cabin of the *Super Cub* to install the camera (that person was also the sailplane pilot). The shoulder harness fault allocation was 8.4% to the injured pilot and 91.6% to Piper. The jury decided that the van driver had no fault for the pilot's injuries. The injured pilot's lawyer argued that judgement against Piper should be entered for 91.6% of the $2.5-million verdict. But the trial court granted judgement against Piper for only 41.7%.

Continued on page 14

Keeping PACE with Safety and Partnership

by Dean Chamberlain, *Associate Editor*

There is a new acronym in the FAA's aviation safety vocabulary: PACE (Pilot and Aircraft Courtesy Evaluation) is the FAA Accident Prevention Program's newest national safety outreach. Instituted formally by the FAA in March 1993, the voluntary PACE program has been under development since 1990. Known in some test areas as "ACE" (Aviation Courtesy Evaluation) and "Operation Fixed Wing" in others, PACE offers pilots and aircraft owners an opportunity to request a non-adversarial FAA review of their piloting techniques and aircraft's airworthiness without risk of FAA penalty. The program's concept is simple. FAA aviation safety inspectors will check pilots and their aircraft for compliance with the appropriate Practical Test Standards and Federal Aviation Regulations (FAR) without risk of penalty. Any inadvertent discrepancies found by the inspectors will be noted, and the pilot or aircraft owner will then be responsible for correcting them. The program's goal is as simple as its concept; to increase aviation safety through the voluntary efforts of airmen and FAA by detecting and correcting any inadvertent non-compliance.

If you are wondering why PACE and why now, the answer is again very simple. PACE is another example of the FAA's ongoing efforts to increase aviation safety through voluntary compliance. This increased voluntary compliance is based on developing more trust between and a greater working partnership with the FAA and the aviation community. PACE is one span to help bridge the gap between FAA's aviation customers and the FAA and to help improve the flow of critical safety information between airmen and FAA. The need to maintain the critical flow of information between airmen and the FAA is why FAA inspectors do not pursue legal enforcement action for inadvertent acts of non-compliance with the FAR or PTS discovered during PACE. PACE's "no penalty" policy gives pilots and aircraft owners the opportunity to have the FAA review their compliance with the FAR and PTS without risk, and it gives them the freedom to ask questions and discuss their problems with the FAA without fear. This "no penalty" aspect also means no one fails an evaluation under the PACE program. Now, if you are wondering what happens if a pilot or aircraft "does not pass" a PACE check, which is not the same as failing, the answer is best illustrated by the following example.

Typically, a pilot and aircraft courtesy evaluation starts with an aviation group such as an FBO or group of pilots coordinating with their local FSDO's FAA Accident Prevention Program Manager to hold an evaluation at a mutually agreeable time and airport. PACE could be part of an aviation safety day, a fly-in or other type of group activity. The idea is to have as many pilots and aircraft as possible participate during the available time. During the planning stage, planners should give some thought about bad weather because PACE is a VFR event. Once a PACE event is scheduled, pilots and aircraft owners need to do some homework before they show up. Pilots will need their pilot's certificate, current medical, and a record or logbook showing currency and appropriate endorsements. This also includes a record of a flight review or equivalent. An FCC radio operator's permit is required if the pilot flies internationally or operates certain types of radio equipment. The pilot/aircraft owner must also have the appropriate aircraft documents such as the aircraft's registration, airworthiness certificate, weight and balance data, FCC radio station license, and appropriate operating limitation/s, such as an aircraft flight manual, or pilot operating handbook, and appropriate maintenance record entries showing compliance with airworthiness directives (AD) and required inspections and equipment installations. Once the appropriate certificates and records are assembled, pilots should also review the appropriate FAA Practical Test Standard (PTS) for their pilot certificate. If all of the above is accomplished, the pilot/aircraft owner should be ready for PACE. A good PACE checklist might be the pilot test checklist in each PTS book. As a final

reminder, current charts will be needed for the flight.

An actual PACE starts with an Airworthiness Safety Inspector checking the designated aircraft's airworthiness. This check should take about 45 minutes. The evaluation of aircraft documents, markings, placards, manuals, equipment, cargo, and general airworthiness will be done using only simple inspection techniques. Since no flight evaluation can be done if the designated aircraft is not airworthy, you might be wondering what happens if the inspector discovers something that makes the aircraft unairworthy. The answer depends upon how serious the problem is. A minor problem might be corrected and signed off by the local FBO's maintenance shop at the airport, and if time permits, the flight portion could then be flown. Another option might be for the inspector to issue a ferry permit so the pilot could fly the aircraft home for repairs. If the aircraft is found unsafe for flight, the aircraft would be grounded until repairs could be made. Regardless of the problem, if any example of inadvertent non-compliance with the FAR is discovered during a PACE inspection, no FAR enforcement action will be taken. But it must be emphasized that the aircraft's owner/operator has the responsibility to ensure the aircraft is in compliance with the FAR before further operation. PACE does not protect pilots or aircraft owner/operators from further operations in non-compliance with the FAR. This means that participation in the PACE program does not provide future immunity for the pilot or aircraft owner/operator from subsequent discovery of non-compliance with the FAR such as during a ramp check on the way home or involvement in an incident or accident. One comment regarding additional airworthiness: Pilots/ aircraft owners/operators should be aware that continued operation of an aircraft that is in non-compliance with the FAR not only subjects you to possible enforcement action, it might also void your insurance coverage in the event of an accident or incident. Many insurance policies require the aircraft to be air-

worthy and the pilot to meet appropriate FAR as a condition of coverage. If it can be proven that an aircraft was not airworthy at the time of an accident or incident, or the pilot was not in compliance with the FAR, the aircraft/ pilot may not be covered by insurance. The only way to be sure is for every pilot/owner/operator to understand the limitations of his or her insurance policy before the policy is needed.

Assuming the aircraft is found airworthy, the operations aviation safety inspector will then brief the pilot on the proposed evaluation flight. The flight will probably consist of a takeoff and area departure, some basic airwork, then a return to the airport followed by one or more landings. During the estimated 45 minute flight, the maneuvers flown and standards used will be those in the Practical Test Standards appropriate to the pilot's certificate. Following the flight, the inspector will debrief the pilot on any areas that might need additional work. If the PACE flight reveals that additional work or training is needed, it is up to the pilot to seek additional training with a CFI of his or her choice. Two important points need to be made regarding a PACE flight, since the flight evaluation is only a courtesy evaluation, the flight cannot be an instructional flight. The FAA inspector is not expected to give dual instruction during the flight. Therefore, the flight can not serve as either a Flight Review or as the dual instruction required for the Pilot Proficiency Award Program (WINGS) program. And like

other flights with FAA inspectors, the pilot being evaluated is the pilot in command during the flight and therefore responsible for compliance with all FAR during the flight. The FAA inspector is only an observer during the flight. The inspector is not an instructor or required crewmember during the flight.

Since PACE is a voluntary no-penalty program promoting safety, no records of the airman or aircraft evaluation are kept for follow-up action by the FAA other than the records normally required to be kept such as file copies of the ferry permit if one is issued. Rather than documenting and following up on discovered discrepancies, FAA is depending upon the airmen participating in the program to correct any discrepancies discovered during PACE.

To recognize the dedication and efforts of the pilots and aircraft owners/operators participating in the PACE program in supporting aviation safety, local FSDO's are authorized to issue certificates to all of those who participate in the program.

To learn more about the PACE program and how you can help promote aviation safety in your area, contact your local FSDO's Accident Prevention Program Manager (APPM). A national list of APPM's with their telephone numbers and addresses was published in the November-December 1992 issue of *FAA Aviation News*.

Set the PACE for Safety in your area, call your local APPM today. ■

Piper Aircraft Corp.

Staying Alert in the Cockpit

by Douglas S. Ritter

Sleep deprivation and its effect on pilot performance

Sometimes the subject for an article just reaches out and shakes you awake to the need to address it. Such was the case a few months back as we flew home late one night after a couple of long days away on business. I was looking forward to getting home and getting to bed. All of a sudden, I was jerked from my thoughts as Center called out traffic. I realized that I had not been paying attention to what I was doing. No danger, but the adrenalin rush served to focus my attention for the remaining 15 minutes of the flight. The long days had obviously taken their toll on my alertness. It turns out that the most common cause of diminished alertness is associated in some manner or other with loss of sleep or interruption of normal sleep patterns. I had not gotten much sleep, and it was well past my normal bedtime.

Most pilots have found themselves in similar situations or worse. Some have succumbed to sleep and flown far beyond their intended destinations before awakening. No doubt, some have fared worse. Studies have shown that accident rates climb precipitously during certain hours as our bodies try to get the sleep they need.

How far can we push ourselves before we pay the price? What can we do to prevent or postpone the inevitable?

Though many of us are loath to admit it, pilots are not superhuman. We are susceptible to the same frailties of the human condition as are all others. Sleep is one of these areas where pilots often fail to acknowledge limits.

Adequate sleep is absolutely vital to maintain alertness and a sound state of mind. Research during the past decade or so has done a lot to illuminate the previously murky condition we refer to as sleep, as well as define its vital role in our health. Simply put, you must have sleep or your mind will fail. Within limits, you can postpone or reduce the sleep you need. Once beyond those limits, performance rapidly deteriorates. Push too far and you lose your rationality and maybe even your life.

We have all grown up with the recommendation that we need eight hours of sleep each day. Like so many other truisms, this one is not exactly true. The average healthy adult may need about eight hours of sleep, but most people need more when they are growing up and less as they age. By late middle age, we are down to an average requirement of seven hours. Many people need less, and many need more. Some get by with as little as four hours' sleep, and others may require nine or 10. What we need is

driven by our own internal biological clock, and there is relatively little we can do to alter that program.

25-Hour Clock

Researchers say the average American in today's whirlwind-paced world gets an hour to one and a half hours too little sleep each night. How can you tell if you are getting enough sleep? Well, if you are awakened by your alarm, have trouble getting going, or just do not seem to function well in the morning, then it is a good bet you did not get enough sleep. Try sleeping a half hour longer for a while and see if you do better in the morning. If not, add yet another half hour. At some point, you will find a remarkable difference in how you feel. That is the amount your body is "programmed" to sleep. Any less, and you pay for it.

Sleep serves as a restorative to both the body and mind. No matter how physically strenuous the day has been, a good night's sleep will allow the muscles to recuperate. This is a relatively simple process. The manner in which our brain reacts to sleep is very much more complicated.

To understand how sleep loss affects our performance, we must first have at least a basic understanding of sleep. Our bodies have a natural biological clock referred to as the circadian rhythm. This internal clock has a period of 25 hours. No one is quite sure why it lasts a full hour longer than a normal day, though many theories exist. There is surprisingly little variation among individuals in the total length of this rhythm.

This 25-hour clock drives our waking and sleeping periods. When we try to operate counter to it, we pay a price. The extra hour is also the reason that it is usually easier to stay up late than to get up early and explains why most of us have more trouble with jet lag when flying from west to east.

Each day when we get up in the morning, we reset our biological clocks. If we did not, every day we would get up one hour later than the day before. It is daylight that does it. Studies of subjects living in isolation, away from any other influences, show they quickly adapt to a 25-hour day, getting up an hour later and going to bed an hour earlier each day.

Our body is influenced by this internal clock in other ways. Our temperatures fluctuate in a cycle that normally has its high during the day and its low late in the night. When our body temperature is low, our brain is inclined toward sleep. "Night people," who are active late into the night and then sleep late during the day, have simply retarded their internal clocks.

Energy Cycle

Within this internal 25-hour cycle exists another cycle of approximately 90 minutes' duration, known as the ultradian rhythm. Our energy level and capacity to perform rises and falls in 90-minute internals as we go through the day. If you make the effort, it is usually easy to recognize these peaks and valleys in your capacity for work and alertness. You are more susceptible to daydreaming or drowsiness during the lowest part of your energy cycle.

Another, somewhat analogous cycle is evident during sleep. Sleep is divided into five stages. The first four stages are known as non-REM sleep and normally occur in ascending and descending cycles (1–2–3–4–3–2–1) lasting a total of 90 minutes on the average. The first cycle can often run

up to 110 minutes. The first stage is a bridge between being awake and asleep. We might just as easily wake up as go to sleep. Stage 2 sleep is true sleep that takes up about 50% of each night's sleep. Stage 3 sleep is deeper than Stage 2 and lasts only a short while, acting somewhat as a transition between Stage 2 and Stage 4 sleep, which is the deepest sleep.

During this stage, you are virtually "dead to the world." It is very difficult to wake someone who is in Stage 4 sleep, and, if awakened, he or she will tend to be nearly incoherent for 10 to 15 minutes. If allowed to resume sleeping before fully awake, there will be no memory of awakening. This stage amounts to about 13% of a young adult's sleep, but it is reduced to nearly zero by late middle age. Many scientists lump Stage 3 and Stage 4 sleep together and call it "slow wave" sleep because the brain's waves are moving at their slowest.

The fifth stage of sleep is REM sleep. REM is an acronym for rapid eye movement. This is the lightest state of sleep and is the stage in which we dream. The first period REM sleep normally occurs at the end of the first sleep cycle, about 60-80 minutes into the cycle, after the second period of Stage 1 sleep. It will last from five to 15 minutes.

Systems Shutdown

As the night progresses, this sequence of stages repeats four or five times. In each subsequent cycle, the portion of REM sleep increases and that of non-REM decreases, especially Stages 3 and 4 sleep. During the last one or two cycles, REM sleep may totally supplant Stage 3 and 4 sleep. REM sleep normally comprises about 25% of the total in adults. Many researchers believe that REM sleep plays an important part in brain development and daily rejuvenation. It is evident in the womb, and babies spend at least half their sleep time in REM sleep, premature babies up to 75%. During REM sleep, the brain is very active, but the body's motor and sensory systems are shut down. REM, or

dream, sleep is absolutely vital to maintain your sanity. It is so important that if you are deprived of it, your brain may try to compensate by daydreaming or increasing the length of any REM sleep it does get. There is another time period when our internal clock seems to encourage us to sleep. Adults have a dip in alertness and a tendency to sleep during the middle of the afternoon. When we are active, we may not notice it so much. When we are less active, or in a susceptible state because of some sort of sleep deficiency, it may be much more evident. The afternoon siesta is a cultural feature in many warmer climates. Its impetus resides within ourselves, and we carry it when it has been socially exorcised.

Sleep Deficit

From a practical standpoint, when we mess with our internal schedule or try to act in contradiction to it, we are asking for trouble. Studies have shown that accident rates rise in mid-afternoon and then rise again significantly at night.

When sleep is postponed, your brain incurs what is known as a sleep debt. Like money owned, it must eventually be repaid. Like interest, it is cumulative. The good news is that you get a pretty good deal. You do not pay it back hour for hour. If your accumulate 10 hours of sleep debt, it may take you only a few nights of good sleep to recover. The more debt you incur, the longer the recovery takes. In extreme instances, it can take weeks to recover fully. This is why it is best to try and deal with it preventively or use naps and other methods to compensate for the sleep loss as quickly as possible. Even a couple of hours of sleep loss can affect your performance to some degree. But we are generally able to cope satisfactorily if that is all that is involved and there is sufficient motivation to perform well. The more sleep you lose, the more sleep debt you accumulate, and the more difficult it becomes to perform acceptably, no matter how strongly you are motivated.

Piper Aircraft Corp.

Jet Lag

Recent studies indicate that the biggest drop in alertness is associated with significant disruptions to circadian rhythm as opposed to simple sleep loss. Jet lag is the best known of these disruptions. It can take many days for you to readjust your internal clock; in the meantime, your performance will suffer. There have been all sorts of strategies suggested for those who want to cope better with jet lag—diets, exercises, special schedules, etc. Researchers say no single method is right for everyone. Generally, the best results come from efforts to adjust your internal clocks before leaving. For very short trips, some find it easier to stay in sync with home time and not even attempt to change. Either way, you are likely to be much better off than if you do nothing.

There have been a lot of media attention to recent reports that very bright lights can be used to adjust your internal clock rapidly. This would be a boon to those who work shifts or travel extensively. Some companies are even offering "jet lag lights" for sale. The problem is that the exciting results have been achieved primarily in the lab or under very controlled conditions, such as with the shuttle astronauts. It is not simply a case of buying a very bright light and turning it on for a while.

So, while light accommodation shows great promise, it has not yet been proven effective in the real world.

Repaying the Debt

Recovery of sleep loss will take place at its own sweet pace. You cannot force it. The best strategy for most people is to go to bed early rather than trying to sleep later in the morning. If you are trying to overcome significant sleep debt by sleeping longer than normal, at some point, say an extra hour or two, you will wake up. If you do not fall back asleep within 30 minutes, it is best to get up and do whatever it is you have to do. But listen to your body. When it tells you it is ready for some more sleep, do not fight it. Find a place to lie down and sleep. This is the quickest way to recover.

Asleep at the Controls

A common problem for pilots flying today's modern aircraft is that there is often little to do. With sophisticated autopilots and navigation equipment, the pilot is left only to monitor the progress of the flight. This is particularly a problem when flying IFR in solid but benign IMC, because there is not even the need to scan for traffic. With little to do, there is a natural tendency to fixate on an instrument or object

and drift off. This tendency becomes more pronounced when you have some sort of sleep deficit.

There is a number of dangers here. One is that you will actually fall asleep and completely lose track of what is going on. Hence the flights that have continued far past their intended destinations. Another danger is that, while you may not fall deeply asleep, you may cease to monitor the instruments adequately and may not catch some deviation from the norm, such as an increasing oil temperature or slipping off your assigned altitude. If something goes drastically wrong, most pilots would be unable to respond immediately. And when they do respond, there is a significant likelihood that the response may not be the best for the situation.

Finally, there is a danger which develops during a normal flight as you transition from the monitoring phase to the active phase; for example, when landing. If you have even somewhat succumbed to the tediousness of the monitoring phase, your performance may suffer as your brain struggles to "spool up" from the monitoring to the action modes.

Strategies for Warding Off Fatigue

Naps between flights can be an effective tool with which to combat sleep deprivation. Unfortunately, for most of us, the idea of taking a nap is accompanied by social stigma left over from the Puritan work ethic. But numerous studies have confirmed the positive influence a short nap can have on productivity. This usually more than compensates for time lost to the nap. At any rate, *a good nap before flying is your best defense against the perils of falling asleep or of diminished alertness in the cockpit.* It is also an important aid in recovering from a sleep deficit.

According to Dr. Mark Rosekind, principal investigator in the Fatigue Countermeasures Program at the NASA-Ames Research Center, a good nap can take two forms. What you want to *avoid,* if possible, is a nap that is interrupted in a deep sleep phase.

Anyone who has been awakened from deep sleep will recall how groggy they felt and how long it took to become effective again. So, the nap should either be quite short (40 minutes or less) or long enough (90–110 minutes) to enable a full cycle of sleep, including Rapid Eye Movement (REM) sleep, to occur. It is in Stage 1 sleep that you are best prepared to awaken with a minimum of problems.

Even when awakened from a light sleep, we carry forward what is called "sleep inertia." You know the feeling. You are groggy, not quite wide awake, not quite ready to deal with anything too complicated. So, after a nap, always wait at least 15 minutes before jumping in the car or plane.

Most of us have read about the recent NASA study that recommended naps for crew members on long-haul flights. A 40-minute "NASA nap," or "power nap" as they have come to be called, taken within a few hours of landing, has proved to be extremely effective. Many long-haul crews already have instituted power naps as a matter of course, and the FAA is preparing an advisory circular covering the matter. Obviously, a nap is a bit impractical for the single pilot, though there are plenty of stories about pilot who intentionally or inadvertently let the autopilot do the flying while they took a catnap. That certainly is not something we can recommend. If fact, you may be better off leaving "George" sleeping to help prevent you from dozing off. Hand flying should keep you more alert.

Seeking Stimulation

Physical or mental activity coupled with outside stimulation is one of the best methods for keeping sleep at bay. An active conversation with your copilot or passenger can be very stimulating during cruise flight when it is not necessary to devote full concentration to flying the aircraft. Simply engaging in mental activity—mind games and the like—will not do it. This withdraws you from the flight environment—exactly what you do not want.

Caffeine is the safest stimulant you can use to stave off sleep. For best results, Dr. Rosekind suggests using it more strategically than many of us tend to. Do not just start drinking coffee, tea, or cola first thing and then continue throughout the flight. All that caffeine is not healthy, but, more relevant to our concerns here, there is a very real danger that you will reach a point where it ceases to be effective at all. When you reach this point, virtually nothing is going to be able to keep you awake. A better bet is to use caffeine judiciously, i.e., only when you need it. If you find yourself getting drowsy, drink something at that time. If you want a little extra perk-up during the approach, take some a half hour before.

It is important to stay hydrated while flying. Dehydration can contribute to tiredness. Caffeine is a diuretic. Besides dealing with the possibility of the need to relieve yourself, you must also be careful not to become dehydrated.

Some pilots swear by oxygen to wake them up, and, indeed, most authorities recommends that supplemental oxygen be used above 10,000 feet during the day and above 5,000 feet at night. If you are drowsy, even mild hypoxia that would not normally cause a problem could be more dangerous. At night, oxygen is a good idea anyway, since our night eyesight can be significantly improved by its use.

Alertness Monitors

Some pilots have reported good results from "doze alarms," which are designed for drivers and offered in catalogs and sometimes on TV. These alarms fit over the ear and are set off by a mercury switch when your head tilts, as it is likely to do when you doze off. Pilots who have tried these alarms say they can be used only during cruise and in smooth air. They do take some getting used to so that you do not set them off while scanning for traffic. Scientists are examining a number of more sophisticated devices that would perform a similar function. These "alertness monitors" would react to our brain waves or some other empirical measurement, but it will be at least a few years before alertness monitors are commercially available.

The cockpit environment can make a difference. It should come as no surprise that a warm cockpit is conducive to drowsiness. Better a bit too cold than too hot. If possible, direct a flow of colder air at your face.

Certainly, there is a lot to be said for moving around as much as possible.

Piper Aircraft Corp.

For the single pilot, this may be limited to adjusting the seat to different positions or engaging in some isometric exercises. For others, it is a good idea to get out of the seat for a while and move around. But do not stay away too long. The other pilot could nod off while you are away. (That is the reason the NASA nap is only recommended when there are at least three flight crew members aboard, so there are always two at the controls.)

Getting to Sleep

For many pilots, getting to sleep, particularly when away from home, is very difficult. Whether recovering from a sleep deficit or trying to prevent it, there are things you can do to help you get to sleep. As with so many other things, a healthy diet and moderate exercise tend to contribute to better sleep. There is little or no scientific evidence that various vitamin supplements or other commercially offered diet supplements promote good sleep.

Contrary to some people's expectations, exercise right before climbing into bed is not helpful. In fact, it is extremely counterproductive, no matter how exhausted you are when you finish. This is because the ideal and necessary precondition for falling asleep is relaxation. After exercise, your body may be tired, but it is not relaxed, and neither is your mind. So, get your exercise earlier in the day.

Relaxation can be accomplished in a number of ways. Some people read; others watch TV. Some pilots have found it advantageous to practice relaxation therapies they have learned.

It is best to avoid eating right before going to sleep. This is not to prevent bad dreams but to prevent the relatively mild action of the digestive process from interfering with relaxation. Liquids are easier to digest and are less of a problem. Many people swear by the soporific effects of a warm glass of milk or chamomile tea. There are actually sound biochemical reasons why these may work.

Researchers discuss the importance of ritual for getting to sleep. Ritual in this sense is nothing more than an habitual activity associated with going to bed and to sleep. Most of us follow certain rituals without being aware of them. They may include brushing teeth, reading, saying prayers. Others may involve the manner in which you undress, what you do with your clothes, and the way you arrange your bed or pillows. The smallest things may play an important role in preparing for sleep. Whenever you interrupt these rituals, you may find it more difficult to get to sleep. This is magnified away from home. If you have or develop rituals which are easily transported, it can make it easier to fall asleep. Some travelers find it helpful to always bring their own pillow along.

Dark and Quiet

For most people, the darker the room, the easier it is to sleep. This is especially important for a pilot trying to sleep during the day. At home, prepare your sleeping quarters ahead of time to be as dark as possible. Some pilots carry a roll of duct tape or Velcro with adhesive backing to enable them to affix curtains and blinds to block as much light as possible in their hotel rooms. Some FBO's have "sleep rooms" for flight crews. Some hotels that cater to airline pilots also have special rooms prepared. It pays to ask around.

Quiet is also very important. While some of us can sleep under any circumstances, most of us are kept awake by loud noise or unfamiliar sounds. Ear plugs can be very helpful. Some people find them discomforting at first, but most get accustomed to them quickly. Another tactic is to use "white noise" to mask sounds. There are a number of commercial products available that are specifically designed to generate a calming background noise. In a pinch, turn on the fan in the room heater or air conditioner or set the radio between stations so all you hear is a static "hiss." Either one of these can do the trick.

Use of Alcohol

Alcohol can be extremely detrimental to good sleep. Though it is a seda- tive, its side effects tend to make it a poor choice for promoting sleep. Further, alcohol-induced sleep tends to be of very low quality with considerably reduced REM sleep. There is also a tendency for insomnia to develop later in the sleep cycle, as sleep often becomes fitful. Alcohol also suppresses normal shifts in posture than accompany transitions between the stages of sleep. This can result in compression of the radial nerve in the upper arm and, ultimately, in so-called "Saturday night paralysis."

Countermeasures

The researchers at NASA-Ames plan to issue an "educational and training module" entitled "Flight Crew Fatigue Countermeasures" some time this summer. It will contain their recommendations for counteracting the effects of sleep deficiency. The free guide will be available from the Fatigue Countermeasures Program, NASA-Ames Research Center, MS 262–4, Moffett Field, CA 94035. For anyone interested in learning more about sleep, an excellent source is *Sleep* by J. Allan Hobson, published in 1989 by Scientific American Library.

Sleep deficiency is a way of life for many pilots. Hopefully, the suggestions here will help you avoid the extreme penalty paid for succumbing to the effects of sleep deprivation. The important point is that each of us is different, and what works for one may not for another. So, try various strategies until you find those that work for you. You cannot make the problem go away, no matter how badly you want to. The best you can hope for is that your chosen strategies will allow you to postpone sleep until your flight is safely completed. ∎

This article has been reprinted courtesy of Aviation Safety *magazine. For further subscription information, contact* Aviation Safety, *Subscription Services, P. O. Box 420234, Palm Coast, FL 32142; (800) 829–9162. The cost is $84 a year for 24 issues; $6 for single copies.*

Piper Aircraft Corp.

Last Leg Syndrome

by Bill Monan, *ASRS Analyst*

This is the fifth and final article in a series reprinted from ASRS Directline, *a quarterly publication that addresses particular areas of safety that appear in pilot reports received by NASA's Aviation Safety Reporting System and which have been identified by safety analysts as "significant."* ASRS Directline *is free from ASRS, NASA-Ames Research Center, Moffett Field, CA 94035. The last leg of a long flight is where fatigue, stress, and "get-home-itis" all seem to combine to make a pilot's life miserable. Knowing the problem is the beginning of making sure that the last leg of a flight is not the ultimate leg.* **—Editor**

One of the routine details frequently noted in pilot incident reports submitted to ASRS is the seemingly innocuous statement, "This was the last leg of the flight." Terminology in other reports varies only slightly: "The last flight of the day," "the final leg," and "the end of a long day."

These air carrier, commuter, and corporate/general aviation pilots were involved in altitude "busts," heading/course deviations, missed crossing restrictions, active runway transgressions, and other, less typical operational incidents.

What is there about the "last leg" that is fundamentally different from any other leg? Let's take a look at some of the factors involved in last-leg operations.

Fatigue

Reporters identified fatigue as an obvious source of error. ASRS narratives included statements such as, "fighting bad weather all day," "multi-approaches to ILS minimums," and "delays" which merged with "end of a long thirteen hour duty day," "the ninth and last leg of a long day." Such descriptions often prefaced complaints such as, "a little tired" and "somewhat fatigued" to "worked out," and "punchy," not to mention "mentally and physically exhausted." "After all," contended one pilot, "some inattention is to be expected at the end of a long duty day."

A good case can be made that fatigue contributed to subsequent breakdowns in discipline and procedures and to attention problems.

Attention Problems

Loss of concentration was referenced in flight crews' explanations of last-leg error such as crossfeeds left on, pressurization switches left off, and misreading of systems gauges and switches. Two flights departed without adequate fuel on board. "I glanced at the fuel gauges," stated one first officer, "but what I was looking at did not register." The second and compounding error came about "when both the

captain and second officer looked at the three fuel gauges, each reading 5,000 pounds, and came up with a total of 30,000."

Forgetfulness plagued the pilots. A number of flight crews "forgot" to call the tower for landing clearances. "Just too many landings for the day," explained one reporter. Flight crew neglected to reduce to 250 knots below 10,000 feet, to make crossing restrictions, to tell the other pilot of the ATC re-clearance, and, on two occasions, "forgot to let down."

> "Last leg of the flight. Driving along at flight level 370, inbound to home, so I'm letting my guard down a bit. The controller gives us a clearance to descend, to cross 35 miles of XYZ at 19,000. . . . A little later, another clearance, this time to cross 5 miles W[est] at 13,000. The controller added, 'See if you can make this one.' What happened? We had stayed at our cruise altitude. The captain didn't catch it, and I missed it because I was so darned tired I was letting him run the store."

Another flight crew failed to read the checklist:

> "We advanced the throttles to takeoff power. Upon hearing the [takeoff] configuration warning horn, I glanced down to verify the warning and was totally surprised to see the flaps in the UP position. I could hardly believe we had forgotten to read the taxi checklist and to extend the flaps!"

Get-Home-Itis

Get-Home-Itis is cockpit jargon for pilot anticipation and eagerness to get finished with the day's work. ASRS analysts include Get-Home-Itis as a diagnostic term when reviewing reports that demonstrate an over-eagerness to get home. "I let my desire to get to the airport overshadow good judgement," stated a commuter pilot who opted to land straight-in at a non-tower airport without bothering to call in on UNICOM. A near-collision occurred. An air carrier first officer, reporting on a runway transgression, stated that "The Captain had home-itis. On our arrival at home base, he was taxiing faster than normal to get to the gate. Next time I'll ask, 'Where's the fire?'" In perhaps the ultimate embarrassment, one chagrined flight crew was informed that they had exited the aircraft with an engine still running at the gate.

General aviation pilots are not immune to the home-itis disease. As one rueful general aviation pilot reported:

"My ground speed dropped off. . . I had a choice of either landing to refuel or to continue. I decided to press on. At 4 miles out, the engine went to idle. At 2 1/2 miles out, the engine stopped."

Get-Home-Itis is a disease that can also afflict a pilot who is fresh and rested, but we are willing to bet that fatigue both occasions and compounds the problem.

Complacency

Perhaps the most welcome sight in aviation is the familiar home airport coming into view on the horizon, especially after a long, hard series of downline flights. However, the subtle slide into psychological letdown (frequently cited in the last-flight-of-the-day narratives), can lead to error, embarrassment, or hazard. Noted one reporter:

"Having the field in sight and being very familiar with local area, I came off the gauges and busted my altitude."

Another reporter, in reflecting on his deviation, noted:

"I was complacent about checking the approach plate and in flying our normal procedures."

A captain who strayed off the route was apologetic:

"Since it was the last leg home, I put away my charts. Next time I'll leave them out."

Cockpit Management

The omission of cross-checking and crew concept monitoring duties was a common factor in last-flight-of-the-trip circumstances. "We were relaxed," admitted one reporter. "We were too relaxed," insisted another. Common errors include selection of wrong VOR and ILS frequencies, radials, and DME distances; incorrect comprehension and readback of clearances; and misinterpreted runway assignments. Pilots frequently cited psychological letdown in vigilance and cross-checking: "Not paying attention to what the captain was doing," "not monitoring the first officer's actions," and "the crew let down their guard. . . [and] lost backup monitoring."

Looking for Solutions

Awareness of the potential for each of us to be a victim of fatigue, complacency, and Get-Home-Itis is the first step in the cure of the disease.

Combatting Fatigue

Fatigue is insidious. Without realizing its progressive impact upon alertness and attentiveness, tired pilots drift toward passivity, inertia, and lethargy. In an increasingly competitive industry, air carrier pilots often cite scheduling as the major contributor to fatigue. There is little advice we can give except to eat well and get as much rest as possible. General aviation pilots often have more control over their schedules but should still plan for adequate rest periods.

Professionalism

By definition, complacency is not recognized a problem in the cockpit while the flight is in progress. Complacency as a factor in flight crew error is identified only in post-incident reflection. None of us is immune to complacency. Working hard to maintain a professional attitude at all times will go a long way in providing a degree of immunity from the affliction. (By the way, you do not have to be a fly-for-hire pilot to strive for professionalism; even the newest student pilot needs to develop a professional attitude.)

Cockpit Management

Maintain proper cockpit and flight crew monitoring and observe duty priorities. Projecting thoughts forward to post-arrival details distracts pilots from the tasks at hand.

It Ain't Over 'til. . .

"The last leg of the flight should be flown in the same way as the first flight of the day, or else it might be the last flight in the pilot's career." ■

The Aviation Safety Reporting System is a cooperative program established by the FAA's Office of the Assistant Administrator for Aviation Safety and administered by the National Aeronautics and Space Administration.

Have You Got That Rhythm?

fatigue

It's more than just a daily clock; it includes flight safety

from *Palmetto Aviation,* a publication of the South Carolina Aeronautics Commission

Body functions are controlled by internal "biological clocks." While the mechanisms of these clocks are largely unknown, their effects are familiar to everyone. Walking, sleeping, eating, and elimination of wastes are regular everyday human experiences. Most people also note daily periods of alertness and periods of dullness. Such periods are normal and are related to swings of one to two degrees in body temperature. People are most alert when the body temperature is highest and least alert when the body temperature is at its low point.

For people who sleep at night and work in the daytime, their body's low temperature occurs about 3 to 5 o'clock in the morning. At this time such people are most prone to errors. Studies of airline pilots confirm that performance failures and human error accidents are most likely to occur early in the morning.

High-speed, long-range aircraft are now commonplace in the general aviation fleet. Crews on such aircraft can be subjected to rapid time zone displacement when traveling in easterly or westerly directions. "Jet lag," or desynchronosis, means that travellers' body

functions remain on home time and, therefore, do not occur at the same times as do those of residents at the destination. Thus, for example, the traveller gets sleepy or hungry at inappropriate times. If the traveller stays at the destination long enough, the biological clock will gradually become reset to the new time. This resetting, or entrainment, takes place at the rate of about one hour per day for each time zone crossed.

Thus, if a California pilot flies to New York (three time zones), he or she requires about three days to adjust functionally to Eastern Time. The same readjustment time will be needed by a New York pilot flying to California, though less difficulty will be encountered adjusting to Pacific Time than to Eastern Time. This is because it is easier to stretch the day (east to west flight) than it is to compress the day (west to east flight). However, in either case the pilot may find it necessary to fly at a time of "circadian low" and should be aware that the tendency to be error-prone is greatest at that time.

Strict adherence to the practice of checklists is the main insurance against error. Two heads are better than one. With two-person crews, the checklist should be used with one pilot reading the items and the other checking the items; only clearly spoken responses should be accepted. Pilots flying alone should read and respond aloud to all checklist items.

Pilots who will not be at the destination long enough to adapt to local time should remain on home time as far as their activities are concerned. In extreme cases this could mean daytime sleep and breakfast at night, but it will, to some extent, prevent fatigue resulting from insomnia.

People experiencing jet lag can force themselves to carry out activities, such as going to meetings, shopping, etc., but they cannot force themselves to sleep when they are not sleepy. Tourists laying awake all night and then dragging themselves about sightseeing the next day is a fairly trivial problem; however, such a situation could be a significant problem for a pilot who must be in top form for a flight. In any case, pilots should never use sedative drugs [without consulting an AME] or alcohol in an attempt to cope with jet lag or insomnia. Likewise, use of stimulants such as amphetamines in an attempt to be "up" at the time of a circadian low period should be strictly avoided. Pilots should also remember that drug effects can wear off in flight, leaving the pilot in a worse condition than he or she might have been otherwise.

If at all possible, pilots should plan departure times to provide a desired arrival time. Of course, terminal or en-route weather forecasts may have powerful influences on departure times. The result may be that a departure or arrival

Continued on page 14

Pilot Decision Making

by Tom Hamilton

A Superior Pilot is One who Stays Out of Trouble by Using Superior Judgement to Avoid Situations which Might Require Superior Skill

This is Part One of a seven part series that first appeared in Balloon Life *magazine in 1989 and was originally written for balloon pilots. We have left the lighter-than-air examples in because the overlying issue of pilot decision making affects all pilots, and the excellent information in these articles can be extrapolated to aviation activities other than ballooning.* **—Editor**

A popular belief is that judgement is good, common "sense" applied to the making of decisions, especially correct decisions. "Sense" involves an intense awareness, realization, and understanding of all the factors involved in making a decision. Sense is generally seen as a person's ability to act effectively and positively in any given situation.

The most significant aspect of pilot judgement and decision making is the outcome. Judgement is not an end in itself but involves both a decision to act and a response—be it an action or even an inaction. Before taking action, pilots must consider all relevant interpersonal, aircraft, and environmental factors which have, or may have, an influence upon the decision-making process. Pilot judgement is thus a pro-

cess which produces a thoughtful, considered decision relating to the aircraft's operation along with the ensuring action/inaction to that decision.

Aeronautical decision making is a combination of our ability and motivation. The former deals with our ability to act like a computer while the latter encompasses the external factors that influence behavior.

Ability is searching for and establishing the relevance of all available information regarding a flying situation, specifying alternative courses of action, and determining expected outcomes from each alternative. We can define ability, then, as *intellectual ability*. It relies on the pilot's capabilities to sense, store, retrieve, and integrate information. This part of judgement is purely rational and, if used alone, would allow problem solving in much the same manner as a computer. Ability comes from training, practice, and continuing education—the learning process. The more knowledge we have, the greater the resources on which we have to draw to evaluate a flying situation and specify a course of action.

The second part of our definition deals with motivation. The motivation to choose and authoritatively execute a suitable course of action within the time frame permitted by the situation. The word "suitable" means an alternative consistent with societal norms, and "action" includes no action, some action, or action to seek more informa-

tion. In this second part is where the decision is made, and indications are that this process can be affected by motivations and *attitudes*. There is an implication that, in part, pilot judgement is based on tendencies to use other than safety-related information when choosing courses of action. Pilots often consider non-safety items such as job demands, convenience, monetary gain, self-esteem, adventure, commitment, etc., before taking action. If properly developed, this part of pilot judgement would eliminate information unrelated to flight safety and direct the pilot's decision to the use of more rational processes.

Most accidents are credited to "pilot error," a large catch-all category to explain the cause of an accident. In Figure 1 is a breakdown by type of pilot error accidents based on information from the National Transportation Safety Board (NTSB) contained in bal-

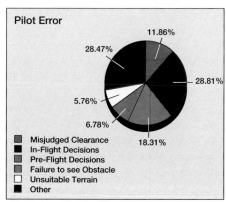

Pilot Error

11.86%
28.47%
28.81%
5.76%
6.78%
18.31%

■ Misjudged Clearance
■ In-Flight Decisions
■ Pre-Flight Decisions
■ Failure to see Obstacle
□ Unsuitable Terrain
■ Other

Figure 1

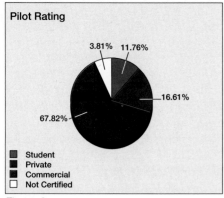

Figure 2

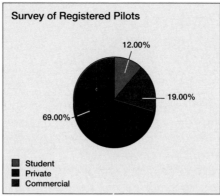

Figure 3

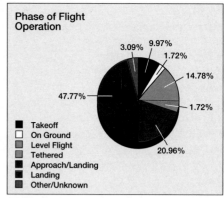

Figure 4

loon accident reports for a recent 20-year period. Pilot error, however, is an oversimplification for the cause of the accident. Pilots, after all, do not *intend* to have accidents. Pilots usually intend to fly safely, but they sometimes make decisional errors. Sometimes skill or luck will be sufficient to get them out of situations. The objective of this and subsequent articles, however, is to provide the pilot with knowledge to avoid situations that require the use of superior skill to overcome.

Accident Characteristics

Before we proceed and look at the risk factors to consider in aeronautical decision making, an examination of accident characteristics is in order.

Figure 2 shows the pilot certificates of those involved in the accidents. At first, it would appear that the commercial pilot is the most guilty of exercising bad judgement. However, the representation of commercial pilots in the figure is the same percentage of total pilots in the population base. Figure 3 represents a survey of current pilot ratings.

Phase of operation statistics can be found in Figure 4. Here one area of flight operation stands out. Approach to landing and landing phases comprise 69% of the accidents reported. [About the same composition for other aircraft.—Editor] This is a clear indication that this phase of operation requires greater ability and can be more adversely affected by motivation.

One other area to consider is recent flight experience in the previous 90 days. Although the statistical data over a recent five-year period would indicate that the fewer hours you had

flown tended to result in a higher degree of risk, the database is too small to draw concrete conclusions because of other factors. Those other factors include the nature of the flight (training, pleasure, for hire, etc.), total pilot experience, and weather.

Elements of Risk

If we look at the decision making process (Figure 5) we find that inadequate skills and procedures and/or inadequate headwork in conventional decision making leads to "Mishaps." A review of accidents involving balloons will reveal that more than 90% of them are "pilot error." These "errors" fall into several categories which include errors of omission—failing to do something one should have done; errors of commission—doing something too soon or too late; and errors involving degrees of response—overreacting or underreacting. It is worth keeping these types of mistakes in mind when examining the decision making process.

Figure 5 shows the four elements of risk involved in a *situation.* The pilot, aircraft, environment, and type of operation combine to create the situation. Situational awareness is the accurate perception of the conditions affecting the balloon and the pilot during a specific period of time. It is knowing what is going on around you. There is a direct relationship between situational awareness and safety.

We have listed below some of the elements for each of the four risk factors. Can you think of others?

Pilot
- **Experience**—total time, last 90 days, type of weather conditions
- **Competency**—ability
- **Health**—minor illnesses, eating properly, alcohol/drug use
- **Fatigue**—lack of sleep, fitness, mental or physical
- **Attitude**—family or work problems, getting married, happy, angry

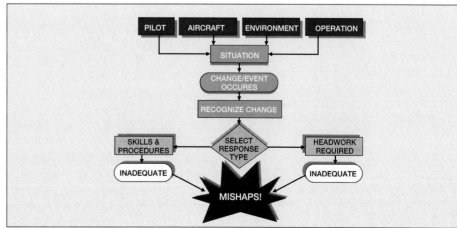

Figure 5

Aircraft
- **Airworthiness**—total time, status of inspections and AD's
- **Type**—single, multiengine
- **Size**—two seater, four seater
- **Accessories**—gauges, avionics, antennas
- **Fuel capacity**—at beginning of flight, end of flight, quality of fuel

Environment
- **Weather**—high pressure system, windy, front nearby, fog, clouds, turbulence
- **Airspace**—over town, agricultural land, near airport
- **Topography**—flat, rolling hills, mountains, sea level, high altitude, desert, trees
- **Takeoff/Landing Area**—grass, dirt, surrounding obstructions, size, weather conditions, accessibility, hazards to flight

Operation
- **Fun**—with friends or solo
- **For hire**—passenger, cargo, banner
- **Day**—visibility
- **Night**—experience
- **Heavy**—full load, high altitude, high ambient temperature
- **Light**—solo, cold weather
- **Instruction**—student and instructor experience, weather

This is certainly not an exhaustive list but a starting point for you to consider. Get together with other pilots and discuss what other elements enter into each of these risk factors. How does each affect the situation? What about the possible combinations?

The situation, of course, does not remain static. Situations are dynamic, and your ability as a pilot to recognize and react to those changes which are occurring is important. In Part Two we will examine Skills and Procedures and Headwork required in managing attitude, stress, risk, and crew.

Thinking about what might happen and planning for it helps the pilot to use superior knowledge to avoid situations that might require superior skill. ■

Our thanks to Mr. Tom Hamilton, publisher of Balloon Life *and author of this series, for permission to reprint this and subsequent articles. For subscription information contact Mr. Hamilton at 2145 Dale Avenue, Sacramento, CA 95815; (916) 922–9648.*

Product Liability: A Case Study
Continued from page 1

Both sides appealed. The appeal court reversed the judgement and sent the case back to the trail court for a new trial, which would permit the jury to find in one "special verdict form" the negligence of the parties and non-parties, whether original or crashworthiness tortfeasors.

Before the new trial, Piper asked the trial court to dismiss the case on the basis of federal preemption. Piper argued that a jury should not be permitted to find that the design of the *Cub* was negligent because the *Cub* met all of the FAA design requirements, including those relating to pilot visibility and seat restraint systems.

The trial court rejected this argument, and Piper again appealed. On appeal, Piper again urged that federal preemption is a bar to the pilot's claims of negligent design. In its appeal brief, Piper also addressed the alleged defectiveness of the tailwheel design by tracing the history of the *Cub* and the tailwheel design.

The lawyers for the injured pilot argued against federal preemption. Recovery for personal injuries because of negligence or product defects has traditionally been a matter of state, not federal, law. That includes injuries arising from air crashes or aviation products. In enacting the Federal Aviation Act, Congress never intended to take this away from the states, the plaintiff's lawyers said.

And so the arguments go.

In April of 1992, the Aircraft Owners and Pilots Association filed a brief amicus curiae (friend of the court) contending that "in the particular circumstances of this case, involving an aircraft design certified by the Federal Aviation Administration and proven over a long history of safe flying, the plaintiff's product liability claim based on an alleged failure of the manufacturer to exceed federal design and safety requirements is preempted by paramount federal law and regulation in the field of aircraft design and safety."

Without federal preemption, juries across the land could, in effect, require the redesign of aircraft whose design has been approved by the FAA. Juries redesigning aircraft is not a good thing.

The FAA also filed a brief as friend of the court, arguing in favor of federal preemption, as did other general aviation organizations. The Association of Trial Lawyers of America submitted a brief to the contrary.

The United States Court of Appeals for the Tenth Circuit on February 16, 1993 filed its opinion in Cleveland v. Piper Aircraft Corporation. The opinion rejects Piper's contention that Federal preemption should bar a state law claim of defective design of an aircraft that met FAA standards. The appeals court said that the plain language of the Federal Aviation Act suggests that Congress intended that the Act have no general preemptive effect. The case will now proceed to a new trial in the United States District Court for the District of New Mexico, based on an earlier appeal in which the trial court was found to have erred in instructing the jury about allocating fault among the potentially responsible parties.

It will be interesting to see how the case is ultimately resolved. ■

Mr. Yodice is AOPA's General Counsel. This article originally appeared in the December 1992 AOPA Pilot and is reprinted with permission.

Have You Got That Rhythm?
Continued from page 11

may be scheduled at a time of circadian low when the likelihood of human error is greatest. At such times errors of confusions and forgetfulness are most common. "Forcing functions" such as checklists, warning horns, stick shakers, flags, and lights are most important in combatting reduced alertness levels. Preflight procedures should always include checks to see that these safety features are present and operating according to specifications.

Checklists are for using! ■

Crew Coordination Problems

by Mary Edwards, Ph.D.

When we speak of Crew Resource Management, we tend to think only in terms of the flight crew. In airline operations flight attendants are part of the crew and, depending on the airline, may participate in CRM training with the flight crew. Many more private operators are using flight attendants, and they need to be trained as part of the crew also. As we see in this article, however, crew coordination problems still exist within the airlines, and we present this article to alert corporate flight departments as well. —*Editor*

Crew coordination problems continue to plague commercial transport aviation despite increased awareness and the development of new training programs. More than 10 years ago, an article published in Flight Safety Foundation's *Cabin Crew Safety Bulletin* described some of the problems encountered in cockpit/cabin communications.

As examples of "rude, discourteous" behavior of the part of some captains, the author listed barring flight attendants from the flight deck unless specifically called there by the captain; keeping flight attendants in ignorance of the progress of the flight by refusing to pass on information about delays or weather conditions; and dismissing the requests of flight attendants for help in dealing with difficult passengers. The author attributed such behavior to a lack of good rapport between captains and flight attendants.

The failure of flight attendants to comply with direct orders from the captain and instances of orders "deliberately disobeyed" were attributed to organizational separation of flight deck crews from flight attendants, the former reporting to flight operations and the latter to a marketing or passenger service division. This separation was considered to be a major factor in the perception by some flight attendants that the captain was peripheral to their chain of command.

These situations also can be aggravated by large aircraft that "create a situation where the flight attendants are distant to the extent that interphone communications are necessary." (B-747's, for example, can have 20 different calling codes for cabin crew handset stations on the aircraft.)

This 10-year old article, based on firsthand experiences, has been followed by several broad-based studies on cockpit/ cabin communication issues. These studies identify two major themes: development of good interpersonal relations and recognition of the organizational context within which these interpersonal relations can be encouraged or modified, if necessary.

An FAA investigation into cockpit and cabin crew coordination conducted in 1988 reported "inadequate crew communication in emergencies, confusion over the sterile cockpit concept, inadequate instruction on the duties of the other crew in training, failure to properly secure the cabin for takeoff and landing, and inadequate support for staffing of the FAA inspector workforce."

Communication problems in emergency situations were linked to inadequate information from the flight deck concerning all the relevant features of the emergency, particularly the amount of time available for preparation of the cabin and its occupants to meet the emergency.

In non-emergency conditions, flight attendants often had insufficient notice from the cockpit of the time available to prepare the cabin for takeoff and landing, according to the FAA report. Communications problems originating in the cabin included violation of the sterile cockpit rule by requesting nonessential information at an inappropriate time and by not reporting to the flight deck matters that could be important for the safety of the flight.

The FAA report emphasized the need for *timely* and *specific* information to be communicated in each direction. Recommendations for action focused on training and procedures to improve communication and increase the awareness of both captain and flight attendant needs and duties.

The FAA report said, "During normal operations each crew needs to have a general idea of what the duties of the other crew are so that they know when that crew is most fully occupied. Such knowledge helps to avoid inappropriate requests and unnecessary friction between the two crews. During emergencies it is imperative that each crew know exactly what to expect from the other crew so that they can work together effectively."

Why should crew coordination problems remain so resistant to solution? The answer may be that the solution has not yet been clearly defined. "Crew coordination" appeared in FAR § 121.417 in relation to emergency training, which must provide "instructions in emergency assignments and procedures, including coordination among crew members."

According to this definition, the regulations do no more than require the coordination of crews in emergencies. They do not include a requirement for coordination under non-emergency circumstances. Moreover, it is not the function of the regulations to describe how this (or indeed any other requirement) may be achieved nor how its success can be measured.

Training manuals (both operator and aircraft-specific) surveyed in FAA's study were found to offer more detail than contained in the FAR, but did little to explain the duties of one group of crew members to the other. Training for coordination was, for the most part, found to be confined to providing verbal instructions rather than providing opportunities for practical exercises. Joint training of flight deck and cabin crews was rare.

According to FAA's report, "All of the flight attendant manuals examined in this study stated that in the event of an emergency, the flight attendant in charge should ask the captain about the nature of the emergency, the time available to prepare the cabin, and special instructions (e.g., what the bracing signal will be). Very little, if any, information is offered on the duties of the flight attendants in the flight operations manuals."

Another possible reason for the failure to solve this problem can abe drawn from the following statement contained in a 1988 advisory circular on the subject: "in certain circumstances it is important for flight crew members and flight attendants to act as one cohesive crew, even though they are trained, scheduled, and generally regarded as two independent crews. When it is necessary to act as one crew, the activities of the cockpit should be coordinated."

But this is precisely where the problem lies. it is very difficult to "act as one cohesive crew" in "certain circumstances" while for the rest of the time there are "two independent crews." Furthermore, the circumstances in which coordination is required extend far beyond relatively rare emergency situations. The FAA report emphasized that coordination is required throughout the flight from takeoff through cruise to landing. Thus it is neither wise nor practical to attempt to confine coordination to one small area.

Organizational Definitions Create Two Crews

The perception of two distinct crews, cooperating only under rare circumstances, is an accurate reflection of reality within some airlines. There are clear organizational differences between the two crews. The flight deck crew reports to the airline's flight operations department while, typically, the flight attendants do not. The working area of the cabin crew is public; the flight deck crew's is private. There are differences in status, power, and salary that favor the flight deck and that are reinforced by the sex differences between the two groups—most pilots are men and most flight attendants are women.

Pilots are perceived to be dealing with state-of-the-art technology in their working lives while flight attendants are perceived to be dealing largely with what could be considered "domestic" activities—serving food and caring for those who are fearful—indeed, confirming the stereotyped feminine images of flight attendants that have been used extensively for marketing purposes. Pilots are thus perceived as essentially proactive—they make things happen.[Indeed, many flight attendants perceive themselves as "left out."—Editor] Flight attendants are perceived as essentially reactive to an agenda determined by others.

While flight attendants would not be expected to share these perceptions, some flight deck crew members may be prone to accept such stereotypes. "In fact, pilots are often surprised to learn the extent of the flight attendant's training and responsibilities," according to the FAA report.

An example deriving from these differences in status might be the reluctance of flight attendants to report to the flight deck any unusual events or difficulties. They may feel that any contribution they could make may appear to be superfluous because they assume that the flight deck crew already has all the information required. In their own difficulties, they may have problems in realizing when it is necessary to seek assistance. The boundary between persistence in the face of odds and foolhardy refusal to seek help at the appropriate time is usually only evident after the fact.

In this context the failure of some of the attempts at joint exercises noted in the FAA report and their subsequent abandonment is not surprising.

An instruction-based training program aimed at improving communication is often not enough to overcome obstacles in cockpit/cabin crew communication. A different approach is required that involves a major reappraisal of the aircraft as an organizational system.

Task Interpretation Can Foster Problems

Status differences are not the sole barrier to effective communication between flight deck and cabin. The way that the primary task of each group is interpreted also creates difficulties.

If the task of those on the flight deck is regarded only as "flying the plane," then this is consistent with the view that the fuselage is just "the piece in the middle that keeps the tail on." Such a view relegates "timely and specific" communication with flight attendants to a low priority.

For flight attendants it is not so much the interpretation of the task as the perception of the task that is the problem. While the statutory function of the flight attendant is to safeguard passengers, service—not safety—is generally by perceived as primary.

This is reinforced by the organizational separation of safety training from service training; by the longer periods of time devoted to service training; and by the image of the flight attendant that emphasizes serving passengers' needs rather than performing an effective safety role. (The use of a video recording rather than the live cabin crew in the aircraft to deliver the statutory safety briefings may serve to distance flight attendants further from the safety role.)

In this context, safety is regarded as separate from the routine activities of the flight and is concerned solely with unusual events involving emergency drills and equipment. An integration of the service role within the context of safety is needed so that safety permeates all flight attendant activities. This would enhance the professionalism of the job of flight attendant and facilitate the communication between the flight deck and the cabin.

These changes in task interpretation would have major implications, not all of which may be welcomed. A greater demand would be placed on the management skills of pilots because of their more direct involvement with the cabin crew. The greater safety awareness developed among flight attendants is likely to lead them to become less tolerant of inadequate or damaged equipment. Above all, such changes would have implications for training and for the relationship between the different organizational functions that provide the training.

Effective decision-making, [one of] the primary objective[s] of CRM, depends on the use of all available relevant information. But it must first be elicited from those who can provide it. The central focus of CRM is therefore on clear and unambiguous communication, on conflict resolution, on self-

Piper Aircraft Corp.

awareness and awareness of others, and on an integrated team performance.

It is well known that there are many obstacles to effective communication, and CRM addresses them. There is a need for listening skills, which in turn demand authenticity on the part of the listener, and for skills in expressing views that may not be popular, which in turn require assertiveness on the part of the speaker.

CRM training is [largely] based on the active participation of trainees in role playing and simulation rather than on passive listening to lectures. The video taping of role playing exercises allows for their subsequent analysis by group members and facilitates the giving and receiving of criticism in a non-threatening environment. The aim is for the attitudes of openness and assertiveness developed in training to be transferred to the operational context.

The problem of cabin/cockpit coordination has a long history of neglect, and the 1988 FAA report documented several serious cases. Practical problems of scheduling and disparities in numbers (typically, there are far more cabin crew than flight deck crew) are often cited as reasons for not implementing joint training.

Only five airlines listed in the FAA report had experience in joint training of crews. Two airlines had discontinued the training because the presence of members of the other crew was found to be either disruptive or inhibiting. In three airlines, however, the joint training experience was positive, lead-

ing to increased mutual understanding of duties and the practical benefit of immediate detection of incompatibilities in manuals.

The FAA report noted that the scheduling of joint training is less problematic for smaller airlines than for larger operators, which may have different training sites for crews and different recurrent training cycles.

There is now an opportunity for a paradigm shift. The increasingly sophisticated technology on the flight deck has led to changes in the pilot's task from the exercise of psychomotor skills to the management of a complex system. These changes have been technologically determined. Therefore, there is a certain lag in the corresponding changes in selection and training, although the adoption of CRM as an important part of pilot training suggests that this situation is improving.

Because the role of a manager as well as a pilot is required on the flight deck, the possibility arises of designating the managerial role in a creative way to take into account all the human resources in the aircraft. This involves integrating the cabin crew within the captain's sphere of operations.

When trained as a manager, the captain is more effective in exercising his or her responsibilities both on the flight deck and in the cabin. This does not preclude the continued delegation of some coordination tasks to senior cabin personnel, although the context within which the delegation takes place will have changed.

The advantage of this approach is that the captain's overall responsibility, already grounded in law, is explicitly recognized in a practical (and safety-directed) way. ∎

This article is reprinted from the November/December 1992 edition of Cabin Crew Safety, *a publication of Flight Safety Foundation, 2200 Wilson Boulevard, Suite 500, Arlington, VA 22201–3306; (703) 522–8300. Dr. Edwards works in the area of human factors and is co-author of a book called* The Aircraft Cabin—Managing the Human Factors.

CORPORATE FLYING
A Different Standard does not Mean Less Safety

by H. Dean Chamberlain and Phyllis Anne Duncan

What comes to mind when you think of corporate aviation? The image of a sleek *LearJet*, Cessna *Citation*, or Beech *Starship* from which executives emerge to attend top-level meetings at places like Aspen or Palm Springs is long-separated from reality. The truth is that not all corporate aircraft are bizjets; many are *King Airs* or *Barons*, *Navajos* or *Senecas*, Cessna 210's or even 172's. And the jobs of most corporate pilots certainly may not be fodder for "Lifestyles of the Rich and Famous." Many corporate executives help themselves to coffee from a thermos or doughnuts from the convenience store (usually picked up by the copilot on his or her way in for the pre-dawn preflight). Many corporate pilots cool their heels in small airport lounges waiting for their executive passengers whose meetings have gone longer than expected, subsisting on peanut butter crackers and colas from the omnipresent vending machines, catching naps on oversprung sofas, and hoping the weather will improve so that he or she won't be faced with a "fly or be fired" dilemma. Not so glamorous a picture at all.

The further reality is that corporate flying, just like any flying done for a living, is hard work, accomplished by professional pilots. The result is that corporate flying as an aspect of general aviation enjoys a safety record envied by some airlines and com-muters. But there are still a number of pressures corporate pilots may be subjected to that could affect that sterling safety record.

One external pressure may be their employer's lack of *aviation* knowledge and experience. Although their business acumen may be legendary, some corporate executives may have little or no experience in the day-to-day operations of a flight department. Some CEO's may view the company aircraft and pilots as a "perk" to be used for their convenience, and many may find it difficult to accept when one of their employees (i.e., the pilot) says that that expensive asset can't move because the weather's not good enough or the MEL won't allow flight with certain equipment inoperative.

Another pressure may be largely internal—pilot attitude. Corporate pilots can be gray-haired captains retired from the airlines or the military and accustomed to calling all the shots in the cockpit. Corporate pilots can be men or women building time to qualify for a commuter or airline job. They could even be those who didn't make the cut for those high-profile flying jobs and who took any flying job that was available. Whatever type they fall into, corporate pilots fly for a living because it is what they want to do, and they know for every one of them there is a newly certificated commercial pilot or laid-off airline pilot ready to take his or her position. Sometimes that leaves a corporate pilot little choice in a "fly or be fired" situation: Whose rules do I follow—the ones the FAA has written down and my own good judgement or the unwritten ones of the person who signs my paycheck? With so many hidden agendas, this is a difficult decision for many of us to contemplate. Making the wrong choice can and has cost lives.

Above all, corporate pilots are professionals as much as any airline pilot. One difference may be corporate structure. Pilots of large airlines know they generally have support for safety decisions all the way up the corporate ladder. When there is any question about a situation or a procedure, the airline pilot consults the company's operating manual—required by the FAR—and there is the answer in black and white. Not all corporate pilots have the luxury of that organizational support or the benefit of written company procedures that all employees must follow. Corporate flight departments may not be the company's primary business; they exist for the company's benefit and efficiency. If the airplane sits in the hangar for a reason management cannot fathom, they see no benefit and little efficiency.

What we have been trying to do up to this point is identify some of the potential problems or questions faced by both flight crews and companies that have small flight departments managed by executives not familiar with aviation: When is it safe to fly? Who is responsible for making that decision? Who is responsible for crew supervision and crew conflict resolution? And who is responsible for safety? These are also some of the questions we will explore as we review the report on an accident that killed nine people. In December 1991, a corporate Beechjet 400 crashed shortly after taking off in VFR conditions and while waiting for an IFR clearance. The accident occurred about 9:40 a.m. EST when the aircraft struck the side of a mountain about six miles west southwest of Rome, GA. At the time of the accident, the aircraft was operating VFR beneath a 1,000-foot overcast and was waiting for an IFR clearance that was on file. Visibility was a reported 10 miles, although another pilot flying an approach to the Rome airport at the time of the accident reported reduced visibility west of the airport.

Before we go in depth into the particulars of the accident, we need to review the regulatory background of corporate flying.

Regulatory Requirements

Because they do not "hold out to the public" for transportation, corporate flight departments operate under FAR Part 91, General Operating and Flight Rules. However, if the corporate aircraft is a large (more than 12,500 pounds), turbine-powered (turboprop or turbojet), multiengine airplane, FAR Part 91, Subpart F provides additional requirements. Furthermore, if that large airplane has a seating capacity of 20 or more or a maximum payload capacity of 6,000 pounds or more, then the operating rules of FAR Part 125 apply in addition to FAR Part 91 (although the requirements of FAR Part 125 supersede Subpart F). The company would have to apply to the FAA and meet the certification requirements for a FAR Part 125 operating certificate. FAR Part 125 is structured along the lines of FAR Part 121, but FAR Part 125 is different from FAR Part 121 in many of its requirements because corporations will be operating the aircraft for *private carriage*. Meeting all the var-

ious requirements of FAR Part 125 might be overly burdensome for a small corporate flight department, so the FAA can issue a letter of deviation authority, which provides relief from all or part of FAR Part 125. Before the FAA issues such a letter, the operator must justify the request and show that the operator can achieve "an equivalent level of safety" when operating solely under FAR Part 91 (full deviation) or appropriate sections of FAR Part 125 (partial deviation).

Consequently, the vast majority of corporate aircraft are operated under FAR Part 91, either by virtue of their configuration or by a letter of deviation authority. FAR § 91.501(b) lists the types of operations that can be conducted under Subpart F. Subpart F operators are also subject to the remainder of FAR Part 91 (unless an exemption permits otherwise); however, aircraft that are *not* large, *not* turbine-powered, *not* multiengine, and *not* airplanes are subject only to FAR Part 91, Subparts A-E and G-J.

Does this mean that corporate aircraft operate under a lesser standard? When reviewing the requirements of FAR Part 121 and FAR Part 91, Subpart F, an initial opinion might be, "Yes." But it is necessary to look at the context of the different types of operations—private versus public carriage. Because they do not provide transportation to the public at large, corporate operators are held to a standard appropriate for private carriage. A corporate flight may involve a half-dozen corporate executives rather than half a thousand vacationers, but the responsibility for a safe operation in the nation's airspace system is the same. For the most part, corporate management and certainly corporate pilots take that responsibility seriously. At a given time, the worth of the executives on board the aircraft, in terms of future productivity for a company, may well exceed the cost of the machine itself. A whole wealth of corporate talent and corporate knowledge could be lost in a single instant, and non-paying passengers are no more expendable than paying ones.

Important Questions

It is not our intention to reprint the entire NTSB report on the Georgia accident, but we do want to highlight some questions the report raises. Before we try to address some of those questions, it is important to iterate that FAR Part 91 VFR rules should have provided adequate protection for this flight while the crew waited for the IFR clearance, but for some reason, the crew failed to maintain a minimum safe altitude in accordance with FAR § 91.119—obvious from the fatal impact with terrain.

The first important question is who is responsible for ensuring safety of a flight? Any pilot will automatically say that the pilot-in-command is responsible. But what might a company executive say about responsibility for his or her expensive aircraft? Would an executive with little knowledge of the FAR be willing to allow the pilot-in-command to make the final decision on that aircraft's operation? What does the FAR say?

FAR § 91.3 states that, "The pilot in command of an aircraft is directly responsible for, and is the final authority as to, the operation of that aircraft."

You can't get much simpler than that. But wait a minute. What if the pilot-in-command fails to fulfill that responsibility? What if the pilot failed in that responsibility because the company president or other highly placed executive felt it was his or her authority? What is the company president's role in the operation of the company aircraft? It seems almost too simple to say the pilot flies and the management takes care of all the other business. Obviously, you can't have the board of directors debating in the cockpit on whether to land the airplane, but you can have that same group in the board room deciding how the company's flight department will operate. Rather than a negative situation, this provides an opportunity for the flight department to educate management on the FAR and the importance of good operating procedures.

This is also an opportunity to go above and beyond the FAR in corporate aviation by establishing written flight operating procedures that all employees agree to and will abide by. Company policies cannot conflict with a FAR requirement, but they can be more strict. For example, FAR Part 91 operations have no requirements for flight/duty time restrictions, but a company policy might go beyond that and require eight hours of rest in a 24-hour duty period. Written procedures can and do establish a "chain of command" and confirm who is responsible for what in a flight department. What the non-aviation people must understand is that the pilots have the flight skills and knowledge and experience, and those cannot be usurped by non-aviators. (It would be like the pilots trying to tell the marketing director how to do his or her job. Imagine how well that would go over.)

Many corporate flight departments have written procedures because of insurance requirements; not following procedures may mean losing coverage. The advisability of small flight departments having written procedures is illustrated by several aspects of the Georgia accident.

Accident Analysis

The company that owned the Beechjet had acquired a flight department when it bought out a chain of rival food stores in Alabama. The flight department then consisted of a Beech *King Air* and the two pilots involved in the accident. The company upgraded to the Beechjet and sent both pilots for company training for that aircraft. At the time of the accident, the two pilots had been flying together for about three years. Both held ATP certificates and had no record of any FAA enforcement action or any other accidents or incidents. The 59-year-old captain had a reported 16,000 hours with about 850 hours in turbojets, all in the Beechjet. The 27-year-old first officer had 3,100 total hours with about the same amount of turbojet time. All of his jet time was also in the company aircraft. Whenever either pilot was not available to fly because of illness, vacation, etc., the company would hire local pilots to fill in for the missing crew member. Some of those pilots pro-

vided statements to the NTSB that reported an apparent conflict between the captain and first officer. According to the statements, the captain reportedly would take chances by going below minimums on an approach to get his corporate passengers into a particular airport, or he would scud run under a ceiling for the same reason. Some said the copilot, whom they described as a professional, "go-by-the-book" type of pilot, felt very uncomfortable flying with the captain.

The substitute pilots also stated the copilot told them that when he was flying or landing, the captain would occasionally override him on the controls for no apparent reason. One statement included an alleged comment from the copilot that he (the copilot) thought the captain's flight habits would kill them.

According to some of the other statements, the copilot had considered going to the FAA about the captain's flying habits but was afraid he would also be implicated since he was aboard as a crew member at the time of the alleged incidents. The copilot thought that an FAA investigation might jeopardize his own chances of becoming an airline pilot. He was also afraid to quit for the same reason. These witnesses also stated that the copilot had felt ignored when he had raised safety issues to company management. However, in his statement to the NTSB, the executive denies the copilot told him anything.

Perhaps a company written procedure for elevating safety concerns that held the respondent accountable for some action might have at least assured the copilot his case was being heard. If the company procedures had included a process for reporting safety concerns, say, through the Aviation Safety Reporting System, the copilot's fears of FAA enforcement action could have been alleviated. There is also the FAA Safety Hotline (1–800–255–1111) which allows people employed by aviation related companies to report unsafe activities or non-compliance anonymously. The FAA is required to investigate every report.

On the day of the accident, the investigation implies that the crew may

have departed VFR to keep to some kind of schedule. Again, the company executive contradicts these statements. In his statement he said that the crew was never under any type of pressure to maintain a schedule. However, employees of the FBO servicing the aircraft, in their statements to the NTSB, overheard the executive passengers talking about having to depart quickly. Company procedures outlining minimums for departure and landing and iterating that safety comes before schedule may have precluded such a contradiction but more importantly may have alleviated imagined pressure from a desire to "please the boss."

VFR Charts

Another interesting point brought out in the investigation where a written company policy may have prevented an accident was that there were no VFR sectionals on board the aircraft although the crew took off VFR. VFR charts would have topographically shown the location and heights of the nearby mountains. Although VFR charts are not required for IFR flights, current VFR charts provide an important safety feature on any flight. VFR charts are the only source of terrain elevation information needed for determining minimum safe altitudes for off-airway IFR direct flights outside terminal areas. If a written company policy had called for the carriage and use of VFR charts, might one of the pilots have noted the specific location of the terrain and been able to avoid it? Impossible to say definitely, but it's a lesson the rest of us can now learn the easy way.

Another consideration is the VFR departure. Apparently, the crew could not contact ATC from the ground to obtain the IFR clearance and so departed VFR to get airborne to have better communications capability—a time-honored and universal practice. But the problems with communicating on the ground may have been caused by the high terrain, and perhaps this should have raised a note of caution before a VFR departure and a flight beneath a 1,000-foot ceiling. If the crew could not communicate directly

with ATC while on the ground, the captain could have requested an IFR departure clearance with a clearance void time by phone. With such a clearance, the flight could have departed IFR and contacted ATC once airborne. ATC specifies that if the aircraft has not departed by the time specified in the clearance, the clearance is canceled. This procedure allows pilots unable to contact ATC from the ground to depart IFR. Once airborne, the pilot checks in with the designated ATC facility. If the pilot does not takeoff within the specified time, the pilot must notify ATC as directed in the clearance. If the pilot fails to notify ATC, ATC considers the flight overdue 30 minutes after the clearance void time and will start search procedures, stopping IFR traffic for one hour in order to locate the "missing" aircraft. A pilot taking off after the clearance void time is operating without an IFR clearance and must remain in VMC or be in violation of FAR § 91.155 and/or 91.173. Would a written company policy requiring pilots to request clearances with void times have kept this flight out of danger?

Assertive First Officers

Although we have commented on the actions and responsibilities of the captain—because he was the PIC—at the time of the accident, the copilot was flying the aircraft. The aircraft's cockpit voice recorder (CVR) provided investigators some insight into the crew's decisions and actions before the crash. It also revealed the captain's comments and directions to the first officer and also the first officer's apparent timidity in responding to the captain. From the recorded conversations, the crew evidently knew they were flying near a mountain and that there were other aircraft flying IFR in the area. Based upon our interpretation of the report, the first officer appeared hesitant to fly in a direction where he could not see clearly, but the captain told him to turn right and to "bring it right on around." The copilot did not voice his concerns further, and a few seconds later the aircraft hit the mountain. The two pilots and all seven executives on board died on impact.

A lack of first officer assertiveness in the face of an intimidating captain has been cited in air carrier accidents and incidents. Air carriers sought to alleviate this with Crew Resource Management (more on that later), and many corporate flight departments have also subscribed to the crew as a team concept. Teamwork is just as important in a two-person flight department. Again, written procedures that support the first officer in safety considerations and an understanding management go a long way toward assuring first officers that they are part of the cockpit team, not just along for the ride.

The NTSB accident report sites the fact that the flight department of this company did not possess (nor were they required to) "... an operations manual, or policies and/or directives addressing the manner in which flights in the Beech 400 were to be conducted, the authority and responsibility of the captain and first officer, and management's support of and respect for the decisions made by the flight crew." We have tried to set forth some specific areas where official company policies and procedures might have prevented an accident.

Developing Procedures

For corporate aircraft operators who want to develop their own FAR Part 91 flight guidelines, the operating requirements in FAR Part 135 (e.g., training programs, operations manuals) could serve as a good example. Also, many manuals are available commercially, and many airlines, commuters, and airline management consultants offer manual production services for a fee. FAA inspectors may provide advice on how to structure or produce policies and procedures appropriate for corporate operations, but they do not approve such documents. Since written procedures are not required for FAR Part 91 operations, company operating policies could only be enforced by company executives or a "chief pilot" in the flight department—not by the FAA. (FAA inspection and surveillance of corporate operators may be included in a FSDO's annual work program; tasks concerning certificated operators take precedence.)

Having a good set of rules is important, but the rules must be developed by aviation professionals (i.e., the company's pilots) and understood by both the flight crews and the executives who use the aircraft. Executives must also know the company's policies and procedures concerning its aircraft because they need to know what operations are permitted so that they do not ask a crew to do something that may go contrary to a FAR.

As noted by NTSB, in addition to the operating guidelines, there should be a procedure for crew members to voice their safety concerns to management. Knowledgeable executive-passengers can then make informed decisions regarding the complaints based upon their own guidelines and their knowledge of the FAR. The need for open and accurate communication is vital for safety. As the FAA has discovered, whenever there is a breakdown in communication among everyone involved in an activity, there is a potential for a breakdown in safety. In the case of this accident, perhaps if there had been some corporate procedure in place to handle the safety issues raised by the first officer, that first officer's statements to his friends might not have been so prophetic.

Corporate CRM

The apparent lack of communication in the cockpit and the lack of assertiveness of the first officer might have been alleviated by a company training policy that required crew resource management (CRM) training. This crew appeared to be operating under the pressure of the ostensible conflict between the captain and the first officer, discussed by many of the witnesses. The FAA and the aviation industry have long cooperated to develop better ways for crews to learn how to work together because studies have shown that human error is a contributing factor in about 70% of all air carrier accidents and incidents. That percentage increases for general aviation, of which corporate flying is a part.

Some of the techniques developed to minimize human error in the cockpit are outlined in FAA Advisory Circular (AC) 120–51A, "Crew Resource Management Training." Available from the FAA, the AC was written to help air carriers and FAR Part 135 operators develop, implement, and evaluate CRM procedures to train crew members how to work as a team instead of as individuals. Most of the CRM concept is adaptable to corporate operations. CRM training also studies how individual crew member attitudes and behaviors impact safety. As the AC says, CRM focuses on communication skills, teamwork, task allocation, and decision making in the cockpit. A vital aspect of learning how to work together is the acknowledgement of the important role the first officer has in safety. Past accident investigations

have shown that an autocratic captain who fails to use the knowledge and skills of his or her first officer (or a first officer who won't speak up) often kills both of them in an accident. CVR tapes have recorded first officers' futile comments regarding their inability to break a chain of events that inevitably led to an accident. The area of first officer authority and responsibility is also discussed in AC 120–51.

Another AC, 60–22, "Aeronautical Decision Making," provides a systematic approach to risk assessment and stress management in aviation. It also illustrates how personal attitudes can influence decision making as well as how those attitudes can be modified to enhance safety and teamwork in the cockpit. There is no reason why corporate flight departments can't make use of the information provided by these resources. Commercial flight training companies offer CRM training for all kinds of flight operations, including corporate aviation.

Another important part of the CRM concept is that the crew trains together as a crew. As noted, the company involved in the accident hired local pilots to replace either the captain or first officer when they were absent. These pilots were likely highly qualified, but they may have lacked the experience of team building. In this instance the second pilot is only along for the ride to satisfy an insurance or a FAR requirement. This is highlighted by another corporate accident, also in 1991, in San Diego, CA. For some reason the copilot of a bizjet flying the band of country singer Reba McIntyre's decided to return home on another company aircraft. Another company pilot was elected to fill in, but there was no evidence that this copilot was type rated in the aircraft, a DH-125. (For a FAR Part 91 operation, the regulations do not require a type rating although he or she would need a check as per the requirements of FAR § 61.55; however, this raises the question of how much help the inexperienced copilot would have been to the captain in an emergency. Consequently, in many corporate flight departments company policy or insur-

ance companies sometimes require type ratings for copilots.) In this accident the type-rated captain with an ATP certificate had over 15,000 total hours with 150 in make and model. The copilot was a commercial pilot with 1,750 total hours; he had a flight instructor certificate and multiengine and instrument ratings. The aircraft's owner described the captain as a very experienced and outstanding pilot. However, he said that the captain had flown many hours solo ferrying aircraft and was the type of pilot to do everything on a flight.

(Ironically, this aircraft also departed VFR to obtain an IFR clearance and also without VFR charts on board, then struck a 3,300-foot mountain 172 feet from its summit. Two crew members and eight passengers died.)

Conclusion

Those of us who write this type of accident analysis article have the benefit of all that 20/20 hindsight. It's sometimes too easy to say the pilots or the company might have, could have, should have done this or not done that. Or the FAA should have, could have, ought to have, ought not to have done a whole host of things. The fact remains that human errors that could have, should have been avoided have cost the lives of talented people in corporate cockpits and passenger compartments. What corporate flight departments must do is learn from these aberrations that occurred in Georgia and California so that the safety record that is so treasured remains enviable.

Developing written operating procedures and/or contracting for CRM training for a corporate flight department might seem tedious and expensive, especially when there is no requirement for any of it. Corporate management, perhaps, needs to consider if that unrequired manual or training program is really superfluous in terms of their safety record and the human resources carried on board that corporate "perk." ∎

[AC's 60–22 and 120–51 are free from DOT General Services Section, M–433.2, Washington, DC 20590.]

FAMOUS FLYER

Augustus Moore Herring
—Genius or Bungler?

by Louise Oertly, *Associate Editor*

The hopes and dreams of many men were shattered on a cold, windy day in December—the 17th day of 1903 to be exact. That was the day when the Wright brothers made their memorable flight and proved that man could fly. Ironically, one of those men whose dreams had been shattered by the first manned, powered flight had been at Kitty Hawk with the Wrights only a year earlier. His name was Augustus Moore Herring.

Herring comes across as a rather an interesting character. He worked with some of the legendary names in early aviation but along the way acquired something of a reputation among them. When Octave Chanute suggested Herring's name as a glider pilot, Wilbur Wright expressed concern since several things he had "heard about Mr. Herring's relations with Mr. Langley and yourself seemed to me to indicate that he might be of somewhat jealous disposition and possibly inclined to claim for himself rather more credit than those with whom he might be working are willing to allow." This characterization aside, his contemporaries labeled him in turn a genius and a bungler.

Beginnings in Aviation

Born in 1865, Herring was 15 when his father, a wealthy Sommersville, GA, cotton broker, gave him a toy helicopter. His interest in aeronautics grew and, by the time his family moved to New York and he entered Stevens Institute of Technology in 1883, designing gliders interested him more than studying mechanical engineering. School records show he never submitted his undergraduate thesis on a design study for a marine steam engine, and his work in mathematics, analytical chemistry, and drafting was incomplete. According to Herring, his failure to graduate was that his thesis on the subject of flight was too visionary for the school to accept. The first of many differing points of view.

After leaving school Herring worked as an engineering consultant. However, in the economic panic of 1893 Herring's successful business went under with many others. He eventually found work as a chainman on the New York Central Railroad. Octave Chanute, who had been corresponding with him about Herring's experiments with a Lilienthal-type glider, tried unsuccessfully to find him a job better suited his talents and finally hired him to build a series of gliders. December 1894 marked the beginning of an eight year on-again-off-again association between Chanute and Herring.

Langley Connection

Barely six months after Herring began working for Chanute, another offer came his way. The Smithsonian's Samuel Langley visited the young New Yorker and was highly impressed by his work. So impressed, in fact, that he made him a job offer of $150 a month as overseer of the work in aerodromics (defined in the dictionary as the art or science of flying). Herring accepted right away—only he forgot to mention that he was already working for Chanute. Within five days of starting his new job in Washington, DC, Herring realized he had made a mistake. Langley was difficult to work for and made of habit of changing the specifications of a design after it left the drafting table. If the design did not work after that it was the fault of the engineer, even if he knew nothing of the changes. Conversely, Langley also took credit for anything that proved successful. By November of 1895 Herring resigned his position and asked Chanute for his old job back.

Back to Chanute

Herring moved this time to Chicago and started construction on two gliders—a Lilienthal-type of his own design and a multi-wing of Chanute's. By late June of 1896 the first trials took place at Miller, IN, about three miles from Chicago. Herring's glider lacked stability and control and, after several crashes, was damaged beyond repair. Chanute's multi-wing design was tested next. The principle of this design was opposite Herring's. Instead of the pilot shifting his weight to achieve stability, the craft's wings would shift on pivots to achieve stability in the wind. After some experimentation, the two men discovered the best combination for stability was five pairs of six by three foot wings stacked in front and one

pair behind at the tail. The glider, affectionately known as because of its bug-like appearance, proved steady and manageable in winds up to 20 miles an hour.

After nearly two weeks of testing Chanute's band packed up and headed back to the Chicago workshop. In late August three gliders were ready for testing—William Paul Butusov's bat-winged *Albatross*, a rebuilt *Katydid*, and a Chanute-Herring designed fixed-wing biplane. The *Albatross* proved to be a disappointment; the improved *Katydid* almost doubled its previous performance; and the fixed-wing glider surpassed all expectations. Flights up to 359 feet in 14 seconds were achieved.

By mid-September of 1896 Herring and Chanute disagreed on how best to proceed. Herring felt powered flight was the next step, while Chanute felt more testing was necessary. Needless to say, the ever impatient Herring struck out on his own. Objective—powered flight.

On His Own

Unable to find other financial support, Herring used $150 of his own money to build a triplane with a compressed air-powered automatic control system. The craft achieved altitudes of 40 feet above his starting point and was capable of making controlled turns. In June of 1897 he shelved his plans when he was unable to raise further funding. Reluctantly, Herring went back to work for Chanute to help develop a five-wing multiplane glider, but after two weeks Chanute dismissed him convinced that Herring's "mind naturally revolts at following other men's ideas."

About the time that Herring accepted an engineering position at the Truscott Boat Yard at St. Joseph, MI, he had also received an order from Matthias Arnot for one of his 1896 gliders. Foreseeing the possibility of future sponsorship by Arnot, Herring upgraded the 1896 design and after successful test flights determined that the design was ready for powered flight. The question was developing the powerplant. Steam was unreliable, and inter-

nal combustion too long term a venture. Herring wanted quick results. The easiest and lightest solution was a simple two-cylinder compressed air powerplant which would power two five-foot propellers—a tractor and a pusher. The finished aircraft weighed 88 pounds and in October 1898 flew 73 feet at a groundspeed of five or six miles per hour. Herring was determine to upgrade the craft and fly it again the following spring. Over the winter he experimented with various types of engines, but his experimentation was all for naught when his workshop caught fire and all his hard work went up in flames.

For the next few years misfortune continued plague Herring. Financial assistance was sparse, and Chanute attempted to take sole credit for the biplane glider design. Herring turned to motorcycle manufacture and the publication of a *Gas Power*, a magazine for motorist, as a more profitable enterprise.

Herring and Chanute would have one more joint venture together when Chanute contracted with him to reconstruct and pilot the 1896 multiplane glider. Joining the Wright brothers at Kitty Hawk in October of 1902, Herring and Chanute soon suspended testing when the superiority of the Wright *Flyer* became evident.

After Kitty Hawk

Herring never totally gave up on aviation. In 1908 he competed against the Wrights for the first military contract and for a short time had a partnership with Glenn Curtiss which ended up in a lawsuit that was finally settled after his death in 1926. Despite Herring's failure to achieve powered flight, he had contributed significantly to the development of aviation. Both Langley and Chanute used his "regulating" cruciform tail in their designs, and the 1896 Chanute-Herring glider descended from Herring's earlier rubberband- and steam-powered scale models. Before the turn of the century, he could also claim the title the most experienced glider pilot in the world.

Genius or bungler? You decide. ■

• Alternate Airport

Is it true that when filing an IFR flight plan, FAR § 91.169(b) requires that if there is no Terminal forecast for the destination airport, even though it has a standard instrument approach procedure, you must specify an alternate regardless of the weather conditions?
Thomas E. Miller
Ballston Spa, NY

The above example is not true. FAR § 91.169(b) states in part, an alternate is not required if the first airport of intended landing has a standard instrument approach procedure and for at least one hour before and one hour after the estimated time of arrival, the weather reports or forecasts, or any combination of them, indicate the ceiling will be at least 2,000 feet above the airport elevation; and the visibility will be at least three statue miles. FAR § 91.l69(b) states weather reports or forecasts, or any combination of them may be used to determine if an alternate airport is required. FAR § 91.169(b) does not require a terminal forecast from the destination airport. The answer provided is for Part 91 operations.

• Measuring Altitude

I have been unable to get a definite explanation of the following question. Several airspace designations have floors stated as above ground level (AGL) such as 3,000 feet, 1,200 feet, 700 feet, etc. About two thirds of the state of Ohio is fairly level with ground elevations of 800 to 1,000 feet mean sea level (MSL). However, along the Ohio River and over most of southeast Ohio the river valleys will be about 500 feet MSL while the surrounding hill tops average about 900 feet MSL. The valleys vary in width. From what point is the above ground level elevation measured when flying over such terrain? Logic would seem to indicate that it would be taken from the ridge tops. However, when flying over a wide valley, what is the base level? How is it figured in areas with mountains rising several thousand feet above valley floors with valleys only a few miles wide. Please help.
Stuart L. Faber
Cincinnati, Ohio

The answer to your specific question is above ground level altitude, or AGL, is the absolute altitude measured perpendicular to a particular point on the earth's surface such as the altitude measured with a radar altimeter. When you are measuring absolute altitude above ground level over a valley with a radar altimeter, the contour of the measurement will vary with the terrain. A measurement of 500 feet AGL over a hill top will be higher than a similar measurement taken in the middle of a valley when both are compared to sea level.

As the FAA's Instrument Flying Handbook says, altimetry involves more than simple measurement of height. The problem is when pilots talk about altitude, they may be talking about several different altitudes such as AGL, MSL, pressure altitude, true altitude, or absolute altitude depending upon how the altitude is measured. This is why it is critical for pilots to understand what altitude is being discussed since a misunderstanding could be fatal. This is also why pilots must know the minimum safe altitude needed for terrain avoidance for their particular operation. Pilots using the typical light aircraft pressure altimeter must also know its operating limitations to ensure an accurate altitude reading. For an interesting discussion on the dangers of incorrectly set pressure altimeters on international flights, please see the September-October 1992 issue of *FAA Aviation News.*

• Testing Standards

Ronald D. Drake's article, "How to Pass Your Next FAA Flight Test" is a good summary of the formal requirements for a test, but because it ignores all except the formal requirements it fails, in the end, to be any help in actually passing the test. It merely shows some ways of failing the test; thus, it in effect says, "all you have to do is get it right, and from now on it's not our fault if you fail."

The reality is that this is a test, and the examiners or inspectors are humans with human defects. I gave up instructing—even

though plenty of evidence showed that I was a superior-quality teacher much in demand—because I have a poor examination temperament, and at my last renewal collapsed into stupidity at the first question. I do not blame my examiner for that: you can scarcely expect better than Clayton Scott. But some examiners and inspectors are destructive to the chances of examinees. I flew twice with one, who, in my opinion and that of several others, is technically fair, with no tricks, but who likes to keep you twitching, on edge. Another was so notorious around here for asking silly trick questions that some highly experienced instructors (including one who has been an Air Force examiner) refused to send candidates to him and, God help us, he has been taken on by the FAA as an inspector.

He is not the first inspector to be known for that, and it must cast severe doubt on the integrity of the FAA's intentions. If the FAA is truly interested in promoting aviation, then it must emphasize fairness in flight tests. A good start might be to find out who are the unfair inspectors and examiners and take them off the job entirely.

Until that happens, Drake's article and similar ones serve merely to emphasize the complacency of an organization that does not have to be responsive to those over whose lives it has so much power.
Name withheld

Thank you for your letter. We deeply regret that your tenure as a certificated flight instructor was not more rewarding. Aviation can ill afford to lose dedicated instructors. Checkrides are in fact tests, and we all react differently to being tested. However, we feel we must take exception to your comments regarding the FAA's testing philosophy. All of us have had checkrides with "good" evaluators and "not so good" evaluators. In many cases, the difference between the good and not so good evaluators was how we reacted to them as individuals. If we liked them, they were good, if we felt uncomfortable with them the moment we met them, we knew the test was going to be bad. And yes, there are a few bad evaluators. Some are either trying to prove their own superiority, or they are simply repeating the bad habits they learned during their own early training and testing. Neither the FAA nor industry is immune from these "not so good" evaluators.

Your comment regarding the fairness of FAA testing perhaps stems from a lack of information about how performance is to be measured during a practical test. FAA designed its current pilot Practical Test Standards (PTS) to be fair and to ensure the consistency of flight testing across the

> FAA AVIATION NEWS welcomes comments from its readers. We may edit letters for style and/or length. We will select one representative letter from those on the same topic for publications, and because of our bimonthly publishing schedule, responses may not appear for several issues. We will send personal replies only upon request. We will not print anonymous letters, but we will withhold names upon request. Address: Editor, FAA AVIATION NEWS, AFS–810, Washington, DC 20591.

country. This was not always the case. The old Flight Test Guides only outlined areas to be tested. The Guides left it up to the evaluators how to do the tests. Some of the "not so good" evaluators used the broad guidelines to ask their trivial questions and to use their various "tricks" to harass the person being tested. Some probably felt these "tricks" eliminated the "less than perfect" pilots out of aviation for the good of all. They may have felt the high-stress testing methods used by the military at the time applied to civilian applicants. Those days are gone. Today, the PTS set the same testing standards for a given test for everyone. Applicants preparing for a test today knows exactly what areas are going to be tested and the standards that are going to be used to evaluate their performance during the test. The applicant's performance either meets the standards or not. If the applicant feels he or she did not receive an accurate evaluation from a designated pilot examiner, the applicant can ask the FAA for a retest with an FAA inspector. As Mr. Drake pointed out in his article, every applicant planning on taking a flight test should review the appropriate PTS to ensure they understand and can meet all of the standards listed.

In addition to redrafting its testing procedures, the FAA trained its inspectors and designated pilot examiners how to use the new testing standards as the new PTS were released. Today, that training is an integral part of FAA inspector training at the FAA Academy in Oklahoma City, OK. All Aviation Safety Inspectors (Operations) and designated pilot examiners are taught how to give practical tests using the PTS.

So, to respond to your statement that the FAA is complacent in its concern for those it tests, the facts prove otherwise. The FAA redesigned its testing procedures to ensure that all applicants receive an objective and realistic practical test which measures only their knowledge and skills necessary to operate an aircraft safely and in accordance with national standards—not those of the evaluator.

We urge you to obtain a copy of the Flight Instructor Practical Test Standards appropriate to the instructor certificates you held and re-evaluate your decision to cease instructing. We need you.

• Legal Approach Plates

Would the FAR be violated if a pilot utilized an instrument approach plate that was still current (latest amendment) but which was contained in an instrument approach bound volume that according to the dates published on the front was no longer effective.
Cyril Toker
Ponte Vedra Beach, FL

Yes, because the pilot may have an out of date instrument approach plate (IAP). IAP amendments reflect only such changes as altitudes, courses to be flown, and final approach minimums on instrument approach plates. Other chart changes can be made without an amendment. Radio frequencies and airport sketches are two items that can be changed without an amendment being issued. You could have a situation where the amendment number is still current, but critical radio frequency information or airport diagram information on the IAP may not be current. Because airport information can change, it is important for pilots to always utilize current IAP's, consult change notices, and check NOTAM's, especially FDC, for the current status of any airport they plan on using.

• Magazine Critique

After seeing several issues, please accept these comments. Use your space to present FAA-related communications to us such as four inspectors saying what they look for most on checkrides, etc. If you try to compete in writing style with regular magazines you not only suffer by comparison with the pros, but also deny us FAA comms. You have eliminated (apparently) the "Instrument Corner." This was, in my opinion, the best ongoing feature you had. It is exactly what I refer to as "FAA comm" to us. No other pub can do this...this is your exclusive property. . . if over half the issue were the "Flight Forum" it would be closer to ideal.

Re the May/June 1992 article on "How to Pass Your Next FAA Flight Test." (By the way, this is the type of article FAA Aviation News *should contain.) Perhaps Mr. Drake should now include in his very pertinent memory aid the fact that the FAA now ramp checks for having the proper charts up-to-date on board. Could his checklist aid then be advanced from ARROW to CARROW?*

C—charts/communications data
A—airworthiness certificate
R—registration (aircraft)
R—radio station license (if needed)
O—operating limits
W—weight and balance
Howie Keefe
Venice, CA

The printing of the "Instrument Corner" depends on the availability of a letter from one of our readers. In the May/June issue that you referred to the "Flight Forum" was expanded to two pages and the "Instrument Corner" required an additional page to answer the question. Admittedly the magazine cannot dedicate three pages

every issue to the "Forum" but it will be expanded as often as space allows. Thank you for your comments. It is alway interesting to know what our readers think of us.

• Requesting SVFR

If a private pilot was sure he could maintain clear of clouds and a mile visibility, would it be plausible for him or her to request a special VFR clearance to spiral up in a control zone to get through a scattered or broken layer of clouds to VFR conditions on top to continue the flight to an airport where a descent could be made under VFR?

According to regulations it should be legal, but I am wondering what the odds are that an air traffic controller would permit it?
Matt Stans
Bloomington, MN

Yes, it is legal to request such a clearance, and the odds are good ATC will approve the request if Special VFR is permitted at that airport. However, the question that must be asked is, though it may be legal, can such a clearance be executed safely. Since we are assuming that the pilot is not instrument rated, we question the safety of such a request by a non-instrument rated pilot because we do not know the answers to some of the old "what if" questions that a pilot must ask before considering such an operation. Will I be able to maintain the basic VFR minimums required in FAR § 91.155 upon exiting the control zone? What if conditions change? What if I get trapped on top? What if the airport of intended landing goes IFR? What if I have an emergency such as an engine failure? What if I lose communications? What if I lose my navigation capability? An air traffic controller will provide available weather information, but it is the pilot-in-command's responsibility to integrate this information with the answers obtained from the above questions before commencing a flight.

AIR SHOWS!

What do Abilene, Brooklyn, Clemson, Davenport, Erie, Ft. Wayne, Galveston, Honolulu, Indianapolis, Jacksonville, Kalamazoo, Lakeland, Marquette, Norfolk, Oshkosh, Paris, Rapid City, San Diego, Tampico, Valdosta, and Yuma have in common? They and some 420 other cities in North America and Europe are hosting air shows this year. Nearly 25 million people will attend these air shows between mid-March and early December this season. That's close to twice the number who will attend NFL football games or auto races. Only baseball, which attracted 55.8 million spectators last year, can expect higher attendance than air shows.

Projected 1993 attendance is based on an annual 2.25% growth rate over the last four years. In 1992 nearly 24.4 million attended festivals that featured aerial events. Of these 346 were "typical" air shows, drawing an average 54,473 fans over a two-day weekend; some 90 were small, largely undocumented events that drew fewer than 8,000; eight were "mega" events that collectively attracted four million or more; and last, but not least, is EAA's annual convention in Oshkosh, WI, which drew 800,000.

Of all North American air shows scheduled for this year, 81% will be held in the U.S. while 19% will be in Canada. Three events will be in Mexico. Civilian air shows account for 74%,

and 26% are military. In the U.S. California leads with 37 shows; next is Florida with 17. Texas, Arizona, and Washington each have 16, and all states except Delaware will have at least one.

In a survey conducted by the International Council of Air Shows (ICAS), the largest trade and professional association representing the air show industry, it seems that the majority of spectators are most interested in seeing military aircraft and demonstration teams like the Canadian Snowbirds, the U.S. Navy Blue Angels, and the U.S.A.F. Thunderbirds.

Air shows are highly visible community events with excellent safety records and traditionally serve as charitable fund raisers. In 1992 alone, air shows contribution an average of $37,242 each to local charities—a combined contribution of $15 million.

If you are interested in the complete schedule of air shows remaining in the season, please contact ICAS at 1931 Horton Road, Suite 7, Jackson, MI 49203; (517) 782–2424—ask for Linda Singer.

Flight Standards Bulletin Board System

Since December 1991 the Flight Standards District Office (FSDO) in Orlando, FL has operated a computer bulletin board system (BBS) which answered more than 10,000 user requests for a variety of FAA-sup-

ported information. The BBS is open for access around the clock, seven days a week, and it is a straight-forward, user friendly system for even the novice computer user. There are no complicated log-on procedures, and once the initial online registration questionnaire is completed, callers obtain "public user" access.

The BBS provides three primary users functions: Electronic Mail messaging, Online Read Files, and a File Transfer Database. An easy-to-follow menu guides the user from one function to the next.

Electronic Mail Messaging allows message exchange among users of the BBS and any registered FAA representative. The "Ask the FAA" message base assures standardization of information among all users of the BBS. The Electronic Mail Messaging primarily supports North Florida as well as certain Flight Standards offices in FAA's Southern Region in Atlanta, GA.

The Read File consists of a variety of North Florida FSDO listings such as Accident Prevention Program safety seminars, air shows, designated examiners, Orlando FSDO personnel, and frequently requested FAA phone numbers at Oklahoma City, OK.

The File Database provides users with a terrific selection of the latest master minimum equipment lists, advisory circulars, Accident Prevention Program "P" pamphlets, and, of course, the latest *FAA Aviation News* [without pictures or graphics, though; to get the full effect, you need to subscribe—Editor's shameless commercial].

The BSS currently serves over 1,000 computer users nationwide, and Orlando APPM Obie Young and Systems Operator Bill Hoenstine want more. Now that the system has a nationwide toll-free number, they should get their wish.

So, don't miss out! Join the growing number of computer-literate airmen who have discovered the benefits of membership in the North Florida FSDO Computer Bulletin Board System. Connect with the BBS via 1–800–645–FSDO (3736).

AVNEWS/BRIEFS

Charles Taylor "Master Mechanic" Award

Hot on the heels of the very successful Aviation Maintenance Technician Awards begun in October 1992 (see September/October 1992 *FAA Aviation News*), FAA's Aircraft Maintenance Division has enacted the Charles Taylor "Master Mechanic" Award Program to recognize the lifetime accomplishments of senior mechanics. The "Master Mechanic" Award is named after Mr. Charles Taylor, the very first aviation mechanic—he worked for the Wright Brothers and is credited with designing and buidling the first successful aircraft engine.

The "Master Mechanic" Award will recognize those individuals who have taken the aviation maintenance industry from radial engines to the space age and have made it the bench mark for safety that other transportation systems strive to imitate. The award will be signed by the FAA Administrator, and FAA Headquaters will maintain a Roll of Honor of all awardees.

To qualify for the award the individual must have at least 50 years in the aviation maintenance profession. At least 40 of those years must have been as a certificated mechanic or repairman. The remaining 10 years can be based on military service as a mechanic or in the aviation maintenance industry before being certificated. Enforcement actions such as civil penalties or suspension or administrative actions such as letters of correction will not be considered sufficient grounds for denying an individual the award. However, if an individual has had his or her certificate revoked at any time, that individual will not be considered eligible.

Qualified individuals may submit their own names, or they can be nominated by others. The request must be in writing to the local FSDO to the attention of the Airworthiness Supervisor. The letter should include a summary of the individual's background and show at least 50 years of aviation maintenance experience. The letter should also include the names of at least three certificated mechanics or repairmen who

recommend the individual for the award. At least once a year the FSDO will assemble a Master Mechanic Award Selection Team made up of an FAA airworthiness supervisor and no fewer than two members of the aviation maintenance community. The team will select the winners from the nominations received, and there is no limit to the number of annual awardees.

The Master Mechanic awardee will receive the award from the local FSDO manager and before his or her peers in the aviation maintenance industry. In that way the Master Mechanic is the perfect role model of professionalism for newcomers to the aviation maintenance community.

For additional information on the program or on the upcoming advisory circular describing it, please contact the Awards Program Manager, Lee Norvell at (202) 257–8616. Her address is FAA, AFS–361, 800 Independence Avenue, SW, Washington, DC 20591.

AIRCRAFT SAFETY REVIEW

AOPA's Air Safety Foundation has just started a new service that will be of benefit to current aircraft owners and prospective buyers. This spring they issued the first of their Safety Reviews, the inaugural one on the Cessna P210.

Foundation safety analysts studied accident and incident reports on the Cessna P210 for a seven-year period and compiled the results in text and graphic presentations. The Safety Review consists of four parts:

Part 1 is a summary of statistical accident data and a comparison to other aircraft of similar configuration (e.g., the P210 is compared to other single engine, turbocharged, retractable gear aircraft).

Part 2 is a compilation of serious accident briefs and a summary of minor accidents.

Part 3 consists of a training outline for instructors and pilots to use in incorporating risk management techniques into transition and recurrent training; emphasis is on areas that have been shown to have a high risk factor.

Part 4 contains articles reprinted from AOPA Pilot magazine on the specific aircraft.

The Cessna P210 Safety Review is available for $19.95 (plus shipping and handling) from the AOPA Air Safety Foundation, 421 Aviation Way, Frederick, MD 21701; (800) 638–3101. The Foundation is currently compiling data for the next Safety Review on all models of the Beech Bonanza. That review should be available later this year.

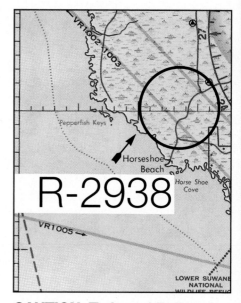

CAUTION: Tethered Balloon!

If you are flying in the vicinity of Horseshoe Beach, FL—on the Gulf Coast west of Gainesville—you need to avoid a restricted area that became effective this past April 1 (no fooling!). R–2038 contains a tethered Aerostat balloon that reaches an altitude of 15,000' MSL. The Aerostat is lighted with white strobe lights, but the tether is NOT lighted or marked.

R–2938 encompasses airspace from the surface to "unlimited," within a three nautical mile radius of a point centered at 29°29'59" north latitude and 83°16'16" west longitude. The restricted area is active continuously 24 hours a day and will appear on the September 16, 1993 edition of the Jacksonville Section Aeronautical Chart. Until you receive your copy, consult the graphic of the restricted area published in NOTAM's.

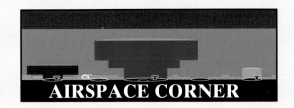

AIRSPACE CORNER

Question: *In reading the new FAR, I read in Section 91.117 that Class B (former TCA's) are going to have a 200 KIAS speed restriction below 2,500 feet AGL within 4-miles of the airport. Is this correct?*

Answer: Our eagle-eyed reader is correct in that is the language in FAR § 91.117(b) effective September 16, 1993. However, this was an administrative error and the Class B inclusion will be deleted prior to the effective date.

Question: *The airport I fly out of has a Class D radius with two Class E arrival extensions. Why are there more than one class of airspace for a single airport?*

Answer: When the airspace reclassification was proposed, the entire control zone at towered airports were going to become Class D. However, based on public comments and the FAA's effort to minimize the number of rule changes, it was decided that if all extensions were two miles or less, the extensions would remain part of the basic surface area and require communications with ATC. However, if any extension was greater than two miles, all extensions would be Class E. This allows the instrument approaches to be contained within controlled airspace without imposing a communications requirement on pilots operating VFR that was not previously required. Remember, if there is an arrival extension, it means that an aircraft executing an instrument approach to that airport is authorized to descend below 1,000 feet AGL. If you are transiting the airspace low level, it would be a good operating practice to contact the

tower and advise them of your presence and intentions.

Question: *I fly out of a satellite airport within the ATA surface area and communications with the tower are not required when taking off or landing. Does this change when the airspace becomes Class D.*

Answer: Yes. The current provision for this exception has been removed from FAR § 91.127(c) effective September 16, 1993. FAR § 91.129, Operations in Class D airspace, establishes a communications requirement for all aircraft operating within the airspace. The FAA made a concerted effort to exclude satellite airports from surface areas to the extent practicable. However, for those satellites that weren't excluded, the legal clause "unless otherwise authorized," has been left in. This allows local FBO's and operators of flying schools to coordinate with the air traffic control manager and develop procedures that would exempt local pilots from communicating with the control tower but not relieve transient pilots of the requirement.

Editor's note: *In the March issue, we replied to a question to the effect that FAR § 91.157(a)(1) had been amended to allow ATC to authorize SVFR operations up to but not including 10,000 feet MSL. This authorization in still in coordination and will be published as a notice of proposed rulemaking soon. We regret any inconvenience this may have caused.*

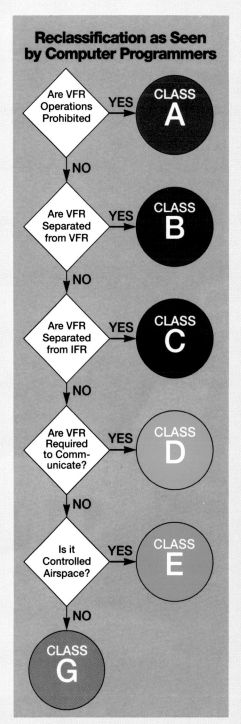

Reclassification as Seen by Computer Programmers

Are VFR Operations Prohibited — YES → CLASS A

NO ↓

Are VFR Separated from VFR — YES → CLASS B

NO ↓

Are VFR Separated from IFR — YES → CLASS C

NO ↓

Are VFR Required to Communicate? — YES → CLASS D

NO ↓

Is it Controlled Airspace? — YES → CLASS E

NO ↓

CLASS G

DO NOT DELAY—CRITICAL TO FLIGHT SAFETY!

NON-CIRCULATING

July-August 1993

FAA Aviation News

A DOT/FAA FLIGHT STANDARDS SAFETY PUBLICATION

U.S. Department
of Transportation

**Federal Aviation
Administration**

Federico F. Peña, *Secretary of Transportation*
Joseph M. Del Balzo, *Acting FAA Administrator*
Carl B. Schellenberg, *Acting Executive Director*
  for System Operations
Anthony J. Broderick, *Associate Administrator*
  for Regulation and Certification
Thomas C. Accardi, *Director,*
  Flight Standards Service
Robert A. Wright, *Acting Manager,*
  General Aviation and Commercial Division
Roger M. Baker, Jr., *Manager,*
  Accident Prevention Program Branch
Phyllis Anne Duncan, *Editor*
Louise C. Oertly, *Senior Associate Editor*
Dean Chamberlain, *Associate Editor*

The FAA's Flight Standards Service, General Aviation and Commercial Division, Accident Prevention Program Branch, AFS–810, Washington, DC 20591, (telephone 202 267–8017) publishes FAA AVIATION NEWS in the interest of flight safety. The magazine promotes safety in the air by calling the attention of airmen to current technical, regulatory, and procedural matters affecting the safe operation of aircraft. Although based on current FAA policy and rule interpretations, all printed material herein are advisory or informational in nature and should not be construed to have regulatory effect. The FAA does not officially endorse any goods, services, materials, or products of manufacturers that may be mentioned. **Certain details of accidents described herein have been altered to protect the privacy of those involved.**
  The Office of Management and Budget has approved the use of funds for the printing of FAA AVIATION NEWS.

SUBSCRIPTION SERVICES

The Superintendént of Documents, U.S. Government Printing Office, Washington, DC 20402–9371, sells FAA AVIATION NEWS on subscription. Use the self-mailer form in the center of this magazine to subscribe. Cost: $8.00 ($10.00 foreign) for one year; $16.00 ($20.00 foreign) for two years. Prices are subject to change by the Government Printing Office without prior notice.
  Change of Address or Subscription Problems: **Send your label with correspondence to Sup Doc, Attn: Chief, Mail List Branch, Mail Stop: SSOM, Washington, DC 20402–9373.**
  To keep subscription prices down, the Government Printing Office mails subscribers only one renewal notice. You can tell how many copies are left in your subscription by checking the number that follows "ISS-DUE" on the top line of your mailing label. For example, when this number is 003, it means you have three issues left in your subscription, and GPO will send you a renewal notice. The number 000 means you have received your last issue. To be sure that your service continues without interruption, please return your renewal notice promptly.

July-August 1993

FAA *Aviation* News

Volume 32   Number 5

FEATURES

DEPARTMENTS

Front Cover: *The ultimate in the efficient application of unpowered flight, but what happens when the pilot contacts ATC? For more information see page 17. Photo by Steve Hines.*

Back Cover: *The FAA is into recycling. A tower that was dismantled, shipped cross country, and re-built now serves Manassas, VA. Photo by Kristine Kjos.*

Looking into General Aviation's Crystal Ball

by Phyllis Anne Duncan, *Editor*

There are a great many aviation soothsayers "out there" who are more than ready to predict there will be no more general aviation. They even attempt to put arbitrary dates for the demise—the year 2000 (which everybody uses now because we're so close; it really renders a prediction, well, predictable); 1995, the year where, if you've read the popular bestseller, the whole country will go bankrupt; there are even those who say any day now.

The cause? It usually comes down to no investment tax credit, tort reform, and "getting the FAA off our backs."

Needless to say, this made the Third Annual General Aviation Forecast Conference an interesting place to be.

For nearly two decades, FAA's Office of Aviation Policy, Plans, and Management Analysis (APO–110), has held conferences where it presents the results of its in-depth analysis of the aviation industry. The two-day event attracts hundreds of interested parties from the industry and many from the FAA itself. Three years ago—because general aviation was taking up so much of the agenda—APO–110 decided to hold a separate two-day meeting for general aviation. Its attendance has grown every year and is now a major event for the general aviation community.

This year the statistics contained in APO–110's conference booklet seemed to support the direst of the soothsayers' predictions. FAA expects the general aviation fleet to grow by less than 1% over the forecast period of Fiscal Years 1993–2004. That modest increase is driven primarily by growth in business use of general aviation aircraft. The number of hours flown should increase only gradually also—up 1.4% annually, reaching 35 million by 2004.

The brightest spot of the general aviation industry is rotorcraft. The active

Robert A. Wright

rotorcraft fleet should reach nearly 9,000 by 2004, with turbine powered rotorcraft (increasing by nearly 5% a year) comprising about 80% of the rotorcraft fleet. The number of overall rotorcraft hours flown should increase by over 6% a year; however, hours flown by turbine helicopters will increase 141% and reach over five million by 2004.

Helicopter Association International President Frank L. Jensen, Jr. echoed these predictions about what he termed aviation's "magic carpet." He expressed the need, however, for more heliports—especially in downtown areas—to service the growing helicopter industry.

Many speakers questioned FAA's predictions and offered their own statistics, which showed general aviation gravely ill, if not terminal. Indeed, speakers expended a great deal of time and talk about how bad things are but provided few solutions, with some exceptions. Two were notable.

One was Dr. Bruce J. Holmes, Assistant Director for Aeronautics at NASA's Langley Research Center in Hampton, VA. The title of his presentation says it all—"U.S. General Aviation: The Ingredients for a Renaissance." The words "general aviation" and "renaissance" have rarely been used together lately, but Dr. Holmes and, apparently, NASA's Task Force see something the rest of the industry can't (or won't?). NASA has formed an Aeronautics Advisory Committee Task Force on General Aviation Transportation, which has been chartered to explore the various opportunities for general aviation of the future and to report its findings to NASA this fall.

The other was Robert A. Wright, Manager of the General Aviation and Commercial Division for the FAA, who offered one of the industry's few strategic plans to address the enhancement

Continued on page 7

Pilot Decision Making

by Tom Hamilton

Decision Making Process and Hazardous Attitudes

This is Part Two of a seven-part series that first appeared in Balloon Life *magazine in 1989 and was originally written for balloon pilots. We have left the lighter-than-air examples in because the overlying issue of pilot decision making affects all pilots.* **—Editor**

As pilots we analyze the elements or risk—pilot, aircraft, environment, and operation—that make up a particular situation. By evaluating those elements of risk we decide on a course of action. In Part One of this series we defined this intellectual ability as the pilot's capability to sense, store, retrieve, and integrate information. In an ideal world the pilot would solve the problem much in the same manner as a computer.

This headwork is the intellectual process used to formulate decision making strategies. The necessary ingredients in good headwork are knowledge, vigilance, selective attention, risk identification and assessment, information processing, and problem solving ability. Headwork, when properly applied, minimizes the negative influence of attitudes and personality traits. The key then is for the pilot to separate the headwork aspect of decision making from the attitudinal part.

Effective headwork requires us as pilots to manage our attitudes, stress, risk, and crew. Those, combined with our skills and procedures—ability to fly the aircraft—results in our responding to a given situation. If our response is adequate, we have a successful operation. If it is inadequate, a mishap occurs.

In this article we will look at how we process information to achieve orderly, timely decision making. We will also look at managing attitude and the five hazardous attitudes to avoid.

Skills and Procedures

If you look at the situation flow chart (Figure 1) you will see that a change or event occurs. The pilot recognizes the change and selects a response using intellectual ability as well as airmanship ability. Airmanship is the procedural, psychomotor, and perceptual skills that are used to control the aircraft and its systems. These skills are learned during the conventional training process until they become automatic reactions. These skills are highly specific to the type of aircraft and are taught in traditional flight training programs using a variety of learning materials.

Decision Making

The traditional approach to pilot decision making has been to teach pilots the capabilities and flight characteristics of an aircraft and its systems, knowledge of the national airspace system, general knowledge of meteorology, regulations, emergency procedures, etc.—the premise being that, if pilots have this kind of information, they will be able to exercise the "good judgement" required to assure safe flight.

Decision making, however, is a mental process. In recent years decision making models have been developed to teach the pilot how to make good decisions. As a pilot considers an action, the consequences of taking, as well as not taking, that action must be considered carefully. To assist pilots in this process, the FAA and AOPA Air Safety Foundation developed a decision making training program based upon previous experience in researching the decision making process. The decision model consisted of 10 steps. For simplicity the model was reduced to a six-element decision process using the acronym DECIDE (Figure 2).

The six elements of the DECIDE model are a continuous loop decision process which has been used during accident analysis and during the instruction of pilots of varying experience levels.

Employing the six elements of the DECIDE model, a pilot uses his or her intellectual abilities and relies on these capabilities to sense, store, retrieve, and integrate information. Earlier we said that this part of judgement is purely rational, and if used alone, would allow problem solving in much the same manner as a computer.

Pilots aren't computers; they are people and are affected by motivations and attitudes. Thus, in part, pilot judgement is based on tendencies to use other than safety-related information when choosing courses of action. It is the management of attitudes, stress, risk, and crew that also play an important role in pilot decision making.

Managing Attitude

How a pilot handles his or her responsibilities as "pilot-in-command" depends to a large degree upon ingrained attitudes—toward safety, toward him- or herself, and toward flying. Attitudes are learned and are not innate behavior. Good attitudes can be developed—again, through training—into a positive mental framework that encourages and produces good pilot judgement. On the other hand, bad pilot thinking habits created by previously learned poor attitudes can be "unlearned" or modified through training.

Descriptions of five hazardous attitudes that each pilot needs to be aware of follow:

Anti-Authority—This is found in people who do not like anyone telling them what to do. They think, "Don't tell me!" In a sense, they are saying, "No one can tell me what to do." They may either be resentful of having someone tell them what to do or may just regard rules, regulations, and procedures as silly or unnecessary. However, it is always your prerogative to question authority if you feel it is in error.

Impulsivity—This is the thought pattern of people who frequently feel the need to do something, anything immediately—a type A personality. They do not stop to think about what they are about to do; they do not select the best alternative—they do the first thing that comes to mind, e.g., "Got to land!" A balloon pilot acting impulsively, for example, when confronted with powerlines at eye level in front of the balloon, might turn on the burner to try and fly over the lines rather than rip out.

Invulnerability—Many people feel that accidents happen to others but never to them. They know accidents

Continued on page 7

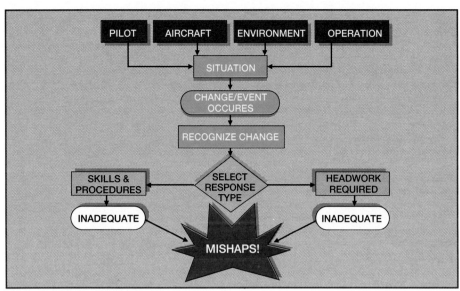

Figure 1 Situation Flow Chart

DETECT
The decision maker detects the fact that change has occurred.

ESTIMATE
The decision maker estimates the need to counter or react to change.

CHOOSE
The decision maker chooses a desirable outcome
(in terms of success) for the flight.

IDENTIFY
The decision maker identifies actions which could successfully
control the change.

DO
The decision maker takes action to adapt to the change.

EVALUATE
The decision maker evaluates the effects of the action countering
the change or reacting to it.

Figure 2 The six elements of DECIDE

Hazardous Attitude	**ANTIDOTE**
Anti-Authority *Don't tell me!*	Follow the rules. They are usually right.
Impulsivity *Do something quickly!*	Not so fast. Think first.
Invulnerability *It won't happen to me!*	It could happen to me. Think about the worst possible accident; it could happen to you.
Macho *I can do it!*	Taking chances is foolish.
Resignation *What's the use!*	I'm not helpless. I can make a difference.

Figure 3 How to avoid hazardous attitudes

Risk Assessment and Management

by Denney L. Bridges, *APPM, Helena, MT*

All activities that we endeavor to undertake involve risk. The more complex an activity becomes, the more opportunity there is for a failure or breakdown and, therefore, the greater the risk. The more an activity allows for "outside" influence, the higher the risk. Also, the greater the complexity of an activity, the more highly regulated that activity will tend to be. Aviation would seem to fall into this described hierarchy as a fairly complex, and therefore, risky activity.

We have been fairly successful in managing the risks associated with flying. We are continually learning from our mistakes as well as the mistakes of others. Our predecessors made mistakes in design, engineering, production, and flight tests. All of us in aviation have actually benefited from those mistakes. Our predecessors made errors, percentage wise, at a much greater rate than we do. That's why they were known as "pioneers." We should thank those pioneers for the heritage they have left with us.

Below are some accident statistics from the days of the pioneers:

Currently, less than seven accidents (fatal and non-fatal) occur per 100,000 flying hours in general aviation. We have learned a lot from the pioneers, but we can improve our risk assessment and risk management skills even more. It's not a bad legacy to leave to the next generation of aviators.

Managing Risk

As pilots, we are taught from our first flying lesson how to manage the risks inherent to flight. We are made aware of a whole range of hazards that can easily be avoided and some that cannot. The system used to verify a pilot's ability to perform the tasks necessary to operate a given aircraft safely is based on that person's risk management skills. We evaluate this skill by developing scenarios in which an individual's *preparation, proficiency,* and *training* are tested and compared to established standards. These scenarios are the certification tests, flight reviews, and proficiency checks that all pilots must undergo.

All three of the elements of risk management are closely related, experience-driven, and equally important. The portion of risk management that is primarily involved with the assessment of how risky a particular event may be in the preparation phase. Preparation can be broken down into three major categories: *mental, physical,* and *mechanical.*

Early Aviation Statistics

1903—First powered flight by the Wright Brothers

1904—Orville had the first wind shear accident

1908—First fatal air crash

1910—First mid-aid collision

1912—First pilot killed as a result of a bird strike

1914—France has 1,400 military air planes, Germany has 1,000, Great Britain 400, Russia 800, the United States 23; wartime losses are tremendous

1918—The U.S. Airmail Service is founded. The U.S. government operates this service for nine years. The airmail pilot's life expectancy is four years. Thirty-one of the first 40 pilots are killed before the Service is turned over to private industry. A forced landing occurs every 20 hours of flight. In the Airmail Service's history, one in every six pilots was killed in a flying accident while delivering the mail.

Each flight begins with an individual assessing his or her mental state. The most convenient method for a non-health professional to use is to evaluate his or her own attitudes. We must decide if we possess an attitude conducive to the safe completion of a planned flight. Consequently, the mental aspect of preflight planning should not be overlooked. How well flight planning is accomplished relates to training in many ways. It also reflects one's mental state.

At the same time we must determine if our physical condition is appropriate for flight.

The final element in the preparation phase involves the aircraft and its mechanical condition. The actual preflight of the aircraft, specifically the thoroughness of the inspection, and the pilot's ability to assess the observed condition of the aircraft correlate directly to the quality of that individual's training.

Proficiency vs. Currency

Proficiency is often confused with currency. A pilot who is legally current may not be as proficient as necessary for a given flight. The amount of current flying experience required to become proficient is as variable as the skill level of each individual who chooses to fly. Each flight that we begin also offers particular challenges unique to that flight. Therefore, we must realize that the proficiency level necessary to complete a flight successfully varies with the complexities or demands of that particular flight. A prudent pilot usually makes a subconscious analysis of the proficiency required for a specific flight. Accident prevention could be enhanced if a conscious effort were made to evaluate one's own ability before each flight (e.g., my instrument skills don't need to be so proficient for a day VFR flight as they might need to be if there is a chance of encountering weather).

Training

When pilots discuss the subject of flight training, the cost of such training usually becomes the focal point. If you think training is so expensive, just wait until you have to pay for an accident.

Even with good insurance coverage, accidents are expensive and painful (in more ways than one) experiences. Training is the least expensive (in some cases the only) alternative to an accident.

Almost all professional pilots receive at least annual proficiency training, with one important exception—general aviation. The FAA's Pilot Proficiency Award Program was designed to encourage general aviation pilots to obtain some annual proficiency training. We believe that pilots who participate in this program have a lower accident rate than those who do not. Completion of any single phase of the "Wings" program also precludes accomplishing a biennial flight review. **Training is worth the expense.** ■

Accident statistical data came from *Normal Accidents* by Charles Perrow (1984) and *FAA Statistical Handbook of Aviation* (1991).

Piper Aircraft Corp.

THE THREE CRITICAL SUCCESS FACTORS

by Larry Schuman, *SimuFlight Training International*

During my aviation career, I have observed pilots in training and line operations who have performed measurably better than others, notably during abnormal and emergency situations. Why is this? We all receive similar initial and recurrent training, simulator training, and checkrides. What, then, makes one pilot outperform another?

In general terms, well-trained aviation professionals share certain attributes and attitudes. These particular qualities are internal. Not only are they present during training, they are present at all times. While excellence in a training environment is no guarantee of excellence during a true emergency, pilots who display these three factors during training and normal line operations consistently display them during actual abnormal and emergency situations. These qualities are called the "Three Critical Success Factors."

1. An Intimate Knowledge of the Business

Professional pilots know much more than the minimum required to complete their training or a checkride. They spend time reviewing the *Airman's Information Manual* and are familiar with proper procedures and techniques for their aircraft and the ATC system. In addition, they have an exceptional understanding of the corporate culture, its policies, and procedures.

These same pilots are extremely resourceful. They are knowledgeable about the information available to them on enroute and approach charts. They understand the symbology. They know their aircraft and its performance capabilities. As "students" of aviation, they are never content with their present knowledge. They are continually searching for more.

However, these pilots are susceptible to making mistakes, but their mistakes are generally less serious and

---

Three Critical Success Factors

1.
An Intimate Knowledge of the Business

2.
A Professional Attitude Embracing Continual Skepticism, Time-Dependent Situational Awareness, and the Conservative Response to Challenge

3.
The Development and Use of Standard Operating Procedures (SOP)

---

acknowledged in time to make the necessary correction.

What part, then, does the "intimate knowledge of the business" play in the day-to-day activities of the professional pilot? The answer is simple. When we are faced with a tough decision, the more knowledge we have about the specific subject, the better the outcome. The best decisions are made by those of us who know our jobs best. Simple, but critically important.

2. A Professional Attitude Embracing Continual Skepticism, Time-Dependent Situational Awareness, and the Conservative Response to Challenge

As professional pilots we must also be professional skeptics. We must not accept status quo for status quo changes quickly at jet speeds. The best among us are constantly alert and always asking ourselves, "What if. . . ?"

A "time-dependent situational awareness" is perhaps the most important of all three factors. The elements of "situational awareness" include knowing the airspeed, altitude, heading, next navigation waypoint, amount of fuel, and present location with regard to a ground reference point. The National Transportation Safety Board (NTSB) accident files include several fatalities where pilots lost situational awareness.

The final part of the second Critical Success Factor is the "Conservative Response to Challenge." A "challenge" is anything that occurs during a flight that compromises safety. For instance, a systems failure or a line of severe storms approach. The "Conservative Response" is any action taken that preserves or enhances our current level of safety.

3. The Development and Use of Standard Operating Procedures (SOP)

First, SOP's provide a structure for operations which gives crew members the ability to anticipate each other's actions. SOP's give us a standard for monitoring and enhance flight safety by keeping pilots "in the loop." Second, and perhaps more important, pilots don't like surprises. SOP's provide us with procedures to manage many situations. In short, SOP's help structure our long-term planning.

Long-term planning is any action taken for which there is an anticipated response. SOP's provide us those anticipated responses and procedures. Examples include the FAR, the Airplane Flight Manual, and company handbooks. Short-term planning is what the crew of UAL 232 at Sioux City, Iowa experienced when they lost all three hydraulic systems. They did not have an SOP for the loss of all hydraulic systems. Therefore, the crew had to create a set of procedures tailored to their immediate situation.

As professional pilots it is vital to be aware of and practice all three critical success factors—if we want to live through our careers. Reviewing NTSB reports and reading aviation statistics tell us that almost 80% of all aircraft accidents are caused by some type of human error. The difference, therefore, between excellent performance and "merely acceptable performance" is extremely critical to all of us. ■

Mr. Schuman is an Advanced Airmanship Instructor for SimuFlite. This article originally appeared in the Summer 1991 issue of SimuFlite's newsletter, Advanced Airmanship.

Looking into General Aviation's Crystal Ball
Continued from page 1

of general aviation. A task force of top-ranking industry organizations (the GAAP Coalition) has adopted the General Aviation Action Plan (GAAP) as the best hope for general aviation. The GAAP Coalition has formed four working groups (Accident Prevention, Training, Maintenance, and Technology) led by industry members and with FAA representation. The working groups will design programs that will ensure the future of general aviation and that support the goals and objectives of the GAAP. (For an overview of the GAAP, see the July/August 1992 *FAA Aviation News* Editorial.)

Both Dr. Holmes' and the GAAP's proposals are material for later articles; we can't do them justice here. You may contact Dr. Holmes at NASA Langley Research Center, Hampton, VA 23681–0001 concerning the Task Force's work and his strategies for general aviation. If you would like a copy of the General Aviation Action Plan, contact the FAA's General Aviation and Commercial Division, AFS-800, 800 Independence Avenue, SW., Washington, DC 20591; (202) 267-8212.

Both Dr. Holmes and Mr. Wright doused the "doomsayers'" flames at the Forecast Conference because they offered solutions and not merely complaints. General aviation will survive and will be viable, but it will take hard work and vision—not whining. ■

Pilot Decision Making
Continued from page 3

can happen, and they know that anyone can be affected; but they never really feel or believe that they will be the one involved. Pilots who think this way are more likely to take chances and run unwise risks, thinking all the time, "It won't happen to me!" Think of the worst accident that you can imagine, and then picture yourself in it.

Macho—People who are always trying to prove that they are better than anyone else think, "I can do it!" They "prove" themselves by taking risks and by trying to impress others. While this pattern is typically labeled as a male characteristic, women are equally susceptible.

Resignation—People who think, "What's the use?" do not see themselves as making a great deal of difference in what happens to them. When things go well, they think, "That's good luck." When things go badly, they attribute it to bad luck or feel that someone is "out to get them." They leave the action to others—for better or worse. Sometimes, such individuals will even go along with unreasonable requests just to be a "nice guy." These are people who can be talked into anything.

Antidotes for Hazardous Attitudes

Being aware of the five hazardous attitudes makes you more alert to them in your own thinking. This is an important first step in eliminating them from your judgements.

In Figure 3 we have provided the antidotes for each of the hazardous attitudes. By telling yourself something different from the hazardous attitude, you're "taking an antidote" to counteract the hazardous attitude. You remove a hazardous thought by substituting the antidote. Recognize a hazardous attitude, correctly label the thought, and then say its antidote to yourself.

By being aware of the hazardous attitudes and applying the antidotes helps to manage or control your attitude and eliminate one of the elements that interferes with headwork during the pilot decision making process. ■

Next issue is Part 3—Managing Stress.

In the March 1993 issue, we wrote about the physiological effects of smoking on flying, and maybe some pilots made the commitment to quit. What is the best way? Cold turkey? Hypnotism? Acupuncture? Studies indicate that sudden nicotine deprivation causes withdrawal symptoms that degrade pilot performance. However, the availability of new programs to help smokers quit the habit while reducing or minimizing withdrawal symptoms may be especially well-suited for flight crews. **—Editor**

Medical Stuff

Adhesive Nicotine Patches Help Pilots Quit Smoking

by Stanley R. Mohler, M.D.

As the detrimental health consequences of smoking become more widely understood, a record number of people worldwide are quitting the use of tobacco products. This change is especially reflected among professional pilots who have developed lifestyles to promote good health and career longevity. Some airlines will not hire a pilot who smokes, and other operators prohibit smoking on the flight deck. [In the U.S., the FAR prohibit smoking on U.S. domestic flights of under six hours, but smoking on the flight deck is permitted if the pilot-in-command authorizes it. Smoking on the flight deck is prohibited during takeoffs and landings.]

Tobacco use results in a powerful addiction to nicotine, which can trigger disturbing withdrawal symptoms. If cigarettes or other tobacco products are not available, addicted tobacco users often become irritable and restless, and they can experience difficulties in mental concentration along with generalized feelings of illness. Quitting tobacco use without some assistance is difficult and often unsuccessful. Relapses occur frequently.

A number of publications and programs provide specific guidance on how to quit smoking successfully. In addition there are audio cassette tapes that can assist smokers to quit. Various approaches have been developed to help those who are "hooked" and want to quit but who cannot stop smoking without assistance. There are now several transdermal nicotine delivery systems using skin-adhesive

patches that can help the smoker move away from the lung-destroying inhalation of nicotine acquisition. More adhesive patch treatment systems can be expected in the future.

At least four companies have conducted research and perfected the use of transdermal nicotine delivery systems for sale in the U.S. These companies offer the products Nicoderm, Prostep, Habitrol, and Nicotrol, which are available by prescription. These systems are available under a physician's guidance, and their use can be tailored to a given person's needs.

Nicotine is absorbed rapidly by the skin, and about half of it is eliminated from the body in one and a half hours. The skin delivery system provides a target blood level of nicotine so that the individual who stops smoking will not experience (during the initial period of not smoking) the withdrawal symptoms that plague most tobacco smokers when they try to quit. This appears especially important for pilots who smoke.

What the Research Says

Research conducted by FAA's Civil Aeromedical Institute (CAMI) suggests that sudden nicotine withdrawal should be avoided on the flight deck. "For some, withdrawal symptoms including tension, depression, irritability, difficulty in concentration, decreased heart

rate, a fall in blood pressure...and impaired performance may occur and more than offset any benefits to aviation safety that are expected from a ban on preflight and inflight smoking," concluded an FAA study on the effects of tobacco on aviation safety. The FAA study said it supported "smoking cessation programs and pharmacologic approaches to nicotine replacement...for improved health, performance, and safety." But the study recommended smoking cessation programs that minimized flight deck withdrawal symptoms. Nicotine patches would achieve that goal by reducing or eliminating withdrawal symptoms.

Another FAA study said experiments of complex pilot performance conducted at a simulated operational cabin altitude of 6,500 feet found "significant adverse effects of smoking withdrawal....When smoking was permitted the overall index of performance was maintained at the initial level or higher over four hours of testing. When smoking was prohibited, however, performance declined with time. The effect was largely a decrement in tracking performance, a psychomotor function important to flying." The study concluded: "Although there were no significant differences between the performance of nondeprived smokers and nonsmokers, smokers who were deprived had significantly inferior tracking and vigilance performance."

A report prepared by the U.S. National Institutes of Health also found that the "fast decline of plasma nicotine and other effects of withdrawal in the habitual smoker are associated with decrements in vigilance and concentration and with increased irritability, anxiety, and aggression."

But that is not a reason to keep smoking.

In addition to identifying long-term health-damaging aspect of smoking, aeromedical studies have established a strong link between smoking and adverse performance effects in the cockpit. Carbon monoxide and nicotine from smoking are known to affect altitude tolerance, vision, and certain judgement and psychomotor skills.

Withdrawal Patchwork

Recent research has shown that many persons find skin patches to be of benefit in getting through the withdrawal period following smoking cessation, which usually lasts two to four weeks. The patches are available in decreasing sizes. As the smoker gradually reduces nicotine addiction, smaller doses of nicotine can be delivered and still alleviate withdrawal symptoms. Symptoms alleviated by the adhesive patch nicotine delivery systems include concentration difficulty, irritability, general feeling of unease, agitation, and headache.

Once the patch is in place, the individual must not smoke. Smoking while wearing the patch would expose the body to a dangerously high dose of nicotine. Nicotine is a deadly poison in high doses. Similarly, nicotine chewing gum cannot be used while the patches are worn.

Studies indicate that smokers who use the patch plus a behavioral modification activity to quit smoking have a higher chance of success without a smoking relapse. It has also been found that after about two weeks of non-smoking and after phasing down with the nicotine patches over four to eight weeks, the individual ex-smoker will experience higher quality sleep, will need less sleep, will be more mentally alert, and will have more energy. In addition, the ex-smoker will have an enhanced sense of smell and taste and will thus use less salt on food, leading to a lower risk of hypertension.

Patch Use

When tobacco is smoked, each inhalation delivers nicotine into the lungs and then into the bloodstream where the nicotine is carried to the brain within eight seconds. The immediate result is to relieve any developing withdrawal symptoms. It creates a feeling of relief for the addicted person. The continual seeking of this relief is one of the causes of continued nicotine dependence and addiction. Patches deliver small, controlled doses of nicotine throughout a sustained period of time, thus working to offset the disturbing symptoms of withdrawal from nicotine.

One of the patch systems, for example, is applied once a day in accordance with the prescription, usually in the morning. The time of application can be varied based on individual preference and the agreement of the prescribing physician. However, the patch should be applied at the same time each day. Some of the patches can be worn while bathing in a tub or shower, while using a hot tub, or while swimming. These patches stick tightly. The user applies a given patch for only one 24-hour time period or for another period as prescribed. Only one patch can be worn at a time. Each patch is applied to some part of the upper body, upper arm, or upper back, and the location of the patches is varied from day to day. This variation is intended to avoid minor skin irritation that could develop by applying the patch in the same place day after day.

Directions that come with the patches tell how to discard them and also emphasize that patches must be kept away from small children and pets because any nicotine exposure would be too high for their body sizes. Pregnant women should be certain their physicians are aware they are pregnant. It is well-established that pregnant women who smoke can cause serious damage to the developing fetus.

Other Considerations

Services are also available that can provide both physical and emotional support during the withdrawal process. Support hotlines that can help an individual understand withdrawal problems are also very important. Such encouragement and assistance have been found to be helpful in preventing smoking relapses.

Persons who quit do not automatically gain weight. In fact, a significant number of persons who have quite do not put on weight. One way to avoid gaining weight is to engage in moderate exercise and to be moderate in food consumption, especially with respect to consuming sweets as a substitute for smoking.

As with any addiction, an approach that targets progress one day at a time is the most successful. Substitute hand actions must be learned to replace the fiddling with lighters, cigarettes, and other smoking materials and paraphernalia that characterize the smoker. Avoidance of alcohol is also an important consideration because it can cause ex-smokers to relapse through impaired judgement or prior association. Alcohol in small amounts can be consumed by ex-smokers without relapsing if the individual is vigilant against relapse tendencies.

Continued on page 16

Four Transdermal Patch Systems

	Nicoderm	Prostep	Habitrol	Nicotrol
Nicotine content (mg)	114 (22 sq. cm)	30 (7 sq. cm)	52.5 (30 sq. cm)	24.9 (30 sq. cm)
Dosage per time period	21mg/24h	22mg/24h	21mg/24h	15mg/16h
Duration of treatment	4–8 weeks	4–8 weeks	4–8 weeks	4–12 weeks

Note: Smaller sizes with lower nicotine doses are available for light smokers (less than one-half pack per day and for persons weighing less than 110 pounds (50KG).

Source: Stanley R. Mohler, M.D.

Aircraft Missing—Or Is It?

by H. Dean Chamberlain, *Associate Editor (and CAP member)*

We need your help.

Actually the U.S. Air Force Rescue Coordination Center (AFRCC) needs your help. Helping the AFRCC means you will also help yourself and other airmen. Helping won't cost you anything except a few seconds of your time, but it could save the Government money.

In these budget-cutting times, does this sound too good to be true?

This is one deal you can't afford to miss. You might even help save a life in the process—maybe even yours. Any way you look at it, it's a great deal.

If you have access to an aircraft frequency radio and about 10 seconds of time, you can do something to reduce excess Government expenditures. All you have to do is use your radio to check your own and neighboring aircraft for possible inadvertent ELT activation. This simple effort can help save the Government, and many dedicated volunteers, both money and time.

That's right. Ten seconds of your time can save the US Air Force (USAF) and others, most notably the Civil Air Patrol (CAP), the cost and time necessary to locate and turn off either your own or someone else's activated ELT that was accidentally (no pun intended) activated—ELT's that may be transmitting to the world their aircraft's' hard landings, bounces, and thumps.

FALSE ALARMS

According to a recent AFRCC activity report for Calendar Year 1992, the AFRCC, which is responsible for coordinating inland search and rescue (SAR) efforts, indicated that one of its biggest problems in 1992 was the high rate of false ELT signals. However, false ELT transmissions are one aviation statistic we could reduce to zero if we would all take just a few seconds to tune our aircraft radios to 121.5 MHz before securing our aircraft. (The (AIM), paragraph 6–15 contains suggested procedures for checking ELT's at shutdown. Some aircraft have expanded checklists that provide a similar procedure, but you could also adapt the AIM procedures for your own shutdown checklist.)

If you were to do this at shutdown and you heard the characteristically raucous ELT signal, that would be a good indication that your ELT, or one nearby, is transmitting. If it turns out to be your ELT transmitting, you should either turn the ELT off or disconnect its battery to verify it's your ELT, then notify the nearest ATC facility about the false signal. (If you turn off or disconnect your ELT, you must ensure that you comply with appropriate airworthiness requirements before your next flight.)

If the signal is not from your ELT, try to locate the transmitting ELT. It might be an emergency signal from an accident site just out of view, since many aircraft crash on or near airports. Probably, you will find just another false alarm. But the only way to tell a false alarm from an emergency is to locate the suspected ELT and turn it off. This is where all the time and effort come in, and this is why we could save the Air Force and everyone who has to go out and try to find a transmitting ELT a lot of work if we do an ELT final check before we secure our aircraft.

We would also help *those in distress* by not tying up valuable resources looking for false alarms. A final ELT shutdown test might also save some pilot the embarrassment of having to go out to the airport in the middle of the night to turn off a transmitting ELT.

Just how widespread is this problem of false alarms?

The AFRCC report states, "This year (1992), 1,994 of 2,562 ELT missions (97%) were false." Incidentally, the report noted that the proposed 406 MHz ELT's may eventually help reduce the work load. According to FAA information regarding the ongoing 406 MHz ELT rulemaking process, the proposed 406 MHz ELT's would offer global coverage, better first satellite-pass signal detection, better reliability, better batteries, fewer false alerts, and each ELT will have a personal identifier that is transmitted upon activation that includes the aircraft owner's data as well as aircraft registration and emergency notification data. As proposed, each 406 buyer would register his or her personal and aircraft information with NOAA's SARSAT Division for later emergency use.

But with all of these benefits for the proposed 406 MHz ELT's, the AFRCC report said it will be years before the high false ELT rate goes down even if the proposed 406 MHz ELT's become widely accepted because the older, less reliable, TSO C91 ELT's will still be in service.

Regardless of the cause, false ELT transmissions could be one of the easiest problems in aviation to eliminate if everyone just would take a few seconds of their time to check their ELT's before leaving their aircraft. Airport operators can also help identify false signals by periodically checking the appropriate frequency on their base station radios. And pilots flying en route should periodically check 121.5 or 243 MHz as appropriate for emergency distress signals. Any pilot receiving an ELT signal should contact ATC immediately. ATC would then take the appropriate action. In some cases, an airborne pilot ELT report may generate a quicker SAR response than if the AFRCC had to wait for a satellite-generated alert. In a real SAR emergency, the time savings might be critical.

According to the 1992 Annual Report, the AFRCC, supporting SAR agencies (local, state, and federal), and volunteer groups such as the Civil Air Patrol (the official Air Force Auxiliary that does the bulk of the Inland SAR missions) all combined to fly 13,131 hours during 6,459 sorties on 2,852 SAR missions in 1992. CAP flew 11,132 of those hours during 5,344 sorties on 2,380 missions. CAP flight time does not include the thousands of ground search hours donated by CAP volunteers. These statistics show the efforts of the many dedicated volunteers and others who are willing to risk their lives on SAR missions each year to help others. Because there is always some risk on any SAR mission for the participants, it is important that they only go out on real missions, not false alarms.

Since 1988, AFRCC has averaged about 7,900 incidents per year.

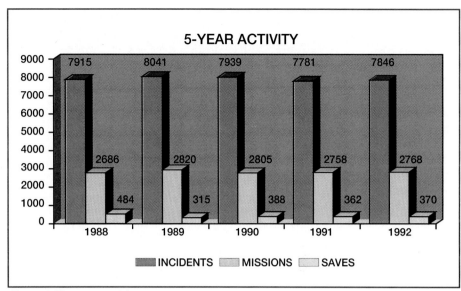

Figure 1 Five-year activity

According to the AFRCC, it responded to 7,846 incidents during 1992. Of that amount, the AFRCC was able to resolve 65% without going to a mission involving other federal agencies. Of the 1,008 people involved in actual distress situations, SAR personnel were credited with saving 370 lives. According to the report, SAR personnel were able to save, assist, or recover 65% of the 1,008 people involved in distress situations. All of us owe a "thank you" to the thousands of dedicated SAR personnel across the country who give their time so others may benefit. This tremendous SAR record is the good news.

The bad news is the continuing problem of finding—or rather not finding—missing aircraft.

FLIGHT PLANS, ETC.

Although the AFRCC is involved in many different kinds of SAR incidents such as missing persons, rescue missions, and aircraft searches, aircraft searches continue to be its least successful type of mission in terms of people saved. The report states, "In 163 aircraft searches, involving 224 persons, only 37 (17%) were saved. Few people survive the type of aircraft crashes we traditionally work at RCC."

How can you help?

It is easy. The report states, "In terms of flying hours and resources used, the most costly missions,

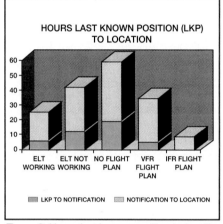

Figure 2 Hours last known position to location

excluding ELT searches, are searches for missing aircraft. In 1992, aircraft searches accounted for only about 6% of our total missions but almost 56% of the total flying hours logged. The reasons for this large investment in flying hours consumed on aircraft searches continue to be:

a. Pilots not filing flight plans

b. Ineffective or inoperative ELT's

c. The intensity of effort required to attain adequate search probabilities of detection in the type terrain aircraft most frequent are lost."

Once again, the annual report states the obvious, "Again this year, the statistics show that on aircraft missions, time from last known position to location is significantly shorter (almost 17 hours on average) for those incidents where the ELT worked. Filing a flight plan decreased time to location by 48 hours for a VFR flight plan and 63 hours for an IFR plan."

As Figure 1 shows, all pilots can help their own survival chances by filing and activating a flight plan. IFR flight plans are easy. ATC activates and closes the IFR flight plan, and pilots are in contact with ATC throughout their flight. VFR pilots must activate and close their own flight plans; however, for whatever reason many pilots don't bother to file flight plans at all. If you want to increase your survival chances your best insurance policy is to file a flight plan and make periodic position reports.

In addition you should periodically test your ELT in accordance with AIM paragraph 6–15 to make sure it works. If you are in an accident, you should, if able, verify your ELT is transmitting by tuning your radio to 121.5 and listening for the ELT signal. If there is no signal and if you have not been incapacitated, check the ELT antenna to see if it is still attached and pointing in an appropriate direction. Failure to verify your ELT transmission may give you a false sense of hope following an accident which may have destroyed your ELT or failed to activate it. (Some accidents may not generate the right kind of forces needed to activate your ELT.) The only way to know for sure is to monitor the emergency frequency.

It might be a good idea to show your passengers how to check and activate the ELT in your aircraft. If the accident incapacitates you, they may be the only ones able to do the check.

Figures 1 and 2 show some of the annual statistics that might be of interest to those planning their next flight. Remember, the best way to help yourself and save Government resources is by filing a flight plan, flying your plan, and closing your flight plan upon landing. And remember to check your ELT before you secure your aircraft. The time—not to mention the life—you save might be your own.

Remember also to practice FAA Eastern Region's Accident Prevention Program safety slogan, "Accident Free in 93." ∎

How to Test Your ELT

(AIM paragraph 6–15)

ELT's should be tested in accordance with the manufacturer's instructions, preferably in a shielded or screened room to prevent the broadcast of signals which could trigger a false alert. When this cannot be done, aircraft operational testing is authorized on 121.5 MHz and 243.0 MHz as follows:

1. Tests should be conducted only during the first five (5) minutes after any hour. If operational tests must be made outside of this timeframe, they should be coordinated with the nearest FAA Control Tower or FSS.
2. Tests should be no longer than three (3) audible sweeps. 3. If the antenna is removable, a dummy load should be substituted during test procedures.
4. *Airborne tests are not authorized*

CHECKING FOR FALSE ALARMS

In addition to the above testing procedure, paragraph 6–15 makes the following suggestions regarding false alarms and in-flight monitoring. It suggests pilots should monitor the emergency frequencies, 121.5 and 243.0 MHz, as follows:

1. In flight when a receiver is available.
2. Before engine shut down at the end of each flight.
3. When the ELT is handled during installation or maintenance.
4. When maintenance is being performed in the vicinity of the ELT.
5. When the aircraft is moved by a ground crew.
6. If an ELT signal is heard, turn off the ELT to determine if it is transmitting. If it has been activated, maintenance might be required before the unit is returned to the "ARMED" position.

If a signal is received in flight, the AIM requests pilots report the following information to the nearest ATC facility:

1. Your position at the time the signal was first heard.
2. Your position at the time the signal was last heard.
3. Your position at maximum signal strength.
4. Your flight altitudes and frequency on which the emergency signal was heard—121.5 or 243.0 MHz. If possible, positions should be given relative to a navigation aid. If the aircraft has homing equipment, provide the bearing to the emergency signal with each reported position.

A Thunderstorm...
...Unites Just About Every Hazard Known To Aviation!

by the Air Traffic Service

Every year this (and every other) aviation publication includes a pertinent article to focus pilot attention on the upcoming thunderstorm season and to remind pilots of the hazardous weather associated with it. This particular article has been reprinted from an internal air traffic publication aimed primarily at air traffic controllers—the Air Traffic Bulletin. *Indeed, the air traffic service has printed it for so many years, its author's name is lost in the annals of bureaucratic obscurity. Although the article was originally written to help controllers understand the severe atmospheric hazards associated with thunderstorms—so that they can better aid pilots in avoiding them—it also presents factors the pilot must consider when flying in the vicinity of nature's most awesome display of power.* **—Editor**

JUST HOW POWERFUL ARE THEY?

The latent heat released by a moderate thundercloud is equivalent to the energy of a nuclear explosion of 400 kilotons! Flight through such clouds should be avoided whenever possible, and, although most commercial and many general aviation aircraft are equipped with airborne weather radar, a pilot should always request up-to-date information concerning the location and extent of any active thunderstorm area that may affect his or her flight. Thunderstorms often reach far greater heights than even the usual cruising levels of commercial aviation. The hazards involved in penetrating a thunderstorm are severe turbulence, hail, icing, extreme water ingestion (turbine engines), and, to a lesser degree, lightning.

Downbursts, the strong descending air current found underneath storm clouds, cause rapid variations in wind speed and wind direction near the ground, both of which have proven to be extremely dangerous to low-flying aircraft. Sometimes violent thunderstorms cause the formation of concentrated powerful vortices, extending from the ground well into the cloud, scattered tornadoes or, when over water, waterspouts. Because tornadoes produce the highest wind speeds experienced near the ground (maximum values are estimated at 460 km/h or 285 mph), an aircraft entering a tornado vortex is almost certain to suffer structural damage. Thunderstorm hazards occur simultaneously in numerous combinations. The following discussions examine these and other thunderstorm phenomena.

TORNADOES

The most violent thunderstorms draw air into their cloud bases with great vigor. If the incoming air has any initial rotating motion, it often forms an extremely concentrated vortex from the surface well into the cloud. Meteorologists have estimated that wind in such a vortex can exceed 200 knots, and the pressure inside the vortex is quite low. The strong winds gather dust and debris, and the low pressure generates a funnel-shaped cloud extending downward from the cumulonimbus base. If the cloud does not reach the surface, it is a funnel cloud; if it touches the land surface, it is a tornado; if it touches water, it is a waterspout. Tornadoes have, at times, occurred with isolated thunderstorms, but more frequently they form with steady state thunderstorms associated with cold fronts or squall lines. Reports or forecasts of tornadoes indicate that atmospheric conditions are favorable for violent turbulence. Since the vortex extends well into the cloud, any pilot on instruments inadvertently caught in a severe thunderstorm could encounter a hidden vortex.

Families of tornadoes have been observed as appendages of the main cloud extending several miles outward from the area of lightning and precipitation. Thus, any clouds connected with a severe thunderstorm carry a threat of violence. Frequently cumulonimbus mammatus clouds occur in connection with violent thunderstorms and tornadoes. These clouds display rounded, irregular pockets or festoons from their bases and are a signpost of violent turbulence. Surface aviation observations specifically mention this and other hazardous clouds.

Tornadoes occur most frequently in the Great Plains states east of the Rocky Mountains; however, they have occurred in every state.

SQUALL LINES

A "squall line" is a nonfrontal, narrow band of active, or very active, thunderstorms. They often develop ahead of a cold front in moist, unstable air, but they may develop in unstable air far from any front. The line may be too long to easily detour and too wide and severe to penetrate. They often contain severe steady state thunderstorms and present the single most intense weather hazard to aircraft. They usually form rapidly, generally reaching maximum intensity during late afternoon and the first few hours of darkness.

TURBULENCE

Hazardous turbulence is present in all thunderstorms; in a severe thunderstorm, it can damage an airframe. The strongest turbulence within the cloud occurs with shear between up- and downdrafts. Outside the cloud, shear turbulence has been encountered several thousand feet above and 20 miles laterally from a severe storm. A low level turbulent area is the shear zone between the "plow" wind and the surrounding air. Often, a "roll cloud" on the leading edge of a storm marks the eddies in this shear. The roll cloud is most prevalent with cold front or squall line thunderstorms and signifies an extremely turbulent zone. The first gust causes a rapid and sometimes drastic change in surface wind ahead of an approaching storm.

It is almost impossible to hold a constant altitude in the turbulence associated with a thunderstorm, particularly if you have inadvertently penetrated the storm cloud. Maneuvering, or attempting to do so, greatly increases the stresses on the aircraft. Stresses will be lessened if the aircraft is held in a constant attitude and allowed to "ride the waves." To date, we have no sure way to pick "soft spots" in a thunderstorm.

MICROBURSTS

Microbursts are small-scale, highly intense downdrafts which, upon reaching the surface, spread outward from the downflow center. This causes the presence of both vertical and horizontal wind shear effects that can be extremely hazardous to all types and categories of aircraft, especially at low, critical flight altitudes. Because of their small size, short life-span, and the fact that they can occur over areas without surface precipitation, microbursts are not easily detectable using conventional weather radar or wind shear alert systems. Parent clouds producing microburst activity can be any of the low or middle layer convective cloud types. Characteristics of microbursts include:

Size—Approximately 6,000 feet in diameter above the ground with a horizontal extent on the surface spreading to approximately 2–1/2 miles outward from the center.

Intensity—Vertical winds as high as 6,000 feet per minute while above the ground, becoming strong horizontal winds with as much as an 80-knot variation when on the surface. The downward airstream may extend as low as tree top level.

Types—In wet areas of the U. S. , microbursts are normally accompanied by heavy rain. However, in dry areas virga is associated with microbursts.

Life—The life-cycle of a microburst from the initial downburst to dissipation will seldom be longer than 10 minutes, with maximum intensity winds lasting approximately two minutes. Multiple microburst activity in the same area is not uncommon and should be expected.

Signs—Dry microbursts often generate a ring of dust on the surface. Opposite direction winds over a short distance, accompanied by cell activity, are also a clear indication of a microburst.

During landing and takeoff, microburst wind shear effects can cause a sufficient reduction in aircraft performance to create a definite possibility of ground contact. Flight in the vicinity of suspected microburst activity should always be avoided.

ICING

Updrafts in a thunderstorm support abundant liquid water. The water becomes supercooled when carried above the freezing level. When temperature in the upward current cools to about –15 degrees Centigrade, much of the remaining water vapor sublimates as ice crystals. Above this level the amount of supercooled water decreases.

Supercooled water freezes on impact with an aircraft. Clear icing can occur at any altitude above the freezing level, but at high levels, icing may be either rime or mixed rime and clear. The abundance of supercooled water makes clear icing occur very rapidly between 0 degrees and –15 degrees Centigrade, and encounters can be frequent in a cluster of cells. Thunderstorm icing can be extremely hazardous.

HAIL

Hail competes with turbulence as the greatest thunderstorm hazard to aircraft. Supercooled drops above the freezing level begin to freeze. Once a drop has frozen, other drops latch on and freeze to it, so the hailstone grows—sometimes into a huge iceball. Large hail occurs with severe thunderstorms that tower to great heights. Eventually the hailstones fall, possibly some distance from the storm core. In fact, hail has been observed in clear air several miles from the parent thunderstorm.

As hailstones fall through the melting level, they begin to melt and precipitation may reach the ground as either hail or rain. Thus, rain at the surface does not mean the absence of hail aloft. You should anticipate possible hail with any thunderstorm, especially beneath the anvil of a large cumulonimbus. Hailstones larger than 1/2-inch in diameter can damage an aircraft in just a few seconds.

LOW CEILING AND VISIBILITY

Visibility generally is near zero within a thunderstorm cloud. Ceilings and visibility can become restricted in precipitation and dust between the cloud base and the ground. These restrictions create the same problem as all ceiling and visibility restrictions, but the hazards are increased manyfold when associated with the other thunderstorm hazards of turbulence, hail, and lightning. In combination, this can make precision instrument flight virtually impossible.

EFFECT ON ALTIMETERS

Pressure usually falls rapidly with the approach of a thunderstorm, then rises sharply with the onset of the first gust and arrival of the cold downdraft and heavy rain showers, falling back to normal as the storm moves on. This cycle of pressure change may occur in 15 minutes. If the altimeter setting is not corrected, the indicated altitude may be in error by over 100 feet.

LIGHTNING

Electricity generated by thunderstorms is rarely a great hazard to aircraft, but it may cause damage and is annoying to flight crews. Lightning is the most spectacular of the electrical discharges associated with thunderstorms.

A lightning strike can puncture the aircraft's skin and can damage communication and electronic navigational equipment. Lightning has been suspected of igniting fuel vapors and causing explosions; however, serious accidents caused by lightning strikes are believed to be extremely rare. Nearby lightning can blind the pilot, rendering one momentarily unable to navigate either by instruments or visual reference. Lightning can also induce permanent errors in the compass. Lightning discharges, even distant ones, disrupt radio communications on low and medium frequencies.

A few pointers on lightning:

- The more frequent the lightning, the more severe the thunderstorm.

- Increasing frequency of lightning indicates a growing thunderstorm.

- Decreasing lightning indicates a storm nearing the dissipating stage.

- At night, frequent distant flashes playing along a large sector of the horizon suggest a probable squall line.

PRECIPITATION STATIC

Precipitation static—a steady, high level of noise in radio receivers—is caused by intense corona discharges from sharp metallic points and edges of flying aircraft. It is encountered often in the vicinity of thunderstorms. When an aircraft flies through clouds, precipitation, or a concentration of solid particles (ice, sand, dust, etc.), it accumulates a charge of static electricity. The electricity discharges onto a nearby surface or into the air causing a noisy disturbance at lower frequencies. The corona discharge is weakly luminous and may be seen at night. Although it has a rather eerie appearance, it is harmless. It was named "St. Elmo's Fire" by Mediterranean sailors, who saw the discharge at the top of ship masts.

ENGINE WATER INGESTION

Turbine engines have a limit on the amount of water they can ingest. Updrafts are present in many thunderstorms, particularly those in the developing stages. If the updraft velocity in the thunderstorm approaches, or exceeds, the terminal velocity of the falling raindrops, very high concentrations of water may occur. It is possible that these concentrations can be in excess of the quantity of water turbine engines are designed to ingest, resulting in flameout or structural failure of one or more engines. Currently, there is no known operational procedure that can completely eliminate the possibility of engine damage or flameout during massive water ingestion. Although the exact mechanism of the water-induced engine stalls has not been determined, it is believed that thrust changes may have an adverse effect on engine stall margins in the presence of massive water ingestion. Avoidance of severe storm systems is the only measure assured to be effective in preventing exposure to this type of multiple engine damage or flameout. During an unavoidable encounter with severe storms, with associated extreme precipitation, the best known recommendation is to follow the severe turbulence penetration proce-

dure contained in the approved airplane flight manual with special emphasis on avoiding thrust changes unless excessive airspeed variations occur.

WEATHER RADAR

Weather radar detects droplets of precipitation by their size. Strength of the radar return (echo) depends on drop size and number. The greater the number of drops, the stronger the echo; and the larger the drops, the stronger the echo. Drop size determines echo intensity to a much greater extent than does drop number. Meteorologists have shown that drop size is almost directly proportional to rainfall rate, and the greatest rainfall rate is in thunderstorms. Therefore, the strongest echoes are thunderstorms. Hailstones usually are covered with a film of water and, therefore, act as huge water droplets giving the strongest of all echoes. Showers show less intense echoes, and gentle rain and snow return the weakest of all echoes.

Since the strongest echoes identify thunderstorms, they also mark the areas of greatest hazard. Radar information can be valuable both from ground-based radar for preflight planning and from airborne radar for severe weather avoidance. Thunderstorms build and dissipate rapidly, and they also may move rapidly. The best use of ground radar information is to isolate general areas and coverage of echoes. Remember that weather radar detects only precipitation drops; it does not detect minute cloud droplets. Therefore, the radar scope provides no assurance of avoiding instrument weather in clouds and fog.

The most intense echoes on weather radar are severe thunderstorms. Since hail may fall several miles from the cloud and hazardous turbulence may extend as much as 20 miles from the cloud, pilots should request separation from the most intense echoes by 20 miles or more.

PIREP's

Since PIREP information may be such a significant factor in both the pilot's and controller's operational decisions, providing and disseminating PIREP information should receive attention. The imminent arrival of thunderstorm season is a good time for pilots and controllers to review and refresh their knowledge of PIREP procedures.

DO'S AND DON'TS OF THUNDERSTORM FLYING

Remember, never regard any thunderstorm as "light" even when radar returns show the echoes are of light intensity. Avoiding thunderstorms is still the best policy. The following are some "Do's and Don'ts" of thunderstorm avoidance:

Don't land or take off in the face of an approaching thunderstorm. A sudden wind shift or low level turbulence could cause loss of control.

Don't attempt to fly under a thunderstorm even if you can see through to the other side. Turbulence under the storm could be disastrous.

Don't try to circumnavigate thunderstorms covering 6/10 of an area or more either visually or by airborne radar.

Don't fly without airborne radar into a cloud mass containing scattered embedded thunderstorms. Scattered thunderstorms that are not embedded can usually be visually circumnavigated.

Do avoid, by at least 20 miles, any thunderstorm identified as severe or giving an intense radar echo. This is especially true under the anvil of a large cumulonimbus.

Do clear the top of a known, or suspected, severe thunderstorm, if possible, by at least 1,000 feet altitude for each 10 knots of wind at the cloud top. This would exceed the altitude capability of most aircraft.

Do remember that vivid and frequent lightning indicates a severe thunderstorm.

Do regard as severe any thunderstorm with tops 35,000 feet, or higher whether the top is visually sighted or determined by radar.

INADVERTENT PENETRATION

If you cannot avoid penetrating a thunderstorm, the following are some "Do's" before entering the storm:

Do tighten your safety belt, put on your shoulder harness if you have one, and secure all loose objects.

Do plan your course to take you through the storm in a minimum time.

Do establish a penetration altitude below the freezing level or above the level of -15 degrees Centigrade, to avoid the most critical icing.

Do turn on pitot heat and carburetor or jet inlet heat. Icing can be rapid at any altitude and cause almost instantaneous power failure or loss of airspeed indication.

Do establish power settings for the turbulence penetration airspeed recommended in your aircraft manual. Reduced airspeed lessens the structural stresses on the aircraft.

Do turn up cockpit lights to highest intensity to lessen the danger of temporary blindness from lightning.

Do disengage the altitude and speed hold modes if using the automatic pilot. The automatic altitude and speed controls will increase maneuvers of the aircraft thus increasing structural stresses.

Do, if using airborne radar, tilt your antenna up and down occasionally. Tilting it up may detect a hail shaft that will reach a point on your course by the time you do. Tilting it down may detect a growing thunderstorm cell that may reach your altitude.

Do keep your eyes on your instruments. Looking outside the cockpit can increase danger of temporary blindness from lightning.

Do maintain a constant attitude; let the aircraft "ride the waves. "Maneuvers in trying to maintain constant altitude increase stresses on the aircraft.

Don't turn back once you are in the thunderstorm. A straight course through the storm will most likely get you out of the hazardous area most quickly. In addition, turning maneuvers increase stresses on the aircraft.

Don't change power settings; maintain settings for reduced airspeed. ■

Medical Stuff
Continued from page 9

Exercise is a very important part of the quitting program. Health spa activities, swimming, walking, hiking, bicycling, and jogging are all excellent forms of exercise that can be used to eliminate the desire to smoke.

The dividends of nonsmoking include greatly diminished risk of emphysema (a crippling lung disease), lung cancer, self-immolation in bed, throat cancer, cardiovascular disease, stroke, aneurysm of the large blood vessels, retinal cell death, and many other serious conditions.

In addition a recent study on the harmful effects of cigarettes smoking on 17,824 U.S. males found that during a five-year period, smokers of 20 or more cigarettes per day developed cataracts at twice the rate of nonsmokers. It is suspected that cigarette smoking changes the nature of the nutrients on which the lens of the eye depends to maintain its transparency. It is also possible that elevated blood carbon monoxide levels may damage the lens of the eye by interfering with the metabolism of the lens cells. Nicotine or the effects of nicotine metabolic products may also injure the lens. Statistics suggest that 20% of cataract cases in the U.S. are attributable to cigarette smoking. As transparency of the lens is an important factor for safe flight, smoking cigarettes is clearly incompatible with piloting aircraft.

There are clear health incentives for pilots to quit smoking, and there are increasingly effective ways to kick the habit successfully. ■

Dr. Mohler is a professor and vice chairman at Wright State University School of Medicine in Dayton, OH. He is also Director of Aerospace Medicine there. A pilot and flight instructor, he is a former director of the FAA's CAMI and former chief of FAA's Aeromedical Applications Division. He has written several books on pilot medications and one on aviator Wiley Post. This article is reprinted from Human Factors *and Aviation Medicine, published bimonthly by Flight Safety Foundation, a non-profit organization that disseminates safety information. For additional information contact FSF at 2200 Wilson Boulevard, Suite 500, Arlington, VA 22201–3307; (703) 522–8300.*

Soaring and Air Traffic Control Can Work Together

by W. G. Hill

"Say again your type aircraft," said the controller.

"I'm in a sailplane," replied the pilot.

There is a slight pause, and the controller replies, "Roger, squawk four six one three."

The glider pilot responds, "What's a 'squawk'?"

This scenario is, of course, a bit of an exaggeration, and the preponderance of sailplane pilots are professional aviators and, therefore, would know exactly what the controller meant when he or she assigned a transponder code.

There are, however, some things glider pilots don't know about ATC and some things ATC doesn't know about gliders.

What are Sailplanes?

They are majestic creatures of the sky who ply their trade on rising air currents created by natural phenomena such as ridges and mountains and by updrafts created by the convective activity of an unstable air mass.

They are the ultimate in the efficient application of unpowered flight.

Had Mother Nature created a flying machine, it most likely would have been a sailplane.

They leave in their passing not a roar but a whisper. They do nothing to violate the environment in which they fly; indeed, they fly because of the environment not in spite of it.

They have been known to share a thermal with hawks and eagles and other soaring birds. Because they mimic the very motions used by soaring birds to gain altitude, they are not perceived as a threat to the safety of such birds.

Sailplanes are one of the few ways in which we can both commune with nature and enjoy the three dimensional activity we know as flight.

Having said all that, it's not hard to understand why some sailplane pilots may view communicating with ATC as an invasion of privacy.

During the course of the last 20 years the National Airspace System has become "FAR" (pun intended) more involved. We have Airport Radar Service Areas (ARSA) and Terminal Control Areas (TCA) where only Control Zones and Airport Traffic Areas existed before. We will soon have the ABC's of airspace [September 1993]. And, of course, uncontrolled airspace at high altitude is almost non-existent in the eastern two-thirds of the lower 48 states.

The airspace, like the air traffic system and associated airborne equipment, has become a very complicated creature, indeed.

Whither the Glider Pilot?

So where has this left the glider pilot whose wood, glue, and fabric sailplane has metamorphosed into the composite thing of beauty you see on these pages?

If that pilot has any intentions of flying his or her sailplane cross country (and a good many do), then he or she must learn the language of the Air Traffic System. More importantly, glider pilots must learn how to communicate the variable of an aircraft that is virtually *never* in level flight to a group of individuals who deal in the constants of assigned headings and altitudes. Therein lies the dichotomy which must be resolved between Air Traffic Control and the sailplane pilot.

Generally, when a controller queries a pilot regarding altitude and receives a reply, the controller tends to think that the pilot will be maintaining that altitude unless the controller receives information to the contrary. Of course, this exchange of information is the key. The controller must know the right questions to ask, and the glider pilot must know how to respond to those questions properly.

For the most part, pilots fly sailplanes because of the freedom associated with the sport. That freedom also includes the desire not to be bothered with the mechanics of dealing with the air traffic system. Because of this, those pilots who have not been reared on such things as control towers and positive control airspace have little knowledge of how to deal with ATC.

Gliders and ATC Contact

Before attempting contact with an ATC facility, be sure you know your position over some clearly identifiable point on the ground. When you transmit, you should be prepared to provide the following information:
- Your aircraft registration number
- The fact that your aircraft type is "glider"
- Equipment code
- The fact that you are operating VFR
- Your location and altitude
- Your request and a statement of your intentions

You should use your aircraft registration number—not a contest number when communication with the ATC facility. The controllers very definitely know what a "glider" is. They may not know what a "sailplane" is. If you identify yourself as a "sail*plane*," they may think you are flying some sort of powered "air*plane*." If you have a Mode C transponder and no other electronic navigation equipment on board, then your equipment code is "/U"—pronounced "slant uniform."

As you are flying along, the controller may ask you to contact another controller on another frequency. This process is called a "handoff" and in theory is carefully coordinated between the two controllers. If no one answers on the new frequency, then change back to the original frequency and tell the controller you were not able to contact the hand-off controller. When you do contact the new controller, you should be sure to mention:
- That you are a glider
- Your entire registration number
- The fact that you are VFR
- Your current altitude
- Your destination

These procedures are exerpted from the article, "Suggested Radio Procedures for Mode C Gliders Flying in and around TCA's," in the October 1992 issue of Soaring *magazine. The author is John O. Graybill. We will reprint the article in its entirety in a future issue.*

For the approximately 11,000 pilots who are rated in gliders and some other powered aircraft, this doesn't pose too much of a problem. For the other nearly 8,000 pilots who are rated in nothing but a glider, the education process is a bit more convoluted.

Gliders are excluded from many of the transponder and Mode C encoder equipment requirements, including those in the airspace between 10,000 feet and flight level 180, and in certain airspace surrounding large airports. The exclusions were granted, in part, because of the power requirements necessary to run the equipment, and the fact is that a sailplane has no other power source save that of a battery, which may be quite small because of the limited space. Additionally, there is no way to re-charge it in flight. However, hand-held transceiver technology seems well-suited to glider pilots.

A recent issue of *Soaring* magazine (November 1992) had an excellent article on suggested phraseology that could be used by glider pilots who are not also rated in powered aircraft and who plan operations in the vicinity of TCA's. What is important is the vast difference between a glider and all the other air traffic that is likely to communicate with ATC.

Operational Considerations

As a rule, controllers are in the habit of dealing with aircraft that operate under a number of constants that make separation and advisories more viable. The average aircraft on an IFR flight plan, for example, will be maintaining a constant altitude, heading, and airspeed unless the route structure or ATC instructions require a change. On the other hand, a glider or sailplane is virtually never in level flight because it is always ascending or descending.

What transforms a gliding (descending) flight into a soaring (ascending) flight is the ability of the pilot to identify and avail him or herself of atmospheric conditions which have a vertical component exceeding the sink rate of the glider or sailplane. When this occurs, the glider can gain altitude.

The majority of cross-country flights in gliders take place using convective

updrafts (thermals), which are often marked by cumulus clouds. For a glider pilot, a cross-country flight is nothing more than an interconnected series of climbs and glides, and those glides must be made to the next source of suspected lift. Rarely do the sources of lift (i.e., clouds) align themselves in an extended straight line which coincides with the point to which the sailplane pilot is attempting to fly. Because of this, the series of climbs and glides associated with cross-country flight in a glider will also be marked with a number of course changes designed to get the glider or sailplane from one lift source to the next. When the glider pilot reaches the next point in space where he or she enters an updraft and initiates a climb, that climb is made by making a series of circles designed to keep the sailplane within the confines of the updraft, which is somewhat cylindrical in shape.

Because the sailplane, and hence the pilot, is in a constant state of flux, it is important that the glider pilot who is in communication with ATC keep the controller appraised of his or her intentions. This is especially true when traffic advisories have been issued.

By the same token, the ATC specialist needs to be aware that the sailplane is either climbing (because it has "stopped" to circle) or is gliding (because it is proceeding on course). If the sailplane is both transponder and encoder equipped (as only a few are), then most of that information is already available to ATC by virtue of the display on the controller's radar scope. But the vast majority of sailplane pilots who are radio-equipped must take on the responsibility of informing ATC of changes.

The bottom line is that of communication: from the controller who has a need to remain aware of the sailplane pilot's intentions and from the sailplane pilot who, when working with ATC, must do the utmost to keep the controller aware of his or her intentions. ■

Mr. Hill is a former ATC specialist from Albuquerque, NM with many years of ATC and sailplane experience.

Wake Turbulence

by the Civil Aviation Authority of the United Kingdom

The following is a reprint of the CAA's General Aviation Safety Sense Leaflet 15. Although its references are to events in the UK and Europe, the information and techniques apply to any general aviation aircraft that shares airspace with its airline big siblings. **—Editor**

Introduction

Recently there has been a fatal accident and a number of serious incidents in the UK as well as at least two fatal accidents in Europe where light aircraft have been severely upset by wake turbulence generated by much heavier aircraft. [Our British cousins do have a gift for understatement.—Editor] The hazard to light aircraft is most likely at airports where general aviation mixes with airline traffic.

All aircraft generate vortices at the wing tips as a consequence of producing lift. **The heavier the aircraft and the slower it is flying, the stronger the vortex.**

Vortices generally persist for up to 80 seconds, but in conducive atmospheric conditions, they can last as long as two and a half minutes. They tend not to decay gradually but come to a sudden end.

In simple terms, the lighter the aircraft you are flying, the greater the degree of upset if you encounter a wake vortex. Thus, microlight aircraft [CAA terminology for ultralights] could be vulnerable to the vortices of all other aircraft, including many general aviation aircraft.

Vortex Encounters

A light aircraft penetrating a vortex from a larger aircraft on the same trajectory and axis can be rolled severely. **For most types it may be beyond the power of the ailerons to counteract fully the roll.**

If the vortex is entered at right angles to its axis, rapid vertical and pitch displacements with airspeed changes are likely. An oblique entry, the most likely event, will of course have symptoms of both.

Ground Effect and Atmospheric Conditions

Although a vortex encounter at altitude is uncomfortable and alarming, it is recoverable. Closer to the ground, there may not be room to recover. A significant proportion of the incidents reported in the UK occur below 200 feet, i.e., mainly just before landing but some were shortly after takeoff. This is when the affected aircraft is most likely to be directly behind a larger aircraft.

Vortices generally persist for about 80 seconds close to the ground where their effect is most hazardous. They tend to move apart at about five knots in still air, so a crosswind component of five knots can keep the upwind vortex stationary on or near the runway; the downwind vortex will move away at about 10 knots. In crosswinds of more than 5 knots it can be seen that the area of hazard is not necessarily aligned with the flight path of the aircraft ahead.

Right Angle Encounter

VERTICAL AND PITCH CHANGES — AIRSPEED CHANGE — VERTICAL AND PITCH CHANGES

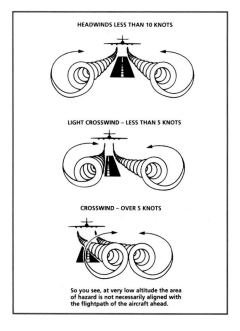

HEADWINDS LESS THAN 10 KNOTS

LIGHT CROSSWIND – LESS THAN 5 KNOTS

CROSSWIND – OVER 5 KNOTS

So you see, at very low altitude the area of hazard is not necessarily aligned with the flightpath of the aircraft ahead.

ATC

ATC is always provided at UK airports where airliners operate, and the controllers will advise pilots of the necessary interval; e.g., "Golf November Tango, you are number two to a 757. The recommended vortex wake spacing is six miles. Report final." (See the sidebar on page 21 for U.S. procedures.)

For VFR arrivals [in the UK] vortex separation is a pilot responsibility, but the recommended spacing will be given by ATC. If in doubt, ask for a greater spacing.

Vortex Avoidance—Approach

• Since the vortices are invisible (except rarely when the cores can be seen in very humid conditions), they are difficult to avoid. There are two techniques which can be employed:

• Distance can be judged visually by runway length—most major airports have runway lengths between one (6,000 feet) and two (12,000 feet) nautical miles long. Thus, if the recommended spacing is six miles, then you need three to six runway lengths between yourself and the airliner ahead.

If the aircraft on approach ahead of you is much heavier than your own type, try to keep it in sight. In general, vortices drift downwards, so **attempt to fly above** and to the upwind side of the lead aircraft's flight path. Obviously as you get closer to the runway any

Landing behind a heavy aircraft – Aim to touchdown beyond the point where the heavy aeroplane landed.

lateral displacement has to be reduced, so land well up the runway—beyond the point where the heavier aircraft touched down. The generation of vortices stops as the [wheels contact] the runway. The heavier the type ahead, the longer the runway is likely to be, so stopping a light aircraft should not be a problem—it may save you some taxi time! Airliners almost always approach on a 3 glide slope; light aircraft can accept steeper angles without difficulty.

Vortex Avoidance—Departure

Vortices start as aircraft rotate on takeoff, so the time interval [in UK air traffic procedures] starts from then. For example, a light aircraft taking off behind a Boeing 737 should allow an interval of at least two minutes if starting from the same point and three minutes if taking off from a point part-way up the same runway.

Vortex Avoidance—General

The simple advice for light aircraft pilots is, "Avoid crossing below or

close behind the flight path of a significantly heavier aircraft."

Helicopters

[U.K. procedures] specify minimum spacing between light aircraft and large helicopters. It is thought that helicopters can generate more intense

vortices than a fixed wing aircraft of the same weight. When following helicopters, pilots of light aircraft should consider allowing a larger spacing than would normally be used behind a fixed wing aircraft of similar size.

Helicopters, with rotors turning, create a blast of air outwards in all directions, the strongest effect being downwind. This effect is not so significant when the helicopter with rotors turning is on the ground. It is very severe during hovering and hover taxing when the rotors are supporting the full weight of the helicopter and this creates the greatest down wash. During your approach it may not be apparent which of the stages the helicopter is at. In these circumstances, pilots of light aircraft should aim to keep as far away as possible. In particular, if there is a helicopter on or near the runway, and if runway length permits, consider landing further down the runway to avoid being caught by rotor wash. If in doubt, make an early decision to go-around.

Summary

• Wake vortices are invisible.

• Vortices last longer and are therefore most hazardous in calm or light wind conditions.

• They are most dangerous close to the ground as there is less recovery room.

• The heavier an aircraft, the stronger its vortex and the greater the risk to following aircraft.

• The lighter the aircraft you are flying the more vulnerable it is.

• On the approach, to avoid vortices, fly above and off-set upwind of the lead aircraft's flightpath.

• Apply the spacing advised by ATC, using runway length as a guide to judging distance.

• Consider allowing a longer gap when following a large helicopter.

• Keep well away from large helicopters with rotors turning, they may be hovering or hover taxiing—it may be difficult to judge. ∎

U.S. Air Traffic Wake Turbulence Separations

FAA Airman's Information Manual
Paragraph 7–49:

A. Because of the possible effects of wake turbulence, controllers are required to apply no less than specified minimum separation for aircraft operating behind a **heavy** jet and, in certain instances, behind large **non-heavy** aircraft.

  1. Separation is applied to aircraft operating directly behind a **heavy** jet at the same altitude or less than 1,000 feet below:
     (a) **Heavy** jet behind **heavy** jet—4 miles.
     (b) **Small/large** aircraft behind **heavy** jet—5 miles.
  2. Also, separation, measured at the time the preceding aircraft is over the landing threshold, is provided to small aircraft:·
     (a) **Small** aircraft landing behind **heavy** jet—6 miles.
     (b) **Small** aircraft landing **behind** large aircraft—4 miles.

(Note: See the AIM's Pilot/Controller Glossary for the definition of aircraft classes.)

  3. Additionally, appropriate time or distance intervals are provided to departing aircraft:
     (a) Two minutes or the appropriate 4 or 5 mile radar separation when takeoff behind a heavy jet will be:
        —From the same threshold
        —On a crossing runway and projected flight paths will cross
        —From the threshold of a parallel runway when staggered ahead of that of the adjacent runway by less than 500 feet and when the runways are separated by less than 2,500 feet.

(Note: Pilots, after considering possible wake turbulence effects, may specifically request waiver of the 2-minute interval by stating, "Request waiver of 2-minute interval" or similar statement. Controllers may acknowledge this statement as pilot acceptance of responsibility for wake turbulence separation and, if traffic permits, issue takeoff clearance.)

     (b) A 3-minute interval will be provided when a **small** aircraft will takeoff:
        —From an intersection on the same runway (same or opposite direction) behind a departing **large** aircraft,
        —In the opposite direction on the same runways behind a large aircraft on takeoff or low/missed approach.

(Note: This 3-minute interval may be waived upon specific pilot request.)

     (c) A 3-minute interval will be provided for all aircraft taking off when the operations are as described in (b) above, when the preceding aircraft is a **heavy** jet, and when the operations are either the same runway or parallel runways separated by less than 2,500 feet. Controllers may not reduce or waive this interval.
     (d) Pilot may request additional separation, i.e., 2 minutes instead of 4 or 5 miles for wake turbulence avoidance. This request should be made as soon as practical on ground control and at least before taxiing onto the runway.
     (e) Controllers may anticipate separation and need not withhold a takeoff clearance for an aircraft departing behind a **large/heavy** aircraft if there is reasonable assurance the required separation will exist when the departing aircraft starts the takeoff roll.

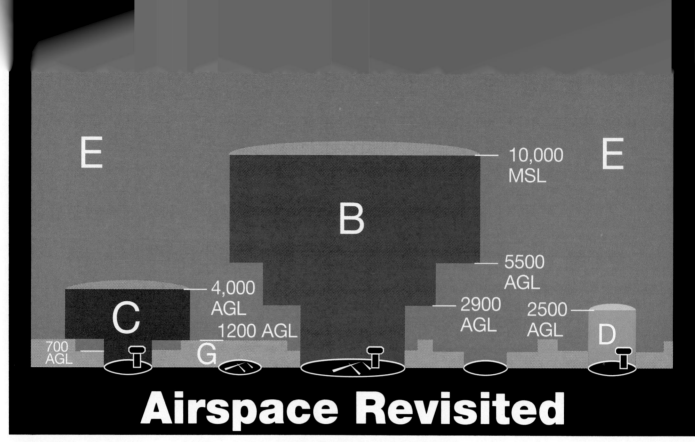

Airspace Revisited

by Louise Oertly, *Associate Editor*

As we get nearer the September 16, 1993 effective date the flying public is beginning to have more questions about what this new system really means to them. At this time it seems appropriate to review just how this reclassification came about and its objectives.

Despite what many people think, the FAA did not arbitrarily adopt the ICAO airspace classification. In 1978 the International Civil Aviation Organization (ICAO) saw the need to study the diverse range of regulations and airspace classifications in use by member states and develop an international standard. Along with such international aviation associations as IAOPA, IFALPA, FAI, IATA, the U.S. as an ICAO member has been among the leaders from the beginning to develop a simplified airspace system.

Paralleling this international effort was our own National Airspace Review (NAR). The FAA published the initial NAR recommendations in 1982 and three initial notices of proposed rulemaking (NPRM) in 1985. The resultant NPRM No. 89–28 was published in the *Federal Register* in October 1989. The NPRM proposed an airspace reclassification. It was not until the following March (1990) that ICAO formally adopted Amendment 33 to Annex 11, Air Traffic Services, which established seven international classes of airspace (A through G). Barely a month after ICAO's November 14, 1991 effective date, FAA's final rule appeared in the December 17 *Federal Register* with an effective date of September 16, 1993.

The airspace reclassification rule established six classes of U.S. airspace, each designated by a letter of the alphabet: A, B, C, D, E, and G. The reason there is no Class F is that the ICAO Class F has no equivalent in U.S. airspace (air traffic control provides separation service to IFR aircraft "so far as practical"). The rule clearly outlined its objectives:

- To simplify the airspace designations.
- To achieve international commonality and satisfy our responsibilities as a member state of ICAO.
- To increase standardization of equipment requirements for operations in various classifications of airspace.

- To describe appropriate pilot certificate requirements, visual flight rules (VFR) visibility and distance from cloud rules, and air traffic services offered in each class of airspace.

This simplification of the airspace will make it easier for pilots to understand the requirements needed to operate in U.S. airspace. In fact, pilots flying IFR will experience very little impact, whereas other pilots will find minimal changes to the operating rules. For example one change permits VFR pilots to remain clear of clouds while operating in Class B (formerly TCA) airspace.

Another way that reclassification will enhance safety and simplify airspace is by eliminating the current difficulty of which requirements apply when several types of airspace overlap around an airport. Within the new airspace reclassification there is a hierarchy; a pilot will know which class takes precedence by simply correlating the class (A, B, C, D, E, and G) of controlled airspace to the airspace surrounding the area—Class A preempts Class B, Class B preempts Class C, etc.

To help clarify some of the questions, comments, or subjects presented by the flying public, the past several issues of the *FAA Aviation News* have featured the "Airspace Corner." The questions have ranged from Airport Traffic Areas to Special VFR to the meaning of surface area (generic replacement for control zones and/or airport traffic area). Another frequent question concerns Terminal Radar Service Areas (TRSA) and what is happening to them. The answer is that they will not become a class of airspace as they do not come under FAR Part 71's definition of controlled airspace nor does the term TRSA appear in FAR Part 91's operating rules. (See "New Terminology for the Pilot/Controller Glossary" in this issue for further description of the TRSA.) The important thing to remember is that they no longer appear on VFR charts in the familiar solid magenta. The new color is solid black. (The color on the chart may vary from black to brown or gray.) The control zone or Class D portion of the TRSA is indicated by a blue segmented line and the remainder of the area overlies other Class E airspace.

The elimination of the Terminal Radar Program that established Stage I, II, and III service is a related and significant change. Basic radar services absorbed Stage I years ago and is now absorbing Stage II services. TCA services replaced Stage III services in the TCA last year and TRSA services are replacing Stage III services in TRSA's. Participating pilots will continue to receive the additional services from TRSA facilities.

To help ease pilots into the new airspace VFR charts began implementing changes last October. The theory is to have all changes in place by the time the new airspace rule goes into effect. By now all the charts have run through their cycle at least once and are now in the process of being fine tuned as errors or conflicts come to light. As with the VFR charts, the IFR charts will also have an insert that explains the new symbology. The only significant IFR chart changes will be going to four colors and deleting the control zones from the charts. [Control zones become part of the Class B (TCA) and Class C (ARSA) surface areas; at towered airports they become Class D; and at nontowered airports they become Class E.] A small boxed [D] next to the airport will be a reminder of a communications requirement should you cancel IFR operations and if the Class D is part-time there will be a star next the boxed [D]*.

For over a year now, the FAA and industry have been educating the flying public about the new airspace system. In meetings with the public one of the most frequent comments regarding the new airspace has been, "It's taken me (you can fill in the number) of years to learn the current system! Why change it now?" It is for this reason alone that the changes were necessary. The FAA believes the simplification of the airspace classifications will reduce existing airspace complexity and thereby enhance safety.

Hopefully, pilots will find it as easy as A, B, C. ∎

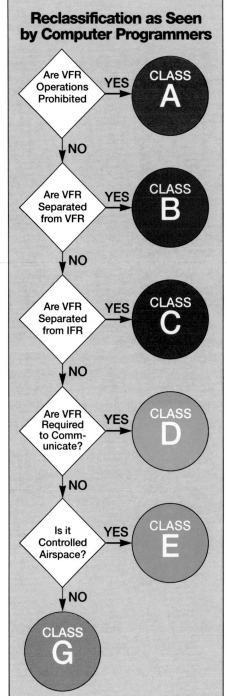

Reclassification as Seen by Computer Programmers

Are VFR Operations Prohibited — YES → **CLASS A**

NO ↓

Are VFR Separated from VFR — YES → **CLASS B**

NO ↓

Are VFR Separated from IFR — YES → **CLASS C**

NO ↓

Are VFR Required to Communicate? — YES → **CLASS D**

NO ↓

Is it Controlled Airspace? — YES → **CLASS E**

NO ↓

CLASS G

NEW AIRSPACE TERMINOLOGY IN THE PILOT/CONTROLLER GLOSSARY

Some of the following terms and definitions are new and others have been revised, but after September 16 this phraseology will be used by controllers in reference to the new airspace.

AIRSPACE HIERARCHY

Within the airspace classes, there is a hierarchy and, in the event of an overlap of airspace: Class A preempts Class B, Class B preempts Class C, Class C preempts Class D, Class D preempts Class E, and Class E preempts Class G.

AIRWAY

Class E airspace area established in the form of a corridor, the centerline of which is defined by radio navigational aids. *(See FEDERAL AIRWAYS). (Refer to Part 71). (Refer to AIM).*

(See ICAO term AIRWAY).

AIRWAY [ICAO]

A control area or portion thereof established in the form of corridor equipped with radio navigational aids.

CLASS G AIRSPACE

That airspace not designated as Class A, B, C, D or E.

CLIMB TO VFR

ATC authorization for an aircraft to climb to VFR conditions within Class B, C, D, and E surface areas when the only weather limitation is restricted visibility. The aircraft must remain clear of clouds while climbing to VFR. (See Special VFR).

CONTROL AREA [ICAO]

A controlled airspace extending upwards from a specified limit above the earth.

CONTROLLED AIRSPACE

An airspace of defined dimensions within which air traffic control service is provided to IFR flights and to VFR flights in accordance with the airspace classification.

Note 1—Controlled airspace is a generic term that covers Class A, Class B, Class C, Class D, and Class E airspace.

Note 2—Controlled airspace is also that airspace within which all aircraft operators are subject to certain pilot qualifications, operating rules, and equipment requirements in FAR Part 91 (for specific operating requirements, please refer to FAR Part 91). For IFR operations in any class of controlled airspace, a pilot must file an IFR flight plan and receive an appropriate ATC clearance. Each Class B, Class C, and Class D airspace area designated for an airport contains at least one primary airport around which the airspace is designated (for specific designations and descriptions of the airspace classes, please refer to FAR Part 71).

Controlled airspace in the United States is designated as follows:

1. CLASS A: Generally, that airspace from 18,000 feet MSL up to and including FL600, including the airspace overlying the waters within 12 nautical miles of the coast of the 48 contiguous States and Alaska. Unless otherwise authorized, all persons must operate their aircraft under IFR.

2. CLASS B: Generally, that airspace from the surface to 10,000 feet MSL surrounding the nation's busiest airports in terms of airport operations or passenger enplanements. The configuration of each Class B airspace area is individually tailored and consists of a surface area and two or more layers (some Class B airspace areas resemble upside-down wedding cakes), and is designed to contain all published instrument procedures once an aircraft enters the airspace. An ATC clearance is required for all aircraft to operate in the area, and all aircraft that are so cleared receive separation services within the airspace. The cloud clearance requirement for VFR operations is "clear of clouds."

3. CLASS C: Generally, that airspace from the surface to 4,000 feet above the airport elevation (charted in MSL) surrounding those airports that have an operational control tower, are serviced by a radar approach control, and that have a certain number of IFR operations or passenger enplanements. Although the configuration of each Class C airspace area is individually tailored, the airspace usually consists of a surface area with a 5 nm radius, and an outer area with a 10 nm radius that extends from 1,200 feet to 4,000 feet above the airport elevation. Each person must establish two-way radio communications with the ATC facility providing air traffic services prior to entering the airspace and thereafter maintain those communications while within the airspace. VFR aircraft are only separated from IFR aircraft within the airspace.

4. CLASS D: Generally, that airspace from the surface to 2,500 feet above the airport elevation (charted in MSL) surrounding those airports that have an operational control tower. The configuration of each Class D airspace area is individually tailored and when instrument procedures are published, the airspace will normally be designed to contain the procedures. Arrival extensions for instrument approach procedures may be Class D or Class E airspace. Unless otherwise authorized, each person must establish two-way radio communications with the ATC facility providing air traffic services prior entering the airspace and thereafter maintain those communications while in the airspace. No separation services are provided to VFR aircraft.

5. CLASS E: Generally, if the airspace is not Class A, Class B, Class C, or Class D, and it is controlled airspace, it is Class E airspace. Class E airspace extends upward from either the surface or a designated altitude to the overlying or adjacent controlled airspace. When designated as a surface area, the airspace will be configured to contain all instrument procedures. Also in this class are Federal airways, airspace beginning at either 700 or 1,200 feet AGL used to transition to/from the terminal or enroute environment, enroute domestic, and offshore airspace areas designated below 18,000 feet MSL. Unless designated at a lower altitude, Class E airspace begins at 14,500 MSL over the United States, including that airspace overlying the waters within 12 nautical miles of the coast of the 48 contiguous States and Alaska. Class E airspace does not include the airspace 18,000 MSL or above.

CONTROLLED AIRSPACE [ICAO]

An airspace of defined dimensions within which air traffic control service is provided to IFR flights and to VFR flights in accordance with the airspace classification. Note-Controlled airspace is a generic term that covers ATS airspace Classes A, B, C, D, and E.

OUTER AREA

(associated with Class C airspace)

Nonregulatory airspace surrounding designated Class C airspace airports wherein ATC provides radar vectoring and sequencing on a full-time basis for all IFR and participating VFR aircraft. The service provided in the outer area is called Class C service which includes: IFR/IFR-standard IFR separation; IFR/VFR-traffic advisories and conflict resolution; and VFR/VFR-traffic advisories and, as appropriate, safety alerts. The normal radius will be 20 nautical miles with some variations based on site-specific requirements. The outer area extends outward from the primary Class C airspace airport and extends from the lower limits of radar/radio coverage up to the ceiling of the approach control's delegated airspace excluding the Class C charted area and other airspace as appropriate.

(See CONTROLLED AIRSPACE).
(See CONFLICT RESOLUTION).

SERVICE

A generic term that designates functions or assistance available from or rendered by air traffic control. For example, Class C service would denote the ATC services provided within a Class C airspace area.

SPECIAL VFR CONDITIONS

Meteorological conditions that are less than those required for basic VFR flight in Class B, C, D, or E surface areas and in which some aircraft are permitted flight under visual flight rules.

(See SPECIAL VFR OPERATIONS).
(Refer to FAR 91).

SPECIAL VFR FLIGHT [ICAO]

A VFR flight cleared by air traffic control to operate within Class B, C, D, and E surface areas in meteorological conditions below VMC.

SPECIAL VFR OPERATIONS

Aircraft operating in accordance with clearances within Class B, C, D, and E surface areas in weather conditions less than the basic VFR weather minima. Such operations must be requested by the pilot and approved by ATC.

(See SPECIAL VFR CONDITIONS).
(See ICAO term SPECIAL VFR FLIGHT).

SURFACE AREA

The airspace contained by the lateral boundary of the Class B, C, D, or E airspace designated for an airport that begins at the surface and extends upward.

TERMINAL VFR RADAR SERVICE

A national program instituted to extend the terminal radar services provided instrument flight rules (IFR) aircraft to visual flight rules (VFR) aircraft. The program is divided into four types of services referred to as basic radar service, terminal radar service area (TRSA) service, Class B service, and Class C service. The type of service provided at a particular location is contained in the Airport/Facility Directory.

1. Basic Radar Service: These services are provided for VFR aircraft by all commissioned terminal radar facilities. Basic radar service includes safety alerts, traffic advisories, limited radar vectoring when requested by the pilot, and sequencing at locations where procedures have been established for this purpose and/or when covered by a letter of agreement. The purpose of this service is to adjust the flow of arriving IFR and VFR aircraft into the traffic pattern in a safe and orderly manner and to provide traffic advisories to departing VFR aircraft.

2. TRSA Service: This service provides, in addition to basic radar service, sequencing of all IFR and participating VFR aircraft to the primary airport and separation between all participating VFR aircraft. The purpose of this service is to provide separation between all participating VFR aircraft and all IFR aircraft operating within the area defined as a TRSA.

3. Class C Service: This service provides, in addition to basic radar service, approved separation between IFR and VFR aircraft, and sequencing of VFR aircraft, and sequencing of VFR arrivals to the primary airport.

4. Class B Service: This service provides, in addition to basic radar service, approved separation of aircraft based on IFR, VFR, and/or weight, and sequencing of VFR arrivals to the primary airport(s).

(See CONTROLLED AIRSPACE). (See TERMINAL RADAR SERVICE AREA).
(Refer to AIM). (Refer to AIRPORT/ FACILITY DIRECTORY).

VFR CONDITIONS

Weather conditions equal to or better than the minimum for flight under visual flight rules. The term may be used as an ATC clearance/instruction only when:

1. An IFR aircraft requests a climb/descent in VFR conditions.

2. The clearance will result in noise abatement benefits where part of the IFR departure route does not conform to an FAA approved noise abatement route or altitude.

3. A pilot has requested a practice instrument approach and is not on an IFR flight plan. All pilots receiving this authorization must comply with the VFR visibility and distance from cloud criteria in FAR Part 91. Use of the term does not relieve controllers of their responsibility to separate aircraft in Class B and Class C airspace or TRSA's as required by FAA Order 7110.65. When used as an ATC clearance/instruction, the term may be abbreviated "VFR;" e.g., "MAINTAIN VFR," "CLIMB/DESCEND VFR," etc.

VFR-ON-TOP

ATC authorization for an IFR aircraft to operate in VFR conditions at any appropriate VFR altitude (as specified in FAR and as restricted by ATC). A pilot receiving this authorization must comply with the VFR visibility, distance from cloud criteria, and the minimum IFR altitudes specified in FAR Part 91. The use of this term does not relieve controllers of their responsibility to separate aircraft in Class B and Class C airspace or TRSA's as required by FAA Order 7110.65.

FLIGHT**FORUM**

• Bonding vs. Grounding

In the May/June 1992 issue the article, "Refueling Considerations" makes no mention of bonding, i.e., connecting the fueling apparatus (truck or hydrant, etc.) and aircraft together with a bonding wire. The article mentions "nozzle bonding wire" which seems to imply that the (hopefully) conductive hose completes the bonding path between the fueling apparatus and the aircraft. This is contrary to the requirements of the National Fire Protection Association Bulletin 407. *The bulletin requires a bonding wire between the fueling apparatus and the aircraft, and for overwing fueling, a nozzle bonding wire as well. The bonding wire eliminates the potential difference in electrostatic charges between the two entities.*

An electrostatic charge is created by fuel (a non-conductive fluid) passing through the pipes. However, much more electrostatic charge potential is created by the filter or filter separator. When fuel flows, the negative (or positive) charge migrates to the aircraft and the opposite polarity charge migrates to the filter vessel and thus into the fuel truck vehicle frame. Bonding eliminates the potential difference in charges between the two entities.

An argument against grounding the fuel truck, hydrant, or fuel station and grounding the aircraft is that the ground wires commonly used are far too small. Imagine what would happen if a ground power unit energized by 3 phase/208 volts AC developed a fault, allowing the AC voltage to be applied to the airframe. The aircraft ground wire would probably "melt down" before the AC circuit breaker would trip. As far as lighting strikes are concerned, have you ever noticed the size of the conductor that lighting rod installations use?

According to a Gammon Technical Products newsletter the National Fire Prevention Association's most recent revision of Bulletin 407 *advises that it is safer not to ground, unless it is an adequate ground cable.*

Is this right or wrong?
Thomas E. Miller
Ballston Spa, NY

Thanks for your comments on bonding and grounding. We contacted the National Fire Protection Association's (NFPA) Technical Committee on Aircraft Fueling Service regarding your letter. Mr. Mark T. Conroy, Staff Liaison, NFPA 407, sent us the following letter.

In response to your request for comment regarding the article "Refueling Considerations" in the May/June 1992 issue I offer the following:

NFPA 407 Standard for Aircraft Fuel Servicing is the industry standard for aircraft fuel servicing. The purpose of this standard is to provide reasonable minimum fire safety requirements for procedures, equipment, and installations for the protection of persons, aircraft, and other property during ground fuel servicing of aircraft with liquid petroleum fuels. Like all NFPA standards, *NFPA 407* was developed and is revised by a Technical Committee made up of industry volunteers in a consensus process.

With regard to "hot" fuel servicing of helicopters (engine running and rotors turning), currently *NFPA 407* paragraph 3–5.1 prohibits fuel servicing while an onboard engine is operating. An exception to this provision permits fuel servicing of jet aircraft during an emergency under certain conditions, but this would not apply to helicopters.

A Subcommittee of the NFPA Technical Committee on Helicopter Facilities has been recently appointed to provide recommendations on whether or not hot fuel servicing can safely be accomplished, under what conditions, and on which aircraft. The Subcommittee is still deliberating on the issue. "The jury is still out."

One of the major changes in the 1990 revision of *NFPA 407* was the elimination of the requirement for grounding of aircraft during fuel servicing. Bonding of the fueling equipment to the aircraft by use of a cable prior to making any fueling connection to the aircraft is still required to provide a conductive path to equalize the potential between the fueling equipment and the aircraft.

You may wish to provide your readers with the following explanation which appears in the Appendix (A–3–4) of *NFPA 407*: "Hydrocarbon fuels, such as aviation gasoline and Jet A, generate electrostatic charge when passing through the pumps, filters, and piping of a fuel transfer system. (The primary electrostatic generator is the filter/separator which increases the level of charge on a fuel by a factor of 100 or more as compared with pipe flow.) Splashing, spraying, or free-falling of the fuel will further enhance the charge. When charged fuel arrives at the receiving tank (cargo tank or aircraft fuel tank)

FAA AVIATION NEWS welcomes comments from its readers. We may edit letters for style and/or length. We will select one representative letter from those on the same topic for publications, and because of our bimonthly publishing schedule, responses may not appear for several issues. We will send personal replies only upon request. We will not print anonymous letters, but we will withhold names upon request. Address: Editor, FAA AVIATION NEWS, AFS–810, Washington, DC 20591.

---

either of two possibilities will occur: (1) the charge will relax harmlessly to ground, or (2) if the charge or the fuel is sufficiently high, a spark discharge may occur. Whether or not an ignition will follow will depend on the energy (and duration) of the discharge and the composition of the fuel/air mixture in the vapor space, i.e., whether or not it is in the flammable range.

The amount of charge on a fuel when it arrives at the receiving tank, and hence its tendency to cause a spark discharge, will depend on the nature and amount of impurities in the fuel, its electrical conductivity, the nature of the filter media (if present), and the relaxation time of the system, i.e., the residence time of the fuel in the system between the filter (separator) and the receiving tank. The time required for this charge to dissipate is dependent upon the conductivity of the fuels: it may be a fraction of a second or several minutes.

No amount of bonding or grounding will prevent discharge from occurring inside of a fuel tank. Bonding will ensure that the fueling equipment and the receiving tank (aircraft or fueler) are at the same potential and provide a path for the charges separated in the fuel transfer system (primarily the filter/separator) to combine with and neutralize the charges in the fuel. Also, in overwing fueling and in top loading of cargo tanks, bonding will ensure that the fuel nozzle of the fill pipe is at the same potential as the receiving tank, so that a spark will not occur when the nozzle or fill tank is inserted into the tank opening. For this reason, the bonding wire must be connected before the tank is opened.

Grounding during aircraft fueling or refueler loading is no longer required because:

(1) It will not prevent sparking at the fuel surface (see *NFPA 77, Recommended Practice on Static Electricity*).

(2) It is not required by *NFPA 77, Recommended Practice on Static Electricity.*

(3) The static wire may not be able to conduct the current in the event of an electrical fault in the ground support equipment connected to the aircraft and could constitute an ignition source if the wire fuses. If ground support equipment is connected to the aircraft or if other operations are being conducted that require electrical earthing, then separate connections must be made for this purpose. Static electrical grounding points may have high resistances and therefore are unsuitable for grounding."

For a more complete discussion of static electricity in fuels see *NFPA 77, Recommended Practice on Static Electricity.*

NFPA 407, Standard for Aircraft Fueling Service and *NFPA 77, Recommended Practice on Static Electricity* and be ordered from NFPA Customer Service at 1–800–344–3555.

Thanks for the opportunity to comment on the article.
Mark T. Conroy
Staff Liaison, NFPA 407

Why Would the Aviation Industry be Interested in Training at the FAA Academy?

The FAA's safety team is responsible for almost every area of aviation, which includes surveillance of operations, maintenance, avionics, and manufacturing. The FAA Academy, located in Oklahoma City, OK, is dedicated to these responsibilities. For example, the Airworthiness Branch within the Regulatory Standards and Compliance Division provides resident courses open not only to FAA employees but also to aviation industry personnel as well as foreign joint aviation authorities who rely on guidance and interpretation of the FAR.

The Academy has a complete avionics section that includes the BE-300 Flight Inspection Aircraft Trainer equipped with a complete avionics complement. The training the Academy provides is widely recognized as some of the finest in the industry. Even though technology constantly changes, the students receive training in the most modern systems, enabling students to apply their skills more effectively and efficiently. The Academy provides training in classrooms, laboratories, aircraft simulators, and actual line aircraft. Course designers continu-

ously update materials in order to provide the student with knowledge of the latest regulatory changes.

The FAA Academy plays a key role in assuring the U.S. airspace system, the busiest in the world, continues to be the safest. The Academy is an accredited institution that meets all the standards of the North Central Association of Colleges and Schools. Many courses offer college credit equivalency from the American Council on Education, which is recognized as a major coordinating body for post-secondary education. Instructors are of the highest caliber and are required to meet stringent experience and educational requirements and, as an added bonus, have at their disposal the very latest technology.

A catalog of airworthiness courses, and a listing of course/class dates, and the cost of each course is available upon request from the Airworthiness Branch, Mike Monroney Aeronautical Center, AMA-250, P. O. Box 25082, Oklahoma City, OK 73125; (405) 954-6952.

Our thanks to Patricia Taylor, Contract/Support Clerk, AMA-250, in Oklahoma City for the above information.

The Year of the Woman— in Aviation History

Members of the Women Airforce Service Pilots (WASP), who fought to use their aviation abilities during World War II and eventually ferried hundreds of airplanes to combat units, will be honored during this year's Experimental Aircraft Association (EAA) fly-in in Oshkosh, WI. The annual fly-in will be held July 29 through August 4 at Wittman Regional Airport in Oshkosh.

As part of EAA's tribute to significant individuals, groups, activities, and engagements during the 50th Anniversary of World War II (1990–1995), the WASP will be recognized throughout the Convention and at a special evening program at the Convention site's "Theater in the Woods" on Saturday, July 31.

The WASP were established in 1942. Their operations were based on

Great Britain's "Air Transport Auxiliary" (ATA), a program that included both men and women who ferried airplanes to bases throughout England. The primary mission of the WASP was to perform flying duties in order to free male pilots for combat missions. The WASP became the first American women to fly military aircraft—testing and ferrying airplanes, towing flying targets, and engaging in other non-combat flying activities.

A tent pavilion near the Convention's "West Ramp" (just south of the FAA tower) will be the focal point for WASP activities during EAA Oshkosh '93. Aircraft representative of those flown by the WASP will be on static display nearby. WASP members will participate in daily seminars at the Pavilion throughout the week.

For additional information contact Dick Knapinski at EAA; (414) 426–4800.

William Kershner, the 1992 CFI of the Year, is shown with his family and FAA Administrator Richards

If You Forgot, Wait 'til Next Year

Nominations for the 1993 Certificated Flight Instructor and Aviation Maintenance Technician of the Year award were due in your local Flight Standards District Office by July 2, 1993. The two national winners will receive awards and honoraria from the FAA and industry at a Washington, DC ceremony in November.

If you can beat the July 2 deadline, contact your local Accident Prevention Program Manager for the nomination forms. If you missed it this year, start thinking about whom you would like to nominate for the 1994 awards.

AV**NEWS/BRIEFS**

Hazardous Materials— Tips for Airline Passengers

Some materials can be very dangerous if carried on an aircraft. Hazardous materials include many common items from the home, workshop, or garage which, because of their physical or chemical properties, can pose a danger when transported. The following is a partial list of common items that are hazardous materials forbidden in carry-on and checked luggage:

- Mace, tear gas, and other irritants
- Aerosols containing flammable material
- Loaded firearms
- Gunpowder
- Loose ammunition
- Gasoline, flammables
- Propane, butane cylinders or refills, lighter refills
- Wet-type batteries (e.g., as used in cars)
- Any equipment containing fuel
- Scuba tanks, if pressurized
- Fireworks, flares
- Safety or "strike-anywhere" matches
- Flammable paint and paint-related material
- Corrosive material
- Poisonous material
- Infectious substances
- Radioactive material

Many other hazardous materials are also prohibited. when in doubt, check with your airline. Violator of Federal hazardous materials regulations (49 CFR Parts 171–180) may be subject to a civil penalty of up to $25,000 for each violation and, in appropriate cases, a criminal penalty.

Think twice before you pack boxes and bags for air transport. These fuel containers were found packed in with household goods, and the boxes had no outside markings indicating their volatile contents. Fortunately, neither the fuel for the camping stove or the Avgas exploded during flight.

Remember, hazardous materials are prohibited in checked or carry-on luggage. However, there are certain exceptions for personal care, medical needs, sporting equipment, and items to support physically challenged travelers. For example:

- Toiletry and medicinal articles containing hazardous material (e.g., flammable perfume) totaling no more than 75 ounces may be carried on board. Contents of each container may not exceed 16 fluid ounces or one pound.

- Matches and lighters may only be carried on your person. However, lighters with flammable liquid reservoirs and lighter fluid are forbidden. (Smoking is prohibited on scheduled air carrier flights of six hours or less within the 48 contiguous states and between certain other locations.)

- Carbon dioxide gas cylinders worn by passengers to operate mechanical limbs and spare cylinders of a similar size for the same purpose are permitted in both carry-on and check luggage.

- Carrying firearms on board aircraft is forbidden. Unloaded firearms can be transported in checked luggage if declared to the agent atcheck-in and packed in a suitable container. Check with your airline representative for other restrictions concerning firearms.

- Ammunition may not be carried on board an aircraft. However, small arms ammunition may be transported in checked luggage but must be securely packaged in material designed for that purpose. Amounts may vary depending on the airline. Check with your airline.

- Dry ice for packing perishables, in quantities not to exceed four pounds, may be carried on board an aircraft provided the package permits the release of carbon dioxide. Further restrictions apply to dry ice in checked luggage. Check with your airline.

- Electric wheelchairs may only be transported as checked luggage. The airline may determine that the battery must be dismounted and packed in accordance with airline requirements. Check with your airline representative.

Some items can be shipped as air cargo. Contact your airline representative for detailed instructions regarding the shipment of hazardous materials.

For a pocket-sized leaflet containing the above information contact FAA, APA–200, 800 Independence Ave., S.W., Washington, DC 20591; (202) 267-3479.

Imagine everyone's surprise when this innocent looking bag exploded during handling. It seems that its owner was carrying butane torches used in the dental industry. One shifted during the flight, causing the explosion.

Koch's Komments

The photo that started it all shows the air-craft is about a half turn into a left spin.

In the September/October 1992 issue we published a letter congratulating us on recovering the camera and film from the aircraft because, he said, the air-craft must have crashed. The photograph showed it spinning at an altitude of 110 feet. We thought his comments would generate some interesting feedback, so we printed it.

The pilot flying the aircraft in question wrote to say he did not crash. In fact he is the current manager of the Scotts-dale (AZ) Flight Standards District Office (FSDO) and our old boss, Mr. Gary D. Koch, Sr., but many pilots may remember him as the former National Program Manager of the FAA's Accident Prevention Program here in Washington. Here is Gary's description of the flight.

The infamous flight occurred back in 1978 while I was assigned to the Denver GADO (General Aviation District Office) as the APS (Accident Prevention Specialist). I managed to talk our avionics inspector, Al Lundquist, who is a private pilot and a darn good

photographer, into going with me to film some "airwork." I kind of soft sold the idea that we would be "spinning." I explained to Al that he would sit in the left seat, with his camera at ready, and using fast shutter technique, capture the instrument readings as we "flopped" around the sky! Al agreed to come along and film this epic.

My goal was to perform a one-turn spin and record exactly how much altitude would be lost during recovery. Also to record the time, in seconds, it took to complete the spin as well as recording altitude, rate-of-descent, and airspeed indications. By the time we got into the spin sequence, Al had figured out he had been duped, and this "airwork" was not quite what he expected. I think Al came close to calling this adventure off and filing a violation of some sort against me!

It took a few takes for Al to adjust to the spinning, as our first pictures turned out showing the rudder pedals, ash trays, and sun visors of the trusty Cessna 150. However, Al hung in and did a great job. After numerous spins, Al captured a good sequence from start to recover. I have used the spin sequence series in numerous spin presentations and the slides have been utilized by the FAA's Accident Prevention Program, the AOPA Air Safety Foundation, and numerous safety related aviation groups.

To put Mr. McLaughlin at ease, we did not crash or burn. We started the spin at 10,200 feet and recovered at

The instigator and pilot of the spin photo mission, Gary Koch. Insert, the unsuspecting photographer, Al Lundquist, before the flight.

9,500 feet. The best I could do was 500 feet to fully recover from a one-turn spin. The slides turned out well and pointed out that a 500 foot altitude loss could occur in approximately 7–9 seconds and the altitude indicator, turn coordinator, rate-of-climb indicator all do their thing as you plummet to the ground. The safety message here is—if you stall and spin on base to final, or in the traffic pattern, "school's out!" In other words, you could be Bob Hoover or any top notch aerobatic pilot, but if you do not have enough altitude to recover, you are dead!

It was a fun project and Al is still alive and well, doing his avionic thing at the Denver FSDO. I think he has forgiven me for "duping" him into filming some "airwork," but he did a great job of filming and hopefully we have prevented some stall/spin accidents through the presentations. ∎

The photographer experiencing post-flight trauma and trying to decide if he could file a violation against the pilot.

BULK RATE
POSTAGE & FEES PAID
GPO
PERMIT NO. G–26

DO NOT DELAY—CRITICAL TO FLIGHT SAFETY!

NON-CIRCULATING
September 1993

FAA Aviation News

A DOT/FAA FLIGHT STANDARDS SAFETY PUBLICATION

NON-CIRCULATING

U.S. Department
of Transportation

**Federal Aviation
Administration**

Federico F. Peña, *Secretary of Transportation*
Joseph M. Del Balzo, *Acting FAA Administrator*
Carl B. Schellenberg, *Acting Executive Director
for System Operations*
Anthony J. Broderick, *Associate Administrator
for Regulation and Certification*
Thomas C. Accardi, *Director,
Flight Standards Service*
Robert A. Wright, *Acting Manager,
General Aviation and Commercial Division*
Roger M. Baker, Jr., *Manager,
Accident Prevention Program Branch*
Phyllis Anne Duncan, *Editor*
Louise C. Oertly, *Senior Associate Editor*
Dean Chamberlain, *Associate Editor*

The FAA's Flight Standards Service, General Aviation and
Commercial Division, Accident Prevention Program
Branch, AFS–810, Washington, DC 20591, (telephone
202 267–8017) publishes FAA AVIATION NEWS in the
interest of flight safety. The magazine promotes safety in
the air by calling the attention of airmen to current technical, regulatory, and procedural matters affecting the safe
operation of aircraft. Although based on current FAA policy and rule interpretations, all printed material herein are
advisory or informational in nature and should not be
construed to have regulatory effect. The FAA does not
officially endorse any goods, services, materials, or products of manufacturers that may be mentioned. **Certain
details of accidents described herein have been
altered to protect the privacy of those involved.**
   The Office of Management and Budget has
approved the use of funds for the printing of FAA AVIA-
TION NEWS.

SUBSCRIPTION SERVICES

The Superintendent of Documents, U.S. Government
Printing Office, Washington, DC 20402–9371, sells FAA
AVIATION NEWS on subscription. Use the self-mailer
form in the center of this magazine to subscribe. Cost:
$8.00 ($10.00 foreign) for one year; $16.00 ($20.00 for-
eign) for two years. Prices are subject to change by the
Government Printing Office without prior notice.
   Change of Address or Subscription Problems:
**Send your label with correspondence to Sup Doc,
Attn: Chief, Mail List Branch, Mail Stop: SSOM,
Washington, DC 20402–9373.**
   To keep subscription prices down, the Government
Printing Office mails subscribers only one renewal
notice. You can tell how many copies are left in your
subscription by checking the number that follows "ISS-
DUE" on the top line of your mailing label. For example,
when this number is 003, it means you have three
issues left in your subscription, and GPO will send you
a renewal notice. The number 000 means you have
received your last issue. To be sure that your service
continues without interruption, please return your
renewal notice promptly.

FAN SMITH 212J ISSDUE003 R 1
JOHN SMITH
212 MAIN ST
FORESTVILLE, MD 20747

FAA Aviation News

Volume 32   Number 6

FEATURES

DEPARTMENTS

Front Cover: *The new airspace rules and aerobatic
flying—what happens after September 16?
See page 26. Photo courtesy of EAA*

Back Cover: *What do the letters in the surface
weather observations really mean?
See page 16. Photo by G. S. Livack*

Looking Back

by Glenn Showalter

In our editorial series you have heard mostly FAA's opinions about things. Time for a break, don't you think? What follows are the musings of someone who loves airplanes and flying. Yet, in his reminiscences, there are a few good lessons. —Editor

Late last year, the McNeil-Lehrer Report had an exciting segment. An older gentleman (over 70) was flying his Piper *Comanche* to see a friend in Kansas. He was still a good pilot and still excited about flying. Seeing that airplane brought back some memories, one being the time I first checked out in this high performance, single engine bird at Billings, MT Airport in 1974. The check pilot required only one landing, since I was plenty current in this type of airplane, and my takeoff, traffic pattern, and landing was something just slightly short of perfection. Actually, I surprised myself because I had never flown this particular model before, and it had a reputation of being a "hot" airplane. The landing was one of those where you really don't know the wheels have touched down until you use the brakes.

Every pilot has those flights once in a while, but it takes a lot of practice and experience to be consistent. I was a commercial pilot fully rated at the time, and even though this was the first time I had flown a *Comanche*, I flew it as though she was a personal aircraft. My sights long set on an airline career received an ego boost that day, for it was one of those career happenings that says you are good, very good. This is necessary if a person is going to sacrifice so much for a goal. Self-confidence is important when flying an airplane. Basic skills are important as well, but I felt that day that if I

Glenn Showalter

could understand and handle an airplane that well, that fast, I could do anything.

Fortunately for my career, such success was not short lived. Later that winter, I served as a charter pilot for a Glasgow, MT family, flying them through the Rocky Mountains to Durango, CO and return. It was a very enjoyable trip and my first in that part of the country. While I had plenty of cross-country experience, this was a challenging trip especially when it came to trying to receive some navigational stations at the "lower" altitudes (12,500' MSL) necessary for non-pressurized airplanes. But the weather was good, the Cessna Turbo 206 performed well, and we all had a great time.

The following spring brought my first flight to the Pacific Coast. The delight of seeing the Pacific Ocean for the first time at about 1,000 feet above the beach was unforgettable. The years of flight training and study had paid off.

Flying does more than get you from one place to another. Both art and science, flight develops in a person the ability to get the big picture, to pay attention to all those flight techniques, principles of science, other aircraft, gauges, possible obstructions, weather, regulations, etc. Dwelling on any one of those aspects to the neglect of the others can cause you problems because the airplane is unforgiving.

The aviation industry is both valuable and noble, doing more for humankind than the Wright Brothers ever dreamed of and certainly more than some of the "junk" industries we have today. A lot of people have served the aviation industry well, but one tends to reflect from time to time on his (or her) own personal efforts and the things he wishes he could have done if only

Continued on page 4

Pilot Decision Making

by Tom Hamilton

Stress

This is Part Three of a seven-part series that first appeared in Balloon Life *magazine and was originally written for balloon pilots. For the most part, we have left the lighter-than-air examples in because the overlying issue of pilot decision making affects all pilots, and the excellent information in these articles can be extrapolated to aviation activities other than ballooning.* **—Editor**

What is stress? The dictionary defines it as, "pressure, strain, esp., a force that tends to distort a body." In this article we will look at types of stress that affect our ability as pilots; stress and pilot performance; how to identify stress; and how to cope with stress.

In our earlier discussions on **Pilot Decision Making** (May/June and July/August issues of *FAA Aviation News*), we defined headwork as the intellectual process used to formulate decision making strategies. Stress interferes with headwork.

The FAA defines stress as the body's response to any demand made upon it by physical, physiological, or psychological factors known as stressors. We'll look at each of these areas.

Physical stressors include conditions associated with the environment. Temperature and humidity extremes, noise, vibration, and lack of oxygen are examples. Think back to when you might have experienced some of these situations: a hot, humid afternoon flight, passengers talking, engine doesn't sound right, static on the radio, etc. Even the physical work of loading/unloading the aircraft can make a pilot pretty edgy.

Physiological stressors include conditions associated with the body, such as fatigue, lack of physical fitness, sleep loss, missed meals (low blood sugar levels), and illness. How late were you up last night? Did you have breakfast before the flight? Do you have a cold or other ailment that might affect your performance?

Psychological stressors are related to social or emotional factors; e.g., death in the family, marriage, divorce, sickness in the family, work-related problems, domestic fights, etc. Or they may be related to mental workload such as analyzing a problem, navigating the aircraft, or making decisions.

One or more of these elements can enter into play and affect your performance. For a balloon pilot for instance: You were up late last night at the welcoming reception at a balloon rally, and this after a long drive. You arrived at the launch field about half-way through the flight briefing because it was so hard to get out of bed, let alone make time for coffee. Now you are two hours into the flight, having miserably missed the target. You are over a heavily wooded area leading to a wide river. The crew will have to drive at least an hour to reach the other side. What if you don't make it across? Can your passengers swim? Will your insurance cover the loss? The burner is beginning to sound funny, your palms are sweating, your mouth is dry, and your heart is pounding!

Now what? You feel a growing sense of urgency and tension. Stress takes control of your normal thought process. You become confused and unfocused on the problems at hand. You begin to give too much attention to "what if" questions which you should be ignoring. You are reaching (or have reached) a state of stress overload. You begin to use poor judgement that can result in a series of bad decisions.

This may be an over dramatization, but stress is a part of our everyday life and can be broken into two components—*static* and *dynamic* stress.

Static stress is what we might call constant, everyday stressors such as financial problems, job pressures, rush hour traffic, "having" to fly, or just flying! Yes, even those things in life that you find enjoyable can be stressors since they represent a change in your environment that must be dealt with.

Dynamic stress involves those stressors that develop as the situation evolves: the engine sounds "off," a passenger is asking too many questions, you're over the water and fuel is getting low, and so on. The effects of these stressors are cumulative. Eventually, they can add up to a level that makes it difficult to deal with the situation at hand.

Stress and Performance

Stress, at least to some degree, is with us at all times. In fact, some people seek stress to make life more interesting. As you can see in the diagram in Figure 1, some stress is good for you. It keeps you on your toes and prevents complacency from setting in. Some stress helps prevent accidents.

Stress helps? We just mentioned that stress, or the effects of stressors, are cumulative. Looking at Figure 1, we see that the relationship between stress and performance has a positive effect up to a point. Performance, then, will generally increase with the onset of stress but only to a point. Beyond a certain level, performance begins to fall off rapidly as stress levels exceed your ability to cope.

At low levels of stress, the pilot experiences boredom and is not taking into consideration all the elements that are necessary to fly the aircraft and make good pilot decisions. At the other end of the spectrum, panic takes control and the pilot's ability to think clearly or think at all is severely impaired.

Task Requirements and Pilot Capabilities

Accidents or mishaps often occur when flying task requirements exceed pilot capabilities. Stress plays an important role by adversely affecting the pilot's capabilities. Figure 2 is an idealized chart developed by the AOPA Air Safety Foundation for the FAA. This chart was adapted to balloon operations.

The top line shows pilot capabilities over the period of the flight. The bottom line indicates the task requirements or degrees of ability needed. The shaded area between the two lines represents what is known as the margin of safety, the difference between our ability and that required by the task.

Over time the pilot's capabilities slowly deteriorate. This deterioration

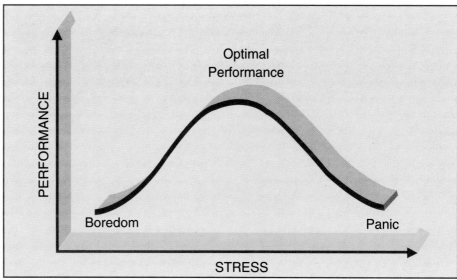

Figure 1. Some stress helps to improve performance up to a point. Beyond a certain level performance begins to fall off rapidly as stress levels exceed your ability to cope.

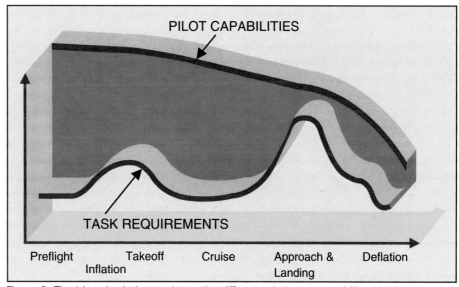

Figure 2. The blue shaded area shows the difference between our ability and that required by the task—the margin of safety.

can come from a variety of sources: the cumulative effects of staying up late, fatigue (physical and mental), low blood sugar, illness, alcohol, etc.

Figure 3 shows the balloon accident statistic chart for each phase of flight from NTSB reports. Notice that 69% of the accidents happen during approach to landing and landing phase of operation—a critical time in terms of ability needed and stress buildup.

We talked about the pilot's capabilities deteriorating over the time line of a flight. What about, for example, over the length of a balloon rally? [Fixed-

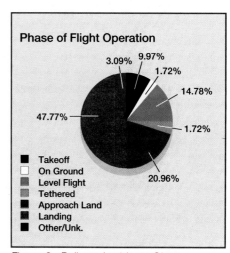

Figure 3. Balloon Accidents Chart

Figure 4

wing pilots who have flown short-hop charters or multiple legs for a commuter can relate to this example.] First, you may have had to drive several hundred miles to attend. There are parties, one or two flights a day, pressure of competition, and so on. Here again, the cumulative effects of stress are building up. Pilots who attend the nine day Albuquerque International Balloon Fiesta often hope for rain or bad weather by mid-week to get a day's rest. Many will take a day or two off to go sight-seeing, and some have more than one pilot registered to fly the balloon so that they can trade off and lessen the stress on each.

Stress Management in the Cockpit

Before beginning any flight you want to make sure that you have planned thoroughly. Receiving and evaluating weather information, flight planning, passenger and crew briefing (if applicable), and preflighting the aircraft are all part of it.

Don't forget to preflight yourself. The "I'M SAFE" checklist in Figure 4 is a valuable tool to use in preflighting yourself. ∎

Looking Back

Continued from page 1

given the chance. There are times in any person's career when you wonder if you should have chosen something else or would have been better off taking over Dad's business. Looking back on my aviation career, I realize it was the right choice

Looking back again on the Piper *Comanche* flight that fall day, I also remembered my first "grease job" landing made while working on my private pilot's license. In 1967 Dulles Airport in Virginia was new, and even on busy days, traffic was light. For general aviation, Dulles was a pilot's dream: Big airport practice and facilities with very little big jet traffic. I occasionally stopped at Dulles for breakfast. The price was reasonable and the food quite good. In those days a general aviation pilot could just taxi up near the tower and zip in for

scrambled eggs, hot cakes, Virginia ham, toast, and OJ.

I visited Dulles not too long ago but this time as an airline passenger. Aside from the thrill of flying there was something special in the air, the feeling of meeting an old friend again. It just seemed that in spite of the problems the airline industry was going through, people realized you were someone who tried to make a contribution. As the engines came up to takeoff thrust, the same warm, overwhelming feeling came over me.

Seattle was my home for many years. I first moved there on a tip for a flying job and stayed. I was flying some people from the mountain region of Montana to Seattle, and an early winter storm had brought rare, light snow to the Puget Sound area. En route, we had enjoyed a beautiful sunset on top of the overcast. The night approach and landing at Seattle Boeing Field gave my copilot/friend his first experience at seeing an instrument landing. The winds were seven knots out of the north so approach control was going to bring us in from the south for the backcourse localizer to 31. I noted to air traffic control that weather was below backcourse minimums and I would accept the ILS 13 with tailwind. The runway was snow covered, and my planned firm touchdown turned out to be a smooth roll on. Such smooth landings tend to be impressive to passengers, but for the sake of the student working on his private pilot's license, I pointed out that while the landing was safe, a firm touchdown allows the tires to make solid contact with the runway surface, important for braking while on wet or snow-covered runways and for reducing the aerodynamic effects of the wings as soon as possible.

As we taxied to the ramp, an MU–2 prop jet landed, nearly spinning out of control. The potentially hazardous situation might have been prevented had the pilots made a firmer touchdown. So, when your airline captain plants those tires on the runway with a "bounce-thud" technique, cut him or her some slack and realize the "old man" up front knows you'd be more impressed with a smooth roll-on. ∎

Parks College of Saint Louis University

Parks College

by Phyllis Anne Duncan, *Editor*

How many institutions of higher learning do you know that were founded because of a succession of rough landings and a profound religious experience?

Only one comes to mind, and that's Parks College of Saint Louis University in Cahokia, IL.

At its inception, the name was simply, "Parks Air College," and it was started by an Illinois automobile salesman who had the flying bug and who became dissatisfied with the short amount of instruction he received when learning to fly. Nearly 70 years later Parks College boasts airline and military pilots, engineers, NASA technicians, teachers, and FAA employees among its graduates.

Oliver Lafayette Parks was born in Minonk, IL and has been described by his biographers as a workaholic and a visionary. Certainly there were others who may have called him a fool until they experienced his success. More than a salesman, he was a promoter who used techniques commonplace now but unheard of in the 1920's. Yet, he was also a man of conviction. After winning a top automobile salesman award and not receiving the promised dealership, he told the company off and left to learn how to fly.

A Marine in World War I, Lafe (he abhorred Oliver or Ollie) had probably seen the aircraft of the day, and perhaps they inspired him in his future endeavors. Most write of him, however, as a man who saw no limits, who overreached himself financially on many occasions, but who succeeded often enough to leave a legacy behind.

In 1925 Parks went to Lambert Field in St. Louis, MO and learned how to fly at Robertson Aircraft Corporation. In the days before federal regulation, pilots could earn certification in a day for about $100. After receiving his license in this manner, Parks began taking people for St. Louis sightseeing flights in a Standard J–1.

Whether the unreliability of the Standard's engine or Parks' fledgling pilot skills, many of these flights ended in forced landings off airport. The one that got his attention was his loss of control of the Standard while making a simple turn around the flagpole of Sportsman's Field, home of Ty Cobb and the St. Louis Cardinals. He recovered before having to crash land, but he realized that the shortness of his pilot training was to blame.

Someone else may have given up flying at this revelation, but Parks the businessman saw it as an opportunity. Parks the pilot wanted to improve his and other pilots' skills.

So, on August 1, 1927 he opened Parks Air College at Lambert Field. The faculty of one (himself) used the Standard and a Laird *Swallow* for instruction. Using his salesman's promotional skills, he soon had several students signed up for the course of training.

However, his own skills may still have been somewhat suspect.

In 1927 while taking a young woman for a thrill ride at the request of her boyfriend, Parks deliberately put the *Swallow* in a spin from which he could not recover. He crashed on the grounds of the St. Stanislaus Jesuit Seminary northwest of the airport. Seminarians rushing to the scene found Parks unconscious, severe injuries to his back and legs, his left eye gone, and his teeth knocked out. (The fate of his passenger was unreported.) In the face of such injuries, the Father Rector blessed Parks and baptized him on the spot. Parks later attributed his recovery to this natural reaction of a Catholic priest, and the incident was to have future importance for Parks Air College.

For the present, its Director and only instructor was in the hospital, and the six students who had given him their money were justly concerned about their and the school's future. When confronted by their spokesman, Parks again used his promotional ability, detailing his plans to move the school to its own 113-acre campus and to increase the number of training hours to 50. Parks was able to sell them on his dream, and many of those early students went on to become faculty and stay with Parks until the end of his life.

Because Parks was a "solid businessman" in the area, he was able to

Charles "Slim" Lindbergh, Oliver L. Parks and Boots Dempsey on the Parks College campus, October 1929

In addition to the basic pilot and mechanic training, Parks added instrument and night flight training. Parks Airfield became the first in the St. Louis area to be fully illuminated and used for night flights. In the 1920's and 1930's aviation's famous came to Parks Air College to visit or to brush up on their skills—Lindbergh, Earhart, and stunt pilot Frank Hawks.

Parks also caught the airplane building bug, perhaps a businessman's natural response to two other airplane manufacturers beginning operations in St. Louis. He formed Parks Aircraft Manufacturing Company on the field, and the students learned design and manufacturing by modifying an open cockpit biplane. They named it the Parks P–1. The P–2 followed shortly after and was used for night training. A third model, called the *Sunbeam,* was short-lived. In fact, the aircraft building venture itself was equally short-lived. The manufacturing company turned out 84 airplanes but managed to lose a quarter of a million dollars.

Parks was forced to sell out most of the College's stock but chafed under the new management. He mortgaged his house, sold his cars, brought his employees in as stockholders, and borrowed money from his friends and more from his existing creditors and bought the company back. This was a gesture to regain control of his school; the company never built another aircraft.

Parks College's association with aviation education is nearly 70 years old. Its association with the FAA and aviation safety is almost as old. In 1929 the Air College received the first Department of Commerce (an FAA precursor) certificate for a Transport and Limited Commercial Ground and Flying School. This prompted Parks to build a three-story, brick dormitory for the increasing numbers of students and to modernize the Mechanic School's equipment. In 1930 the College received its 14th certificate from the Department of Commerce, this for a Repair Station, and soon planes from all over the country were arriving for overhauls and rebuilding. The school became a refueling stop for the Bendix

make a better impression on prospective investors than the "here today, gone tomorrow" barnstorming pilots who usually came through the St. Louis area. He was able to convince the owner of a field in Cahokia, IL to give him land for his college campus. Initially, the landowner may have felt he had put something over on Parks. The site was described universally as a "mud hole," politely as a swamp. It was bottom land, just a mile from the Mississippi that had not yet been controlled by levees.

Impressed by a nationwide blitz of advertising for an "air college," the students came in droves.

More students meant more flight hours on the training planes, which were now *Travelaires.* (Parks also sold

Travelaires from the new Parks Airfield.) The college began getting behind in its maintenance and so Parks founded the Mechanics School of Parks Air College. This was immediately promoted as "Learn to fly them and fix them!"

Enrollment increased to the point where a dormitory had to be built. Students had a well-rounded air education, but they were also expected to work. Parks told them this up front, and the students expected to wash and fuel airplanes—which they did. But they also cleared land, built hangars, cleaned the grounds, and put out the boundary light smudge pots at night— all for a 50¢ per hour credit against their lessons. They did it happily.

Air Race in 1929, and the first racer to land there was Roscoe Turner. It was also a landing spot for the first all women's transcontinental air race (1929). All this success occurred at the onset of the country's Great Depression.

This is not to say that the school was not affected by the Depression. Its enrollment plummeted from 400 to 33 over a three-year period. Despite the loss of students, Parks fired none of the faculty; indeed, they outnumbered the student body at one point. Occasionally, he skipped paydays, but no one seemed to care as long as they had a job. Parks never skipped out on his debts though. He wrote explanatory letters, made apologetic phone calls, and borrowed from friends to pay the bills. Everybody was eventually reimbursed when Parks College was one of the few aviation schools that survived the depression.

This success, ironically enough, is attributed to Parks' approach to aviation education. Most aviation schools of the 1920's and 1930's emphasized their few entrance requirements, simple enrollment process, low cost, and quick graduation. They failed, and Parks College with its requirements of a high school diploma, lengthy course of study, and well-rounded curricula that took time to master succeeded. Its pilots and mechanics were better prepared at all aspects of aviation when they graduated. Parks also kept in touch with the growing aviation industry and was able to adjust programs at the school to keep up. Eventually, the school offered four two-year courses all of which led to a Bachelor of Science Degree: Professional Flight and Executive Training, Aviation Operations and Executive Training, Maintenance Engineering, and Aeronautical Engineering. Even if a student selected one as a major, he (and in those days it was all "he's") still had to cross-train somewhat in the other three.

As Parks College graduates went out into the aviation business world, the success of Parks' approach was evident. Enrollment continued to increase, and the school continued to grow. To teach students how to man-

Women in Aviation Conference

by Dr. Peggy Baty, *Parks College*

Women in aviation today are still a rare commodity. Although their numbers have improved dramatically during the past decade, the percentage remains small. Often women in aviation feel isolated; i.e., they may be one of a few, if not the only, professional women in aviation in their group or organization.

One of the tasks facing the aviation industry today is the need to encourage young people to consider aviation as a career option to meet the human resource needs of tomorrow. Too many times only males receive this kind of counseling because often their teachers and guidance counselors still believe in the stereotype of aviation being only for men.

In response to these two issues, Parks College of Saint Louis University has hosted the second through the fourth National Women in Aviation Conferences when Dr. Baty came to Parks. The first was held in 1990 in Arizona and was a success with its 150 participants, primarily women, from 17 states. The response to the conference was so enthusiastic that 98% of those attending asked that it be made an annual affair. Parks College stepped in as sponsor to assure that.

The second conference held in 1991 in St. Louis, MO boasted approximately 300 attendees from 22 states and a few participants from Canada. In 1992 the conference moved to Las Vegas, NV where nearly 500 men and women from all parts of the aviation industry attended. Thirty-five states were

represented. This year's conference, back in St. Louis, had 535 participants, representing 40 states and three foreign countries. The name has now officially changed to the International Women in Aviation Conference.

The annual conference served the following three objectives:

1. Educates the general public regarding women's contributions to aviation, past and present.

2. Allows women in various aviation occupations (pilots, controllers, mechanics, engineers, etc.) to network.

3. Provides role models and information to young women of high school and college age about aviation careers.

The conference continues to be timely because of the concerns for the under-representation of women in traditionally male-dominated careers and the upcoming human resource needs of the aviation industry. From what began as an idea for a one-time, single-state meeting, the conference has grown beyond anyone's dreams. It has evidently filled a need in the aviation community—the reason for its success.

Next year's (1994) conference will be held March 10–12 at the Walt Disney World Contemporary Hotel in Orlando, FL. The conference's emphasis will be on networking and other career development skills. For more information, contact Dr. Peggy Baty or Hilda Ramage at (618) 337–7500, extension 203.

Parks College

Parks College

moon. von Braun also donated a rocket engine to the school. Willi Ley, another of the German rocket scientists the U.S. had employed after World War II, also visited the college, and its students and faculty quickly began considering how the college could contribute to this new frontier. New departments were instituted—General Sciences, Basic Engineering, and, from the Jesuit influence, Humanities and Social Sciences. Many Parks College graduates held significant positions in NASA, planning and designing the Apollo program and providing operational management for the Space Shuttle project.

Financial setbacks in the 1960's and 1970's caused the Jesuits to consider closing Parks College. Amid the rumors and confusion over the school's fate, enrollment dropped, and a woman director of public relations, Marjorie Rose Beintker, designed a recruitment campaign that rivaled the big sports schools of today. Another area she reached out to were women, long a shortage on the campus. As a result, the college met its goal of "710 in 1971," and now includes women airline pilots among its alumni. The number of women attending the school has steadily increased in the past two decades. Parks College at Saint Louis University for the past three years has sponsored a unique convention, the Women in Aviation Conference (WIAC). Conceived by Dr. Peggy Baty, Academic Dean at Parks and an avid pilot and instructor, WIAC has become a mainstay in the international aviation convention scene. The 1993 conference, held across the river from the college in St. Louis, featured practical, operational workshops on thorough preflighting, panel discussions on the role of women military aviators in combat, and seminars on job opportunities with airlines, the military, and the FAA. (*See the sidebar on p. 7 for more on the WIAC.—Editor*)

Parks College is now thriving. Its flight school has 28 aircraft: One of the surviving P–1's, a 1961 DeHavilland *Beaver,* a Cessna 310, four Mooney 201's, 14 Cessna 152's, and 7

Continued on page 11

age an airline, he started one, Parks Air College Airline. The school was one of the first to qualify for the Civilian Pilot Training Program and the newly established CAA subsidized 30 students from the Works Progress Administration. Eventually, Parks Air College would train 15% of the World War II aviation cadets.

Parks himself, and perhaps incongruously, was an intensely spiritual man. The near fatal accident that led him to start an air college also led him to convert to Catholicism, and he maintained a close spiritual and personal relationship with the Jesuits—a relationship with led him to "give" Parks Air College to the Jesuits' Saint

Louis University in 1946. He would remain as Dean of the school at a salary of $1 a year. Theology and ethics taught by Jesuits joined courses on flying and maintenance, and the G.I. Bill brought scores and scores of new students to the campus.

Although Parks' direct involvement was not as evident as in early years, by the college's 25th anniversary in 1952, its functional Dean, Niels Beck, was showing himself as visionary as Parks had been two and a half decades before. Beck was looking forward to the space age. In 1954, Beck invited Werner von Braun, father of America's space program, to speak at Parks College about a possible flight to the

The First Non-stop Transcontinental Flight in the U.S.

by Sally Macready Wallace

Part 1

In the years following World War I, the fledgling U.S. Army Air Service was fighting for its very existence. The Government was looking for ways to cut spending, and the public saw aviation as an unnecessary frill and a luxury. Air Service pilots knew that the public needed some tangible evidence of the commercial value of aviation and proposed an ambitious plan: to fly across the U.S. *non-stop*, thereby demonstrating, irrefutably, the feasibility of commercial flying as a means of transportation.

The idea for a non-stop flight evolved from the strategic goals of reducing the time needed to deploy military airplanes crosscountry and proving that it could be done within a 24 hour period. Eventually, a few pilots such as the air mail pilots and Jimmy Doolittle would succeed in a transcontinental flight, but they had made at least one stop along the way. It was late 1921 when rumors of a proposed non-stop transcontinental flight spread among the Air Service pilots at McCook Field, OH. Many considered the idea impractical, since they believed neither man nor airplane was equipped for such a trip.

To overcome the first obstacle of an appropriately equipped airplane, First Lieutenants Oakley G. Kelly and Muir S. Fairchild researched the cruising speed, load-carrying capacity, fuel consumption, reliability, and other characteristics

John A. Macready

of several aircraft. They finally decided on the Fokker IV, a Dutch passenger plane which the Army then designated as the Fokker T-2 for the transcontinental flight. Originally, the monoplane accommodated eight passengers plus crew and carried 130 gallons of fuel. When the Army finished its modifications the aircraft had more oil and water capacity, an auxiliary radiator, an oil radiator, larger and stronger wheels, a door between the cockpit and cabin (we'll see why later), a set of controls in the cabin, and a fuel capacity of 737 gallons (increased by adding tanks in the wings and cabin). These modifications made maneuvering rather difficult inside the cabin, to say the least. Fully loaded, the airplane grossed at 10,580 lbs. According to engineering calcula-

tions, 11,000 lbs. was the maximum gross takeoff weight.

The cast of characters changed in 1922 when First Lieutenant John A. Macready replaced Fairchild, who had been injured in an airplane crash. The two pilots (Kelly and Macready) expected to fly out to San Diego, CA about 10 days before the full moon to bask in the sun at Coronado Island and take a few swims in the Pacific—a little R and R before the trip. The actuality was a bit different. In Dayton they had the entire Engineering Department behind them. In San Diego they and two mechanics had to do all the preparation themselves, which included installing a new engine and preparing the plane in general for the long trip. The biggest job was clearing a two-mile runway across North Island so they could take off. Their airport of choice, Rockwell Field, had been inactive for several years and was covered with clumps of brush, bunch grass, and small hummocks of sandy soil.

Although Macready and Kelly received splendid cooperation from the U.S. Weather Bureau, traditional weather forecasting in the 1920's was still aimed at farmers and was not what was needed for transcontinental, non-stop flights. At first there was some confusion as to their needs, i.e., storm fronts or winds aloft? The plan was to fly from San Diego to New York City, since the prevailing winds would favor a flight from west to east. The flip side of

Fokker T–2 plane in flight

that was that they would have to climb over the Sierra Nevada mountains while the plane was at gross weight, which could prove a problem.

The weather report on Wednesday, October 4, at 8:30 p.m. was favorable for an early start the next morning. The two pilots were out at the field before dawn. There were high clouds overhead. Blocks were removed from the wheels of the plane, throttle applied. The big plane hesitated, then slowly moved forward. After a run of about a mile, it slowly lifted off the ground, and Kelly and Macready were airborne. So heavily loaded was the big monoplane, they made two complete circles of the island before they reach 200 feet.

The T–2 had climbed to 1,700 feet by the time they reached the Temecula Pass, about 50 miles from San Diego. Then, they flew straight into a cloud bank. "We dived blindly into the white mass and came through the cloud and pass with a short stretch of lower, open rolling country ahead," said Macready. Their route was northeast of San Jacinto, then over a narrow stretch of mountains and foothills to Banning at an elevation of 2,700 feet. At San Jacinto they ran into more thick fog and low clouds. After dodging foothills for one hour hoping the fog would dissipate or break, they decided any attempt to fly through those winding mountain passes in a heavily loaded plane with visibility no more than 50 feet ahead was not a viable plan. After a quick consultation, they decided to return to Rockwell Field to try for an endurance record. Macready said later, "The primary reason for staying in the air for two long days and a night on an endurance flight was because we did not have the nerve to return to San Diego at once after being hand-shaked, slapped on the

back. . .and started for New York with all proper ceremony and eclat!"

The pilots took turns of six hours each, flying the plane from the open cockpit out front just eight inches from the engine. When it was shift change time, the front pilot wiggled the stick and the pilot in back flew until the front pilot crawled back through the narrow tunnel to the rear, taking the controls while the relief pilot crawled forward. There was no sleep for either flyer during the entire 35-hour endurance record flight. They broke the world record by over eight hours and gained invaluable data on fuel, water, and oil consumption for future transcontinental tries.

Although disappointed at the failure of their original plan, Macready and Kelly were ready for another transcontinental attempt shortly after landing, and again were watching the weather closely for another takeoff. On November 5, armed with a more favorable weather report, they arrived at Rockwell Field in the 5:00 a.m. darkness. As they had to arrange for their own food and

beverage for the trip, they came complete with tins of chicken sandwiches, soup, and hot coffee for the long flight. The weather was clear, and this time they cleared Temecula and Banning passes without effort.

Their route took them to Tucson, AZ but, as they approached the area, it became a continuous struggle with the plane to cross over the high passes, mountains, and elevations. The air was very rough and bumpy; numerous air currents lifted the airplane 100 feet, then plunged it down sharply. For long periods the T–2 was flown within 40 to 50 feet of the ground, unable to gain altitude. To make matters worse, a terrific wind came up from the south, making flying the heavily loaded plane difficult and fatiguing. It finally became obvious if they continued their route they would fly right into the ground, so they turned south over New Mexico's salt marshes and ancient volcanic lava beds, a very picturesque portion of the flight, according to Macready. Almost certainly, no planes had ever flown over this area.

As they approached the Colorado Divide, climbing over the mountains looked doubtful. However, with each gallon of fuel burned, the plane rose a few more feet and finally they reached an altitude of 150 feet above the terrain. Then, just as they reached the divide, a sudden downdraft hit them, and the T–2 went diving toward the ground at terrific speed, missing the cactus and

Fokker T–2 plane, pilots Kelly and Macready, and gasoline drums used on flight.

shrubbery by inches. The plane flew for miles not more than 20 feet above the ground, both pilots expecting to crash at any moment. But once again, as the aircraft burned fuel, they were able to gain altitude, and the flight continued.

Clouds began to form, and darkness came on, and the pilot flying at this point (Macready) needed a known point of reference to start the night portion of the flight. Weather conditions continued to deteriorate, and the clouds were so low Macready had to either fly through them or fly dangerously close to the ground. Consequently, he displayed great flying skill in avoiding the farmhouses, trees, and buildings in the inky, black night.

That first night they followed train tracks when they could see them, and occasionally the strong headlights of a train would appear to guide them. Thunderstorms and lightning were in all quadrants; rain clouded up the pilot's goggles, impairing vision. Their morale was very low at this point, but they pressed on even though their navigation reliance was entirely upon the magnetic compass. "The people of Kansas and Oklahoma apparently retire early," Macready said later. "There were no cottage lights after 10:00 or 11:00 p.m., no lights of any kind to steer by." (Newspapers the next day reported a severe storm raged and a tornado swept through Oklahoma and Kansas killing 12 people and injuring 80.)

The pilots changed positions at Missouri, Macready crawling back through the narrow passageway, Kelly coming up front. Dawn was breaking and the storm was abating—things were definitely looking up. However, over Illinois, their hopes were dashed once again when Kelly sent a note back to Macready, indicating a forced landing looked like a definite possibility, because of cracked cylinder jackets on the engine. The pilots again changed places, and Macready, now up front, noted conditions were, indeed, extremely bad. Water was shooting from both sides of the engine. About 50 miles from Indianapolis the engine temperature began to rise very rapidly, and Macready turned back to a field previously picked out for an emergency land-

ing. Kelly was in back pouring everything liquid—drinking water, coffee, consomme—into the radiator, and with these additions, the airplane made it to the Indianapolis Speedway. The engine froze solid as they touched down.

When the pilots jumped out of the T–2 at Indianapolis, they were through—no more talking about transcontinental flights. They flew to Dayton and had a few days rest, but it wasn't long before the U.S. map once again went up on the wall in the pilot's lounge and before they knew it, they were planning a third attempt. ■

To be continued in the October issue.

Sally Macready Wallace is the daughter of John A. Macready. She is the President of the Macready Foundation and is currently serving on the Board of Directors of Castle Air Museum at Merced, CA.

Parks College
Continued from page 8

Tampico's with 7 more to come this fall. The schools also uses sophisticated Frasca flight simulators connected to air traffic simulators to give student pilots and controllers "experience" in the airspace environment. Its mechanic school develops skills in all engines and is teaching composite construction. It has its own wind tunnel in the Aerospace Engineering School for testing the design model each student of that school must develop and build. Recently, the college opened an avionics school for training in the development and repair of modern navigational equipment.

The school continues to add degree programs to reflect changes in the aviation industry and in business in general. In addition to its undergraduate degrees in Aeronautical Administration, Aerospace Engineering, Aircraft Maintenance Engineering, Aircraft Maintenance Management, Airway Science (five separate bachelors degree programs), Aviation Science/Professional Pilot, Avionics, Electrical Engineering, Logistics, Meteorology, and Travel and Tourism Management, Parks College also offers a Master's in Aerospace Engineering. In addition to numerous

associate degree programs, the school has introduced two, new bachelors degree programs for 1993: Software Engineering and Applied Computer Science.

Dr. Baty describes Parks College as a "unique environment where students can have the best of both worlds—a quality, personalized education with the advantages of a large university." The faculty-to-student ratio is 1/14, and class size is usually less than 30 students. The Cahokia campus has over 1,000 students from 47 states and several foreign countries (19% of the students are foreign). The school also has a sister campus in Madrid, Spain.

In addition to receiving the first FAA (then CAA) approved school certification, Parks College is a frequent host of FAA safety seminars on campus, not just for its students but for the Cahokia and greater St. Louis communities. In 1986, Parks College was the first FAA Teacher Resource Center. Its safety relationship with the FAA is firmly grounded.

What, in all this, happened to Oliver Parks?

Ill health forced him to retire from the school's board in the late 1960's, although he was a sometime, familiar figure at school events—graduations and homecomings. In February 1985, having witnessed aviation from its birth and nursed its growth through to the space age, Oliver Lafayette Parks died, but, according to Dr. Baty, "his legacy has not. Parks College is alive and well.

"Down through the years, Parks College personified its founder. It reflected his vision, his genius, his capacity to see goals and to reach them, to anticipate the future, to know what lay beyond the edges of this earth, and to study the outer reaches of our universe. He stands in the pioneering tradition of famous aviators.

"Parks College is his monument."

No one could ask for a better epitaph. ■

This article is based in large part on the book, Parks College—Legacy of an Aviation Pioneer *by William Barnaby Faherty, S.J. Additional information came from Dr. Baty and Parks College's Office of Public Relations.*

Suspected Unapproved Parts
They may look the same, but. . .

by the FAA Aircraft Certification Service

- **Improperly** overhauled fixed-wing aircraft starters
- **Unauthorized** alteration of helicopter main rotor blades
- **Re-identification** of certain AN and MS fittings
- **Unapproved** 4½" bearing seal spacers
- **Counterfeit** marking, labeling, and packaging

WHAT CAN YOU DO TO PREVENT THEIR USE?

Unapproved parts may not be of the same high quality or be as fully compatible as those approved by the FAA. Unfortunately, unapproved parts are not easy to detect because those who manufacture and distribute them go to great lengths to duplicate materials, part numbers, and serial numbers to coincide with the approved parts.

To make matters even more difficult, some of these parts may be available from the same suppliers who provide parts to FAA Production Approval Holders under the original design. Therefore, without a detailed inspection or material analysis, unapproved parts can go undetected and enter the aviation supply system.

Definition

An unapproved part is a part, component, or material—

- that has not been manufactured in accordance with the approval procedures in FAR § 21.305 or repaired in accordance with FAR Part 43;

- that may not conform to an approved type design; or

- that may not conform to established industry or U.S. specifications (standards parts).

Such unapproved parts may not be installed on a type certificated product, unless a determination of airworthiness can otherwise be made.

Examples of unapproved parts include, but are not limited to:

- "counterfeit" or fraudulently marked parts, components, or materials

- parts shipped directly to users by a manufacturer, supplier, or distributor who does not hold or operate under the authority of a production approval for the part; e.g., parts that the manufacturer produces in addition to those authorized by the production approval holder

- parts that have been maintained or repaired and returned to service by persons or facilities not authorized under FAR Part 43 or 145

Who is Responsible for Airworthiness?

The performance rules for replacement of parts and materials used in the maintenance and alteration of U.S. certificated aircraft are specified in FAR §§ 43.13 and 145.57.

Continued airworthiness of the aircraft, which includes the replacement of parts, is the responsibility of the owner/operator per the requirements of FAR §§ 91.403, 121.363, 125.243, 127.131, and 135.413.

To ensure continued safety in civil aviation, it is essential that great care be used when inspecting, testing, and determining the acceptability of all parts and materials. Particular caution should be exercised when the identity of parts, materials, and appliances cannot be established or when their origin is in doubt.

How Unapproved Parts Get Into the System

Most aircraft parts distributors, aircraft supply companies, aircraft electronic parts distributors, etc., are not subject to certification or surveillance by the FAA. They are not required to establish the airworthiness of parts they advertise and/or sell.

In some cases subcontractors have overproduced a production approval holder's part, and these subcontractors later offer the surplus parts to a distributor, repair station, or airline as replacement parts. These parts are

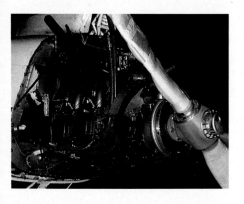

usually cheaper and delivered faster than if purchased from the authorized manufacturer. As a result, these parts bypass the certificated production approval holder's quality control system and become "unapproved parts." New components or parts may be manufactured for the production approval holder but fail to meet the approved design; they, too, can enter the spare part distribution system.

Used life limited parts may be offered for sale with falsified records. This makes it difficult to determine or verify the actual time remaining limits for safe operation. These parts usually come from a cannibalized or damaged aircraft. Life limited parts that have exceeded their time limit or that have nonrepairable defects are sold to part dealers where they are reworked or camouflaged to give the appearance of being serviceable. A salvaged part may be accompanied with a counterfeit operating history or records that falsely account for its life limits.

Inadequate mutilation of unsalvageable and life limited parts by aircraft repair stations or owners/operators allow some of these parts to be cosmetically doctored for resale. Inadequate methods of mutilation may include marking, spray painting, hammering, or identification tagging. Failure to remove and report data plates from aircraft or components when declared unsalvageable may also allow their reuse. These data plates should be removed and the information reported to the FAA.

An FAA-approved part or standard part (manufactured to an industry or U.S. specification) illegally modified by an aircraft replacement parts distribu-

tor/broker would also be considered an unapproved part.

Guide to Detection of Unapproved Parts

Procedures should be established before purchasing parts to establish qualified suppliers who are authorized to manufacture or distribute FAA approved parts. The following criteria would help to identify and screen out potential unapproved parts suppliers:

1. The quoted price or the advertised price is significantly lower than the price quoted by other suppliers of the same part.
2. A delivery schedule that is significantly shorter than that of the same part when existing stocks have been depleted.
3. The inability of a supplier to provide substantiating data demonstrating the conformity of the part.
4. The inability of a supplier to provide evidence of FAA approval for the part.

Regulation and Guidance

An approved aeronautical part conforms to an FAA type design and is in condition for safe operation because of—

- FAR Part 21, Certification Procedures for Products and Parts, specifically:
- FAR § 21.125, Approved Production Inspection System
- FAR § 21.143, Production Certificate
- FAR § 21.303, Parts Manufacturing Approval, Standard Parts

- FAR § 21.305, Approval of Materials, Parts, Processes, and Appliances
- FAR § 21.500, (Import) Approval of Engines, Propellers
- FAR § 21.502, Materials, Parts, and Appliances
- FAR § 21.605, Technical Standard Order Authorization
- Authority and responsibility to repair and install approved parts:
- FAR Part 43, Maintenance, Preventive Maintenance, Rebuilding, and Alteration
- FAR Part 121, Certification and Operations: Domestic, Flag, and Supplemental Air Carriers and Commercial Operators of Large Aircraft
- FAR Part 127, Certification and Operations of Scheduled Air Carriers with Helicopters
- FAR Part 135, Air Taxi Operators and Commercial Operators
- FAR Part 145, Repair Stations

Aeronautical replacement parts not produced, repaired, or installed in accordance with the above requirements are questionable because the parts' approved design and quality are unknown.

Guidance includes:

1. Advisory Circular 21–29, Detecting and Reporting Suspected Unapproved Parts
2. Advisory Circular 20–62, Eligibility, Quality, and Identification of Approved Aeronautical Replacement Parts

Continued on page 25

AIRWORTHINESS—
Pilot or Owner's Responsibility?

by Donald E. Small, *Aviation Safety Inspector*

We've all heard of the pilot's "prerogative" which is effectively nothing more than a demonstration of good judgement. It's the ability to make a decision which assures the safest possible continuation of the flight. Good judgement guarantees the positive aspects of flying, the ability to preflight your aircraft, go flying, and return to earth safely.

In the process of becoming a certificated pilot, training may be accomplished by a well-qualified, FAA certificated flight instructor and/or may be part of an approved school's programmed curriculum. Consider this: Most new pilots entering aviation are not skilled in the maintenance of aircraft and are not expected to be. They also may not be aware of the contents of the aircraft, engine, and propeller logbooks, what the documents represent, or what they should contain.

Whose responsibility is it to know that the aircraft has had a recent 100 hour/annual inspection and that all Airworthiness Directives (AD) have been complied with?

Where in the "pilot training curriculum" are aircraft preflight inspections covered, and how much time is dedicated to this process?

The answer to the second question is found in Advisory Circular (AC) 141–1, "Pilot School Certification." Among other things, this AC explains the required time and subject matter for the private pilot course. A closer look in the AC will reveal that Lesson No. 5 is a "two hour" course that covers airplane structures, propellers, engines, hydraulic systems, electrical systems, pitot static and vacuum systems, and the magnetic compass.

The subject matter is certainly all inclusive; however, the amount of material would seem to be too great to cover and comprehend thoroughly in such a short amount of time. Is a two-hour lesson enough to gain the experience necessary to make a judgement call for airworthiness? And what about those who learn from a FAR Part 61 school, where curricula are not approved nor required by the FAA?

The answers can be found in the regulations, namely FAR §§ 39.3, 91.7, 91.403, 91.405, 91.407, 91.409, 91.411, 91.413, and 91.417.

A quick review of these FAR would reveal language that states either "No person may" or "each owner or operator shall." It's important to understand exactly "whom" these regs apply to. That is, if you were to look up "person" in FAR Part 1, you would find that it reads as follows:

"Person means an individual, firm, partnership, corporation, company, association, joint stock association, or governmental entity. It includes a trustee, receiver, assignee, or similar representative of any of them."

So you can see that the "owner/operator" as well as the pilot of the aircraft is indeed included under the umbrella of this definition.

Okay, so now that we know these rules apply to pilots, what basic responsibilities go along with them?

The best place to start might be with the definition of the term "airworthy." Now most would probably agree that the term means "safe for flight;" however, that's only half of it. The remainder of the definition is generally the one that gets most folks into trouble, and that is that the aircraft conforms to its FAA approved type design data. In addition, close examination of the aircraft's airworthiness certificate will reveal that it is effective as long as the aircraft is maintained in accordance with FAR Parts 21, 43, and 91. Therefore, a pilot performing a preflight needs to consider many things in evaluating whether or not an aircraft is airworthy.

The obvious issue here is the "safe for flight" condition of the aircraft. No one in his or her "right mind" would want to fly away in an unsafe aircraft, so this condition is probably always observed.

The not-so-obvious other issues here deal with conformity to the type design data and the aircraft's being maintained in accordance with the appropriate regulations. In meeting these conditions, the aircraft must have had all required inspections and maintenance accomplished, including AD's, and must have been returned to service in its original or "properly altered" condition by a person authorized in FAR § 43.7 (FAR §§ 91.407 and 91.409) As for conformity to its type design the aircraft must conform to its original or properly altered condition, and that includes all installed components, accessories, and replacement parts.

Preflight—Records

So, how does one verify all of the above, you ask? Enter FAR Part 91, Subpart E, "Maintenance, Preventive Maintenance, and Alterations," specifically maintenance record keeping requirements. Part of the "preflight requirements" should include reviewing the aircraft's maintenance records and within these records you will find out whether all required inspections have been accomplished. These should include the 100-hour/annual inspections, and the 24-month recurring altimeter and transponder inspections, and the ELT battery inspection interval, as appropriate and if the aircraft is so equipped. (Refer to FAR §§ 91.207, 91.409, 91.411 and 91.413 for more detailed information.)

The records would also indicate to the pilot whether any open maintenance entries exist. An aircraft with an "open" maintenance item is technically "unairworthy" unless it is repaired or deferred via FAR § 91.213 or a minimum equipment list (MEL).

AD accomplishment is checked via the records and is usually contained on

a separate "AD Compliance List." This list, if properly completed, will identify each applicable AD and state the "next time due." The "persons" who own, rent, or lease an aircraft must know if AD's have been complied with and when any additional inspection is due.

Preflight—Aircraft

The more familiar phase of the preflight inspection is of course the "walk around" where the pilot looks for obvious damage that in his or her mind would "affect safety." Let's stop here and review another regulatory requirement.

FAR § 91.405, with the exception of paragraph (c), requires that all discrepancies must be repaired between inspections in accordance with FAR Part 43. FAR § 43.13 states in part that the aircraft must be returned to

service after maintenance in its "original or properly altered condition."

So there you are looking at that dent you've seen numerous times and that you know hasn't affected the safety of the aircraft. As a matter of fact, it's been flying like that for years. Don't be fooled into thinking the airplane's airworthy for those reasons alone. To take that aircraft is to assume the liability for flying it in an unairworthy condition. When in doubt, check with a mechanic, who will be in the best position to judge the extent of the dent.

Part of the reason for offering this information is that pilots and owner/operators are often unaware of their responsibilities regarding aircraft airworthiness. Most pilot recurrent and upgrade training is lacking when it comes to airworthiness. Hopefully, this article will help to bridge that gap.

As a pilot you may now know enough to ask the right question the next time you talk to your mechanic. Adhering to the above in performing your preflight and checking with your mechanic for any observed deficiencies will go a long way in keeping you safe—and out of trouble. ∎

Mr. Small is an airworthiness inspector in FAA's Flight Standards District Office in Bedford, MA. This article originally appeared in the April 1993 issue of "FSDO 1 Communicator," the newsletter published by Bedford's Accident Prevention Program Manager, John F. Hemmes.

A Few Remarks about
Surface Weather Observations

by Richard McDonald

Several jump-seat rides ago the Captain of the flight handed me a computer print-out of a surface weather observation from ATL.

ATL SA 1351 CLR 3 262/39/28/0305/029/ SFC VSBY 7 TWRINUN

The Captain asked me what does the remark TWRINUN mean? I guessed it had something to do with the surface visibility; however, like everyone else on the flight deck who never saw the remark before, I did not know what information the surface observer was trying to relay to the aviators.

The crew and I knew the Atlanta aerodrome, and knew the control tower and weather office were about fourteen floors above the surface. At that time, the weather office was about one-half mile north of runway 26R and on a line normal to the control tower, but none of us could connect surface visibility with INUN. The crew and the aircraft, an L1011, were CAT 3 qualified; the weather at landing was CLR 7 271/37/28/3206/031, well above everyone's minimums. The aircraft was landed and everybody went home.

About a month later, I visited the ATL weather office and found out that the remark TWRINUN means "tower in unknown." This remark was added to the ATL observation because the control tower determined the surface visibility was lower than the weather office had determined it to be, and according to paragraph 2.13.5 page A3–16, of the *Federal Meteorological Handbook*

Number 1, "If the tower visibility is 3 miles or less and the surface visibility is 7 miles or more, enter the reason for the tower's reduced visibility. . . ." On the day and the hour of the TWRINUN observation, the weather office could not determine why the control tower could not see as far as it could and was required to affix the remark TWRINUN at the end of the observation.

As a refresher course for people in the aviation industry, I put together 50 remarks commonly used in surface observations along with their meaning. So if you have 20,000 hours at the yoke or 20,000 hours at the boards and never saw the remark before, welcome to the review.

Surface Weather Observation Remarks

1. /FEW CU
Few Cumulus (less than $\frac{1}{10}$ covering the sky).

2. /HIR CLDS VSB
Higher clouds visible through breaks in the overcast.

3. /BINOVC
Breaks in the overcast not classified as thin.

4. /BRKS N
Breaks or an area absent of clouds in a layer below 1,000 feet which covers $\frac{6}{10}$ but less than $\frac{10}{10}$ of the sky.

5. /BKN V OVC
Broken layer variable to overcast.

6. /CIG 14V19
Ceiling variable 1,400 to 1,900 feet (used only when the ceiling is below 3,000 feet).

7. /ACCAS ALQDS
Altocumulus castellanus clouds all quadrants.

8. /ACSL SW–NW
Altocumulus standing lenticular clouds southwest through northwest.

9. /VIRGA E–SE
Vertical or inclined trails of precipitation attached to clouds but not reaching the surface east through southeast.

10. /CUFRA W
Cumulus factus clouds west.

11. /TCU N–E
Towering Cumulus north through east.

12. /K20 SCT
Scattered layer of smoke at 2,000 feet above the surface.

13. /IC4
Ice crystals obscuring $\frac{4}{10}$ of the sky.

14. /PRESRR
Pressure rising rapidly (at a rate of 0.06 inch or more per hour, e.g., 29.92 to 29.86).

15. /WND 23V33
Wind direction varying from 230 to 330 degrees. The variation must be 60 degrees or more during the period of the observation and the wind speed must be more than 6 knots).

16. /RADAT 87120

Contraction for freezing level data. (The first two numbers indicate the relative humidity at the freezing level; the last three numbers indicate the height, (MSL), in hundreds of feet of the freezing level. e.g., 12,000 feet MSL).

17. /RADAT ZERO

This means the freezing level, zero degrees centigrade, was at the surface or below it.

18. /F5 TWR VSBY 2

Fog obscuring 5/10 of the sky, the control tower determined the surface visibility to be 2 miles.

19. /CB MOVG E RWU E

Cumulonimbus moving east, rain showers of unknown intensity east.

20. /TB08 S MOVG E OCNL LTGIC

Thunder began eight minutes after the hour; the sound of thunder was south moving east with occasional lightning in the cloud where the thunder was heard.

21. /TB10 N MOVG N FQT LTGCCCA

Thunder began ten minutes after the hour it was north moving north with frequent lightning cloud to cloud and cloud to the atmosphere.

22. /T S MOVG W OCNL LTGCGCW

Thunder was south moving west with occasional lightning cloud to ground and cloud to water.

23. /VSBY ¼V1 SB50 PRESFR

Surface visibility variable between ¼ of a mile and 1 mile. (The remark is used only when the prevailing visibility is less than 3 miles and varies by one or more reported values.) Snow began falling 50 minutes after the hour; the pressure was falling rapidly— at a rate of 0.06 inch or more per hour. e.g., 29.92 to 29.86.

24. /WSHFT 33

The wind shifted at 33 minutes past the hour.

25. /KOCTY

Smoke over the city.

26. /CBMAM 10W MOVG SE

Cumulonimbus Mama 10 miles west moving southeast.

27. /LWR CLDS APCHG STN

Lower clouds approaching the station.

28. /SFC VSBY ½

Surface visibility (visibility at the weather station) ½ mile.

29. /LOWEST PRES 631 2345

The lowest sea level pressure in tens, units and tenths of a millibar and the time of occurrence (963.1 millibar recorded at 2345 GMT)

30. /PRJMP 8/1012/18

Pressure jump, 8 was the magnitude of the jump to the nearest 0.01 inch omitting the decimal and zeros preceding the first significant digit. The time in hours and minutes when the jump began and the time in minutes when it ended follow.

31. /FUNNEL CLOUD B16E19 NW DSIPD

A funnel cloud was first seen at 16 minutes after the hour and last seen at 19 minutes after the same hour northwest of the station where it dissipated.

32. /TWRINUN

Control tower in unknown.

33. /TWRINC

Control tower in the clouds.

34. /TWRINK

Control tower in a layer of smoke.

35. /TWRINH

Control tower in a layer of haze.

37. /TWRINP

Control tower in precipitation.

38. /AB13E20 HLSTO ½

Hail began falling at 13 minutes after hour and ended 20 minutes after the same hour; the size of the hail stones were ½ inch in diameter.

39. /SU N

Snow of unknown intensity falling north.

40. /SHLW GFDEP 4

Shallow ground fog 4 feet deep.

41. /DRFTG SNW

Drifting snow (height less than 6 feet in depth). Do not confuse with blowing snow, BS. Blowing snow, BS, is when the snow is lifted by the wind to moderate or greater heights, visibility is 6 miles or less and the sky may become obscured when the snow is raised to great heights. BS is always reported in the body of the observation right after the visibility e.g. SA W1X 1/16BS.

42. /RWU E–S

Rain showers of unknown intensity

43. /WET SNW

Wet snow (snow that contains a great deal of water).

44. /SNOINCR 1/4/8

Snow depth increase in the past hour, 1= one inch of new snow in the past hour, 4= four inches of new snow since the last six hourly (00Z, 06Z, 12Z, and 18Z are six hourly observation times), 8= total snow on the ground in inches.

45. /PCPN 103

Fallen precipitation exceeded ½ inch (water equivalent) during the past hour, 103= 1.03 inches.

46. /F BANK N–S

Obscuring phenomena at a distance. Fog bank north through south not at the weather station (airport).

47. /TE55 MOVD E AB12E52 HLSTO ¾ PK WND 3548/20

Thunder moved east and ended 55 minutes past the hour. Hail began 12 minutes past the hour and ended 52 minutes past the hour; the hail stones were ¾ of an inch. The peak wind "PK WND" is the greatest peak wind in excess of 35 knots observed or recorded during the hour of the observation. In the example above the peak wind occurred 20 minutes past the hour, the wind was from 350 degrees, the speed 48 knots.

48. /VSBY NW½S2

When the visibility sector is less than 3 miles or when it is operationally significant and differs from the prevailing visibility, it is disseminated as a remark. In the example, visibility in the northwest was ½ mile, and in the south it was 2 miles.

49. /OCNL RW

The precipitation falling, in this example rain showers, was varying in intensity during the period of the observation.

50. /ROTOR CLOUDS S

Rotor cloud south.

Always read every item in a surface weather observation in the past tense. e.g., was seen, was heard, were falling. For example, at 1351 the sky *was* clear, the prevailing visibility *was* 3 miles, the sea level pressure, temperature, dew point, wind, altimeter *were* 262/39/28/0305/029, the surface visibility was 7 miles, the control tower *was* in an unknown phenomena and so on.

Additional Explanatory Notes

The following cloud types are especially important and should be reported whenever the pilot sees them; they are listed in remarks 7, 8, 19, 26, 31, and 50.

Altocumulus Standing Lenticular, ACSL, (Standing means almost stationary) look like smooth lenses or almonds. They are the result of lee waves (barrier in the wind flow, a mountain) and are associated with turbulence.

Cirrocumulus Standing Lenticular, CCSL, is also associated with lee waves and turbulence. CCSL is higher up in the atmosphere than ACSL and it is white throughout, ACSL has shadowed parts.

Cumulonimbus Mama, CBMAM, this cloud has hanging protuberances, like pouches on the under surface of the cloud (easy to identify). The cloud is associated with turbulence.

Funnel Cloud is a cloud column or inverted cloud cone pendent from cumulonimbus or cumulus, mostly cumulonimbus. If the funnel reaches the ground or water it is classified as a tornado or waterspout respectively.

Rotor Cloud, sometime called roll cloud, is a turbulent cloud found on the lee of some large mountain barriers. The air in this type of cloud rotates around an axis to the mountain range and is associated with turbulence. Rotor Clouds are lower in the atmosphere then CCSL and ACSL.

The examples in remarks 12, 13, 18, and 28 are given further explanation below.

Remark 12: In the remark K20 SCT, K is the obscuring phenomena (smoke)

aloft, 20 is the height above the ground, and SCT is scattered. The observer wants you to know its a layer of smoke, so the next time you see XYZ SA 0150 20 SCT 15 123/23/20 /0205/999/ K20 SCT you will know the 20 SCT is a layer of smoke and not a layer of clouds.

Remark 13: IC4 is used when ⅒ to ⁹⁄₁₀ of the sky is obscured by ice crystals. When the sky is partially obscured, ⅒ to ⁹⁄₁₀, by surface based phenomena (see the list below) a –X is disseminated at the beginning of the observation. e.g., XYZ SA 0150 –X 20 SCT 15 123/23/20/0205/999/IC4. The 4 after IC is the amount of sky obscured by the ice crystals.

Here is the list of other types of surface base phenomena that could obscure the sky.

L D̲rizz̲le any form and intensity including frozen drizzle ZL

R R̲ain any form including RW and ZR

S S̲now any form including SW, SP, and SG (sho̲w̲ers, p̲ellets, g̲rains)

BS Blowing S̲now

BY Blowing Spra̲y̲

F F̲og any form including GF and IF (G = ground, I = ice)

D D̲ust including blowing dust

H H̲aze

N Sa̲n̲d including blowing sand

K Smo̲k̲e

Remark 18 and 28: When the control tower and the weather station have visibility values that differ and either or both are 3 miles or less, the location where the highest visibility was observed and that value are disseminated in the remarks section of the observation. e.g., XYZ SA 0150 -X 20 SCT 11/2F 233/44/33/2205/999/ F5 TWR VSBY 2. In this example, the weather office determined the **prevailing visibility** to be 1½ miles and the control tower determined it to be 2 miles; therefore, the TWR VSBY 2 was added to the observation as a remark. The lower visibility determined by the weather office was place in the body of the observation and used as the prevailing visibility.

Prevailing visibility is the greatest visibility equaled or exceeded throughout at least half the of the horizon circle, which need not necessarily be continuous. The number after the surface based obscuration, in this example fog (F5) can be any number from 1–9, indicating ⅒ to ⁹⁄₁₀ of the sky is obscured.

Another note about surface weather observation rules: The Air Force, Army, and Navy have observation rules that differ from civilian rules. If you are a weekend warrior, check with the Base or Post Weather or Aerology Office before you assume.

That said, I leave you with the last example and one question. It is 1610Z, you are on a 15 mile final for runway 27, here is the 1551Z observation, XYZ SA 1551 M2 BKN 15 OVC ½TRW 123/90/75/2515G20/999/ TB45 S MOVG N

Where is the thunderstorm now? ∎

This article was originally printed in the Delta Air Lines' Up Front in 1990 under the title "999 Remarks." Mr. McDonald is a pilot and an Air Traffic Control System Command Center Meteorologist for the FAA.

The One Moose Airplane

by John Steuernagle

The author of this piece was a flight instructor and charter pilot (and a fine one of both) at an airport where I worked on and received several certificates and ratings. The airport has been replaced by the modern-day bane of pilots—the housing development—but the lessons I and hundreds of others learned there I carry with me every day on every flight I make. The anecdotes provided here contain some of those lessons that we can pass on to others who didn't have the wonderful opportunity to learn at a little airport in Northern Virginia we called "Woodbridge International." **—Editor**

Some time ago I was asked to speak at an FAA seminar—topic to be my choice. I chose complacency. I didn't get around to choosing a title for the presentation, so the Accident Prevention Program Manager did it for me: "Some Thoughts for Those Who do not Intend to be Involved in an Accident." The title didn't appeal to me at first, but the more I thought about it the more sense it made. Nobody intends to be involved in an accident, but we have them just the same, and the pilot is usually at fault. It's often easy to see what went wrong after the fact, especially if the pilot survives. Knowing when things are about to go to pieces is more difficult. Hence, the following

THE ONE MOOSE AIRPLANE

The story is told of an Alaska bush pilot who contracted with a group of hunters to transport them and their gear to a remote lake. They agreed that the pilot would return in 10 days to fly the hunting party back to civilization. The pilot was as good as his word, and 10 days later he taxied up to the dock where the hunters had assembled their gear and trophies.

Looking over the cargo, the pilot announced, "You fellas have a problem here. I know I told you when I dropped you off that this is a one moose airplane. You've got two moose here, so you'll have to leave one behind."

The hunters were understandably reluctant to abandon half of their trophies. They tried to reason with the pilot with arguments like, "They're unusually small moose, don't you think?" and "They were a matched set. We can't take one without the other."

The pilot stood his ground, countering, "In the first place I'll grant you that some moose are smaller than others but there's no such thing as a small moose. I'm sorry about the matched set, but you were told that this is a one moose airplane. Now, if you'll just agree on which moose to leave behind, we'll be on our way."

In an attempt to appeal to the pilot's avarice, the hunters said, "If it's a matter of money, we're willing to pay."

"It's got nothing to do with money," the pilot said, "It's a problem of weight and balance and airplane performance; the length of this lake, the obstruction on the shore, and a number of other things, such as density altitude. All of which add up to one thing: Flying out of here with two moose is unsafe, and I'm not about to do it at any price. Now, if you'll just pick the lucky moose, we'll get it into the airplane and be off."

Not to be dissuaded, the hunters voiced the ultimate argument, "Oh, all right. If you don't think you can do it, we'll have to agree, but your friend Joe flew us out of this very spot last year with two moose that were bigger than these."

Knowing that Joe flew the same type of airplane, the pilot reconsidered his decision, "Joe flew you out of this lake last year?"

"Yep."

"With two moose?"

"That's right, and they were lots bigger than these scrawny things."

The pilot thought for a moment, then said, "Load 'em up. We'll give it a try."

The floats were nearly under water as they staggered away from the dock. The pilot taxied the airplane to the downwind end of the lake and circled at full throttle, going a little faster with each turn. At last he headed for the far end of the lake and at the last possible moment, the airplane crawled into the air. They flew no more than a foot or so above the water, in what I guess you would call "lake effect," but the airplane didn't climb. Presently the lake ended, and they crashed into some low scrub growth near the tree line.

Everyone survived with minor injuries, but the pilot was knocked unconscious. When he came to, in a daze he asked, "Where are we?"

One hunter looked back toward the lake and then at the tree line. "I'm not absolutely sure," he said, "but it looks as if you got us about a quarter mile further than Joe did last year."

What Went Wrong

It's easy to see where our pilot went wrong. The concept of pilot-in-command is important, and it means just what it says. We can't allow passengers to influence our command decisions. The pilot in the story was being paid to make those decisions. He was the only one qualified to make them, and he did a pretty good job, too, until he heard about Joe. Then, a macho, I-can-do-it attitude surfaced. He wasn't about to let Joe show him up.

The thing to remember here is this. There will always be someone who makes it through, who takes off in terrible weather, or overloaded—you name it. That's no reason for us to compromise what we know is right. We must show our students by word, which is easy, and by example, which often is not so easy, that we make our decision in light of all available information. Then, we stand by those decisions. Of course, we have to be flexible enough to modify our plans to accommodate changing conditions.

With the exception of the One Moose Airplane story, all of the events described in the following pages are true. they come from my personal experience and that of others well know to me. As you read these stories try not so much to understand what went wrong, which is easy enough; but why the pilot made the decisions that led to the incident. Look for early indicators that point to trouble and see if some of the attitudes described mirror your own or your student's or your friend's.

THE SOLO CROSS COUNTRY FLIGHT

In order to understand what went wrong on my second student pilot solo cross country flight, it's necessary to tell you a little bit about my first one. It was almost 25 years and 8,000 hours ago when I made my first solo flight from DuBois, PA to Franklin, PA. I had spent most of the night before planning in exquisite detail each checkpoint along the way. The morning of the flight I computed and double checked the courses, constructed a detailed flight log, and filed my flight plan. The flight itself was perfect. I hit each checkpoint just as planned and arrived at Franklin in the very minute I had predicted an hour before. The return flight was just as wonderful, and I left the airport filled with pride in my accomplishment and feeling as if I

were just about the best student pilot there ever was. This cross country flying business was easy.

The second solo cross country flight was planned from DuBois to Johnstown, PA, about 60 miles south. Looking forward to the day when I would be a full fledged private pilot, I asked my flight instructor to permit a landing at Ebensburg, PA on my way to Johnstown. There were a couple of airplanes for sale there, and I wanted to take a look at them. My instructor agreed, and I booked the airplane. My planning for this flight was almost as exhaustive as that for the first. Each checkpoint was selected with care and the dead reckoning calculations were checked and rechecked. There was a VOR on the Johnstown airport but, in my mind, VOR was for those who were unsure of their pilotage skills. I knew it was available but I didn't plan to use it.

The flight from DuBois to Ebensburg was just was wonderful as the first solo cross country flight to Franklin. I arrived precisely at the time predicted on my flight log and strode off in search of bargain airplanes. Then, as now, there are no bargain airplanes, but I enjoyed the tire-kicking experience and presently found myself number two for the runway, waiting my turn to launch for Johnstown about 10 miles away.

The trip should have taken about five minutes. My first clue that all was not right with the world came about 10 minutes out of Ebensburg. I knew Johnstown should be dead ahead, but there were no airports between me and the horizon. "Must be one heck of a headwind," I mused and pressed on.

Fifteen minutes out of Ebensburg and still no Johnstown. "It's a good thing I'm so experienced," I thought. "Other students might not recognize the terrific wind. All the same I'll have a word with Flight Service when I get on the ground. Their winds aloft forecast was really off."

Just then I spotted Johnstown right in front of me and about 10 miles away. I radioed the FSS for an airport advisory and began my descent into the ferocious headwind. Nearing the airport my keen senses detected an

anomaly. "What do you know," I thought, "There are only two runways at Johnstown, and the chart indicates three. They must be planning an addition and somehow it's already charted. Now that could be really confusing."

This last bit of evidence finally caused me to question my position, and I called Johnstown to ask how many runways they had. "Three," they replied. "Why do you want to know?"

Admitting that my position was temporarily in doubt elicited an impressive offer of flight assist options from Flight Service, who were no doubt prepared to scramble a flight of interceptors from Pittsburgh if they felt it would help in getting this incompetent student out of the sky without doing damage to himself or others. I declined their offer for the time being, extended my flight plan, and got very busy in the cockpit. For the first time in the flight I tuned and identified Johnstown on the VOR receiver and took up the heading indicated. It was a relatively simply task to navigate to Johnstown after visually confirming my position over the famous horseshoe curve of the Pennsylvania Railroad near Altoona.

What Happened

As many of you will have guessed, I shut the airplane down on one heading at Ebensburg. Later we moved the plane to another heading beside the hangar, and when I started the airplane again, the heading indicator was incorrect. A casual attitude toward the pretakeoff checklist allowed me to omit the setting of the heading indicator and voila! I was on my way to Altoona.

Why What Happened Happened

I was so embarrassed by this incident that years passed and I had students of my own before I could discuss it with anyone other than my amused flight instructor. It was my first brush with cockpit complacency and, in retrospect, it couldn't have come at a better time.

Complacency has many faces, but it is often simply an expectation of success. I didn't expect to have any difficulty navigating 10 miles to Johnstown. After all, I'd just come almost 60 miles to get to Ebensburg.

Impressed with my flying ability and skill, I took a casual attitude toward the checklist and missed an important item. A small error, and with plenty of fuel on board and good weather, embarrassment was the worst I had to suffer. But the same error before an instrument takeoff has led to unsurvivable encounters with obscured terrain, sometimes known as "cumulogranite."

THE CHECK-OUT

Another face of complacency is a lack of respect for the airplanes we fly. This may come from over-familiarity with the machine or may indicate the way the pilot views most things in life. Either way it can have some interesting consequences. There are some indicators that flight instructors can use to identify potential attitude problems. One of the most reliable indicators I've found is the adjective "Li'l Ole." Just about every pilot I've flown with who referred to his or her airplane as a li'l ole Cherokee, Baron, or even li'l ole King Air was, at the best, sloppy and, at the worst, downright dangerous.

One memorable check-out involved flying with an itinerant airplane salesman who was amazed that our company would require him to check out in our rental planes. After all, he was just going to take his girlfriend for a li'l ole airplane ride. As we went through the preflight inspection, I discovered that he had flown a Cherokee "once or twice" but preferred his li'l ole Baron back home. As the three of us piled into the airplane and headed for the runway, the salesman made me aware that because of his "tight schedule" he couldn't afford to spend the whole morning on this "check-out thing."

The pilot was sloppy but not particularly dangerous. I noted, with interest, that he flew all the maneuvers with his feet flat on the floor. I knew if I were uncomfortable sliding around in my seat, the woman in the back must be feeling the strain as well. I asked the pilot if he had most of his time in "li'l ole" LearJets. "Well, no, not really," he said, "only a couple of hours. Why?"

"Oh, just curious," I said. "I thought a lot of jet time would explain your lack of coordination."

His rudder control improved markedly after that, and we successfully completed the check-out.

A word of caution here: It's much easier to identify complacent attitudes in others than it is to see them in ourselves. Instructors strive to project calm and competence, and that's good. We need to listen to what we're saying from time to time though, and we need to make absolutely clear our profound respect for flying.

THE CHECKLIST

When I first started flying charter, our company's insurance required 100 hours of multi-engine time before a pilot could be designated as a charter captain. With about 98 hours of multi-engine flying logged, a flight instructor in our employ scheduled his first charter check ride with an FAA inspector at a nearby airport. Because the would-be captain didn't meet the insurance requirements, our chief pilot went along for the ride.

The oral portion of the check gave the FAA inspector ample opportunity to evaluate the pilot's personality as well as his knowledge. He was quite capable but also arrogant to a fault. when the questioning came to checklists, he correctly answered that the aircraft operator was required to provide checklists for normal and emergency operations. He added, incorrectly, that the pilot was not required to use them. The inspector probed deeper, "Are you sure you don't have to use those checklists?"

"Absolutely," he replied, "I've committed the checklists for all the airplanes I fly to memory. That way I can keep my head where it belongs—out of the cockpit, scanning for traffic."

The flight portion of the check was not successful, and the pilot was encouraged to try it another day. Needless to say, tension was high on the flight home. The pilot was furious with the inspector and went to great length to explain her inadequacies to our chief pilot. "I know she busted me on that checklist thing, and I know I'm right. I've never used checklists. That's what my memory is for!"

The long-suffering chief pilot nodded and said, "I couldn't agree with you more. I've always maintained that checklists are for the weak-minded. By the way, do you think we'd go any faster if you raised the landing gear?"

Familiarity Breeds Contempt

Most of us have some mindless, routine activities in our lives—a morning waking, bathing, shaving (for some!) ritual, for example, that we can, and sometimes do, do in our sleep. The same is often true with checklists. A new or complex airplane demands our complete attention, and we're grateful for the checklists provided. But even the most complicated machine becomes too familiar after a while, and that's when we most need to have a checklist and to use it. Unfortunately, that's also when we may feel so comfortable that the checklist becomes more of a bother than an important component of the airplane.

Students, always quick to mirror their instructor's habits, will note how we approach flying the training airplanes in the fleet. If we rely on memory to configure these airplanes for flight, no amount of urging will persuade our students to use the checklist. If we don't insist on a thorough line check before each flight, they won't either. As soon as they're able, they'll fly the way their instructor does. Once again our actions speak louder than our words. We must set the example every flight, every day.

A TALE OF TWO PILOTS

This story happened some time ago, but I've remembered it all these years because the pilots involved made two different decisions based on the same information. One was a VFR renter pilot who flew regularly at our airport and who often took one- or two-day cross country flights. The other was a young corporate pilot employed by a construction firm. He was responsible for a nearly new Beech Baron, and he took his job very seriously. The aircraft, lavishly equipped with good avionics, anti-ice, and weather avoidance gear was kept in top shape and clean as a whistle.

The renter pilot, his wife, and another couple had just taken off on a day trip to Atlantic City when the corporate pilot landed with his boss and two associates. They would spend the day in the city and leave for home in late afternoon. It was a typical July day in Washington, DC: hot in the morning with the promise of rising temperatures throughout the day. Relief in the form of a fast-moving cold front was expected in the early evening, and that was causing the corporate pilot some concern.

Over lunch he explained to me that his boss was on a very tight schedule and had to be home for an important meeting first thing in the morning. Leaving on time was imperative, but that would involve penetrating the approaching front. The pilot knew that severe weather was likely to accompany the front and dreaded having to delay his boss' departure. He told his boss the longer they waited to depart the more likely they would encounter thunderstorms enroute. The boss agreed to call the pilot for a weather update before leaving the job site.

The pilot checked the weather every hour throughout the afternoon, and as the day wore on, the front became more and more active. By the time his boss called, a well-developed squall line had formed along the front, and even though the weather was fine at the departure point, it was impossible to conduct flight safely.

The pilot was rightfully concerned. Corporate jobs can hang in the balance of go/no-go decisions, and he knew his boss had to get home. I only heard half the conversation, but it was obvious that his boss was upset, asking the pilot to explain why they had spent all that money on radar if they couldn't fly in thunderstorm weather. Nevertheless, the pilot prevailed, and it was agreed that they would leave at dawn the next morning. Arrangements were made to store the airplane for the night, and I agreed to be at the airport early the next morning to get it out of the hangar.

Decisions like these are never easy, but they must be made. Maybe that

explains the "lavish" salaries we pilots command.

Later that same evening, the renter pilot got a weather briefing from Flight Service, filed a VFR flight plan, and departed Atlantic City for home. Shortly thereafter, he contacted a flight service station reporting that he was in IFR conditions with heavy rain and extreme turbulence. Flight service coordinated with Atlantic City Approach to identify the airplane and provide vectors out of the weather.

I've often wondered what compelled that pilot to launch into such severe weather. Was he pressured by his friends? Did he feel compelled to demonstrate his ability to complete the flight? Did he fail to understand his weather briefing? Perhaps he was taken in by the weather at his departure point, which was still VFR. Unfortunately, we'll never know.

The next day was beautiful, as it usually is after a squall line passes. In the morning the airplane was found in a tidal marsh on the north shore of Delaware Bay. It had crashed nearly vertical and buried itself up to the baggage door. Rising out of the marsh, the tail was a monument to four lives lost and five children orphaned.

Conclusion

Although we become comfortable as we gain experience and proficiency, we must always remember that flying is serious business. A seemingly insignificant error in procedure or lapse in judgement can lead to disastrous consequences. Aviators work hard to improve their flying skills and take great pride in their accomplishments. Unfortunately, many fail to realize that how and when we apply those skills is often more important than the level of proficiency we possess.

Skill and experience have time and again proven to be no match for complacency and contempt. ∎

Mr. Steuernagle is the Director of Program Development with the AOPA Air Safety Foundation. This article originally appeared in the January 1993 issue of the Foundation's Flight Instructors' Safety Report *and is reprinted with permission.*

Communication and Coordination Are the Keys to Safe and
Effective Winter Operations

Airports in areas that experience regular and substantial snowfall and icing conditions need to develop comprehensive snow and ice control programs to minimize winter operational risks.

Coordination and timely communication are the keys to effective airport winter operations, recent reports compiled by the FAA say.

Airports faced with substantial snow and ice removal tasks, FAA says, need to develop clearly defined procedures to ensure that ramps, taxiways, and runways are safe for aircraft operations. These procedures and strategies are also echoed by other aviation and regulatory agencies.

According to advisory circular (AC) 150/5200–30A on airport winter safety and operations, "All airports subject to annual snowfall of several inches or more or icing conditions should have a snow committee." FAA also suggests that every airport in frequent and heavy snowfall areas establish a snow control center to coordinate all snow and ice control activities.

In addition, FAA recommended that every airport in such areas should have a written snow and ice control plan that "state the procedures, equipment, and materials to be used by the airport in removing snow and ice."

Committees and Plans

The airport snow committee "expedites decision-making, reduces the response time for keeping runways, taxiways, and ramps operational, and improves the safety evaluation process that determines when or if a runway should be closed."

Such a committee would be comprised of representatives from airport management, operational staff, airline flight operations, air traffic control, fixed-base operators, flight service stations, and weather services.

A *snow control center* is designed to be a prime source and clearing house of field condition information. The snow control center would also inform air carriers and ATC of expected runway closing and opening times.

A *written snow and ice control plan* should "set out. . . objectives and the priorities assigned to airport movement areas." The plan should also "define areas of responsibility, establish operational requirements and procedures, and define relationships with contractors (if used)." The plan should address "any unique environmental, climatic, and physical conditions affecting the airport. Elements. . . included are pre-season preparation, snow committee composition, snow control center location, equipment, personnel training, weather reports, field condition reports, clearance criteria, clearance priorities, supervision, and communications."

Each plan must be flexible enough to adapt snow and ice removal operations quickly to changing weather con-

ditions and operational changes. Two-way radio communication between snow and ice control crews and the coordination centers is essential.

Pre-Season Preparation

Pre-season preparation should include review and checks in the following areas.

• *Equipment and supplies:* Snow and ice removal equipment should be repaired and spare parts ordered; ice control chemicals and abrasives should be ordered and stockpiled.

• *Training and communications:* Practice runs should be made with the equipment in typical operational scenarios; crews should be trained in proper communications procedures and terminology.

• *Installation of snow fences:* Fences should be set up *before* the onset of the snow season; they should be placed in areas where previous observation has shown their effectiveness in reducing accumulation.

• *Identification of disposal areas:* Snow storage areas should be chosen with careful consideration given to drainage characteristics; storage areas must not interfere with aircraft operations and navigational aids.

Weather and Runway Condition Reporting

The AC underscores the importance of accurate reporting of weather and runway conditions.

"Appropriate response to a snow or ice removal event depends on accurate information about an approaching storm and the likely effect of precipitation on airport surfaces," says the AC. "The snow or ice removal task can be reduced and costs lessened by a prompt, effective response to a storm warning."

Pavement surface condition sensors are also recommended. The sensors, embedded in the pavement, provide accurate measures of the pavement temperature and indicate the presence of moisture, ice, and the ambient air temperature near the pavement. The sensors also transmit this information directly to the snow control center, thus helping shape snow and ice control strategy, especially in the area of timing the application of anti-icing chemicals.

Runway friction testing is also crucial: "Airports serving turbojet aircraft during winter operations should have trained personnel and approved equipment to carry out runway friction testing."

Pilot braking action reports sometimes are not representative of actual runway braking conditions, so "many airports use runway friction-measuring equipment to provide an indication of the existing friction on runways contaminated by snow or ice during aircraft operations and during snow removal operations."

The testing is done by using either continuous friction-measuring equipment (self-contained or towed) or decelerometers. Use of continuous-measuring equipment is more precise, although neither device gives reliable data if operated on more than two inches of loose snow or ½-inch or slush.

Communications and Coordination

Accurate runway friction testing requires close coordination between ground crews, ATC, airlines, and the snow control center. The airport operator must furnish appropriate communications equipment and frequencies on all vehicles used in conducting snow and ice control operations. This will ensure that operations personnel at both controlled and uncontrolled facilities can monitor appropriate ground control and/or airport advisory frequencies.

Snow removal operations also require close cooperation between the snow control center, ATC, FSS, and airport management to ensure a prompt and safe response.

When weather conditions begin to deteriorate, NOTAM's should be issued immediately, advising airport users of unusual airport conditions.

Reducing Drifts and Removing Snow

In addition to snow fences, snow trenches also are effective in reducing the amount of drifting snow on runways. (Figure 1) Multiple trenches spaced about 10 feet apart can reduce further drifting and be used to store more snow. Trenches should be excavated no nearer than 50 feet from a runway.

Snow clearance from runways is best accomplished by operating plow teams in echelon, using a number of displacement plows to move the snow, with a minimum of rehandling, into a "windrow that can then be cast beyond the edge lights by a rotary plow." The edge lights should not be obstructed by blown or cast snow.

An effective snow removal program must also ensure:

• Equipment movements (on runways) are carefully timed and coordinated to ensure safety and operational efficiency.

• Snow bank height adjacent to runways, taxiways, and aprons must be limited to provide wing overhang clearance and to prevent operational problems caused by ingestion of ice into turbine engines or propellers striking the banks.

• Movement areas where aircraft operate at high speeds (such as turnoffs) should receive the same snow and ice control attention as runways. Says the AC, "Areas of low speed operation such as taxiways and ramps can also be critical under some conditions. Directional control and braking action should be maintained under all conditions."

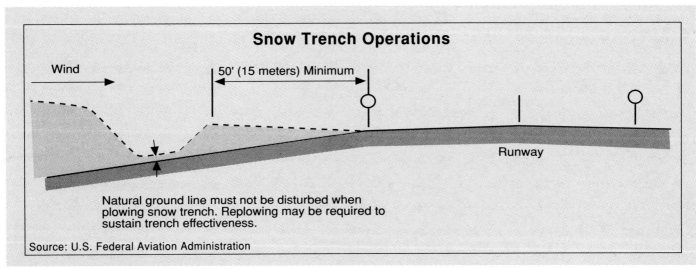

Figure 1.

- Great care must be taken while removing snow from arresting barriers, which airports with joint military operations may have installed near the end of the active runway or at the beginning of the overrun area.

- The faces of all signs and all lights must be kept clear of snow and in good repair. Priority should be given to signs and lights associated with hold lines and the instrument landing system (ILS).

Anti- and De-icing

Anti-icing [of pavement surfaces] is preferable to deicing whenever possible. [Ice melting is called deicing, while anti-icing lowers the freezing point of water and thereby prevents the formation of ice for a period of time.] Dry snow does not often form a strong bond with the runway surface even under freezing conditions and heavy and frequent wheel passes. However, wet snow and ice quickly develop such a bond so that "mechanical removal is either difficult, slow, or damaging to the pavement. Thus, the primary effort should be directed at bond prevention."

Anti-icing is accomplished by concentrating either thermal or chemical energy at the pavement surface. According to the AC, "Because of the high cost of installing pavement heating systems and the large amounts of energy required to maintain the surface above freezing [before] the onset of precipitation, deicing/anti-icing with approved airside chemicals is generally more economical." All such chemicals should be applied based on pavement temperature rather than air temperature.

Deicing chemicals should be applied on ice 1/16-inch or less in thickness. The AC adds, "The recommended chemical form for anti-icing is liquid, although solid chemicals can also be effective in this application. A dry, solid chemical has the disadvantage that if applied to a cold dry surface it may not adhere and, therefore, may be windblown or scattered by aircraft movements. However, certain physical properties of a solid, such as its bulk density, particle shape, etc., may reduce these tendencies. Regardless, wetting a dry anti-icing chemical, either during distribution or

before or after loading into the application vehicle, improves the ability to achieve uniform distribution and improved adhesion."

U.S. standards for airside chemicals are either established by the FAA or based on specifications outlined by professional organizations such as the Society of Automotive Engineers (SAE) Aerospace Material Specifications.

Approved fluids for runway and taxiway operations are either glycol base or potassium acetate base. Solid compounds include airside urea, calcium magnesium acetate, and sodium formate.

The most effective landside chemicals used for deicing/anti-icing are from the chloride family, e.g., sodium chloride (rock salt), calcium chloride, and lithium chloride. But these chemicals are highly corrosive to aircraft and cannot be used in aircraft operational areas.

Airport operators need to monitor closely the environmental impact of chemicals used in snow and ice removal programs.

Summary

Successful and accident-free winter operations on airports require pre-season planning, guidelines and procedures to follow, training and practice, and plenty of communication and coordination among all parties involved in using, maintaining, or managing the airport. ■

This article is based on an "Editorial Staff Report" that originally appeared in the January/February 1993 issue of Airport Operations *published by the Flight Safety Foundation, 2200 Wilson Blvd., Suite 500, Arlington, VA 22201–3306; (703) 522–8300. Advisory Circular 150/5200–30A, "Airport Winter Safety and Operations" can be obtained by contacting the Office of Airport Safety Standards, AAS–100, 800 Independence Avenue, S.W., Washington, DC 20591.*

Detecting and Reporting Suspected Unapproved Parts

Continued from page 13

Buyers are advised to:

✔ Inspect product containers for damage, another supplier's name, or absence of markings.

✔ Cross check purchase orders with the delivery receipts for proper part number or component history card.

✔ Develop a means of ensuring the shelf or service life has not expired.

✔ Verify that part identification requirements have not been tampered with (e.g., serial numbers stamped over, label improper or missing, vibroetch or serial numbers at other than normal locations).

✔ Inspect parts for visual defects or abnormalities (e.g., altered or unusual surface, absence of required plating, evidence of prior usage, scratches, new paint over old, attempted exterior repair, pitting, or corrosion).

✔ Perform supplier audits to ensure suppliers establish and maintain the quality requirements specified in the purchase order. The following are examples of subsystems that should be included in an audit program:

- *Design data control to include latest revision*
- *Supplier control*
- *Material handling/control*
- *Evidence of a production approval*
- *Manufacturing/assembly control*
- *Tool and gauge control*
- *Tests and inspections*
- *Records*

Reporting Suspect Parts

There are two formal procedures for reporting suspected unapproved parts:

1. FAA Form 8120–11, Suspected Unapproved Parts Notification (from your local FAA office or from AC 21–29) should be forwarded immediately to FAA, System Surveillance and Analysis Division, AIR–300, P. O. Box 17030, Washington, DC 20041.

2. Suspected unapproved parts may also be reported via the toll free FAA Aviation Safety Hotline (1–800–255–1111). ■

This article is based on FAA Advisory Circular 21–29, "Detecting and Reporting Suspected Unapproved Parts," available from the Aircraft Certification Service, Aircraft Manufacturing Division, 800 Independence Ave., S.W., Washington, DC; (202) 267–8361. Copies of a brochure on the same subject may also be obtained from the above address.

FLIGHT**FORUM**

AIRSPACE CORNER

Question. I heard that the Airspace Reclassification is going to result in a major escalation in the prohibition of aerobatics by denying aerobatics in Class E airspace. Is this true?

Answer. Absolutely and unequivocally NOT TRUE! In trying to ascertain how this misconception came about, we reread FAR § 91.303(c) effective September 16, 1993 and came to the conclusion that some folks are confusing "a Class E surface area designated for an airport" with Class E airspace period. Not only is there NOT an escalation, the new classes significantly increase the amount of airspace where aerobatics can be performed. For years, a major prohibition has been in control zones which used to extend upward to 14,500 feet MSL or, in the case of Hawaii, infinity. Under airspace reclassification, FAR § 91.303(c) has been revised, and the term "control zone" has been replaced with "within the lateral boundaries of a Class B, Class C, Class D, or Class E airspace designated for an airport." Additionally, the FAA will continue its prohibition of aerobatics: (1) over any congested area of a city, town, or settlement; and (2) over an open air assembly of persons; and (3) within 4 nautical miles of the centerline of a Federal airway; and (4) when flight visibility is less than 3 miles. The accompanying graphic (see inside back cover) depicts the airspace in which aerobatics are prohibited without a waiver and provides an excellent illustration of "within the lateral boundaries" of the Class B and Class C airspace.

What this means is that aerobatics can be performed over the top of Class B (former TCA's) which typically are 10,000 feet MSL, over the top of Class C (former ARSA's) which typically are 4,000 feet AGL, over the top of Class D (former control zone with airport traffic area) which typically are 2,500 feet AGL, and over the top of Class E (former control zone at nontowered airport). Class E airspace does not have a defined vertical limit; therefore, the restriction on aerobatics would be 1,500 feet AGL [Ref: FAR 91.303(e)] in the absence of a waiver. Since only four Class B's (TCA's) exceed 10,000 feet MSL and none exceed 12,500 feet MSL, we can say that we have reduced the vertical limit of *every* control zone in the United States, which is another way of saying we have otherwise *increased* the amount of airspace that is available for aerobatics. Thanks for the opportunity to clear this up.

Question. What is the rule regarding aerobatics in what used to be arrival extensions to control zones?

Answer. The arrival extensions are controlled airspace extending upward from the surface, and they meet the definition of "within the lateral boundaries of the surface areas of Class B, Class C, Class D, or Class E airspace designated for an airport" discussed in the answer to the preceding question. Most of the extensions are Class E and, therefore, the operating rule becomes the 1,500 foot AGL limit, in the absence of a waiver. If the extension is other than Class E, the vertical limit of the higher class and associated restriction will be as charted.

As an aside, we would like to use this forum to remind everyone that arrival extensions are established to contain instrument approach procedures to airports and are also extensions of arrival and departure paths to the airport. These areas are probably not the best place to practice that Immelmann, eight point roll, or to do spin training. Again from a safety viewpoint, while it will now be legal to perform aerobatics as low as 1,500 feet above an airport with a Class E surface area, it would certainly be prudent to determine the VFR traffic pattern altitude, and a good operating practice would be to provide a vertical safety buffer between you and your fellow airmen operating in that traffic pattern. Letting others know what you are doing, via CTAF or UNICOM, is also a good idea.

Editor's note: We are planning to continue the Airspace Corner through the November/December issue. Please let us know if you want this column beyond that issue. As always, we invite questions on airspace.

• VFR Conditions

Thank you for the clarification of ceiling reporting criteria within control zones ("Weathering CZ's," September/October 1992). The response, while answering the writer's question, stopped short of explain- ing the whole issue. The other element in determining weather minimums is visibility.

For example, a control zone was recently established at the Pitt Greenville, NC, airport utilizing AWOS 3 for official weather reporting. Being located adjacent to a river, within a shallow valley, the airport is often blanketed by patchy morning ground fog. When one of those fog patches forms over the AWOS visibility sensors, the airport reports less than VFR conditions. Meanwhile, three miles away at a launch field used by the local hot air balloonists, it is clear blue.

In this case, do the balloonists (or any other pilots operating within the control zone, but not at the airport) need a special VFR clearance to launch?

I say, "no," as per FAR § 91.155(d)(2). Are we in agreement?
    Kent Yoest
    Atlanta, GA

No. We cannot agree. A special VFR clearance may be needed. The answer depends upon how the AWOS is reporting conditions at the airport. If it reports the fog conditions as a ceiling of less than 1,000 feet AGL, then the balloonists will need a clearance to operate "beneath" the reported ceiling. If the AWOS reports the fog as a visibility restriction then the balloonists can launch if the flight visibility is at least three statute miles. As we said in our September/October 1992 issue, the key to operating VFR within a control zone without a special VFR clearance is a reported ceiling of 1,000 feet AGL or more at the airport for which the control zone was established and visibility of at least three statute miles. If a ceiling of less than 1,000 feet at the primary airport is reported then no aircraft can operate VFR within the control zone beneath the reported ceiling without a special VFR clearance. Pilots can operate VFR on top of a ceiling when the reported ceiling is 1,000 feet AGL or above, within a control zone as long as VFR conditions can be maintained.

Visibility is also a factor. FAR § 91.155(d) states "Except as provided in § 91.157, no person may take off or land an aircraft, or enter the traffic pattern of an airport, under VFR, within a control zone: (1) Unless ground visibility at that airport is at least three statute miles; or (2) If ground visibility is not reported at that airport, unless flight visibility during landing or takeoff, or while operating in the traffic pattern, is at least three statute miles."

In summary, if the AWOS is reporting the ceiling as 1,000 feet AGL or greater and the balloonists have a flight visibility of three statute miles or more at their launch site and can comply with FAR § 91.155, they can take off without a special VFR or IFR clearance.

Former Airline Executive Nominated as FAA Administrator

President Bill Clinton has nominated David R. Hinson to be the next Administrator of the FAA. Hinson is a former FBO owner, airline pilot, and founder of Midway Airlines who has 35 years of experience in aviation.

After three years as a Naval Aviator, Mr. Hinson joined Northwest Airlines in 1958. Throughout his aviation career, Mr. Hinson has also been a flight instructor and fixed base operator. He has logged over 9,000 hours of flying time and is typed in 10 different aircraft ranging from a DC–3 to an MD–11, one of the latest wide-body jets; he also has flown many types of military aircraft, including the F–4 *Phantom* and F–18 *Hornet*. His personal aircraft is currently a Beech *Baron*. He has also held flying and management positions with West Coast Airlines and United.

In 1978, along with several airline pilot colleagues, Hinson started Midway Airlines, based out of Chicago's downtown Midway Airport. He became chairman and chief executive officer of Midway in 1985, remaining in that position until Midway went out of business in November of 1991, a victim of the airline recession. McDonnell Douglas named him Vice President of Marketing and Business Development for its Douglas Aircraft Division in early 1992. He has served on the board of the Washington-based Air Transport Association, whose president, James Landry, said, "The airline industry has been waiting for years for an FAA Administrator who

is committed to safety and also understands the issues facing commercial aviation."

According to the *Wall Street Journal*, "Mr. Hinson's appointment won praise from many in the industry, including top executives at airlines and rival companies such as Boeing Corp." His general aviation experience as a CFI and FBO owner add to his balance for the Administrator's job.

Mr. Hinson was "on board" at the FAA in early June as a consultant. As of press time, his confirmation by the U.S. Senate is pending.

All Flight Reviews are Biennial Again

Effective August 31, FAA cancelled the annual flight review requirement for recreational pilots and noninstrument-rated private pilots with less than 400 hours. To date these pilots have not had to comply with the annual flight review requirement because the FAA delayed the rule's implementation date pending a review of the documents and data used to justify the adoption of the annual flight review. Based upon that review, the FAA determined that the data used to develop the annual flight review was insufficient. As a result, Acting FAA Administrator Joseph M. Del Balzo signed an amendment to FAR Part 61 deleting the annual review requirement on July 19, 1993.

Several changes to FAR § 61.56, Flight Review, the rule that requires all pilots to complete a flight review, become effective August 31, 1993.

First, the new amendment deletes the annual flight review, as discussed. Then it establishes a minimum requirement of one hour flight and one hour ground instruction for the biennial flight review (BFR) required of every pilot every 24 calendar months. (The BFR requirement can be met through other acceptable means such as any required flight test, proficiency review, or completion of any phase of the FAA's Accident Prevention Program Pilot Proficiency Award Program, commonly known as "Wings." The FAR lists acceptable alternative means of meeting the BFR requirement.)

The amended rule also states that flight instructors who complete an approved flight instructor refresher course (FIRC) need not accomplish the one hour of ground instruction required by the current FAR since they receive ground instruction in the FIRC.

Finally, the amendment allows glider–rated pilots the option of substituting three instructional flights in a glider, each with a 360° turn, for the one hour of required flight instruction.

FAA/Education Partnership Chartered

The National Coalition for Aviation Education (NCAE) signed a formal charter and established a partnership with the FAA at the recent National Congress on Aviation and Space Education in Orlando, FL. Before an audience of more than 1,000 educators, NCAE Chairman Tyson Whiteside and FAA Assistant Administrator for Human Resource Management Herbert R. McLure signed the partnership agreement, symbolizing the beginning of a formal relationship between the two organizations.

In partnership with the FAA, NCAE members will provide teaching materials to FAA Teacher Resource Centers across the country. Together the organizations will actively promote aviation education while supporting school initiatives at the local, state, and national levels.

"This new partnership indicates a cooperative spirit between industry and the FAA and emphasizes the importance of aviation education," said Chairman Whiteside. "As association representatives, we have joined together to present a united voice on aviation education issues. We need to work with aviation educators, government officials, and or own industry representatives to marshall education resources and to use aviation to train America's young people."

The NCAE, composed of 14 aviation industry and labor associations has produced *A Guide to Aviation Education Resources*. The guide, designed to be a clearinghouse of aviation education materials for teachers, lists the

AV**NEWS/BRIEFS**

resources available from each member organization. Copies are available at no charge by writing to NCAE, P. O. Box 28086, Washington, DC 20038.

Accident Prevention Counselors Provide Production Crew Support for Sun 'n Fun

The Sun 'n Fun Fly-In 1993 at Lakeland, Florida is over, and the show and the FAA Safety Forums Series were tremendous successes. According to Obie Young, the Accident Prevention Program Manager for the North Florida Flight Standards District Office, the FAA Forums series increased their attendance by more than 100 percent compared to last year. He attributes the success to improved programming, improvements made to the FAA Aviation Safety Center building including additions to the sound, lighting, and audiovisual systems, and a trained volunteer Production Crew to support the forums.

A major part of the North Florida FSDO–15 Accident Prevention effort is directed toward motivating the local aviation community to become involved in the safety program. One of the groups supporting the Program is the Accident Prevention Counselor Production Crew that was formed to support Special Projects at the FAA Aviation Safety Center at the Lakeland Airport, Lakeland, Florida. The Production Crew supports the project with a financial commitment and many hours and long days of work.

The Production Crew Accident Prevention Counselor members were Diego Alfonso, Bill Ball, Eric Bolves, Larry Enlow, David Garner, Tom Hennessy, Joe Hinson, Harry Kimberly, Dave Lawson, Steve Moore, Mike McCormick, Ed Rice, Meredith Rob-

bins, Tom Savage, Kay Schuttler, Vicki Sherman, Ernie Strange, Jack Tunstill, and Dave Whitman. The Production Crew FAA Members were Gail Davis, Larry Freiheit, Bill Hoenstine, Ellen Spillane, and Obie Young. Expenses born by the Accident Prevention Counselors on the Production Crew for their food and lodging alone reach over $4,700, and they contributed over 750 hours of time to support Safety Forums during Sun 'n Fun Fly-In 1993.

You might ask how this support and effort from the folks at Sun 'n Fun Fly-In, the FAA, businesses, organizations, individuals, and Accident Prevention Counselors on the Production Crew were obtained. The answer is easy. . . They all believe in aviation and wanted to give "The Gift of Flight" by supporting aviation safety. What a good example of the FAA/industry partnership! And they had fun, too!

FAA Approves Use of GPS

Acting FAA Administrator Joseph Del Balzo has approved use of the Global Positioning System (GPS) for navigation in the U.S. In a recent statement he said, "We are moving rapidly to make wider use of this revolutionary new navigational system. Last year, we established standards for GPS aviation equipment, and now, we are approving its use for all phases of flight down to non-precision approaches."

Although FAA-approved GPS receivers are not on the market yet, Del Balzo said, "We expect that aircraft owners will be able to purchase cockpit GPS receivers by sometime this fall." According to his statement, this first approval will allow pilots to fly direct with approved GPS units and to fly non-precision approaches into about 2,500 airports.

In his statement, Del Balzo thanked both the Aircraft Owners and Pilots Association (AOPA) and Transport Canada for their help in testing GPS procedures.

Although the satellite-based navigation system has not been declared operational by the Department of Defense, which developed and oper-

ates the system, that announcement is expected by this fall.

GPS, like LORAN–C, is rapidly evolving from a military system into the navigation system of choice for general aviation. GPS was first adopted by general aviation pilots using non FAA-approved receivers for VFR use. And like LORAN–C, GPS has now evolved into an IFR compatible system with FAA and industry standards for IFR receivers and their installation. As the GPS program matures and operators and the FAA gain experience with it, it is conceivable that GPS will be approved for precision IFR approaches in the future.

Owners wanting to meet FAA-approved, non-precision IFR equipment and installation standards should review some FAA publications before installing a GPS unit for IFR use. The first one is Technical Standard Order (TSO) C–129, dated 12/10/92, *Airborne Supplemental Navigation Equipment Using the Global Positioning System (GPS).* TSO C–129 sets the minimum performance standards for GPS and lists other important GPS references. [TSO C–129 can be ordered from the U.S. Department of Transportation, Utilization and Storage Section, M–443.2, Washington, DC 20590. It can also be ordered by FAX from the Publications Office by calling (202) 366–3911.] Information on ordering other TSO's is available by writing for the *Index of Aviation Technical Standard Orders*, at the same address. The Index is also available by FAX at the same number. Two FAA Notices will also help: N–8110.47, *Airworthiness Approval of Global Positioning System (GPS) Navigation Equipment For Use As A VFR and IFR Supplemental Navigation System*, dated 4/23/93 and N–8110.48, *Airworthiness Approval Of Navigational Or Flight Management Systems Integrating Multiple Navigation Sensors*, dated 4/23/93. Each lists references that may help an owner/operator install an FAA-approved GPS system. Both notices are available free from the FAA Aircraft Certification Service, Aircraft Engineering Division (AIR–130), 800 Independence Ave., SW, Washington, DC 20591.

Airspace for Aerobatics

(See page 26 for the Airspace Corner)

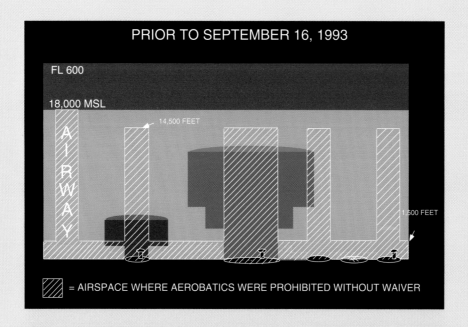

PRIOR TO SEPTEMBER 16, 1993

FL 600

18,000 MSL

14,500 FEET

AIRWAY

1,500 FEET

///// = AIRSPACE WHERE AEROBATICS WERE PROHIBITED WITHOUT WAIVER

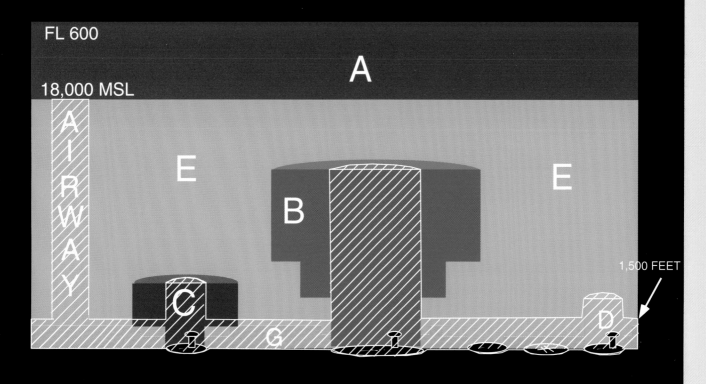

EFFECTIVE SEPTEMBER 16, 1993

FL 600

18,000 MSL

A

AIRWAY

E

B

E

C

G

D

1,500 FEET

///// = AIRSPACE WHERE AEROBATICS ARE PROHIBITED WITHOUT WAIVER

DO NOT DELAY—CRITICAL TO FLIGHT SAFETY!

FAA Aviation News

October 1993

A DOT/FAA FLIGHT STANDARDS SAFETY PUBLICATION

U.S. Department
of Transportation

**Federal Aviation
Administration**

Federico F. Peña, *Secretary of Transportation*
David R. Hinson, *FAA Administrator*
Monte R. Belger, *Acting Executive Director
    for System Operations*
Anthony J. Broderick, *Associate Administrator
    for Regulation and Certification*
Thomas C. Accardi, *Director,
    Flight Standards Service*
Robert A. Wright, *Acting Manager,
    General Aviation and Commercial Division*
Roger M. Baker, Jr., *Manager,
    Accident Prevention Program Branch*
Phyllis Anne Duncan, *Editor*
Louise Oertly, *Senior Associate Editor*
Dean Chamberlain, *Associate Editor*

The FAA's Flight Standards Service, General Aviation and
Commercial Division, Accident Prevention Program
Branch, AFS–810, Washington, DC 20591, (telephone
202 267–8017) publishes FAA AVIATION NEWS in the
interest of flight safety. The magazine promotes safety in
the air by calling the attention of airmen to current technical, regulatory, and procedural matters affecting the safe
operation of aircraft. Although based on current FAA policy and rule interpretations, all printed material herein is
advisory or informational in nature and should not be
construed to have regulatory effect. The FAA does not
officially endorse any goods, services, materials, or products of manufacturers that may be mentioned. **Certain
details of accidents described herein have been
altered to protect the privacy of those involved.**
    The Office of Management and Budget has
approved the use of funds for the printing of FAA AVIA-
TION NEWS.

SUBSCRIPTION SERVICES

The Superintendent of Documents, U.S. Government
Printing Office, Washington, DC 20402–9371, sells FAA
AVIATION NEWS on subscription. Use the self-mailer
form in the center of this magazine to subscribe. Cost:
$8.00 ($10.00 foreign) for one year; $16.00 ($20.00 for-
eign) for two years. Prices are subject to change by the
Government Printing Office without prior notice.
    Change of Address or Subscription Problems:
**Send your label with correspondence to Sup Doc,
Attn: Chief, Mail List Branch, Mail Stop: SSOM,
Washington, DC 20402–9373.**
    To keep subscription prices down, the Government
Printing Office mails subscribers only one renewal
notice. You can tell how many copies are left in your
subscription by checking the number that follows "ISS-
DUE" on the top line of your mailing label. For example,
when this number is 003, it means you have three
issues left in your subscription, and GPO will send you
a renewal notice. The number 000 means you have
received your last issue. To be sure that your service
continues without interruption, please return your
renewal notice promptly.

FAN SMITH 212J ISSDUE003 R 1
JOHN SMITH
212 MAIN ST
FORESTVILLE, MD 20747

October 1993

FAA Aviation News

Volume 32   Number 7

FEATURES

DEPARTMENTS

Front Cover: *This United Express DeHavilland
Dash 8 was on a training flight as part of the air
carrier's certification program for operating the
Dash 8. See page 4 to see how FAA is involved.
Photo by Dean Chamberlain*

Back Cover: *How current is your night flying?
See page 8.*

GENERAL AVIATION POLICY STATEMENT

General aviation is critically important to the Nation's economy and to the national transportation system. General aviation plays a crucial role in flight training for all segments of aviation and provides unique personal and recreational opportunities. It makes vital contributions to activities ranging from business aviation, to agricultural operations, to Warbird preservation, to glider and balloon flights.

ACCORDINGLY, IT IS THE POLICY OF THE FAA to foster and promote general aviation while continuing to improve its safety record. These goals are neither contradictory nor separable. They are best achieved by cooperating with the aviation community to define mutual concerns and joint efforts to accomplish objectives. We will strive to achieve the goals through voluntary compliance and methods designed to reduce the regulatory burden on general aviation.

The FAA's general aviation programs will focus on:

1. **SAFETY**
   To protect recent gains and aim for a new threshold.

2. **FAA SERVICES**
   To provide the general aviation community with responsive, customer-driven certification, air traffic, and other services.

3. **PRODUCT INNOVATION AND COMPETITIVENESS**
   To ensure the technological advancement of general aviation.

4. **SYSTEM ACCESS AND CAPACITY**
   To maximize general aviation's ability to operate in the National Airspace System.

5. **AFFORDABILITY**
   To promote economic and efficient general aviation operations, expand participation, and stimulate industry growth.

David R. Hinson
Administrator

September 8, 1993

Pilot Decision Making

by Tom Hamilton

Risk and Crew Management

This is Part Four of a seven-part series that first appeared in Balloon Life *magazine and was originally written for balloon pilots. For the most part, we have left the lighter-than-air examples in because the overlying issue of pilot decision making affects all pilots, and the excellent information in these articles can be extrapolated to aviation activities other than ballooning.* **—Editor**

In this issue in our continuing look at pilot decision-making, we will review the elements of risk in flying and examine risk assessment. Part 1 of this series looked at the four elements of risk that are involved in a *situation*: the pilot, the aircraft, the environment, and the type of operation.

Risk Assessment

As pilots, when we evaluate flying risks, we must first recognize a developing or potential hazard situation, analyze the situation, and finally resolve what action should be taken. In risk assessment the pilot reviews the elements (pilot, aircraft, environment, and operation), determines the risk associated with each, and evaluates the situation to determine what action is necessary.

And because a situation does not remain static, but changes continually, a pilot must constantly reevaluate the situation and its probable influence on the safe outcome of the flight.

Here is a brief review of the elements of the four risk factors:

Pilot: experience, competency, health, fatigue, attitude

Aircraft: airworthiness, type, size, accessories, fuel capacity

Environment: weather, airspace, topography, departure and arrival airports

Operation: for fun, for hire, day, night, heavy or light load, instruction

The question the pilot faces is, "How do I evaluate this risk?"

You might start by asking yourself, "What is the probability that if I do not do a fuel capacity check before takeoff that I will have enough to finish the flight?" Or, "If I don't use a checklist what is the probability that I will have to land in an area that might not be considered appropriate?"

By asking questions of this type and determining a probability of risk, you begin to establish the amount of risk that you are willing to take as a pilot. After you have accumulated several of these risk assumptions, the next question you can ask yourself is, "Is this amount of risk acceptable?"

What we have started to do here is establish some thoughts about our attitudes toward risk and what would be acceptable parameters under which you would make or continue a flight. By reviewing these various risk factors the pilot is able to arrive at a more informed decision.

A Practical Exercise

A technique that has been used at safety seminars is to pass out file cards in four different colors, one for each element described above. Half the participants indicate what they think would be a good example of each element on a different color card and the other half indicate what they think would be a bad example of each element. The cards are then grouped by color, shuffled, and then placed in four stacks. By drawing one card from each stack you have created a situation with four elements of risk defined. Now, what is your decision—to make the flight or not?

You will find some of the situations clear cut go or no/go. But, what about the grey areas? Should the flight be made or continued? Why?

Getting together with other pilots and conducting these types of exercises will provide practice in making decisions. The discussions that follow each decision will allow the group to explore additional items, methods of dealing with the situation, and build the participants' reference base for future decision-making. The goal here is to stimulate thinking about decision-making and risk assessment.

The effects of change and its probable influence on the safe outcome of a flight must be continually evaluated. An assessment of the risks created by that change helps to focus on those alternatives which are realistic and which will produce a safe outcome. By conducting these exercises, a projection of the events that are likely to flow from each possible alternative to a situation, hopefully, results in a realistic approach.

As the pilot you have the capability and responsibility for determining the risks associated with a particular flight. Accident statistics indicate that 80–85% of all general aviation accidents involve "pilot error." Thinking about what might happen and planning for it helps the pilot to use superior knowledge to avoid situations that might require use of superior skill.

Crew Management

Crew resource management is the method of making the best use of all crew members (when others are present) through proper communication and coordination techniques.

Utilization of crew begins in the preflight phase of operation and continues through the inflation [or takeoff in an airplane—*Editor*], flight, landing, and recovery phases. How you utilize these people and communicate with them is an important element in conducting a safe flight.

A good place to start is by making a checklist of all the activities that you went your crew to participate in, what you want them to do or accomplish, and how you intend to communicate with them whether it is on the ground or in the air.

Involving the crew in this process will help to stimulate ideas on how to best accomplish various tasks and allows them to participate in the process and become an integral member of the team. ■

Answers to Quiz: 1–N, 2–M, 3–L, 4–K, 5–J, 6–I, 7–H, 8–G, 9–F, 10–E, 11–D, 12–C, 13–B, 14–A

Controller Is Dismayed When Student Obeys

The following incident actually happened to an FAA controller at a busy airport where a great deal of pilot training is conducted.

The traffic pattern had several trainers conducting "touch-and-go" landings. Several newly soloed students were in the landing sequence. Two of the students had been sequenced *number one* and *number two* for the runway.

The student *number one* ground-looped after landing and came to rest squarely in the middle of the runway. The controller immediately transmitted to student *number two*, who had already been cleared for a touch and go, "Go around! Disabled aircraft on the runway."

Student *number two* dutifully "rogered." The alert tower operator noticed , however, that student *number two* was continuing his approach. He repeated his previous transmission with a firmer voice, "Go around! Disabled aircraft on the runway."

Again, student *number two* obediently and quickly "rogered." But the tower man was something less than reassured when he noticed that student *number two* was about to cross the runway threshold, still in a landing attitude.

Student *number two* landed, taxied slowly around his companion's disabled aircraft, and then took off while the tower controller looked on in stunned silence.

On reflection, the tower controller realized that the student had complied to the letter with his instructions. He had landed, *taxied around the disabled aircraft on the runway*—and then took off again.

This article originally appeared in the June 26, 1967, issue of FAA Horizons, *the long-time defunct FAA employee publication. Our thanks to our Alaska Region for bringing it to our attention.*
If anyone would like to share a story with our readers, send it to us. Our budget precludes payment but we can give you a byline.

Fight Standards Service

Small Service—Big Job

by Dean Chamberlain, *Associate Editor*

Aviation Safety Inspectors
Part One

Two past issues of *FAA Aviation News* discussed the important role Flight Standards Aviation Safety Inspectors (ASI) play in aviation safety by highlighting two of the many types of jobs inspectors do—issuing safety waivers and conducting the Accident Prevention Program.

These articles told only part of the Aviation Safety Inspector's job. There are many, other, important aviation services available from the ASI's at your local FSDO, services that protect you in the air as well as people on the ground. Public safety is one of the Flight Standards Service's most important responsibilities. This concern for public safety is one of the reasons for regulations concerning minimum safe altitudes, dropping of objects from aircraft, and airshow safety, among others.

Flight Standards Service

Within the FAA, the Flight Standards Service is a small service with only about 3,400 employees, but it is a Service with a big job. The name says it all. The "first name" tells what we do, i.e., Flight Standards sets the aviation standards for airman and aircraft operations in the United States and for American airmen and aircraft around the world. The "last name" is *Service*.

Combine the two and you have an organization that *serves* the needs of U.S. airmen by setting safety standards in the United States that also serve as examples around the world.

Flight Standards, like other FAA organizations, has a national director, Mr. Thomas C. Accardi, and a headquarters staff at FAA Headquarters in Washington, DC, which is broadly organized into divisions based upon work function (Air Transportation, Aircraft Maintenance, Technical Programs, Field Programs, the Regulatory Support Division based in Oklahoma, and the General Aviation and Commercial Division—the titles are self-explanatory). Regional Flight Standards division managers, one at each of the FAA's nine regional offices, coordinate Flight Standards activities within their respective regions.

But many inspectors will say the "real" day-to-day Flight Standards' work of serving the aviation public is done in the 90 Flight Standards district offices around the country and the four overseas international field offices.

Flight Standards District Offices

As many airmen and operators know, their local FSDO is their primary Flight Standards office for all of their aviation concerns or, to paraphrase a common advertising term, it's your one-stop shopping center for all your aviation needs. Whether you are a new student pilot with a question about

your certificate or you are a seasoned professional aviator wanting information about starting an air carrier or charter operation, your local FSDO is there to serve you. Its services are as close as your nearest telephone or FAX machine.

This article is also about one of the FSDO's most important public safety services that usually goes unnoticed by the public, and that is the safe departure and arrival of thousands of flights, both air carrier and general aviation, with their many passengers. This is also the story of the men and women who work in your local Flight Standards District Office and their efforts to both protect and serve you. (We'd like to call it, "A day in the life of a FSDO," but the editor doesn't like clichés.) We will highlight some of the typical work activities done by field inspectors and support specialists at a FSDO, and we will talk to a FSDO manager about how the public and FAA can work together for the benefit of all. By doing so, we hope to point out some of the ways your local FSDO can help make your aviation experience more enjoyable.

If you find the term "aviation experience" somewhat convoluted, it is. If you are wondering why we simply did not say "flying experience," the answer is simple. FSDO's serve all airmen—pilots, maintenance technicians, amateur-built aircraft builders, flight engineers, flight attendants, air carrier executives, and all others as defined in the FAR as "airmen." Too many people only think of pilots when they think of aviation, but without the hard work, professionalism, and dedication of many others in the industry, pilots and aviation in general would never get off the ground.

We will also point out some ways for airmen to save time and effort in dealing with their local FSDO by emphasizing some of the common problems airmen have in dealing with the FAA.

The best way for all airmen to avoid being buried in needless bureaucratic paperwork, unnecessary corrections, and long delays is to learn what is required in order to simplify the approval process. By eliminating unnecessary extra work, everyone benefits.

A Typical FSDO

Much of this article is based upon the activities at the Washington Flight Standards District Office located at Dulles International Airport in northern Virginia. The Washington FSDO is fairly representative of FSDO's nationwide and the types of services each provides.

During an interview with the Washington FSDO Manager Kent D. Stephens about the services provided by the Washington FSDO and similar FSDO's he wanted to make one point very clear. "One of the popular misconceptions many airmen have about FAA aviation safety inspectors is that they are policemen or policewomen. That is not true. Flight Standards is a service organization that has a public trust for developing aviation standards for the public good. It is not a police force," he said.

According to Stephens the FAA depends upon the voluntary cooperation of all airmen in its efforts to fulfill its statutory role of promoting and regulating aviation, and the idea of inspectors being cops does not support that voluntary compliance attitude. Having said that, he was quick to point out that inspectors will take appropriate action to protect the public when pilots or operators fail to comply with appropriate regulations. "The key to aviation safety is the mutual respect and coop-

eration between FSDO inspectors and the airmen, aircraft owners, and operators they work with," Stephens said.

Inspector Tasks

According to Stephens, "Inspectors are responsible for accomplishing five tasks. They are required to do certification, surveillance, accident investigation, enforcement, and promotional work." Many of the tasks are self-explanatory. For example, certification deals with both individual airman and operators such as airlines, air taxis, and maintenance facilities. Surveillance means checking those same airmen and operators for compliance with appropriate regulations. Accident investigation involves both work on behalf of the FAA, and when requested by NTSB, on behalf of NTSB. The enforcement part of an inspector's job involves investigating incidents of alleged non-compliance of the FAR or FAA procedures. Promotional work involves supporting aviation growth and development as well as promoting public confidence in the world's safest aviation system through effective regulatory programs.

Air Carrier Certification And Safety

"If you ask the average passenger how his or her flight was, the typical answer will probably either be, 'It was bumpy,' or 'The airline lost my bag.' In a sense from a safety standpoint, neither relates to safety, but isn't it interesting when passengers talk about

their flights, they discuss how smooth the flight was or the status of their bags? Seldom do they discuss how safe the flight was," Stephens said.

"No one truly sees what goes on in the background as far as crew training, people having to meet simulator requirements, hours and hours of review by both FAA and the company developing manuals and procedures for deicing, flight attendants, pilots, ground servicing personnel, proving flights, evacuation drills, and the hundreds, if not thousands of hours that go into certification. It really is praise for the FAA when someone is asked how his or her flight was, and all they can say is the air was a little bumpy or it took a while to get my bag. We know we have done our job at that point if that is the most significant activity that took place on that flight," he said.

Stephens provided another example of Flight Standards' dedication to service by using a recent air carrier certification process at his office. "At times, I counted 13 inspectors from this office involved in one manner or another in the certification of that airline," he said, "and that certification only involved a new aircraft, not a new airline."

Starting a new airline involves developing procedures, manuals, and operations specifications among other things. "There is no cookbook that tells someone how to start a new airline," he said.

"The process involves taking a lot of procedures and regulations and

Washington FSDO Manager Kent D. Stephens discusses FSDO procedures in his office.

compiling a list of related tasks that must be accomplished. Certification is designed for people who know what they are doing. It also requires certain experience requirements to be met by the key management individuals involved, and it requires a lot of money. It also involves a lot of time both by the company and the FAA. It is a massive amount of work. You would think with just one rule [FAR Part 121] for air carriers, certification would be easy, but that is not the case," he said.

For example simple questions such as, "How much training is needed for the pilots," or, "Who trains the first instructor," can become major questions that must be resolved during the certification process. Certification takes a lot of time, energy, and effort. The main task is to ensure that that airline's first flight is a safe one.

"Passengers may never realize all that went on in the background to get them there," Stephens said, "but, the purpose of all of that work is to get the passengers to their destination safely."

FSDO Organization

To serve the different aviation needs of airmen and operators within its area and to better use the experience of its inspectors, the Washington FSDO is organized into four primary sections. One is an administrative section to support the FSDO administrative needs. The other three are operational sections made up of inspectors based upon the type of work and parts of the FAR each group works with. The office manager, the administrative officer, the Accident Prevention Program Manager, a Cabin Safety Specialist (more about this unique position later), and administrative support personnel make up the administrative section. As the name implies, this section provides several important services.

The manager, besides providing the guidance for the office, also participates in the certification work done within the office. Many certification actions require the manager's or acting manager's signature. And like managers everywhere, the manager is responsible for the training and personnel actions for all of the assigned staff.

Assisting the manager in many of these activities, especially when dealing with Regional and FAA Headquarters' matters, is the administrative officer who is an expert in FAA administration policies and procedures. Supporting the administrative and operational functions of the office are the administrative support personnel. Without the secretarial, data entry, and clerical support provided by the support specialists, many of the functions done by the office would come to a screeching halt.

Another important part of the administrative team is the Accident Prevention Program Manager (APPM), whose duties were outlined in the article on the Accident Prevention Program in the November/December 1992 issue of *FAA Aviation News*.

The final person in the administrative section is the office's cabin safety specialist. One of only a handful of such specialists in the FAA, the Washington cabin safety specialist plays an important role in helping to protect passengers in commuter and air carrier operations by ensuring the air carriers comply with appropriate FAA cabin safety requirements. Together all of these people play a key role in the day to day operation of the FSDO.

Operations Unit

The remaining three sections within the office are identified by the type of work the assigned aviation safety inspectors do. As the name implies, the Operations Unit serves the operational needs of both airmen and operators based within the District. Some of the assigned "Ops" inspectors work with air carrier and scheduled commuter operators operating under FAR Parts 121 and 135, while other Ops inspectors work with general aviation operators and pilots operating under FAR Parts 135, 133, 137, 141, and 91. All Ops inspectors deal with FAR Part 61 matters. One Ops inspector at Washington FSDO is a specialist in air crew training and advanced simulation instruction and training.

Typical Ops inspector duties range from giving pilot certification check rides, to giving air carrier crew check rides, to going on air carrier or air taxi proving flights during which the pilot or crew must demonstrate their ability to safely fly the route and/or aircraft as part of a required certification program. Ops inspectors also work with flight schools and air carrier training facilities. Ops inspectors also get involved in many investigations. An important part of their job is answering questions about all aspects of pilot and air crew certification and aircraft operating procedures. For example, an Ops inspector can spend a significant amount of time working with a FAR Part 121 air carrier or Part 135 commuter or air taxi operator in developing operating specifications for the operation as part of the certification process. For those not familiar with the term "operational specifications," or as they're more commonly called "ops specs," ops specs define or limit the types of operation or under what conditions an operator can operate under FAR Parts 121 or 135. As you can see, like other inspectors within a FSDO, the duties of an Ops inspector are varied both in content and detail.

And like other inspectors, Ops inspectors have both a required training program they must complete as well as ongoing recurrent training. One of the constant challenges for all inspectors and FSDO managers is keeping up with the rapidly changing aviation industry which requires continued refocusing of the organization's energies.

Airworthiness Unit

The Airworthiness Unit, like the Operations Unit, is divided into specialties based upon the type of work performed. There are airworthiness (AW) inspectors who work primarily with FAR Part 121 air carrier operators and FAR Part 135 Scheduled Commuter operators while others work primarily with general aviation operators. The office's Avionics Inspector is part of the Airworthiness Unit at Washington.

Like their Ops inspector counterparts, airworthiness inspectors are involved in a wide-range of aviation community activities. In many cases they work as part of a FSDO team,

Richard F. Belle (left) a Supervisory Aviation Safety Inspector talks with United Express crewmembers following their flight at Dulles International Airport. Belle was monitoring the air carrier's operations as part of the air carrier's new aircraft certification program.

one or more Ops inspectors and one or more AW inspectors, on many certification or certification renewal projects. AW inspectors play a key role in the certification of air carriers, air taxis, flight schools, and maintenance shops. They take the lead in inspecting and certificating maintenance facilities and maintenance training facilities and schools. They are involved in the certification of airframe & powerplant (A&P) maintenance technicians and those A&P's with inspection authorization (IA's) within their areas as well as refresher clinics for IA's. And as explained in Part 2 of this series, AW inspectors are involved in certificating amateur-built aircraft and their builders. AW inspectors also play a critical role in accident and incident investigations.

Geographic Unit

A group of inspectors are assigned to the unique Geographic Unit. This unit contains both operations and airworthiness inspectors. They are responsible for ensuring that air carrier operators who use airports and facilities within the Washington FSDO's area, but whose main-base of operation is located in another FSDO's district, comply with appropriate regulations and procedures. Although, the certificate holding district office, the "home-based" FSDO, is responsible for servicing the needs of all of the operators based within its area and ensuring those operators are in compliance with appropriate FAR, Geographic inspectors work with the certificate-holding FSDO to ensure its

operators are in compliance with regulations and approved procedures while they are flying into and through Washington FSDO's area of responsibility.

Geographic units also provide an important national service. They give Flight Standards the mechanism to monitor the operational safety of air carriers throughout the nation regardless of the location of their supervising FSDO or certificate holding office. Geographic units help provide the flying public a vital safety net by ensuring the same safety standard is applied throughout an air carrier's system.

How to Help Yourself

Obviously, not everyone wants to start an airline or an air taxi operation, a flight school, etc., but for those who do, there are ways to speed up the application process. You could hire an aviation consultant or contract with a company to help you develop the necessary documents and training manuals. But one of the easiest ways is simply to call your local FSDO for an appointment to meet with an inspector specializing in your particular operation. The inspector will provide guidance in what has to be done and in many cases will provide you a list of references and instructions you must follow to start the application process.

For major projects such as starting an air taxi operation or a FAR Part 141 flight school, you might want to purchase copies of the appropriate FAA inspector manual or manuals that pertain to your intended operation. An

inspector at your local FSDO can tell you what documents you might be interested in. The various inspector handbooks will show you what items an inspector must look at and approve for any operation. The handbooks also show examples of how to fill out the required FAA forms correctly for each specific application. Copies of the various inspector handbooks can be ordered from the U.S. Government Printing Office (GPO) in either Washington, DC, or from select GPO bookstores in some major cities. In addition, the FAA publishes Advisory Circulars on many procedures that outline many application processes. Also, many trade organizations produce "how to guides" on significant FAA application processes. Knowing what is expected is one way to help yourself during any certification process. Another way is by completing all applications properly. Many applicants fail to complete their various application forms properly. Missing information not only delays the processing of the form and adds to the amount of time an airman must wait for his or her certificate, it also adds to the workload of the inspector trying to get the application corrected. The time and effort spent on the telephone discussing the status of the application and in trying to correct the incomplete application is like a snowball rolling down hill. And no one likes to get buried in an avalanche of paperwork or delays, especially an inspector or an airman waiting for his or her certificate.

Another way of learning how to work with the FAA and its inspectors is by understanding how a typical FSDO is organized and the job requirements of the various types of inspectors assigned at a typical FSDO. ∎

Part 2 of this article in the FAA Aviation News *will present a "typical" day in the life of an inspector. During that "day" we will tell you how to prepare yourself for a check ride, show some of the steps in air carrier certification including cabin safety, discuss the "bogus" parts issue, and explain how amateur-built aircraft are certificated among other things. For those interested in becoming an FAA aviation safety inspector, we will list some of the job requirements and briefly outline how to apply for a job with the FAA.*

Flying Safely at Night

by Thomas N. Jones, *APPM, Winston-Salem, NC FSDO*

My first inclination was to title this article "Night Flight," but that title was taken long ago by a pioneer aviation writer, Antoine De Saint-Exupery. His book was a largely romanticized account of flying mail planes at night using very primitive navigational facilities.

What I want to do is more practical than romantic: To acquaint the pilot with precautions to take while flying at night or to refresh the pilot's knowledge of aircraft operations at night. In order to use your aircraft fully and get the most out of all the bucks you put into it, there will be times when it may be necessary to fly in less than ideal conditions. When appropriately current and qualified, we may have to fly in instrument meteorological conditions (IMC) or at night or both.

In night flight, as in all flight operations, there are several distinct components that are required for safe flight. Individually identified they are:

- **The Pilot**
- **The Aircraft**
- **Useful Equipment**
- **The Atmospheric Environment** (i.e., weather)
- **Airport Facilities.**

The Pilot

First, let's look at pilots, you and me. Of course, to fly at night, you can't have a night flying restriction on your certificate. Furthermore, to be pilot in command while carrying passengers at night, you have to have had three takeoffs and three landings at night to a full stop in category and class within the preceding 90 days.

Currency and qualification aside, one thing that is absolutely essential to be a pilot is vision. We may be able to fly an aircraft with many illnesses that would disqualify us to pass an FAA medical examination, but without vision it is physically impossible—at least as I'm writing this it is.

It is important for pilots to have a good understanding of how the vision system works. (Just like airplanes, we pilots have systems also!) Nearly everything we do and many ailments, illnesses, etc., affect our vision. A rule of thumb would be anything that reduces the amount of oxygen going to the eye will have a detrimental effect on vision.

Consequently, smoking is detrimental to vision for several reasons:

1. Smoke obscures vision.

2. Carbon monoxide (CO), a by-product of smoke, combines with the oxygen-carrying red corpuscles of the blood approximately 200 times greater than oxygen, thus displacing oxygen in the bloodstream and decreasing the amount of oxygen to the eyes.

3. Smoking nicotine constricts the blood vessels, allowing less blood and less oxygen to reach the eyes.

Our eyes see when light entering the pupil strikes the retina, the light sensitive layer of tissue at the back of the eye that is analogous to the film in a camera. The retina contains two kinds of light sensitive receptor cells—rods and cones. The cones are responsible for daytime and color vision. Rods are responsible for vision in dim light.

The central region of the human eye (the fovea), on which we depend most for vision, is tightly packed with cones but contains no rods. The rest of the human retina contains both rods and cones, and the ratio of rods to cones increases in the periphery of the human retina. Could this be one of the reasons that we can see things better at night or in dim light in our peripheral vision?

As winter approaches the days get shorter, and the hours of darkness increase. Consequently, we need to be aware of how the environment affects our vision. For example, winter is the time for respiratory illnesses—colds, flu, allergies—to be more prevalent. Most of us treat our symptoms of these maladies with the many medications that can be purchased "over the counter." *No pilot acting as a "required crewmember" should ever use a medication that has not been approved by an aviation medical examiner (AME)*

Why not? The obvious reasons such as inducing nervousness or sleepiness aside, one of the many reasons is the possibility of histotoxic hypoxia. This is a condition in which certain chemicals inhibit the cells of the body to assimilate oxygen. No matter how much supplemental oxygen is used, the body cannot absorb it. Alcohol is one of the offending chemicals that causes histotoxic hypoxia. The FAA Office of Aviation Medicine recently published a brochure containing a chart that shows some of the symptoms associated with the use of "over the counter" medication. (The January/February 1993 issue of *FAA Aviation News* reprinted the information in that brochure, including the chart.) If you are taking ANY medication, obtain approval from your AME. Your family physician may not be familiar with the problems associated with using a certain drug and flying an aircraft. AME's receive special training in this area.

Winter also brings on colder weather. In many cases the aircraft is heated by air blown directly off the aircraft exhaust system. If there are any leaks in this system, carbon monoxide will be introduced directly into the aircraft and, thus, directly into the pilot. This can and does cause unconsciousness and ultimately death. Symptoms of carbon monoxide poisoning include headache, drowsiness, or dizziness. Carbon monoxide is odorless, but because it is mixed with exhaust fumes, a smell of exhaust in the cockpit could mean CO is present.

Some of the ways to deal with suspected carbon monoxide poisoning are to use supplemental oxygen, breathe outside air, close heating vents, and land as soon as possible. Do not expect to recover from CO poisoning for a while. It takes time for the bloodstream to become saturated with oxygen again. A CO detector in the aircraft cabin is a good investment.

The Aircraft

Of course the aircraft must have an electrical system for night flight. One necessary question before your night flight is, "How healthy is the electrical system on the aircraft that you propose to fly at night?" Is the alternator/generator in good repair? How about electrical connections, drive belts, battery condition, etc.? An ounce of prevention is truly worth a pound of cure! (In the event of a discharged battery, a common problem in the winter time, the use of an automotive-type battery charger is not recommended. If the battery is charged improperly, it may deteriorate more rapidly than if properly charged. An excessive charge rate is also not recommended; it may cause the battery to explode.)

Good maintenance procedures and an extra careful pre-flight inspection are essential for safe flying at any time, and ESPECIALLY in the dark! Be sure all the lights—inside and out—work. Landing lights are very often used during daylight hours to increase visibility for collision avoidance and may be burned out. A spare bulb or two might be a good investment!

If you routinely fly above 5,000' MSL at night, supplemental oxygen could be a wise investment. A few minutes on pure oxygen will do wonders! For improved night vision, corporate and airline pilots routinely use supplemental oxygen before making an approach at night. I have found that after a long flight at night if I use supplemental oxygen before an approach, lights appear to grow brighter—just as though I turned up a rheostat! It is especially important when fatigued to use supplemental oxygen. Hypoxia again! Of course any oxygen system installed in the aircraft must have routine maintenance as well as the rest of the aircraft systems. Follow manufacturer's recommendations for carry-on systems.

Useful Equipment

Some of the items that should be included in the pilot's equipment for a night flight are flashlights; spare batteries and bulbs for the flashlights; current charts; airport diagrams with taxi charts; a CO detector; blankets, etc.

For example, carry at least one flashlight, but remember, flashlights break, bulbs burn out, batteries discharge. Spare flashlights, bulbs, and batteries are not that expensive. The disastrous effects of an electrical failure at night will be greatly diminished by having emergency lights. Pre- and post-flight procedures are greatly enhanced with light—it is very difficult to check the oil and fuel levels and look for contaminants in the dark!

There are other light sources that can be used in emergencies. Light sticks that glow in the dark are good for a one time use, and their use could save flashlight batteries while enroute and leave the flashlight for use later during the approach. Pilots have come up with some innovative ways of holding a flashlight when they only have two hands—one flying the airplane and one holding a chart or tuning a radio. Between the teeth or under the chin are the most popular places. But flashlights that have a cord attached to one end to hang around the neck or ones with flexible necks and that clip to your clothes are now available.

Another form of "equipment" is having the proper publications available.

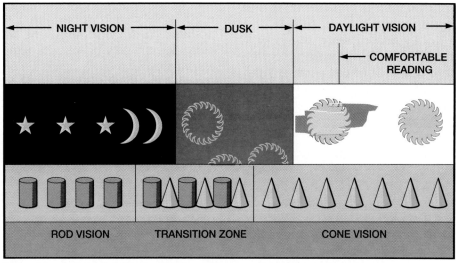

The retina contains two kinds of light sensitive receptor cells—rods and cones.

Current sectional charts are important because they show altitudes of obstructions and the location of airports and roads. Having a "road map" of the airport taxiways and runways is very helpful. Airport taxi charts are contained in NOS and Jeppesen approach charts. There are also other publications with airport diagrams. The *Airport Facility Directory* has a veritable wealth of information about airports, ATC frequencies, etc. The *Airman's Information Manual* is an excellent resource. An explanation of airport lighting and a section on flight physiology is contained in this very important publication.

A blanket may also be an important item to have along. With the cooler temperatures at night, passenger comfort is a very important ingredient to a successful flight. It would also be good to have along in the event of a precautionary landing off airport or at an airport with no facilities.

The Atmospheric Environment—Weather!

"Everybody talks about the weather, but no one does anything about it!" is an old saying that holds true today. With all of our technology, satellites, radar, meteorologists with PhD's, we still cannot tell with a great degree of accuracy what the weather is going to do. We use all the weather information sources available to us, then make an educated choice based on what we learn from the weather services. Our experience level, our equipment, and our preparation are large determining factors in whether or not we operate an aircraft safely.

Night weather is especially tricky. A big problem is fog. At night the temperature/dew point spread narrows. When the spread is less than 5°, some type of fog is likely. The dew point is the temperature to which air must be cooled to become saturated by the water vapor already present in the air. A dew point spread of 4° or 5° with no wind or a very light wind will most likely produce fog. A thin layer of ground fog can be very deceptive. You may be able to see down through it and think it is thin enough to fly in, but once you get into it all visibility could very well be lost.

Clouds are also difficult to see and avoid at night. A good idea is to be sure the ceiling and visibility are adequate if planning VFR flight. Another is to attend an Accident Prevention Program seminar dealing with disorientation and take a ride in the "Barony Chair." Learn about vertigo. Some recurrent instrument training could be an excellent precaution, *especially* some training on "partial panel." Knowing how to make a 180° turn solely by reference to instruments is one of the most important skills a pilot can possess.

While flying at night, if you see the lights on the ground start to "twinkle," landing at the nearest suitable airport may be called for. Fog forms rapidly in the cool night air. When it starts to form, the first indication may well be when the lights are diffused by moisture in the air. Remember, the dew point is the temperature at which the moisture in the air will most likely become visible.

With all the limitations of the weather forecasts, a good weather briefing, and an *understanding* of the briefing is essential to safe flight. It is also required by FAR § 91.103!

Airport Facilities

Airports come in a wide variety—Everything from a small grass strip with no lights to behemoths like JFK, DFW, LAX, ORD, etc. Approaches to different airports require different skills. An approach to an airport with a VASI, a glide slope, REILS, sequential discharging lights, centerline lights, green lights in the center of taxiways, etc., is far different from a "black hole" approach to a barely lighted runway in a sparsely populated area with obstructions all around.

General aviation pilots routinely operate at airports with minimal facilities. How do we maximize resources at such airports? One way is to learn how to make a stabilized, steep approach. Practice this first during the day. Try to visit more remote and "primitive" airports during daylight hours before attempting an approach at night. Look up the airport in the Airport/Facility Directory to determine what lighting aids may be available. Many of the smaller airports have pilot controlled lighting. Learn how to activate the runway lights from the airport's entry in the Airman's Information Manual (AIM).

You might also contact the airport operator before attempting a flight into a strange airport at night. (This might be a good idea in daylight also!) If you know someone who has an airplane based there, call them and ask about special procedures. You can also call the nearest FSDO, talk to the APPM, and find out if there is an Accident Prevention Counselor at that airport who may be able to give you hints on how to approach and land safely at night.

While on approach to an airport at night be particularly observant of the runway lights. If they start to "blink," "twinkle," or appear to "flash" near the end of the runway—GO AROUND! More than likely what you are seeing is some kind of obstruction between you and the runway, i.e., trees, powerlines, fences, etc. Remember one of the basic laws of physics: "No two objects can occupy the same space at the same time!"

When flying anytime, but especially at night, use every resource you can think of. The more information you have, the more skills you acquire, the better your equipment, all these increase your chances of having a safe successful flight.

Remember the five P's:

Proper Preparation Prevents Poor Performance! ∎

Three Hundred Moving Parts

by Ivan J. Jaffe

"You fly one of those things!? Three hundred moving part waiting for something to go wrong, and then you fall like a brick."

If I've heard this once about helicopters, I've heard it a thousand times. Not from an uninformed, clueless wannabee pilot, but from experienced and knowledgeable fixed-wing captains. The helicopter, for this vocal observer, may as well be a Martian flying saucer, using extraterrestrial aerodynamics to stay in the air, precariously on the edge of obliteration at the slightest hiccup.

Not so, of course. The helicopter is a safe efficient flying machine with the unique capacity of flying without moving over the ground—an advantage that opens innumerable opportunities of access and ability in countless facets of life, such as sightseeing and photography, movie making, and air ambulence services.

So why such comments from people who should know better? The truth about helicopters and the good that they do has too often taken a back seat to the sensational publicity of the daring low-level antics and ensuing helicopter crash so often depicted in today's entertainment media. This is an image we in the helicopter industry are not entirely blameless of because of our deficiency in disseminating the real facts about our machines and our pilots.

Clearly, this false view of the helicopter is not limited to the general, non-flying public but rather, it seems, to almost everyone outside of helicopter pilots. We are beginning to understand our distorted image as viewed from the cockpit of the airplane, and I would like to highlight some of the misunderstandings surrounding our flying machines.

"Where is That Crazy Eggbeater!"

A common problem is that we are not easy to spot from the airplane cockpit, especially in the traffic pattern. We're small, slow, low, and often below the horizon, not following conventional traffic patterns, contending with wings and instrument panels obstructing view and, in fact, do not even look like an "aircraft."

Conversely, the visibility from a helicopter cockpit, windshield cleanliness and sun position notwithstanding, is excellent, and spotting traffic is usually not a problem for us. This, coupled with our ability to slow down or even stop, keeps us well away from potential collision areas.

If you're looking for a helicopter in the traffic pattern, we will usually be flying unconventional patterns, i.e., right side and approximately 800 feet AGL. Our approaches will usually be to a point other than the runway—often a helipad or taxiway on the airport.

"When that Engine Fails, the Fan Stops, and You Really Begin to Sweat!"

Have you ever heard of "autorotation?" Do you know what autorotation is? No? Well, it is simply a glide in a helicopter. Yes, we can glide, and in fact we can do even better than that. We can terminate the autorotation (remember, no engine) in a safe landing in the space of 20 feet or less, very often in a hover landing! Very different flying characteristics from a brick. We offer far more safe forced landing opportunities than even a Cessna 152. Next time you're on a cross-country flight, note how many 20–foot clearances you can see along your route.

"Helicopter N1234, Hold Your Position on Final for One Departure"

What a great aircraft we fly; we can stop in midair and wait. A Controller's dream! Did you know, however, that a successful autorotation for many helicopters is impossible if it is initiated from the hover anywhere between 20 and 400 feet AGL? Helicopters can and are often required to operate in the hover within this envelope. However, for engine failure considerations, we would prefer to have some airspeed below approximately 400 feet AGL. Today's advanced engine reliability statistics allow safer flight in these areas, but you can be assured that the helicopter pilot hovering below 400 feet AGL has thoroughly assessed and is constantly monitoring the engine's operations and is well aware of the options he or she has in the event of an emergency.

Continued on page 14

Unusual Attitudes: Helicopters and Instrument Flight

by Hillman E. Bearden

While attempting to remain under visual flight rules (VFR) in marginal weather conditions, an instrument-rated pilot flying an instrument-equipped helicopter crashes into a hillside. There are no survivors.

Within a month a similar accident occurs. This time the aircraft collides with a power line. Aviation statistics show that this deadly scenario continues to occur with tragic frequency. Despite training and awareness programs, pilots operating legally under VFR continue to collide with obstructions or terrain because poor visibility prevents avoidance or because inadvertent instrument meteorological conditions (IMC) induce spatial disorientation from which the pilot cannot recover in sufficient time to regain aircraft control.

There are many reasons why a pilot on a VFR flight will continue flying into deteriorating weather conditions while depending on visual references to navigate and maintain aircraft control. Some of these reasons are practical in nature while others are personal and vary among pilots.

Options Have Advantages and Disadvantages

The only other options to continuing the flight under VFR are landing in a suitable open area or climbing into IMC. These options are often dismissed because both require a major change in the original flight plan and create complications that the pilot has little time to contemplate fully. Having to plan a new course of action completely would require the pilot to dilute his or her concentration with matters other than safely flying the aircraft. An in-flight mission change is no small task—even when everything is going well.

The option of landing short of the destination runs counter to the pilot's purpose for flying in the first place. The importance of the flight has already been established before takeoff, and the pilot has the intention of completing the flight. External pressures, from passengers or others involved in the operation, add to the pilot's own internal pressure to complete the flight with as little direction as possible.

The second, and [perhaps] least desirable, option requires transitioning to instruments and continuing under instrument flight rules (IFR) without adequate preparation. Even a pilot proficient in instrument procedures is at a serious disadvantage when confronted with the prospect of climbing into instrument conditions when no planning for an IFR operations has been made.

Mission Compatibility

For most helicopter pilots, instrument flights are not compatible with their missions and, although they may be required by their employers to possess instrument ratings, they may not have had the opportunity (or been required) to maintain instrument competency. Therefore, a pilot may not be inclined to venture into an IFR environment because of a lack of confidence in his or her ability to control the aircraft adequately by reference to instruments. The pilot would, at the same time, have the tasks of navigating to an airfield for an instrument letdown to visual conditions and communication with ATC to allow for proper separation from other aircraft.

Ego and Go/No-Go Decisions

Ego can also influence go/no-go decisions. The pilot elected to take off when the weather conditions were supposedly forecast and known. Could the pilot be considered guilty of poor judgement if flight under VFR could not be continued? It may be that the pilot had gotten through bad weather many times before. Would landing short of the destination make it appear that the pilot was frightened or lost or lacking in pilot skills?

A natural conclusion is that good judgement was used when the decision was made to take off and that the flight can somehow be completed. Any other conclusion might threaten to undermine the self confidence all pilots must have in order to compete in their chosen profession. Still, objective self-evaluation is imperative when facts begin to suggest that potentially dangerous pilot attitudes are at work.

Aeronautical Decision Making

An FAA publication, *Aeronautical Decision Making for Helicopter Pilots*, concluded:

"Pilots, particularly those with considerable experience, as a rule try to complete a flight as planned, please passengers, meet schedules, and generally demonstrate the 'right stuff.' [But] this basic drive can have an adverse effect [sic] on safety and impose an unrealistic assessment of piloting skills under stressful conditions. Even worse, these repetitive patterns of behavior, based on unrealistic assessments, produce piloting practices that are dangerous, often illegal, and will ultimately lead to mishaps."

Aircraft accidents cannot simply be accepted as the cost of doing business. While accident prevention can be expensive in terms of dollars lost when flights are cancelled because of weather and [in terms of] the cost of recurrent training for pilots, it is worth the price when it prevents loss of life and aircraft.

Another FAA publication, *Aeronautical Decision Making for Air Ambulance Helicopter Pilots: Situational Awareness Exercises*, said weather-related accidents involving low visibility or spatial disorientation are the most serious and easily prevented types of accidents. The publication, which focused on accidents involving helicopters on emergency medical missions, said that 67% of all fatal aeromedical accidents were weather-related.

"The vast majority (71%) of these [accidents] occur during the hours of darkness and during the en route segment of flight."
[The report] said that 40% of all emergency medical flight operations are at night. [The] study concluded:
"Pilots either are not being adequately trained, are forgetting their training or are not maintaining their proficiency in those special skills and knowledge demanded by flying in the dark. The prudent aeromedical pilot must be proficient in keeping the helicopter upright by reference to instru-

ments, even if he [or she] is not instrument rated."

The studies also conclude that weather-related accidents involving low visibility and spatial disorientation are among the most serious and easily preventable kinds of accidents in other less specialized kinds of helicopter operations.

Reasonable minimums for VFR operations can reduce but not eliminate the risk of encountering inadvertent IMC. Recurrent instrument training can greatly improve a pilot's ability to avoid unsafe situations or safely recover from IMC that cannot be avoided.

Risk Assessment, Pilot Judgement, and Weather

Accurate risk assessment and pilot judgement also play key roles. The FAA study said,

"One bad decision often leads to another (in the decision chain). One poor decision, e.g., inaccurate assessment of deteriorating weather, increases the availability of false information that may then negatively influence decisions that follow. As time progresses, the alternatives available may decrease, and the option to select the remaining alternatives may be lost. For example, if a pilot elects to fly into hazardous weather, the alternative to circumnavigate the weather is automatically lost."

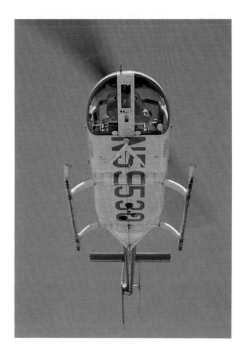

Considering the difficulty of accurately forecasting precise weather conditions, especially in areas remote from weather observing stations, it is likely that pilots flying in those areas will sometimes encounter reduced ceilings and visibilities, although the forecast is generally favorable for VFR flight. Weather phenomena are seldom uniform even over short distances.

FAR § 91.155 allows helicopters to operate in uncontrolled airspace below 1,200 feet above ground level (AGL) with no specified visibility as long as clearance from clouds is maintained and the aircraft is flown at a speed that will allow the pilot to avoid obstacles. Many obstacles, however, are difficult to see at any speed even when there is no atmospheric restriction to visibility. It requires little deterioration of ceiling or visibility to create a dangerous environment while flying within several hundred feet of the ground.

Operating close to the ground, even helicopters with their superb maneuvering capabilities cannot always enable pilots to avoid obstacles such as wires or antennas. Abrupt maneuvers to avoid these and other obstacles in low weather conditions may prevent collision but may also place the helicopter in an unusual attitude. If the pilot subsequently encounters IMC, and it requires more than just a few seconds to regain visual meteorological conditions (VMC), spatial disorientation may cause the pilot to lose control of the aircraft and impact terrain or obstacles.

A National Transportation Safety Board (NTSB) report, *Commercial Emergency Medical Service Helicopter Operations*, noted:

"Even if the pilot is instrument rated, current, and proficient in helicopters, success in coping with inadvertent instrument flight is not guaranteed. The FAA has reported that in tests with qualified instrument pilots, it took as long as 35 seconds for some of the pilots to establish full control of the aircraft by instruments after the loss of visual contact with the surface. These tests were conducted with fixed-wing aircraft, which are inherently more stable than helicopters."

Helicopter cruise speeds, the NTSB said, can also easily overrun the pilot's ability to see and avoid hazards or deteriorating weather.

"The effect of speed on the ability of the pilot to recognize a hazard (such as a cloud bank) and to react can be significant. It takes a helicopter pilot an average of 5 seconds to recognize a hazard, to determine what corrective action is needed, and to respond. A helicopter traveling at 120 knots (138 mph) will cover 1,012 feet in these 5 seconds. If the pilot reverses course and starts a turn, the helicopter continues to move toward the hazard for a distance equal to the radius of the turn. In a 30° banked, coordinated turn at 120 knots, this is 2,208 feet. Therefore, a pilot flying at 120 knots who recognizes a hazard and initiates a course reversal will travel 3,220 feet before starting to move away from the hazard. It should also be recognized that a 30° banked turn in marginal visibility can induce spatial disorientation in pilots if they are relying on outside visual cues to control the aircraft."

Accident Prevention

What can be done to prevent accidents that occur when it becomes impractical or perhaps even impossible to continue flight under VFR? Normal precautions in preflight planning cannot eliminate the risk of weather encounters completely. Virtually every professional pilot will eventually find him- or herself in a situation in which weather threatens the safety of a flight.

The following recommendations will significantly reduce the risk of weather-related accidents for VFR flights: [Note that the parameters suggested in the following may be more restrictive than minimums or requirements established by the FAR but NOT less restrictive.—*Editor*]

• Each operator should have weather minimums for VFR operations that are sufficient to provide reasonable assurance that pilots will not inadvertently encounter unsafe low ceilings and visibilities while en route.

• Pilots should be provided with a company-approved procedure to guide them if they encounter an inadvertent IMC situation. This procedure should specify minimum safe altitudes for obstacle clearance, current instrument navigation charts, and ATC facilities that a pilot can contact for assistance.

• [Operators should] provide recurrent pilot instrument trainingμ even if normal flight operations include frequent IFR operations. Without practice, the skills and knowledge necessary to prepare a pilot for successfully handling adverse weather degrade over time. In addition, maintaining instrument proficiency is more complex than simply satisfying the FAA requirement for recency of instrument flight experience. Among other things, it includes studying regulations, the *Airman's Information Manual*, and flight or simulator training with a qualified instructor.

Conclusion

The NTSB safety report also concluded:

"Spatial disorientation or vertigo can be so overpowering that even when pilots are aware that it is occurring and are trained to rely on instrumentation, they may have difficulty in controlling an aircraft. The importance of spatial disorientation cannot be overstated, [because] 90% of general aviation accidents involving disorientation as a cause or factor are fatal. Special training and proficiency maintenance are required to reduce the risks involved in flying in IMC."

A flight operation that emphasizes flight safety and provides thorough instrument recurrent training for its pilots [may] experience a reduced risk of accidents while maximizing the use of flying hours. ∎

Mr. Bearden is a ground/simulator instructor at FlightSafety International's Fort Worth, TX facility. This article originally appeared in Helicopter Safety, *a publication of the Flight Safety Foundation (not affiliated with FlightSafety International), 2200 Wilson Boulevard, Suite 500, Arlington, VA 22201–3306; (703) 522–8300.*

Three Hundred Moving Parts
Continued from page 11

"Perpetual Pilot Motion Machine"

If you have ever taken a helicopter flight (and I suggest that you do), you will see that the pilot's hands are continuously occupied. The controls are in constant motion to maintain stability in the helicopter. For this reason, among others, the helicopter pilot must master some fine and sensitive control touches. The helicopter pilot must essentially become a highly skilled and competent flyer and, contrary to popular belief, be a safe, conservative aviator. You would too if you controlled "300 moving parts!" Unfortunately, because of the occasional sensation-seeking reporter and a very few irresponsible pilots, you may have the wrong idea of our abilities and intent.

Similarly the noise of helicopter flight all too often drowns the lifesaving, knowledge-gathering good helicopters do. Rather than being known as a converter of aviation fuel to noise, I would like to see the air ambulence flight or the mountain rescue flight or the essential supply flight or the news-gathering flight dominate our image.

So, yes, we do good work, and we are responsible, competent pilots flying safe, able, and reliable machines. I know you are, too.

Let's get together some time and talk. ∎

Mr. Jaffe is the Chief Pilot for Boston Helicopter Company and an Accident Prevention Counsellor for the Bedford, MA FSDO. This article originally appeared in the Bedford FSDO's newsletter, FSDO 1 Communicator, published by APPM John Hemmes.

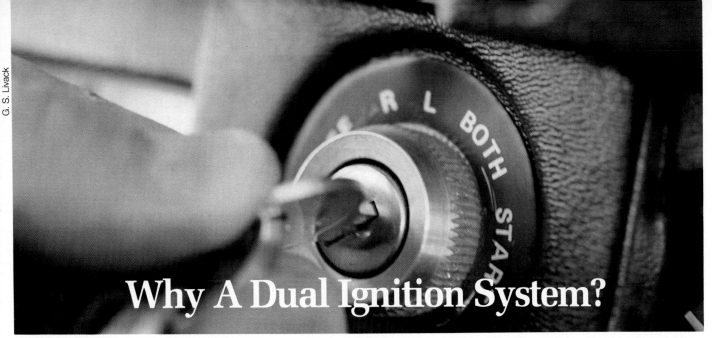

Why A Dual Ignition System?

by Henry Davison

Standard aircraft engines (Lycoming, Continental, etc.) have independent, dual ignition systems. However, false logic prevails when most general aviation pilots respond to the question, "Why dual ignition?" The usual answer is "For safety—in case one system fails, the other takes over." No doubt; however, safety covers a wide spectrum of definitions, but this logic is not the main reason for dual ignition. Normal engine operation requires that both ignition systems function properly and simultaneously. This is not to be construed as both mags firing at the same instant. Not so—on some engines the mags are timed two degrees apart as prescribed by the engine manufacturer. As this article progresses, we will see why a pilot should not elect to take off with one magneto inoperative or otherwise malfunctioning. Remember—it's a lot better when you are down here wishing you were up there than when you are up there wishing you were down here.

Theory of Operation

Once normal ignition occurs in a cylinder, the fuel/air mixture burns at a relatively slow rate, providing continued expansion of kinetic energy that pushes against the piston throughout its power stroke. Although less intensive, this same fuel/air mixture still continues to burn as it passes through the exhaust port on the return trip of the piston (exhaust stroke). At night a blue flame would be visible emitting from the exhaust stacks if the mufflers were omitted. The fuel/air mixture burns at a rate comparable to that of a gas stove.

The dual magnetos produce prolonged ignition for a period of time (measured in micro-seconds) that starts two flame fronts when the piston is well advanced of top-dead-center (TDC). More specifically, this ignition event occurs approximately 28 to 30 degrees before top-dead-center (BTDC) as it relates to crankshaft rotation. By the time the piston arrives at TDC, the expanding gas has reached maturity and is ready to do its thing. During the power stroke the piston actually accelerates from zero movement at TDC to its fastest movement at midpoint of travel, then decelerates back to zero at bottom-dead-center (BDC). This phenomenon is because of the rotating crankshaft throw position and the connecting rod reciprocating action. The fuel/air combustion process is very much in harmony with this piston movement, providing a graceful transition of power to the crankshaft.

If only one ignition system is operative and producing a single flame front, the combustion process is retarded. This retarded energy is just the opposite of what is required as the piston accelerates to its peak velocity at midpoint cylinder travel. Instead of the energy being depleted gradually during the second half of piston travel when decelerating, the delayed-burning gas is still prosperous. The piston then is unable to absorb the prolonged energy, and the suppressed burning gas results in higher combustion temperature, causing uncontrolled burning (detonation). This condition usually does not present a real problem during cruise flight at 75% or less power for a normally aspirated engine, provided the mixture has been leaned properly. On the other hand, the condition intensifies during takeoff and climb-out. With insufficient cooling at slower airspeeds, detonation could cause severe engine damage.

If one magneto is functioning normally, but the other abnormally, it is conceivable that the defective magneto could ignite the fuel/air mixture prematurely negating the good magneto. Consequently, an aggravated assault by detonation could be devastating to the engine. When severe detonation occurs, it usually burns a hole right through the piston adjacent to the cylinder wall. Then all of the crankcase oil makes a fast exodus through the breather tube. As Paul Harvey might say, "You can predict the rest of the story."

Spark Plugs

The spark plugs have the final say when converting magneto electro motive force (EMF) to ignition spark; therefore, the plugs should be at their best behavior. A few factors to be cognizant of concerning spark plug integrity are as follows:

1. Spark plug/engine compatibility
2. Heat range of plug
3. Electrode gap setting
4. Condition of electrodes

Spark Plug/Engine Compatibility

Both spark plug and engine manufacturers working together determine the proper type plug suitable for each engine model. Extensive flight testing is conducted through a wide range of operating conditions and at different power settings. To eliminate any possibility of error in spark plug selection, both manufacturers provide spark plug data charts as a guide. It makes safety sense then to take full advantage of their combined expertise.

Heat Range (Hot and Cold Running Plugs)

For specific operating conditions, you may have the option of selecting a hot or cold running plug. The terms "hot" and "cold" refer to the plug's ability to transfer heat from the firing end to the engine cylinder head. A cold running plug transfers heat more readily; therefore, it is normally recommended for a relatively hot running engine. Conversely, a hot running plug transfers heat more slowly; therefore, it is recommended for a relatively cold running engine.

Operating temperature of the plug insulator core tip is one factor that governs the function of troublesome combustion deposits, namely carbon and lead. Plugs are susceptible to these deposits when the operating temperature of the insulator core tip is at or below 800 degrees F, but an increase of just 100 degrees F is sufficient to vaporize such deposits. By employing the proper heat range plug when applicable and by avoiding prolonged idle rpm on the ground and in the air, spark plug fouling should succumb.

Electrode Gap Setting

The size of the electrode gap has a definite effect on spark plug service life and on engine performance. An incorrect gap setting will not only cause misfiring during idle but will also misfire during cruise power when the mixture is leaned. This intermittent firing lowers the plug insulator tip temperature to such an extent that combustion deposits may not vaporize sufficiently to keep the plugs from fouling.

Condition of Electrodes

The spark plug center electrode tip should be flat with a relatively sharp edge instead of being rounded with an indefinite edge. The ground electrodes should be hefty instead of being eroded thin. On fragile ground electrodes, a correct gap setting cannot be maintained for long. Even though the plugs seemingly fire okay in this deteriorated condition, the spark burn time is shortened considerably, degrading engine performance and wasting fuel. When the electrodes are eroded as described, it is time to make a change. As the saying goes, "You can pay now, or you can pay later."

Magneto Periodic Inspections

When it comes to magneto periodic inspections in the way the factory recommends, false logic again intervenes: "If it ain't broke—don't fix it!" When performing 100-hour or annual inspections, maintenance personnel check the magneto timing to the engine and run the engines to determine satisfactory performance regarding power output, static idle rpm, magneto grounding check, and the rpm drop when checking the mags during the run-up. The magnetos are not usually removed and inspected unless a problem is evident. Consequently, magneto integrity and longevity are compromised.

Teledyne Continental Motors (TCM) recommend that its product lines of Bendix magnetos be disassembled and given a detailed inspection at 500-hour intervals. TCM's Service Bulletin No. 632, "Maintenance Intervals for all TCM and Bendix Aircraft Magnetos," issued in November 1989, further emphasizes several important inspection/overhaul intervals. In its manuals, Slick Magneto Division also recommends periodic inspections and overhaul maintenance. The maintenance schedules are varied according to the magneto model and serial number.

Since 1985, the National Transportation Safety Board (NTSB) has cited magnetos as a cause or factor in 92 accidents involving 22 fatalities and 21 serious injuries. A multitude of Service Difficulty Reports concerning magnetos have also been submitted to the FAA during this period. These reports include 130 instances of cracking, burning, arcing, leaking, or other deficiencies in certain magneto ignition coils.

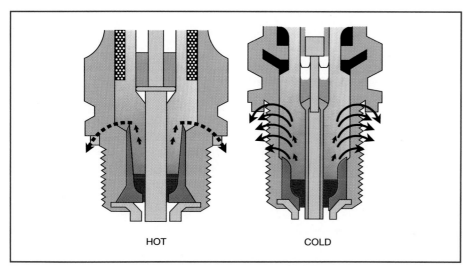

HOT   COLD

The length of the nose core is the principal factor in establishing the plug's heat range. "Hot" plugs have a long insulator nose that creates a long heat transfer path, whereas "cold" plugs have a relatively short insulator to provide a rapid transfer of heat to the cylinder head. (from the Airframe and Powerplant Handbook*)*

I have experienced an engine failure on an aborted landing because of magneto problems. The aircraft had been purchased a couple of months earlier in northern New Mexico where sandstorms are prevalent. Both magnetos, when removed after the engine failure, were found to be infected with very fine, pulverized dust. The dust wore down the breaker point cam block to the extent that the maximum point opening was only .003 when it should have been approximately .016 to .018. In addition, the foreign dust had mixed with the carbon brush dust to form a carbon track around the distributor block. This could have resulted in a premature firing in a cylinder next in the firing order. This is because of the lower compression cylinder offers less electrical resistance at the spark plug.

The FAA believes that periodic inspections, overhaul, and replacement of critical components are important fundamental facets of magneto preventive maintenance. An examination of accident reports and Service Difficulty Reports make it clear that the current level of magneto inspection, maintenance, and service is much too infrequent.

There are unknown numbers of airplanes that have been stored or otherwise used infrequently and may not have accumulated sufficient total flight time to require that obsolete magneto ignition coils and/or rotating magnets be replaced with more reliable parts in accordance with AD 73–07–04 or other service information. Ignition coils are adversely affected by the environment over relatively long periods of time. They should be replaced and subsequently inspected at conservative intervals of calendar and flight time.

Such severe environmental operating conditions as engine overspeeds, sudden stoppage, immersion in water, and any other circumstances that require complete or partial engine overhaul before the regular overhaul time can and do adversely affect engine operation. The magnetos are an integral part of the engine and are subject to the same degenerating

forces as the engine. In such circumstances the magnetos, regardless of in-service time, should be overhauled with particular attention focussed on all rotating parts, bearings, and electrical components. I have seen a magneto rotating magnet that was sheared in two by an engine backfire where the crankshaft reversed direction for several revolutions.

It must be remembered that any maintenance performed on magnetos must be done by a certificated power-plant mechanic or certificated repair station. Also, the periodic inspections and overhauls require special tools mentioned in the factory maintenance manuals. A seemingly insignificant task such as adjusting or changing the breaker points requires a special timing device to set up the magneto internal timing. The rotating magnet must be positioned precisely with respect to the field magnets for the maximum build-up of magnetic flux. This set-up is called "E gap." With E-gap established, the points are set to open at .0015 (based on standard atmosphere of 29.92" Hg) which collapses the magnetic field to initiate the ignition spark at the appropriate spark plug. There is quite a wide range of maximum point gaps allowed in most magnetos, but the important thing is when the points break (.0015) at E-gap, not the maximum opening gap, so long as it is within specified maximum/minimum settings stipulated by the manufacturer.

Conclusion

Here are a few final considerations about the care and feeding of the magnetos in your dual ignition system.

Magneto Bearing Lubrication

Who would ever think that the magneto bearings require a special lubricant that helps prevent flash-over? If regular bearing grease is used, flash-over could pit the bearing surfaces, shortening component service life.

Handling Magnetos

It is an awful temptation to spin over a freshly overhauled or new magneto while watching the spark jump across the high tension outlets to the housing

ground. When you do this, you just voided the warranty, and most of all you may cause a coil breakdown at the most inopportune moment. The EMF energy buildup in the coil seeks an escape route wherever it may be at the point of least resistance. Eventually, the secondary winding insulation could break down rendering the coil inoperative or intermittent when heated up in service. Secondly, the magneto should be handled with care. A sudden jolt caused by hammering on its components or dropping it could degrade the magnetism in the field and/or rotor magnets affecting magneto performance.

Live Magnetos

A parked airplane without continuity between the mag switch and the magneto, regardless of whether the switch position is at OFF, has a hot (live) mag; therefore, every propeller coupled to an engine must be handled with as much respect as a loaded gun. The propeller does not have to be rotated very much to activate and discharge the magneto impulse coupling. This coupling mechanically retards the magneto-to-engine timing and spins the magneto's rotor over quickly to generate enough EMF to start the engine easily. Even if the mixture is in idle-cutoff, there could be enough fumes in the cylinder to give one more swift kick to an unfortunate and complacent individual.

Run-up/Mag Check

If the mags are accidentally turned off during the run-up mag check, the throttle should be returned to idle before the magneto switches are turned back on. [Consult your pilot operating handbook or flight manual for the manufacturer's recommended procedure.—*Editor*] This procedure negates the afterfiring event that is sure to follow otherwise. Afterfiring could be violent and result in damage to the exhaust system. ∎

Mr. Davison is an A&P mechanic, a flight and ground instructor, and an Accident Prevention Counsellor for the FAA's Baltimore, MD Flight Standards District Office.

GPS, Looking Towards the Future

by Dean Chamberlain

The Aircraft Owners and Pilots Association (AOPA) recently conducted demonstrations of Differential GPS (DGPS) precision instrument approaches at its Frederick, MD headquarters. The media were invited to participate in approaches comparing both DGPS and ILS, flown in AOPA's A–36 Beech *Bonanza*. AOPA used the same *Bonanza* in the FAA/AOPA GPS non-precision approach test program earlier this year at the FAA Technical Center at the Atlantic City (NJ) International Airport.

The briefing and flight demonstration by AOPA's Drew Steketee highlighted the ease with which pilots could be flying DGPS precision approaches, just as they will soon be flying GPS non-precision approaches regularly once GPS receivers meet the FAA's new Technical Standard Order (TSO) C–129 for IFR certification.

As reported in the September issue of *FAA Aviation News,* the FAA approved the supplemental use of GPS in June. Initially, GPS may be used to fly current non-precision approaches pending development of GPS specific approaches. Research is ongoing regarding the future use of GPS for precision approaches, which provide descent guidance as well as navigation to the runway.

During its ongoing test program, AOPA will use two means to provide Differential GPS information to the A–36. During the recent demonstration

flight, AOPA used an FAA-provided differential ground station that uses a one-way VHF radio frequency data link to transmit information to the aircraft. Later, AOPA will lease the sub carrier on a local commercial FM radio station to transmit differential corrections to the aircraft.

For those not familiar with Differential GPS, it uses a ground-based, survey-quality GPS receiver and associated communications equipment to transmit differential information to GPS-equipped aircraft in the transmitter's local area. The airborne receiver then uses the information to make precise corrections to satellite navigation data. As a result, differential GPS can increase the accuracy of commercial GPS receivers from their normal hori-

zontal positional accuracy of about 100 meters to within a few meters. The vertical positional accuracy is also improved dramatically

AOPA President Phil Boyer emphasized AOPA's long-term endorsement of GPS and its advantages for general aviation in particular and aviation in general. Key points included the potential of a single GPS receiver being able to replace many different navigation boxes in a cockpit while providing more information to the pilots; the potential ability for the FAA to design GPS approaches for every airport; and the potential monetary savings governments may realize from having a space-based navigation system that does not require some type of transmitter to be purchased, installed,

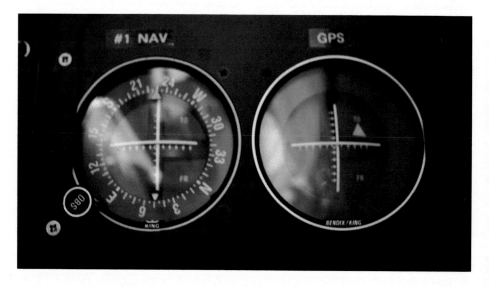

and maintained at each approach site as the current ground-based system does.

During the demonstration flight, two instrument approaches were flown. One approach, emulating the published Frederick ILS 23 approach, was flown to show a comparison between the ILS guidance and those of a GPS-derived guidance. The other approach demonstrating the versatility of GPS was established on Frederick's runway 12 where nearby mountain ranges would make ILS impossible. The GPS approach featured a customized four degree "glide path" designed to overfly nearby mountains and noise sensitive neighborhoods.

In both approach demonstrations, the *Bonanza* with ILS and GPS displays for both the pilot and copilot showed little variation between its ILS and GPS indicators as the aircraft flew the two approaches. The major differences between the two displays were in the display needles' sensitivities and projected touchdown points on the approach. An ILS indicator displays angular course guidance to touchdown; ILS course sensitivity increases as the aircraft gets closer to the ILS transmitters.

The GPS display starts out angular, but it switches to a linear sensitivity mode within 2,000 feet of the runway. Linear course guidance keeps the GPS needles' sensitivity constant to touchdown. Course guidance is not overly sensitive or erratic as the aircraft gets closer to the runway, making for easier and smoother approaches.

In comparing GPS to ILS/VOR, some of the benefits that production FAA-approved GPS approach receivers should provide pilots may be the ease and reduced workload needed to fly an approach. Approved IFR GPS receivers will be programmed to provide sequential navigation steering information automatically from the initial approach fix through the missed approach point and on to the missed approach holding fix. The potential for a pilot's being able to fly a complete published approach without having to tune, adjust, or set in any other navigation information may be the greatest

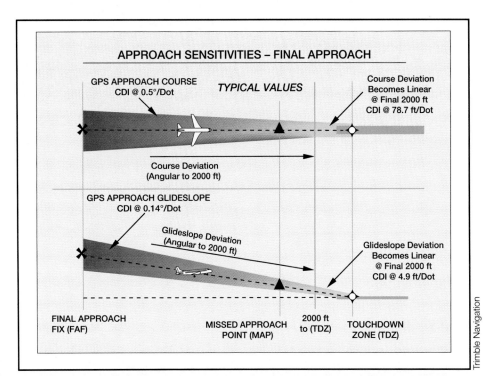

A pie-shaped GPS receiver antenna and mast-mounted DGPS transmitter antenna were installed on the roof of AOPA's headquarters at Frederick Municipal Airport MD.

benefit of GPS, especially for single pilot IFR. Another important benefit may be the constant position and other flight and airspace information available to a pilot throughout the approach. Why, we may reach the point where it might become impossible for a pilot to get lost in flight.

No, on second thought, some pilots will probably forget to turn their GPS receivers on. As history has proven, there will always be room in a cockpit for Murphy and his laws.

But all joking aside, GPS has the potential of being the greatest thing to happen to aviation since the Wright Brothers first flew. Time and GPS operating experience will tell how great.

The work of AOPA and others within the industry with the FAA in developing the DOD-funded and operated GPS for civil aviation use is an example of how the aviation industry and the FAA are working together for the benefit of all. ■

FAMOUS**FLIGHTS**

The First Non-stop Transcontinental Flight in the U.S.

Lt. John A. Macready & Lt. Oakley G. Kelly

by Sally Macready Wallace

Part 2

In the years following World War I, the fledgling U.S. Army Air Service was fighting for its very existence. In an effort to prove the worth of aviation, a non-stop transcontinental flight was proposed. **—Editor**

On November 5, 1922 Lieutenants John Macready and Oakley Kelly jumped out of the engine-damaged Fokker T–2. They were *through*—no more talking of transcontinental flights after this second failed attempt. They left Indianapolis and returned to Dayton for a few days rest. However, it was not long before the U.S. map was once again up on the wall in the pilot's lounge and before they knew it, they were planning a third attempt.

While waiting for favorable weather, Macready and Kelly attempted another endurance record to test the engine and plane, but even these flights were beset with frustrations. On the first try, the mayor and influential citizens of Dayton, were out en masse to bid them "Godspeed." The movie cameras were rolling, they were slapped on the back and wished good luck as they climbed in the plane for the two day flight. Macready said later; "We waved to the multitude, 'gave 'er the gun' and rolled down the runway. . . only to get stuck in the mud up to the hubs 50 feet down the runway."

The second try was not a whole lot better. They got off the ground with an experimental high compression engine and remained in the air for approximately eight hours, at which point the engine quit. It was pitch black with temperatures of eight degrees above zero in very bad weather. They were not sure of their exact position in relation to the field; there were no lights and they were losing altitude fast. Luck was with them. Macready spotted a light on top of a building and headed for it, landing with a thud. The only damage, other than to their egos, was a bent spreader between the landing gear.

Finally the weather reports looked favorable. By this time they had made a drastic change in their route, reversing the direction of flight and flying from east to west to take advantage of the Hudson Bay High during which the prevailing winds blow east to west. Flying the T–2 to Washington, DC, the two pilots put in their weather order. Without a good tailwind, the success of the flight was questionable as fuel exhaustion would occur before they reached their destination.

At 10:00 a.m. May 1, 1923, they received this weather report:

New York to Dayton, Ohio, northeast and east winds, clear sky; Dayton, Ohio to Kansas-Missouri line, low clouds and rain, east winds; Kansas-Missouri line to San Diego, clear sky, variable winds.

They hesitated. The idea of low clouds and rain at night over the Ozark Mountains was not an appealing one. These were conditions to avoid, but the rest of the weather looked good and they decided to go for it. Here again, the first roll-out down the runway, with a crowd of well-wishers waving them off, ended in ignominious defeat. After rolling at top speed for almost a mile over the ground, the huge, heavily laden transport displayed no sign of rising into the air and trees and wires lay directly ahead.

They aborted takeoff and the T–2 taxied back to another position. Roosevelt Field, Long Island (now a racetrack) was a plateau about one mile square. Hazelhurst Field was about the same size and adjacent, but 20 feet below. They pointed the nose of the airplane toward the aerial mail hangars on the far side of Hazelhurst Field, some two miles distance, and again waving goodby to the group of now-anxious spectators, pushed the throttle forward and the plane lumbered heavily over the ground. "It bounced and bounced down the runway but did not rise," Macready wrote later in the *National Geographic Magazine*. It was still on the ground when they came to the 20 foot dropoff between Roosevelt and Hazelhurst Fields. Over they went, and the plane settled back toward the ground, but not quite to earth. The T-2 was flying, but without any apparent climb, and the big hangars were still directly ahead. When they got to the hangars the plane "just sort of flopped over them."

The heavily loaded plane only just maintained level flight. For 20 minutes over Long Island their climb was hardly appreciable. In fact, for the first few miles they barely cleared the poles and wires. They were over Pennsylvania before they could climb above 400 feet. During the daylight hours they navigated by the compass, section lines, and railroad tracks and checked the wind direction by bonfires or chimney smoke. At night it was a different story. Navigation was solely by compass and the occasional flicker of automobile lights on national highways. Lights from cities helped to orient the flyers.

Over Terra Haute they were only 800 feet above the ground. It was nighttime but they could distinguish the river going through the center of the city. They were flying in a light mist under heavy cloud cover as they pressed on toward St. Louis, MO. Macready up front noticed a faint flicker on the propeller that seemed to come regularly and grew stronger as they flew on through what was now a full fledged storm with rain, thunder, and lightning.

A few months before the flight, the new Sperry high intensity aviation beacon had been developed and was being tested on this flight. The Sperry Beacon proved to be a real aid to air navigation and helped make aviation history on this flight as Macready's own words attest: "Approximately 50 miles from Belleville, IL, in total darkness at 2,000 feet altitude, we were thrilled by the sight of a huge beam of light projecting up through the clouds. It was a veritable beacon along a rocky and dangerous shore to us, for otherwise we were trusting solely to the compass to keep on a straight course. Aided by this beam of light, which we knew came from Belleville, we continued straight as an arrow for the Missouri River."

A little after midnight the plane suddenly came out from under the dark, dismal clouds into bright moonlight, a very welcome sight. Kelly now took the controls and flew during the night to

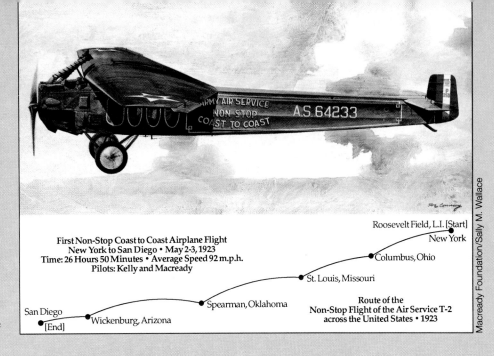

First Non-Stop Coast to Coast Airplane Flight
New York to San Diego • May 2-3, 1923
Time: 26 Hours 50 Minutes • Average Speed 92 m.p.h.
Pilots: Kelly and Macready

Roosevelt Field, L.I. [Start]
New York
Columbus, Ohio
St. Louis, Missouri
Spearman, Oklahoma
San Diego [End]
Wickenburg, Arizona

Route of the
Non-Stop Flight of the Air Service T-2
across the United States • 1923

Macready Foundation/Sally M. Wallace

Santa Rosa, NM. Their first positive navigation point after the long night flight was Tucumcari. NM. They reached it at daybreak and recognized terrain they had flown over on a previous flight. They were right on course! It looked as if they were really going to accomplish their goal at last.

Macready took over at Santa Rosa, NM. Being a San Diego boy, he would fly the final leg and land at San Diego to give the hometown folks a treat. Once he reached the Rio Grande he knew he was seven hours from touchdown. There was nine hours of fuel left. If he could just get over the upcoming mountains, success was assured.

The T–2 was struggling for altitude as each gallon of gas burned off. Once more they were confronted with the Continental Divide and once more they were unable to push the Fokker high enough to clear the mountains. As before, they had to look for a new route, a gap in the divide. Flying south, Macready found the opening he needed and with 100 feet to spare, cleared the highest point of the flight.

As they approached San Diego there was a feeling of elation in the cockpit, but they were eager to land and planned no flourishes over the city. According to Macready's note: "Diving down from 8,000 feet with power on, we reached San Diego, cocked the T–2 up on one wing to swing down the main street and passed about 100 feet

above the tops of the buildings. I noticed something black on top of those buildings and was greatly surprised to observe that it was people. People waving sheets, coats, hats, anything they could get their hands on." Sirens were blaring from fire engines, ships in the harbor tooted their horns, as did automobiles on the streets, and there was a general din below of which the pilots were unaware. They wasted no time. The Army Air Service Fokker T–2 made one turn of North Island to head into the wind and landed exactly 26 hours 50 minutes after taking off from Long Island, NY, thus accomplishing their goal of the first non-stop transcontinental flight.

After three attempts, two crack military pilots had achieved the impossible with the help of elaborate preparations (including a specially equipped airplane) and shear determination. Of course the Air Service chose to forget these facts when they extolled the virtues of aviation and how both the military and businessmen could travel faster and further by air. According to the Air Service this flight proved that commercial aviation was "born" and off and running!   ■

Sally Macready Wallace is the daughter of John A. Macready. She is the President of the Macready Foundation and is currently serving on the Board of Directors of Castle Air Museum of Merced, CA.

"Will It Or Won't It Quit?"

by Robert J. Hawkins, *CFII*

Student pilots spend endless hours practicing emergencies, but it doesn't end there. Instructors chop the power and say "Surprise!" to licensed pilots during their biennial flight reviews, pilots working on their commercial or ATP rating, or just pilots who want to brush up on their procedures. And those instrument students—much of what they do is "what do you do if. . . ."

Collectively we spend countless hours thinking and worrying about emergencies. Many of us fly for years or our whole careers without ever having a real emergency.

Over the last 30 years of flying I have encountered my share of vacuum pump failures, electrical system failures, ice—both on the wings and in the carburetor, "bad gas," plugs that just don't run smoothly, and a myriad of other problems. Some situations are memorable, and most have been forgotten, but I think I have learned a little something from each one.

In every case, I believe, I took the time to calmly look, evaluate, and determine the course of action to be taken. None of the situations were a true "emergency." That is, until last night.

A Real Emergency

My student and I were in an airplane and we were shooting a practice ILS at Frederick (FDK) Airport (Maryland). However, it could have been any-

where, since this approach is a typical ILS. The approach itself went well, but during the initial climb-out portion of the missed approach the engine started running roughly, *very* roughly.

This time there was no calm analysis of the situation. Somehow I knew we didn't have a lot of time. Immediately I switched fuel tanks, just in case the problem was contaminated fuel, and told the student to turn on the fuel pump and to declare an emergency on the CTAF. Then I made sure the mixture, throttle, and prop were forward; took the controls; and turned toward the airport. In my mind the engine was sounding worse with each second, but it continued to run through the landing and we were able to taxi to the ramp, shut down, get out, and sit down to consider our good luck.

I found out the next day that the rocker arm assembly on the number 1 cylinder had failed and taken the push

The first major decision was to fly the airplane in the first place.

rod and valve with it. The mechanic told me that when he removed the rocker arm cover parts came spilling out. The entire rocker arm assembly had been destroyed.

A Postmortem

In reviewing this situation I saw that there were many questions calling for decisions. The first was: Would the plane make it back to our home base some 17 miles away? I didn't want to try and find out, even though the mechanic said it would probably have run for at least another 10 or 15 minutes! More importantly, we were within two miles of a 5,000–foot runway. What would you do?

Now let's look at what we did. A review of the events brings to light the decision points that occurred. At the time I was not particularly conscious of having made them; they were almost instinctive. In reality, however, they were the result of training and discipline taught me by my instructors and my students and reviewed frequently by my peers.

The Decision Process

The first major decision was to fly the airplane in the first place.

Next, could we have found this mechanical problem during the preflight? No. The reality for all of us is that in some situations we just don't know something will happen until it happens. Should we forego the preflight just because we wouldn't find this type of problem? Again, no.

Let's move ahead to the actual start of the failure, or rather just before it. Most instructors and pilots who take flying seriously are subconsciously aware of the possibility of engine failure, and we tend to evaluate the situation constantly. This, by the way, may be what makes many CFI's a pain in the behind when it comes to following checklists and procedures in general. In this case, while the student was flying the missed approach, I was doing several things: looking for traffic both conflicting and in relationship to our position, listening to and watching the student, and making a mental note of where we were in relationship to the airport in general. These points, and I am sure many others, are the result of many hours of being drilled by instructors in "position awareness"—know where you are and what's around you.

When the engine started to run roughly, we had to decide what to do or whether to do anything at all. Many times I have encountered carburetor ice, bad gas, or fouled plugs, and each of these occurrences has a distinctive and subtly different sound and feeling and requires a different solution from the pilot. When I saw the RPM's drop and felt the whole plane vibrate, I didn't care what the problem was.

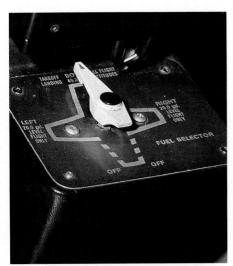

"Immediately I switched fuel tanks, just in case the problem was contaminated fuel, and told the student to turn on the fuel pump and to declare an emergency on the CTAF."

> **Don't upset your passengers, don't create panic, be decisive and definitive, and give clear and concise instructions.**

Such sensations are the basis for the decision to *get it on the ground NOW.*

Fly the Airplane

How can you teach these concepts? You can't. My student and I now know what an eminent engine failure sounds and feels like. I am not sure I can pass that sense and feeling on to my other students. What I can try to teach them is that when the moment comes to decide, make the most conservative decision possible and make it fast. If you have to think about it, it may be too late. In an instant I decided to return to the airport and land—no quibbling, no thinking, just reaction based on "pilot instinct."

Yet, at this point several things were also happening. There were other aircraft in the pattern, and we needed to notify them that we thought we had a problem. Declare the emergency! Other pilots would collectively prefer to get out of your way when you are experiencing an emergency, but they are not mind readers and you need to tell them what is going on. This is not a time to be shy or macho. Your ego, possible sense of embarrassment, or even the thought of "crying wolf" have no place in a shaky, noisy, possibly broken airplane.

Next was the decision to maintain altitude, establish the best attitude with the remaining power for as long as it lasts, and prepare to pitch for best glide when the powerplant fails. Textbook, all the way, but the feeling was nothing like the descriptions in the books or those easy-going simulated engine-outs I've practiced so often.

Getting It on the Ground

Making an inside entry to the downwind leg of the traffic pattern is not one of my favorite maneuvers. Although it is not actually illegal, I don't think this type of entry is good operating practice. However, in this case we had an emergency, and the decision to make that entry was part of the overall decision to get on the ground. This was not the time to go out and make the standard 45–degree outside entry to the downwind. The key factors here were to be careful and not waste position, airspeed, or altitude.

As we were turning from a short downwind to final I was thinking about how putting the gear down early could create a lot of drag and could keep us from a successful landing, especially if the engine quit. So we held off on the gear until we were on final and were confident we could make the runway as a glider. Meanwhile, we maintained our altitude and made shallow banked turns toward the end of the runway, lining up for final approach.

Within a few seconds the runway was under our nose, and we had gear down and full flaps. It is surprising how quickly a manually-activated gear comes down when you are under stress. The next issue was whether to

"When I saw the RPM's drop and felt the whole plane vibrate, I didn't care what the problem was. Such sensations are the basis for the decision to get it on the ground now."

"Meanwhile, we maintained our altitude and made shallow banked turns toward the end of the runway, lining up for final approach."

reduce power. With a sick engine, this can be a critical point. It's highly probable that when you change the power setting on an ailing engine, it is going to quit. When you pull that throttle back, you need to be prepared for an engine failure! I clenched my teeth and eased the powerback. My sweaty hand was so wet it almost slipped off the throttle, but to my relief that prop kept turning.

We were properly positioned and had the runway made, but, believe it or not, there were still more decisions to be made. Go back in your mind to all your training. What else is there to be done? Well, for one, unlatch the door and make sure your seat belt and shoulder harness are secure. For another, be prepared to get out of that plane ASAP! We could have had an engine fire and not known it. I don't even remember unlatching the door, but when we touched down I was not surprised when the door popped open.

Taxiing to the ramp was uneventful. I turned off all the electronics except for one radio and the intercom. When we shut the engine down, smoke billowed out of the engine from oil on the exhaust stack. I got out of the plane quickly and encouraged the others to do the same. There was no panic, just common sense with a bit of urgency. The others followed quickly and calmly, although in my mind there was still the potential for danger. I remembered the

drill: Don't upset your passengers, don't create panic, be decisive and definitive, and give clear and concise instructions.

All these rules apply to decisions which must be made by the private pilot as well as the grizzled old ATP. They are all the result of training, repetition, and acquired habits. So the next time your friendly CFI simulates some emergency, remember that it is part of the overall learning process and is designed to develop in you the reaction process that is so vital to safe aviation. These are the circumstances where actions should occur without much thought.

Conclusion

A retrospective look at what happened vividly points out the need to practice procedures. I currently have

about 50 hours in Mooneys and probably 500 in similar high performance retractables, but in the last 30 years of flying I've only got two to three minutes of eminent engine failure time, all in the last 24 hours. And during those two or three minutes, I was convinced that the engine was going to quit any second, and the decisions I made were based on that gut feeling.

In discussing this situation with some of my peers there was the observation that it might have been better to have let the student/owner land the plane so he could get the experience. This was a good point, but not one which I considered at the time. An emergency in progress is not necessarily the place to start your training. My wife said that she would be glad to speak with anyone who disagrees with this decision. She also said, "I know you. I don't know this other guy. I'd rather have you at the controls." (I pay her to say things like this.)

I hope I'll go more than another 30 years without another failure. Maybe I will, but the issue is that some of us will have these failures and, unfortunately, some of us will not handle the situation effectively. Each of us has to know our airplane and practice the procedures so that when something goes wrong we can make a decision and take the action we have been trained for. ∎

Mr. Hawkins is a CFI and Accident Prevention Counsellor for the Baltimore, MD FSDO. This article originally appeared in the December 1992 issue of IFR Refresher *and is reproduced with permission, © IFR Refresher.*

"When you pull that throttle back, you need to be prepared for an engine failure!"

AIRSPACE CORNER

Question: *Does the 250 knots (288 mph) speed restriction apply throughout Class B airspace?*

Answer: No, only that portion below 10,000 feet MSL. Unless otherwise restricted by ATC, on departure you can automatically accelerate when passing 10,000 feet at those airports (Atlanta, Denver, Los Angeles, and San Diego) with Class B airspace above 10,000 feet. Likewise, you can hold your airspeed until descending through 10,000 feet.

Question: *Does the 200 knots (230 mph) rule under the Miami Class B shelves apply outside of 12NM?*

Answer: Yes. FAR § 91.703, Operations of civil aircraft of U.S. registry outside the United States, specifically states that FAR § 91.117c is applicable.

Question: *I'm still a little confused about Class E airspace, can you clarify it?*

Answer: One way to think of Class E, the general class, is by a default process. If it (the airspace) isn't Class A, Class B, Class C, or Class D, and it is controlled airspace, it is Class E. The variable with Class E is where does it start. Class E may begin at the surface (nontowered control zone), 700 and 1,200 feet (transition areas), Federal airways (VOR, colored, and Hawaiian), enroute domestic control areas, offshore control areas (low), and the former Continental Control Area, which has been redefined as Class E airspace extending upward from 14,500 feet MSL. By the way, in the western states, the Class E airspace beginning at 14,500 feet can be the floor of controlled airspace.

• ?°F =?°C

In the September/October 1992 issue of your magazine was an article written by TSgt. Rand M. Sanders about carburetor icing. First of all let me compliment the author as this subject is not always clearly understood by quite a few airmen. Under the heading "What causes carburetor ice?" it is mentioned that the temperature drop in the carburetor can be as much as 40° but is usually 20° or less. That is correct. Between brackets is mentioned the equivalent in degrees Fahrenheit and here a mistake occurs. When we just compare Celsius with Fahrenheit then—only then!—1°C is equivalent to 1.8°F. To add the usual

32 degrees is only done when we compare a temperature, but not when we compare just the value of the two degrees to each other as is done in this article. A drop from 40° to 20° Celsius is a drop from 72° to 36° Fahrenheit as the outside temperature is not important and irrelevant.

> Rt. Hon. Capt. A.J.H. Cornelis BSc
> Nonthaburi Province
> Suanyai, Thailand

Thank you for pointing out an important fact about the two temperature scales. In reviewing your letter we found an interesting point in Webster's Ninth New Collegiate Dictionary regarding thermometric scales for our budding scientific buffs. There is a subtle difference between the Celsius and Centigrade thermometric scales although most Americans use the terms interchangeably. Celsius' interval between the triple point of water (the point where a substance exists as a gas, solid, or liquid) and boiling is divided into 99.99° with the triple point being .01° and the boiling point being 100°. The Centigrade scale has an interval scale of 100° with 0° as the freezing point and 100° as the boiling point. Either way one looks at it, .01° Celsius or 0° Centigrade, cold is cold.

• Did You Know

A friend gave me a copy of the July/August 1992 issue containing your story on the early days of crop dusting. I enjoyed the article and am happy to see that John A. Macready is getting credit for his fine contributions to early aviation. I would like to offer a few corrections and additions:

1. Mr. Neillie was head of the Cleveland Ohio Parks Service and contacted Entomologist J.S. Houser of the Ohio Agricultural Experiment Station in Wooster with the idea of dropping insecticide on the tall trees of the Cleveland Parks.

2. Director Charles Thorne of the Experiment Station arranged the original contract with the Army Air Corps at McCook Field in Dayton.

3. The Catalpa grove was owned by Mr. H.B. Carver of Troy, OH, who approached Macready and Houser on his own asking them to try out this idea on his trees.

4. Army report records state the hopper contained 135 lbs. of lead arsenate and the total dusting time for the six acre plot was 54 seconds.

5. The entire test was photographed from the air by Lt. Kelly and Capt. A.W. Stevens using a DeHavilland airplane.

6. J.S. Houser noted in his report that Macready made a walking inspection of the entire woodlot prior to taking the plane up.

It's always interesting how different memories remain of the same event. . . makes our jobs more interesting, I guess.

> E. E. Whitmoyer
> Historical Records Officer
> Ohio Agricultural Research and
> Development Center
> The Ohio State University
> Wooster, OH

Thanks for sharing your information. Digging up historical facts is a lot like solving a mystery. You have to weigh the information you find and come up with your own conclusion.

As Macready is featured in this issue's "Famous Flights," it seemed appropriate to addendum one of his other aviation accomplishments.

• Straight-in Approach

What constitutes a straight-in approach at an uncontrolled airport? In other words, how far out from the airport do you have to be lined up with the runway to be considered straight-in? Advisory Circular (AC) 90–66, page 2, paragraph (d), states that pilots should be particularly alert for air carrier operations as they may execute a straight-in approach.

> Gary S. McBride
> Fayetteville, GA

The *Airman's Information Manual* (AIM) defines a straight-in VFR approach as "Entry into the traffic pattern by interception of the extended runway centerline (final approach course) without executing any other portion of the traffic pattern." Because each airport is different, there is no definition for how far out you have to be to be on a straight-in approach. For your

FLIGHT**FORUM**

INSTRUMENT CORNER

• Safely Departed

Four of us have a question that we cannot agree upon. The question is about published IFR departure procedures for select airports. First of all why are they there? Then when do I have to follow them and under what conditions?

Gary S. McBride
Fayetteville, GA

The published IFR take-off minimums and departure procedures exist for those airports where the standard IFR minimums in FAR Part 91 do not provide the required level of safety. You are expected to follow the procedures when operating IFR. Conditions where the procedure is not required are published for specific airports and runways.

• Safety Pilot Update

I am enclosing a page from your old FAA General Aviation News dated May/June 1985. The article is about when a safety pilot needs a medical. I would like an update on your agreement that the safety pilot does not need a current medical certificate. In 1992 I was informed by someone from the FAA that I could not ride as safety pilot with an already instrument rated pilot current and qualified for the airplane and conditions of flight.

James A. Whitley, CFII
Shreveport, LA

The answer in the old issue is correct. A safety pilot who does not act as a required crewmember, as in the original question, does not need a current medical certificate. But if a safety pilot is a required crewmember, as in the case of being the safety pilot on a simulated IFR flight when the pilot flying is wearing a view restricting device, the safety pilot must possess at least category and class rating for the aircraft being flown and have a current medical certificate in case the safety pilot must assume control of the aircraft and act as PIC.

• Logging of Instrument Time

FAA Aviation News has received four letters asking about how to log instrument training in a ground training device. Rather than print the individual letters from Nolan G. Beck, Mark K. Walter, Howard G. Soloff, and Lloyd J. Probst,

we will summarize their questions and answer them.

Each asked about logging time in a ground training device or simulator and if that time had to be signed off by an appropriately rated instructor. Several questions dealt with the question of maintaining instrument currency in a training device or simulator and if that time had to be signed off by an appropriately rated instructor.

Dean Chamberlain
Associate Editor

Since one writer also said we do not always answer the question asked, we will do our best to be direct. All instrument training and instrument currency training conducted in FAA approved simulators, airplane flight training devices, and ground training devices must be signed off by an appropriated rated instructor and logged as received in the specific device used for that training to count towards meeting any FAA requirement. FAR § 61.51(b)2,v, Pilot ground trainer instruction, describes this type of pilot experience or training received, and FAR § 61.51(c)5, Instruction time, states in part that pilot ground trainer instruction must be certified by an appropriately rated instructor. Pilots may not log ground training instruction time as either PIC or solo time. No one can solo either a simulator or training device. Nor can instrument instructors sign themselves off. Everyone can play to their heart's content, but for the time to be credited toward meeting any FAA requirement, the training device or simulator used must be FAA approved and the time signed off by an appropriately rated instructor

Finally, a significant point must be cleared up regarding ground instrument training. It appears that many pilots (and occasionally this magazine) have used the term FAA-approved simulator, airplane flight training device, and ground training device to mean the same thing. The terms are not interchangeable. Advisory Circulars (AC) 120–40, Aircraft Flight Simulator Qualification, and 120–45A, Airplane Flight Training Devices Qualifications dated February 5, 1992, describe the various types of such devices, the qualification requirements for each, and how each can be used in pilot training. AC 120–45A paragraph 14, also outlines the five year moratorium on the generic training devices described in the AC that have not been determined to meet the "level" standards listed in AC 120–45A.

information, AC 90–66, "Recommended Standard Traffic Patterns for Airplane Operations at Uncontrolled Airports," is being rewritten and straight-in approaches will be addressed in the proposed AC.

The FAA/industry Aviation Rulemaking Advisory Committee was actively involved in the rewrite, and the committee considered many industry ideas on straight-in approaches. Although the new AC will recognize straight-in approaches, the FAA recommends the standard left-hand traffic pattern as defined in the FAR and AIM. Because pilots may use different procedures, either intentionally or by error, all pilots must be alert for traffic conflicts near any airport.

• Veiled Comments

Recently a speaker at an EAA chapter meeting claimed that everything within the 30NM "transponder veil" of a TCA was "controlled airspace." I argued that the limits of controlled airspace were defined by the blue and magenta shaded areas on a

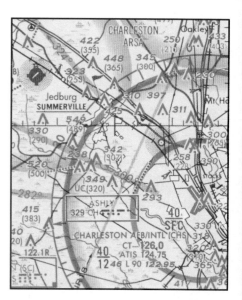

sectional chart and by the dashed boundaries of airport areas. I felt that the 30NM circle defined an equipment requirement and not controlled airspace.

Which one of us knows what we are talking about?

Jack Bennett
DeKalb, IL

You are correct. The 30NM TCA (now Class B airspace) veil is only a transponder requirement. FAR § 91.215 applies. By the way, the blue shading is no longer used with the magenta to indicate controlled airspace *(now Class E)* and solid magenta is used for ARSA's *(now Class C)* on sectional charts. An insert explaining the new symbology is included with each sectional.

Aerobatic Champion Donates Aircraft to the National Air and Space Museum

During ceremonies at Andrews Air Force Base on June 1, 1993, National Aerobatic Champion Patty Wagstaff and her husband Robert donated her *EXTRA 260* to the Smithsonian Institution in memory of the late Robert W. Wagstaff of Kansas City. Following a brief Aerobatic demonstration by Patty in the *EXTRA 260,* she presented the aircraft to Dr. Martin Harwit, Director of the National Air and Space Museum.

The *EXTRA 260* in which she won the overall 1991 and 1992 National Aerobatic Championships will be displayed in the Pioneers of Flight Galley next year.

Open Doors

Recently the Transportation Safety Board of Canada issued a safety recommendation that applies to pilots on both sides of the border. The Board is concerned about the number of Canadian accidents resulting from in-flight openings of doors on small aircraft. In its statement the Board said it reviewed accident data from 1977 to the present in the hope of identifying why pilots were having accidents when a passenger or baggage door opened on takeoff or in flight.

In its report, the Board reviewed 33 accidents in which a door opened either on takeoff or in flight. Ten people were killed in the accidents. Several interesting points were discovered during the Board's review. One was that the pilot experience level was generally high. Another was in 30 of the accidents the door was either not properly secured or was left open during preflight. The Board noted that most small aircraft do not have a conspicuous visual indication that a door is not secured nor are such aircraft equipped with a "door-open" warning device in the cockpit. *The most important fact the Board noted in its investigation was that in all 33 accidents the aircraft should have been capable of controlled flight with the door open.*

Part of the Board's recommendations concerned hardware recommendations. One recommendation is to encourage manufacturers to add secondary door latches and to design better visual indicators of unlatched doors. The Board noted some manufacturers and after-market manufacturers sell kits to modify doors for more security.

Most of the Board's comments concerned pilots and their training. The Board recommended to Canada's Department of Transport that because of the inadequate pilot response to a door opening on takeoff or in flight that all pilots receive training on how to handle such a problem either as part of their student training or as part of their refresher training.

A door ajar on the ground is easier to close than one in flight so be sure all doors are securely shut before you leave the ground.

The Board said in part, "An open door in flight can generate extensive noise, airframe buffeting, loss of lift, increased drag, and adverse aircraft stability. In the data sample, all 33 aircraft should have been capable of controlled flight with the door open. However, the distraction, pre-occupation, channelized attention, panic, etc., associated with a door opening in flight apparently affected 17 of the accident pilots to such an extent that aircraft control was significantly degraded. This resulted in the pilots either stalling the aircraft, landing with the gear up, landing hard, inadvertently flying into the ground or an object, or losing control of the aircraft while attempting to close the door. In 11 of these 17 accidents, the pilot-in-command had over 500 hours total flying time.

"A pilot who is not mentally prepared for an unfamiliar situation, such as a door opening in flight, may take inappropriate actions to deal with the situation. The stress inherent in such emergencies could cause pilots to narrow their normal scanning pattern, resulting in failure to monitor critical flight parameters or to perform essential actions.

"Individuals are less susceptible to distraction-induced errors and erroneous decision-making if they are prepared for an emergency or unusual event by having a pre-determined plan of action. Guidance on the handling of open doors on take-off or during flight is not consistently provided to pilots during initial training, nor is such training required by regulation. The study and reference materials currently used by student pilots provide little discussion on this subject." The Board followed this comment with its recommendation regarding pilot initial and recurrent training. [*Editor's Note:* Pilot distraction has been identified as a cause of many accidents in the U.S. over the years. As a result, the U.S. Practical Test Standards (PTS) for pilot certification requires that applicants be trained and tested on their ability to safely handle an aircraft system or equipment malfunction such as a door opening in flight or other common distractions listed in the PTS. The question is how many pilots think about and review emergency procedures after they get their certificate.]

The Board concluded its recommendations with the following observation. "The flight characteristics of an aircraft with an open door vary by aircraft type; consequently, type-specific procedures may be required in order to land safely with an open door. Some manufacturers already provide specific procedures in their safety supplements; however, the pilots' primary reference document, the Aircraft Flight Manual (AFM), normally does not contain this type of information. . ." The Board then went on to ask manufacturers to include this type of information in their flight manuals.

In summation, the Board's comments can be reduced to three simple comments. Pilots should be prepared for the possibility of a door opening at any time. Pilots should check that all doors are secured as part of their preflight check. And the final comment involves the first rule of aviation, pilots must always fly their aircraft.

U.S. Customs Service Reminders to Private Flyers

For those of you who plan to take a vacation outside the U.S. here are a few reminders from the U.S. Customs Service to make the trip easier.

Advance Notice of Arrival

All aircraft, before coming into any area from any place outside the United States, for security reasons, and in order to avoid the penalties applicable to aircraft, shall furnish a timely notice of intended arrival. This may be done either by or at the request of the commander of the aircraft through the FAA or other flight notification procedures or directly to the District Director or other Customs officer-in-charge at the nearest intended place of first landing in such area. Check the U.S. Customs' "Guide for Private Flyers" or your local Customs office for specific advance notice requirements.

Advance Notice Requirements

Your advance notice or notice of intended arrival to Customs must contain the following information:

1. Aircraft registration number
2. Name of aircraft commander
3. Number of U.S. citizen passengers
4. Number of alien passsengers
5. Place of last departure
6. Estimated time and location of crossing U.S. border/coastline
7. Name of U.S. airport of first landing
8. Estimated time of arrival

Private aircraft that are coming from a foreign place are required to furnish the notice of intended arrival in compliance with these special reporting requirements and must land for Customs processing at the nearest designated airport to the border or coastline crossing point unless an overflight exemption has been granted. Check with the Customs district office having jurisdiction over the airport you wish to fly to for overflight exemption application requirements.

Emergency Landings

Pilots should report as promptly as possible by telephone or most convenient means

to the nearest Customs office. All merchandise and baggage should be kept in a segregated area. No passengers or crew should be permitted to depart the place of arrival or come in contact with the public without official permission, unless other action is necessary for the preservatio of life, health, or property.

Required Aircraft Documents for U.S. Customs Inspection

1. Aircraft registration
2. Pilot license
3. Medical certficate
4. Airworthiness certificate
5. FAA Form 337 (Major Repair and Alteration) on board for additional fuel tank installation in baggage/cargo compartments
6. Radio license

Other Reminders

- Overflight exemption and landing rights permissions if applicable
- Required survival equipment
- Current navigational charts
- Required insurance
- Proof of U.S. citizenship (current passport,original or notarized copy of birth certificate, voters registration card)
- If in possession of over $10,000 in monetary instruments, you must report to U.S. Customs the international movement of monetary instruments in excess if $10,000)
- Agricultural pests? (fruits, vegetables, plants, plant products, soil, meats, meat products, birds, snails, or other live animals or animal products)

This information is from a U.S. Customs handout. For your own copy of "Guide for Private Flyers," which lists all the airports serviced by the Service, write to U.S. Customs Service, P.O. Box 7407, Washington, DC 20044.

FAA Commissions First Precision Runway Monitor System

The FAA has just commissioned a new radar system at Raleigh-Durham International Airport, designed to enable simultaneous approaches to closely spaced parallel runways during low visibility weather. Called a precision runway monitor(PRM) system, it is the first of its kind to become operational in the United States.

The new radar system allows air traffic controllers to monitor aircraft making parallel

Roger Myers

approaches to runways during low visibility weather conditions. Equipped with electronically scanned radar and high resolution displays, it allows simultaneous landings on parallel runways, resulting in increased capacity, reduced delays, and fuel savings.

The precision runway monitor system enables landings on parallel runways as close as 3,400 feet apart. The parallel runways at Raleigh-Durham are 3,500 feet apart. Parallel runways operating without the benefit of the new radar system must be at least 4,300 feet apart for simultaneous landings in inclement weather.

The system scans a 360-degree area, providing air traffic controllers with a visual display of each aircraft's position, updating the information once per second. Automatic alerts—both visual and audio—are provided to assist controllers in assuring the required separation of traffic. The system also displays aircraft identification and position, along with a ten-second projected position of the aircraft.

Twenty-six of the top 100 airports have, or plan to have, parallel runways with spacings between 3,000 and 4,300 feet.

The precision runway monitor system will not only significantly increase airport capacity, but will maintain a high level of safety in aircraft operations. Costing about $6 million for each system, the FAA plans to install five of these new radar systems at airports around the country in the near future.

This article originally appeared in the FAA's Headquarters Intercom.

TEST YOUR PILOTING IQ:
Surface Weather Observations Quiz

by Louise Oertly

In the September 1993 issue of *FAA Aviation News* Mr. Richard McDonald did an article entitled, "A Few Remarks About Surface Weather Observations." In this issue we are going to test your knowledge and see how many of these weather remarks you can translate. Match Column A with Column B. For the answers see page 3.

Column A

1. /FEW CU
2. /HIR CLDS VSB
3. /ACSL SW–NW
4. /CIG 14V19
5. /PRESRR
6. /F5 TWR VSBY 2
7. /TB08 S MOVG E OCNL LTGIC
8. /RADAT 87120
9. /BINOVC
10. /KOCTY
11. /VSBY NW½S2
12. /F BANK N–S
13. /TWRINUN
14. /WET SNW

Column B

____ A. Wet snow (snow that contains a great deal of water).

____ B. Control tower in unknown.

____ C. Obscuring phenomena at a distance. Fog bank north through south not at the weather station (airport).

____ D. When the visibility sector is less than 3 miles or when it is operationally significant and differs from the prevailing visibility, it is disseminated as a remark. In the example, visibility in the northwest was ½ mile, and in the south it was 2 miles.

____ E. Smoke over the city.

____ F. Breaks in the overcast not classified as thin.

____ G. Contraction for freezing level data (first two numbers indicate the relative humidity at the freezing level, the last three numbers indicate the height, MSL, in hundreds of feet of the freezing level. e.g., 12,000).

____ H. Thunder began eight minutes after the hour, the thunder (the sound of thunder) was south moving east with occasional lightning in the cloud where the thunder was heard.

____ I. Fog obscuring 5⁄10 of the sky, the control tower determined the surface visibility to be 2 miles.

____ J. Pressure rising rapidly (at a rate of 0.06 inch or more per hour, e.g., 29.92 to 29.86).

____ K. Ceiling variable 1400 to 1900 feet (used only when the ceiling is below 3000 feet).

____ L. Altocumulus standing lenticular clouds southwest through northwest.

____ M. Higher clouds visible through breaks in the overcast.

____ N. Few Cumulus (less than 1⁄10 covering the sky)

DO NOT DELAY—CRITICAL TO FLIGHT SAFETY!

November/December 1993

FAA *Aviation News*

A DOT/FAA FLIGHT STANDARDS SAFETY PUBLICATION

U.S. Department
of Transportation

**Federal Aviation
Administration**

Federico F. Peña, *Secretary of Transportation*
David R. Hinson, *FAA Administrator*
Monte R. Belger, *Acting Executive Director
for System Operations*
Anthony J. Broderick, *Associate Administrator
for Regulation and Certification*
Thomas C. Accardi, *Director,
Flight Standards Service*
Robert A. Wright, *Acting Manager,
General Aviation and Commercial Division*
Roger M. Baker, Jr., *Manager,
Accident Prevention Program Branch*
Phyllis Anne Duncan, *Editor*
Louise Oertly, *Senior Associate Editor*
Dean Chamberlain, *Associate Editor*

The FAA's Flight Standards Service, General Aviation and
Commercial Division, Accident Prevention Program
Branch, AFS–810, Washington, DC 20591, (telephone
202 267–8017, FAX 202 267–9463) publishes FAA Aviation News in the interest of flight safety. The magazine
promotes safety in the air by calling the attention of airmen to current technical, regulatory, and procedural matters affecting the safe operation of aircraft. Although
based on current FAA policy and rule interpretations, all
printed material herein is advisory or informational in
nature and should not be construed to have regulatory
effect. The FAA does not officially endorse any goods,
services, materials, or products of manufacturers that
may be mentioned. **Certain details of accidents
described herein have been altered to protect the
privacy of those involved.**
    The Office of Management and Budget has
approved the use of funds for the printing of FAA AVIA-
TION NEWS.

SUBSCRIPTION SERVICES
The Superintendent of Documents, U.S. Government
Printing Office, Washington, DC 20402–9371, sells FAA
AVIATION NEWS on subscription. Use the self-mailer
form in the center of this magazine to subscribe. Cost:
$15.00 ($18.75 foreign) for one year; $30.00 ($37.50
foreign) for two years. Prices are subject to change by
the Government Printing Office without prior notice.
    Change of Address or Subscription Problems:
**Send your label with correspondence to Sup Doc,
Attn: Chief, Mail List Branch, Mail Stop: SSOM,
Washington, DC 20402–9373. (Or call GPO Customer Service at 202 512–2303.)**
    To keep subscription prices down, the Government
Printing Office mails subscribers only one renewal
notice. You can tell how many copies are left in your
subscription by checking the number that follows "ISS-
DUE" on the top line of your mailing label. For example,
when this number is 003, it means you have three
issues left in your subscription, and GPO will send you
a renewal notice. The number 000 means you have
received your last issue. To be sure that your service
continues without interruption, please return your
renewal notice promptly.

November-December 1993

FAA *Aviation News*

Volume 32   Number 8

Features

Departments

Front Cover: *The Washington FSDO played a
key role in this external load operation, but you
won't get the details until next issue. See page 11.
Photo by David K. McDaris*

Back Cover: *When winter arrives you have
to remember a different set of flying rules,
especially in mountainous areas. See page 17.
Photo by G. S. Livack*

A New Voice, A New Policy for General Aviation

by David R. Hinson, *Administrator, FAA*

Let me say straight off how deeply honored I am that President Bill Clinton and Secretary of Transportation Federico Peña have chosen me to lead the world's foremost aviation agency. I'm still getting acquainted with the job, but I hope to meet as many aviation people—inside and outside the FAA—as I can in the next few weeks.

I think it's clear to all of us that the general aviation industry is at a critical juncture. I'm not going to write a long dissertation about what's happened over the last 10 years. You know all that because you've lived through it. We in the FAA have taken a number of steps to give you the opportunity to share that experience with us and to give us your ideas on how we can revitalize general aviation.

We all know there are no easy solutions. But I believe we have an opportunity now to bypass the gridlock, to pry open the deadlock which has stalled progress for so many years. Already there are signs of movement enough to build real momentum. The Clinton Administration is committed to the idea of reinventing government. The FAA and the aviation community—through the partnership that has been flourishing for the past several years —have already taken steps which I believe will help general aviation reinvent itself as a thriving, vital industry.

First, we now have four new standards that weren't available to the industry a year ago for certifying small airplanes—a step which should greatly stimulate product innovation.

Second, this past June the FAA approved the supplemental use of the Global Positioning System (GPS) for all phases of flight, including non-precision approaches at 2,500 U.S. airports. It's been estimated that the move to GPS technology may reduce the cost of on-board avionics in general aviation aircraft by as much as 75%.

And in October 1992, the Flight Standards Service issued the first ever General Aviation Action Plan (GAAP). This isn't just an FAA plan. It was developed jointly with a coalition of eight trade and industry associations that represent general aviation's interests. The plan addresses five broad concerns of the general aviation community: Safety and Certification Services, Product Innovation and Competitiveness, System Access and Capacity, and Cost.

I wholeheartedly support each of these initiatives and the work which has already been done by the FAA and the coalition. But it's only a beginning. If we are to halt the forces that are steadily eroding the economic viability of general aviation, we must take even stronger measures.

All of us are aware of the close link between a strong general aviation industry and the economy. We recognize it as a source of jobs for over half a million people and a mainstay of the U.S. export trade. Like our highways, bridges, and tunnels, general aviation is a national resource. If we let it die, an essential part of our transportation infrastructure will die with it. It's up to all of us to see that this doesn't happen.

At a recent meeting of FAA and general aviation industry representatives in Kansas City, I released a General Aviation Policy Statement adopting the GAAP's five-point program as goals for the *entire* agency. Underlying that Policy Statement is our bedrock concern for safety.

During my Senate confirmation hearings, fully half the questions directed to me concerned general aviation safety and prosperity. I assured the Senators, as I now assure everyone who reads this, that general aviation will be a major focus of my tenure with the FAA. This new policy is the initial down payment on my promise. You will find a copy of that policy printed on the inside back cover of this, the FAA's safety publication for airmen. I hope you read it and take it as a contract between the FAA and the general aviation industry for better things to come. I hope also that you'll reproduce it and post it in your FBO's, your airport lounges, anywhere general aviation airmen can see it and take heart.

I am looking forward to the months and years to come and to the ideas which will help shape our agenda. ∎

FAA Administrator David R. Hinson

Rebuilding General Aviation

by Phyllis Anne Duncan

"If you build it, he will come."

A fictional character named Ray Kinsella heard those words in his sleep and, to the derision of his neighbors and bankers, decided to level part of a money-crop cornfield to build a baseball field. When he finished it, legendary Shoeless Joe Jackson of Black Sox infamy and a host of other problems for Kinsella arrived, threatening him with the loss of his farm. But at the end of the movie, "Field of Dreams," hundreds of cars are seen on their way to a new tourist attraction in Iowa, and Kinsella was vindicated.

James "Jim" Haight, FAA Central Region Administrator, is not Kevin Costner and far more down to earth than a Hollywood fantasy. Whether or not he heard a nocturnal voice is uncertain, but what was clear to him was the declining state of general aviation—the same thing obvious to everyone in the industry. Haight decided that action not words was needed. So, perhaps his inner voice said something like,

> "If you propose a national meeting of FAA and general aviation industry representatives held away from the politically charged atmosphere of Washington, DC where everyone can participate in an open dialogue and come up with meaningful action items for general aviation, they will come."

He did. They did. Twice.

Upon his selection as the Regional Administrator a year and half ago, Haight wanted to reach out to the aviation community in the Central Region, which consists of the states of Nebraska, Iowa, Kansas, and Missouri and which also headquarters FAA's Small Aircraft Certification Directorate. (He explained his reasoning for meeting with aviation interests in an interview conducted during the second general aviation conference held this past September. That interview appears on pages 8 and 9 of this article.)

Basically, what started out as a meeting with aircraft manufacturers in the region became a meeting with the general aviation industry to find out what could be done to save what some have termed a dying industry.

The doomsayers have certain statistics on their side: New pilot starts are down, certificate upgrades are down, hardly any—you might as well say no—new entry level training aircraft are being built; airports are being bought by developers and covered with houses; FBO's are going out of business. The only bright spot is the fact that exports of turbojets used for corporate or business flight continue to be high. However, an industry which, slightly more than a decade ago, churned out tens of thousands of new aircraft a year last year built just under a thousand.

While this downturn occurred simultaneously with a general downturn in the overall economy, it struck close to so many, and it certainly appeared as if general aviation were headed for the same place in history occupied by the denizens of Jurassic Park and the carrier pigeon.

Consequently, at the request of local industry representatives, Jim Haight convened not just a meeting where aircraft manufacturers would be preached to by their new FAA Regional Administrator, but rather a forum where the industry and FAA could discuss the state of general aviation and what could be done to help it. The meeting was held May 25, 1993.

Identifying the Problems

The attendees' discussion resulted in a "grocery list" of concerns and issues that required change before general aviation could improve. Those issues were:

- Increase production of affordable small airplanes.
- Promote liability reform to reduce costs for new aircraft and components.
- Reduce the burden of regulations (state and federal).
- Increase the number of general aviation airports.
- Reduce the cost of parts.
- Improve the accessibility of replacement parts.

- Increase the transfer of technology to general aviation airplanes.
- Increase the capital necessary to rebuild general aviation.
- Increase the FAA's desire to foster and promote general aviation.
- Improve the coordination between state aviation departments.
- Further refine the term "general aviation" into segments that better represent the different constituencies.
- Foster change in the "way FAA does business."
- Improve the level of trust between the FAA and industry.
- Reduce costs for the existing general aviation pilot/owner.
- Promote self-signing medical certification for private pilots.
- Promote the global perspective of general aviation.
- Reduce the tax burden on general aviation owners.
- Reduce the amount of airspace from which general aviation is restricted.

It was immediately clear to the May attendees that a follow-on meeting was necessary and that some fairly high-level decision-makers from FAA needed to attend to hear recommendation on the issues this conference had identified. A tentative date was set for Fall 1993, but everyone had to go back and do some homework, for this follow-on meeting could not be more talk on defining the problem. Everyone knew what the problem was and that both industry and FAA had to work together to solve it.

By now, what had started as a regional listening session in Kansas City had attracted a great deal of attention within the FAA and among the grassroots of general aviation.

In the industry, the idea received some Kinsella-like scorn:

"Not another committee meeting on general aviation."

"Don't we have enough committees?"

"Right, and you know what a camel is?"

"A horse designed by a committee!"

"Image what general aviation redesigned by a committee will look like."

Joe Del Balzo (left) and Rick Weiss (center) of FAA, with Dave Higdon (right) of Witchita Eagle during a break at the conference.

"I'd rather not."

"But, if the FAA is there, at least we get a chance to talk to them, to let them know what's really happening out here."

In the FAA, the sentiments were somewhat similar:

"Why do we need another meeting about general aviation?"

"Right, we already have the General Aviation Action Plan."

"It's been in place for nearly a year, and the industry helped develop it."

"Exactly. What more do they want?"

"They want the FAA to just go away and let them regulate themselves. Hah!"

"Well, let's think about this. Maybe there are some areas where that's feasible. The least we can do is sit down with them and talk about it, maybe enhance the scope of the GAAP."

The General Aviation Action Plan (GAAP)

The FAA's Flight Standards Service, under the direction of Thomas C. Accardi, the Service Director, has been in the process of strategic planning for the past few years. Accardi recognized that in a government of dwindling and unrenewable resources, government agencies had to learn how to plan ahead carefully and strategically. In late 1991, Flight Standards published its first Strategic Management Plan for the years 1992–1997. With its mission statement, "To provide the public with accident-free aircraft operations through the highest standards in the world," as a working philosophy, the plan set forth eight specific goals:

PEOPLE

Goal 1 Build an organizational culture which promotes both empowerment and accountability.

Goal 2 Assure a well-trained, skilled, and qualified workforce.

Goal 3 Provide quality facilities and resources to perform our job.

SAFETY

Goal 4 Develop and maintain current regulations and policies.

Goal 5 Develop an effective and efficient global surveillance and certification safety system.

Goal 6 Achieve compliance through partnership.

QUALITY SERVICE AND PRODUCTIVITY

Goal 7 Improve the quality of service by anticipating the customer needs and responding in the public interest.

Goal 8 Create and implement a flexible, dynamic, visible, and responsive management philosophy to support the ever-changing environment.

Some of the terminology and philosophy outlined in the publication were unheard of for a government agency. Flight Standards was now in the business of supplying "quality services" to its "customers." We were to respond in the "public interest." We were to form "partnerships" and work toward "voluntary compliance" and look for "alternatives to enforcement." It sounded almost too good to be true, and if the Strategic Management Plan had remained simply a philosophical document, it would have been just another publication from a government agency—released with accompanying fanfare then forgotten.

However, the plan spelled out specific objectives for each goal, objectives which all of Flight Standards were committed to over the next five years. Each of the headquarters Flight Standards policy divisions (Air Transport, Aircraft Maintenance, Technical Programs, Field Programs, Regulatory Support, and the General Aviation and Commercial Divisions) had to come up with annual operating plans which reflected the division's objectives toward achieving these goals.

In early 1992 the then Manager of the General Aviation and Commercial Division, which sets all the policy and divines the regulations for general aviation airmen and operations, W. Michael Sacrey and his Assistant Division Manager, Robert A. Wright, wanted not only an operating plan for the division but a blueprint for rebuilding and revitalizing general aviation. What was needed was some sort of action plan—not rhetoric, not typical Washingtonian, politically motivated oratory.

Sacrey tasked Wright to devise the plan, but Wright decided that in order for this plan to be a success among the people it should help, he could not write it in an FAA vacuum. Industry had to participate. He came up some general goals and a skeleton of an outline and then contacted representatives from all aspects of the general aviation industry, a who's who, so to speak—AOPA, EAA, NBAA, GAMA, SAMA, HAI, NAFI, and so on. They helped him flesh out the plan and give it life.

In October 1992, Flight Standards published the General Aviation Action Plan and touted it as "an agenda for the 90's." The Plan indicated general aviation's importance to not only the nation's transportation system but to its economy as well: General aviation supports 100% of the nation's 17,500 civil airports while scheduled air carriers provide services to only 700 airports—

roughly 4%; general aviation contributes more than $38,000,000,000 (that's nine zero's or *billion*) and more than half a million jobs to the economy. Former FAA Administrator James Busey stated that, "even if general aviation did only one thing—provide basic training for future pilots—it would be essential."

The plan also explained why the FAA had a vested interest not only in its safety role, as defined by the Federal Aviation Act of 1958, but also in its "fostering and promoting" role (also outlined in the Act). The two roles are not mutually exclusive, and the GAAP is committed to the accomplishment of its objectives through "education, training, and partnership with the general aviation community with less emphasis on rulemaking."

The five GAAP goals are:

Goal 1 SAFETY: Protect our Recent Gains and Aim for a New Threshold

Goal 2 CERTIFICATION SERVICES: Provide the General Aviation Community with Cost-Effective Certification Services

Goal 3 PRODUCT INNOVATION AND COMPETITIVENESS: Ensure the Technological Advancement of General Aviation

Goal 4 SYSTEM ACCESS AND CAPACITY: Maximize General Aviation's Ability to Operate in the National Airspace System

Goal 5 AFFORDABILITY: Promote Economical and Efficient General Aviation Operations, Expand Participation, and Stimulate Industry Growth

Again, these goals—in support of Flight Standards goals—list specific objectives, distinctive actions the General Aviation and Commercial Division can take to improve the lot of general aviation. However, since this was a document forged in partnership, it also needed partnership to achieve these goals. The general aviation organizations, which had helped Bob Wright in defining the General Aviation Action Plan, decided that in order for the Plan to succeed, it needed support not only in the FAA but in the industry and that

both had to work together to achieve the goals. In November of 1992, AOPA, EAA, GAMA, HAI, NATA, NASAO, NBAA, and SAMA formed the General Aviation Action Plan Coalition, an organization dedicated to working with the FAA as equal partners to "support, nurture, enhance, and promote general aviation."

The Coalition identified the 1993 GAAP objectives it could help with and formed four working groups to address the areas of accident prevention, flight training, maintenance, and new technology. By spring of 1993, the working groups—composed of industry people with FAA in an advisory role only—were well into the work of designing programs and making changes. What, then, was going on in Kansas City? What was going to happen when the new Administration finally got around to appointing a new FAA Administrator? What if he or she couldn't care less about general aviation?

A New Administrator

While all the GAAP Coalition working groups were meeting and while the Kansas City conference planning was going on, Congress finally confirmed President Clinton's choice to be the new FAA Administrator. David R. Hinson is well-known in the aviation industry as the founder of Midway Airlines, and his nomination received universal acclaim from the airline and general aviation industry. Here was a civilian aviation enthusiast, former airline captain, and general aviation aircraft owner (a Beech *Baron*) who had been selected to head the FAA. Hopefully he would be not only receptive to the general aviation community, but he was also representing an administration which had committed itself to improve the way government does business.

Bob Wright, now the Acting Division Manager for the General Aviation and Commercial Division, lost no time with the new Administrator. At general aviation's foremost showcase, the annual EAA convention at Oshkosh, WI, Wright "got to" the Administrator first, presented him with a copy of the

GAAP, and sat down over lunch to discuss it with him.

Administrator Hinson agreed that general aviation was important to the nation not just from a historical perspective but as a source of potential growth in technology and exports. He agreed with Wright that the GAAP had to be an FAA-wide agenda, not just for Flight Standards, but what could he, as Administrator, do? Wright responded, "Issue a policy statement."

Policy statements are traditional throughout the government at the beginning of new administrations. Agency and department heads issue policy statements in flowery language which declare their utmost devotion to certain issues; e.g., support of EEO policies and directives, prevention of sexual harassment. FAA has seen its share, but there had never been one issued on such a direct issue. This required not only some thought but the right springboard as well.

Kansas City—Here We Come!

In the interval between the Central Region's May meeting and the proposed September conference, FAA's Central Region polled the attendees and other aviation concerns and asked them to prioritize the issues which had emerged from the original meeting. From that prioritization, Haight's staff grouped the issues under the general headings of:

• Airmen Certification
• FAA Business Practices and Services
• Aircraft Certification
• Operations Regulations
• General Aviation Promotional Policies/Activities
• Maintenance Standardization
• Non-Regulatory Ways to Promote and Improve the Safety of General Aviation
• Increasing the Level of Knowledge among FAA Inspectors and Other Employees
• Ways the FAA Can Foster and Promote General Aviation
• Airspace/Airport Access

FAA Central Region Public Affairs

FAA Central Region Administrator James Haight addressing the September meeting of FAA and general aviation industry representives.

• Promoting Product Innovation and Integration of Technology for General Aviation
• Increasing Standardization of FAA Service Delivery to General Aviation
• Non-Regulatory Ways to Increase the Affordability of General Aviation Products and Services
• Parts Certification
• Marketing the Social/Economic Value of General Aviation

Obviously, this would an untenable agenda for a large group, and Haight was beginning to see that it was going to be a large group, judging from the response to the announcements being sent out. Again, the theme of "reinventing government" provided a solution. Each of these topic areas would have a work group to address it, and attendees could sign up for the work group they desired. The meeting would consist of a short, general session, then the attendees would divide up into their work groups and, well, get to work defining the specific problem and resolving it. The work groups would consist of industry attendees and FAA subject matter experts. Neither the industry nor the FAA would chair any group; rather, independent facilitators would control the flow of discussion and assure that personal or organizational agendas did not take over.

And all this would be done in a day and a half.

Anyone who has ever participated in any type of committee work knows that group dynamics have to go through certain stages before the

group can effectively function. That takes time, and some groups never become effective for various reasons. Was Haight expecting too much from such a diverse group of people?

Motivation can speed up the formation of a cohesive group, and this was a very motivated bunch of people whose, in Haight's words, "mutual love of aviation. . . transcends our agendas."

A Message from the Administrator

At the opening session on Wednesday, September 8, there were some maudlin references to general aviation as a "troubled child we all love" and "a losing team we all root for." But Jim Haight went straight to the real importance of the gathering—that the FAA and industry were in this together. Meetings like this, he said, "increase the FAA's desire to foster and promote aviation. But we all have to be part of the cure." Many other opening session speakers from the FAA and industry followed, each seeking to be optimistic about the outcome of the meeting and inspirational to those who were actually going to do the work.

It apparently worked. Over 200 aviation enthusiasts began to feel they held the future of general aviation in their hands. Then, FAA Administrator Hinson spoke to them via videotape.

"I think it's clear to all of us that general aviation is at a critical juncture," he said. "You don't need a speech from me about what's happened over the past 10 years. You know that, because you've been through it. We've invited you here to share that experience with us and to give us your ideas on how we can help revitalize this great industry. We know there are no easy solutions. But this conference gives us a chance to take a new look at the way we attack these problems."

Hinson cited some new ways of FAA business: the new aircraft certification rules, the FAA approval of the supplemental use of GPS (". . . the move to GPS may reduce the cost of your on-board avionics by as much as 75%.), and the GAAP. He cited the link between a strong general aviation industry and the economy—half a million jobs and a mainstay of our export trade. "Like our highways, bridges, and tunnels, general aviation is a national resource. I feel so strongly about this issue that today I am releasing a general aviation policy statement adopting the Action Plan's five-point program as goals for the entire FAA."

(Signed on September 8, 1993, the General Aviation Policy Statement was published on page 1 of the October 1993 issue of *FAA Aviation News* and on the inside back cover of this issue. This issue's editorial is based on Administrator Hinson's videotaped message.)

Administrator Hinson concluded by saying, "I'm looking forward to this conference for the ideas which will help shape our agenda in the decisive months ahead. It's very important to us."

The pep rally was over; it was time to get to work.

The Process and the Results

Also at that initial, general assembly, there was a great deal of consternation about this "work group thing." Sitting around jawing wasn't going to get things done—let's just get to work. John Colomy, Manager of the Standards Office of the Small Aircraft Directorate, kept urging everyone to "trust the process" and to ask for help when needed. "If you want something different for general aviation," he said, "you've got to try something new." Furthermore, if this process didn't work, they would try another.

By the end of the first half-day, jackets and high heels came off, and ties and hair pins were loosened. By the next day, everyone was in casual working attire, and the avenues of communication had become boulevards. At after-hours "conferences" in the hotel lounge, everyone voiced pleasure at the fact that general aviation and FAA could sit down and talk with each other as if, well, as if they were hangar flying. They discovered mutual experiences in Vietnam, with operators, flying air taxis, and so on, and this seemed to convince everyone they were working for the same thing.

It was, in the vernacular of today, awesome.

But not as awesome as the results. The day and a half of talking, discussing, and even wrangling resulted in meaningful ideas, definitely food for thought for the FAA. FAA senior management in the form of Acting Deputy Administrator Joseph Del Balzo and Deputy Associate Administrator for Regulation and Certification Daniel C. Beaudette listened intently to the following recommendations for a new way for FAA to do business:

Airman Certification:

- Analyze the safety record of training flights and low-time pilots and determine if the FAA needs to reassess the training process.
- Implement more comprehensive testing at flight instructor refresher training courses.
- Develop a training manual for flight instructors and emphasize the ability to teach.

FAA Business Practices and Services

- Institute a 90-day moratorium on ramp checks.
- Develop an immunity program for airmen who turn themselves in or voluntarily request a compliance check.
- Develop a "code of conduct" towards the regulated.
- Enhance the customer service philosophy.
- Issue warning "tickets" in lieu of enforcement action for non-injury/non-criminal infractions.
- Increase the delegation of compliance functions.

Aircraft Certification

- Return management to the field for two weeks out of every year.
- Expose management to general aviation as users.
- Participate in cross-training with the industry.

Operations Regulations

- Update and simplify mailing lists and NPRM format and distribute NPRM's to the public for comments in a timely manner.
- Thoroughly automate the process so that NPRM's go to the part of the

industry best qualified to comment; e.g., FAR Part 135 NPRM's to FAR Part 135 operators.

Lack of Standardization Among Maintenance Inspectors

- Place the development of maintenance inspectors handbook back into the policy division in FAA headquarters.
- Develop a procedure for industry involvement in policy development.
- Establish a communication system for interpretation resolution in a industry accessible database.
- Define a consistent policy for STC approval versus field approval.
- Establish a database that contains all STC's.

Increasing the Level of Knowledge Among FAA Inspectors and Employees

- Continue and expand the Quality Measurement Implement Plan [an ongoing customer service survey that has been tested in three regions and which will eventually extend to all FAA regions].
- Establish an outreach program to provide policy implementation guidance for the lowest level.
- Encourage field inspectors to get more involved with local programs—the three I's concept: Involvement Increases Interest.
- Make time for field inspectors to do general aviation duties.
- Standardize handbook guidance.
- Change FSDO's back to GADO's to emphasize general aviation.

Ways the FAA Can Foster and Promote General Aviation

- Obtain and continue funding for the Accident Prevention Program.
- Consolidate various entities within the FAA into one general aviation office.

Access to Properly Located Public-Use Landing Areas

- Accelerate the development of GPS approaches at general aviation landing areas.
- Revise and update the advisory circular for the State Airport System Plan.

John Colomy, Manager of the Standards Office of the Small Airplane Directorate.

Promoting Product Innovation and Integration of Technology for General Aviation

- Encourage greater FAA acceptance of new technology.
- Improve the certification process by eliminating artificial constraints, expanding delegated certification authority, and allowing more flexible means of compliance.
- Complete plans for transition to advanced systems so that industry can plan its investments accordingly.
- Provide uplink graphical weather information.
- Organize the FAR by category of aircraft.

Non-Regulatory Ways to Promote and Improve the Safety of General Aviation.

- Increase the emphasis on the Accident Prevention Program by assuring the Accident Prevention Program Manager has the human resource support and fiscal resources to make the program proactive; rename the program to place emphasis on safety education and promotion.
- Improve the selection criteria for Accident Prevention Program Managers and place a priority on communication and sales ability as well as management of volunteers.
- Improve the Accident Prevention Counselor Program by developing improved criteria for selection, by providing quality control and management by the Accident Prevention Program Manager, and by conducting initial/recurrent counselor training.
- Expand the outreach of the Accident Prevention Program to all aspects of general aviation.

- Recognize industry contributions on joint safety programs.

Maintenance

- Establish an industry/FAA task force to revise FAR Part 43, Appendix 3 to expand the amount of preventive maintenance a pilot/owner can do.
- Consider extending aircraft inspection intervals from annual to biennial and from 100 hours to 200 hours.
- Simplify the replacement parts certification process.

Increasing the Standardization of FAA Service Delivery to General Aviation

- Establish a process for timely resolution of differences in interpretations and establish a follow-up procedure to all FAA offices to prevent recurrence.
- Educate general aviation on FAA processes.
- Establish an Associate Administrator for General Aviation or designate a Regional General Aviation Administrator.

Non-Regulatory Ways to Increase the Affordability of General Aviation Products and Services

- Participate aggressively in aircraft litigation to defend the federal preemption position.
- Fund a study to investigate the merits of mandatory liability insurance for all FAA airman certificate holders.
- Review the certification process as a key cost driver in the affordability of general aviation products and services.
- Help promote general aviation through public awareness programs and marketing.
- Explore new ways to encourage pilot starts.
- Work with the Department of Commerce to promote international sales.

Parts Certification

- Review PMA design approval process and determine appropriate action.
- Speed up the design approval process.
- Expand the use of DER's for design approvals.

The Aftermath

Not bad for a day and a half's work.

Deputy Associate Administrator Beaudette's personal favorite was the 90-day moratorium on ramp checks. "Maybe," he said, "it should be 120 days—120 days we could devote to the promotion of general aviation."

Deputy Administrator Del Balzo added, "If we can find a way to do only some of the things suggested, we can make a difference in general aviation." He continued, "We owe you a response, a short term response by November 1 and something more substantive by early 1994."

To paraphrase what they used to say in the serials, "Join us next month to find out just what the FAA's commitment was."

Some of the recommendations from the Kansas City General Aviation Conference have already been incorporated into the annual management plans for all of Flight Standards and for the General Aviation and Commercial Division. More of the recommendations will be incorporated into an upcoming revision of the GAAP. Consequently, we—FAA and general aviation—can look forward to interesting times over the next four years.

Jim Haight closed the conference by stating, "We asked for honesty, and we got it. We wanted to see if we could form a partnership to save something we all love, and we did."

Did we save general aviation? The attendees' consensus was that at least the resuscitation had begun but that the rehabilitation could be long and involved, requiring therapy for both the industry and the FAA. But it's a start.

The terms "reinventing government" and "changing the way we do business" have been bandied so much lately that they are already near-clichés. This conference was a different way for FAA to get things done, but what is key here is that the voice of the people not only must be heard; it must be heeded.

Said Jim Haight, "Aviation symbolizes humanity's continual striving to reach beyond our grasp. We can't let the dream die." ■

REBUILDING GENERAL AVIATION

An Interview with Central Region Administrator James Haight

The General Aviation Conference was not the only thing going on in the Central Region the first week of September—after all, a Regional Administrator has to manage the entire region. However, it became quickly apparent that this conference was close to the heart of James Haight, a former U.S. Air Force pilot who joined the FAA as an aviation safety inspector and moved up the "ranks" to his current position. He was present physically and devoted many hours of time and energy to it. Why? The issue was important to him, service to his customers was important to him, and both of which are evident from the talk—too impassioned to be called an interview—I had with him on the second day of this ground-breaking meeting.

Duncan: What happened to "stir this up?" Was there a specific event?

Haight: When I came to the Central Region a year and a half ago, I knew that the FAA was turning toward a customer focus. The customers here are primarily small airplane manufacturers.

Duncan: You wanted to reach out to them?

Haight: It was important for me as the new Regional Administrator to do just that. I decided to use something that had been successful in other regions—specifically by [Acting Deputy Administrator] Joe Del Balzo when he was Eastern Region Administrator—the listening session.

Duncan: Listening sessions are very broad in scope. How did a listening session become a conference on the future of general aviation.

Haight: As we were setting up the listening session for manufacturers, we began to get feedback from within the

FAA and from the general aviation community here that perhaps we needed to broaden the horizon somewhat and address *general aviation.* Basically, we wanted to be responsive to the needs of the customers in the Central Region, and when I proposed this to the various division managers in Central Region, Ben Tollison, the Flight Standards Division Manager, volunteered to take the ball and run with it. All the concerns in the region worked to put together the listening session, but Flight Standards was the focal point.

Duncan: Why did you feel the issue of general aviation revitalization was so important?

Haight: General aviation benefits everyone—they just don't know it yet!

Duncan: What do you feel is the state of general aviation?

Haight: Actually, there is some disagreement about the state of general aviation. From the input we were getting when we set up the first meeting in May [1993], we learned that some people think it's dead, some people didn't want FAA involved because we could only make it worse—leave it alone, in other words—some people were crying for help, ours included. Consequently, we wanted last May's meeting to be something different.

Duncan: What do you mean 'different?'

Haight: We wanted speakers from the FAA and from industry who would challenge some of the complaints and the complainers and who would stimulate some thought about general aviation's condition and what we could do about it. That certainly happened.

Duncan: Give an example.

Haight: Well, I concluded May's meeting by asking everyone a rather direct question: 'Is general aviation worth saving?'

Duncan: That's pretty direct! What was the answer?

Haight: The answer was clearly, yes, but action rather than words was needed.

Duncan: What do you mean 'action rather than words?'

Haight: The FAA already had the General Aviation Action Plan as a policy document, but what the FAA needed was a more specific focus on its general aviation customers.

Duncan: In other words, the words look good on paper, but what are we going to do about it?

Haight: Exactly.

Duncan: And what came out of the May meeting that falls under 'action?'

Haight: We identified 15–20 general aviation issues that needed to be addressed—product liability, new technology, costs, even how the FAA does business.

Duncan: Let me guess, one meeting was not enough?

Haight: We immediately realized we needed another meeting to flesh out some of these ideas we had. Our original intent was for one meeting, the results of which we would turn over to industry for action, but the issues we identified were of a scope that meant we had to meet again. And here we are.

Duncan: I'll be the Devil's Advocate here. What would you say to people inside and outside the FAA—or the industry for that matter—who might say that commercial air travel is where it is and that general aviation should be allowed to die a quiet, dignified death?

Haight: I disagree that commercial air travel is 'where it is.' In the FAA and in the media that is certainly where the focus is. General aviation is not in the media focus until there's an accident, but that's only part of its story. General aviation doesn't have its story told.

Duncan: What part of it doesn't get told?

Haight: That everyone benefits socially and economically from general aviation. Just as importantly, general aviation has not told its own story. We need to do that.

Duncan: Does the industry agree with that?

Haight: This need to get the word out on general aviation became apparent to everyone at the May meeting, and people are beginning to come around to the concept of spreading the word about general aviation to the public—not just preaching to the choir.

Duncan: Why was it so important to include industry in this endeavor?

Haight: The customer focus, of course, but also there are some things that are beyond the scope of the FAA, beyond what is appropriate for an agency in the executive branch of government to do.

Duncan: Such as?

Haight: Such as tax relief, product liability reform. Lobbying for these things is where industry is its most powerful. This is where we need their help.

Duncan: In setting up both of these general aviation meetings, did you encounter skepticism from the industry?

Haight: The people from industry who were in on planning the May meeting were working with us, but there was skepticism in the room. But, by their presence and their response to the evolution of this process, they showed they wanted the opportunity to try. That was what mattered.

Duncan: Is that what has brought them here in great numbers?

Haight: Interestingly enough, I think what was most attractive to them was the fact that the meeting, the inviting of national representatives from industry, was not going to be held in Washington, DC. That was a real draw, an indicator that, at last, FAA in the field was becoming involved in customer service.

Duncan: The "inside the beltway" politics certainly are refreshingly missing. What are your feelings about this second meeting?

Haight: It's what I hoped it would be and better than I anticipated, if that makes sense.

Duncan: Try to explain it a little.

Haight: For example, the level of enthusiasm among the participants is better than I hoped, but it's exactly what I hoped for. The people here really wanted to work, and they rolled up their sleeves and did just that—enthusiastically.

Duncan: What happens next?

Haight: There will probably be another follow-on, judging from the action items that are coming out of the working groups.

Duncan: In your opening remarks you indicated that you wanted "action not plans for another meeting."

Haight: Right, but we are going to get so many good recommendations, specific recommendations that we—FAA and industry—have to analyze them before presenting them to FAA senior management.

Duncan: Are you optimistic about any of the recommendations being accepted?

Haight: I am convinced that steps will be taken, positive steps, but they have to evolve. There is one definite possibility, and that is here in the Central Region we have supplied a model to be shared with the rest of the regions. That is, it is time now to focus on specific issues. Meetings like this may be the mechanism. What might follow on is that the specific recommendations are not taken up at one big meeting but at several smaller ones across the country.

Duncan: Was that the intent from the beginning?

Haight: Absolutely. Our intent was not to spotlight the Central Region but rather to try to put the resources and thought toward an agency-wide model. If it worked we wanted to hand it off to other regions to use; if it didn't we would take the hits.

Duncan: It is quite a monumental effort and is certainly a success thanks to a great many Central Region employees.

Haight: I need to give credit to a wide variety of people in the Central Region, but if I try to list them I'll invariably leave someone out. Central Region employees from all the disciplines worked very hard to make both these meetings a reality. It was not a one-person or one-organization show. Central Region personnel rallied around the concept with enthusiasm and gave so much of themselves. They should get the credit they so rightly deserve.

Duncan: They just did.

FAA Central Region Public Affairs

FAA Aviation News Editor Phyllis A. Duncan *interviewing FAA Central Region Administrator James Haight at the September General Aviation Conference.*

Pilot Decision Making

by Tom Hamilton

Errers

This is Part Five of a seven-part series that first appeared in Balloon Life *magazine in 1989 and was originally written for balloon pilots. We have left the lighter-than-air examples in because the overlying issue of pilot decision making affects all pilots.* —*Editor*

Over the last four issues our continuing series on Pilot Decision Making has examined the elements of risk, crew management, stress, hazardous attitudes, accident statistics, and making decisions. Utilizing sound judgement to make decisions leads to safer flight habits and fewer mishaps. In our earlier discussions it was pointed out that the National Transportation Safety Board attributes most accidents to pilot error.

Pilot error, as mentioned before, is an over simplification. This article is about why people make mistakes. It is about all of us, for we all make errers.

Errors are sometimes deadly. The NTSB attributes more than two-thirds of all fatal aircraft accidents to pilot error. On the average, one private pilot per day executes a surprise belly landing (fixed wing) simply because the pilot forgot to lower the wheels.

What causes someone who is trained to error? To be human, you have to possess the capability of mak-ing random deviations. When those deviations are beneficial, we call it genius. When they are not beneficial, we call it error. The human mind is called upon to perform such a voluminous array of tasks that the opportunities for error become great. Ford Motor Company once estimated that its assembly personnel face three billion opportunities for error every day.

The process of error is better understood when the human mind is viewed as a complex information-processing system: a supercomputer. The mind accomplishes a task by means of plugging into a series of subconscious components, much like a computer program utilizes a series of subprograms. One psychologist calls these schemas.

For example, when you go to fly in a balloon race, you rarely think to yourself, "Now I am going to pull the balloon out of the truck, then lay it out, attach the cables, put the baggie in the basket, start the fan. . ." Instead, you think in a broader agenda: "Now I am going to inflate the balloon." Pulling the balloon out of the truck is a subprogram, or schema, and since it is a common task, your brain plugs into it automatically. That schema in turn is composed of a number of more detailed subprograms that coordinate the actions of your hands and feet and receive input from your eyes and ears.

Suppose you face a difficult task of a high wind inflation during competition. You prepare the aerostat for inflation without a second thought, turn on the fan, and light the burner. Musing upon the situation that faces you during the flight, you take off and suddenly realize that you forgot to bring along the baggie to drop on the target. What happened? You activated the schema that dealt with the high wind inflation and it, at least momentarily, dominated your normal "take the baggie along" schema. Since that schema became temporarily inoperative, it threw your larger "Now I am going to inflate the balloon" schema out of whack.

We tend to use previous experiences as a guide as much as possible. We process new information only enough to figure out where it fits into the structure of previous knowledge. This is done, in part, by forming a description of the information, a description that characterizes things at as high a level of abstraction as possible, because that form of abstraction takes less mental effort.

This mental laziness is generally beneficial because it saves our resources for more important tasks. But it also fosters a tendency to see what we expect to see instead of being receptive to reality. When, early last January, you wrote 1992 on a check, you erred because you plugged into your familiar "write the year of 1992" schema.

Continued on page 16

Dean Chamberlain

Flight Standards Service
Small Service—Big Job

by Dean Chamberlain, *Associate Editor*

A Typical Day of An Inspector
Part Two

This is the second of a two-part series on the FAA's Flight Standards Service. For those who did not see Part One in our October issue, the series is designed to help everyone work more effectively with the Flight Standards Service, its local Flight Standards District Offices (FSDO), its aviation safety inspectors (ASI), and its support staff nationwide. Part One introduced the series by providing an organizational overview of Flight Standards and a typical FSDO. Our representative FSDO is the Washington FSDO located at Dulles International Airport in northern Virginia near Washington, DC.

In this part, we will take a more in-depth view of a "day" in the life of an inspector, albeit a "very long" day based upon some select inspector activities at the Washington FSDO.

A Flight Standards District Office (FSDO) determines the resources it dedicates to specific projects in large part by the needs of the aviation community it serves. Although the Washington FSDO is a representative FSDO, some of the activities discussed in this article may or may not be done at all FSDO's. For example, some FSDO's work more

with air carriers, while others work with agricultural operators or repair stations as a primary activity.

All FAA aviation safety inspectors (operations, airworthiness, and avionics) share certain duties in addition to their primary duty of ensuring flight safety within their respective areas of expertise. For example, FAA inspectors investigate accidents or incidents as well as public complaints involving inappropriate aircraft operations or inadequate maintenance practices.

Operations Inspector

For those new to aviation, operations (ops) inspectors work primarily with pilots and aircraft operators to ensure their compliance with appropriate Federal Aviation Regulations (FAR) and FAA operating procedures such as FAR Parts 91, 121, 133, 135, 137, and 141. Ops inspectors, like all other inspectors, are classified into one of two categories: air carrier related operations or general aviation operations which include corporate, small air carriers, agricultural, and external load operators among others.

Both types of ops inspectors share certain duties. Their responsibilities differ only in the unique requirements of the particular section or sections of the FAR they work with. For example, although there are certain common rules between FAR Part 121 and FAR Part 135 operations there are enough differences between the two FAR parts

to make them separate inspector job tasks. All ops inspectors perform required pilot and air crew flight check rides for their respective operators. However general aviation inspectors also conduct various initial airman certification flights including the important initial flight instructor applicant check ride.

Remedial Training

Ops and airworthiness inspectors also work with pilots and maintenance technicians in the FAA's Remedial Training Program. Remedial Training is a program for airmen who have been involved in certain, inadvertent acts of non-compliance with the FAR. For those airmen who qualify for Remedial Training, an inspector can recommend that they be offered the option of remedial training as the best way to ensure their future voluntary compliance with the FAR. For example, if a pilot is offered the program and accepts Remedial Training, an ops inspector works with the pilot and a flight instructor to design a training program that will increase the pilot's knowledge and/or skill level to a point sufficient to prevent a similar act of non-compliance in the future. The flight instructor provides the training at the pilot's expense and then certifies to the FAA that the training has been completed. After all conditions have been met, the ops inspector notifies the pilot that the FAA considers the matter

closed. Two years after satisfactory completion of the Remedial Training course of study, the FAA expunges the incident from the pilot's FAA records. For airworthiness issues, an airworthiness inspector would follow the same procedure to design a training program for the maintenance technician involved. For additional information about the program, you can contact your local FSDO.

Meeting an Inspector

Today, it is possible for a pilot to fly a lifetime and never meet an FAA safety inspector. A pilot can be trained, certificated, and add ratings through designated pilot examiners who act for the FAA aviation safety inspector. Safety inspectors assure that pilot examiners carry out their responsibilities professionally and serve the airman community efficiently.

If you do meet an inspector it is important to know that inspectors carry FAA Form 110A, which is the FAA Inspector's Identification card. The "110A" contains a photograph identifying the individual. If an inspector fails to show you his or her identification card, you should ask to see it. Although 50,000 people work for the FAA, only 2,500 are Flight Standards aviation safety inspectors.

Tip number one is for you to always check for proper identification of anyone who says he or she in an FAA aviation safety inspector. If you are still in doubt, you should ask for the "inspec-

tor's" name, and call your local FSDO to verify the person's identity.

An inspector might ask to see your airman's certificate or medical certificate, as well as appropriate required aircraft documents. Unless you have been involved in an accident or incident, an inspector meeting you on an airport ramp is probably simply conducting a routine, random spot check of airmen and aircraft to ensure that the pilots and aircraft on the ramp are properly certificated and meet current safety requirements. Random ramp checks should be viewed by both inspectors and pilots as an opportunity for safety education. They are only one of the ways the FAA and airmen can work together for voluntary compliance with the FAR.

PACE

Another way the FAA is working to ensure everyone's voluntary compliance with the FAR is through its new Pilot and Aircraft Courtesy Evaluation Program. More commonly known as PACE, the program is a joint effort by both operations and airworthiness inspectors to provide a courtesy review of a pilot's flight skills and aircraft's airworthiness. During a no-fail PACE inspection, pilots and aircraft owners make an appointment at the PACE site for the FAA to inspect their aircraft and to fly with those pilots whose aircraft have been found in compliance with all appropriate regulations. An important part of the program is the fact that no FAA enforcement action or 609 pilot

checkrides will result from any discoveries made during the voluntary PACE Program. The program is designed to identify and correct safety problems before they can cause an accident. For more information on PACE, you should read the story of how PACE originated in the FAA's Great Lakes Region on page 18 of this issue.

Information

Another benefit of getting to know your local inspectors is for the information they have access to. For example, an inspector can help you identify accident trend information for your type of activity or aircraft. Your local Accident Prevention Program Manager (APPM) is also one of the inspectors every airman should get to know. That's right; your friendly, local APPM is also an experienced aviation safety inspector. This is why your local APPM can not only provide you with information about scheduled safety seminars, but he or she can also provide you with important safety and operational information. Access to timely FAA safety information is probably one of the best reasons for everyone to get to know his or her local ASI or APPM.

NASA

Besides knowing the pertinent sections of the FAR, every airman should also know about the NASA Aviation Safety Reporting System and its reporting rules. Depending upon circumstances, filing a timely NASA safety report might protect you in case of an alleged act of non-compliance involving the FAR. If you do not know about the NASA ASRS, call your local APPM. He or she will be glad to send you a copy of the NASA reporting form which explains the program if one is available. You can also write to the Office of the NASA Aviation Safety Reporting System, P.O. Box 189, Moffett Field, CA 94035–0189 for more information.

Information and help are two important reasons for contacting the FAA, but what happens if you are involved in an alleged reportable accident or incident. (Remember only those accidents or incidents that meet the appropriate FAR or NTSB definition need be reported.) If you are involved in a reportable event and an ASI does not meet you at the scene, you will either be contacted by telephone or certified mail to arrange a meeting to discuss the event.

Customer Satisfaction

Most meetings with aviation safety inspectors should be positive, productive, and educational, but if you have any concerns about any meeting with an inspector, you should call the FSDO manager and discuss the issue. Each FSDO manager reports to a Regional Flight Standards division manager. (There are nine division managers who report to the Director of Flight Standards.)

A "Typical" Day

After having spent days working with inspectors at Washington FSDO, this writer can say with conviction, "There is no such thing as a typical inspector day!" Part of the reason is because inspectors have many responsibilities. Another reason is inspectors work with a number of different operators. As a result, inspectors may work with different people every day. One day an inspector might be scheduled to give an initial flight instructor check ride. The next time the inspector does a flight check it might be with a FAR Part 135 operator, or an airline transport pilot applicant, or with an air carrier for an en route check. Some days the inspector might have to drive miles across the district to work with one of his or her assigned operators. Other days the inspector might be working in the office. At other times the inspector might be working on one of the various programs mentioned in the article such as at a PACE site, or working with a pilot developing a Remedial Training course of study. Regardless of their daily schedule, all inspectors also have to meet all FAA annual assignments as well as meeting the needs of their

assigned operators and keeping up with all unscheduled, "walk-in" projects. The requirement to coordinate the needs of many airmen and operators makes having the ability to manage time and limited resources efficiently an important inspector asset. Another is the ability for all potential inspectors to be able to work well and effectively with all members of the aviation community and the public.

That ability is important because in the course of a "typical" day, an inspector may work with seasoned aviation professionals who know the industry, to young people just entering the profession, to someone complaining about a low flying aircraft. All of whom deserve the same attention, courtesy, and professional service regardless of their aviation experience, knowledge, or comments.

Some of the types of work an inspector may do was discussed in Part One of this article, which appeared in our October 1993 issue. One example was the Washington FSDO's involvement in approving the use of a new type of aircraft for both a regional commuter airline and a charter air carrier earlier this year. For those not familiar with the approval process, or who did not read Part One, an equipment upgrade involves more than just adding a new type of aircraft to a company's flight and maintenance schedules. A typical upgrade can involve hundreds of hours of work on the part of many FAA operations and airworthiness inspectors as they review, approve, and monitor the training and operating experience that the operator and crews need to demonstrate to the FAA before receiving FAA approval. The following example illustrates one of the unique jobs done by ASI's during one of the certifications.

Cabin Safety

Normally, when we think of inspectors, most of us think of either ops or airworthiness inspectors. But there is a small group of inspectors within the Flight Standards Service that many airmen may not think about when they think about an air carrier certification. Two FAA cabin safety specialists, one

from Washington and one from New York, were an important part of the FSDO certification team. The approval process for the FAR Part 121 charter operator required that its cabin attendants as well as its flight deck and ground crews for the new aircraft be trained and tested to FAA standards. That requirement resulted in several cabin safety tests. The tests included both ground and airborne testing. One ground test was done in California. Another test was done at Washington Dulles International Airport. FAA inspectors spent many hours on the ground and in flight working with, inspecting, and monitoring the air carrier during the certification process. In both cases, the operators and crews had to demonstrate to the FAA their ability to safely operate their respective aircraft under the conditions of their operating certificates before they could fly with paying passengers.

It was dark. It was cold. And it was wet. Melting piles of dirty snow from the Storm of '93 stood along the edge of the ramp. An aircraft taxied in the background as a group of FAA inspectors stood waiting in the passenger area of one of the FBO's at Dulles International Airport. They were waiting for the right amount of darkness. Then, with special flashlights in hand they quietly surrounded an aircraft on the ramp. Several entered the aircraft and could be seen moving about its interior. Noise from the generator connected to the aircraft added to the aircraft sounds on the ramp and to the jet engine sounds heard in the distance. A small group of interested onlookers watched from a distance. Then someone shut the door on the giant, 409-passenger-aircraft. Carefully, the truck-mounted boarding ramp used by the FAA inspectors and others going in and out of the aircraft moved back from the aircraft. Cabin attendants could then be seen moving about the darkened interior preparing the aircraft for departure. Suddenly, some of the giant aircraft's eight doors flew open. Cabin attendants could be seen standing in the doorways yelling evacuation instructions.

TEST PREPARATION

One of the best ways for a pilot applicant to prepare for any check ride with an inspector or FAA designated examiner is to buy a copy of the current FAA Practical Test Standards (PTS) for the intended test. The PTS not only outlines what knowledge and performance areas you will be tested on, they list the standards you must demonstrate. The PTS also provide a checklist of required documents, testing materials, and type of aircraft needed for your respective test. If more pilot applicants knew, used, and could meet the standards in their respective PTS for the rating or certificate sought, there would be fewer failures and more satisfied pilots, designated pilot examiners, and FAA inspectors. See page 20 for more information about PTS.

Another important training tip is the fact the PTS are also a good checklist for evaluating your instructor's teaching ability. If your instructor is not training you to meet *all* of the tasks and objectives listed in the PTS for your rating then it may be time for you to hold a serious student to instructor talk to find out why you are not being trained to meet those standards. It may be time to find a new instructor. As you prepare for your test, both the oral and flight, remember the appropriate PTS are the only standards you must meet. Gone are the days when an inspector or designated pilot examiner could broadly determine their own standards. Today, you know what you are going to be tested on and the standards you must meet before you go for the test. Now, your fate is in your own hands, and your ability to meet the PTS requirements.

Another important reference you should review before a check ride or before filling out an application are the appropriate FAR that pertain to whatever you are applying for. You need to make sure you meet all the FAR requirements such as age, flight experience, training, medical qualifications, required certificates, etc., before you schedule a meeting with your local testing center or FSDO. You can bet the inspector has a copy of the FAR and will use it to review your qualifications.

Application Forms

Checking the PTS and the FAR are just two of the ways you can save yourself time and effort during any certification process. The final check all applicants need to make may be the hardest. In talking to several inspectors about this article, they said some of the most common errors applicants make are not following directions and completing all of the required spaces. One critical question for all applicants is the question about drug or alcohol related convictions. A wrong answer or deliberate falsification could jeopardize your certificate and your aviation career. Read the question and answer it correctly.

Your final check should be for any required endorsements that an instructor or designated pilot examiner must make. Instructors and examiners have been known to make an occasional mistake in signing off an applicant's paperwork.

The important thing for everyone is to avoid any mistake that can delay your check ride, test, or application. Discovering a problem at the FSDO or designated examiner's office is a waste of everyone's time. If you are an initial flight instructor applicant, it is not a good way to start your evaluation as a potential flight instructor with the authority to sign off other applicants' paperwork if your own paperwork is incorrect!

Another paperwork tip for all pilots is to list all of your flight experience on your application form. Although you are only required to record those hours required to show currency or those required for a specific certificate or rating in a reliable record, it is a good idea to record all hours and to list those hours on your next airman application form. This builds a record of your experience with the FAA in case you ever lose your records. This FAA record could save you both flight hours and much personal aggravation if you ever have to reconstruct your flight time after losing your flight records.

Flight Tests

The final tip for check rides is for every pilot to remember that he or she is pilot in command. As discussed in FAR § 61.47, Flight tests: Status of FAA inspectors and other authorized flight examiners, an inspector or examiner is only PIC by prior arrangement or if required by safety to take control. Applicants are expected to plan for and comply with all appropriate regulations when planning their check flight as well as during the check ride. An inspector or examiner does not have the authority to ask any applicant to violate any rule or FAR. Every applicant and for that matter every pilot should always resolve the question of PIC and what role any pilot sitting in the other seat is expected to play during any flight. As PIC, you cannot expect another pilot to act or react as you might expect in a tense situation without prior coordination. On a check ride, applicants who expect the inspector or examiner to perform specific tasks during the flight must brief them before the flight and get their concurrence. The final check ride tip is, to paraphrase an old cliché, to plan your flight based upon the Practical Test Standards then fly your plan. If you do, you should have a successful check ride.

A scene from the latest Hollywood movie? No, it was just another night in the "day" of a FSDO inspector doing his or her job. This night, inspectors and cabin safety specialists were conducting a mini-evacuation test at Dulles as part of the new aircraft certification process described earlier. The inspectors, led by the air carrier's principal operations inspector and the Washington FSDO's cabin safety specialist, were testing the airline's cabin attendants training and training program by seeing if newly trained attendants on the aircraft could safely evacuate the 409-passenger jet in a specified amount of time or less using prescribed procedures. The test, designed to evaluate the cabin attendants and their training without the use of passengers, was part of the airline's certification process to operate the McDonnell-Douglas MD-11 aircraft the air carrier wanted to add to its fleet.

The late-night evacuation test was only part of the air carrier's certification process. Like other types of air crew training, the airline had to get FAA approval for its flight attendant training program before it could conduct the required training with FAA monitoring. And like other certification items, the final cabin safety test was an airborne one that had to be successfully completed before the cabin crews could fly with passengers. Timed evacuation tests are only one example of the required flight attendant training and recurrent training all cabin crews must complete before they can fly with passengers with any airline. Because of their important safety role in the event of an incident or accident, flight attendants are trained to handle many kinds of emergencies ranging from helping a choking child or heart attack victim, to fighting a cabin fire or quickly evacuating an aircraft following an emergency.

Airworthiness Inspectors

Participating with their office counterparts in all of this work were the airworthiness (AW) inspectors. As explained in Part One, like operations (Ops) inspectors, AW inspectors and avionics inspectors tend to specialize in either air-carrier or general aviation airworthiness areas. And like Ops inspectors, airworthiness inspectors are involved with more than just aircraft airworthiness issues. They monitor the training

SO YOU WANT TO BE AN FAA INSPECTOR

The following is a summary of some of the minimum qualifications needed by someone wanting to be an FAA operations, airworthiness, or avionics aviation safety inspector. Since cabin safety specialists are recruited so infrequently, their position requirements are not listed. For specific Federal Government employment application requirements, you should contact a Federal Jobs Information Office in your area, your local Flight Standards District Office, FAA Regional Office, or FAA Headquarters in Washington, DC. You can check your local telephone directory under U.S. Government for the telephone number of your local Federal Jobs Information Center or FAA Flight Standards office, or you can send inquiries to the Federal Aviation Administration, Human Resource Management Division, Operations Branch, AHR-150, 800 Independence Ave., S.W., Washington, DC 20591.

Operations Inspectors

General aviation inspectors: 1,500 flight hours, 300 hours within the last three years, and 1,000 hours within the last five years; hold either an airline transport pilot certificate or a commercial pilot certificate with instrument, single and multi-engine land airplane ratings; and have a valid flight instructor certificate with instrument, single, and multi-engine airplane ratings. The applicant cannot have had more than two flying accidents within the last five years.

Air carrier inspectors: 1,500 flight hours; pilot in command time in large (over 12,500 pounds gross takeoff weight); 100 hours in large aircraft within the last three years; and 1,000 hours within the last five years.

Maintenance Inspectors

General aviation inspectors: work experience on aircraft under 12,500 pounds gross takeoff weight; work experience in a repair station, airline

repair facility, or military repair facility; and three years supervisory experience. Applicants must have an Airframe and Powerplant (A&P) rating.

Air carrier inspectors: work experience similar to that required for a general aviation inspector except experience must be on aircraft with a gross takeoff weight of 12,500 pounds or larger.

Avionics Inspectors

General aviation inspectors: avionics work experience similar to general aviation maintenance inspector except an A&P rating is not required.

Air carrier inspectors: avionics work experience similar to air carrier maintenance inspector except an A&P rating is not required.

Federal Government Employment

In addition to meeting the aviation work experience requirements for a specific type of inspector position, all aviation safety inspector applicants must meet current Federal employment requirements. In addition, select individuals must submit to urinalysis for illegal drug use before and after employment.

Equal Opportunity

As a Federal Government agency, the FAA is an equal opportunity employer. All qualified candidates will be considered regardless of race, color, religion, sex, or national origin. As an equal opportunity employer, the Flight Standards Service encourages qualified minorities and women to apply for inspector positions.

Hiring Freeze

At the moment, there is a hiring freeze at the FAA. This information gives you an outline of the minimum qualifications needed to be an inspector when the register opens after the hiring freeze is lifted.

FAA Airworthiness Inspector Dale Allen checking an engine for fuel at a crash site.

and certification of maintenance technicians, inspect and certify maintenance training programs, inspect and certify repair facilities, and approve the designation of maintenance technicians with inspection authorization (IA) authority. Designating IA's is an important inspector function because, although a maintenance technician with an Airframe and Powerplant (A&P) certificate can work on an aircraft, only an IA can approve certain types of aircraft maintenance work and the required annual aircraft inspection.

Airworthiness and Safety

AW inspectors are also important members of any FSDO certification team involved in the certification of either a new operator or an established operator adding new aircraft to its fleet. AW inspectors ensure the aircraft and maintenance personnel meet appropriate airworthiness standards and that they use operating procedures designed to ensure the public's safety. This safety role is especially important. History has shown some troubled air operators may try to save money by skimping on maintenance or simply not doing it. If such practices are not discovered by AW inspectors,

public safety could be jeopardized. To prevent this problem, or to minimize its impact, the FAA conducts major safety inspections on certain airlines when they go into or are operating under bankruptcy procedures. The FAA wants to make sure that as long as the airlines are operating, they were maintaining the minimum level of safety required of all airlines.

Suspected Unapproved Parts

AW inspectors also play an important safety role in investigating the distribution, sale, and use of suspected unapproved parts on certificated aircraft. This role is critical because not only is public safety at risk, but aircraft owners and operators can lose thousands of dollars when unscrupulous dealers sell them unapproved parts that cannot legally be used on certificated aircraft. Compounding the problem is the fact that whenever an unapproved part is installed on a certificated standard aircraft, that aircraft becomes unairworthy because it no longer meets the requirements of its original type certificate. For an in-depth look at the unapproved parts issue, you can read the article, "Suspected Unapproved Parts" in the September 1993 issue of *FAA Aviation News*.

Repair Stations

Another important function AW inspectors are involved in is the certification of FAA-approved repair stations. For those not familiar with repair stations, they are FAA-approved facilities that can within the limitations of their FAA operating certificates maintain or alter; airframes, powerplants, propellers, or appliances. After certification, AW inspectors ensure that repair stations continue to perform their vital repair functions according to the FAR and appropriate procedures.

This is just one example of the many types of jobs that ASI's perform during a "typical" day.

Aviation Safety Inspectors

Aviation safety inspectors do many things during a day from answering questions about aviation to monitoring over 13,000 certificated operators world-wide! Although they do many

different things during a typical day, the one thing they all strive to do is to provide the public with accident free aircraft operations with the highest standards in the world! So the next time you see or meet an ASI on or off the job, stop and say hello. They are there to serve all airman in the prevention of accidents and in the promotion of safe flying. ■

Editor's Note: Information about inspector involvement in the certification of amateur-built aircraft and helicopter external-load operations will be published as separate articles in future issues.

Errers

Continued from page 10

Errors can also occur when a familiar schema reaches out and grabs us because we strayed too close. For example: very absentminded persons in going to their bedroom to dress for dinner have been known to take off one garment after another and finally get into bed, merely because that was the habitual issue of the first few moments when performed at a later hour. Have you ever been driving down a familiar road going to a different location than normal only to make the wrong turn towards that "usual" place that you go to?

Fatigue, distracting noises, and emotional stress are well-known factors that cause us to plug in the wrong schemas, but they do not account for all occurrences. The fact is, random "schematic" errors will be with us always, for they are part of the system that makes us human. Recognizing that error is a byproduct of thinking, you can work to reduce the consequences.

Planning, practice, goal-oriented flying, and thinking "what if?" are elements that help to make for safer flying and avoidance of "errers." ■

Next issue is Part 6—Do You Remember How? Our thanks to Mr. Tom Hamilton, publisher of Balloon Life *and author of this series, for permission to reprint these articles. For subscription information contact Mr. Hamilton at 2145 Dale Avenue, Sacramento, CA 95815; (916) 922-9648.*

Mountain Flying in Winter
GO/NO GO Decision

by Ken Watters

I am the co-editor of the Seattle Flight Standards District Office's aviation safety newsletter, *AeroSafe*. Almost every fall, we run at least one article reminding pilots to be cautious about flying over the Cascade Mountains in the winter. And almost every year, there is at least one airplane lost in the Cascades because of icing and weather.

For me the go/no go decision over mountains in the winter has always been relatively easy—ever since I flew for an air taxi firm that would not permit charter flights over the mountains in non-deiced airplanes in anything less than strict VFR, period. If that policy was good enough for them, it was good enough for me.

So, what prompts pilots to head off into dangerous conditions? It can't be ignorance of the dangers; after all, Flight Service does a good job of trying to tell us about turbulence and icing, and

they've taken criticism for trying to discourage flight into adverse weather. All one has to do is read the newspapers after one of these crashes to find out more than you want to know about the dangers of mountain flying in the winter.

In trying to recall the thoughts that have gone through my own mind when planning winter flights, and in my experience with some of my students and other pilots, I thought I would try to examine some "critical attitudes."

Flights at Risk

It seems that the flights most often at risk are those made by privately owned and flown aircraft, as opposed to corporate or FBO owned and rented planes. I am sure there is good reason for this: Corporate flight departments have policies regarding when flights may be dispatched, as do many FBO's. Pilots operating their own aircraft have to make all of these decisions on their

own. There is little or no support—other than what might be obtained at a weather briefing and those are rarely performed in person.

The Routine Activity Trap

A common pitfall when flight planning is what I will call "routine." This is the feeling that flying is really a routine activity; i.e., one flight is much like the next. Since nothing has ever gone wrong before, why should it now? After all, this airplane has always gotten me there before—no reason for that to change now.

Any pilot who has ever flown in a high-risk environment such as combat, traffic-spotting, medevac, etc., will tell you how foolish that attitude is. They have learned to expect trouble on every flight and are relieved when it doesn't happen.

It's All a Matter of Perspective

Another dangerous attitude is what I will call "perspective" or actually, lack of perspective. A pilot with this attitude will lose sight of what is really most important about every flight—his or her life and the lives of the passengers. Ridiculous though it may sound, I've heard it expressed many times: "I didn't buy a (fill in the blank with any expensive, deiced, turbo, multiengine, whatever airplane) to stay on the ground. This should handle anything I encounter."

Talk to test pilots who check out deicing systems or who fly in Alaska in the winter or who do thunderstorm research if you really believe there's enough

Continued on page 19

SIDE-SLIPS
by Dale Martin, APC, SEA FSDO

"Just a little light rime icing, my foot!"

Great Lakes Region Sets the "PACE"

by Bill Coons

On May 1,1993, at Aurora Airport, Illinois, some pilots were heard to make these comments:

"My friends told me that if I took my airplane to be examined by the FAA that the next thing to be examined should be my head. So, I did it anyway. They actually did find that my transponder and Mode C were inoperative, but they got me a waiver to get back home and have it repaired."

"I didn't have the octane decals on the tanks, so quick as a wink, they made me decals on a machine, stuck them on, and now I'm legal again."

"I've always had problems holding a heading, but after 30 minutes with an FAA operations inspector, I was flying as steady as a rock and straight as an arrow."

By way of explanation, let's back up a bit in time—to June 9, 1990, to be exact. That's when FAA Accident Prevention Program Manager Denis Caravella and the staff at the DuPage FSDO came up with the idea to offer pilots a courtesy evaluation of their flying skills and, at the same, time look at the airworthiness of their airplane. This was the classic and truest example of "We're from the FAA, and we're here to help." And at no charge the idea was certainly affordable. However, that old fear of punitive action was still in the minds of those who mistrusted the FAA.

The program was called "Operation Fixed Wing," and it actually caught on despite those who thought the idea was too good to be true.

Denis got things rolling, and soon more and more pilots were bringing their airplanes in to be evaluated. The program got so popular that the FAA Administrator endorsed it. Now it is operating nationwide, but one thing has changed.

Now it's called "PACE"—Pilot and Aircraft Courtesy Evaluation. (It seems that the Helicopter Association International thought the name might confuse some people into thinking they couldn't bring their helicopters in.) The

PACE is designed for all categories of aircraft from balloons to jets.

game is the same; only the name has changed.

Back to May 1, 1993, and the PACE operation at Aurora Airport. Airplanes started arriving well in advance of their appointed times. Three teams of inspectors met 14 airplanes and 16 pilots.

The first step was an airworthiness document review: airworthiness, weight and balance, equipment list, flight manual, current maintenance status, and AD record. This was followed by a walk-around that emphasized propeller nicks, worn tires, or anything visible that might be or become a flight hazard.

The next step involved a check of the ELT, transponder, and communications/navigation equipment, including GPS or Loran units. The final step was a flight evaluation—but only after the airworthiness portion had been completed and the aircraft judged to be airworthy. (In case of an airworthiness problem, a ferry permit may be issued to enable the pilot to return to his or her home airport for repairs.) The inspectors examined the pilots' logbooks, medical certificates, and pilot certificates. The actual flight evaluation consisted of a take off, basic air work, and several landings. A nice twist here is that you could "confess" the area in which you may be deficient, and time was spent on that area.

PACE is designed to be a skill evaluation not a flight check. In fact, you

Most aircraft soar through PACE with flying colors. In this case, a propeller A.D. needed to be complied with. The pilot was happy with the discovery.

CANNOT fail. You may, however, ask for an evaluation of your flight and any observations from the inspector.

Fourteen airplanes flew in that day, and 14 airplanes flew out. Not too bad. A few discrepancies were noted, but that's pretty good for the supposedly "bad guys."

FAA policy on PACE states, "No enforcement or administrative action will be taken as a result of any evaluations conducted under the PACE program." True or not? Well, while I was gathering information for this story, I asked the DuPage FSDO for a list of people who participated. Imagine my

surprise when Denis told me that except for the inspector activity log, all of the records had been destroyed.

This went over so well, that we had another one in October. They are starting up all over the country. So, don't be surprised when you sign up if you are greeted by smiling people who say, "Hi, there. We're from the FAA and. . ." ∎

Mr. Coons is an Accident Prevention Counselor for the DuPage FSDO. Our thanks to DuPage FSDO manager Michael J. Nowicki for sending us the article.—Editor.

An aircraft records check is made before any flying is done in PACE.

GO/NO GO
Continued from page 17

money to buy your way out of inconvenience. You'll be convinced. Again, put it in perspective: How much is your life and your passengers' worth?

"Get-there-itis"

A subset of the perspective trap is one I'll call "importance," otherwise known as "gotta get there." It has several forms, from a need to be at work Monday morning to a need to be at any "important" event, such as a meeting or even a sports event. Of course, perspective is lost when the pilot forgets what is REALLY important here (all together now: his or her life and the lives of the passengers). There is ALWAYS an alternative to making a dangerous flight, no matter how inconvenient.

"Air-Headed?"

Finally, something seems to happen to some pilots' judgement when they are actually in the air. It seems as if, having committed to making the flight, there is no turning back. They've made the decision to go, and that's that. They will then sometimes wind up in conditions so bad that had they known about it before leaving the ground, they never would have taken off. Somehow, the thought of an alternate plan or playing the game of what I call "what if?" doesn't happen. Like the battery-powered bunny, they just keep on going and going and going. . .

Should you find yourself in a situation where you are not really comfortable about making a flight, slow down a bit and think, hard. There are some risk situations that some airplanes and pilots are just not meant to handle. I've often been tempted to compare flight in instrument conditions to the ultimate video game, where you get only one chance.

The difference—and it's a big one—is that in this game if you die, the game's over—no extra lives. ∎

Mr. Watters is an Accident Prevention Counselor and publishes AeroSafe *for the Seattle FSDO at his own expense. In May 1992, Mr. Watters received the first annual "Friend of Flight Standards" Award at Flight Standards national awards program. The cartoonist, Dale Martin, is also an Accident Prevention Counselor in the Seattle area. You'll see his amusing and thoughtful cartoons in upcoming issues.*

The Practical Test Philosophy

by E. Allen Englehardt

The Practical Test Standards (PTS) publication has been jointly created by the FAA and industry and represents the FAA standardized tests for certification. The Practical Test Standards are the essential part of FAA's intent to assure the public of a fair and objective evaluation process. All examiners and FAA inspectors are required to test applicants in accordance with the procedures and standards found in the PTS.

The practical test is the final step in the FAA certification process. It serves the dual purpose of determining that the applicant has completed the required training to a level of proficiency required by the FAA and that the applicant can safely perform the tasks required for the certificate or rating sought.

The process of the practical test is to observe the applicant as he or she completes the routine, non-routine, and emergency tasks that are required of the applicant in order to operate safely. The examiner or inspector evaluates these tasks through both oral questioning and the observation of ground and in-flight procedures. Oral questioning may be used at any time throughout the test. Questions will always be of a practical nature and should generally be referenced to the respective sources shown in the PTS for the particular task.

Evaluating pilot technique, procedures, or answers to oral questions,

based on reference sources other than those shown in the PTS, may be inappropriate and inconsistent with a sense of fairness to the applicant and the recommending instructor. Such procedures or questions should be avoided. Likewise, requiring an applicant to state seldom used aircraft limitations and procedures from memory, without the use of normally available placards, markings, and aircraft limitation material, is also inconsistent with the philosophy of an objective practical test. A sense of fairness to the public during the conduct of the practical test is of the very highest priority for the FAA.

The examiner's role is to represent the FAA fairly and objectively during an applicant's final evaluation process. This role requires the proper use by examiners of the PTS. Following are some "philosophical notes" that examiners could and should keep in mind when conducting practical tests in accordance with the PTS.

Simulating Emergencies and Inoperative Equipment

A designated pilot examiner conducts the flight test of an applicant for the purpose of observing the applicant's ability to perform satisfactorily. FAR § 61.47 explains that the examiner's status during flight tests is that of an observer and states that:

"... the inspector or other examiner is not pilot in command of the aircraft during the flight test unless he or she

acts in that capacity for the flight, or portion of the flight, by prior arrangement with the applicant."

Such an arrangement would be required in order to conduct a flight test under instrument flight rules when the applicant is not instrument rated or when an unsafe situation develops that requires examiner intervention.

When a practical test requires an examiner to test emergency procedures, such as failures of equipment or loss of engine power, the examiner should discuss with the applicant before the flight the preferred method to be used in order to simulate the particular emergency safely. Examiners must keep in mind that only the pilot in command can authorize the examiner to disable engines or other components and systems of the aircraft intentionally. Notwithstanding the authority of the pilot in command, examiners are expected to use good judgement while administering tests and must avoid intentionally disabling any component or piece of equipment that can not be done so safely.

Cross Country Flight Planning

The private and commercial pilot practical tests both require the applicant to plan a cross country flight to the maximum range for the particular aircraft used during testing. Evaluation of this task permits examiners the opportunity to test the applicant's judgement as well as performance by observing and checking the pilot's computation of fuel requirements following his or her consideration of weather reports and forecasts, reserve fuel, and alternates available if the planned flight cannot be completed as planned. This task can best be evaluated by allowing the applicant the responsibility to determine the range of the aircraft by their selection of a cross country destination. It is the applicant's decisions regarding his or her determination of aircraft range that is an important part of the examiner's evaluation of judgement during the testing of this task.

Short Field/Maximum Performance Landings

The private and commercial pilot practical tests also require applicants to demonstrate a short field/maximum performance landing. During this demonstration the applicant is responsible for the selection of a suitable runway touchdown point. Selection of the touchdown point is based on required aircraft stopping distance, existing obstructions, and available landing distance for the particular runway. If a simulated short field is used, examiners must inform the applicant of the simulated length of the runway. The applicant's pilot judgement may then be evaluated based on his or her selection of a safe touchdown point.

Partial Panel

The instrument rating PTS require the demonstration of a partial panel non-precision approach procedure. Examiners are required to place special emphasis on fundamental attitude-instrument partial panel skills. This area of special emphasis testing is the result of FAA concern over increases in fatal aircraft accidents involving spatial disorientation of instrument rated pilots following the loss of the aircraft's gyroscopic instruments.

For most instrument rating applicants using typical general aviation aircraft, a loss of the aircraft vacuum system is the most likely cause of a simultaneous failure to the attitude indicator and heading indicator. This failure is one of the in-flight emergency (loss of radio communications or navigation radio is another) that must be tested during the instrument rating practical test. The failure of the aircraft vacuum system can be tested in two ways: Fundamental Skills and Partial Panel Approaches.

Fundamental Skills

The fundamental skills associated with this emergency are tested by observing the applicant demonstrate partial panel air work such as timed turns and compass turns to headings, climbs and descents at constant airspeed and rate, and unusual attitude recovery without the use of the attitude indicator.

Partial Panel Approach Procedure

The demonstration of a partial panel non-precision approach procedure will provide an opportunity for the examiner to test the applicant's fundamental skills as applied to a practical problem. It will also test the applicant's judgement relating to loss of the aircraft's vacuum system and the associated gyroscopic instruments. Applicants should demonstrate their knowledge of resources that may be available during emergencies and should demonstrate judgement in resource management.

Following a loss of the aircraft's vacuum system, a pilot would be expected to inform ATC as to the nature of the

Dean Chamberlain

The PTS are the only standards an applicant must meet for both the oral and the flight test.

emergency and to advise ATC if any Special assistance may be needed. special assistance in this case may include a request for ATC help in coordinating with an FSS in locating the closest area of VFR weather. If VFR weather cannot be located, applicants should request assistance from ATC in locating the closest airport with a suitable instrument approach procedure. Other assistance, if radar is available, may include special considerations from ATC concerning radar-vectored turns to specified headings, special requests for no climbing or descending turns, wide radar intercepts for the instrument approach course, and special radar assistance and surveillance during the conduct of the approach.

Since ATC's normal workload will only permit special assistance and consideration during actual emergencies, during testing examiners may wish to simulate ATC response to pilot requests.

As a point of clarification, it should be understood that while good judgement would always dictate a pilot's selection of an ILS approach when available, the instrument rating PTS specifically require the demonstration of a partial panel non-precision approach (VOR or NDB) as the standard for evaluation. This requirement is not intended as a suggestion or recommendation for the use of such procedures during actual emergencies but only as a means to encourage training in that area.

Conclusion

Examiner's should keep in mind that it is the nature of a practical test that encourages the applicant to demonstrate good judgement and use all available resources during the flight. The successful conclusion of an in-flight emergency is always the pilot's primary objective, and the applicant's use of all resources available is consistent with the philosophy of a practical test. ∎

Mr. Englehart is also an Accident Prevention Counselor in the FAA's Great Lakes Region and a first officer for United Airlines. He gave this presentation at Sun'n Fun and Oshkosh.

Flying to Alaska Addendum

Once in a while a letter needs more than just a small space on the Flight-FORUM page. This is such a letter. As you read it you will see why.

The City of Dawson Creek and the citizens of our community who are interested and dependent on activities and movements at our Airport are concerned with the information contained in the above mentioned publication. (Editor's Note: The above mentioned publications are the FAA Aviation News-*Flying to Alaska article and reprint.*)

Dawson Creek is very proud of the services provided at the Airport and strive to have people stop here, especially American itinerants.

Some of the services we provide and do not charge for are parking, camping, and hospitality.

I am including a copy of the information contained in our Canada Flight Supplement and draw your attention to the fact that we have a Flight Service Station in Dawson Creek and the FSS staff can give you all the information needed to fly the Alaska Highway.

　　　Bob Trail
　　　Mayor
　　　City of Dawson Creek,
　　　British Columbia, Canada

Everyone planning on flying to Alaska via the Alaska Highway should take note of the Mayor's comments. In our article, we stated although Milepost

Zero is in Dawson Creek, flight planning is better accomplished at Fort St. John, a short 47-mile hop away to the northwest and on the highway, where there is a flight service station and weather office for flight planning assistance and weather briefings. Although we contacted Transport Canada and our FAA counterparts in Alaska about the accuracy of our information, we did not contact individual communities or airports listed in the article regarding their services.

Although each pilot must make his or her own flight planning decisions based upon all available information, pilots flying the Alaska Highway may want to stop at Dawson Creek to start their trip at Milepost Zero. Dave Carpenter, when contacted at the Dawson Creek FSS about this reply, described his FSS as, "Just the darn nicest little Flight Service Station in western Canada." According to the Airport Manager, Mr. Harald Hansen, the year and a half old, 2.5 million dollar Dawson Creek Flight Service Station is the newest FSS in Western Canada. To find out more about the Dawson Creek FSS, you can contact it by calling (604) 782–5375 during the hours of 1345Z to 0515Z. You should contact the Fort St. John FSS at (604) 787–0434 during other times. For additional information

about Dawson Creek airport or community, you can contact City Hall from 8:30 a.m. to 4:30 p.m. at (604) 782–3351. After those hours you can contact the Airport Manager, Mr. Harald Hansen, at home by calling (604) 782–7628 or Mayor Bob Trail at home by calling (604) 782–2352. Dawson Creek, BC, airport information is listed in the Canadian Aerodrome/Facility Directory. The Dawson Creek airport identifier is CYDQ. ■

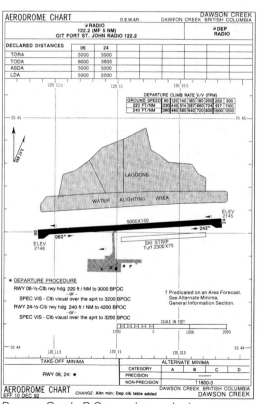

Dawson Creek, B.C.,aerodrome chart

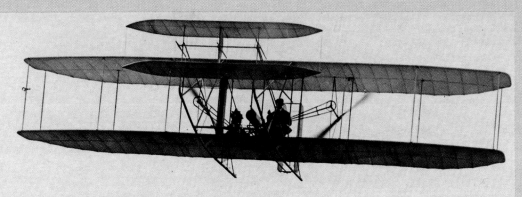

The Wright Questions

This is an unusual Famous Flight but an appropriate one as this December marks the 90th anniversary of the Wright brothers' first powered flight. It begins with a letter and a search to find the answers to some intriguing questions. **—Editor**

Your July/August issue contains many of the informative articles that I look forward to. Your magazine is a fine publication and I wish you continued success. However, being a history buff—especially aviation history—and a career police officer I could not pass over your early aviation statistics on page four without a few questions.

Your first entry that the Wright brothers made their first powered flight in 1903 is a given. Your second entry regarding Orville's wind shear accident brought me to a halt. Several questions came to mind.

Where did the accident occur?

Who investigated the accident and determined "wind shear?"

Was the term wind shear actually used in 1904?

As far as the investigation goes, I can surmise that the Wright brothers did their own since the NTSB, FAA, or anyone else was not around at that time. If they did investigate their own, I can see why they blamed it on the weather. If Glenn Curtiss had done the follow up it would have been pilot error.

I realize that none of this means a hoot eighty-nine years later in our now very complex aviation world, but if your article on early aviation stats was meant to arouse my interest, it did.

Dave Miner
Reno, NV

Your first question is easy to answer. The accident occurred at Huffman's field near Dayton, OH in the summer of 1904. The other questions are a bit more difficult to answer.

The term wind shear was not used at that time. The Wrights blamed the accident on wind gusts. According to Fred C. Kelly's book, *The Wright Brothers,* Orville was piloting the airplane when it hit a gust of wind and began to rise rapidly. Just as quickly the wind suddenly stopped sending the airplane towards the ground at a steep angle. Orville was thrown from the plane before it hit the ground and the upper wing spar came to rest across the middle of Orville's back. The only thing that saved him from serious injury was a damaged two foot section of the spar was missing and just happened to coincide with Orville's position on the ground.

Another interesting fact discovered while researching this incident was that Wilbur coined the term "stall." In a letter to Octave Chanute he described their flights on June 21, 1904:

"Today we had our first decent chance [to fly], but as the margin was very small, we were not skillful enough to really get started. The first two flights were for a distance of a little more than a 100 feet and the third 225 feet. On this one Orville almost got away, but after about 200 feet he allowed the machine to turn up a little too much and it stalled it. He had a speed of about 18 miles on leaving the track, but the rise necessary to gain a little room for maneuvering reduced this to about 16 miles, and as the wind was blowing only 8 miles, and unsteady at that, the resistance was too high to permit rapid acceleration, owing to the great angle of incident required. To get started under such conditions requires perfect management. We are a little rusty. With a little more track and a little more practice we hope to get a real start before long and then we will see what the machine can really do in the way of flying. The machine landed nicely each time without any injury at all." ∎

FLIGHT**FORUM**

• Question of Visibility

I am writing this letter to request a clarification of a question published in the Flight-FORUM of the FAA Aviation News magazine.

The question involves an answer that was given in the April 1993 issue entitled "Visibility Defined." I believe your answer here is incorrect. I am enclosing an excerpt from the FAR "P" pages, specifically Amendment 91–173, effective May 8, 1981 ("Thus §§ 91.116(c)(2) and 91.116(d) retain the concept of pilot determination of specified visibility and clarify the frequently misunderstood point that the visibility referred to is flight visibility), which will provide a basis for my opinion.

Thanks as always for publishing a great and informative magazine.
>   Robert Anderson
>   Scottsdale, AZ

Thanks for the compliment. The answer in the April issue is correct. Landing and takeoff visibility are ground-based measurements.

• Important—not Critical

After reading your response to "Legal Approach Plates" in the May-June issue, I find I must ask some further questions. You stated, "You could have a situation where the amendment number is still current, but critical radio frequency information or airport diagram information on the IAP may not be current." If the information is critical, it is clear that the amendment number should change. What can I do to rectify this potentially hazardous situation? Who should I write?
>   Bruce Miller
>   Prosper, TX

There is no need to write to anyone. After reading your letter, we wish we had used the word important rather than critical. But regardless of the word used, the most important thing you and everyone else can do is to use current instrument approach procedures (IAP) and check Notices to Airmen (NOTAMS) for possible changes to the IAP'S you plan on using. Government IAP's are published with current information every 56 days with an update issued at the 28 day point. NOTAMS are issued as required. In addition to changes to IAP's, NOTAMS may also be used to inform that the IAP is not authorized.

• Left Hander Special

I always enjoy your magazine. There is something of value and informative interest in every issue. Even humor is present for the observant.

Your September 1993 article on Winter Ops on page 23 features a Grumman AA5A unlike any I have ever seen before. Must be a special for left handers. I like your magazine.
>   Emil Duchay (Grumman Owner)
>   Minneapolis, MN

We try to have something for everyone. Seriously though, the photograph was reversed in printing. Thanks for pointing out our mistake. We wonder how many other pilots recognized the error.

• Outer Marker Requirement

I am writing this letter to request a clarification of a question published in the Flight-FORUM section of the FAA Aviation News magazine.

The question involves an answer that was given in the March 1993 issue entitled "Outer Marker Approach." I believe that it is not a requirement to have an outer marker (or authorized substitution) in order to conduct a full ILS approach. The GSIA marks the beginning of the final approach segment of a full (using the glide slope) ILS approach.

FAA AVIATION NEWS welcomes comments from its readers. We may edit letters for style and/or length. We will select one representative letter from those on the same topic for publication, and because of our bimonthly publishing schedule, responses may not appear for several issues. We will not print anonymous letters, but we will withhold names or send personal replies upon request. Address: Editor, FAA AVIATION NEWS, AFS–810, Washington, DC 20591.

The outer marker, by itself, provides very little information to the pilot. However, when flying an ILS approach with an inoperative glide slope (localizer approach) the outer marker (or legal substitution) normally would serve as the FAF and therefore be required.
>   Robert Anderson
>   Scottsdale, AZ

Outer markers or an authorized substitute are required. Paragraph 1–10 of the *Airman's Information Manual* and FAR § 91.175(k) apply.

• Cross Country Endorsement

Assume a student pilot holds a valid medical and student pilot certificate which has been endorsed by an authorized instructor for a specific make and model aircraft to be flown in solo flight. In addition, the student's logbook has been endorsed within the 90 days prior to the student operating that make and model aircraft in solo flight. The instructor has attested that instruction has been given and proficiency obtained in areas of FAR §§ 61.87(d), (e), and (m), and 61.93(c)(1) and (2).

For a specific cross country flight greater than 50 nautical miles from the original departure point, I have assumed it is legal if the logbook endorsement attesting that the student can make the flight safely under known circumstances is given by an authorized instructor under FAR Part 61 who has reviewed the student's preflight planning and preparation, but is a different instructor from the one who has endorsed the student's certificate after having given the student instruction in FAR areas § 61.93(c)(1) and (2).

Under FAR § 61.93(d)(1) and (2), it might appear that the instructor who endorses the student's logbook for a specific cross-country flight must be the same instructor who has endorsed the student's pilot certificate. Yet, under Far § 61.193(b)(3), flight instructor authorizations, it would appear that, providing all other endorsements are given, any authorized instructor may sign off a student's logbook for a specific cross-country flight after reviewing preflight planning and preparation procedures, although they have not given that student instruction in areas FAR § 61.93(c)(1) and (2). Am I correct in assuming that the instructor who has endorsed the student's logbook for a specific cross-country flight in accordance with FAR § 61.93(d)(2)(i) may be different from the one who has endorsed the student's certificate?

Seth Rosan
Saratoga Springs, NY

Yes.

• Chandelle Pitch-up

What degrees of nose up pitch attitude are indicated respectively, by the two short horizontal lines placed, one above the other, above the horizon bar of the attitude indicator? In performing a chandelle, which of these two lines should indicate the highest pitch-up attitude to be attained during the maneuver?

Cyril Toker
Ponte Vedra Beach, FL

We can't say without access to the aircraft or instrument manufacturer's instrument information. Each manufacturer decides how to mark its attitude indicators for pitch according to the guidelines in the following reference. The reference, the Society of Automotive Engineers Inc.'s Aerospace Standard, AS 8001, Minimum Performance Standard for Bank and Pitch Instruments (dated September 1975 and reaffirmed October 1984) does not specify the number of degrees that must be indicated by any pitch graduations. It only requires that pitch be marked to display a range of at least plus or minus 50 degrees in both normal and inverted attitudes with markings to at least 20 degrees nose up and down. AS 8001 does require that a zero pitch reference be provided.

Regarding your question about flying a chandelle, neither mark should be used as a chandelle is a visual maneuver and should be accomplished by reference to outside references. Due to all of the variables in flying a chandelle with various aircraft, the FAA pilot Practical Test Standards (PTS) does not specify a specific pitch indication such as you suggest. The PTS only talks about maintaining a constant pitch attitude and rolling out of the maneuver at the 180° point just above a stall airspeed

and momentarily maintaining that airspeed without stalling. Stalling is disqualifying.

• Complex Endorsement

In regard to FAR § 61.31, should there be a log book endorsement for a pilot receiving instruction and demonstrating competency in an aircraft with greater than 200 horsepower and a separate endorsement for instruction and demonstration of competency in a complex aircraft regardless of horsepower?

There appears to be some debate as to whether or not a person can act as PIC of an aircraft with greater than 200 horsepower with a complex endorsement received in an aircraft with less than 200 horsepower.

John A. (Jack) Ford
West Jordan, UT

No. Either endorsement meets the requirement for both endorsements.

• Second-in-Command Time

I would like to ask you a question about the logging of flight time.

FAR § 61.51(c)(3) says that a pilot may log as second in command time all flight time during which he acts as second in command of the aircraft on which more than one pilot is required under the type certificate of the aircraft, or under the regulations under which the flight is conducted. I am curious whether time logged while acting as a crew member in a foreign air transport operation should be logged under the regulations of that country which the company is registered in, or whether the compatible U.S. regulation should be consulted, in the case where an airman plans to use his or her flight experience to apply for a U.S. airman certificate? For example, a pilot acting as second in command (SIC) in a Piper Navajo in Canada for an Air Taxi Operation would consult the applicable Canadian regulations or FAR Part 135 to decide which time logged could be apply towards the U.S. ATP certificate?

Uwe Goehl
Prescott, AZ

The FAA has no jurisdiction over the logging of flight time by an airman serving as second in command of a Canadian Air Taxi aircraft operation. However, in general, flight time gained by an airman as a crewmember of an aircraft in foreign aircraft operations, when logged in accordance with the specific requirements of FAR §

61.51, (for example, as second in command) is creditable toward meeting U.S. airman certification requirements. It should be noted that any specific instruction or endorsement specified under the FAR for the U.S. certificate or rating applied for must be made by a person authorized under the FAR to provide the instruction and/or endorsement.

• NORDO Procedures

I can't get a consistent answer to this question from anyone, including Flight Standards. Perhaps you can give me "the official word." If I am NORDO, (no radio) and IMC and I arrive at the IAF of my destination airport early, do I immediately shoot the approach and land, or do I hold until my ETA and then shoot the approach and land?

Name withheld
by request

As per FAR § 91.185(c)3, you would hold until such time as you could commence your descent or descent and approach as close as possible to the expect further clearance time if one has been received, or if one has not been received, as close as possible to your estimated time of arrival (ETA) as calculated from the filed or amended (with ATC) estimated time en route. In other words, you hold until you only have enough time left to fly the published approach procedure and touchdown at your ETA. The Airman's Information Manual (AIM) provides guidance on this and other procedures such as lost communication transponder procedures you may want to review before operating IMC.

AV**NEWS/BRIEFS**

Maintenance Technician Awards Program Takes Off

The Federal Aviation Administration's Aviation Maintenance Technician Award Program (AMT) celebrated its first birthday on October 1st. During this time over 35,000 awards were handed out nationwide to general aviation and air carrier maintenance technicians and their employers. The intent of this highly successful awards program is to foster professionalism and provide FAA recognition for initial and recurrent training that a technician has received or their employer has provided.

The Awards program for both technician and employers is divided into five award categories: Bronze, Silver, Gold, Ruby, and Diamond. Each award starting with Bronze is more difficult to achieve than the one before it. However, the technician or employer is not locked into a repetitive lock step process of acquiring the Bronze award before earning the Silver, Silver before the Gold, etc. This awards program is flexible and runs for 12 calendar months from October 1 to September

30. The training requirements for each award must be met within that one year period. If you meet the requirements for the Diamond award the first year, you then apply through the local Flight Standards District Office and they will be glad to issue you one. Technicians receive a Certificate of Training and a lapel pin. Employers receive a Certificate of Excellence.

Technicians must meet the training requirements based on classroom hours of attendance. The training requirements are not easy. The Bronze award requires six hours of training, but the Diamond award requires 100 hours of training including 40 hours of college or college level courses in mathematics, English, science, management subjects, or related courses.

The Employer's award is based on the percentage of technicians who earn a Certificate of Training. For a Bronze Certificate of Excellence an employer must have five percent of the work

force awarded a Certificate of Training. The Silver Certificate of Excellence requires 10 percent; the Gold, 15 percent; the Ruby, 20 percent; and the Diamond, 25 percent.

For further information contact FAA, Awards Program Manager, AFS-361, 800 Independence Ave., SW, Washinton, DC 20591. Telephone 202 267–8616. This program is designed for all Aviation Maintenance Technicians. To provide you with a better perspective of what is happening in the aviation maintenance community, here are examples of three different participants:

Air Carrier Participation:

Recently, USAir, Boston Maintenance Department, was presented a FAA Diamond "Certificate of Excellence," because 93 percent of its maintenance technicians earned their own individual AMT awards. The award was accepted on behalf of the 120 member technical staff by Mr. Ron Danner, USAir-Boston, Maintenance Manager. The awards were presented by Mr. Gary S. Lopez, Manager, and Mr. Thomas A. Welman, Geographic Unit Supervisor, of the New England Flight Standards District Office, and Mr. Barry Otto, Aviation Safety Inspector, Flight Standards at Logan Airport, Boston. USAir says the AMT Awards program will help enhance recognition of the importance of safety training, and USAir is proud to take a leadership role in this effort.

Aviation Gulf Coast Helicopter Company Presentation

The Baton Rouge, Flight Standards District Office, recently presented AMT awards and Employer awards to Aviation Gulf Coast Helicopter company a division of ERA Helicopter in Lake Charles, Louisiana. As of April 1993, Aviation Gulf Coast has provided at least 40 hours of training to 103 technicians or 97% of their maintenance work force. For this accomplishment Aviation Gulf Coast Helicopters was awarded the FAA "Certificate of Excellence" Award. Mr. John E. Able, Team B—Certification, Mr. James A. Jackson, Principle Aviation Safety Inspector Operations, and Mr. Laurel W. Johnson,

USAir Maintenance Department personnel at Boston's Logan Airport received Ruby (above) and Bronze (below) awards.

AV**NEWS/BRIEFS**

Aviation Safety Inspector Airworthiness of the Baton Rouge FSDO presented the Diamond "Certificate of Excellence" to Mr. Mark Jones, Director of Maintenance with Mr. Bob Gillespie, Chief Inspector, also in attendance.

General Aviation participation in the State of Ohio

Sixteen aviation technicians who work for the State of Ohio, Department of Aviation, Division of Aviation Bureau of Aircraft Support Services will receive the Silver "Certificate of Training" award from Flight Standards District Manager Hortense M. Vick. Jerry Wray, Director of Transportation for the State of Ohio, and John B. Cornett, Deputy Director, Division of Aviation, will accept the "Certificate of Excellence".

The State of Ohio has an FAA approved Repair Station to maintain its 15 plus general aviation aircraft. As one of the largest FAR Part 91 operators in the state, it goes beyond the minimum safety requirements.

Avionics Safety Check

A review of an NTSB accident report safety recommendation to the FAA revealed several important safety items that might be of interest to all pilots. The 1992 report concerned the crash of Alitalia Flight 404 on November 14, 1990, in Switzerland. The crash occurred when an Italian-registered McDonnell Douglas DC–9–32 hit the side of a mountain about five miles north of Zurich-Kloten Airport in controlled flight. According to the report, the accident investigation indicated the possible failure of the VOR/ILS system on the aircraft. The report said, "The investigation has disclosed a possible failure mode of the very high frequency omnidirectional range (VOR)/ILS system, which was installed on the airplane, that could have contributed to this controlled flight into terrain. This failure mode could have led the flightcrew into believing they were on course and on the glidepath when they were not."

NTSB reported that, "According to Douglas Company engineers, it is possible that a short circuit or an open cir-

cuit in certain models of VOR/ILS receivers could cause navigation instruments to indicate 'zero deviation.' Thus, raw data deviation information on the attitude direction indicator, displayed by the flight director bars, and the horizontal situation indicator could center and remain centered with no failure or warning flag in view. In addition, this short circuit or open circuit could prevent the autopilot and the ground proximity warning system (GPWS) from receiving the proper course and glidepath deviation signals. The autopilot would continue to guide the airplane according to previously established crew inputs, and the GPWS would not sound an alarm due to glideslope deviation or descent below a safe altitude. This could occur if the VOR localizer (LOC) or glideslope signals to the autopilot were interrupted by an open circuit.

"As a crosscheck of the system, the captain and first officer would normally use two separate VOR/LOC receivers for navigation information that would be displayed on their respective instruments. However, without warning flags indicating system failure, the pilots might accept as accurate centered indications and then use the 'NAV' switching function to select the malfunctioning VOR/LOC receiver on both panels."

The report listed the following VOR/ILS receivers that Douglas said did not have an expanded self-monitoring capability to detect this type of failure. The receivers are: Collins model 51RV-1 and model 51RV-4; Wilcox model 806; King model KNR6030; and some versions of Bendix model RNA 26C.

Douglas first reported this potentially hazardous problem in 1984 in two letters to all its operators using the identified equipment. According to Douglas records, Alitalia received the letters. According to NTSB, Alitalia pilots did not receive the information until after the crash. In 1991, Douglas again sent a letter to all of its operators using the equipment restating its 1984 warning.

NTSB also asked the FAA to distribute the warning through its notification system and to foreign governments.

The FAA made the appropriate notifications.

One Douglas recommendation in the NTSB report is appropriate for all pilots regardless of the equipment they are using. Douglas recommended that, ". . . if a discrepancy exists between deviations displayed on the indicators of the same type of instrument, the pilots should carefully compare the VOR/LOC or glideslope deviation information with other navigational aids, such as distance measuring equipment, VOR bearing, radio and barometric altitude, marker beacon, automatic direction finding bearing, and vertical speed. Also, if 'NAV' switching is used, it should be accomplished before localizer and glideslope capture on an instrument approach to allow positive verification of all deviation information that will be used for that approach. Douglas further recommends that if one VOR/ILS receiver is inoperative, the other receiver should be temporarily turned to a nearby VOR station and the selected course varied to ensure that the course deviation indicator moves in accordance with the selected course."

Based upon this report, *FAA Aviation News* believes that several important safety items should be brought to the attention of all pilots and operators. First is the need for all owners/operators to be able to receive and disseminate received safety information about their aircraft and installed equipment to all of their pilots and crews in a timely manner. Although the major aircraft manufacturers and FAA have established means of notifying owners/operators about safety issues, especially air carrier operators, individual general aviation aircraft owners/pilots may not receive important safety information as timely as other operators if they do not keep their current addresses and other required information on file with their respective aircraft/equipment manufacturer and the FAA. The need to be able to receive timely safety information underlines the need for all operators and flight crews to know and understand their equipment and its limitations. Regardless of the type of equip-

AV**NEWS/BRIEFS**

ment in an aircraft, Douglas's comments about the importance of cross-checking all navigational equipment before starting an instrument approach is a good reminder for all pilots. This is as important to the VFR pilot as it is to the IFR pilot. Although a VFR pilot is not going to fly an instrument approach to minimums, we have all heard stories of VFR pilots who have been lost after failing to properly check or operate their navigational equipment when they were not following good visual navigational practices. It is important for all pilots to know how to not only use their equipment, but also for them to know when it is not operating properly.

ASOS Booklet

A booklet that explains the National Weather Service's Automated Surface Observing System (ASOS) is now available from your local Accident Prevention Program Manager or nearest Flight Service Station.

The booklet, titled, *ASOS Guide for Pilots*, explains how the automated weather reporting system works as well as its limitations. The booklet provides a detailed explanation of the terminology and symbology used to report the observed weather. It also explains the differences between a manual weather observation and an automated observation. The booklet's back cover has a key printed on it to help pilots read ASOS printed reports.

ASOS units provide weather information to on-site airport users, national communication networks, and for computer-generated voice reports for pilots either by radio or telephone. It is a joint project of the National Weather Service, FAA, and Department of Defense.

A separate five by eight inch card is also available with keys for both the ASOS and the FAA Automated Weather Observing System (AWOS) reports.

Award winners Kenneth Medley (CFI) and Anthony Saxton (AMT) with Bruce Landsberg, Executive Director of the AOPA/Air Safety Foundation, and FAA Adminstrator David Hinson.

And the Winners Are...

The General Aviation Industry selected its General Aviation Maintenance Technician (AMT) and General Aviation Flight Instructor (CFI) of the Year for 1993 in September. Mr. Anthony R. Saxton of Defiance, OH, was selected as the AMT of the Year. Mr. Kenneth W. Medley of Arlington, VA, was selected as the CFI of the Year. A panel of industry and FAA representatives selected the winners from a list of nominees submitted by the various FAA regions. The winners were honored at an awards presentation and luncheon in Washington, DC, on October 25.

Mr. Saxton is the president and manager of TAS Aviation, Inc., A 1976 graduate of Parks College, he is also the manager of the Defiance Memorial and Van Wert County airports. During his 17 year maintenance career, he has been an active supporter of general aviation. Besides being the maintenance manager for a Part 135 operation, he has become an expert on Cessna light twin aircraft. He shares his knowledge of light twin maintenance through safety seminars and by being an FAA Accident Prevention Safety Counselor. He is also the technical advisor for the "The Twin Cessna Flyer," a magazine published for piston Cessna twin pilots.

Mr. Medley, a flight instructor since 1943, has given more than 7,000 flight instruction hours and has more than 12,000 flight hours total. A World War II military pilot and instructor, he has been a supporter of the FAA's Accident Prevention Program since its founding. As

a designated pilot examiner, AOPA Air Safety Foundation flight instructor refresher clinic instructor, FAA Safety Counselor, a founding member of the Capital Area Association of Flight Instructors, and Gold Seal instructor, Mr. Medley has played an important role in flight training and safety in the Washington, DC, area. In addition to his other aviation activities, he also produces the Accident Prevention newsletter for the Washington Flight Standards District Office.

The General Aviation Industry Awards Program is an annual program sponsored by the General Aviation Manufacturers Association, the National Business Aircraft Association, the AOPA Air Safety Foundation, and the FAA. The concept is simple. Each FAA Flight Standards District Office (FSDO) can nominate one AMT and CFI district award winner for its respective region's regional award. Then regional winners compete for the national AMT and CFI awards. The national award winners are brought to Washington for an exciting tour of Washington, the opportunity to meet industry and FAA leaders, and the distinction of being the National AMT and CFI of the Year. Now is the time for everyone to think about next year's program. Anyone can nominate an AMT or CFI to their respective FSDO Accident Prevention Program Manager (APPM) for the annual program. You should contact your local APPM now about next year's program. Application forms for the 1994 program should be available by late spring.

GENERAL AVIATION POLICY STATEMENT

General aviation is critically important to the Nation's economy and to the national transportation system. General aviation plays a crucial role in flight training for all segments of aviation and provides unique personal and recreational opportunities. It makes vital contributions to activities ranging from business aviation, to agricultural operations, to Warbird preservation, to glider and balloon flights.

ACCORDINGLY, IT IS THE POLICY OF THE FAA to foster and promote general aviation while continuing to improve its safety record. These goals are neither contradictory nor separable. They are best achieved by cooperating with the aviation community to define mutual concerns and joint efforts to accomplish objectives. We will strive to achieve the goals through voluntary compliance and methods designed to reduce the regulatory burden on general aviation.

The FAA's general aviation programs will focus on:

1. **SAFETY**
   To protect recent gains and aim for a new threshold.

2. **FAA SERVICES**
   To provide the general aviation community with responsive, customer-driven certification, air traffic, and other services.

3. **PRODUCT INNOVATION AND COMPETITIVENESS**
   To ensure the technological advancement of general aviation.

4. **SYSTEM ACCESS AND CAPACITY**
   To maximize general aviation's ability to operate in the National Airspace System.

5. **AFFORDABILITY**
   To promote economic and efficient general aviation operations, expand participation, and stimulate industry growth.

David R. Hinson
Administrator

September 8, 1993

DO NOT DELAY—CRITICAL TO FLIGHT SAFETY!

January-February 1994

FAA *Aviation News*

A DOT/FAA FLIGHT STANDARDS SAFETY PUBLICATION

U.S. Department
of Transportation

**Federal Aviation
Administration**

Federico F. Peña, *Secretary of Transportation*
David R. Hinson, *FAA Administrator*
Monte R. Belger, *Acting Executive Director
for System Operations*
Anthony J. Broderick, *Associate Administrator
for Regulation and Certification*
Thomas C. Accardi, *Director,
Flight Standards Service*
Robert A. Wright, *Acting Manager,
General Aviation and Commercial Division*
Roger M. Baker, Jr., *Manager,
Accident Prevention Program Branch*
Phyllis Anne Duncan, *Editor*
Louise Oertly, *Senior Associate Editor*
Dean Chamberlain, *Associate Editor*

The FAA's Flight Standards Service, General Aviation and
Commercial Division, Accident Prevention Program
Branch, AFS-810, Washington, DC 20591, (telephone
202 267-8017, FAX 202 267-9463) publishes FAA Aviation News in the interest of flight safety. The magazine
promotes safety in the air by calling the attention of airmen to current technical, regulatory, and procedural matters affecting the safe operation of aircraft. Although
based on current FAA policy and rule interpretations, all
printed material herein is advisory or informational in nature and should not be construed to have regulatory effect. The FAA does not officially endorse any goods,
services, materials, or products of manufacturers that
may be mentioned. **Certain details of accidents described herein have been altered to protect the privacy of those involved.**
The Office of Management and Budget has approved the use of funds for the printing of FAA AVIATION
NEWS.

SUBSCRIPTION SERVICES
The Superintendent of Documents, U.S. Government
Printing Office, Washington, DC 20402-9371, sells FAA
AVIATION NEWS on subscription. Use the self-mailer
form in the center of this magazine to subscribe. Cost:
$15.00 ($18.75 foreign) for one year; $30.00 ($37.50
foreign) for two years. Prices are subject to change by
the Government Printing Office without prior notice.
Change of Address or Subscription Problems:
**Send your label with correspondence to Sup Doc,
Attn: Chief, Mail List Branch, Mail Stop: SSOM,
Washington, DC 20402-9373. (Or call GPO Customer Service at 202 512-2303.)**
To keep subscription prices down, the Government
Printing Office mails subscribers only one renewal notice. You can tell how many copies are left in your subscription by checking the number that follows "ISSDUE"
on the top line of your mailing label. For example, when
this number is 003, it means you have three issues left
in your subscription, and GPO will send you a renewal
notice. The number 000 means you have received your
last issue. To be sure that your service continues without interruption, please return your renewal notice
promptly.

January-February 1994

FAA *Aviation News*

Volume 33   Number 1

Features

Departments

Front Cover: *A canopy formation team joins up
over Wisconsin. The largest formation record, held
by the U.S, is 38 canopies (parachutes). Photo by
Andre Jesmanowicz, U.S Parachute Association*

Back Cover: *This Sun 'N Fun photograph is a
reminder that spring time flying activities are just
around the corner. Photo by H.D. Chamberlain*

Another Step Toward Rebuilding

Photos and story by Phyllis Anne Duncan, *Editor*

"Hi, I'm David. What do you fly? A *Skyhawk*? Great airplane. Me? A *Baron*, but I had to sell it. I'm without my own airplane for the first time in 20 years. I miss it. How about you, what do you fly? A *Mooney*? Another great bird. . . "

What else do pilots who meet for the first time talk about except what each flies? The snippet of conversation above seems fairly typical, then, until you know that the speaker is FAA Administrator David R. Hinson.

The occasion was his speech before the 38th Annual Convention of the Aircraft Owners and Pilots Association, held in Orlando, FL, this past November and attended by a record 7,000+. Hinson was late beginning his speech because he spent several minutes "working the room," going from pilot to pilot, shaking hands and "hangar flying." Bearing no visible identification of his role, he strolled almost anonymously among the attendees who had gathered to see him, his presence given away only by the number of photographers cataloging his walk for posterity.

One perplexed pilot turned to another and asked, "Who did I just shake hands with?"

"Administrator Hinson."

"The FAA Administrator? Why, he seems like a regular guy."

Hinson began his "speech" by saying he was pleased to be among "real pilots who fly real airplanes for real fun." He then set aside his prepared speech and spoke for over an hour off the cuff, reminiscing about his "40 years as a customer of the FAA." During his tenure as an airline pilot, airline president, Fixed Base Operator (FBO), and airplane owner, he indicated he had encountered the occasional problem with an individual in the FAA, but he was now proud to head "the world's finest aviation safety organization with the world's leading fund of aviation knowledge." The United States, he said, "offers more opportunities for flying in a safe environment than anywhere in the world. We have the finest general aviation environment anyone could want." All this stems from the FAA doing its job.

However, he added that organizations like AOPA need "to make a lot of noise" because FAA must compete with many other agencies and departments for federal resources. This "noise" also makes FAA sensitive to the concerns of general aviation. He added, "I want to be and will be an advocate for general aviation. I believe in general aviation."

Airline Commission and National Program Review

Hinson briefly covered the results of the President's Commission on Airlines and the Vice President's National Program Review and their possible effects on the functions of FAA. The one of most concern to the people in the room was the privatization of the air traffic service. AOPA has gone on record opposing the suggestion of the National Program Review that the air traffic system be changed to either a private, public, or government corporation.

Problems with the procurement and budget processes have slowed air traffic modernization, and privatization would alleviate a great deal of red tape involved in budgeting and procurement. A non-government air traffic service would also not be subject to government personnel practices, meaning controllers could be hired—and fired—without the process of appeal granted to government workers.

On the other hand, some sort of user fee for a private air traffic service would probably have to be charged. Hinson cited the example of many other countries around the world who have private air traffic control.

Hinson reported that the FAA is currently studying the feasibility of privatizing air traffic, but that the look will be "a long, hard" one. Given the current safety record, "you have to think a long time about changing a system that works so well." For example, in a recent year, "there were 144,000,000 operations in the air traffic system with a delay rate of .075%, of which .4% were weather-related."

FAA Administrator David R. Hinson

Continued on page 20

U.S. Parachute Association

by H. Dean Chamberlain, *Associate Editor*

According to the United States Parachute Association's training manual, "The first rule for all skydivers is to land with an open parachute." *The Skydiver's Information Manual* then goes on to list another rule, "Don't hit an obstacle upon landing." Like other aviation rules, they both state the obvious. The problem is, like other aviation rules, getting everyone to learn and to obey the rules.

Although the two skydiving rules seem very basic, there is nothing basic about today's sport of skydiving. For those who have not kept up with the sport, skydiving is as different today from the old images of World War II paratroopers leaping from C-47's as today's automobiles are from the cars of that era. Like today's cars, today's skydivers and their equipment come in a wide variety of colors, styles, and shapes. Today, you see skydivers dressed in multi-colored florescent jump suits landing beneath rainbow-colored square parachutes. Quite often that skydiver is a woman. Today, skydivers range in age from teenagers and young adults to senior citizens. Not only is skydiving open to men and women, young or old, it is open to many physically challenged persons. Although there are certain minimum physical requirements that should be met, just about everyone can skydive today using some of the new techniques developed over the last 10

years or so. In many cases, skydiving is a family affair.

Gone are the days when your basic macho male ex-military parachutist jumped surplus military round chutes in classic government white, orange, or green. Today, like other active sports such as skiing or scuba diving, skydiving has undergone a technological evolution involving new and safer designs, lighter materials, better training, and the addition of exciting colors such as vibrant reds, yellows, pinks, and blues. For the daring, they can now buy hot florescent colors to match their spirit. For the more conservative skydiver, equipment in classic black is still available.

This change in equipment and its resulting increase in the sport's safety record has contributed to the increased numbers of people trying the sport. This change in the sport has been highlighted in some recent movies and television commercials. Some commercials feature skydivers sky surfing for today's soft-drink generation. All of these changes and the increased media exposure resulting from the changes have resulted in a dramatic increase in the

number of people taking that first leap. Helping to make that first leap more exciting and safer is a technique called tandem parachute jumping.

During a tandem jump, a qualified, experienced instructor is attached to a student by a harness that is then connected to a parachute system built for two. The advantages are many. For those who only want to make one jump, they can make that jump with a minimum amount of training because the tandem instructor is there to teach and help the student during the entire jump from exit to landing. In the past, first-time jumpers had to spend hours training for any anticipated emergency before they could make their jump. Now, using the tandem technique, they can enjoy that jump with only about a 30 minute to one hour training period before they jump, knowing that if they have a problem an expert is there to handle it. The technique is also used for student training beyond the first jump. It accelerates student learning as a student prepares for his or her first solo jump. Before a student's first solo jump though, the student should be trained to handle normal emergencies as part of the student's training. Proper training is important. Expert training is needed because like other active sports such as flying, scuba diving, or mountain climbing, skydiving has risks. Death or serious injury is possible. Like pilots, scuba divers, or mountain climbers, skydivers can substantially reduce their accident risk through the use of good equipment, use of available safety devices, proper training, and by following established and accepted rules and safety procedures.

Like the other articles in our FAA/Industry Partnership Series, we are recognizing one of the major membership groups within sport parachuting that is dedicated to promoting safety within the sport. It does this by working with the FAA and by setting standards and operating requirements for its member skydivers and drop zone (DZ) operators that make up part of the largely self-regulated sport of skydiving. That membership group is the United States Parachute Association (USPA) headquartered in Alexandria VA. Located just across the Potomac River from Washington DC, the not-for-profit USPA Inc., has an interesting history in sport parachuting. Since its founding, USPA has been a division of the National Aeronautic Association (NAA) in the United States and is the official U.S. representative of the Fédération Aéronautique International (FAI) in the U.S. For those not familiar with FAI, it is the international aviation organization based in France that oversees sport aviation and recognizes aviation records set world-wide. As a recognized representative for parachuting and skydiving activities in the U.S., USPA plays an important role in developing rules and safety procedures for its members that are recognized throughout the sport and world.

Sport parachuting or skydiving is somewhat like the ultralight vehicle movement in the U.S. Although the FAA has specific regulations that deal with both, FAA considers both to be self-regulating sports. As a result, FAA regulations are designed more to protect those on the ground than those in the sport. FAA sets only minimum standards for the sport. FAR Part 105, Parachute Jumping, only outlines where and under what conditions intentional parachute jumping may occur, what FAA-approved equipment is required, and the responsibilities of the skydiver and/or jump-plane pilot. FAR Part 105 and other rules that deal

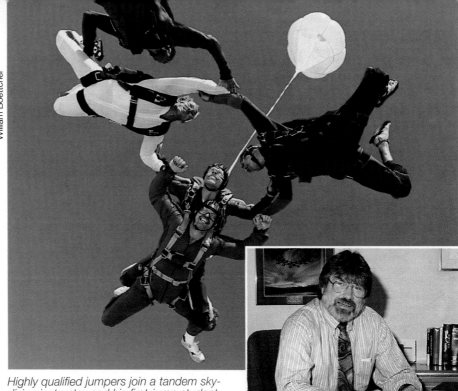

Highly qualified jumpers join a tandem skydiving instructor and his first-jump student.

USPA Executive Director, Jerry Rouillard

with parachuting do not get involved in the specific training of skydivers and certain other aspects of the sport.

Because FAA considers skydiving a self-regulated sport, individual skydivers are responsible in large part for their own safety and training. This self-regulating, individual responsibility aspect of the sport can create a potential problem for someone not familiar with the sport. In a sport where there is a possibility of death or serious injury, the question becomes one of how can someone who wants to make a jump learn what is safe and not safe without knowledge of the sport.

The answer is USPA. As one of the two widely recognized industry groups, the other being the Parachute Industry Association (PIA) which represents primarily parachute manufacturers, USPA is recognized by the FAA as the industry group that sets training standards, issues USPA parachute licenses and ratings accepted by the industry, recognizes drop zone (DZ) operators who follow USPA standards, and promotes safety in the sport. With a membership of more than 27,000 jumpers, USPA officials believe their organization represents most of the dedicated skydivers in the U.S. According to USPA Executive Director Jerry Rouillard, only about 10 percent of all first-time

jumpers continue in the sport. Many people only make one jump just to see what skydiving is like. In discussing first time jumpers, he made one point very clear. "No one should ever jump unless that person really wants to jump. No one should feel forced to jump as a result of a dare, bet, or because their spouse or significant other wants them to jump," he said. "Skydiving should be a personal decision made because you want to jump, not because of someone else."

During an interview with Rouillard and Jack Gregory, USPA's Director of Training, at USPA headquarters, they discussed many aspects of USPA. Both are proud of USPA's current growth rate. For the last several years, USPA's membership has grown at a rate of about 12 percent per year, and this past year is no exception. They attribute USPA's growth rate to several factors. One is the public's increased awareness of the sport. Another is the technological advances made in the sport. Today's new, light-weight equipment makes it easy for more people to participate in the sport. Both men believe the major change in the sport has been the development of tandem jumping.

Skydiving Flight Safety

Many skydivers think mainly about their next jump, not how they are going to get to their jump altitude. Recently, FAA has identified a safety problem related to skydiving that both USPA and the FAA are working to solve. The problem is the safe operation of jump aircraft used by skydivers. For example, two aircraft accidents in the recent past killed 27 people. That number includes both jumpers and pilots. Over the years, incidents of fuel starvation, mechanical problems and other aircraft-related problems at drop zones indicate that pilots, drop zone operators, and skydivers may not have been paying as much attention to the safe operation of their jump aircraft as they should. Part of the problem may be a desire to get as many people in an aircraft as possible and drop them as quickly as possible. In the process certain Federal Aviation Regulations (FAR) dealing with safety may be compromised. Part of the problem may be the pilot-in-command's failure to comply with appropriate Federal Aviation Regulations. Part of the problem may be skydivers' and especially first-time skydivers' lack of knowledge of safe aircraft operating requirements.

One of the factors identified in the above crashes was that some of the jumpers were not wearing seatbelts.

In the past, some skydivers were reluctant to wear seatbelts in jump aircraft because they believed that they needed to be unrestricted so they could jump out of the aircraft in case of trouble. At jump altitude this idea might work, but at low altitudes such as during takeoff where most aircraft accidents occur there is normally not enough altitude for a parachute to function. FAA believes that some aircraft accidents have been caused by the pilot's loss of aircraft control because of the rapid change in aircraft weight and balance as skydivers tried to exit the aircraft. Another problem with jumpers not wearing a restraining device in an aircraft involved in either an accident or during a quick stop on the runway on takeoff is the fact non-restrained jumpers can interfere with the pilot or the controls and cause loss of aircraft control, or the jumpers can

be seriously injured when they impact the aircraft's structure when the aircraft stops suddenly. In either case, skydivers increase their risk exposure to serious injury or death in a survivable accident by not wearing a restraining device. Like an automobile driver or passenger, parachutists are statistically safer restrained in an aircraft than when they do not wear a restraining device.

For those wondering why we are using the awkward term, restraining device, the answer is simple. Not all aircraft have seats for skydivers. In most aircraft, the seats have been removed to aid jumpers exiting the aircraft. Jumpers sit on the floor. The question now is for the FAA and the parachute industry to develop a restraining device that is both safe and non-binding that jumpers will wear. Devices are available. The problem is getting jumpers to wear them. A non-binding restraining device is important because some skydivers fear that a seat belt or restraining device might get tangled in their equipment and either jeopardize the safety of their jump or result in their parachute opening in the aircraft. The problem facing the industry is developing a restraining device that provides the required level of safety needed and one that all jumpers will use.

Finally, although it is not the intention of FAA to make skydivers into pilots so they will know how to preflight and operate a safe jump aircraft, there are some common sense things that all skydivers should consider before going for that next one-way plane ride. Also, it is important for skydivers to remember that the FAA does not consider parachutists as aircraft passengers in the same way it defines passengers under FAR § 91.111(c) or in commercial operations and under FAR Part 121 or 135. FAA considers parachutists as aircraft occupants rather than as passengers as defined in the FAR. Occupants, although not considered aircraft crew members by the FAA, are considered by the FAA to be part of the operation, and therefore, they should be knowledgeable of aircraft and parachuting

operations. The following are a few helpful tips for being an informed occupant.

1. Does the aircraft look safe. Aircraft used to fly jumpers take a lot of abuse. Although looks may not be a true indicator of the quality of maintenance an aircraft receives, generally speaking, an operation that takes care of an aircraft's appearance also takes care of its problems.

2. How well is the aircraft being maintained? If you have any doubts, you should talk to the aircraft's pilot.

3. How experienced is the pilot? Although jump pilots are not required to have a commercial pilot certificate unless flying for hire, the unique requirements of flying jumpers requires a level of experience that some new pilots may lack. Aircraft handling can change as jumpers move to the door and exit.

4. Is the plane only carrying the number of jumpers authorized. The number may be found in the aircraft's operating handbook and certification paperwork. That number may be modified by an authorized supplemental type certificate (STC) change or FAA field approval change made to that aircraft. Some aircraft require FAA-approved changes for skydiving. Aircraft weight and balance requirements must be within approved limits for safe flight.

5. Are restraining devices provided for the authorized number of jumpers?

6. What is the role of the jump master in aircraft operations.

7. What type of pilot briefing is provided jumpers before takeoff?

These are only some of the types of questions jumpers should ask about their jump aircraft and the pilots who fly them. As we said in our article, although the FAA and USPA work to promote safety in sport parachuting, ultimately, each skydiver is responsible for his or her own safety. A responsibility that starts on the ground and does not end until that jumper is safely back on the ground again. To paraphrase two of USPA's rules, to be safe you should always land with an open parachute and don't hit any objects upon landing.

Safe jumping.

Tandem parachuting was developed by two parachute manufacturers. Tandem jumping was authorized under an FAA exemption to FAR Part 105 issued in 1984 and subsequently renewed. The exemption authorized the companies and their respective employees, representatives, and other volunteer experimental parachute test jumpers under their direction and control to make tandem parachute jumps as part of an ongoing test program. Because of the importance of tandem jumping to the industry and the expiration of the current exemption in 1994, USPA is part of an ongoing industry/FAA group reviewing the status of tandem jumping. The outcome of the group's review could be a proposed rulemaking change to FAR Part 105 authorizing tandem jumping.

WHY USPA

Safety is the most important reason for joining USPA or training at a USPA member drop zone. As we stated earlier, in this largely self-regulated sport, FAR Part 105 does not require a skydiver to have an FAA license to jump. What this really means is that the only industry licensing system that recognizes any "level of demonstrated skill, knowledge, and experience, ranked according to the level of accomplishment" is that of USPA. USPA's minimum training standards for licensing its members, its instructors, and participating DZ operators are internationally recognized by FAI member countries and by the FAA. Not having a USPA issued parachuting license will not prevent anyone from skydiving if they want to jump. But if they want to compete in international competition or instruct at USPA Group Member Training Centers, they must have a USPA license. The reason they need a USPA license is because someone having one of USPA's four parachuting licenses, A, B, C, or D license with D being the highest, has demonstrated his or her ability to safely skydive. The same is true of someone having one of USPA's instructional ratings such as its jumpmaster, instructor, or instructor/examiner rating. The rating identifies someone who has not only demon-

Jonny Goss and Graham Godding record a straddle stand-up during Skyblazin' 92's compulsory round over Skydive Arizona.

Mike McGowan

Steve Scott

A 4-way freefall formation team exits from a Cessna over Perris, CA.

strated his or her skydiving ability, but also his or her ability to teach skydiving.

This is important for potential skydivers because it provides them with a basis for comparing training programs as well as verifying an instructor's skill, knowledge, and teaching ability. Since skydiving is one of those sports where a serious error can be fatal, proper training is critical to all involved in the sport. USPA provides a recognized industry standard for that training. Another benefit of USPA membership is the fact that USPA not only sets standards for its members, it also requires USPA drop zone operators to operate according to specific standards both in terms of skydiving training and related activities as well complying with responsible business practices as a condition of membership. What all of this means for someone interested in learning how to skydive is that they can look to USPA and one of its Group Member USPA drop zone operators and USPA instructors as a means of getting good training. If the operator and instructor follow required USPA guidelines, you should receive training designed to minimize your accident risk and make you a safe jumper. Training that is recognized both by the sport parachute industry and the FAA.

Because every jump carries a certain amount of risk, every jumper needs good training to reduce that risk to an acceptable level. If you do not feel comfortable making a jump, don't jump. Only the individual jumper knows how he or she feels about any particular jump. When in doubt, don't jump. To minimize the inherent risk involved in the sport, all new and non-current jumpers need to get quality training or recurrent training at a reputable drop zone before they jump. USPA Group membership is an industry recognized way of finding such an operator. ∎

To learn more about the exciting sport of skydiving or benefits provided by USPA, you can visit a USPA Group skydiving center near you, or you can contact USPA headquarters in Alexandria, VA, for additional information. Upon request, USPA will send anyone who asks, a "Dear Friend" skydiving information packet. USPA can also provide you a list of the USPA Group Member drop zones near you. USPA's address is United States Parachute Association, 1440 Duke Street, Alexandria, VA 22314. USPA's telephone number is (703) 836-3495. Its FAX number is (703) 836–2843.

Pilot Decision Making

by Tom Hamilton

Do You Remember How?

This is Part Six of a seven-part series that first appeared in *Balloon Life* magazine in 1989 and was originally written for balloon pilots. We have left the lighter-than-air examples in because the overlying issue of pilot decision making affects all pilots.　　**—Editor**

You have made the commitment to ballooning, bought the balloon, taken the flight instruction, passed the written exam, passed the oral exam, and passed the flight check. Now you are a licensed pilot—it says so in black and white. What a way to enjoy those lazy days just floating in the skies. As time goes along how much of what you learned do you remember?

This issue of our continuing series on Pilot Decision Making examines skill retention. A few years ago the Federal Aviation Administration conducted studies on pilot skill retention. In this article we will take a look at some of the information that was gathered.

Some pilots find it difficult to believe that human learning, once acquired, is not stored permanently in the mind—as is possible with computers. But the fact is that human intelligence retention is selective; we retain both skills and knowledge in proportion to their use

and apparent importance to our survival. The process of forgetting can begin almost the moment we walk off the landing site with a newly acquired certificate or rating in hand. This is certainly true for general aviation pilots who may fly infrequently and irregularly, in between work and family demands on their time, i.e., those who fly for pleasure or recreation, or for occasional business convenience.

Some understanding of how rapidly the night skills of pilots can erode resulted from a study conducted at the FAA's Technical Center in Atlantic City, New Jersey. The study was designed to track the retention or loss of pilot skills over a 24 month period following certification as a private pilot (fixed wing); and to observe the effect of additional training on retention of the initial skill level. A secondary objective was to learn how accurate recently certificated private pilots were in predicting their ability to carry out basic flying tasks and in evaluating their actual performance.

The group of pilots studied consisted of 42 subjects, with an average age of 25. At intervals of 8, 16, and 24 months they were individually tested and rated on their performance of 29 basic flight tasks. Some were given additional training towards instrument and multi-engine rating in the intervals between flight checks. The pilot subjects were all told in advance exactly which tasks they would be tested on.

They were also invited to predict how well they thought they would do on each task, and to comment later on their performance. During the 24 months of the study the pilots as a group average about three hours of flying per month. However. those who received no advanced training flew less than one hour a month.

In scoring the subjects' performance on the 29 basic flight tasks, the investigators used as a base line the score recorded during their private pilot testing on these same tasks. Over the 24 month test period the group as a whole averaged a 33 percent increase in flight task errors. Pilots who had performed at least nine out of ten flight tasks correctly during their initial testing now completed only six out of ten tasks correctly, on the average. (Their written test scores also dropped by about 16 percent.)

The study concluded that recently certificated pilots who do not fly regularly undergo a rapid and significant deterioration of their ability to perform flight tasks. (No definition of what it is to "fly regularly" was attempted.) Some pilots in the study logged as many as six or more hours a month in the first eight months, including instrument and multi-engine training, yet committed nearly as many errors in the test at the end of the period as other pilots who flew less than one hour per month and received no advanced training.

The study observed that some types of advanced training were helpful in reducing skill erosion, but the effects were temporary in any case. (See Figures 1 and 2) Not only recently certificated pilots, but the majority of the general aviation pilot population was considered susceptible to rapid skill erosion—i.e., "forgetting"—in the absence of some form of continuation training.

The self-prediction and self-evaluation forms completed by the subject pilots largely failed to conform to the errors in their actual flight task performance. In other words, their assumed level of competence was much higher than their demonstrated performance.

In this connection the FAA-required Biennial Flight Review (BFR) serves an important purpose in calling attention to unsuspected skill weaknesses in the basket. However, the responsibility for taking appropriate remedial actions, following the completion of a BFR, rests with the individual. Many pilots apparently assume that they can improve their skills by resolve alone, rather than by means of scheduled practice or training—which is illusory.

Skill retention or loss in flying is generally divided into two kinds; cognitive/procedural and control oriented—or, more simply put, mental versus manual tasks. The study confirmed the widely held belief that the most serious skill loss is in the mental area.

It should be noted that these errors did not necessarily constitute an unsafe flight condition, insofar as the pilots were able to complete the maneuver without incident, but there was clear evidence that flight skills had eroded since certification, and presumably would continue to erode given the present pattern of flight activity.

Some of the flight tasks which in this study showed the greatest and least degree of skill loss during the 24 month test period are shown in Figure 3. Note that those with minimal skill loss are primary control-oriented, with sources of immediate feedback.

Ideally, skill retention is best reinforced with continued flight practice, training, and testing.

Next issue will look at some programs that pilots can participate in to improve their skill retention. ■

Our thanks to Mr. Tom Hamilton, publisher of Balloon Life *and author of this series, for permission to reprint this and subsequent articles. For subscription information contact Mr. Hamilton at 2145 Dale Avenue, Sacramento, CA 95815; (916) 922–9648.*

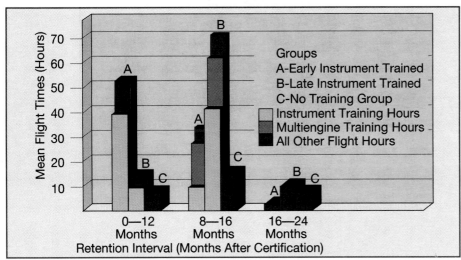

Figure 1. Mean flight times of the groups by eight month intervals

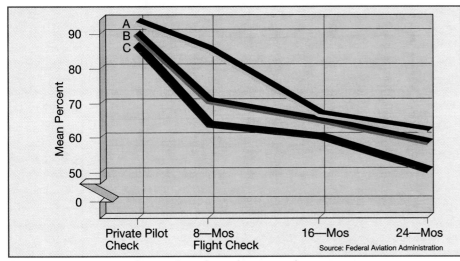

Figure 2. Mean percent of correctly performed measures by groups

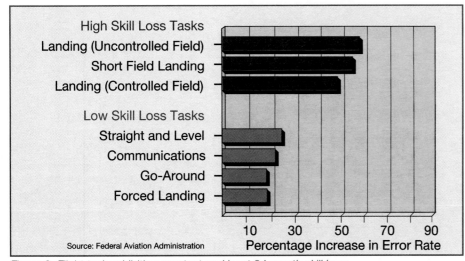

Figure 3. Flight task exhibiting greatest and least 24 month skill loss

HELICOPTER SAFETY

by H. Dean Chamberlain, *Associate Editor*

It is not often that a helicopter crew receives the kind of attention this crew did on what they described as a relatively simple job. For them the job was easy, but then making a job look easy is the mark of a true professional, and this crew was professional. If the job was routine, the attention the job received was anything but routine. Few jobs get the national exposure this one did when phase one was done, let alone the attention the job received when phase two was completed months later.

The first part of the job was done on Mother's Day 1993 as a few thousand spectators and several news media camera crews gathered to watch what many believed would be a historical moment. A helicopter was going to take off from the Plaza area in front of the U.S. Capitol and pluck the 15,000 pound, 19 and a half foot Statue of Freedom from its perch on top of the Capitol where it had stood for the last 130 years. Then the helicopter would lower the statue to the Plaza for months of restoration work. Finally, the helicopter would land back on the Plaza before departing. According to the crew, the job was simple compared to some of their typical jobs of moving heavy, external loads around buildings and hazardous construction sites. But this was not one of their typical jobs at some out of the way construction site.

Not only was the Statue on top of the U.S. Capitol in Washington, DC, but as everyone knows, nothing in Washington, DC is ever simple. According to Mr. James Cieutat, Project Director for the Architect of the Capitol's office, there were many agencies, contractors, and workers with some role in the project. The FAA was one of the agencies involved. Then like many Washington projects, the selection of what helicopter organization was going to remove and later replace the statue was controversial. First a National Guard unit was supposed to do the lift. Then the President of Helicopter Association In-

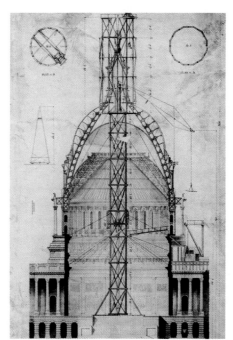

An 1863 architectural drawing shows how Statue of Freedom was originally installed.

ternational, Mr. Frank L. Jensen, Jr., and Erickson Air-Crane Company of Central Point, OR protested that this type of service was available in the private sector and that a civilian company should get the job. In the end, Erickson Air-Crane which specializes in this type of work was awarded the contract for the job. Erickson demonstrated again the unique abilities of general aviation helicopters to perform those special missions that helicopters can do so well. The company, using a Sikorsky *Skycrane* (S-64F) helicopter, quickly picked up the statue and gently lowered it onto a special mount built near the entrance to the Capitol. According to Max Evans, the pilot in command, the ease with which the job was done was a reflection of the experience of the crew and workers involved and the planning that went into the job. Part of that planning involved the FAA's Washington Flight Standards District Office (FSDO). Why was the FSDO involved? Its involvement can be summed up in one word "Safety." According to Mr. Bill Osborne, the FAA aviation safety inspector assigned the project, he was there to ensure the job was done according to safe operating procedures described by the operator and approved by FAA. Procedures designed to primarily protect those on the ground in case of an accident involving either the helicopter or the external load. FAR Part 133, Rotorcraft External-Load Operations, lists the certification requirements

FAA Safety Inspector Bill Osborne (Right) checks Larry Pravecek's pilot certificates.

FAA Safety Inspector Bill Osborne (Left Front) watches as "Bubba" is prepared for the day's job.

for operators, crew members, and aircraft used in external load operations. The FAR also lists the required equipment as well as procedures for working with external loads.

One of those requirements is that, whenever a helicopter is going to carry an external load in a congested area, a congested area plan must be developed for FAA approval before the job can be done. From verifying the qualifications of the crew to reviewing the emergency plans for dropping the load in case of a problem, to inspecting the job site, FSDO inspectors are frequently involved in many aspects of a congested area job.

This job was no exception. Inspector Osborne met with government and company representatives days before the mission to review the plans and to conduct an on-site inspection. He would later check and monitor the actual operation. Throughout the planning and actual job, the FAA's emphasis was placed on flight safety, including the safe entry and exit of the helicopter in the Prohibited Area (P-56) surrounding the Capitol Area, the development of contingency plans in case of a problem either with the helicopter or load, the safety of spectators watching the lift, and the safety of workers on top of the Capitol and those on the ground. As part of the area plan, a detailed inspection was made of the Capitol and surrounding area to ensure that all loose objects were secured to prevent them from becoming projectiles that could endanger the flight crew, the workers working with them on the project, or the

spectators. The inspection also included structures that could be damaged by the rotor wash from the helicopter.

The project went off without a hitch including all of the resulting publicity.

What a difference five months makes in Washington.

For the October 23 reinstallation, company employees and crew members now wore custom-designed hats and shirts promoting the company's part in the restoration project as Inspector Osborne reviewed the company's confined area plan the day before the job. Again, he toured the grounds and Capitol with the crew and other Government personnel to ensure that no safety factor dealing with the actual external load was overlooked. This was one job where flight and load safety were critical. This job was special. After all, no one wanted to see the 15,000 pound Statue of Freedom go crashing through the Capitol Dome. Another factor was that although the removal and restoration of the statue received national attention when it was done, the reinstallation of the statue on top of the Capitol was going to receive Presidential attention. President Clinton and the leaders of the House and Senate were to be present to view the operation along with other members of Congress. On the morning of the job thousands of spectators went through security checks to gain access to the Capitol grounds to view the event as workers and the helicopter crew prepared for the reinstallation. National media representatives were on hand to record the

operation. Everyone waited for the President's arrival. Once he arrived, the helicopter crew and workers placed the statue on top of the Capitol with the same ease and care with which they had removed it. Following a meeting with the crew, the President commemorated the bicentennial of the Capitol with a public ceremony on the West Front or Mall side of the Capitol.

Although the actual operation was comparatively easy, according to the crew the job only took about 13 minutes, the historic value of the operation was immeasurable. The operation demonstrated to the world that a professional crew using the right equipment and following prescribed safety rules can make even a Washington job look easy. Once more, aviation demonstrated that for those special jobs that aviation is uniquely qualified to do, it can not only do it safety, it can do it even when the President is watching. ∎

President Clinton and Congressional leaders observed the reinstallation of the statue.

H. Dean Chamberlain

Amateur-built Aircraft

by H. Dean Chamberlain, *Associate Editor*

How many ways can you tell when spring is coming? Melting snow is one way. Another is the sound of small aircraft taking flight after a long winter on the ground. For some, the best way of all may be the sound of aircraft construction as amateur-aircraft builders try to finish their projects in time for Sun 'n Fun. For those not familiar with Sun 'n Fun, it is the large, annual, spring time, Experimental Aircraft Association (EAA) fly-in in Lakeland, FL. In case anyone is wondering why we are talking about Sun 'n Fun, the answer is simple. It is the first, large, EAA event of the year and, like other EAA events, it is the gathering place of many amateur-built aircraft which is the subject of this article.

As many first-time builders work to complete their amateur-built aircraft in time for either Sun 'n Fun in April or Oshkosh later in the summer, it seems like a good time to review some important information about building and certificating such aircraft. We also want to point out some important information for those who go to either event and decide to build an aircraft.

In our recent series on FAA aviation safety inspectors (ASI's), we described some of the responsibilities of the airworthiness ASI's. As we said, airworthiness ASI's do more than just monitor the health and well-being of the commercially produced aircraft fleet. AW inspectors play an important role in the amateur-built aircraft community. They inspect and issue FAA experimental airworthiness

certificates for amateur-built aircraft that meet applicable FAA standards under FAR Part 21, *Subpart H-Airworthiness Certificates.* They also can issue Repairman Certificates to those builders who qualify. These two ASI functions are the foundation of the amateur-built movement.

A quick review of Federal Aviation Regulation (FAR) § 21.191(g), *Experimental certificates, Operating amateur-built aircraft,* states in part that persons who have fabricated and assembled the major portion of an aircraft for their own education or recreation can request FAA certification of that aircraft as an experimental amateur-built aircraft. Then FAR § 21.193, *Experimental certificates: general,* outlines what a builder must do and what an FAA inspector must check before the inspector can issue an experimental airworthiness certificate for an amateur-built aircraft. To help builders meet the FAR requirements, the FAA has published several Advisory Circulars (AC) to help builders safely construct and fly their aircraft. One of these is the important AC 90–89, *Amateur-Built Aircraft Flight Testing Handbook,* which discusses important safety recommendations for those preparing for their amateur-built aircraft's first flight. Another AC, AC 20–27D, *Certification and Operation of amateur-built aircraft,* provides guidance and information about airworthiness certification and operation of amateur-built aircraft. In addition to the various AC's produced by the FAA, another important item pub-

lished by the FAA's Flight Standards Service's Manufacturing Standards Section (AFS-613) in Oklahoma City, (405) 954–4103, is the *Revised Listing of Eligible Amateur-built Aircraft Kits* that lists the kits that meet the FAA's major portion requirement of FAR § 21.191(g). The latest issue, dated October 1, 1993, is available upon request from AFS-613. The list is important. If an aircraft kit is listed as having met the FAA's major portion requirement, this will assist the FAA inspector in determining that the kit meets the rule at certification time. This makes the certification process easier. Each builder should check the list for his or her specific model kit. Not all models of a given manufacturer may be approved.

Repairman Certificates

AW inspectors also can issue qualified aircraft builders a Repairman Certificate that allows them to maintain the amateur-built aircraft they built as well as perform FAA-required inspections on that aircraft. For those who qualify, it is a great deal. There are restrictions. For example, the certificate is only issued to a specific builder for a specific aircraft identified by make, model, and serial number. The Repairman Certificate does not allow the builder to do required inspections on any other aircraft. The exceptions are if the builder is a certificated pilot, that person can do preventive maintenance on another aircraft under FAR Part 43, and if the person is a certificated A&P maintenance technician, he or she can work on other aircraft on the basis of the A&P certificate.

The theory behind issuing a Repairman Certificate to a person who builds an FAA-certificated experimental aircraft is simple. The person who built the aircraft or the major portion of that aircraft should be the most knowledgeable of that aircraft and its systems. Each amateur-built aircraft is unique, and there are no repair stations authorized to perform repairs on amateur-built aircraft. Before everyone runs to their local Flight Standards District Office (FSDO) claiming to be an aircraft builder, there are a few requirements that must be met. Repairman Certificates are only issued to builders who can document they have constructed the aircraft. If more than one person constructed the aircraft, only the team leader or the person who did the majority of the construction would be eligible for the Repairman Certificate. This is another good reason for keeping your builder's log up to date. For those individuals who are thinking about buying a partially constructed aircraft, if you cannot establish through the builder's log that you are the primary builder of that aircraft, then you will not be eligible for a Repairman Certificate. Repairman Certificates are not transferable to the new owners of an amateur-built aircraft. But, the person who holds the Repairman Certificate for that aircraft may continue to perform the condition inspections on that aircraft after it is sold. The only other person who can sign off a condition inspection is a certificated Airframe and Powerplant mechanic.

Potential builders thinking about building a kit aircraft should check with their local FSDO, FAA Manufacturing Inspection District Office (MIDO), or the following FAA electronic bulletin board (EBB) for amateur-built aircraft information before buying a particular kit and during construction. One reason is not all kit aircraft meet the FAA's major portion requirement for experimental, amateur-built aircraft certification. Some kits are too complete. Buyers of such kits are assemblers, rather than builders. Another reason is the certification and safety information either the offices or the EBB can provide anyone planning on building and certificating an amateur-built aircraft. (The bulletin board is the Safety Data Exchange Bulletin Board operated by the FAA Small Airplane Certification Directorate in Kansas City, MO. The EBB's telephone number is 1–800–426–3814. The password is SAFETY. The protocol is ANSI/VT100/300–9600 Baud/8/N/1. The EBB operates 24 hours per day.)

Construction Tips

Potential builders should check with their local FSDO, MIDO, or EAA chapter before and during any construction project because each can provide important construction tips. For example, builders should maintain a photographic and written record of construction to show compliance with the major portion requirement of FAR § 21.191(g). They should keep all material receipts. And they should develop a safe test flight program for their aircraft in preparation for their aircraft's certification. All of these and other construction and safety tips are designed to make certificating an aircraft easier and safer.

MINI PROJECT CHECKLIST

Since most airmen like checklists, the following mini checklist is a few representative ideas potential builders may want to consider before starting a project.

• Do you have the experience and ability to do the work. In the case of the Lenn brothers, they had already built one aircraft as well as a 60-foot motor yacht.

• Do you have the resources to complete the project. Many would-be builders start, stop, and then sell their projects when they either run out of money or time or both.

• Where are you going to build the aircraft? A living room is not the best place. Hangers can be expensive construction sites until needed for final assembly.

• Do you have your family's support for the project. Building an aircraft takes time, patience, money, hard work, labor and, if you have a family, family support. Is your family willing to help you when you need help? Are they willing to share "their" house or garage with "your" aircraft parts? Are they willing to share you and your time with the project?

• Building an aircraft does have its good points. One hot air balloonist whose family helped him make a balloon said the time the family spent working together on the balloon was worth more than the balloon.

These are only some ideas all builders may want to consider before starting a project. For more information, interested builders can contact their local FAA office, talk to other pilots, visit their local airports and look for builders, join local flying clubs, review the EAA video tape discussed earlier or contact one of their local EAA chapters to talk to members building or who have built an aircraft. You just might decide to build the project of your life.

H. Dean Chamberlain

H. Dean Chamberlain

Certification

Certification involves many things. Although the FAA's amateur-built aircraft certification information packages provide detailed instructions on the certification process, here are a few of the items an inspector will check for during any certification procedure. The builder must apply for and have an aircraft registration number (N-number) from the FAA in Oklahoma City for the aircraft before it can be certified. The inspector will check the aircraft for acceptable construction based upon FAA/industry standards. Many of these standards are listed in the various FAA maintenance manuals available for sale from the Government Printing Office. Being able to show that these standards have been used is where a detailed builder's log or construction manual with good construction records becomes very important. The log should detail each step used in the construction of your aircraft. Each step should identify any materials (glues, wood, metal, etc.) or special tools used (jigs, alignment tools, etc.). This includes any tools you made to accomplish these tasks. All these items are taken into account when determining eligibility for certification. Again, a photographic history is also important. The photographs will be used to verify proper construction techniques and materials were used in hard to see or closed up areas not accessible by inspection holes. A photographic history of construction is a great help. The inspector will check for weight and balance information for the aircraft. And one of the most important segments of the certification process is the development of a safe flight test program for each amateur-built aircraft. As part of the certification process, a specified number of flight hours must be flown within a designated test area. The flight hour requirement is designed so a pilot can check the flight characteristics and construction of the aircraft in a safe area with minimal risk to those on the ground or to other aircraft in the air. Obviously in the interest of safety, passengers are not permitted on the proving flights. The flight requirement is important because although the FAA AW inspector can check the aircraft for such things as the use of acceptable construction techniques, and that the aircraft's weight and balance information have been computed, and other required items have been complied with, only a flight check can show that a particular aircraft's flight characteristics are safe. In essence, the aircraft's first pilot becomes its first test pilot.

Although a particular aircraft design may have hundreds of completed aircraft flying, each amateur-built aircraft is unique. Probably, no two models of the same aircraft design are ever constructed or equipped exactly the same. Upon certification, each amateur-aircraft builder becomes his or her aircraft's original manufacturer. As a result, although home-built models may look alike, because of possible undiscovered construction problems or changes made by its "manufacturer" during construction that might affect the aircraft's flight characteristics, every pilot flying a newly constructed aircraft on its first flight and later required certification flights must be prepared for any possibility. That is why a parachute, helmet, and appropriate safety gear are good things to wear during that first test flight because not every amateur-built aircraft survives its first flight unscratched. As outlined in the AC on testing amateur-built aircraft, a careful pilot will also have help standing by in case emergency assistance is needed as he or she flies off the required FAA flight test hours.

Flight Testing

To help builders and pilots test their aircraft, not all builders are pilots, the FAA's flight hour requirement will be listed as an operating limitation on the aircraft's experimental airworthiness certificate. The number of hours that must be flown is determined in part by the type of engine and propeller installed. (We are assuming a single-engine aircraft.) An aircraft with an FAA certificated engine and propeller requires less operating hours for example than one with non FAA certificated equipment. The reason is the FAA certificated engine-propeller combination does not have to reprove its airworthiness. That work was done during the combination's original certification process. Non-certificated equipment must be flown more hours to prove its reliability during a longer flight test period. The goal is to discover any potential safety problems in the aircraft or its systems before passengers are allowed to fly in the aircraft. The AC on flight testing amateur-built aircraft provides detailed ideas on how to develop a safe flight test program. Local EAA chapters can also provide builders guidance on safely testing newly constructed aircraft.

Any discrepancies discovered during the FAA certification inspection and flight hour requirement must be corrected and proper notification made to the FAA as part of the certification process. The inspector signing off the aircraft will outline how discrepancies must be corrected and notification made. The certification process also requires that future modifications to the aircraft be approved by the FAA. This is one reason it helps if detailed construction and test records are kept to verify that required actions have been completed and when.

Pilot Experience vs Risk

It is important that all pilots testing amateur-built aircraft know what they are doing and have a detailed plan for

testing the aircraft. History has shown that test flying amateur-built aircraft can be a high risk area for unqualified pilots. Qualification is not necessarily a function of total flight hours either. High-time pilots not familiar with a particular amateur-built aircraft's handling characteristics can have problems flying the aircraft the same as low-time pilots. The National Transportation Safety Board (NTSB) and FAA have the accident statistics to prove the risk factor. A casual review of an NTSB summary of more than 300 amateur-built aircraft accidents from January 1990 through December 1991 showed that only 38 pilots of those with reported pilot total flight time and time in type had less than 200 total flight hours. Only seven of those 38 pilots had less than 10 hours in type. The reason we call this review a casual one is because, in the summary, not every accident reported types of pilot time such as total time and time in type or the causes of the accidents. Some accidents had no pilot flight times reported. In many of the accidents, the pilots had thousands of flight hours with varying amounts of times in type. In one fatal accident the pilot had a reported 15,000 hours, but only 5 in type. In other accidents the pilots had many hours in type. Our point is anyone can have an accident. High-time pilots are not immune, nor is the number of hours in type a safety factor. What is apparent in looking at the summary is the number of reported accidents, fatal, serious, minor, and non-injury ones, that show one to five hours in type listed. The total is 38. This is approximately 10 percent of those accidents with flight hours listed. Although our safety review is not a scientific study of amateur-built aircraft accidents and their causes, we, *FAA Aviation News*, are saying that all pilots should exercise a greater degree of care when flying an amateur-built aircraft for their first few hours and especially if it is the aircraft's first flight. We are not saying that amateur-built aircraft are unsafe. We think that in some cases, the pilots, in the excitement of finishing their aircraft, may try to fly their new amateur-built aircraft without

benefit of an adequate checkout. Some aircraft are hard to get checked out in. After all, where do you find someone to check you out in a one-place aircraft model that only has a few models flying. To minimize everyone's risk, we are suggesting that everyone flying any aircraft for the first time should exercise due caution. Particularly, if your first flight in the aircraft is the aircraft's first flight. Enough said.

Flight Experience

The key we believe is for any pilot planning on making the first flight in an amateur-built aircraft to have experience testing and flying amateur-built aircraft. Ideally, the pilot should have some experience flying the same make and model amateur-built aircraft before making that first flight in a new aircraft. At a minimum the pilot should have some experience in a similar design or type of

aircraft. That experience could be in either an amateur-built or commercial aircraft with similar handling and speed characteristics. At a minimum, the pilot should talk to someone who flies similar equipment. This is one reason why joining a group such as EAA can benefit a builder or pilot planning on flying an amateur-built aircraft. The key is trying to learn from someone who has already done whatever you are trying to do.

As previously stated, to help reduce a pilot's first-flight risk exposure, the FAA has published guidelines on how to test new homebuilts that include pilot, aircraft, and equipment safety items, how to do high speed taxi tests, and how to develop a step-by-step test program. In addition, EAA and its local chapters can also provide pilots and builders a lot of information on constructing and safely flying amateur-built aircraft. Help is available for the asking. Needless to say, every first flight should be preceded by the best preflight the pilot has ever done. Crossed control cables can ruin the best pilot's day.

For more information on building and testing home-built aircraft, interested builders can contact their local FSDO, MIDO, or EAA chapter. They will all be glad to help anyone interested in building and testing amateur-built aircraft. EAA Headquarters also sells a 45-minute video titled *Building Your Own Aircraft, How to get Started*. The video provides some good ideas and suggestions for prospective builders to consider before buying their first kit part. EAA's telephone number is 1–800–843–3612. ∎

A TALE OF THREE BROTHERS

The following brief story illustrates a few of the construction and certification steps that Mr. Kaye (Boots) Lenn and his two brothers, Edwin and Wayne, of Culpeper, VA, went through in building and certificating their amateur-built Wheeler Express *in the spring of 1993. Like many others last spring, they too were trying to complete their aircraft in time for Sun 'n Fun 1993. Their story shows some interesting (typical?) problems or challenges that can develop between the time a decision is made to build a particular aircraft and its certification. Their story also highlights some of the important safety points that other builders may want to consider when building their own aircraft.*

Building an Aircraft

With an aviation background that dates back to World War II, and with one completed homebuilt aircraft project behind them, the Lenn brothers decided to build a *Wheeler Express* after Oshkosh 1988. After visiting the aircraft's factory in Washington state to get a feel for the company and looking at the aircraft's construction manuals, they bought their first two aircraft kits in October 1988. After starting to work on the kits, they discovered the construction manuals they had been impressed with at the factory were not as complete as they had thought. They said the factory kept revising the manuals during the project. This problem was eventually resolved.

They also had problems getting parts. "Parts were always slow in coming," Kaye said. To help others avoid similar problems, the brothers said that builders should check out what type and level of factory support is and will be available during a long term project. They pointed out that if someone is building a kit aircraft and if money and storage space are no problem the builder might want to buy all of the aircraft's kits at one time. Buying the complete aircraft kit package eliminates the possibility that required kits might not be available when needed in the future.

While waiting for additional kit parts in late 1989, the first prototype *Wheeler Express* crashed in Long Beach, CA. "We were a little hesitant to proceed," Kaye said. In their search for what caused the crash, the brothers wrote the Long Beach newspaper for details of the crash. According to the newspaper article and its photographs they were sent, the aircraft's engine apparently seized right after takeoff and the plane hit a house. "It was quite dramatic the way the aircraft was torn up, but the pilot and passenger just walked away from the fiery

crash. By the time the emergency crew arrived, the pilot and passenger had exited the wreckage and were sitting on the curb with only minor injuries. It made us feel good that the aircraft could take such a beating and the passengers could survive," Kaye said.

Then in 1990 with their fourth kit on the way, the second factory aircraft crashed in Wyoming with three fatalities. The aircraft had been on its way to Oshkosh for the EAA convention. Kaye said the NTSB would later attribute the cause of the crash of the 200 MPH aircraft to pilot error. The crash had a major impact on the brothers' project. The publicity, legal, and business concerns surrounding the two crashes of the factory aircraft caused the factory to shut down. "We were a little apprehensive that we would not be able to finish because of a lack of parts. We stopped working for almost a year because of the lack of parts," he said.

Then in 1991, a group of about 40 *Wheeler Express* builders, a few at a time, starting going to the Tacoma Narrows Airport (WA), the home of the *Wheeler Express* factory to try to build the third factory demonstrator. Slowly kit parts became available. Finally, in March 1993, the Lenn brothers certificated their aircraft. Since then they have flown it about 60 hours.

Although this article is a short summary of a completed amateur-built aircraft project that spanned several years, we think the Lenn brothers did several important things during their project. First they compared various models and made their selection decision based upon their skills, experience, and desired aircraft performance. Then they got involved in what was happening to their aircraft's design both before and after they decided on which aircraft to build. They visited the factory, met and talked with other builders, and kept track of the prototype aircrafts' accidents. They searched for information about the accidents and made decisions regarding completing their aircraft based upon that information. They even went to North Carolina to fly for more than an hour in a completed *Wheeler Express* to learn how the aircraft flies. And when it came time to certificate their aircraft, they worked closely with their local FAA airworthiness safety inspector. Throughout their project they had kept detailed parts and kit receipts, complete construction records, and a photographic scrapbook showing the project's history. Their record keeping and docu-

mentation efforts made it easy for the FAA Airworthiness Inspector from the Washington (DC) Flight Standards District Office to certificate their aircraft.

When asked if they had any advice for anyone thinking about building an aircraft, the Lenns' had several suggestions. First they believe pilots thinking about building an aircraft should determine why they want to build an aircraft. Their point is if a pilot wants to fly *now*, then that person should take the money he or she will spend on building a homebuilt aircraft and buy a good used aircraft. If a pilot enjoys building things, wants to learn more about aircraft, and is in no hurry to fly the completed homebuilt, then they said a homebuilt may be the right choice. They said a good kit aircraft will probably cost as much if not more than a good used production aircraft with similar performance. An aircraft built from plans will probably take much longer than a kit project.

Then they pointed out there are many types of construction materials available for building an aircraft. From the traditional wood or metal tubing and fabric to metal to space age composite or any combination, each material has its advantages and disadvantages. They said there are aircraft with similar performance specifications available in each type of material so a builder is not limited to a certain type of material just to get a certain type of performance. The key they said is for each builder to look at all of the various designs, talk to other builders, compare the various options and then decide what aircraft design best meets his or her needs and ability. They also said some kit manufacturers offer starter kits for new builders so that they can test their skills. The starter kit provides a relatively inexpensive way for new builders to see if they can do the type of work needed to build the aircraft. The starter kit item built will be used in the construction of the aircraft so the project is not a waste of time or money.

Finally, they said builders should start their projects as young as possible because projects often take longer to complete than initially planned. They said older pilots may run out of 'runway' [life] before they complete their projects.

When asked if they would do it again, they all said yes. They did say though that building the aircraft was more enjoyable than flying it. The comments of true builders.

*Freedom
"Flying"*

The Statue of Freedom "flies" from the Capitol dome with a little help from a Sikorsky Skycrane. The insert shows the rigging used to help Freedom "fly" safely.

Today, lifting a 15,000 pound load to the top of a building is no big deal especially with our modern technology and external load-carrying helicopters. But after reading the preceding article, I started wondering about our "Famous Flyer's" history and her first flight 130 years ago.

In the early 1850's the U.S. Congress decided that the Capitol's small wooden dome sheathed in copper was unsafe. It was also out of proportion with the extensions on either side of the main building. When Architect of the Capitol Thomas U. Walter's offered a design for a much larger cast-iron dome topped by a monumental statue, Congress approved and commissioned its construction in 1855. The task of designing the statue was given to Thomas Crawford, who was in Italy working on other neoclassical sculptures for the Capitol. His proposal was for an allegorical figure of "Freedom triumphant in War and Peace."

The Statue of Freedom stands 19 feet 6 inches tall on a cast-iron globe encircled with the national motto, *E Pluribus Unum*. She is depicted as a classical female figure robed in flowing draperies which are secured by a brooch inscribed "U.S." In her right hand she holds a sheathed sword and in her left a laurel wreath of victory and the shield of the United States with thirteen stripes. Her headgear proposed in an earlier design was a liberty cap—the emblem of freed slaves in Ancient Greece and a symbol of liberty during the American and French Revolutions. However, Secretary of War Jefferson Davis, who was in charge of the project, objected to that idea. In a January 15, 1856, letter he wrote, ". . . its history renders it [the cap] inappropriate to a people who were born free and would not be enslaved." The sculptor conceded to his suggestion that a helmet be used instead and replaced the liberty cap with a crested Roman helmet encircled by stars and topped by a crest composed of an eagle's head, feather, and talons (this crest leads many to believe the statue is a Native American). Tragically, Crawford would never see his statue crowning the U.S. Capitol. He died in 1857

by Louise Oertly, *Associate Editor*

at age 44 before the plaster model left his studio in Rome.

In the spring of 1858 Freedom finally left Italy. However, her transport soon proved to be unseaworthy. The small ship had to stop in Gibraltar to repair leaks and later in Bermuda where her journey ended. The model's six crates were put in storage until another ship could be arranged. It was nearly a year later, March of 1859, when all six crates finally arrived in Washington, DC, via New York. In 1860 the plaster model was sent to Clark Mills' bronze foundry located on the outskirts of Washington where the casting of the five main sections of the Freedom would begin.

Progress on the new Capitol dome was slow. Plagued by financial problems and the outbreak of the Civil War, it looked as if the whole project would be stopped. Secretary of War Edwin Stanton argued that the iron and manpower would be better utilized elsewhere. As it was, the Capitol building had become a barracks and after the Second Battle of Bull Run and then Antietam (August and September 1862) it was pressed into duty as a hospital. After Freedom's bronze casting was completed in 1862, her fate was still undecided. She was assembled and for nearly a year displayed on the east grounds of the Capitol silently watching the troops around her. In 1863 President Abraham Lincoln finally decided that the Capitol's construction would continue. He said, "If people see the Capitol going on, it is a sign we intend the Union to go on."

Continued on page 21

Does the tower controller usually sound like a kid with a mouthful of marbles? Do you always have to ask Clearance Delivery to repeat everything after, "ATC clears"? Do you miss Center's calls a lot, even though the radios are turned to max volume? Maybe it's time to run the radios into the shop for a little look-see, huh? Well, that may help, but the trouble may not lie with the equipment—the airplane's equipment, that is. Even though you may have been freshly blessed by your local, friendly, neighborhood Aviation Medical Examiner (AME), *you* could be the one with the problem.

Your hearing may not be bad enough to bust the medical, but a significant hearing loss, particularly in certain frequency ranges, may have occurred. How does this happen? Exposure to high levels of noise, that's how! Those of us in the bifocal set may have acquired our loss of audio acuity over many years. Some younger types may have picked up their affliction a little more quickly, especially if they are heavy metal music fans. (Judging from the sound level heard outside the auditorium, I'd guess that ONE Grateful Dead concert would produce a measurable hearing loss in most people!)

All kidding aside, much of the aviation business exists in a pretty noisy environment, and if you spend any significant amount of time in and around aircraft, it is almost certain to affect your hearing. Is this some new discovery? Nope! How come people intentionally, knowingly, put themselves into this hazardous environment, then? Good question, and one without any simple answers. Maybe everybody just accepts this as an occupational hazard. Perhaps it's economics. A regimen for protection from and/or reduction of noise hazards can sometimes be quite expensive. Perhaps the student in a Cessna 150 figures his or her exposure will not be enough to worry about, but even an occasional hour of instruction can make a difference. Could be it's just macho, too; the old, it-can't-happen-to-me syndrome, right? Well, folks, it can hap-

Medical Stuff

Say Again?

by Bruce Edsten
APPM, Louisville, KY

pen, and it does happen, so we all need to think about it.

What can we do about it? Reducing the noise level in the environment is probably beyond the control of most of us. Out on the ramp, there is nothing you can do at all. Inside the airplane, it's a bit easier. Just about any airplane can be quieted down by installing sound proofing material and devices. Things like thicker windows, foil-backed foam batting, improved door and window seals, etc., are readily available but not cheap. And, what if it's not your airplane?

Realistically, most of us won't be able to materially affect the environment, so our only choice is protection *from* that environment. My first encounter with hearing protection was in the Army. Hanging around a *Huey* is a mighty fine way to get a big time hearing loss, so we all got helmets. Inside were some heavy-duty ear cups with speakers in them, and the whole thing seemed like it protected the head pretty well. I say "seemed" because it still allowed some damage to occur. Now, you would think that the military would have nothing but the best, and that these helmets would have saved my ears, but after three years in Army Aviation I had a fairly substantial high-frequency loss. I hate to think what

would have happened without the helmet.

During the next 11 years, I got all my tickets and instructed for about 4,000 hours, all without any protection. No doubt that hurt me. I spent the next couple thousand hours with a commuter airline in very noisy cockpits, and I quickly opted for a good headset. Since we had no intercom, however, a lot of time was spent with one ear cup half off. More damage! Eventually, I'll probably need a couple of those itty-bitty hearing aids.

So, what's available today? Check the ramp at your average airline-type airport. Most of the folks out there will have ear protection consisting at least of a headband with pointed plugs on the ends, which will block out some of the racket. In almost all cases, the hearing protectors with cups that go over the ears will provide better protection, however. These are the ones that look like headphones and are frequently called "Mickey Mouse Ears." Several kinds of earplugs are available, also. Some, like the cylindrical foam type, are quite inexpensive.

All of the above are somewhat impractical if you need to listen to the radio or other occupants of the aircraft, though. Some of the earplugs reportedly do not cut out much in the range of normal speech, but they may not be terribly effective at blocking the harmful noise, either. Best bet? Head phones!

Oh, boy. Here it comes: Head phones = BIG BUCKS! No, not really. Of course, if you really want to, you could blow a major bundle on a set of head phones, but it simply isn't necessary. Like everything else, of course, performance carries a price, but a quite serviceable headset can be had for less than the price of an hour of dual.

What do you want to look for? Probably comfort should be high on your list. The best rig in the world won't be worn much if it weighs a ton or squeezes your head like a C-clamp! Next is noise attenuation, which is usually shown in dB or decibel rating. Most head phones will be rated around 15–20 dB at least, and many are higher. You may have to compromise a bit, trading comfort for dB ratings, or vice versa. You must also be sure that the rig is compatible with your radio set-up, particularly if you are including a boom mike. Your radio shop can be a big help here.

Of course, any of these headsets will help by putting a couple of little speakers virtually on top of your ears. Aircraft speakers, especially original equipment in light planes, leave a lot to be desired even when new. After a few years of exposure to the elements, they are even less efficient, and the headset might be a worthwhile investment for this reason alone.

If you have a few more rubles to spare, an intercom is a truly great investment. Again, features and performance can drive the price up, but reasonably good units are quite affordable. Generally, these rigs allow you and up to three others to converse in normal conversational tones without missing any radio calls. These rigs can be portable or fixed and may be powered by an internal battery or plugged into the cigarette lighter. Permanently installed ones could be connected to normal ship's power, of course. The benefits of this arrangement are obvious: noise attenuation without any loss of communication inputs. As a result many flight instructors are now using a portable system consisting of the intercom box and two headsets with boom microphones. They take the whole rig with them to each training aircraft they use, and most students I've talked to really love it.

At present, the pinnacle of hearing protection technology is "noise cancellation." In these systems a microphone picks up the noise and sends the signal to a computer, which analyzes it. The computer then develops a counter-signal designed to "oppose" the input signal and sends it out through an amplifier and speaker. I have seem some demonstrations of this technology in controlled situations, and it is most impressive. And it's cheap, too, right? Wrong. It also doesn't work quite as well in headsets as it does in big, fixed installations, but it does work.

So, assuming that Ed McMahon just brought you one of those sweepstakes checks, you could go out and invest in one of the new noise canceling headsets and get some really great protection. (Some of these systems retail for over $1,000!) Now that there are three or four manufacturers of noise canceling headsets in the market, the prices will come down, and if you dig through that big yellow classified newspaper (you know the one I mean), you can find some of them for about half that figure. It might well be worth it, too. Even at full retail, it could be worth the extra dB protection if you have an especially noisy environment to deal with.

In any case, if you spend a lot of time in airplanes, you could be asking for trouble if you don't protect your ears!

Say again . . . . ■

This article orginally appeared in the March 1993 issue of the Louisville FSDO's Accident Prevention Program Newsletter.

IN THE **HANGAR**

Hooked in Nashville

by Brian M. Jacobson

The weather conditions for the flight from Houston back to Providence, RI, were fair with lots of humidity pumping its way from the Gulf of Mexico to the Northeast. We flew on instruments in the old DeHavilland *Dove* to Nashville where we had planned a fuel stop. Henry, a recent instrument pilot, did the navigating and radio work, and I flew.

Just before reaching Nashville we were talking to Memphis Center, and approximately 30 miles from our destination the controller handed us off to Nashville Approach Control and gave us the correct radio frequency.

"Memphis Approach, DeHavilland Six Three Zero Hotel at five thousand," Henry called. The controller answered, "Cherokee Six Three Zero Hotel, Nashville Approach. Maintain five thousand and present heading for vectors to the final for runway two zero right."

Henry and I looked at each other and shrugged. We figured the controller was busy and got our type wrong.

"Cherokee Six Three Zero Hotel, Nashville, turn left 040 and maintain 4,000 feet."

"Memphis," Henry said, "Three Zero Hotel would like two zero left for landing today."

"Cherokee Six Three Zero Hotel, Roger. Will keep you informed."

It went on for quite a while that way. Finally Henry decided to straighten the controller out on the type of aircraft we were flying.

"Memphis Approach be advised that Six Three Zero Hotel is a DeHavilland *Dove.* We are not a Piper *Cherokee.*"

The controller's drawl came back loud in our headsets.

"Tell ya what, Six Three Zero Hotel. I'll make ya a deal. You stop calling me Memphis, and I'll stop calling you Cherokee."

Henry's face turned beet red, and we both laughed. He put his thumb in his mouth simulating a hooked fish. After that the correct terminology was used on both sides of the mike.

In the years since I have been to Nashville many times and always remember the first time I landed there. It is interesting to note that the people of Nashville are always friendly and happy to see those who visit their city for whatever reason they may have. They are rightfully proud of their city and will let a wayward visitor know that should he confuse Nashville with Memphis.

STATUS OF THE FAR

As promised, the *FAA Aviation News* is publishing an annual listing of the Federal Aviation Regulations (FAR) in loose-leaf form and their latest changes and prices. Many of the FAR are reprinted commercially, some in book form. It is important to keep in mind that the rules are amended often in some cases, and existing provisions may be nullified or changed by this process unless they are updated continuously. Commercial publications may or may not provide updates.

The FAR are sold in two ways by the Superintendent of Documents—subscription and single sales. When you order a subscription, for which there is an annual change, the changes will be sent to you automatically as they are issued. Single sales are a different matter. The changes to these parts are infrequent, and no direct notice of a change is sent out. Therefore, you must order and pay for each change as it is issued.

Another way of obtaining the FAR is to purchase the bound volumes of the U.S. Code of Federal Regulations. These three volumes of Title 14 contain the Federal Aviation Regulations of interest to most airmen:

Parts 1–59	(SN 869–017–00042–6)	$25.00
Parts 60–139	(SN 869–017–00043–4)	$22.00
Parts 140–199	(SN 869–017–00044–2)	$11.00

These volumes are only updated annually, so the latest changes would have to be obtained from another source.

The following pages contain the current status and price list for the loose-leaf FAR. Color highlighting indicates those rules considered of special interest to general aviation pilots. To order any of the FAR parts, send check, money order, or credit card number to the Superintendent of Documents, U.S. Government Printing Office, Washington, DC 20402–9325. Add a 25% charge for foreign mailing on the single sale items. Remember to use the stock number.

Parts Sold on Subscription Service

Part	Title	Code Letter	Price Domestic	Foreign	Changes Issued
1	Definitions and Abbreviations	FA001	36.00	45.00	
11	General Rule-making Procedures	FA011	30.00	37.00	1
13	Investigative and Enforcement Procedures	FA013	30.00	37.50	12
21	Certification Procedures for Products and Parts	FA021	38.00	47.50	—
23	Airworthiness Standards: Normal, Utility, Acrobatic, and Commuter Category Airplanes	FA023	36.00	45.00	
25	Airworthiness Standards: Transport Category Airplanes	FA025	32.00	40.00	1
27	Airworthiness Standards: Normal Category Rotorcraft	FA027	35.00	43.75	
29	Airworthiness Standards: Transport Category Rotorcraft	FA029	36.00	45.00	25
33	Airworthiness Standards: Aircraft Engines	FA033	27.00	33.75	9
36	Noise Standards: Aircraft Type and Airworthiness Certification	FA036	26.00	32.50	—
43	Maintenance, Preventive Maintenance, Rebuilding, and Alterations	FA043	32.00	40.00	1
45	Identification and Registration Marking	FA045	33.00	41.25	—
61	Certification: Pilots and Flight Instructors	FA061	38.00	47.50	—
65	Certification: Airmen Other Than Flight Crewmembers	FA065	36.00	45.00	—
71	Designation of Federal Airways, Area Low Routes Controlled Airspace, and Reporting Points, Jet Routes, and Area High Routes[3]	FA071	29.00	36.25	2

Parts Sold on Subscription Service

Part	Title	Code Letter	Price Domestic	Foreign	Changes Issued
91	General Operating and Flight Rules	FA091	47.00	58.25	2
	*Preamble		free		
93	Special Air Traffic Rules and Airport Traffic Patterns	FA093	36.00	45.00	2
103	Ultralight Vehicles	FA103	12.00	15.00	—
108	Airplane Operator Security	FA108	29.00	36.25	10
121	Certification and Operations: Domestic, Flag, and Supplemental Air Carriers and Commercial Operators of Large Aircraft	FA121	60.00	75.00	—
125	Certification and Operations: Airplanes Having a Seating Capacity of 20 or More Passengers or a Maximum Payload Capacity of 6,000 Pounds or More	FA125	25.00	31.25	—
127	Certification and Operations of Scheduled Air Carriers With Helicopters	FA127	35.00	43.75	—
129	Operations:Foreign Air Carriers and Foreign Operators of U.S.-Registered Aircraft Engaged in Common Carriage	FA129	26.00	32.50	—
135	Air Taxi Operators and Commercial Operators	FA135	45.00	56.25	—
137	Agricultural Aircraft Operations	FA137	12.00	15.00	—
139	Certification and Operations: Land Airports Serving Certain Air Carriers	FA139	29.00	36.25	—
145	Repair Stations	FA145	34.00	42.50	—
150	Airport Noise Compatibility Planning	FA150	22.00	27.50	—
159	National Capital Airports	FA159	17.00	21.25	—
161	Notice and Approval of Airport Noise and Access Restrictions	FA161	29.00	36.25	—

* Not included with subscription. For a particular FAR Part 91 preamble, write to DOT, M–443.2, Washington, DC 20590.

Parts Sold on Single Sale Basis

Part	Title	Price[1]
31	Airworthiness Standards: Manned Free Balloons (SN 050-007-01020-6)	5.50
34	Fuel Venting and Exhaust Emission Requirements for Turbine Engine Powered Airplanes (SN 050-007-00883-0)	1.00
35	Airworthiness Standards: Propellers (SN 050-007-01016-8)	6.00
39	Airworthiness Directives[2] (SN 050-007-00229-7)	1.75
47	Aircraft Registrations[5]	
49	Recording of Aircraft Titles and Security Documents (SN 050-007-01021-4)	2.75
	Change 1 (050-007-00336-6)	2.00
	Change 2 (050-007-00792-2)	1.00
63	Certification: Flight Crewmembers Other than Pilots[5]	
67	Medical Standards and Certification (SN 050-007-00999-2)	3.50
73	Special Use Airspace[3] (SN 050-007-01007-9)	2.00
75	Establishment of Jet Routes and Area High Routes[3] (SN 050-007-00275-1)	2.75
	Change 1 (050-007-00326-9)	2.00
	Change 2* (050-007-00941-1)	1.75
77	Objects Affecting Navigable Airspace (SN 050-007-00978-0)	2.75
95	IFR Altitudes[3] (SN 050-007-00277-7)	1.75
	Change 1 (050-007-00285-8)	1.75
97	Standard Instrument Approach Procedures[4] (SN 050-007-01002-8)	1.75
99	Security Control of Air Traffic (SN 050-007-01022-2)	4.00
101	Moored Balloons, Kites, Unmanned Rockets, and Unmanned Free Balloons (SN 050-007-00964-0)	3.25
105	Parachute Jumping (SN 050-007-00965-8)	4.25
107	Airport Security (SN 050-007-01017-6)	5.00
109	Indirect Air Carrier Security (SN 050-007-00512-1)	1.75
	Change 1 (050-007-00856-2)	1.00
133	Rotorcraft External-load Operations (SN 050-007-00998-4)	6.00
141	Pilot Schools (SN 050-007-00322-6)	3.50
	Change 1 (050-007-00620-9)	2.25
	Change 2 (050-007-00844-9)	1.75
	Change 3 (050-007-00900-3)	2.75
143	Ground Instructors (SN 050-007-00249-1)	3.00
147	Aviation Maintenance Technician Schools	3.75
151	Federal Aid to Airports (SN 050-007-01018-4)	6.00
152	Airport Aid Programs[5]	

Parts Sold on Single Sale Basis

Part	Title	Price[1]
155	Release of Airport Property from Surplus Property Disposal Restrictions (SN 050-007-00270-0)	1.75
	Change 1 (050-007-00550-4)	1.75
157	Notice of Construction, Alteration, Activation, and Deactivation of Airports (SN 050-007-01023-1)	2.25
158	Passenger Facility Charges (SN 050-007-00906-2)	1.25
169	Expenditure of Federal Funds for Non-Military Airports or Air Navigation Facilities Thereon (SN 050-007-00280-7)	2.25
	Change 1 (050-007-00851-1)	1.00
170	Establishment and Discontinuance Criteria for Airport Traffic Control Services and Navigational Facilities (SN 050-007-01019-2)	2.50
171	Non-Federal Navigation Facilities (SN 050-007-00967-4)	9.00
183	Representatives of the Administrator (SN 050-007-00233-5)	3.00
	Change 1 (050-007-00352-8)	1.75
	Change 2 (050-007-00398-6)	1.75
	Change 3 (050-007-00503-2)	1.75
	Change 4 (050-007-00527-0)	1.75
	Change 5 (050-007-00634-9)	3.50
	Change 6 (050-007-00862-7)	1.00
185	Testimony by Employees and Production of Records in Legal Proceedings and Service of Legal Process and Pleadings (SN 050-007-00237-8)	1.75
	Change 1 (050-007-00859-7)	1.00
187	Fees (SN 050-007-00234-3)	2.75
	Change 1 (050-007-00618-7)	2.75
189	Use of Federal Aviation Administration Communication System (SN 050-007-00235-1)	2.75
	Change 1 (050-007-00867-8)	1.00
191	Withholding Security Information From Disclosure Under the Air Transportation Security Act of 1974 (SN 050-007-00359-5)	1.75
	Change 1 (050-007-00502-4)	1.75.
	Change 2 (050-007-00857-1)	1.00

[1] Add 25% for foreign handling.

[2] Due to their length, complexity, and frequency of issuance, individual Airworthiness Directives (AD's) are published separately in the Federal Register. Microfiche or paper copies of the AD's in summary form are sold by DOT/FAA for the Superintendent of Documents. Ordering information is in Advisory Circular 39-6P, "Announcement of Availability—Summary of Airworthiness Directives," (free from DOT, M-443.2, Washington, DC 20590) or call 405-680-6901 for an order form.

[3] Due to their length, complexity, and frequency of issuance, individual airspace designations, airways descriptions, restricted areas, jet route descriptions, and IFR altitudes are not included in the publication of these basic Parts. Such descriptions are published in the Federal Register and depicted on appropriate aeronautical charts. Aeronautical charts can be obtained from the Distribution Branch, N/CG33, NOS, NOAA, Riverdale, MD 20737-1199.

[4] Standard Instrument Approach Procedures are published in the Federal Register by reference to FAA documents which are available for examiniation in the Rules Docket (AGC-10) and the National Flight Data Center, FAA Headquarters, Washington, DC, and at the appropriate FAA regional offices and Flight Inspection District Offices. These Instrument Approach Procedures Charts can be obtained from the Distribution Branch, N/CG33, National Ocean Service, NOAA, Riverdale, MD 20737-1199.

[5] Formerly sold as subscription items. At time of magazine publication the price and stock numbers were not available.

* This change incorporates Amendment 75-5 which removes and reserves Part 75, effective December 1991.

Another Step Toward Rebuilding

Continued from page 1

Technology

"Technology will act on us [the FAA] whether we like it or not," Hinson said, "It forces us to change." He spoke specifically of the recent FAA approval of non-precision GPS approaches. The switch-over to GPS "will be gradual evolution with a phase-out of existing ground-based systems." FAA has yet to determine what will be the back-up for GPS, but "we're working hard on that and other concerns with GPS." Until such time as approved receivers are available, Hinson asked his fellow pilots, "Please don't use your hand-helds for instrument approaches. Right now it's illegal, but more importantly, you might get hurt." FAA approval of receivers is moving along, and "we're getting to the point where soon you'll be able to make GPS approaches safely with standardized equipment." He added, "GPS is a marvelous tool for general aviation."

General Aviation and the Kansas City Conference

Hinson began to talk about general aviation by listing some positive changes under the current administration; namely, an improving economy and the repeal of the luxury tax. He reiterated the "General Aviation Policy Statement" he signed as one of his first official acts as FAA Administrator (November/December 1993 *FAA Aviation News*) and the redraft of the General Aviation Action Plan as a result of a precedent-setting meeting between general aviation industry interests and the FAA last September. (See "Re-

building General Aviation" in the November/December 1993 *FAA Aviation News*. If you missed it, call (202) 267–8017 for a copy.)

Next came the awaited response from the FAA to the recommendations presented at the Kansas City Conference. The Administrator announced that he had directed FAA Associate Administrator for Regulation and Certification Anthony J. Broderick to form a special general aviation team. "I have asked this team to revise the General Aviation Action Plan to incorporate my policy statement and to incorporate and develop strategic goals for *implementing the recommendations* [emphasis added] developed by the Kansas City group. The revised plan is to be completed by March 1, 1994."

The administrator went on to announce that, "in response to your expressed concerns about the lack of replacement parts for your aircraft, the FAA will continue to pursue the definition of a parts policy. . . by July 1, 1994."

Next, he announced, "In order to fully implement the new Primary Category rule, I have asked [Mr.] Broderick to expedite the publication of a new policy expanding owner maintenance in over 20 areas for operators of primary category aircraft. . . by no later than February 1, 1994 or the date the first production primary aircraft is available, whichever comes first."

"Next month [December 1993]," he continued, "we will implement a one-year program at the Denver Flight Standards District Office to test a new, proactive education compliance approach to Accident Prevention and safety compliance. If the techniques

are successful, we will implement the program nationwide."

Finally, he concluded, "I am placing a high priority for the evaluation of AOPA's petition to extend the term for third-class medical certificates from two to four years. I also will seek this same high priority for the Experimental Aircraft Association's petition to replace the third-class medical for recreational pilots [with self-certification]."

Hinson then broke away from his prepared speech again to talk pilot-to-pilot. "In 1979 and 1980 when I was the owner of a Beech distribution center, general aviation delivered 17,000 airplanes. In 1993, we're going to deliver less than 700. General aviation has had difficulty staying alive, and the causes for that have been varied. The market will come back—I am certain of that—but it will be in a different form from that of the 1970's."

Customer Service and Safety Issues

"FAA has taken a big step forward in incorporating customer service in its actions," Hinson said. "We will still regulate and enforce when we have to, but we all must be professionals about it. Also, we ought to be looking at anything that will safely alleviate your costs."

Hinson then began to talk about how every morning he receives preliminary reports of all the accidents and incidents that have occurred in the preceding 24 hours. He has noted that "general aviation fatalities have been slowly and steadily getting better, but I don't like to see every morning that someone has died in a general aviation aircraft." The aircraft, he notes, are highly reliable—contrary to the public's

FAAers Obie Young (Left) and Larry Randall.

Phil Boyer, President, AOPA.

belief. "What we find after investigating is that 90% are mental errors—in other words, preventable. Think about that when you fly home. The key to safety is right here," he said, pointing to his head.

"An old instructor of mine," he continued, "summed it up this way: 'The airplane flies in two directions. If you don't like where you're going, you can go back to where you were.'"

Every pilot in the room had heard that same thought expressed in a multitude of ways, and it was sobering coming from an Administrator who could so easily relate to his audience.

Hinson concluded the formal portion of his speech by promising to "use the assets of the agency to further general aviation. After all, you are the customer."

Q and A

The Administrator next fielded questions from the floor and ones that AOPA had video-taped from pilots unable to attend.

"The FAA is too airline-oriented. What can you do about that?" asked one pilot.

"I quarrel with that conclusion," answered Hinson. "We in general aviation just haven't done a very good job of telling our story. But that will change."

"How will we pay for privatizing ATC, if that happens?" asked another.

"We could use a portion of the current ticket tax or issue bonds," responded Hinson. "There is a committee within FAA looking at a number of such issues. Other countries, such as Germany, have user fees, but, then, there's not much flying in Germany. They only have nine control towers."

"What's the FAA going to do about communities closing airports?" asked another pilot.

"This year the FAA will provide money to help in converting six military airports to civilian use. That's not much, but it's a start. Basically, closing airports is really a local issue, and the grassroots of aviation have to make themselves heard at that level. Tell general aviation's story, clear up the misconceptions about safety, and the FAA will be right there with existing rules that preclude the capricious closing of airports," Hinson replied.

"Real Pilots... Real Airplanes... Real Fun"

His speech wasn't the only thing the Administrator put aside. The opportunity to be among people he considered his peers was not one to be passed up. He set aside his schedule and wandered among the vendor booths in the exhibition area, stopping to chat with vendors and attendees and answering questions. He seemed reluctant to leave and opted to stay and spend more time with those real pilots.

The reaction to this new Administrator and his taking on the revitalization of general aviation as a major project for his tenure ("I'm in for the full four years," he said.) has been almost overwhelmingly optimistic. For those who pre-supposed that the recommendations of the Kansas City Conference would be swept under some vast, bureaucratic rug in Washington were wrong. "Just remember," Hinson said, "this is still a bureaucracy and one in the midst of transition. Things may not happen as quickly as you and I want them. But they will happen."

The word of another bureaucrat? No, the word of a pilot. ∎

Freedom "Flying"

Continued from 15

It was near the end of 1863 before dome construction was ready for installation of the statue. Using the scaffolding which rose through the center of the Rotunda (see diagram), each section of the statue had to lifted by a steam hoist and a hand-cranked winch and then assembled. At noon on December 2, 1863, the last section, Freedom's head and shoulders, was lifted to her perch 288 feet above the Capitol's east front plaza and bolted in place. Her completion was announced by a 35-gun salute (one for each state in the union including the states that had seceded) and the answering guns from the 12 forts ringing Washington.

For the next 130 years the Statue of Freedom stood guard atop the U.S. Capitol facing the ravages of time and the environment. However, the day finally came when extensive restoration of Freedom and her cast-iron pedestal became necessary. Thankfully, today's technology allowed a relatively painless way to get the statue on the ground and back on top again as was told in the preceding pages. Which leave me with the intriguing thought—imagine it is 1863 and someone suggested that it was possible to move the whole statue (remember it weighs 15,000 pounds) within a matter of minutes. The person would most likely have been declared a candidate for the new Government Hospital for the Insane (another structure designed by Architect of the Capitol Thomas Walter, and now known as St. Elizabeth's) or a storyteller rivaling Jules Verne. ∎

Editor's Note: *We want to thank the Architect of the Capitol's office for information and photographs for this article and the Surratt House Museum in Clinton, MD for the use of its library for information on Lincoln and Washington, DC, during the Civil War. The Architect of the Capitol's brochure,* The Statue of Freedom, *the* In Commemoration of The Bicentennial of the United States Capitol 1793–1993 *program, and the various releases provided by the Architect's office were used in preparing this article.*

FLIGHT**FORUM**

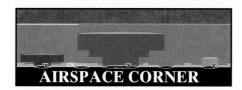

AIRSPACE CORNER

Question. *The new classes of airspace, a, bee, cee, dee, e, and gee, all sound pretty much the same; especially, during congested times in the cockpit, on the edge of ATIS reception, or busy ATC periods. Why can't we use the phonetic alphabet to avoid confusion?*

Answer. We can. FAA Order 7110.65, *Air Traffic Control,* paragraph 2–85, instructs controllers to use the ICAO pronunciation of numbers, and as necessary to clarify individual letters; paragraph 2–90, Airspace Classes states, "Classes A, B, C, D, E, and G airspace are pronounced in individual letter form. Only use ICAO phonetic pronunciation of letters to clarify the class of airspace. Examples:"Cessna 1–2–3 Mike Romeo cleared to enter Class B airspace." "Sikorsky 1–2–3 Tango Sierra cleared to enter New York Class Bravo airspace." Similar guidance can be found in paragraph 4–37 of the *Airman's Information Manual.* The criticality of pilot/controller communications demands complete understanding by all parties. Regardless of what method the controller uses, you are authorized to use the geographic and phonetic designators during your request and again during your acknowledgement. For example, you call San Antonio approach for clearance through the Class C, "San Antonio approach, Cessna two-three-four-six-Victor fifteen miles east, request clearance through the Class Charlie westbound at two-thousand five-hundred." San Antonio responds with: "Cleared through the Class C." You may reply, "Roger, Cessna four-six-Victor is cleared through the San Antonio Class Charlie." Thanks for flying safe.

Question. *What is the purpose of a Class E extension to a Class C or D surface area? I heard that if the airport in the Class D was IMC, then the Class E extension is also IMC and radio communications are required. Is this correct and how would the pilot of an aircraft without radios be able to comply?*

Answer. A Class E extension to a higher class of surface area airspace is simply an extension designed to contain IFR arrivals in controlled airspace. If, when executing an instrument approach, the pilot is authorized to descend below 1,000 feet AGL outside of the basic surface area, an "arrival extension" is created. By making these extensions Class E, we are containing the

instrument approaches in controlled airspace and making the cloud clearance and flight visibility provisions of FAR § 91.155 apply without establishing a communications requirement.

Which leads to your second question. No, the Class D airport being IMC does not automatically make the Class E portion IMC! What it does do is make FAR § 91.155(c) and (d) applicable. FAR § 91.155(c) states, "Except as provided in § 91.157, no person may operate an aircraft *beneath the ceiling* under VFR within the lateral boundaries of controlled airspace designated to the surface for an airport when the ceiling is less than 1,000 feet. FAR § 91.155(d) states, "Except as provided in § 91.157, *no person may take off or land an aircraft, or enter the traffic pattern* of an airport, under VFR, within the lateral boundaries of the surface areas of Class B, Class C, Class D, or Class E airspace designated for an airport, (1) Unless ground visibility at that airport is at least 3 statute miles; or (2)If ground visibility is not reported at that airport, unless flight visibility during take off, landing, or while operating in the traffic pattern is at least 3 statute miles."

What does all that legalese mean? If you are flying through the Class E airspace at or above 1,000 feet AGL AND are able to maintain the required cloud clearance of 500 feet below, 1,000 feet above, and 2,000 feet horizontal AND have at least 3 statute miles of flight visibility, then the official weather at the airport meets basic VFR requirements. Again, there is not a communications requirement for VFR flight in Class E airspace. However, if you are flying beneath an official ceiling that is less than 1,000 feet, a special VFR clearance is required for flight within the surface area, including the Class E extension. If the official visibility is less than 3 miles, a special VFR clearance is required for take off, landing, or while operating in the traffic pattern. Thanks for the complex question, we hope our answer, while lengthy, is helpful.

FAA AVIATION NEWS welcomes comments from its readers. We may edit letters for style and/or length. We will select one representative letter from those on the same topic for publication, and because of our publishing schedule, responses may not appear for several issues. We will not print anonymous letters, but we will withhold names or send personal replies upon request. Address: Editor, FAA AVIATION NEWS, AFS–810, Washington, DC 20591.

• Computer Catch

Although I enjoyed your recent article on Embry-Riddle, the caption on the lower photograph on page 4 (March 1993 issue) is a little misleading. Everyone in the picture is playing a video game called TRACON. I know, since I am a TRACON addict (and a pretty good one, if I do say so myself). The student in the foreground is wearing a dismayed expression because his screen is displaying the dreaded red box that indicates that he has just crashed a couple of airplanes. Oops!
> *Bennett E. Taber*
> *San Francisco, CA*

Thanks for the catch. We just used the slide caption that Embry-Riddle provided and didn't notice what was on the screen.

• Simple ELT Check

In your July/August issue, your article concerning ELT's and the number of false signals that are transmitted caused me to put my thinking cap on. I feel that there can be a very simple cure for the problem.

I fly a Beechcraft Baron, always IFR and generally the cockpit is too busy to monitor 121.5 on a regular basis. When I reach my destination, I, like most, am running short on time, and at large airports everything is moving pretty fast so we can't always check 121.5 before shut down.

I suggest a small, very inexpensive radio receiver that would remain on at all times, for all aircraft, FBO's, towers, or other airport facilities. With this very inexpensive radio a pilot would know without checking when his ELT was transmitting, also an airplane on the ramp or in the hangar would be very easy to locate.

A radio receiver similar to the Radio Shack weather band (retails for around 20 bucks) with the 121.5 frequency might be a very easy solution to a very costly problem. If this receiver was available I would have one in the aircraft and also one at home.
> *Gary F. Jones*
> *Paris, TN*

Your idea sounds great. Mr. Jones has already contacted Radio Shack-Tandy Corporation about his idea. We will wait and see what happens. As long as the radio meets FAR § 91.21, Portable Electronic Devices, requirements when used in an aircraft, it could save rescue people, especially Civil Air Patrol volunteers, a lot of wasted effort on needless ELT searches. Although the FAA cannot endorse a particular company or product, this idea would be a great help in reducing the number of false ELT signals.

There are two other items that pilots and aircraft owners might want to consider. One is the installation of a remote ELT switch in the cockpit for those units that are designed for one. The switch allows a pilot to turn a unit off after a flight if the unit was inadvertently activated. The only problem is the pilot must remember to arm the unit before takeoff or after an ELT test. If not armed, the unit will not transmit in case of an accident. The other item is the cockpit use of activation monitors such as the aural or visual monitor explained in Technical Standard Order TSO-C91a, Emergency Locator Transmitter (ELT) Equipment, which sets the standards for ELT equipment. The monitors indicate when the unit is transmitting.

Thank you for your suggestion.

• Koch's Komments Kontinued

I noticed in the pictures accompanying the article, Koch's Komments, (page 28 of the July-August 1993) that there are no parachutes as required by FAR § 91.303(c). This operation could not come under the rules of flight instruction as the purpose of the flight was photography.

Does the FAA consider the photographer a crew member, or is the FAA exempt from their own rules.

> Chuck Jamieson
> Metairie, LA

According to Mr. Koch, the flight met the appropriate rules when the flight was made. As a matter of information, although the FAA chooses to operated its aircraft, owned, leased, and rented, under FAR Part 91 rules, it, like other government agencies, could operate its aircraft as public use aircraft. FAA employees are not exempt from complying with the FAR.

• Lack of Definition

Editor's Note: The following is a verbatim transcript of the letter we received.

I'm in my tenth year as a subscriber to FAA Aviation News, and during that span I've found the magazine informative and unique. Its uniqueness stems from its being, as it were, "official" (notwithstanding the relatively recent appearance of distended disclaimers inside the front cover): straight from the source where rules and interpretations are concerned.

In this sense, one expects the editors to know the terminology. After all, your outfit invented it.

Yet in the March 1993 issue, Harold Bogin of the NWS (editor's note: National Weather Service) refers in the article "ASOS. . . ." to "Surface Aviation Observations (SAO)." I assume he's referring to the 'sequence reports" traditionally identified by the letters SA, and if this is the case, I beg to differ. "SA" has stood, for at least the twenty years I've been flying, for "scheduled airways." If you take a step back and regard the question logically, it's reasonably evident that "A" would not stand for "aviation": there's no necessity to include this word in the name of a particular report that belongs to the whole family of reports and forecasts (FT, FA, SA, UA, etc.) that are all produced specifically if not exclusively for aviation.

If the FAA (or the NWS) has officially changed the meaning of the abbreviation, I guess I didn't hear about it. But I suspect that instead, those closest to the source know less about their roots than one who values the ideal of expertise would hope for.

Though I can cite an official FAA source identifying "SA" as "scheduled airways" (IFR Pilot Exam-O-Gram #5, 2/71,) I've never tracked down a print reference to "UA" as other than "pilot report," which implies nothing concerning the genesis of the two-letter abbreviation. Now, however, it dawns on me that it must stand for "unscheduled airways." The hallmark of the sequence report is its hourly appearance on the weather network; the pilot report, on the other hand, is strictly ad hoc. (Now if only someone call tell me what "FD" stands for.)

Another terminological problem is your reference to "towered airports." The officially correct terms are controlled *and* uncontrolled*. A controlled airport will almost certainly have a tower, and if by "tower" we mean function rather than form, then the correspondence is 100% (by definition).*

But having a tower does not by itself make an airport controlled. The tower has to be on the air. A lot of towers operate only part-time, which renders their associated airports uncontrolled *for a portion (usually at night) of each and every day.*

Accordingly, the term "towered" lacks precision, unless you're talking about structures. We owe this bastard term mostly to commercial publishers, and genesis lies, I support, in an irrational discomfort with the word "uncontrolled," which is perceived wrongly by the ill-informed as connoting disorder or even chaos.

No pilot is supposed to receive an airman certificate unless he (or she) understands the explicit rules and procedures to use at an uncontrolled field; an editor of aviation material ought to know at least as much as a private pilot about such things and has no business polluting the lexicon with misleading and inexact popularisms, whether attempting to stem perceived pub-

lic misperceptions or (worse) because of lacuna in his (or her) training.

There's also scant excuse for outright grammatical errors, such as lack of agreement between subject and verb. Since your disclaimer inside the front cover is likely to be reprinted a few more times, I'd suggest you correct the sentence that says "all printed material. . . are advisory." Notwithstanding the presence of "all," material is a singular noun. (And in the sentence on the inside back cover of the May-June issue, where you employ the term "towered," the sentence reads "the entire control zone. . . were going to become Class D." It were? Some readers is not amused by such lapses. . . .

Finally, I don't care for the sans serif typeface you're now using. I find the serifed font in use years ago more readable and pleasing to the eye than your current choice.

> N.W. ("Nick") Miller
> Redlands, CA

Thank you for being a loyal subscriber.

Regarding Mr. Bogin's article, the Automated Surface Observation System (ASOS) does generate a Surface Aviation Observation (SAO). The term was correctly used. The *Airman's Information Manual* (AIM) explains both ASOS and the Automated Weather Observing System (AWOS) and their associated reports. The term "sequence report" is communicators or briefers lingo or "jingoism" for Surface Aviation Weather Report (SA) because it was transmitted in teletype sequence format. A practice that, hopefully, will change with the advent of high speed transmission capability—perhaps we can go to clear text, tabular formats. By the way the *VFR* and *IFR Exam-O-Grams* can no longer be considered an official FAA source as the series was canceled several years ago.

Concerning routine aviation weather reports, you need to prepare for change. METAR is coming January 1, 1996. Just about the time you think you have the system figured out, the system changes.

Regarding abbreviations, you can check on the latest meanings of the alphanumeric combinations in FAA Order 7340.1. Certain combinations can have more than one meaning. In many cases, the meaning depends upon how the word is used.

When talking about weather, F stands for *F*orecast (e.g.: FD, Win*D*s and Temperatures Aloft *F*orecast; FT, *T*erminal *F*orecast; FA, *A*rea *F*orecast, etc.) and generally S stands for ob*S*ervation.

We appreciate your comments about the terms, towered, non-towered, controlled, and uncontrolled. We understand your concern for precise word usage, however, word usage changes with the times. Today, the general aviation industry is using the terms towered and non-towered to avoid the illusion in the non-flying public's mind of chaos in the sky at uncontrolled airports. And yes, the staff of *FAA Aviation News* knows the difference between controlled and uncontrolled airports and the explicit rules for operating at both. The problem is most Americans do not. They may also be the voters controlling the fate of their local non-towered airport. They, and other voters like them, are the ones who may decide whether your local general aviation airport survives or not.

Regarding subject verb agreement, you can take heart. Both my editor and I agree with you that subjects should agree in number with their verbs, our problem is we seldom agree on the number. She *are* a tough editor.

Sorry you don't like our type style. We hope you keep subscribing in spite of it.

• How to Get Your A&P

I would like to get some reactions from your readers regarding the different ways someone can earn a mechanics (A&P) license. For those that aren't aware of the differences in the way to earn an A&P, let me explain. There are three ways to obtain an A&P: You can get it through military competency; work for a maintenance facility for 30 months; or, go to an approved school for two years. Well, it doesn't sound too bad concerning these three methods, but there is a world of difference in each of the three and therein lies my complaint.

A service man or woman who can prove to the FAA that they served as a mechanic in the military simply takes the FAA written and practical tests and that is it. The person who works in a maintenance shop for 30 months obtains a written request from his employer stating that he or she has completed the specified time and he or she takes the FAA written and practical tests.

These two methods are quite similar. In both of them you are getting paid while you are learning. You have no exams to pass throughout your maintenance career and you don't have to make up missed time on your days off.

The third method of obtaining your A&P is by far the most demanding of the three. You must pay many thousands of dollars for your mechanics school. If you arrive at class late, you must make up the time you were tardy, and only on a day off. The person that decides to attend formal school must sit in class or lab (hangar) eight hours a day, four days a week for two years. Whenever a subject is completed a test is given and you must get the FAA 70 percent or take a make up test. If you fail the make up you could be out of the course. Some instructors make their own tests. Others use some of the hundreds of FAA questions that can be obtained from the government or private sector. It is a

good idea for the instructor to give the FAA questions as they appear on the government books because it affords the student a look at the questions that will be asked on the FAA exam. Some instructors change these stock questions or answers just in case you have memorized them. This is a bad practice. When the instructor was asked why he changed the question or answer, his reply was, in my test the answer is B, on the FAA exam you had better mark C. This course is most demanding and memorizing two sets of answers is uncalled for.

As I stated before, every subject in the three large manuals, General, Powerplant, and Airframe, requires a test and you must get 70 percent. Well, since you have hopefully passed all subjects with a minimum grade of 70 percent you are all set. Not so with the tricky FAA. You must take the FAA tests and get a 70 percent in all sections. Why is this in effect, when you have all ready gotten your tests in each subject and passed with a 70 percent or you wouldn't be in school.

Not only is it ludicrous to make you take the same tests twice, but to add insult to injury you have to take a practical test, and an oral exam with an FAA designated examiner. This might last two days and cost you $300. Why is it necessary for a strange person to ask you questions for two days and watch you perform maintenance tasks in the hangar when your instructor for the past two years knows more about what you can do on written exams and work in the hangar than a stranger who is going to charge you $300.

It would seem to me that the lion's share of the schooling should be performed in a hangar working on real aircraft. This is not so. Over three quarters of your schooling is devoted to classroom studies on physics, math, punching a calculator and learning many things that have no practical use to an A&P. More time should be spent with dirty hands taking components apart. Do you think that you would be qualified to time a magneto after working on only one magneto? Or, would you feel qualified to rebuild an engine, if you only took one apart? I think not.

In essence, since the first two methods of obtaining your license are so lax, it behooves the FAA to give the people who attend a school for two years some slack. There is no need for them to take the same tests twice, they should get their hands soiled in the hangar rather than working with a calculator, and when they have finished their two-year hitch in the classroom, they should not only get a diploma, they should get their license.

Brian Power-Waters XIII
Church Hill, MD

We need to correct some of your comments. No one ever said becoming an A&P was easy. In fact, some people would like to make it harder. They believe in today's hi-tech world of glass-cockpits, computerized wide-bodied jets, and composite airframes, maintenance technicians must know more now than ever. For them, the question might be, "Are the FAA's A&P certification standards too low?" We are also not going to discuss whether an instructor is teaching how to pass a test through memorization of the answers rather than teaching understanding of a process that can be applied to future situations. These issues are subjects for future articles. This article is a brief outline of how someone can obtain an A&P certificate.

Application Process

Applicants for a mechanic certificate must meet the requirements of Federal Aviation Regulations (FAR) Part 65, Subparts A and D for certification. FAR § 65.77 requires an applicant to have practical experience in maintaining airframes and/or powerplants. The FAR requires at least 18 months of practical experience for one rating. For a certificate with both ratings, the requirement is for at least 30 months experience concurrently performing the duties appropriate to both ratings. (NOTE: Practical experience, both military and civil requirements, is based on a standard 40-hour work week. A standard work week is 8 hour per day for 5 days per week which totals 40 hours per week and approximately 160 hours per month.)

An applicant can verify his/her experience for an Airframe & Powerplant (A&P) certificate by several methods:

(1) Graduate from an FAA-approved Aviation Maintenance Technician School
(2) Practical experience gained by maintaining airframes and/or powerplants
(3) Military experience. Experience gained by maintaining civilian and military aircraft, as an airframe or powerplant mechanic helper, will be evaluated on its own merits to determine whether it fulfills the experience requirements of FAR § 65.77.

Military Experience

Applicants who have not graduated from an FAA-approved Aviation Maintenance Technician School and are applying based on military experience must prove their military aviation experience. The applicant should supply the following documents:

(a) A properly completed Form DD-214, which lists the total time in service and the Military Occupational Specialty (MOS) codes the applicant was assigned.
(b) A letter from his/her maintenance officer, or classification officer that certifies the applicant's length of military service, the

amount of time the applicant worked in each MOS, the make and model of aircraft and/or engine on which the applicant acquired the practical experience, and where the experience was obtained.

(c) Training records showing the type of aviation schools the applicant attended.

(d) Record of on-the-job training.

(e) Performance Appraisal (PER) documenting performance in that career discipline.

Military experience can only be used, if it is applicable to the certificate and ratings sought.

Civil Experience

Applicants who have not graduated from an FAA-approved Aviation Maintenance Technician School and are applying based on civil experience must also produce documents to establish the required record of time and experience. These records must show the applicant has the basic knowledge and skills with the procedures, practices, materials, tools, machine tools, and equipment used in aircraft construction, alteration, maintenance, and inspection. The applicant should supply the following documents:

(a) A letter from his/her employer stating the amount of time the applicant worked at the facility. The letter should list the make and model of aircraft and/or engine on which the applicant acquired the practical experience, and where the experience was obtained.

(b) Training records showing any type of aviation schools the applicant attended.

(c) Record of on-the-job training.

Maintenance School Graduates

An applicant who graduates from an FAA-approved Aviation Maintenance Technician School may present a certificate of graduation or completion to demonstrate training appropriate to the rating(s) sought. The Aviation Maintenance Technician School must ensure that each graduate possesses the minimum knowledge for the certificate(s) sought. They accomplish this by testing the individuals in all subject areas taught.

Written Test

After an FAA airworthiness safety inspector is satisfied that the applicant is eligible to take the written test, the applicant must fill out FAA Form 8610–2, Airmen Certification and/or Rating Application. The FAA inspector signs the form and issues the applicant FAA Form 8060–7, Airman's Authorization for Written Test. If the applicant is authorized to take both the Airframe and Powerplant tests the applicant receives three separate authorizations. One authorization is for the General test, one is for the Airframe test, and one is for the Powerplant test.

The applicant presents these authorizations to a Written Test Examiner, who administers the test to the applicant. After successful completion of the written test (70% to pass) the applicant is qualified to take the oral and practical test. The results of the written test are good for 24 months.

Oral and Practical Test

The applicant must present a valid AC Form 8080–2 to show successful complete of the written test. The applicant will also need a valid copy of FAA Form 8610–2 to arrange to take the oral and practical tests with an FAA designated maintenance technician examiner. Applicants can locate designated maintenance examiners by checking the current edition of FAA Advisory Circular, AC 183–32, FAA Designated Maintenance Technician Examiners Directory, which lists the name and address of each designated examiner and the types of tests each is authorized to give. Upon successful completion of the oral and practical tests, the designated examiner can issue the appropriate certificate.

As you can see from this brief outline, attending an approved maintenance school only provides the experience necessary to start the A&P certification process. The final certification check is the FAA written, oral, and practical test.

For additional information on A&P testing procedures, interested readers can contact their local Flight Standards district office (FSDO). In addition to their local telephone directories, the addresses and telephone numbers of the various FSDO's are listed in the FAA Airport/Facility Directory for their respective region.

Jan Monroe

Creve Couver, MO, airport

Flood Damaged Aircraft Pose Potential Threat

FAA's Aircraft Maintenance Division reports that during the recent floods in the midwestern part of the United States some aircraft suffered water damage. The flood water not only did damage to the aircraft,but it also deposited a layer of mud, organic matter, and various chemicals (some possibly toxic) into and upon everything it touched.

The FAA has received reports of aircraft not receiving thorough cleaning after the flood waters receded and of aircraft being flown after a cursory washing. Proper cleaning and restoration of the airframe, engines, propellers, and all the other appliances after a flood is a complex endeavor. Manufacturers do not list cleaning or restoration instructions for aircraft submerged in flood water. Although the following is not complete and comprehensive for all aircraft, some areas of concern are listed below:

1. The structures in metallic aircraft have very little access for cleaning, so gaining access to every compartment or bay of the wings, fuselage, tail, and control surfaces may be difficult or even impossible. Once the area is rinsed, how are the contaminants removed? Many aircraft with internal and/or external stiffeners have only small drain holes at the ends. There may be no sure way to clean some structure short of total disassembly.

2. Wooden structure aircraft were built with casein glue, which is not waterproof. Some glues are water resis-

tant, but were never meant to withstand long-term immersion. How to decide the strength of wooden glue joints after submersion in flood water may be very difficult. Cracks or other defects in wood finishes may allow mud and/or other contaminants to contact the wood, also wood is dried to a specific moisture content and normally remains at a fairly constant value afterwards. The moisture content may increase dramatically after immersion, especially if the finish is not totally waterproof. Several conditions can develop from being submerged in flood water such as *dry rot* (which actually occurs in wet wood), and corroded hardware. Some bolts and bushings in direct contact with wooden structures have surface corrosion with reasonable protection from the elements. After being submerged in flood water, corrosion will be accelerated.

3. Steel tube and fabric structure aircraft can have many problems. Mud and slime may become trapped in the fabric forming a moisture trap, water can find its way into the tubing structure, and corrosion from the inside may be difficult to locate until severe damage has occurred. Aircraft covered with cotton or linen may have its life shortened dramatically. Synthetic fabrics are less likely to show damage, but any defects in the finish may accelerate the chance of the finish peeling.

4. Flexible wire control cables are susceptible to corrosion and wear from grit and moisture soaking in and re-

moving lubrication. Cables usually consist of thin wires braided together and any damage could cause loss of those control surfaces. The acceptable way of checking cables is to remove the tension and "birdcage" to see cable strands inside. (See Advisory Circular 43.13–1A, Acceptable Methods, Techniques and Practices—Aircraft Inspection and Repair, a U.S. Government Printing Office sale item.) New cables may be the only sure way to eliminate the possibility of damaged cables.

5. Rod end bearings, bearings in pulleys and, hinge points on control surfaces are all subject to failure, and/or restricted use from corrosion, grit, and lack of lubrication.

6. Aircraft engines may pose problems after water immersion and cleaning can be a complex operation. An oil change and a general wash may result in extensive damage if grit and dirt are not removed from the many tiny, hard to get to crevices. (Example: piston ring grooves, etc.)

7. A fixed pitch wooden propeller is subject to absorbing moisture, and being submerged in flood waters could have a disastrous effect on the strength of glue joints. This also could effect the static and dynamic balance of wooden propellers. Constant speed propellers have blade bearings and pitch change mechanisms which operate under variable loads. Foreign materials (grit, rust, contamination) could lead to catastrophic failures of the units.

8. Aircraft engines have a number of driven accessories, each having an important function that contribute to safe operation. Magnetos, starters, generators, alternators contain precision bearings and other parts that are used to produce electrical energy for the operation of an aircraft engine and could fail if foreign materials are present.

9. Fuel systems need a clean supply of proper type fuel for dependable operations. An aircraft submerged in flood water could have contamination in the entire fuel system.

10. Instruments and avionics are critical to the operation of any aircraft. I tems installed in aircraft submerged in flood water may not operate freely or properly if contaminants are not completely removed.

11. Landing gears submerged in flood water are susceptible to corrosion (especially those with air/oil struts). The possible damage is loss of fluids and nitrogen due to contaminant damage by flood waters.

12. The electrical system on an aircraft is not immune from flood water damage. Corrosion in circuit breakers, switches, relays, and other connections can cause problems, and loss of systems essential for an aircraft operation.

An aircraft properly cleaned, lubricated, and maintained can be expected to give long and safe service after an incident as the flood of 1993. A flood damaged aircraft, misrepresented as "no damage history" may result in tremendous expenses, or even worse, a catastrophic accident.

Flight Standards District Office personnel should advise mechanics performing inspections on aircraft domiciled in the midwest where the flood of 1993 occurred to question the service history of aircraft and aircraft parts. Those performing inspections should be advised to inspect aircraft and aircraft appliance and parts for possible flood damage using this guidance and appropriate manufacturers guidance.

Hand Prop

Recently, a hand propping propeller accident was reported to the FAA. According to the report, when the aircraft would not start, the pilot decided to hand prop the aircraft. The pilot barely moved the prop before the engine fired. The prop then struck and killed the pilot. The pilot's wife, who was in the aircraft, had to stop the engine.

In an effort to prevent similar accidents, we want to review some safety tips for being near propellers in general and hand propping specifically. Everyone, and especially non-airmen, should treat all propellers with great respect. Each propeller has the potential of being able to start an engine with a minimum of movement such as in our tragic example. A defect in the grounding wire on your engine's magneto system could make your magneto "hot" even though the magneto switch is turned off. The important thing to remember is that whenever you are around an aircraft with a propeller, you must be prepared for that propeller to become a deadly threat. Because of this threat, the most important tip we can offer anyone is that no one should hand prop an aircraft if hand propping can be avoided. Yes, we know there are many aircraft without electrical systems and starters, but the following safety tips are as important to the operators of those aircraft, as the tips are to new pilots of aircraft with electrical systems who have never hand propped an aircraft. Standing in front of an aircraft trying to hand prop it is not an experience that anyone can take lightly. One mistake can be fatal.

The best way to avoid having to hand prop an engine is to keep the battery and starter system in good operating condition. This is especially important during cold weather. A new, warm, fully charged battery is the ideal. An old, cold, weak or dead battery in a snow-covered aircraft is the worst case. Most batteries are somewhere in between. The following ideas can make it easier for your battery to start your aircraft. You should: Keep your battery warm and fully charged; use the proper grade of oil for your local operating conditions; if needed, preheat your engine compartment if your aircraft is not kept in a heated hangar; make sure your charging system is working properly; and maintain your battery according to its manufacturer's recommendations. These are only some of the things you can do. You can ask your local maintenance technicians for more helpful hints. If you routinely "pull your prop through to limber up your engine," always remember to treat your prop as "alive" whenever you are near it.

If your battery cannot start your aircraft, you should ask your maintenance technician for help. It is safer to either replace a bad battery or to jump start an aircraft with a low battery than to hand prop the engine.

If you are determined to hand prop your aircraft, consider the following:

1. Make sure the aircraft is tied down securely. More than one aircraft has gotten away from its owner after being started by hand propping.

2. Make sure chocks are under the main wheels for the reason given for Number 1. Then do not walk into a prop trying to remove the chocks. More than one person has been killed by a prop strike trying to remove a chock. Recently a passenger walked into a rotating prop while trying to remove a nose-wheel chock after the pilot started the engine. Passengers are especially vulnerable around any type of aircraft. Because of the dangers of rotating props and jet blast on a flight line, all pilots should brief their passengers on flight line safety procedures before taking their passengers out on the line. Children should not be allowed to walk around the line without adult supervision. Non-airmen should not be asked to hand prop an aircraft or help start an aircraft without proper training.

3. Have someone in the pilot's seat who knows the recommended procedure for hand propping an aircraft and how to safely start your aircraft. Coordinate all activities with that person before attempting to start the aircraft.

4. Verify and re-verify all engine control settings and magneto switches before touching the propeller. An open throttle has resulted in more than one runaway aircraft that was not tied down.

5. Check your footing. You do not want to slip near a rotating prop and fall into the prop. You should wear clothing that does not restrict your movement. You should not wear clothing that might get caught on the prop.

6. Position your body so that your momentum from pulling the prop through moves you clear of the prop's path. A test is you want to have to reach into the prop's path to grasp the prop.

7. We suggest you loosely grasp the prop with your finger tips only. Avoid wrapping your thumbs around the blades. That way, if the engine starts, your thumbs are out of the way.

8. Be prepared for the engine starting. You do not want to be startled into moving into the prop path. For those who have not hand propped an engine, standing that close to a rotating prop takes a while to get use to.

9. If your first attempt fails, take your time trying again. You do not want the engine to suddenly start when you are not prepared for it.

10. The last tip is, if you are still determined to hand prop an aircraft after reading steps one through nine, and if you are not experienced at hand propping, you should find someone who is experienced and ask him or her to show you the safe way to do it. As always, you should ask yourself the question, "Is the risk of an accident worth what I am trying to accomplish."

Pilot Killed by Main Rotor

The following safety article appeared in the Civil Aviation Authority's GASIL (the United Kingdom's General Aviation Safety Information Leaflet). It was reprinted from Transport Canada's Aviation Safety Vortex. **—Editor**

The owner of a fishing lodge, located 30 miles north of Bella Coola, British Columbia, took off on a VFR flight from his Dean River base camp to another camp, located 30 miles west on the Kitlope River. He landed his Hughes 500C, picked up four sport fishermen, and continued 20 miles northwest to the Tsaysis River. He dropped off his passengers at three sites along the river, returning to the center location to join one of the fishermen.

After shutting down the engine, the pilot got out of the 500 and retrieved a cleaning rag and some solution from behind the passenger seat. With the rotor still turning, the pilot climbed on to the left side of the helicopter, intending to clean the windscreen. As he raised himself to a standing posture, on the left cockpit door sill, his head passed into the plane of the main rotor. He was killed when his head was struck by three of the four blades.

The pilot had about 2,500 hours of helicopter time, the majority of which was in the Robinson R22. Four months before the accident he had sold his R22 and about three weeks prior to the accident he had stared flying the 500. In the three week period before the accident, he flew 32 hours on the new machine. He was type rated on the Hughes.

The pilot was reported to have been meticulous about the cleaning of the windscreen, primarily to enhance flight visibility for safety reasons, but also to accommodate passengers who wished to take photographs. On this occasion, the windscreen needed cleaning.

The landing area was level and was located about 150 feet from the Tsaysis River.

The cyclic was found in a nearly neutral position, laterally centered and inclined slightly forward. The cyclic trim actuator motors were found to operate properly through the normal range of travel.

The helicopter was not equipped with a rotor brake. So after engine shutdown in a no-wind condition, the rotor system would continue to turn for about three minutes.

On the Hughes 500C with high skid gear, the distance between the ground and the rotor blades, with the disc level, is 8.3 feet. While the distance from the ground to the top of the windscreen, is 6.3 feet, it is 4.3 feet from the cockpit door sill to the top of the windscreen and 5.7 feet from the door sill to the rotor blades. The pilot was 5.8 feet tall. When the pilot was standing upright on the door sill, his head extended slightly more than one inch into the plane of the main rotor.

On the other hand, on the Robinson R22 (the helicopter he was more familiar with), the distance from the ground to the rotor is 8.8 feet and the distance from the ground to the top of the windscreen is 5.7 feet.

Editor: One can see that a pilot of average stature can clean the windscreen of an R22 without getting his/her head into the main rotor. This is true only as long as the pilot keeps his/her feet on the ground, but I don't think its a good idea to be doing anything to the helicopter until all the parts stop moving. Why not wait the short time it takes for the blades to stop?

To Whom It May Concern

Effective January 6, 1994, pilots operating in the San Juan Islands, WA, area should monitor 128.25 MHz for air traffic activity reports within the area. Air traffic congestion in the San Juan Islands has increased to the point where pilots have recommended that a single discrete radio frequency be assigned for the islands area. The intent is for all pilots in the island area to be aware of activities which may affect their operations. This would also provide a frequency which is protected from interference from distant sources.

Please call (206) 227–2536 if more information is required.

The FAA Needs Your Help

FAA Advisory Circular (AC) 90–89, *Flight Testing Amateur-built Aircraft,* is scheduled to be revised starting January 3, l994.

The FAA plans to enhance and enlarge the popular AC by including flight testing information on high performance and ultralight/micro-light aircraft.

The FAA is requesting that amateur-built aircraft test pilots share their expertise in flight testing techniques and good common sense practices. Please submit your ideas or comments in writing to:

Federal Aviation Administration
AFS-310
800 Independence Avenue S.W.
Washington, DC 20591
Attention: Bill O'Brien

You can FAX your comments by calling (202) 267–1551.

Pilot Puzzle

ACROSS

1. Load vs. weight (2 words)
5. Parasol
7. Engine-less aircraft
8. Psuedo military ILS
9. Flight Standards District Office
10. Forward control wing
11. Little wing (Fr.)
13. Updraft
14. Propeller driven rotorcraft
16. Your choice
17. Will comply
18. Required above FL240
19. Minimum enroute altitude
21. Inflight advisory
22. Airport
24. Controllers abrv.
26. New NAV system
27. Franklin's airship
29. Radio detection and ranging
30. Motion lotion
33. O'Hare's old name
34. Above ground level
35. Not VFR
36. Class B entry requirement
37. Third Class, e.g.
38. _____ rating

DOWN

1. Over 12,500 pounds (2 words)
2. Hydrometeor
3. Broken or overcast
4. Aviator
6. Cloud like streamer
12. Course reversal (2 words)
15. Weather hazard
18. Great circle route
20. Horizontal wind at altitude
22. Substitute
23. Narrow band of weather (2 words)
25. Long range NAV system
28. Precision approach
31. Visual rules
32. Homing device
35. Good in drinks only

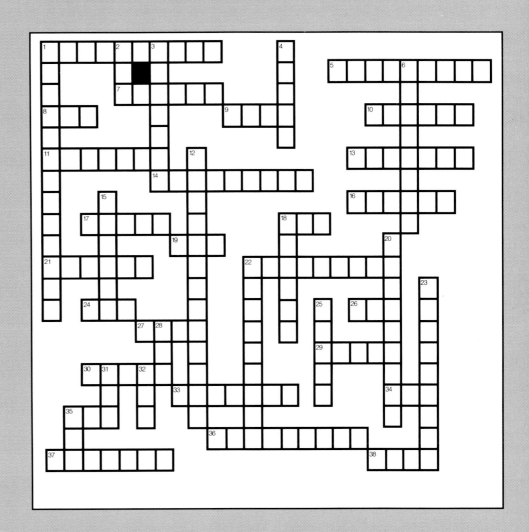

The first 10 correct crossword puzzles submitted to the Cleveland FSDO will win an FAA video tape. The correct answers will appear in the next issue of the *FAA Aviation News*. Submit your completed pilot puzzle along with your name and address to:

Timothy Lett and Ron Drake
c/o Cleveland FSDO
Federal Facilities Office Bldg., Room 131
Cleveland Hopkins International Airport
Cleveland, OH 44135

DO NOT DELAY—CRITICAL TO FLIGHT SAFETY!